Contents

A NOTE TO READERS

At Rough Guides, we always strive to bring you the most up-to-date information. This book was produced during a period of continuing uncertainty caused by the Covid-19 pandemic, so please note that content is more subject to change than usual. We recommend checking the latest restrictions and official guidance.

Introduction to
Cuba

For the last two decades, the popular refrain on visiting Cuba has been "Go now before it changes forever". There have been some startling developments in that time, but the Cuban story, and the country itself, never ceases to captivate and enthral. This is an island that lurches forward, then crunches into reverse with such regularity that change, in some senses, is a constant. Yet it is also a place renowned for its stagnation over the last six decades, since the 1959 Revolution stopped the clocks and turned everything upside down. Vintage radios, refrigerators and lamps furnish the average home and swinging neon signs hang over storefronts; on the same streets are antique pharmacies and traditional barbers, and iconic classic American cars are everywhere. But this is no retro trend, it's make-do-and-mend, frozen-in-carbonite Cuba.

In spite of all this living history, the pace of modernization in Cuba is increasing exponentially. Rampant hotel building is throwing up new, swish places to stay all over the island and particularly in the mesmerizing capital, Havana, which celebrated its 500th anniversary in 2019. In the past decade, Cuba launched its first mobile internet service and wi-fi is now common throughout the country – though it's in public parks and squares, rather than in the privacy of their own homes, that most Cubans get online. Like so much of life in this remarkably sociable nation, accessing the internet is often a shared, outdoor experience.

The changes affecting Cuba are not just technological. In recent years this communist stronghold in the Caribbean has lost its titanic patriarch, Fidel Castro, celebrated the first US presidential visit in 80 years and sworn in a new president of its own, Miguel Diaz-Canel, the first person outside the Castro family to lead the country since 1959. All of these events have been transformative in a number of ways, but the uniqueness of Cuba is unwavering. Salsa still bubbles through the veins of every citizen, roadside billboards still proclaim "Socialism or death", world-class ballerinas and baseball players dazzle for the same meagre state salary as the ordinary workers, who pay

THE ROUGH GUIDE TO
CUBA

ROUGH
GUIDES

This ninth edition upda
Joanne Owen

CUBA

ATLANTIC OCEAN

Feet — Metres

Feet	Metres
5000	1524
4000	1219
3000	914
2000	610
1000	305
500	152
250	76
0	0

0 — 100 kilometres

N

Gulf of Mexico

Straits of Florida

Florida Keys

THE BAHAMAS

Eleuthera
Cat Island
San Salvador
Crooked
Acklins
Long Island
Great Exuma
Little Exuma
Great Guana Cay
Andros

Great Bahama Bank

CARIBBEAN SEA

Archipiélago Jardín del Rey
Archipiélago Jardines de la Reina
Archipiélago de Sabana
Archipiélago de los Canarreos

Cayo Santa María
Cayo Las Brujas
Cayo Guillermo
Cayo Coco
Cayo Romano
Cayo Largo

Cayman Brac
Little Cayman
Grand Cayman

ISLA DE LA JUVENTUD
Nueva Gerona
Julio A. Mella
La Fe
Cocodrilo

PINAR DEL RÍO
Cordillera de Guaniguanico
Península de Guanahacabibes
Cabo de San Antonio
María La Gorda
Isabel Rubio
Guane
San Juan y Martínez
Pinar del Río
Viñales
Cayo Levisa
Las Terrazas
Mariel
Artemisa

CIUDAD DE LA HABANA
HAVANA
Cojímar
Guanabo
Jibacoa
San Antonio de los Baños
Bejucal
Batabanó
MAYABEQUE

MATANZAS
Varadero
Cárdenas
Canasí
Matanzas
Jovellanos
Bay of Pigs
Península de Zapata
AUTOPISTA NACIONAL

VILLA CLARA
Santa Clara
Remedios
Sierra del Escambray
CIENFUEGOS
Cienfuegos
Topes de Collantes
Trinidad

SANCTI SPÍRITUS
Sancti Spíritus

CIEGO DE ÁVILA
Ciego de Ávila
Morón
Florencia
Júcaro

CAMAGÜEY
Camagüey
Nuevitas
Santa Lucía

LAS TUNAS
Las Tunas
Playa Covarrubias
Puerto Padre

HOLGUÍN
Holguín
Gibara
Guardalavaca
Banes
Mayarí
Moa
Sagua
Cayo Saetía

GRANMA
Bayamo
Manzanillo
Media Luna
Niquero
Cabo Cruz
Pilón
Marea del Portillo

SIERRA MAESTRA

SANTIAGO DE CUBA
Santiago de Cuba
Contramaestre
Chivirico

GUANTÁNAMO
Guantánamo
Baracoa
Maisí
Bacanao
US Naval Base

Inset map

ATLANTIC OCEAN

USA
THE BAHAMAS
CUBA
GREATER ANTILLES
HAITI
DOMINICAN REPUBLIC
PUERTO RICO
JAMAICA
LEEWARD ISLANDS
WINDWARD ISLANDS
LESSER ANTILLES
CARIBBEAN SEA
HONDURAS
NICARAGUA
COLOMBIA
VENEZUELA

FACT FILE

- Cuba's 11,300,000 inhabitants and 110,861 sq km of land make it the **largest island in the Caribbean** by both population and area.
- The eastern province of **Granma** and one of Cuba's national newspapers are both named after the boat which carried Fidel Castro and 81 other rebels from Mexico to Cuba to start the revolutionary war in 1956. The boat itself was named after the original owner's grandmother.
- **Christmas was abolished** as a public holiday in Cuba in 1969 and officially reinstated in 1998.
- Cuba has a **99.7 percent adult literacy rate**, among the highest in the world.
- The world's **smallest bird**, the bee hummingbird, is indigenous to Cuba.
- Cuba has the only functioning public passenger **railway service** in the Caribbean. The first steam railway line in Latin America was built on the island in 1837.

next to nothing to watch them, earn themselves – and the island's breathtaking beaches, unspoiled seas and forest-covered mountains haven't gone anywhere.

Despite President Trump's determination to reverse so much of the progress that the Obama administration made in normalizing US-Cuban relations (in his last week in office, Trump placed Cuba on the US list of countries supporting terrorism), US travellers needn't feel despondent. Though the Biden administration has upheld the sanctions of the previous administration, Cuba is back on the agenda.

Getting there remains relatively straightforward as commercial airlines take off for Cuba every day from various cities around the US. Only a small amount of imagination is needed to stay within the fairly flexible restrictions set by US law, and the Stars and Stripes continue to flutter above a US Embassy in Havana, closed in 1961 but reopened in 2014.

The decision makers of the authoritarian government in Cuba continue to grapple with just how much change to allow. And while the ongoing process is both maddening and hopeful for the local population, it does provide a fascinating narrative. Among the biggest dilemmas is how much freedom to give to the private sector, as Cuban entrepreneurs relentlessly push the boundaries and become ever more inventive, professional and determined, even going on strike, as taxi drivers did in 2018 – an unprecedented event in modern Cuba. In addition, food and medicine shortages, and the government's response to the Covid-19 pandemic, sparked protests in July 2021.

First-class, family-run boutique hotels, many of them still at the affordable end of the price spectrum, are flourishing, while shoestring budget options are expanding too as dorm-based hostels, not long ago a rarity in Cuba, are popping up all over the island. House-based restaurants – paladars – are slowly putting Cuban cuisine on the culinary map and confining the once-deserved infamy of Cuban food to history. You can meet Cuban artists in their own front-room galleries, learn how to dance rumba or salsa in home-based studios, take a city tour in a 1956 Chevrolet and learn how to kite surf, rock climb, play the conga and ride a horse. Highly educated individuals – doctors, lawyers and civil engineers – frequently run these ventures, stalwarts of the hospitality industry ever since tourism took over the economy in the 1990s. Though increasingly professional, these domestically run businesses remain small scale, making close-up contact with the locals

CLASSIC AMERICAN CARS

Perhaps the most clichéd image of Cuba is of a **classic American car** rolling past a crumbling colonial building, and you don't have to spend long in the country to see why this image has become so ubiquitous. There are said to be around 60,000 vintage American cars in Cuba, known as *almendrones*, most of them still on the road and almost all of them imported from the factories of Detroit during the 1940s and 1950s, when the US was Cuba's most significant trade partner. After President Kennedy cut off all trade with Cuba via the 1962 economic embargo that exists to this day, car owners were compelled to keep their Buicks, Oldsmobiles, Chevrolets and Fords running. Unable to source replacement parts, proud owners have over the years become the most ingenious on the planet, culling pieces from Eastern Bloc Ladas, household appliances and even old tanks to keep their cars alive.

a common feature of a trip. It is possible to peel back more layers of life in Cuba than you might have imagined in a relatively short visit. By doing so, you'll discover that for most Cubans, waiting lists for trains and buses, prices way out of proportion with wages and free-speech restrictions still characterize their lives, as do the long-held and cherished achievements of the Cuban Revolution: free education and cradle-to-grave healthcare, providing literacy rates and life-expectancy figures that are among the highest in the world.

Cuba is undoubtedly undergoing a great transformation, but it is still like nowhere else on earth.

Where to go

No trip to Cuba would be complete without a visit to the potent capital, **Havana**, a unique, personable and pedestrian-friendly metropolis with largely traffic-free streets away from the main thoroughfares. Its time-warped colonial core, Habana Vieja, is where so much of what is excitingly new as well as fascinatingly old is found, crammed with architectural splendours dating as far back as the sixteenth century and some of the freshest, most interesting restaurants, bars, boutique hotels and *casas particulares*. Elsewhere there are handsome streets unspoiled by tawdry multinational chain stores and fast-food outlets: urban development here has been undertaken sensitively, with the city retaining many of its colonial mansions and numerous 1950s hallmarks.

To the west of Havana, the nature-tourism centres of **Artemisa** and **Pinar del Río** are popular destinations with day-trippers but also offer more than enough to sustain a longer stay. The most accessible resorts here are **Las Terrazas** and **Soroa**, focused around the subtropical, smooth-topped Sierra del Rosario mountain range; but it's the peculiarly shaped *mogote* hills of the prehistoric **Viñales valley** that attract most attention, while tiny Viñales village is a pleasant hangout frequented by a friendly traveller community. Beyond, on a gnarled rod of land pointing out towards Mexico, there's unparalleled seclusion and outstanding scuba diving at **María La Gorda**.

There are **beach resorts** the length and breadth of the country but none is more complete than **Varadero**, the country's long-time premier holiday destination, two

STATUE OF CUBAN HERO J. MARTINEZ MOLES IN SERAFIN SANCHEZ PARK

CUBAN RUM

When Carlos V issued a royal order in 1539 formalizing rum production, it secured **Cuban rum**'s place on the map. Today Cuba produces some of the world's most respected brands of rum, silky smooth modern varieties that have little in common with the harsh drink enjoyed by sixteenth-century pirates and renegades. Quality ranges from the most basic **white rum** widely used for mixing in cocktails (famously the *mojito*, the Cuba libre and the daiquiri), to various **dark rums** aged in oak casks for different lengths of time, from around three years to as many as thirty, and are best enjoyed neat or over a chunk of ice. Though Havana Club is the best known of all Cuba's rums, browsing will reveal tempting but lesser-known varieties such as **Cubay**'s pleasantly sweet dark rum and **Ron Palma Mulata**, a good white rum slightly cheaper than its Havana Club equivalent. Among the finest Cuban rums are **Havana Club Gran Reserva** and **Santiago de Cuba Extra Añejo** – reputed to be the favourite tipple of Fidel Castro himself.

hours' drive east of Havana in **Matanzas province**. Based on a highway of dazzling white sand that stretches almost the entire length of the 25km **Península de Hicacos**, Varadero offers the classic package-holiday experience. For the tried-and-tested combination of watersports, sunbathing and relaxing in all-inclusive hotels, there is nowhere better in Cuba. On the opposite side of the province, the **Península de Zapata**, with its diversity of wildlife, organized excursions and scuba diving, offers a melange of different possibilities. The grittier **Cárdenas** and provincial capital **Matanzas** contrast with Varadero's made-to-measure appeal, but it's the nearby natural attractions of the **Bellamar caves** and the verdant splendour of the **Yumurí valley** that provide the focus for most day-trips.

Travelling east of Matanzas province, either on the Autopista Nacional or the island-long Carretera Central, public transport links become weaker, and picturesque but worn-out towns take over from brochure-friendly hotspots. There is, however, a concentration of activity around the historically precious **Trinidad**, a small colonial city brimming with symbols of Cuba's past, which attracts tour groups and backpackers in equal numbers. If you're intending to spend more than a few days in the island's centre, this is by far the best base, within short taxi rides of a small but well-equipped beach resort, the **Península de Ancón**, and the **Topes de Collantes** hiking centre in the **Sierra del Escambray**. Slightly further afield are a few larger cities: lively **Santa Clara** is best known for its Che Guevara connections, while laidback **Cienfuegos**, next to the placid waters of a sweeping bay, is sprinkled with colourful architecture, including a splendid nineteenth-century theatre. Further east, historic **Sancti Spíritus** and modest **Ciego de Ávila**, both workaday cities in their namesake provinces, will appeal to anyone looking to escape the tourist limelight without having to work hard to find a memorable and comfortable place to stay. With a mix of luxury and family-oriented options, the expanding resorts of **Cayo Coco** and **Cayo Guillermo**, off the north coast of Ciego de Ávila province, feature wide swathes of creamy-white beaches, while the tranquil countryside nearby, with its pretty lakes and low hills, is best enjoyed from the small town of **Morón**, the most popular base for independent travellers in the province.

Heading eastwards back on the Carretera Central into **Camagüey province**, romantic, attractive and underrated **Camagüey**, the third most populous city in Cuba, is a sightseer's delight, fully meriting its Unesco Heritage Site award, with numerous intriguing buildings and a half-decent nightlife. In the north of the province, the small, rather remote resort of **Santa Lucía** is a much-promoted though modestly equipped option for sunseekers; while there's an excellent alternative north of here in tiny **Cayo Sabinal**, with long empty beaches and romantically rustic facilities. Another 200km east along the Carretera Central is the amiable city of **Holguín**, the threshold to the province of the same name, containing the biggest concentration of pre-Columbian sites in the country. On the northern coast of Holguín province, **Guardalavaca** (together with the neighbouring playas **Esmeralda**, **Pesquero** and luxurious **Turquesa**) is one of the country's liveliest and most attractive resorts, spread along a shady beach with ample opportunities for watersports.

Forming the far eastern tip of the island, **Guantánamo province** is best known for its infamous US naval base, but the region's most enchanting spot is the jaunty coastal town of **Baracoa**. Isolated from the rest of the country by a high rib of mountains, this quirky, friendly town – freckled with colonial houses – is an unrivalled retreat popular with long-term travellers, and offers ample opportunities for revelling in the glorious outdoors.

Santiago de Cuba province, on the island's southeast coast, could make a holiday in itself, with a sparkling coastline fretted with golden-sand beaches such as **Chivirico**; the undulating emerald mountains of the **Sierra Maestra**, made for trekking; and **Santiago**, the home of traditional Cuban music and the country's most vibrant and energetic city after Havana. Host to Cuba's most exuberant **carnival** every July, when a deluge of loud, rhythmic and passionate sounds surges through the streets, you can hear some of the best Cuban musicians here year-round. Trekkers and Revolution enthusiasts will want to follow the Sierra Maestra as it snakes west of here along the south coast into **Granma province**, with various revolutionary landmarks and nature trails.

Lying off the southern coast of Artemisa province, the **Isla de la Juventud** is an inconvenient three-hour ferry ride or a forty-minute flight away from the mainland but its remoteness is part of its appeal and it feels even more time-warped than the rest of the country. Easily explored over a weekend, the island promises leisurely walks, some of the best diving in the country and a personable, very low-key capital town in Nueva Gerona. There is also the luxurious **Cayo Largo**, the southern coastline's only sizeable beach resort.

CYBER CUBA

Take a stroll through the parks and squares of the country's towns and cities and you will see thick clusters of Cubans staring intently at smartphone screens. Groups of students jostle around laptops while entire families crowd into the frame of phone cameras and gesticulate at relatives elsewhere in the world. They are all online, accessing the country's public wi-fi hotspots. Using the internet, like so many aspects of life in Cuba, is riven with idiosynchronicity. This very social scene is a microcosm of urban street life: music plays, touts trade cards with practised sleight of hand while street vendors with rusting shopping carts ply the crowds with freshly roasted peanuts, served in paper cones. In December 2018 Cuba launched its first 3G mobile network and domestic wi-fi connections are on the increase, most prevalent in *casas particulares*, the Cuban version of B&Bs. But most Cubans remain reliant on the public hotspots and, for now at least, Facebook and Instagram in Cuba are still very much sociable media. See page 57 to find out how to get online in Cuba.

When to go

Cuba has a hot and sunny tropical climate with an average temperature of 24°C, but in the winter months of January and February the mercury can drop as low as 15°C, and even lower at night. This is during the **dry season**, which runs roughly from November to April. If you visit in the summer, considered the **wet season**, expect it to rain on at least a couple of days over a fortnight. Don't let this put you off, though; although it comes down hard and fast, rain rarely stays for very long in Cuba, and the clouds soon break to allow sunshine through to dry everything out. Eastern Cuba tends to be hotter and more humid during this part of the year, while the temperature in the area around Trinidad and Sancti Spíritus also creeps above the national average. September and October are the most threatening months of the annual **hurricane** season that runs from June to November. In September 2017, Hurricane Irma struck Cuba as a Category 5 storm with 200 mph winds, rain and flooding affecting 200,000 households, particularly along the north central coast. In June 2022 heavy rains from the remnants of Hurricane Agatha caused widespread flooding in western and central Cuba, killing three people in Havana. That said, compared with other Caribbean islands and some Central American countries, Cuba has so far held up relatively well even in the fiercest of hurricanes.

The **peak tourist season** in Cuba runs roughly from mid-December to mid-March, and all of July and August. Prices are highest and crowds thickest in high summer, when the holiday season for Cubans gets under way. As much of the atmosphere of the smaller resorts is generated by tourists, Cuban and foreign, out of season they can seem somewhat dull – although you'll benefit from lower prices. The cities, particularly Havana and Santiago, are always buzzing and offer good value for money throughout the year. Compared to the all-out celebrations in other countries, **Christmas** is a low-key affair in Cuba, with the emphasis on private family celebration. **New Year's Eve**, also the eve of the anniversary of the Revolution, is much more fervently celebrated.

AVERAGE TEMPERATURES AND RAINFALL

	Jan	Feb	March	April	May	June	July	Aug	Sept	Oct	Nov	Dec
HAVANA												
Min/Max (°C)	18/26	18/26	19/27	21/29	22/30	23/31	24/32	24/32	24/31	23/29	21/27	19/26
Min/Max (°F)	64/79	64/79	66/81	70/84	72/86	74/88	76/90	76/90	76/88	76/84	70/81	66/79
Rainfall (mm)	71	46	46	58	119	165	125	135	150	173	79	58
PINAR DEL RÍO												
Min/Max (°C)	18/26	18/26	19/27	20/28	22/30	24/31	24/32	24/32	24/32	23/30	21/28	19/26
Min/Max (°F)	64/78	65/79	66/80	68/82	71/85	75/88	76/90	76/90	75/89	73/86	70/83	66/79
Rainfall (mm)	21	24	32	26	52	118	75	121	88	66	47	22
SANTIAGO DE CUBA												
Min/Max (°C)	20/30	20/30	22/30	23/31	24/32	25/32	25/33	25/33	25/33	24/32	23/32	22/30
Min/Max (°F)	69/86	69/86	71/86	73/87	75/89	77/90	77/92	77/92	77/91	75/90	73/89	71/87
Rainfall (mm)	74	43	53	58	140	102	69	94	107	193	94	81

Author picks

Our hard-travelling authors visited every corner of Cuba, from the sandy beaches of the western tip to the verdant interior of the eastern rainforests. Here are some of their favourite things to see and do in Cuba.

Antique and vintage collectables The land that not only froze in time but simultaneously got frozen out of numerous global markets has accumulated a mountain of antiques and vintage memorabilia, which Cubans can now legitimately sell. Find the best places to uncover a gem in Havana (see page 132) and Trinidad (see page 278).

Our favourite casas particulares Whether it's eating a home-cooked meal, hanging out on the family veranda or marvelling at a precious domestic interior, a homestay grants access to all that is idiosyncratic about Cuba. The owners of *Casa Muñoz* in Trinidad (see page 275), *Alojamiento Maite* in Morón (see page 303) and *Casa 1932* in Havana (see page 118) all go the extra mile.

Alternative music venues All over the island, away from the spotlight that falls on the Casas de la Música and their ilk, are fantastically quirky venues like *El Mejunje* in Santa Clara (see page 254), artsy auditoriums such as the *Casa de las Américas* (see page 103) and backstreet live music spots like *El Jelengue de Areito* in Havana (see page 129).

Mountain vistas Trekking through the pine-thick Sierra del Escambray (see page 283), the cloud forests of the Sierra Maestra (see page 402) or ascending the squared-off summit of Baracoa's El Yunque (see page 363) gives a glimpse of historic revolutionary rebel hideouts, unique fauna and breathtaking views over waterfalls, land and sea.

Private art galleries Original Cuban contemporary art, much of it strikingly expressive, is experiencing unprecedented exposure now that the artists themselves are free to sell and exhibit their work in their own galleries. Havana (see page 88) and Cienfuegos (see page 234) are two of the best cities to visit to see for yourself.

> Our author recommendations don't end here. We've flagged up our favourite places – a perfectly sited hotel, an atmospheric café, a special restaurant – throughout the Guide, highlighted with the ★ symbol.

EL NICHO WATERFALL

INTI ALVAREZ PAINTINGS ON DISPLAY IN HAVANA

25

things not to miss

It's not possible to see everything that Cuba has to offer in one visit, and we don't suggest you try. What follows is a selective taste of the country's highlights, from lively festivals to natural wonders and stunning architecture. All highlights are colour-coded by chapter and have a page reference to take you straight into the Guide, where you can find out more.

1

1 BARACOA'S COUNTRYSIDE
See page 363
Jewel of coastal eastern Cuba, tiny Baracoa makes an ideal base for exploring the verdant rainforest, mountain peaks and tranquil rivers dotted about this part of Guantánamo province.

2 JARDINES DEL REY
See page 306
One of Cuba's most popular resorts has miles of beaches, including one of the country's best in Playa Pilar, its largest coral reef and its top kitesurfing spot.

3 TRINIDAD OLD TOWN
See page 271
This much-visited sixteenth-century town is packed with colonial mansions and churches, threaded together by cobbled streets and compact plazas.

4 MUSEO PRESIDIO MODELO
See page 420
Tour the isolated prison where Fidel Castro and his cohorts were incarcerated.

5 VIÑALES
See page 164
Particularly enchanting in the morning when mist rises from the valley floor, Viñales' is unforgettable.

6 VILLA CLARA NORTHERN CAYS
See page 260
The cays' stunning white-sand beaches sit in isolated splendour at the end of a narrow causeway.

7 ALEJANDRO ROBAINA TOBACCO PLANTATION
See page 175
This small but highly successful tobacco plantation offers refreshingly down-to-earth tours.

8 FÁBRICA DE ARTE CUBANO
See page 108
A club, arts centre and gallery space rolled into one, this slick converted peanut-oil factory is the place to experience Cuba's counterculture arts scene.

9 HAVANA JAZZ FESTIVAL
See page 45
This lively festival is the perfect showcase for Cuba's jazz musicians.

10 HOTEL NACIONAL
See page 98
Wander around the cliff-edge gardens of this majestic hotel in the capital, or sip cooling cocktails on one of its elegant terraces.

9

10

11 LAS TERRAZAS, PINAR DEL RÍO
See page 153

Thickly wooded hillsides, grassy slopes and natural swimming pools make this idyllic eco-resort a great base for a few days' exploration.

12 CIGAR FACTORIES
See pages 94, 160 and 247

World-renowned Cuban cigars are made by hand in workshop-factories all over the island. Look in on the rows of nimble-fingered workers on fascinating factory tours in Havana, Pinar del Río, Santa Clara and elsewhere.

13 HABANA VIEJA
See page 67

This well-preserved colonial centre boasts perfectly restored centuries-old buildings throughout its narrow streets and historic plazas.

14 HAVANA'S MALECÓN
See page 95

All the idiosyncrasies of Havana are on display here: the majestic and crumbling buildings, beatbox salsa, kissing couples and *jineteros*.

15 CASA DE LA TROVA, SANTIAGO
See page 390

Given Santiago's heritage as the birthplace of trova, it's unsurprising that the *Casa de la Trova* here is the country's top spot to listen and dance up a storm to traditional music, banged out by veteran and up-and-coming musicians alike.

16 SANTIAGO IN JULY
See page 378
This is the best time to visit Cuba's second city, when its vibrant music scene boils over and the annual carnival brings fabulous costumes, excitement and song to the streets.

17 LA GUARIDA RESTAURANT
See page 123
Dine in style in Havana's most atmospheric paladar, where the excellent food is matched by Baroque surroundings, pre-revolutionary memorabilia and the aura of another age.

18 PUNTA GORDA, CIENGUEGOS
See page 235
The magnificently decorative Palacio del Valle is the icing on the cake during a wander around the broad avenues of this bayside district in laidback Cienfuegos.

19 NATIONAL LEAGUE BASEBALL
See page 48
Take a seat alongside the exuberant crowds at one of the country's timepiece baseball stadiums.

20 HERSHEY TRAIN
See page 208
This antiquated electric train slowly winds through the gentle countryside from Havana to Matanzas.

CASA BLANCA

21 LA PLATA MOUNTAIN TRAIL
See page 402

Bring Cuba's history to life with a day of mountain trekking to explore Fidel Castro's revolutionary base camps.

22 CAVERNA DE SANTO TOMÁS
See page 174

A guided walk through these narrow underground chambers is a thrilling Tolkien-esque outing.

23 DIVING OFF THE SOUTHERN COASTLINE
See page 48

The diving at María La Gorda, Punta Francés and the Jardines de la Reina is world-class.

24 CLASSIC AMERICAN CAR RIDE
See page 33

Ride around Havana or Varadero in one of Gran Car's classic 1950s cars, a testament to both US engineering and Cuban ingenuity.

25 COLONIAL CAMAGÜEY
See page 314

The most overlooked of the country's Unesco World Heritage Sites, the 500-year-old heart of Camagüey, with its tangle of streets, abundant churches and lovely squares is a great place to wander around and to stay, with an outstanding set of boutique hotels and *casas*.

Itineraries

It's not possible to see everything that Cuba has to offer in one trip – and we don't suggest you try. What follows is a selective taste of the country's highlights: historic plazas, bewitching mountain ranges and tempting beaches. All highlights are colour-coded by chapter and have a page reference to take you straight into the Guide, where you can find out more.

HAVANA GRAND TOUR

You could cram this tour of Havana's major sights into two days, but allow yourself three and there'll be plenty of time to soak up the atmosphere.

❶ Plaza de Armas The oldest and most animated of Habana Vieja's squares is where Havana established itself as a city in the second half of the sixteenth century – and it's been the barrio's heartbeat ever since. See page 71

❷ Obispo A microcosm of all that is changing in Havana, this pedestrianized thoroughfare is brimming with a lively mix of street vendors, open-fronted bars, neighbourhood hairdressers, secondhand bookstalls and artists' ateliers. See page 83

❸ Museo Nacional de Bellas Artes The country's most spectacular museum houses its largest art collection: revel in the history of Cuban art (and Cuba itself) seen through Spanish colonial portraits, Cuban painting and sculpture and Revolution-inspired work. See page 87

❹ Plaza de la Revolución Visit when the plaza is brimming with patriotic Cubans waving a sea of flags against a backdrop of sculptural tributes to Che Guevara, José Martí and Camilo Cienfuegos, and you'll have yourself the ultimate revolutionary photo opportunity. See page 104

❺ Casa de la Música Miramar One of the city's best music venues, hosting Cuba's most popular musicians. See page 129

❻ La Guarida The atmospheric beauty, on-point menu and slew of celebrity guests all keep this as Havana's number-one paladar. See page 123

❼ Gran Teatro ballet Watch some of the world's finest prima ballerinas give mesmeric performances in an ornate building on the Parque Central; Carlos Acosta regularly takes to the boards here, too. See page 131

MOUNTAINS AND MOGOTES

Inland Cuba has natural treasures galore, and you could easily dedicate two weeks to trekking through the country's glorious forests, mountains and countryside.

❶ Las Terrazas A variety of birdlife flits through the fertile mixture of semitropical rainforest and

---

Create your own itinerary with Rough Guides. Whether you're after adventure or a family-friendly holiday, we have a trip for you, with all the activities you enjoy doing and the sights you want to see. All our trips are devised by local experts who get the most out of the destination. Visit **www.roughguides.com/trips** to chat with one of our travel agents.

evergreen forest on the slopes of the Sierra del Rosario mountain range. See page 153

❷ Viñales The jewel in the crown of western Cuba is the landscape in this striking national park, where rich red earth and lush tobacco fields contrast with the almost eerie Jurassic rock formations. See page 164

❸ Cuevas de Bellamar Venture over 50m below the surface and along hundreds of metres of atmospheric passageways in these awe-inspiring underground caves. See page 211

❹ Topes de Collantes This beautiful national park in the steep forested slopes of the Sierra del Escambray mountains has some excellent hiking trails. See page 283

❺ Pinares de Mayarí Few venture into this beautiful pine forest, with a placid lake, majestic waterfall and intriguing caves. See page 352

❻ Baracoa Cradled by lush green mountains and threaded with swimmable rivers, Baracoa is the perfect place to immerse yourself in the great outdoors. See page 356

HAVANA TO TRINIDAD BY BIKE

Outside the cities, the roads in Cuba, are remarkably free of traffic, making it a fantastic country to cycle around. This week-long tour is based on a pace of between 40 and 90 kilometres a day. Flip the order around to avoid the headwind.

❶ Playas del Este A gentle start to the tour allows you to get used to cycling in the humidity with a short hop from the capital to the nearest

beaches, where you can cool off and relax before the longer leg tomorrow. See page 140

❷ Matanzas via the Yumurí valley It's around 80km from the beaches to the provincial capital of Matanzas, a tatty but culturally interesting city on a bay with a colonial past – but the real pleasure is cycling through the idyllic Yumurí valley on the approach to the city. See pages 203 and 211

❸ Varadero An easy ride along a coastal road leads to the country's largest beach resort, where there's an abundant spread of excellent *casas particulares* and paladars. See page 182

❹ Península de Zapata Head south, down through Matanzas province, via the forgotten, picturesque village of San Miguel de los Baños through the sugar cane fields and citrus orchards to the northern tip of the Península de Zapata. See page 217

❺ Playa Girón This leg of the tour takes in most of the Península de Zapata's sights and ends up at the Bay of Pigs, where a modest beach and museum mark one of the key events of the Revolution. See page 223

❻ Cienfuegos 85km from Playa Girón, either along a coastal track and then a ferry at the Castillo de Jagua or along country roads, is the laidback capital of Cienfuegos. See page 228

❼ Trinidad Follow the Circuito Sur along the coast to Trinidad. With beaches just down the road, mountains not much further away and a glorious nearby valley, you can do some day-tripping if you have any energy left before popping your bike on a bus back to Havana. See pages 244 and 266

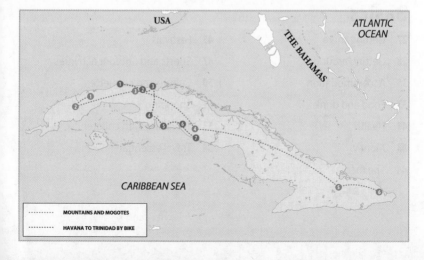

COCOTAXI IN HAVANA

Basics

Getting there

Getting to Cuba from the US has never been easier and though only a few airlines operate direct flights from the UK, there are plenty flying direct from elsewhere in Europe. Canada has had more flights to Cuba than any other country for years but there are no direct flights at all from Australia.

The point of entry for the vast majority of international scheduled flights is Havana's José Martí airport, though some flights, and in particular from Canada and the US, go direct to a number of the much smaller regional airports, most commonly Varadero, Santa Clara, Holguín and Santiago de Cuba. These same airports are served by charter flights from Europe, Canada, the US and elsewhere, as are the tiny resort-based airports at Cayo Coco and Cayo Largo del Sur and, to a lesser extent, the airport in Cienfuegos.

FLIGHT SEASONS

The **high season** in Cuba, when flights are at their most expensive, is broadly December to March and all of July and August. You'll usually get the best prices for flights during the **low season**, from April to June and September to November.

relatively inexpensive flights, they have a justified reputation for overbooking, overzealous enforcement of the baggage weight limit and a very poor safety record; an internal flight crashed in May 2018.

No airline flies nonstop **from Ireland** to Cuba, and you'll usually fly via London, Paris, Madrid or Toronto. For example, Air France flies from Dublin via Paris. Otherwise the best option is to buy a flight from one of the European cities mentioned above and arrange separate connecting flights from Ireland to that city.

Flights from the UK and Ireland

From the UK, Virgin Atlantic offer two direct flights a week from London Gatwick to Havana. For a cheaper option, TUI operate flights from Manchester to Varadero. At the time of writing, TUI flights from London Gatwick to Havana, Cayo Coco and Varadero have yet to resume since the Covid-19 pandemic. Check airline websites for updates on the changing situation.

It's often cheaper to fly to Cuba **from the UK via other European cities**, typically Madrid, Paris and Amsterdam. Air Europa is consistently one of the least expensive options, while **Air France** is the most versatile option, with daily flights from London Heathrow to Havana via Paris. **Iberia** and **KLM** also fly from Heathrow, via Madrid and Amsterdam respectively. Other airlines flying direct from Europe include Blue Panorama from Rome and Milan to four different Cuban airports; Aeroflot from Moscow to Havana; and the national Cuban carrier, Cubana, from Madrid and Paris to Havana and Santiago and from Moscow and Rome to Havana only. Though Cubana tends to offer

Flights from the US

Despite the embargo that Washington still maintains on trade with Cuba and the continued obligation for visitors to adhere to the terms of a "licence to travel" (see page 29), it is now possible for US citizens to take direct scheduled flights from the US to Cuba. In the autumn of 2016, for the first time in over fifty years, major American airlines began flying commercial, non-charter flights from several cities throughout the US to cities around Cuba. The uptake of consumer flights was less than expected, and many of these routes have already been cut or reduced. That said, there are still enough flights to make passage between the two countries a mere hop, skip and a jump away.

The main airlines that fly from the US to Cuba are JetBlue (Ⓦjetblue.com), who fly daily to Havana from Fort Lauderdale, Orlando, JFK New York and Boston. American Airlines (Ⓦamericanairlines.com) fly from Miami to Havana six times a day. Southwest Airlines (Ⓦsouthwest.com) fly from Fort Lauderdale to Havana three times daily, and from Tampa twice daily.

A BETTER KIND OF TRAVEL

At Rough Guides we are passionately committed to travel. We believe it helps us understand the world we live in and the people we share it with – and of course tourism is vital to many developing economies. But the scale of modern tourism has also damaged some places irreparably, and climate change is accelerated by most forms of transport, especially flying. We encourage all our authors to consider the carbon footprint of the journeys they make in the course of researching our guides.

Prior to this breakthrough, US travellers flying direct were restricted to more complicated, relatively expensive charter flights and of course charters are still an option. Traditionally the preserve of specialist tour companies, booking a charter flight through one of these Cuba specialists, though sometimes more expensive, does still have some advantages. Most of these tour operators are themselves licenced to take groups of US citizens to the island, so by signing up for a flight and tour with them you don't need to concern yourself with a licence at all, and you are likely to be well protected from, or at the very least guided through, any nasty bureaucracy. Two reputable travel and charter agencies are Marazul (Wmarazul.com) and Cuba Travel Services (Wcubatravelservices.com).

Flights from Canada

Cuba and Canada are very well connected. Air Canada flies to Varadero, Santa Clara, Holguín, Cayo Coco, Cayo Largo del Sur and daily to Havana **from Toronto**, with plenty of direct flights from Montréal and some from other Canadian destinations. Cubana, generally cheaper but less reliable and comfortable than Air Canada, flies regularly from Toronto and Montréal to Havana, Varadero, Cienfuegos, Santa Clara, Camagüey and Holguín. Westjet and the Panamanian carrier COPA Airlines also operate regular direct services from Toronto to Cuban airports. Air Transat, Skyservice and Sunwing Airlines fly direct chartered flights from all over Canada to a number of Cuban airports.

Flights from Australia and New Zealand

There are no direct flights from Australasia to Cuba. The most easily available route **from Australia** is via Toronto with Air Canada. A trip **from New Zealand** will involve a stopover in either Canada, South America or Europe.

Getting around

Though there is a reliable, good-value long-distance bus service, public
transport in Cuba is generally slow, complicated and subject to frequent cancellations and delays. Getting around the country efficiently means using buses, long-distance taxis or planes and, within cities, taxis in their myriad forms.

By bus

Given the relatively low percentage of car owners, Cuba's **buses** – known as *guaguas*, or omnibuses when referring to long-distance services – are at the heart of everyday Cuban life and by far the most commonly used form of transport, both within cities and for interprovincial journeys.

Interprovincial buses

The long-established **Víazul** service (Wviazul.com) connects all of the mainland provincial capitals and a number of smaller, touristy cities like Trinidad and Baracoa. In general, the service is reliable and though some routes only function sporadically, notably those to the northern cays in Villa Clara and the Jardines del Rey in Ciego de Ávila, it's one of the two quickest, most reliable and most hassle-free ways to get about the country independently – the other is in long-distance taxis (see page 30).

Buses are equipped with air-conditioning, occasionally usable toilets and, in some cases, TV sets. They can get very cold, so remember to take a sweater with you; it's also worth bringing your own toilet paper. **Booking tickets** can be complicated and the process often changes; best to ask at a travel agent like Havanatur or Cubatur (see page 34) or the official tourist information centre, Infotur (see page 60). Demand often outstrips supply, so to guarantee a seat you should buy tickets from the station at least 24hr before departure or a week in advance if booking online (and remember to print tickets). It's possible, though unadvisable, to book a seat on the day, but you'll probably have to wait till the bus arrives to see if there's space. Havana to Santiago; children free, under-12s half price.

The **Conectando Cuba** service, whose buses are marked with the **Transtur logo**, currently only runs along routes connecting Havana, Cienfuegos and

Havana – the service to and from Viñales is currently suspended with no indication of whether it will be reinstated or not. It differs from Víazul in that it picks you up and drops you off at hotels in the cities and towns it serves. While this means you avoid the hassle and expense of getting to and from the bus stations, it also means journey times can be much longer, as buses make more stops picking up passengers, especially in Havana where there could be stops at up to a dozen hotels. You can buy **tickets** at Cubanacán no later than noon on the day before travel (no tickets are available on the day of travel), and you can specify the hotel from which you want to be picked up – note that it needn't be a hotel you're actually staying in.

US LAW AND TRAVEL TO CUBA

US citizens travelling to Cuba, no matter how they get there, must ensure their trip falls under at least one of the **twelve categories of authorized travel** as outlined by the Office of Foreign Assets Control (OFAC), an agency of the US Treasury Department. Travelling for "tourist activities" is not legally permitted. The categories, which are defined under the terms of a "licence to travel", as described in detail on the US Treasury Department website (🅦 treasury. gov), include travelling for educational, journalistic, diplomatic or religious purposes. The law was changed in November 2017 to prohibit independent travellers from using the "people-to-people" category (though this can still be used by people travelling with a group or tour). Despite this, what these kinds of trips look like in practice is becoming increasingly blurry. At the time of writing, the Biden administration announced "measures to support the Cuban people" which may impact travel regulations – be sure to check for updates (see page 56).

TRAVEL LICENCES

There are two categories of licence: general and specific. Almost everyone now travels under the terms of a **general licence** for which, confusingly, no application is necessary. However, you are expected to keep a record and collect evidence of what you do in Cuba, ensuring that it complies with the terms of the licence. If you are travelling within the "people-to-people" educational travel category and therefore with a tour operator that itself has permission to take groups to Cuba under the terms of the licence, travelling with them is considered evidence enough that your trip complies with the rules. There are now innumerable tour operators of this kind (see page 34). While as of November 2017 independent travellers can no longer use the same category, they may use any of the other 11 categories. "Support for the Cuban people" is often considered the most appropriate. The main points to note are that you must avoid any transactions with military-owned businesses (including hotels) and that you must actively engage with "supporting" the Cuban people. Such activities might include visiting independent museums, staying in *casas particulares*, taking a dance class and discussing Cuban society with locals. Some independent travel does still require a **specific licence**, which means completing an application form and sending supporting documentation to the Office of Foreign Assets Control (US Department of the Treasury, Treasury Annex, 1500 Pennsylvania Ave. NW, Washington, DC 20220; ☎ 202 622 2480). You can find out more and get the latest rules and definitions, which have changed a number of times over the last couple of years, on the Cuba Sanctions pages of the Treasury's website (🅦 treasury.gov). All US visitors to Cuba will also need a **visa** from the Cuban Embassy (see page 57)..

TRAVELLING WITHOUT A LICENCE

For US citizens, travelling to Cuba without adhering to the terms of a travel licence is **illegal**, whether you fly direct or via another country. Some travellers still do try to bypass the licence system by travelling via Canada, Mexico or other countries and buying **tourist cards** (see page 56) in those destinations to meet Cuban entry requirements, just like citizens of any other country. However, Cuban immigration officials, who previously obligingly stamped only the potentially incriminating and disposable tourist cards, now routinely stamp the passports themselves on entry to and departure from the country. Technically, the penalty for travelling without a licence is a fine of up to US$250,000 and a possible prison sentence.

Local bus services

While large numbers of foreign travellers use long-distance buses, very few use **local buses** as a means of getting around the country's towns and cities. The almost complete lack of information at bus stops, absence of timetables and the overcrowding are more than enough to persuade most visitors to stay well away.

The only written **information** you will find at a bus stop is the numbers of the buses that stop there (and sometimes not even that). The front of the bus will tell you its final destination, but for any more detail you'll have to ask. Once you know which bus you want, you need to mark your place in the queue, which may not even appear to exist. The unwritten rule is to ask aloud who the last person is; so, for example, to queue for bus #232 you should shout *"¿Ultima persona para la 232?"* When the bus finally pulls up, make sure you have change.

Camiones

Supplementing the bus system are large numbers of converted trucks – *camiones* – which tend to run along relatively short routes between towns and within provinces. Aimed squarely at Cubans, they are nevertheless an official part of the public transport system and even have their own timetables at some bus stations, where most of them gather unless there is another transport hub in town. Be aware that not all drivers allow non-Cubans on board.

By taxi

Taxis are one of the most popular expressions of private enterprise in Cuba and it sometimes seems that merely owning a car qualifies a Cuban as a taxi driver. There are plenty of state-run and even greater numbers of privately-owned taxis. Though there are no visible characteristics to distinguish between the two, neither have meters. Almost all the American classics in Cuba, popularly referred to as *almendrones*, or sometimes *maquinas*, are used as taxis or by tour agencies in a similar capacity.

Local colectivos

Communal taxis, or **taxis colectivos**, taxis operating within towns and cities, are more like bus services than regular taxis. They are usually privately-owned vehicles, though there are some state-run *colectivos*, and generally they run along **specific routes**. There is no official mark or sign used to distinguish a *taxi colectivo* from the other kinds of taxi, or the route which it is operating along, but they are almost always classic American cars, whose larger capacities

are ideally suited to this kind of service. If you see an old American car packed with passengers, it's most likely a *colectivo* – to catch a ride and find out where it's going you'll need to flag it down – destinations are not displayed. There are fixed **fares** for most routes. You may find it hard to flag down a *colectivo* if you're carrying a lot of luggage as drivers want to pack their cars with people, not suitcases.

Long-distance taxis and colectivos

Arriving at any Víazul bus station in the country you will be greeted by taxi drivers offering to take you wherever you are going for the same price as the Víazul ticket. Though sometimes you will need to negotiate a little, these offers are usually reliable, particularly if there are several of you travelling in the same direction. These are often excellent alternatives to the bus and, depending on the car, might well get you to your destination quicker. Make sure you see the car you will be travelling in before you finalize the deal with the driver, as they sometimes park older less reliable models out of sight.

Some long-distance taxis are *colectivos* and in most towns and cities they also congregate at the bus station, though if there are separate stations for Víazul buses and the Cubans-only Omnibus Nacionales buses they tend to gather at the latter, while in some cities, such as Santa Clara, there are **long-distance taxi** stations. Drivers tend to wait with their car at the start of their route and shout out their final destination. Like the local equivalents, most long-distance *colectivos* operate along fixed routes, usually within a province (though there are interprovincial routes too) and charge fixed fares.

Tourist taxis

Though by no means exclusively for tourists, the official metered state taxis are usually referred to as **tourist taxis** (or *turistaxis*), and are often modern Japanese and European cars as opposed to old American or Russian ones. Though most state taxis have a **meter**, many taxi drivers do not use them, not always for legitimate reasons. There are several other kinds of state-run taxis, many of them Ladas, but they are rarely used by foreign visitors and less likely still to stop for you if you're obviously not Cuban.

Private taxis

Some classic American cars (*almendrones*) function as straightforward taxis known as *taxis particulares*, literally **private taxis.** The type of car used in this way varies more than the *colectivos* and are as likely to be old Russian and Eastern European cars as American classics. These are the minicabs of Cuba, not neces-

---

HITCHHIKING

Hitching a lift is as common in Cuba as catching a bus, and is the main form of transport for some Cubans. The petrol shortages that followed the collapse of trade with the former Soviet Union in the early 1990s meant every available vehicle had to be utilized by the state, effectively as public transport. Thus a system was adopted whereby any private vehicle, from a car to a tractor, was obliged to pick up anyone hitching a lift. The yellow-suited workers employed by the government to hail down vehicles at bus stops and junctions on main roads and motorways can still be seen today, though their numbers have decreased significantly. Nevertheless, the culture of hitching, or **coger botella** as it is known in Cuba, remains, though drivers often ask for a few pesos these days. Crowds of people still wait by bridges and junctions along the major roads for trucks or anything else to stop. Tourists cannot hitch lifts themselves as any Cuban who transports a tourist must have a taxi licence to do so.

---

sarily cheaper than state taxis, and if you don't haggle the chances are you'll end up paying over the odds. The essential thing is that you **establish a price** before you start your journey.

Bicitaxis and cocotaxis

Bicitaxis (also known as *ciclotaxis*) are three-wheeled bicycles with enough room for two passengers, sometimes three at a squeeze. In use all over the island, there are legions of these in Havana, where you won't have to wait long before one crosses your path. **Fares** are not all that different from tourist taxis, but again, negotiation is part of the deal.

Less common **cocotaxis**, sometimes called *mototaxis*, are aimed strictly at the tourist market and offer the novel experience of a ride around town semi-encased in a giant yellow bowling ball, dragged along by a small scooter. **Fares** are, again, negotiable. They should be used with caution as they don't have the best safety record.

By train

At present, Cuba is the only country in the Caribbean with a functioning **rail system**, and although trains are slow (average top speed is 40km/hr) and subject to long delays and cancellations, they nevertheless provide a sociable form of travelling and a great way of getting a feel for the landscape as you journey around. You'll need your passport to **buy a ticket**, which, depending on which town you're in, you should do between an hour and five days before your date of departure, direct from the train station. (If you show up less than an hour beforehand, the ticket office will almost certainly refuse to sell you a ticket.) You cannot buy tickets online or by phone, only in person at stations.

The **main line**, which links Havana with Santiago de Cuba via Santa Clara and Camagüey, is generally reliable and quite comfortable, though it will prove less appealing if you fail to bring your own toilet paper. Most of Cuba's major cities are served by this route, and while there are branch lines to other towns and cities and a few completely separate lines, any service not running directly between Havana and Santiago will be subject to frequent delays and cancellations, and even slower trains. The state tacitly discourages tourists from using some lesser-used branch lines, from cities such as Cienfuegos and Sancti Spíritus, as standards are so much lower than on the mainline, and instead nudges travellers toward the more profitable bus services.

The quickest of the two mainline services, from Havana to Santiago, is known as the **Especial**. Sometimes referred to as the Tren Francés, it uses air-conditioned coaches imported from France, and offers two classes of seats. It leaves Havana once every three days and calls only at Santa Clara, Camagüey and Cacocum in Holguín province on the fifteen-hour journey to Santiago. An alternative service, the **Regular**, with no air-conditioning and just one class of seating, leaves more frequently, usually four or five times a week. The two most notable routes beside the mainline and its branch lines are the **Havana–Pinar del Río line**, one of the slowest in the country, and the **Hershey line** (see page 208), an electric train service running between Havana and Matanzas. Children under 4 travel free and children aged 5 to 11 travel at half fare.

By car

Given the infrequency of buses on many routes and the fact that some significant destinations are completely out of reach of the bus and train networks, it makes sense to consider **renting a car** if you intend to do a lot of travelling around. Though it's relatively expensive to hire a car, traffic jams are almost unheard of and, away from the cities, many roads – including the motorways – are almost empty, meaning you can get around quite quickly. That said, driving on Cuban roads can be a bit of an anarchic experience.

Renting a car

All **car rental firms** in Cuba are state run, making the competition between them somewhat artificial: the two principal firms, Cubacar and Havanautos, now operate more or less as the same company from the same offices. Internationally recognized companies like Avis and Hertz do not exist in Cuba, but there are plenty of privately-run online agencies, like CarRental Cuba (☎ 52 83 4721, Ⓦ carrental-cuba.com), acting as middlemen between the state firms and customers.

Havanautos and Cubacar have the largest number of rental points throughout the island, though the other major rental company, REX, generally has flashier cars. It's well worth reserving a car at least a month in advance if you can – especially if you want one of the cheaper models, which tend to run out fast. You make a reservation with any of the state agencies through Ⓦ transturcarrental.com.

All agencies require you to have held a **driving licence** from your home country (or an international driving licence) for at least a year and that you be 21 or older. You will usually be required to provide a **deposit**.

CAR RENTAL AGENCIES

Transtur Ⓦ transturcarrental.com.

Havanautos Ⓦ havanautos.com.
Vía Rent a Car Ⓦ gaviota-grupo.com.

Driving in Cuba

Driving in Cuba is hazardous and patience-testing. **Road markings** and **street lighting** are rare and usually nonexistent on side roads, neighbourhood streets and even motorways, while the majority of roads, including the Autopista Nacional, have no cat's eyes either. **Potholes** are common, particularly on small country roads and city backstreets. Take extreme care on **mountain roads**, many of which have killer bends and few crash barriers. **Driving at night** anywhere outside the cities is dangerous, and to mountain resorts like Viñales or Topes de Collantes it's positively suicidal. Bear in mind also that push-bikes are very common on most roads in Cuba and rarely have any lights of their own. Most Cuban drivers use their **car horn** very liberally, particularly when overtaking and approaching crossroads. There's a brief glossary of driving terms in this book's "Language" section (see page 467).

To add to the confusion, away from the most touristy areas there is a marked **lack of road signs** which, coupled with the absence of detailed road maps, makes getting lost a probability. On journeys around provincial roads you will almost certainly have to stop and ask for directions, but even on the motorways the junctions and exits are completely unmarked. Be particularly vigilant for **railroad crossings**, common throughout the country, with a

---

CAR RENTAL, SCAMS AND HAZARDS

The most common hidden cost when renting a car in Cuba is a charge for the cost of the **petrol** already in the vehicle; if you are charged for this, however, then logically you should be able to return it with an empty tank. In general, it pays to be absolutely clear from the start about what you are being charged for to avoid any nasty surprises on returning the car.

Tampering with the **petrol gauge** is another popular trick – it's sometimes a good idea to take the car to a petrol station as soon as you've rented it and make sure the tank really is full before setting off on a long journey. By the same token, if you want your deposit back you should check the car over thoroughly before setting off to make sure every little scratch is **recorded** in the logbook by the agent.

You may find that if you pay by **credit card** – widely accepted in all rental agencies – the agent will ask you to pay for a small part of the overall cost (usually the insurance or petrol in the tank) in cash, as this will be the only way they can cream anything off; though note that this "scam" won't necessarily cost you anything extra.

You should also be aware that all rental cars come with easy-to-spot **tourist number plates**, so there is no hiding from *jineteros* and street entrepreneurs on your travels. However, these plates make it far less likely that anyone will steal your car, as Cubans driving tourist cars are more likely to attract the attention of the police. The plates are less of a deterrent, though, to people stealing your wheels or anything you have left inside the vehicle, so be particularly careful where you park (see page 34).

RENTING CLASSIC AMERICAN CARS

On the whole, **classic American cars** can only be rented with a chauffeur, effectively as taxis, many from a state firm called **Gran Car**, part of the Cubataxi group, based in Havana (☎7 648 7338) and Varadero (☎45 66 2454). The easiest way to do this is to go direct to their well-established taxi ranks (see pages 115 and 192). Since liberalization of private enterprise laws, however, individual car owners can rent out their pride and joy as a legitimate business. The best way to track them down is online as advertising or leafletting is all but non-existent.

few actually sited on motorways. They are marked by a large X at the side of the road but otherwise you will be given no warning since there are no barriers before any crossings in Cuba. The accepted practice is to slow down, listen for train horns and whistles and look both ways down the tracks before driving across. Other things to look out for are permanently flashing yellow traffic lights at junctions, which mean you have right of way; a flashing red light at a junction means you must give way.

Petrol stations are few and far between (you can drive for up to 150km on the Autopista Nacional without passing one), and with no emergency roadside telephones it's a good idea to keep a canister of petrol in the boot, or at the very least make sure you have a full tank before any long journeys. Petrol stations are manned by pump attendants and tipping is common practice.

Major roads

Cuba's principal **motorway**, the **Autopista Nacional**, is split into two sections: the shorter one runs between Havana and the provincial capital of Pinar del Río and is marked on maps as the **A4**; the longer section between Havana and the eastern edge of Sancti Spíritus province is shown on maps as the **A1**. However, both are referred to simply as *el autopista*, literally "the motorway". The **speed limit** on the Autopista Nacional is 100km/hr.

The main alternative route for most long-distance journeys is the two-lane **Carretera Central**, marked on maps as **CC** – an older, more congested road running the entire length of the island, with an 80km/hr **speed limit**. This tends to be a more scenic option, which is just as well, as you can spend hours stuck behind slow-moving tractors, trucks and horse-drawn carriages. It is also the only major road linking up the eastern half of the island, and on a drive from Havana to Santiago de Cuba it becomes the nearest thing to a motorway from the eastern side of Sancti Spíritus province onwards.

There are more options for alternative routes in the western half of Cuba, where there are two other principal roads: the **Circuito Norte (CN)**, the quickest route between some of the towns along the northern coast, and the **Circuito Sur (CS)**, linking up parts of the southern coast. The Circuito Norte runs between Havana and Morón in Ciego de Ávila and is the best road link between the capital and Varadero, a stretch better known as the **Vía Blanca**.

By plane

Tip to tip, Cuba is 1200km (745miles) in length and given the relatively slow road and rail routes, **domestic flights** offer a temptingly quick way of getting around. Of the two state-owned domestic airlines, Cubana de Aviación operates the most routes. Almost all internal flights take off or land in **Havana** and there are very few cities or resorts that connect directly to anywhere other than the capital, though you can fly direct from Varadero to Cayo Largo. Outside Havana the main **regional airports** are in Varadero, Santa Clara, Camagüey, Holguín and Santiago de Cuba, while Cayo Largo, Cayo Las Brujas and Cayo Coco all have their own airports handling flights specifically for the tourist industry.

Cuban airlines have had a **poor safety record** over the last couple of decades. Many domestic routes use planes built in the 1970s and 1980s, some old Russian Antonov aircraft with a capacity of about fifty passengers. A crash in May 2018 resulted in several passenger and crew fatalities, and the Cuban authorities responded by suspending all Cubana de Aviación internal flights. These have since resumed, along with several inter-Caribbean routes.

DOMESTIC AIRLINES

Aerogaviota Ⓦ aerogaviota.com.
Cubana de Aviación Ⓦ cubana.cu.

By bike

Cycling tours are very popular in Cuba. However, though basic Chinese bikes are a common sight in all towns and cities, cycling for recreation or sport is

PARKING

Car parks with meters are non-existent in Cuba, and car parks themselves, outside of Havana, are few and far between. In the capital, there are a significant number of state- and privately-run car parks, the latter often makeshift affairs, sometimes in the ruins of old buildings – you could easily pass one without realizing it. Most of the large and luxurious hotels have their own car parks and they are often prepared to let non-guests use them if there's room.

Cuban car parks are always manned by **attendants**, to whom users pay a fee. A couple of pesos are usually enough to cover a nightshift, but it makes sense to establish a price beforehand and to find out when the attendant's shift ends. If the car park is particularly crowded you may be asked to leave your keys in the event that your car needs to be moved to allow another driver out.

If you're staying in a *casa particular* or a smaller hotel, it's a good idea to ask where you can and should park your vehicle. Leaving it on the street is of course an option, but bear in mind that few (if any) car rental firms in Cuba offer insurance covering the cost of your wheels if they are stolen – a distinct possibility if you leave your car unattended overnight. Furthermore, the police have a tendency to look less favourably on any theft or damage to a vehicle if it is left anywhere other than a garage or a car park. At the very least you should look for someone who will watch your car for a fee; in most places even remotely touristy there will usually be someone in the habit of doing just that.

not particularly popular among Cubans themselves. There are no proper cycling shops but privately-run bike rental agencies are beginning to appear, while a few hotels also rent out bicycles. On the other hand, there are makeshift bicycle repair workshops all over the place and you'll rarely have to travel far within the cities before coming across what is known in Cuba as a *ponchera*.

The most straightforward long-distance cycling opportunities for visitors are **prepackaged cycling tours**. Several of the national tour operators offer *cicloturismo* packages, but you're generally better off booking with a foreign company. McQueen's Island Tours (𝕎 macqueens.com) is an experienced operator, and are also the best equipped agency when it comes to **renting bikes in Cuba** for independent touring – though as with touring packages, you'll need to book your bike in advance. McQueen's has an office in the Kohly district of Havana and rents out mountain bikes and hybrids.

If you do intend to cycle in Cuba it's worth bringing your own padlock, as they are rarely supplied with rental bikes and are difficult to find for sale. Most Cubans leave their bikes in the commonplace *parqueos de ciclos*, located inside houses, ruined buildings or sometimes in outdoor spaces, where the owner will look after your bike for a peso or two until you get back.

Also worth packing if cycling around Cuba independently is a copy of the excellent *Bicycling Cuba* by Wally and Barbara Smith.

AGENTS AND OPERATORS IN CUBA

Cubamar Viajes ☎ 7 833 2523. One of the smaller operators, responsible for running most of the country's *campismos*, offers some of its own unique off-the-beaten-track tours including cycling, trekking and birdwatching.

Cubanacán 𝕎 viajescubanacan.cu. Among the largest tourism entities in the country, Cubanacán has its fingers in almost every aspect of the tourist industry and has a suitably impressive portfolio of organized excursions and tours.

Cubatur 𝕎 cubatur.cu. One of the most comprehensive programmes of excursions, with offices and *buros de turismo* all over the country; has the best website of all the tour operators, too.

Gaviota Tours 𝕎 gaviotahotels.com/en/cuba-trips. With jeep and truck safaris in Matanzas province, or a helicopter trip from Havana to Cayo Levisa, Gaviota can provide something a little different as well as the more run-of-the-mill day-trips.

Havanatur 𝕎 havanatur.cu. Featuring offices all over Latin America, Europe and Canada, Havanatur is the only national Cuban travel agent that comes with an international reputation. Wide range of excursions and tours in every corner of the country. Those interested in bird watching should contact for Edelso (✉ edelso@nauta.cu) at Havanatur who is an expert in nature tourism. He also specialises in city tours.

Paradiso 𝕎 paradisoonline.com. Specialists in "turismo cultural". In addition to historically and culturally oriented excursions, Paradiso provides music and dance classes, and stages special events such as music festivals.

Trinidad Travels ✉ trinidadtravels@gmail.com. One of the best privately run travel agents. As well as assistance with every aspect of visiting Cuba, it offers tours all over the country, and can tailor them to individual tastes in a way the state-run agencies can't.

Accommodation

Broadly speaking, accommodation in Cuba falls into two types: hotels and *casas particulares* – literally "private houses". The hotels themselves divide into two relatively distinct groups: those run by wholly Cuban-owned chains, which are therefore state-run and -owned; and those run by international chains.

Cuban hotel chains

The principal **Cuban-owned chains** run most of the hotels in the country's cities and towns, and a fair few at beach resorts, particularly in Varadero. With any state hotel, knowing which hotel chain it belongs to will give you a fairly decent idea of what to expect, though in general the star ratings that the Cuban state assigns to its own hotels are very generous and may not tally with your experience of international ratings. **Islazul** (Ⓦislazulhotels.com) operates most of the budget hotels, which are generally poorly maintained, sometimes with broken fixtures and fittings, leaky and noisy air-conditioning units and mediocre food. They compare very unfavourably with *casas particulares*, and usually cost at least twice as much. **Cubanacán** (Ⓦhotelescubanacan.com) runs the mid-priced options, but some of their hotels (particularly the excellent Encanto-branded establishments) are better

---

ACCOMMODATION PRICES

All accommodation listed in this guide has been coded into four categories, with prices based on the cost of a standard double room per night in high season – November to mid-March. During low season, generally June and July, some hotels lower their prices by roughly 10–25 percent. Advance online booking for hotels will often secure a significantly lower price, too.

$\bar{\underline{\$}}$ – under $1500 CUP
$\bar{\underline{\$\$}}$ – $1500–$3000 CUP
$\bar{\underline{\$\$\$}}$ – $3000–$6000 CUP
$\bar{\underline{\$\$\$\$}}$ – over $6000 CUP

---

than the more expensive chains; Cubanacán is also responsible for most of the new or recently renovated hotels in the provinces, making them fairly dependable. The **Gran Caribe** (Ⓦgrancaribehotels.com) and military-owned **Gaviota** (Ⓦgaviota-grupo.com) portfolios consist mainly of large, supposedly more upmarket hotels, most of which are past their best but still offer a stay in a prestigious building or a prime location. **Habaguanex** (Ⓦhabaguanexhotels.com) hotels, which only exist in Havana and which became a subsidiary of Gaviota in 2017, are the most reliably attractive and well-appointed state-run places, almost

---

ADDRESSES

Most **addresses** in Cuba indicate both the street on which the building is found and the two streets which it is between. For example, the address of a building on Avenida de Bélgica between the streets Obispo and Obrapía would be written Avenida de Bélgica e/ Obispo y Obrapía, e/ being an abbreviation of *entre* (meaning between). If a building is on a corner, then the abbreviation esq. (short for *esquina*) is used. So the address of a building on the corner of Avenida de Bélgica and Obispo would appear as Avenida de Bélgica esq. Obispo. You may also see this written as Avenida de Bélgica y Obispo. Occasionally, you will see the word "Final" included in an address, which denotes a house or building that is at the end of a row on a given street. You should also look out for the use of the words *altos* and *bajos*, which indicate top-floor and ground-floor flats, respectively. When an address incorporates the Autopista Nacional or the Carretera Central, it may often include its distance from Havana. Thus the address Autopista Nacional Km 142 is 142km down the motorway from Havana. These distances are often marked by signs appearing every kilometre at the roadside.

Following the 1959 Revolution, streets in towns and cities throughout Cuba were **renamed** after people, places and events held in high esteem by the new regime. The old names continued to be used, however, and today most locals still refer to them. Where a name appears on a street sign it will almost always be the new name. Wherever addresses are written down they tend to also use the new name, though some tourist literature has now returned to using the old ones. Where an address incorporating a renamed street appears in this book the new name will be used, with the old one in brackets.

all of them in beautifully restored colonial buildings in the old town.

All these chains often offer very good deals via their websites and it's almost always worth **booking online in advance**.

Hostales

Run mostly by Habaguanex and Cubanacán, state-owned **hostales** are in fact boutique hotels, and often represent the best options in Cuba's provincial cities, though there are quite a few in Havana as well. Small, stylish and competitively priced when compared with standard state hotels, they are often housed in beautiful old buildings, and though rarely luxurious, they usually offer all the facilities you'd expect in a good-quality hotel, including decent restaurants and concierge services.

International hotel chains

Hotels operated by **international chains** are mostly found in Cuba's major beach resorts but there are a few in Havana and other very touristy places. Though non-Cuban does not always mean better, the more upmarket foreign-run hotels tend to offer a more attentive level of service.

Casas particulares

For many visitors, staying in Cuba's *casas particulares* is an ideal way to gain an insight into the country and its people. Many offer conditions far superior to the cheaper hotels and usually represent better value for money, while an increasing number are out and out luxurious. Their nearest equivalents are bed and breakfasts, but there is usually a stronger sense that you are staying in someone's home, most notably outside Havana. That said, a small number are more like boutique hotels, with as many as eight guest rooms, a clutch of staff and some truly impressive furnishings.

Casas particulares are found throughout Cuba – and they'll often as not find you, with **touts** (called *jineteros* or *intermediarios*) waiting in many towns to meet potential customers off the bus (see page 36). You can identify a *casa* by the blue insignia (shaped like a capital I or sideways H) usually displayed near

---

ACCOMMODATION TOUTS

The biggest drawback of staying in *casas particulares* is that you might have to run the gauntlet of the **touts**, also known as *jineteros* or *intermediarios*. Ostensibly, these are locals who work as brokers for a number of houses. In return they collect a commission, which usually gets added to your nightly bill. In tourist hotspots, groups of local *casa* owners greet every Víazul bus arrival with pictureboards of their houses. Most are perfectly legitimate, but be aware of touts among them who, in the event that you say you have already booked a place, claim that it is full or has closed down – it's always a scam.

Touts will often demand their commission from any *casa particular* to which they have taken customers – even when they have done little more than given directions. There is no way to avoid the attention of these people outright when you arrive in a town, and it can be incredibly frustrating when you feel besieged by people hassling you at every turn. There are, though, several ways to avoid falling prey to touts and thus having your accommodation bill increased unnecessarily.

- Always **book ahead** and **ask your hosts to meet you** at the bus station with your name on a sign – many *casa* owners do this anyway.
- If you are approached by a tout, **state that you have already organized accommodation**, but don't disclose where. Often touts will arrive at your chosen house first and tell the owners that they have sent you themselves.
- One of the best ways of finding a *casa particular* in another town is by **referral**. Most owners have a network of houses in other towns which they will recommend, and will often phone and make a reservation for you, or at the very least give you that house's card, though they may well collect a commission themselves for passing you on.
- If you need to ask for **directions**, ask for the street by name rather than the house you want to get to. Another trick to watch for is that *intermediarios* will pretend to direct you to the house of your choice but will actually take you to a totally different one, where their commission is better.

the front door; the same insignia in orange indicates that the owners rent out rooms to Cubans only.

Given that most *casas particulares* rent out just a couple of rooms, you should always book in advance. In popular areas demand always outstrips supply. Almost all houses have phones or mobiles and most have email addresses too, with a small but growing number also investing in a website. Booking ahead, however, is not always a guarantee that you will secure a room in the house of your choice. Some house owners will not tell you when they're full; instead, they will allow you to turn up, and then escort you to another *casa particular* from which they will usually collect a commission. There's little you can do to circumvent this; however, the practice is becoming less common. Two useful websites are Ⓦcuba-junky.com, a comprehensive directory of houses, and Ⓦcubacasas.net, which has been operating for many years and is generally reliable and up to date. Some package tours also offer homestays as part of their offerings and you can also book *casas particulares* through certain branches of Cubanacán, Havanatur and Cubatur in Cuba. As these options will be prepaid, your room will be guaranteed. Airbnb (Ⓦairbnb.com) also has a wealth of properties on the site, with many in Havana.

The law requires proprietors to register the names and passport numbers of all guests, and you are expected to enter your details into an official book as soon as you arrive. All payments are in cash, generally taken at the end of your stay.

Most *casas particulares* offer **breakfast** and an **evening meal** for an extra cost. Make sure that you are clear about the cost of meals and agree to the rate at the start of your stay. Drinks will also be added to your bill, including those that you drink with your evening meal. You'll also be charged for any bottled water (provided by the house) you drink.

Campismo

Often overlooked by visitors to Cuba, **campismos**, quasi-campsites, are an excellent countryside accommodation option. Although not prolific, all provinces have at least one, often set near a river or small stretch of beach. While a number of *campismos* have an area where you can pitch a tent, they are not campsites in the conventional sense, essentially offering basic accommodation in rudimentary concrete cabins. Some have barbecue areas, while others have a canteen restaurant. They are all very **reasonably priced**. Although foreigners are welcome, this is one accommodation choice where Cubans actually have priority, and *campismos* are sometimes block-booked in June and July for workers' annual holidays. For more details contact **Cubamar Viajes** (☎7 833 2523). Cubamar also handles the hire of camper vans.

Food and drink

While you'll often be able to eat your fill of simply prepared, good food in Cuba, meals here are generally not a gastronomic delight. Spices are not really used in cooking, and most Cubans have a distaste for hot, spicy food altogether. There is also a marked lack of variety and after two weeks in Cuba you'll be very familiar with the national cuisine. A few green shoots are poking through the culinary undergrowth, particularly in Havana, as a new wave of privately-owned restaurants shakes things up.

Fluctuations in the food supply caused by Cuba's economic situation mean that restaurants and hotels can sometimes run short on **ingredients**; equally, imports of some foodstuffs are restricted due to the US embargo. As a consequence, you'll find the same platters cropping up time and again, and it's rare to find a restaurant that can actually serve everything on the menu. Perhaps in compensation for this, portion sizes tend to be massive, so large in fact that those visitors on a tight budget would do well to order one main between two.

Local produce is usually fresh and often **organic**. There is little factory farming in Cuba, and the food is not pumped full of hormones and artificial fertilizers. Partly as a result of the constraints of the Special Period, Cuba was a pioneer in the use of ecologically sound farming, all of which means that the ingredients do tend to be full of flavour.

As a general rule, always carry enough money to pay for your meal in **cash**. Although some of the top-end restaurants take credit cards, using this form of payment results in problems (real or created) so often, that it's best avoided entirely.

EATING OUT PRICES

All restaurant and cafés listed in this guide have been coded into four price categories that reflect the typical cost of a two-course meal for one.

$\overline{\underline{S}}$ – under $200 CUP
$\overline{\underline{SS}}$ – $200–500 CUP
$\overline{\underline{SSS}}$ – $500–800 CUP
$\overline{\underline{SSSS}}$ – over $800 CUP

State restaurants and cafés

State restaurants and cafés differ greatly in quality – ranging from tasty meals in congenial settings to the simply diabolical. The other viable option for decent meals are restaurants in tourist hotels, although the food they serve is sometimes quite removed from Cuban cuisine – with pizza and pasta dishes figuring heavily. **Service** in any kind of state restaurant is often characterized by a somewhat strained formality, even in some of the cheaper places.

One of the most idiosyncratically Cuban **café chains** are the popular *Coppelia* ice-cream joints found all around the island. They are usually large, semi-outdoor affairs and dole out decent ice cream for a handful of pesos.

Paladars

Legalized by the state in the 1990s in response to demand from Cubans keen to earn money through private enterprise, **paladars** (*paladares* in Spanish) originally offered visitors a chance to sample good Cuban home-cooking in private residences, often the proprietor's house. A whole new wave of paladars have opened in the last few years following laws that lifted all kinds of restrictions on where and how Cubans could run them. This has certainly raised the bar in terms of quality, as chefs previously shackled by laws banning all kinds of foodstuffs are now free to flex their skills and ideas in public. Though most paladars still stick to Cuban cooking, there are signs of diversification too, with Japanese, Mexican and Swedish places becoming more popular. The most striking improvement has been in the dining atmospheres and environments, from authentic and stylish 1950s themes in spacious apartments to moody little grottos in old colonial buildings, though equally notable is the vast improvement in service and professionalism.

Although the menu will have few (if any) vegetarian options, paladars are more accommodating than state restaurants to ordering off the menu.

Cuban cuisine

Known as **comida criolla**, Cuban cuisine revolves around roast or fried pork and chicken accompanied by rice, beans and *viandas*, the Cuban word for root vegetables.

Popular national dishes include **ropa vieja**, shredded beef (or sometimes lamb) served as a kind of stew, prepared over a slow heat with green peppers, tomatoes, onions and garlic; **ajiaco** is another rich stew whose ingredients vary from region to region, but always includes at least one kind of meat, corn and usually some green vegetables; and **tasajo**, a form of fried dried beef. One particularly divine delicacy is **lechón**, or suckling pig, commonly marinated in garlic, onions and herbs before being spit- or oven-roasted. Meat and seafood is often cooked **enchilado**, meaning in a tomato and garlic sauce with mild chilli.

Invariably accompanying any Cuban meal are the ubiquitous **rice and beans** (black or kidney), which come in two main guises: **congrís**, where the rice and beans are served mixed (also known as *moros y cristianos*), and **arroz con frijoles**, where white rice is served with a separate bowl of beans, cooked into a delicious soupy stew, to pour over it. Other traditional accompaniments are **yuca con mojo** (cassava drenched in an oil and garlic sauce); fried **plantain**; mashed, boiled or fried **green bananas**, which have

---

AVOIDING HIDDEN COSTS AND EXTRA CHARGES

Overcharging, particularly in state restaurants, is widespread in Cuba. Common-sense precautions include insisting that your bill is itemized, asking for the menu with your bill so you can tally the charges yourself, and always asking to see a menu that has prices listed alongside the dishes.

Paladars are less likely to get their maths wrong than state-run places, but are prone to **adjusting their prices** according to the type of customer (although this isn't an unheard-of practice in state restaurants either). There's often not a lot you can do about this, but bear in mind that it's most likely to occur if you've been guided to a restaurant by touts, who collar a commission from the owners; or sometimes if you're seen pulling up in a state taxi, so try to get dropped off a short distance away.

It's common for waiters to talk you through the menu, as opposed to showing you a **printed menu**, and though this might simply mean that the food on offer changes daily, it can also be a sign that you're being charged more than other diners – at the very least clarify prices when ordering.

VEGETARIAN AND VEGAN FOOD

Vegetarianism does not come naturally to a country where cuisine is largely about the more meat the better. As a vegetarian your staple diet will be rice and beans, eggs, fried plantain, salads, omelettes and pizzas. Cubans often class *jamonada* (Spam) as not really meat and will often mix pieces into vegetarian dishes, so always remember to specify that you want something without meat (*sin carne*) and ham (*sin jamón*). There are however a handful of inventive vegetarian restaurants cropping up around the country with dishes including pumpkin tart, falafel and bean crêpes, and vegetarian paella putting in an appearance.

Vegans will find that they will be extremely limited in what they can eat in Cuba. You'll generally be better off in paladars, where ordering off-menu is easier and most places serve rice, black beans (though check to make sure they don't contain meat) and root vegetables such as potato and malanga.

a buttery, almost nutty taste; **boniato**, a type of sweet potato; and a simple **salad** of tomatoes, cucumber, cabbage and avocado, the latter in season around August.

Lobster, **shrimp** and **fish** make it onto a lot of menus and are usually superbly fresh. As a rule of thumb, the simpler the dish the better it will be. Grilled or pan-fried fish is usually a safe bet, but a more complex dish like risotto will most often disappoint.

Fruit is generally eaten at breakfast and rarely appears on a lunch or dinner menu. The best places to buy some are the *agromercados*, where you can load up cheaply with whatever is in season. Particularly good are the various types of mangos, oranges and pineapples, while delicious lesser-known fruits include the prickly green soursop, with its unique sweet but tart taste, and the mamey – the thick, sweet red flesh of which is made into an excellent milkshake.

Street food

Street food is all the result of private enterprise. It's usually sold from front gardens, porches, windows, driveways and street trolleys, and these places are invariably the cheapest places to eat and an excellent choice for snacks and impromptu lunches, usually freshly made and very tasty. Dishes to look out for include **corn fritters**, **pan con pasta** (bread with a garlic mayonnaise filling), and cheap **pizza** is a good basic option though quality varies wildly. **Tamales** are prepared from cornmeal, peppers and onions, then wrapped in the outer leaves of the corn plant and steamed until soft. The somewhat bland taste is enlivened with a piquant red pepper sauce served on the side.

It's wise to avoid home-made soft drinks, and ice cream, or at least ask if either has been prepared with boiled water (*agua hervida*) before sampling.

Meals

Breakfast in Cuba tends to consist of toast or, more commonly, bread eaten with fried, boiled or scrambled eggs. Fresh fruit is often served alongside. The better hotels do buffet breakfasts that cover cooked eggs and meats, cold meat and cheeses, fruits and cereals; while the majority of *casas particulares* serve an ample breakfast. It goes without saying you can expect to find *café con leche* – made with warm milk – on every breakfast table too. Most restaurants generally don't differentiate between lunch and dinner menus though lunchtime meal deals which will include a main, dessert and drink are becoming more common in the capital.

Cubans tend to eat their main meal in the evening, usually a hearty dose of meat, rice, beans and *viandas*, but restaurant and paladar menus are pretty much the same at any time of the day.

Sweets and snacks

As you might expect from a sugar-producing country, there are several delicious **sweets** and **desserts** that you are more likely to find on a street stall than in a restaurant. Huge slabs of sponge cake coated in meringues are so popular at parties that the state actually supplies them free for children's birthdays up to the age of 15, to make sure no one goes without. Also good are **torticas**, small round shortcake biscuits; **cocos** or **coquitos**, immensely sweet confections of shredded coconut and brown sugar; and thick, jelly-like **guayaba** pasta, like a Cuban quince, often eaten with cheese.

Grocery stores and supermarkets stock **snack foods** of varying quality. You might find that you have more variety (and better quality) in the larger ones where you can get decent Western potato chips, cookies, olives, canned fish for sandwich fillers and some fruit,

CLASSIC CUBAN COCKTAILS

The origins of many **cocktails** are hotly disputed, from where they were first created to their proper original ingredients. There are, nevertheless, undoubtedly plenty of bona fide Cuban cocktails. The five Cuban classics listed here appear time and again on drinks menus throughout the country.

• **Cuba Libre** The simplest of Cuban cocktails, no more than white rum with cola and a twist of lime, is second only in popularity to the *mojito*. It was given its name ("Free Cuba") in 1902 after the country had broken free from Spanish colonial rule.

• **Daiquiri** There are countless variations on the daiquiri but the classic – as popularized by *La Floridita* and championed by Ernest Hemingway, who regularly visited that renowned bar in Old Havana – is made with white rum, maraschino liqueur, sugar syrup, lime juice and crushed ice.

• **Mojito** The most famous Cuban cocktail, which came to prominence in *La Bodeguita del Medio* bar in Havana, is a refreshing combination of white rum, sugar, lime juice, soda water and mint.

• **Presidente** Gained fame during the years of US Prohibition in the 1920s and named in honour of Mario García Menocal, president of Cuba from 1912 to 1920. There are lots of recipes but the basic components are dark rum, curacao, white vermouth and a dash of grenadine.

• **Ron Collins** This is the Cuban version of the gin-based American Tom Collins, made here with white rum, sugar, lime, soda water and ice.

in addition to UHT long-life milk, breakfast cereals, sweets and chocolate.

Drink

If you like **rum** you'll be well off in Cuba: the national drink is available everywhere and is generally the most inexpensive tipple available. Havana Club reigns supreme as the most widely available brand, but also look out for Caribbean Club, Siboney and Santiago de Cuba; vintage editions of the latter are considered by many connoisseurs to have the edge over Havana Club. White rum is the cheapest form, generally used in cocktails, while the darker, older rums are best appreciated neat.

Apart from cigars and rum itself, Cuba's most famous export is probably its **cocktails**, including the ubiquitous **Cuba Libre**. Spirits other than rum are also available and are generally reasonably priced in all bars and restaurants, other than those in the prime tourist areas. The bottles on sale usually work out cheaper than in Europe.

Lager-type **beer** (*cerveza*) is plentiful in Cuba. The best-known brands are Cristal, a smooth light lager, and Bucanero, a darker more potent variety. These are usually sold in cans and, less commonly, in bottles. Beer on draught is less common in Cuba, although you can find it in some bars and all-inclusive resorts.

When drinking **water** in Cuba, it's a good idea to stick to the bottled kind, which is readily available

from shops and hotels – or follow the lead of prudent locals and boil any tap water you plan to drink (see page 41).

Canned **soft drinks**, called *refrescos*, are readily available, and in addition to Coke and Pepsi you can sample Cuba's own brands of lemonade (Cachito), cola (Tropicola, refreshingly less sugary than other cola drinks) and orangeade (the alarmingly Day-Glo Najita). Malta, a fizzy malt drink, is more of an acquired taste. Popularly sold on the street, *granizado* is a slush drink served in a paper twist and often sold from a push-cart; *guarapo* is a super-sweet frothy drink made from pressed sugar cane and mostly found at *agromercados*; while Prú is a refreshing speciality in eastern Cuba, fermented from sweet spices and a little like spiced ginger beer. If you are in a bar, fresh lemonade (*limonada natural*) is rarely advertised but almost always available.

Coffee, served most often as pre-sweetened espresso, is the beverage of choice for many Cubans and is served in all restaurants and bars and at numerous coffee stands dotted around town centres. Cubans tend to add sugar into the pot when making it, though you are usually able to order it unsweetened. Aromatic packets of Cuban ground coffee and beans are sold throughout the country, and it's well worth buying a few to take home.

Tea is less common but still available in the more expensive hotels and better restaurants – usually as an unsuccessful marriage of lukewarm water and a limp tea bag, or a very stewed brew.

Health

Providing you take common-sense precautions, visiting Cuba poses no particular health risks. In fact, some of the most impressive advances made by the revolutionary government since 1959 have been in the field of medicine and the free healthcare provided to all Cuban citizens. Despite all the investment, Cuba's health service has been hit hard by the US trade embargo, particularly in terms of the supply of medicines. It's essential to bring your own medical kit from home, including painkillers and any prescription drugs you use, as availability is limited in Cuba.

No **vaccinations** are legally required to visit Cuba, unless you're arriving from a country where yellow fever and cholera are endemic, in which case you'll need a vaccination certificate. It is still advisable, however, to get inoculations for hepatitis A, cholera, tetanus and to a lesser extent rabies and typhoid. A booster dose of the hepatitis A vaccination within six to twelve months of the first dose will provide immunity for approximately ten years.

Bites and stings

Despite Cuba's colourful variety of fauna, there are no dangerously **venomous animals** on the island – the occasional scorpion is about as scary as it gets, while the chances of contracting diseases from bites and stings are extremely slim. Cuba is not malarial and **mosquitoes** are relatively absent from towns and cities due to regular fumigation. They are, however, prevalent in many rural areas. Basic, common-sense **precautions** include covering your skin, not sitting out at dusk, closing windows at this time, and using DEET repellent.

There are occasional outbreaks of **dengue fever**, a viral infection spread by the Aedes mosquito. It can occasionally be fatal, though usually only among the very young or old or those with compromised immunity; reported numbers of deaths in Cuba have been in single figures, and serious cases are rare. There's no vaccine, so prevention is the best policy. Avoid getting bitten by mosquitoes, and be aware that though more common after dusk, mosquitoes can strike throughout the day. **Symptoms** develop rapidly following infection and include extreme aches and pains in the bones and joints, severe headaches, dizziness, fever and vomiting. Should you experience any of the above symptoms, seek medical advice immediately – early detection and access to proper medical care eases symptoms and lowers fatality rates to below 1 percent.

Cuba has also reported cases of **Zika**, a virus which is also spread by the bite of the Aedes mosquito (and to a lesser degree through sexual intercourse.) For most people it's a mild infection with few or no symptoms that may include aching joints, an itchy rash, headache and high temperature. It can be dangerous to pregnant women as it can cause neurological abnormalities in unborn children. As with dengue fever, there is no vaccine so prevention is the best policy.

A third viral infection spread by infected mosquito bites has also been reported in Cuba. **Chikungunya** is non-fatal and produces flu-like symptoms accompanied by intense aching in the bones which ease after a few days. Cases in Cuba are, however, rare.

More widespread wherever there is livestock, **ticks** lie in the grass waiting for passing victims and burrow into the skin of any mammal they can get hold of. Repellent is ineffective, so your best form of defence is to wear trousers tucked into socks. It is possible to remove ticks with tweezers, but make sure that the head, which can easily get left behind, is plucked out along with the body. Smearing them first with Vaseline or even strong alcohol leaves less of a margin for error. Minuscule **sand flies** can make their presence felt on beaches at dusk by inflicting bites that cause prolonged itchiness.

Food and water

Due to the risk of parasites, drinking tap water is never a good idea in Cuba, even in the swankiest hotels. Whenever you are offered water, whether in a restaurant, paladar or private house, it's a good idea to check if it has been boiled – in most cases it will have been. **Bottled water** is available in shops and most tourist bars and restaurants.

Although reports of **food poisoning** are few and far between, there are good reasons for exercising caution when eating in Cuba. Food bought on the street is in the highest-risk category and you should be aware that there is no official regulatory system ensuring acceptable levels of hygiene. Self-regulation does seem to be enough in most cases, but you should still be cautious when buying pizzas, meat-based snacks or ice cream from street-sellers. Power cuts are common and there is no guarantee that defrosted food is not subsequently refrozen.

Cholera

A cholera outbreak in eastern Cuba in 2012 caused three fatalities, while another in Havana in early 2013 was the country's biggest outbreak in decades; dozens of people were infected, but none fatally so. Since then there have been a handful of reported cases. The disease is carried by contaminated water or food and is characterized by sudden attacks of diarrhoea with severe cramps and debilitation. Cholera can prove fatal if untreated, but foreign visitors are at very low risk of contracting it.

Covid-19

At the time of writing, Cuba has reported over 8,500 Covid-19 fatalities, and 88% of the population have been double vaccinated with the country's home-grown vaccines, making it the smallest country in the world to successfully develop and produce its own. According to Cuban clinical trials, the vaccines are over 90% effective, and, after a surge in cases through summer 2021, infection rates are now extremely low.

Post-pandemic, Cuba opened to tourism on 15th November 2021. As of 6th April 2022, the country removed the requirements for visitors to have a Covid-19 vaccination certificate or a negative Covid-19 test. However, at the time of writing, visitors must still complete an online Health Declaration (Declaracíon Jurada de Sanidad) 72 hours prior to arrival, random PCR tests may be carried out at airports, and face masks must be worn in airports and while travelling by bus, taxi, and private hire vehicles. Be sure to bring your own supply of masks and hand sanitiser as they might not be easy to come by on the island.

Sun exposure and heat issues

Cuba's humid tropical climate means you should take all the usual common-sense precautions: drink plenty of **water**, limit exposure to the **sun** (especially between 11am and 3pm) and don't use a sunscreen with a protection factor of less than 15, and if you're fair-skinned or burn easily, no lower than 30. You may find sunscreen difficult to find away from hotels, so be sure to pack some before taking any trips into less-visited areas.

Hospitals, clinics and pharmacies

Don't assume that Cuba's world-famous **free health service** extends to foreign visitors – far from it. In fact, the government has used the advances made in medicine to earn extra revenue for the regime through **health tourism**. Each year, thousands of foreigners come to Cuba for everything from surgery to relaxation at a network of anti-stress clinics, and these services don't come cheap. There are specific **hospitals** for foreign patients and a network of clinics, pharmacies and other health services targeted specifically at tourists, run by Servimed (Ⓦ servimedcuba. com). The only general **hospital for foreigners**, as compared to the smaller clinics found in around half-a-dozen cities and resorts across the island, is the Clínica Central Cira García in Havana (see page 137).

If you do end up in hospital in Cuba, one of the first things you or someone you know should do is contact **Asistur** (❼ 7 866 4499, ✉ asistur@asistur.cu), which usually deals with insurance claims on behalf of the hospital, as well as offering various kinds of assistance, from supplying ambulances and wheelchairs to obtaining and sending medical reports. However, for minor complaints you shouldn't have to go further than the **hotel doctor**, who will give you a consultation. If you're staying in a *casa particular* your best bet, if you feel ill, is to inform your hosts, who should be able to call the family doctor, the *médico de la familia*, and arrange a house call. This is common practice in Cuba where, with one doctor for every 169 inhabitants, it's possible for them to personally visit all their patients.

There is no single **emergency number** for ringing an ambulance, but you can call ❼ 105 from most provinces and ❼ 7 838 1185 or ❼ 7 838 2185 to get one in Havana. You can also try Asistur's emergency Havana numbers (❼ 7 866 8339 and ❼ 7 866 8527).

Pharmacies

There are two types of **pharmacy** in Cuba: those for the population at large; and **Servimed pharmacies** aimed primarily at tourists, usually located within a *clínica internacional*. Tourists are permitted to use the antiquated national establishments but will rarely find anything of use besides aspirin, as they primarily deal in prescription-only drugs. The Servimed pharmacies only exist in some of the largest towns (as detailed throughout the Guide), but even these don't have the range of medicines you might expect.

MEDICAL RESOURCES

Canadian Society for International Health Ⓦ csih.org. Extensive list of travel health centres.

CDC Ⓦ cdc.gov/travel. Official US government travel health site.

Hospital for Tropical Diseases Travel Clinic UK Ⓦ thehtd.org/TravelClinic.aspx.

International Society for Travel Medicine US Ⓦ istm.org. Has a full list of travel health clinics.

MASTA (Medical Advisory Service for Travellers Abroad) UK Ⓦ masta-travel-health.com for the nearest clinic.

The Travel Doctor Ⓦ traveldoctor.com.au. Lists travel clinics in Australia, New Zealand and South Africa.

Tropical Medical Bureau Ireland Ⓦ tmb.ie

Money

In 2021 Cuba abolished its dual-currency system of the Cuban peso (CUP), which was used by Cuban nationals, and the Cuban convertible peso (CUC), which was used by tourists. Today, both nationals and non-nationals use CUPs, *moneda nacional* – the only legal cash currency in the country. CUCs were converted at the rate of 24 CUP/CUC, and a single official exchange rate of 24 CUP/USD.

The Cuban peso is divided into 100 centavos. Banknotes are issued in denominations of 500, 200, 100, 50, 20, 10, 5, 3 and 1. 1000 notes exist, but are rare. The lowest-value coin is the virtually worthless 1c, followed by the 5c, 20c, 1-peso and 3-peso coins, the last adorned with the face of Che Guevara.

Hard currency is king in Cuba, and wherever you are it always pays to have at least some money in **cash**. It's best to carry cash in **low denominations**, as many shops and restaurants simply won't have enough change. Be particularly wary of this at bus and train stations or you may find yourself unable to buy a ticket. If you do end up having to use a larger denomination note you will usually be asked to show your passport for security. The slightest **tear** in any banknote means it is likely to be refused.

Scottish, **Northern Irish** and **Australian** banknotes and coins cannot be exchanged in Cuba.

Credit cards, debit cards and ATMs

Visa and, to a slightly lesser extent, MasterCard **credit cards** and **debit cards** are more widely accepted than travellers' cheques for purchases. However, Maestro and Cirrus debit cards are not accepted at all. No credit and debit cards from US banks are currently accepted at all at the time of writing.

Although you'll generally be OK using cards in upmarket hotels, restaurants and touristy shops, when dealing with any kind of private enterprise, from paladars to puncture repairs, anything other than cash isn't worth a centavo. For most Cubans, plastic remains an unfamiliar alternative, and in most small- to medium-sized towns, cards are absolutely useless. Bear in mind also that power cuts are common in Cuba and sometimes render cards unusable.

The number of **ATMs** in Cuba is slowly increasing but there are still relatively few, and some of them only accept cards issued by Cuban banks. Among those that do accept foreign cards, very few take anything other than Visa. Most ATMs display stickers stating clearly the cards they accept. Those that take foreign cards are generally found in top-class hotels, branches of the Banco Financiero Internacional, the Banco de Crédito y Comercio and some CADECA *casas de cambio*.

All transactions (including cash withdrawals) involving a foreign credit or debit card in Cuba will be converted into US dollars, for which a commission will be charged. While some ATMs have a withdrawal limit, there is no such limit if you withdraw cash through a bank teller, but the commission for this type of transaction is sometimes around one percent higher. Credit cards are more useful for obtaining **cash advances**, though be aware of the interest charges that these will incur. For most cash advances you'll need to deal with a bank clerk.

Travellers' cheques

Travellers' cheques are less convenient in Cuba than they are in many other countries. Although they are exchangeable for cash in many banks and bureaux de change (*cambios*), subject to a commission charge which ranges from three to six percent, a significant number of shops and restaurants refuse to accept them. Complicating matters further, most banks and *cambios* require a receipt as proof of purchase when cashing travellers' cheques. Also, make sure that your signature is identical to the one on the original cheque submitted: cashiers have been known to refuse cash cheques with seemingly minor discrepancies.

Banks and exchange

Banking hours in Cuba are generally Monday to Friday 8am to 3pm, while a tiny minority of banks are open Saturday mornings. However, in touristy areas opening hours are sometimes longer for foreign currency transactions, referred to at banks as the "*servicio de caja especial*". Not all Cuban banks readily handle foreign currency transactions; those most accustomed to doing so are the Banco Financiero Internacional and the Banco de Crédito y Comercio, both with branches in all the major cities. Whether withdrawing money with a credit or debit card or cashing travellers' cheques, you'll need to show your passport for any transaction at a bank.

The government body CADECA runs the country's bureaux de change, known as **casas de cambio**, found in hotels, roadside kiosks and buildings that look more like banks. These establishments are where you can exchange foreign currency, and use a Visa card or MasterCard to withdraw cash. They have more flexible opening hours than the banks – generally

Monday to Saturday 8am to 6pm and Sunday 8am until noon.

Black-market salesmen often hang around outside *casas de cambio* and may offer a favourable exchange rate or, sometimes more temptingly, the opportunity to buy pesos without having to queue. Although dealing with a black-market salesman is unlikely to get you into any trouble, it could result in a prison sentence for the Cuban. You may also be approached by people on the street offering to exchange your money, sometimes at an exceptionally good rate. This is always a con.

Current exchange rates can be checked at ⓦxe. com.

Financial difficulties

For any kind of money problems, most people are directed to **Asistur** (ⒺAsistur@assistur.cu), set up specifically to provide assistance to tourists with financial difficulties, as well as offering advice on legal and other matters. Asistur can arrange to have money sent to you from abroad as well as provide loans or cash advances. There are branches in a few of the big cities and resorts (see Directory in respective chapters).

Other than Asistur, the firm to contact if you have problems with your credit or debit cards is **FINCIMEX**, which has offices in at least ten Cuban cities and can provide records of recent card transactions and shed light on problems such as a credit card being declined in a shop.

The media

All types of media in Cuba are tightly censored and closely controlled by the state. While this means that the range of information and opinion is severely restricted and biased, it has also produced media geared to producing (what the government deems to be) socially valuable content, refreshingly free of any significant concern for high ratings and commercial success.

Newspapers and magazines

There are very few **international newspapers** available in Cuba, and your only hope of finding any is to look in the upmarket hotels. Tracking down an English-language newspaper of any description, even in the hotels, is an arduous, usually unrewarding task and you're far better off looking online.

The main **national newspaper**, *Granma* (ⓦgranma.cu), openly declares itself the official voice of the Cuban Communist Party. The stories in its eight tabloid-size pages are largely of a dry political or economic nature with some arts and sport coverage. The international news has a marked Latin American focus. Articles challenging the official party line do appear, but these are usually directed at specific events and policies rather than overall ideologies. Hotels are more likely to stock the weekly *Granma Internacional*. Printed in Spanish, English, French, German, Italian, Turkish and Portuguese editions, it offers a roundup of the week's stories, albeit with a very pro-Cuban government spin. There are two other national papers: *Trabajadores* (ⓦtrabajadores. cu), representing the workers' unions, and *Juventud Rebelde* (ⓦjuventudrebelde.cu) founded in 1965 as the voice of Cuban youth. Content is similar, though *Juventud Rebelde*, in its Thursday edition, features weekly listings for cultural events and has more articles that regularly critique social issues.

Among the most cultured of Cuba's **magazines** is *Bohemia* (ⓦbohemia.cu), the country's oldest surviving periodical, founded in 1908, whose relatively broad focus offers a mix of current affairs, historical essays and regular spotlights on art, sport and technology. The best of the more specialized publications are the bimonthly *Revolución y Cultura* (ⓦwww.ryc.cult. cu), concentrating on the arts and literature, and the tri-monthly *Artecubano*, a magazine of book-like proportions tracking the visual arts. There are a number of other worthy magazines, such as *La Gaceta de Cuba*, covering all forms of art, from music and painting to radio and television; *Temas* (ⓦtemas.cult.cu), whose scope includes political theory and contemporary society; and *Clave*, which focuses on music.

US-based *On Cuba* magazine and website (ⓦoncubamagazine.com) is one of the best resources for up-to-date impartial news and views on Cuba and particularly Cuban–US relations and cultural projects. Many journalists are Cuban based and articles give a welcome insight into the intricacies, pleasures and anomalies of life on the island.

Havana Live website (ⓦhavana-live.com) is a good resource for of-the-moment news stories about the capital and beyond, plus listings and tourist information.

Radio

There are nine national **radio** stations in Cuba, but tuning into them isn't always easy, as signal strength varies considerably from place to place. You're most likely to hear broadcasts from **Radio Taíno** (Ⓦwww.radiotaino.icrt.cu), the official tourist station, and the only one on which any English is spoken, albeit sporadically. Playing predominantly mainstream pop and Cuban music, Radio Taíno can also be a useful source of up-to-date tourist information such as the latest nightspots, forthcoming events and places to eat. Its FM frequency changes depending on where you are in the country; in Havana, it's at 93.3FM.

Musically speaking, other than the ever-popular sounds of Cuban salsa, stations rarely stray away from safe-bet US, Latin and European pop and rock. The predominantly classical music content of Radio Musical Nacional is about as specialist as it gets; in Havana, it's at 99.1FM, but the frequency varies around the country.

Of the remaining stations there is little to distinguish one from the other. The exception is **Radio Reloj** (Ⓦwww.radioreloj.cu), broadcasting on 101.5FM, a 24hr news station on air since 1947, with reports read out to the ceaseless sound of a ticking clock in the background, as the exact time is announced every minute on the minute; and **Radio Rebelde** (Ⓦradiorebelde.cu), the station started in the Sierra Maestra by Che Guevara in 1958 to broadcast information about the rebel army's progress.

Television

There are five national **television channels** in Cuba: Cubavisión, Telerebelde, Canal Educativo, Canal Educativo 2 and Multivisión, all commercial-free but with a profusion of public service broadcasts, revolutionary slogans and daily slots commemorating historical events and figures. Surprisingly, given the hitherto strained relationship between Cuba and the US, **Hollywood films** are a TV staple, sometimes preceded by a discussion of the film's value and its central issues. The frequent use of Spanish subtitles as opposed to dubbing makes them watchable for non-Spanish speakers.

Cubavisión hosts a long-standing Cuban television tradition, the staggeringly popular **telenovela** soap operas, both home-grown and imported (usually from Brazil or Colombia). There are also several weekly music programmes showcasing the best of contemporary Cuban music as well as popular international artists. Saturday evenings are the best time to catch live-broadcast performances from the cream of the national salsa scene.

Telerebelde is the best channel for **sports**, with live national-league baseball games shown almost daily throughout the season, and basketball, volley-ball and boxing making up the bulk of the rest. As the names suggest, both **Canal Educativo** channels are full of educational programmes, including courses in languages, cookery and various academic disciplines.

The newest channel, **Multivisión**, began broadcasting in 2008 with a schedule of predominantly foreign-made programmes, including films, Latin American soap operas, National Geographic documentaries and US cop shows and comedies. It has become enormously popular with Cubans.

Officially, **satellite TV** is the exclusive domain of the hotels, which come with a reasonable range of channels, though you won't find BBC or VOA. Cuba's international channel is Cubavisión Internacional, designed for tourists and showing a mixture of films, documentaries and music programmes.

Festivals

Cuba has some of the most highly regarded festivals in Latin America, and events like the Festival Internacional del Nuevo Cine Latinoamericano continue to grow in prestige and attract growing numbers of visitors. There are also plenty of lesser-known festivals celebrating Afro-Cuban dance, literature, ballet and other arts, and a whole host of smaller but worthwhile events in other provinces. Catching one of these can make all the difference to a visit to a less-than-dynamic town.

Cuba's main **carnival** takes place in Santiago de Cuba in July and is an altogether unmissable experience. As well as numerous parades featuring dramatically costumed carnival queens waving from floats, and more down-to-earth neighbourhood percussion bands, several stage areas are set up around the town where live salsa bands play nightly. Also worth checking out are the smaller carnivals held in Havana and other provincial towns, such as Guantánamo in late August, which feature parades and boisterous street parties as well. Below are listings for the main festivals and a selection of smaller events.

JANUARY

Liberation Day (Jan 1). This public holiday celebrates the first day of the triumph of the Cuban Revolution as much as the first day of the year, with street parties and free concerts throughout the country.

Havana International Jazz Festival Havana (mid-Jan; ☏ 7 862 4938). Organized by the Cuban Institute of Music and Cuban jazz legend Chucho Valdés, this is the powerhouse event in the local international jazz calendar. It consistently attracts an excellent line-up: Dizzy Gillespie, Charlie Haden and Max Roach have all played in the past, alongside Cuban luminaries such as Bobby Carcassés, Roberto Fonseca and of course Chucho Valdés himself. Venues across the city include Teatro Mella, Teatro Karl Marx, Teatro Amadeo Roldan, Teatro América and the Casa de la Cultura de Plaza.

FEBRUARY

Feria Internacional del Libro de La Habana (Havana International Book Fair) Havana (mid/late Feb–early March). You'll find more books on Cuban politics and ideology at this citywide festival than you can shake a stick at, as well as new fiction and poetry, at the Fortaleza San Carlos de la Cabaña in Habana del Este (as well as at several bookshops across the capital). Events include discussions, poetry readings, children's events and concerts. Havana's Casa de las Américas also presents its literary prize during the festival period.

Festival del Habano (Cuban Cigar Festival) Havana and Pinar del Río (late Feb; ⓦ festivaldelhabano.com). A commercialized festival promoting the Cuban cigar industry, but still a great event for any cigar enthusiast with visits to cigar factories and tobacco plantations, a trade fair and plenty of tastings.

MARCH

Festival Internacional de la Trova "Pepe Sánchez" Santiago de Cuba (usually March 19–24). Commemorating the life of the great nineteenth-century Santiaguero trova composer José "Pepe" Sánchez, this festival fills the town's streets, parks and most important music venues with the sounds of acoustic guitars and butter-smooth troubadours.

APRIL

Festival Internacional del Cine Pobre Gibara (mid-April; ⓦ cinepobre.org). Small coastal town Gibara hosts the annual International Low Budget Film Festival. As well as public screenings in the local cinema and on outside projectors, there's a competition for fiction and documentary films as well as an assortment of captivating exhibitions, recitals, seminars and concerts. See page 343.

International Urban Dance Festival: "Old Havana, City in Motion" Havana (mid-April; ⓦ danzateatroretazos.cu). Rather than displays of breakdancing and body-popping, this festival, organized by the well-respected Retazos Dance Company, uses sites around Habana Vieja to show off contemporary dance choreography, with accompanying master classes, lectures, workshops and night-time jazz jams.

Bienal de La Habana (April–May; ⓦ bienalhabana.org). This month-long biennale focuses on Cuban, Latin American, Caribbean, African and Middle Eastern artists. It takes place in dozens of galleries, museums and cultural centres all over the city, such as Pabellón Cuba and the Museo Nacional de Bellas Artes. Though called a biennale, the event generally takes place every three years.

MAY

International Workers' Day (1 May). Known in Cuba simply by its date, Primero de Mayo is vigorously celebrated in this communist country. A crowd of around twenty thousand, waving banners and paper flags, march past dignitaries in front of the José Martí memorial in Havana, with similar parades taking place across the country, in a quintessentially Cuban celebration of national pride and workers' solidarity.

Romerías de Mayo San Isidoro de Holguín (May 2–8). A yearly pilgrimage, Mass and three-day celebration of performing arts in this eastern city. See page 338.

Feria Internacional Cubadisco Havana (mid to late May; ❶ 7 832 8298). A celebration of the local recording industry, in which Cuban musicians who have released albums in the preceding year compete for the title of best album. The finale is held at Salón Rosado de la Tropical Benny Moré.

JUNE

Festival Internacional "Boleros de Oro" Havana (late June; ⓦ uneac.org.cu). The siren song of bolero, a musical genre born in Cuba in the nineteenth century, draws singers from all over Latin America for this week-long Havana festival organized by UNEAC. Concert venues usually include Teatro Mella and Teatro América in Havana as well as venues elsewhere in the country.

Camagüey Carnival Camagüey (mid- to late June). With over thirty outdoor stages and party areas set up throughout the city, and big stars like Adalberto Álvarez and his Orchestra in attendance, this is one of the worthier provincial carnivals. See page 322.

JULY

Fiesta del Caribe Santiago de Cuba (first week of July). Santiago's week-long celebration of Caribbean music and dance culture takes place at the beginning of July, with free concerts and dance displays in Parque Céspedes and throughout the city. See page 390.

Carnaval de Santiago de Cuba Santiago de Cuba (mid-July). Cuba's most exuberant carnival holds Santiago in its thrall for the last two weeks of July, with costumed parades and congas, salsa bands and late-night parties. Official dates are 18–27 but the week-long run-up is often just as lively. See page 378.

Carnaval de La Habana Havana (late July to early Aug). Usually lasting a week or so, the Havana carnival is a jubilant affair with many of the country's top bands playing to packed crowds throughout the city, and a weekend parade of floats working its way along the Malecón.

OCTOBER

Festival Internacional de Ballet de la Habana Havana (late Oct to early Nov). Held in even-numbered years and presided over by Alicia Alonso and the Cuban National Ballet. Recent highlights have included performances by visiting Cubans Carlos Acosta and José Manuel Carreño. Performances take place at the Gran Teatro and Teatro Mella.

FESTIVAL AND LISTINGS INFORMATION

It can still be frustratingly difficult to find accurate **information** on festivals, particularly away from the resort areas. The UNEAC website (Ⓦ uneac.org.cu) is a useful resource, as are hotels, especially concerning events they are hosting. To get information on events that have no dedicated website or email address, contact the local branches of Infotur in relevant towns and provinces.

Although the free monthly **listings magazine**, *Cartelera* – only available sporadically in Havana from the larger hotels and branches of Infotur – carries information on a variety of Havana goings-on, it is far from comprehensive and many local events, particularly those organized principally by and for Cubans, don't get a mention. *La Papeleta* (Ⓦ lapapeleta.cult.cu) listings website has a good crop of forthcoming visual and performing arts exhibitions and events across the country. The site is clunky and slow at the best of times so you're better off checking it when you have a strong internet connection – possibly before you arrive in Cuba.

A welcome addition to the newsstands (and online) is the listings magazine *Excelencias*, (Ⓦ guiaexcelenciascuba.com) published by a collaboration of the main Cuban hotel chains and operators. This comprehensive, annually published title has information and maps for all types of accommodation, eating and drinking and is intermittently available at the higher-end hotels.

Granma newspaper has details of baseball games and is one of the only sources of television programming schedules, while *Juventud Rebelde* publishes cultural listings in its Thursday edition. Radio Taíno often broadcasts details of major shows and concerts as well as advertisements for the tourist in-spots. For less mainstream events the principal method of advertising is word of mouth, with posters and flyers rare.

Festival de Matamoros Son Santiago (mid- to late Oct). This three-day festival, a tribute to the Santiago de Cuba nineteenth-century musician Miguel Matamoros, draws music stars from around the country for concerts, dance competitions, workshops and seminars. While the focus is on son, expect to see many other traditional styles of music, including salsa.

Havana International Theatre Festival Havana (Oct–Nov; ☎ 7 833 4581). Excellent ten-day theatre festival showcasing classics and contemporary Cuban works as well as productions by theatre groups from Latin America, Europe and the US, with plenty of free street theatre in the city's open spaces as well.

NOVEMBER

Festival de la Habana de Música Contemporánea Havana (late Nov, Ⓦ musicacontemporanea.cult.cu). A festival of classical and chamber music staged in venues around the city, such as the Casa de las Americas and the Convento de San Francisco de Asís.

Baila en Cuba – Encuentro Mundial de Bailadores y Academias de Baile de Casino y Salsa Havana (late Nov; Ⓦ baila-en-cuba.de). A commercial event consisting of a week of concerts, workshops and classes showcasing and teaching Cuban dance styles. There's usually an impressive line-up of salsa bands too.

DECEMBER

Festival Internacional del Nuevo Cine Latinoamericano Havana (early Dec; Ⓦ habanafilmfestival.com). One of Cuba's top events, this ten-day film festival combines the newest Cuban, Latin American and Western films with established classics, as well as providing a networking opportunity for leading independent directors and anyone else interested in film. Information, accreditation and programmes are available at the *Hotel Nacional*, from where the event is managed. It's well worth paying the accreditation fee, which gains you access to all screenings, seminars and talks, and many after-parties.

Parrandas de Remedios Remedios, Villa Clara (Dec 24). An unusual and exuberant carnivalesque display of floats, fireworks and partying. See page 258.

Sports and outdoor activities

Cuba has an unusually high proportion of world-class sportsmen and -women but its sporting facilities, for both participatory and spectator sports, lag some way behind the standards set by its athletes. Nevertheless, you can catch a game in the national baseball, basketball and soccer leagues for next to nothing, while Cuba is endowed with countless outstanding scuba-diving and fishing sites. Hiking and cycling are both popular outdoor activities for foreign visitors but access to either requires some advance planning.

Baseball

For some outsiders, the national **Cuban baseball league**, the Serie Nacional de Béisbol, is not only one of the best leagues outside of the US to see world-class players in action, but represents a nostalgic version of the game, harking back to a time when the sport elsewhere – particularly in the US – wasn't awash with money and spoiled by celebrity and commercialism. Every province has a team and every provincial capital a stadium, most of which were built in the 1960s or early 1970s, and are relatively intimate affairs, with the exception of Havana's 55,000-capacity Estadio Latinoamericano. Free of mascots, cheerleaders, obtrusive music blasted through PA systems and any form of commercial distraction, all the attention is instead on the game and the skill of the players.

The national league adopted a new **season structure** in 2012. The first half of the season begins in late summer or autumn depending on the year (in recent years start months have ranged from August to November), as the sixteen teams play the first of their forty-five regular season games in an all-against-all contest. In March the top eight teams play a further forty-two games to qualify for play-offs, semifinals and finals in May. Traditionally, games start around 8pm during the week, but in recent years there have been plenty of 2pm and 3pm start times, both throughout the week and at weekends. Some stadiums have special seating areas and higher admission costs for non-Cubans.

Dominant **teams** over the last decade have included Ciego de Ávila, Industriales of Havana, Pinar del Río, Villa Clara and Santiago de Cuba. By far the best resource for anything relating to Cuban baseball, including season schedules and tournament information, is the website Ⓦ baseballdecuba.com.

Other spectator sports

The national **basketball** league, the Liga Superior de Baloncesto, generates some exciting clashes, even though most of the arenas are on the small side. There are only eight teams in the league, with Ciego de Ávila the dominant force over the last decade. The timing of the basketball season, played over a 28-round regular season followed by semi-finals and finals, is inconsistent from year to year but most recently has taken place between January and April.

There is a national **football** (soccer) league as well, with its season running from October to February, followed by play-offs and finals in March. Pinar del Río, Villa Clara and Cienfuegos have been the most consistently strong teams over the last three decades. There are very few custom-built football stadiums, with many games taking place in baseball stadiums or on scrappy pitches with very little enclosure.

Scuba diving

Cuba is a **scuba-diving** paradise. Most of the major beach resorts, including Varadero (see page 198), Cayo Coco (see page 308), Santa Lucía (see page 325) and Guardalavaca (see page 346), have at least one **dive centre**, with numerous others all over the island, including several in Havana (see page 137). The most reliable dive sites are generally off the south coast where the waters tend to be clearer, away from the churning waves of the Atlantic Ocean, which affect visibility off Cuba's northern shores. For the **top dive spots** head for María La Gorda (see page 178) in southwestern Pinar del Río, Punta Francés (see page 425) on the southwestern tip of the Isla de la Juventud, and the Jardines de la Reina (see page 314) off the southern coastlines of Ciego de Ávila. All three have been declared National Marine Parks by the Cuban government and as a result are protected from man-made abuses, particularly commercial fishing.

Diving in Cuba is worthwhile in any season, but during the hurricane season (June to November)

SPORTS LISTINGS AND INFORMATION

Finding out in advance about sporting events in Cuba is notoriously difficult. Most locals rely on word of mouth or are in-the-know fans, but for the foreign visitor there are very few publications carrying any useful **information**. The daily newspapers *Granma* and *Juventud Rebelde* usually have a page dedicated to sport, and you can sometimes garner information on forthcoming events from these. However, your best bet is to go **online**, even though Cuban sports websites are frequently out of service. The web-based sports publication *Jit* (Ⓦ jit. cu) is the official mouthpiece of INDER (National Institute of Sport, Physical Education and Recreation), and covers all Cuban plus some international sports.

and particularly in September and October, there is a higher chance that the weather will interfere and affect visibility. Among the **marine life** you can expect to see in Cuban waters are nurse sharks, parrotfish, turtles, stingrays, barracuda, tarpon, moray eels, bonefish, snapper and tuna. The best time to see whale sharks, arguably the highlight of any diving trip to the island, is in November, while in the spring the fish are in greater abundance. On the other hand, from late April to late May there is an increased chance of swimming into what Cubans call *el caribe*, invisible jellyfish with a severe sting, found predominantly off the southern coast of the island. To counter this, you can either wear a full wetsuit or simply make sure you dive off the northern coastline at this time of year.

The principal **dive operator** in Cuba is Cuba Nautica (Wcubanautica.travel), which runs most of the dive centres and many of the marinas. Other significant players are Gaviota (Wgaviota-grupo.com), which operates five marinas, including the Marina Gaviota in Varadero, and Cubanacán (Wcubanacan. cu). Most dive centres are ACUC certified, but a few are SSI or SNSI certified, and all offer courses accredited to one or more of these diving associations. There are countless opportunities for all levels of diving, from absolute beginners to hardened professionals, but the best place to start is in a hotel-based diving resort, where you can take your first lesson in the safety of a swimming pool.

Kitesurfing

Kitesurfing in Cuba is a rapidly growing sport. The last few years have seen the country's first clutch of kitesurfing schools and centres set up, though currently only the one in Cayo Guillermo (see page 311) is operating. The northern coast is where you'll get the best winds (commonly 14–20 knots). The premier months for wind are between November and April.

Fishing

Cuba is now firmly established as one of the best **fishing** destinations in the Caribbean, if not the world. Largely free from the voracious appetite of the huge US fishing market and discovered only relatively recently by the rest of the world, Cuba's lakes, reservoirs and coastal areas offer all kinds of outstanding fishing opportunities.

Inland, bass are particularly abundant, especially at Embalse Hanabanilla (see page 263) in Villa Clara, Embalse Zaza in Sancti Spíritus and the lakes in Ciego de Ávila province (see page 304), which between them provide the best locations for **freshwater fishing**. The top Cuban destination for **fly-fishing** lies south of the Ciego de Ávila and Camagüey coastlines at the Jardines de la Reina archipelago. This group of some 250 uninhabited cays, stretching for 200km at a distance fluctuating between 50km and 80km from the mainland, is regarded by some experts as offering the finest light-tackle fishing in the world. With commercial fishing illegal here since 1996, other than around the outer extremities, there are virtually untapped sources of bonefish and tarpon as well as an abundance of grouper and snapper. To get a look-in at the Jardines de la Reina archipelago, you will have to go through Avalon (Wcubanfishingcenters.com), a specialist foreign operator granted exclusive rights to regulate and organize the fishing here, in conjunction with the Cuban authorities. Fly-fishing is also excellent at the Peninsula de Zapata (see page 221). There are numerous other opportunities for saltwater fishing around Cuba, with **deep-sea fishing** popular off the northern coastlines of Havana, Varadero and Ciego de Ávila, where blue marlin, sail fish, white marlin, barracuda and tuna are among the most dramatic potential catches.

There is no bad time for fishing in Cuban waters, but for the biggest blue marlin, July, August and September are the most rewarding months, while April, May and June attract greater numbers of white marlin and sail fish. The best bass catches usually occur during the winter months, when the average water temperature drops to 22°C.

Other than the considerable number of foreign tour operators who now offer specialist fishing trips to Cuba, hotels and marinas are the main points of contact for fishing in Cuba. Before you start, you will need a **fishing licence**.

Equipment for fishing, particularly fly-fishing, is low on the ground in Cuba, and what does exist is almost exclusively the property of the tour operators. Buying anything connected to fishing is all but impossible, so it makes sense to bring as much of your own equipment as you can.

Golf

Its associations with the pre-1959 ruling classes made **golf** something of a frowned-upon sport in Cuba once Fidel Castro took power. The advent of mass tourism, however, has brought it back, and though currently there are only two courses on the island there are plans for more. The biggest, best-equipped and most expensive is the eighteen-hole course run by the Varadero Golf Club (see page 198), established in 1998. Less taxing are the nine holes of the

Club de Golf Habana (see page 136), just outside the capital, the only course in the country that survived the Revolution.

Hiking

All three of Cuba's mountain ranges feature resorts geared toward hikers, from where **hiking routes** offer a wonderful way to enjoy some of the most breathtaking of Cuban landscapes. Designated hikes tend to be quite short – rarely more than 5km – and trails are often unmarked and difficult to follow without a guide, while going off-trail is largely prohibited. Furthermore, orienteering maps are nonexistent. This may be all part of the appeal for some, but it is generally recommended, and sometimes obligatory, that you hire a **guide**, especially in adverse weather conditions. In the Cordillerra de Guaniguanico in Pinar del Río and Artemisa the place to head for is **Las Terrazas** (see page 155), where there is a series of gentle hikes organized mostly for groups. The **Topes de Collantes resort** (see page 284) in the Escambray mountains offers a similar programme, while serious hikers should head for the **Gran Parque Nacional Sierra Maestra** (see page 402), host to the tallest peak in Cuba, Pico Turquino. To get the most out of hiking opportunities at these resorts you should make bookings in advance or, in the case of the Sierra Maestra, turn up early enough to be allocated a guide, as independent hiking is severely restricted.

Birdwatching

With such a diversity of habitats – cloud forests, tropical rainforests, pine forests, mangrove forests and swamp forests; coastal thickets and savannas; freshwater vegetation and cactus shrub – Cuba is incredibly biodiverse. As such, it's also among the Caribbean region's most rewarding destinations for birders, with 354 species recorded on the island. 285 of these species are seen regularly, 149 breed here, and 26 of them are endemics, In addition, Cuba is home to a further 22 species that are endemic to the West Indies. Of the endemics, the Cuban tody, Cuban trogan, Cuban pygmy owl and the bee hummingbird (the world's smallest bird, no less) could be said to sit top of the must-see tree.

Throughout this Guide we've highlighted top bird-watching sites and what you can expect to see when you visit. For more information, the Club de Observardores de Aves Cubanas (Cuba Birders Club) Facebook group shares a wealth of detail on sightings and events. The friendly, informed members will also be able to recommend bird guides around the country. See also the Contexts chapter for the best books on Cuban ornithology and birdwatching in Cuba.

Cycling

Though cycling isn't particularly popular among Cubans, many tourists take to the saddle to explore cities and travel long distances across the country (see pages 25 and 33).

Culture and etiquette

Tipping

Many Cubans take jobs in the tourist and service industries for the tips that so significantly top-up their salaries. In general, it's appropriate to tip waiters, hotel cleaners and baggage carriers, car park attendants, toilet attendants and tour guides, but be aware of the differences between people who own their own business and those who work for the state. For example, a taxi on the meter means the driver works for the state and a tip is appropriate; most taxis don't have a meter as they are privately owned and paying your fare is enough. Similarly, the hosts at a *casa particular* wouldn't expect a tip, though if they employ cleaning staff a tip for them is always a nice gesture. **Service charges** of 10–12 percent are now fairly common in state restaurants and in smarter paladars.

BATHROOM BREAK

Public toilets are few and far between in Cuba, and even fast-food joints often don't have a bathroom. You're more likely to find bathrooms in hotels and petrol stations, but don't expect toilet paper to be supplied – carry your own. Train and bus stations usually have toilets, but conditions are often appalling. Cuban plumbing systems, be they in a *casa particular* or hotel, cannot cope with waste paper, so to avoid blockages remember to dispose of your paper in the bins provided.

LGBTQ+ travellers

Homosexuality is legal in Cuba and the age of consent is 16, though same-sex marriage remains illegal. Changes to the constitution to allow same-sex marriage were proposed in 2018 but were quickly dropped as a result of public pressure. There are still plans for its legalization through a Family Code amendment, with a public consultation on marriage equality law underway, and a referendum to be held in autumn 2022. Despite a very poor overall record on gay rights since the Revolution, there has been marked progress in the social standing and acceptance of gay men and women in Cuba since the early 1990s, and there are now significant numbers of openly gay men in Cuba, though gay women are far less visible. That said, police harassment of gay men and particularly of transvestites is still quite common. There is still a strong stigma attached to same-sex hand-holding or similar displays of sexuality, but freedom of expression for gay people is greater now than at any point since 1959. There are no official LGBTQ+ clubs and bars as such in Cuba but there are a few gay-friendly venues, particularly in Havana and Santa Clara.

Mariela Castro, the daughter of former President Raúl Castro, has emerged as a champion for gay rights in Cuba. As director of Cenesex, the National Centre for Sex Education, she has been instrumental in a number of initiatives designed to increase tolerance and awareness of LGBTQ+ issues. In 2007 Cenesex was behind the country's first official recognition and celebration of the International Day Against Homophobia.

There is no **pink press** in Cuba. The only magazine in which gay issues are regularly discussed is the rather academic *Sexología y Sociedad*, the quarterly magazine published by Cenesex.

Shopping

Though the range of consumer products available in Cuba's shops is slowly expanding, quality and choice are still generally poor – cigars, rum, music and arts and crafts remain the really worthwhile purchases here. The late 1990s saw the first modern shopping malls emerge, predominantly in Havana, but outside of these and a few of the grandest hotels, shopping comes with none of the convenience and choice you're probably used to.

That said, it's still possible to unearth the odd antique camera or long-since-deleted record, while others specialize in imported second-hand clothes. The most worthwhile are the **casas comisionistas**, the Cuban equivalent of a pawnbroker. These can be delightful places to poke around, frequently selling vintage and sometimes antique items, from furniture to pocket watches and transistor radios.

Cigars

With the price of the world's finest tobacco at half what you would pay for it outside Cuba, it's crazy not to consider buying some *habanos* (the term for **Cuban cigars**) while on the island. The national chain of **La Casa del Habano** stores accounts for most of the cigars sold in Cuba, with around ten outlets in Havana and lots more around the country, often in classy hotels; cigars are also sold in airports, gift shops and many of the less classy hotels, too. The industry standard is for cigars to be sold in boxes of 25, though you can find them in boxes of ten or fifteen, and miniatures in small tins too.

There are currently around thirty different **brands** of Cuban cigar. The biggest names and generally the most coveted are Cohiba, Montecristo, Partagás, Romeo y Julieta, H. Upmann and Hoyo de Monterrey, with Cohiba Esplendidos and Montecristo A the top dogs and rarest smokes. Like most *habanos* brands, these are all hand-made, but if you're buying cigars as souvenirs or for a novelty smoke, you'd do just as well with one of the less expensive, machine-made brands. The most widely available are Guantanameras. First-time smokers should start with a mild cigar and take it from there; it makes sense to try a machine-made brand given the lower cost, but of the hand-made brands Hoyo de Monterrey is relatively light.

If you leave Cuba with more than **fifty cigars**, you're theoretically required to make a customs declaration, and must also be able to show receipts for your purchases. Sometimes you may be asked to show receipts even for fewer than fifty cigars; if you can't, you risk having them confiscated. Although most travellers are not checked when leaving, you're obviously more at risk of having cigars confiscated if you've bought them on the black market (see page 53).

Rum

Along with cigars, **rum** is one of the longest-established Cuban exports and comes with a worldwide reputation. Although there are a few specialist rum shops around the island, you can pick up most of the recognized brands in any large supermarket without fear of paying over the odds. Rum is available in several different strengths, according to how long it was distilled; the most renowned name is Havana

Club, whose least expensive type is the light but smooth Añejo Blanco. The other, darker types increase in strength and quality in the following order: Añejo 3 Años, Añejo Especial, Añejo Reserva, Añejo 7 Años, Cuban Barrel Proof and the potent Máximo Extra Añejo. Other brands to look out for include Caney, Mulata and a number of regional rums, such as Guayabita del Pinar, from Pinar del Río, and the excellent Santiago de Cuba. The maximum number of bottles permitted by Cuban customs is six.

Coffee

First introduced to the island by French plantation owners fleeing the 1798 Haitian revolution, **coffee** is one of Cuba's lesser-known traditional products. It's easy to find and excellent quality, mostly grown and cultivated without the use of chemicals in the rich soils and under the forest canopies of the three principal mountain ranges. Supermarkets are as good as anywhere to find it, but there are a few specialist shops in Havana and elsewhere. The top name is Cubita, but there are plenty of others like Turquino, from the east of the country, Serrano, and even a couple produced under cigar brand names Montecristo and Cohiba.

Books and music

Bookshops in Cuba are generally disappointing, with a very narrow range of titles. Stock is often characterized by nationalist and regime-propping **political texts**, from the prolific works of the nineteenth-century independence-fighter José Martí to the speeches of Fidel Castro, and other titles unwavering in their support of the Revolution. Perhaps more universally appealing are the **coffee-table photography books** covering all aspects of life in one of the most photogenic countries in the world.

English-language books are few and far between, but two or three bookshops in Havana and at least one in Varadero and Santiago de Cuba have a handful of Cuban fiction in translation as well as foreign-language titles, usually crime novels and pulp fiction.

Some of the most comprehensive catalogues of **CDs** are found in Artex stores, the chain responsible for promoting culture-based Cuban products. Most provincial capitals now have a branch, and there are several in Havana. Look out also for Egrem stores, run by one of the country's most prolific record labels and sometimes stocking titles hard to find elsewhere.

Arts and crafts

One of the most rewarding Cuban shopping experiences is a browse around the arts and crafts – or **artesanía** – markets. Cuba has its own selection of tacky tailored-to-tourism items, but if you want something a bit more highbrow there are plenty of alternatives, like expressive African-style wood carvings, a wide choice of jewellery, handmade shoes and everything from ceramics to textiles. **Haggling** is par for the course and often pays dividends, but shopping around won't reveal any significant differences in price or product.

Look out also for the **BfC logo**, a seal of above-average quality and the trademark of the Fondos Cubanos de Bienes Culturales, shops selling the work of officially recognized local artisans. Artex shops also make a good port of call for crafts, though they tend to have more mass-produced items.

Antiques and vintage memorabilia

In recent years, with the expansion of private enterprise, Cuba's immensely rich bounty of **antique** and **vintage** furniture and memorabilia has come onto

---

SHOP SECURITY MEASURES

In any shop where the locals outnumber the tourists you should be prepared for some idiosyncratic **security measures**. Don't be surprised to be asked to wait at the door until another customer leaves, and don't assume you'll be allowed to enter carrying a bag – chances are, you'll have to leave it at a *guardabolso*, with some identification, to be collected afterwards. These *guardabolsos* are similar to left-luggage offices and are usually located at the entrance to the building, but sometimes you'll have to search them out. If you purchase anything, make sure you pick up your receipt at the cash till, as your shopping will be checked against it at the exit. It's also possible that your carrier bag will be sealed with tape at the till only to be ripped open when you get to the door so that the contents can be checked – ripping it open yourself will leave not only your bag but the whole precious system in tatters. Bear in mind that there are **no refunds or exchanges** on any goods purchased anywhere.

BLACK MARKET CIGARS

The biggest business on the black market is selling **cigars** to foreign visitors, with the average price of a box representing at least as much as the average monthly wage. If you spend any time at all in a Cuban town or city you will inevitably be offered a box of cigars on the street. Ideally you should ask someone you know, even just the owner of a *casa particular*; even if they don't have a direct contact, chances are they will be able to help you out – everyone knows someone who can get hold of a box of Cohibas or Monte Cristos.

SPOTTING FAKES

What makes a Cuban cigar a **fake** and what makes it **genuine** can be fairly academic, especially for smoking novices, and some fakes are so well made that it's difficult to tell the difference even once they're lit. If your cigars pass the following checks you'll know that you at least have some well-made copies.

- Genuine boxes should be sealed with three labels: a banknote-style label at the front, a smaller one reading *Habanos* in the corner and a holographic sticker.
- The bottom of the box should be stamped: *Habanos SA*, *Hecho en Cuba* and *Totalmente a mano*.
- A factory code and date should be ink-stamped on the base of the box.
- All the cigars in a box should be the same colour, shade and strength of smell.
- When the cigar is rolled between the fingers, no loose tobacco should drop out.
- There should only be extremely slight variations in the length of cigars, no more than a few millimetres.

---

the open market. Though still quite hard to track down, the rewards for doing so are some extraordinary collections of books, maps, ceramics, glassware and jewellery, as well as Art Deco furniture and all sorts of 1950s memorabilia, from postcards and magazines to cabaret coasters, glasses and swizzle sticks. Look out also for 1970s revolutionary posters and collectable 1990s Cuban baseball cards. You'll find the richest vintage pickings in Havana (see page 132) and Trinidad (see page 278).

Travelling with children

Beach and placid waters aside, Cuba is not a country with an ample stock of entertainment for children. But what the country lacks in amenities, it makes up for in enthusiasm. By and large Cubans love children and welcome them everywhere, and having a kid or two in tow is often a passport to seeing a hidden side of Cuban social life. Practically speaking you'll be able to find things like nappies in the department stores of bigger towns and some of the hotel shops, though the quality might not be what you're used to and you may not always find the size you need readily available. Baby wipes and nappy bags are less common so it's wise to bring your own. To get hold of baby food you may need to visit the larger supermarkets. The only milk widely available is UHT.

Make sure your **first-aid kit** has child-strength fever reducers, diarrhoea medicine, cold remedies, plasters, antihistamines and other medicines. These are available throughout the country but not always readily so and tend to be more expensive than at home. Plenty of child-friendly **sunscreen** is essential; the Caribbean sun is very hot, particularly during the rainy season (May–Oct). Remember also to bring lots of loose cotton clothing, plus a few long-sleeved tops and trousers to combat the brutal air-conditioning in restaurants and buses. It's also a good idea to pack a raincoat and appropriate footwear, as sudden downpours are common even outside the rainy season. Bear in mind that with limited **laundry facilities** you may be hand-washing many garments, so take items that are easy to launder and dry.

Public **toilets** are scarce in Cuba (see page 50), and there are few places with dedicated **baby-changing facilities**; hand-washing facilities can be patchy so antibacterial hand wipes are useful.

In terms of **accommodation**, children under 12 can stay for half-price in many hotel rooms and if no extra bed is required they may stay for free. Staying

CAPTIVE DOLPHINS IN CUBA

Cuba has a number of dolphinaria, popular among families with young children. There are serious concerns about the wellbeing of marine mammals like whales and dolphins being kept in captivity. Studies suggest that restricted space, limited social interaction, loud noises, lack of environmental enrichment and behavioural restrictions can contribute to stress, aggression, ill health and sometimes death in captive dolphins. Read up before you visit a dolphinarium on Ⓦ responsibletravel.com.

in a *casa particular* is a great way to give children a taste of Cuba beyond the tourist belt. Rooms often have extra beds for children and many households have pets and courtyards where children can play. However, be aware that most houses, even those with steep narrow stairs and high balconies, do not have child gates or safety restraints.

Eating out, children are made very welcome pretty much everywhere. Children's menus are on the rise but generally still scarce. Places with high chairs are similarly rare – most children sit on their parents' laps. Discreet breastfeeding in public is fine.

When travelling around Cuba with children, it's important to remember you'll often be dealing with long queues and sporadic schedules. Long bus journeys can be particularly exhausting and uncomfortable. If you plan on renting a car, bring your own **child or baby seat**, as rental companies never supply them and there are none in Cuba. Newer cars are fitted with three-point seat belts in the front and seat belts in the back. Poor-quality pavements make using a buggy or pram difficult, so it's a good idea to consider an alternative like a baby sling or backpack.

Travel essentials

Accessible travel

Away from the package holiday resorts, life for **travellers with disabilities** in Cuba is very tricky: there are very few amenities or services provided for people with physical disabilities; pavements are generally poor, paths uneven and dropped kerbs extremely scarce. Wheelchair users would do well to use a Freewheel attachment or similar to cope with the uneven terrain. Accessible toilets are more or less non-existent outside the resorts and public buses are not modified for wheelchair users, while the tourist buses do not have ramps. To get around, using a taxi is the best option, as accessible car hire is difficult to find. On the brighter side, Cubans are generally very helpful and accommodating. Many *casas particu-*

lares are located on the ground floor which makes access easier. It's worth calling ahead and asking for doorframe and passageway measurements to make sure that specialist equipment can be accommodated. Most upmarket hotels are well equipped for travellers with disabilities, each with at least one specially designed room and all the necessary lifts and ramps.

Costs

In general, Cuba is not a particularly cheap place to visit. However, with some considerable effort and a willingness to sacrifice some quality and comfort, it is possible to get by on a budget. Given the prevalence of fresh-food markets, street vendors and house-front caterers, the biggest savings can be made when buying **food and drink**.

You're unlikely to find a hotel room for less than the equivalent of $25, though some of the older, more basic hotels that cater to Cubans as much as foreign visitors may offer lower rates. Rooms in *casas particulares*, which are always doubles, range from around $270CUP to $1400CUP, though for long stays in some places outside the capital, you may be able to negotiate a lower nightly price.

If you travel by Víazul bus, expect to pay between $200CUP and $1500CUP – for example, Havana to Varadero is $200CUP, Havana to Trinidad $500CUP and Havana to Santiago de Cuba $1350CUP. Long-distance private taxis can sometimes work out cheaper than buses if you share them with three or four other travellers. The cost of **public transport** is more flexible within the towns and cities, where local buses cost next to nothing, though most foreign visitors use taxis or tourist buses.

Crime and personal safety

Crimes against visitors are on the rise in many Cuban cities, particularly Havana (including some violent crime), so it pays to be careful. That said, gun crime is virtually unheard of and murder rates are estimated to be way below those of most Latin American countries, though official crime statistics are kept under wraps by the Cuban government. In the vast majority of cases, the worst you're likely to experience is incessant attention from *jineteros*, but a few simple **precautions** will help ensure that you don't fall prey to any petty crime. While there's no need to be suspicious of everyone who tries to strike up a conversation with you (and many people will), a measure of caution is still advisable. You should always carry a photocopy of your **passport** (or the passport itself), as the police sometimes ask to inspect them.

The most common assault upon tourists is **bag-snatching** or **pickpocketing** (particularly in Habana Vieja and Centro Habana), so always make sure you sling bags across your body rather than letting them dangle from one shoulder. Unfortunately, bag snatches in which cross-body straps have been slashed are becoming more common; the ultimate self-protection is to carry no visible bag at all. Keep cameras concealed whenever possible, don't carry valuables in easy-to-reach pockets and always carry only the minimum amount of cash. A common trick is for thieves on bicycles to ride past and snatch at bags, hats and sunglasses, so wear these at your discretion. Needless to say, don't leave bags and possessions unattended anywhere, but be especially vigilant on beaches, where theft is common.

Other than this, watch out for **scams** from street operators. Never accept the offer of moneychangers on the street, as some will take your money and run – literally – or palm you off with counterfeit notes. Exercise extra caution when using unofficial taxis,

POLICE

The **emergency number** for the Cuban police differs from place to place, though ☏ 106 has now become standardized in most provinces; see Directory listings throughout the Guide.

particularly when riding in a cab where "a friend" is accompanying the driver. Although you're unlikely to suffer a violent attack, you may well find yourself pickpocketed. This is a particularly common trick on arrival at the airport, where you should be especially vigilant. Even if you are on a tight budget, it's well worth getting a tourist taxi into the centre when you're loaded with all your valuables and possessions.

Some **hotels** are not entirely secure, so be sure to put any valuables in the hotel security box, if there is one, or at least stash them out of sight. Registered *casas particulares* are, as a rule, safe, but you stay in an unregistered one at your peril.

At airports, thefts from luggage during baggage handling both on arrival and departure are a significant possibility, so consider carrying valuables in your hand luggage, using suitcase locks and having bags shrink-wrapped before check-in.

Car crime

Though car theft is rare, **rental-car break-ins** are much more common. Take all the usual sensible

JINETERISMO AND THE ESCORT INDUSTRY

As a general definition, the pejorative term **jinetero** refers to a male hustler, or someone who will find girls, cigars, taxis or accommodation for a visitor and then take a cut for the service. He – though more commonly this is the preserve of his female counterpart, a **jinetera** – is often also the sexual partner to a foreigner, usually for material gain.

Immediately after assuming power Castro's regime banned prostitution, which was rife. It was officially wiped off the streets, with sex workers and pimps rehabilitated into society. The resurgence of the tourist industry has seen sex work slink back into business since the mid-1990s; however, in Cuba this entails a rather hazily defined exchange of services.

In the eyes of Cubans, being a *jinetero* or *jinetera* can mean anything from sex worker to paid escort, opportunist to simply a Cuban boyfriend or girlfriend.

As an obvious foreign face in Havana, you will often be pursued by persistent *jineteros* and *jineteras*. Many Cubans are desperate to leave the country and see **marrying a foreigner** as the best way out; while other Cubans simply want to live a more materially comfortable life within the country and are more than happy to spend a few days or hours pampering the egos of middle-aged Westerners in order to go to the best clubs and restaurants and be bought the latest fashions.

Police sometimes stop tourists' cars and question Cuban passengers they suspect to be *jineteros* or *jineteras*, and *casas particulares* must register all Cuban guests accompanying foreigners (foreigners themselves are not penalized in any way).

precautions: leave nothing visible in your car – including items you may consider worthless like maps, snacks or CDs – even if you're only away from it for a short period of time. Furthermore, thieves are not just interested in your personal possessions but will break into and damage cars to take the radios, break off wing mirrors, wrench off spare parts and even take the wheels. To avoid this, always park your vehicle in a car park, guarded compound or other secure place (see page 34). Car rental agencies will be able to advise you on those nearest to you, or, failing that, ask at a large hotel. *Casa particular* owners will also be able to tell you where to park safely. If the worst happens and you suffer a **break-in**, call the rental company first, which should have supplied you with an emergency number. They can advise you how to proceed from there and will either inform the police themselves or direct you to the correct police station. You must report the crime to be able to get a replacement car and for your own insurance purposes.

Women travellers

Though violent sexual attacks against female tourists are virtually unheard of, women travellers in Cuba should brace themselves for a quite remarkable level of attention. Casual sex is a staple of Cuban life and **unaccompanied women** are often assumed to be on holiday for exactly that reason. The nonstop attention can be unnerving, but in general, Cuban men manage to combine a courtly romanticism with wit and charm, meaning the persistent come-ons will probably leave you irritated rather than threatened. If you're not interested, there's no sure-fire way to stop the flow of comments and approaches, but decisively saying "no" and avoiding eye contact with men you don't know will lessen the flow of attention a little. Even a few hours of friendship with a Cuban man can lead to pledges of eternal love, but bear in mind that **marriage to a foreigner** is a tried-and-tested method of emigrating. Aside from this, women travelling in Cuba are treated with a great deal of courtesy and respect. The country is remarkably safe and you are able to move around freely, particularly at night, with more ease than in many Western cities, and you should encounter few problems.

Emergencies

Should you be unfortunate enough to be robbed and want to make an insurance claim, you must report the crime to the **police** and get a **statement**. Be aware, though, that the police in Cuba can be surprisingly uncooperative and sometimes indifferent to nonviolent crime – they may even try to blame you for not being more vigilant. You must insist upon getting the statement there and then, as there is little chance of receiving anything from them at a later date. Unfortunately, the chance of your possessions being recovered is equally remote.

Following any kind of emergency, whether medical, financial or legal, you should, at some point, contact **Asistur** (☏ 7 866 5560, ☏ 7 866 8339 or ☏ 7 866 8920, ✉ asistur@asistur.cu), the tourist-assistance agency. It has branches in most provincial capitals and can arrange replacement travel documents, help with insurance issues and recover lost luggage as well as provide a host of other services. In the case of a serious emergency, you should also notify your foreign consul or embassy (see page 57).

Electricity

The **electricity supply** is generally 110V 60Hz, but always check, as in some hotels it is 220V, and in a significant number of *casas particulares* there is both. Plug adaptors and voltage converters are almost impossible to buy in Cuba, so if you intend to use electrical items from the UK or the rest of Europe, Australia or New Zealand, then you should, as a minimum, bring a plug adaptor and maybe voltage converter too.

Entry requirements

To enter Cuba, you must have a ten-year **passport**, valid for two months after your departure from Cuba, an onward or return plane ticket and health insurance. Though rarely checked, visitors may be required to present an insurance policy at immigration valid for the period of their stay in Cuba – if you do get checked and you do not have proof of insurance you may be required to purchase a Cuban health insurance policy. US insurance companies do not currently provide coverage for Cuba. You'll also need a **tourist card** (*tarjeta del turista*), essentially a **visa**. Although you can buy tourist cards from Cuban consulates outside Cuba, some tour operators, airlines and travel agents also sell them (or include them as part of your package) and you can purchase them online. Consulates can usually sell tourist cards instantly, but in some countries you may have to wait for a week. In addition to the completed application form, you'll need your passport (and sometimes a photocopy of its main page) plus confirmation of your travel arrangements, specifically a return plane ticket and an accommodation booking, though the latter is rarely checked. They are valid for thirty days for UK, US and Australasian citizens, and ninety days for Canadians, and must be used within 180 days of issue.

You will need to show your tourist card at customs on arrival and departure.

Once in Cuba, you can **renew a tourist card** for another thirty days. To do this consult a *buro de turismo*, found in the larger hotels, or one of the immigration offices in various provinces (listed throughout the Guide). There is an office in Havana dedicated specifically to visa extensions (see page 138). When renewing your visa, you will need details (perhaps including a receipt) of where you are staying.

Should you wish to stay longer than sixty days as a tourist (120 if you are Canadian) you will have to leave Cuban territory and return with a **new tourist card**. Many people do this by island-hopping to other Caribbean destinations or Mexico and getting another tourist card from the Cuban consulate there.

For full details of import and export regulations, consult the Cuban Customs website: Ⓦ aduana.gob.cu.

EMBASSIES AND CONSULATES IN CUBA

There are no consulates or embassies in Cuba for Australia or New Zealand. The local Canadian Embassy and the Australian and New Zealand embassies in Mexico provide consular assistance to Australians and New Zealanders in Cuba.
British Embassy Calle 34 no.702–704 esq. 7ma, Miramar ☎ 7 214 2200, Ⓦ www.gov.uk/government/world/organisations/british-embassy-havana.
Canadian Embassy Calle 30 no.518 esq. 7ma, Miramar ☎ 7 204 2516, Ⓦ canadainternational.gc.ca/cuba.
South African Embassy Avenida 5ta no.4201 esq. 42, Miramar ☎ 7 204 9671 or ☎ 7 204 9676.
US Embassy Calzada e/ L y M, Vedado ☎ 7 839 4100, Ⓦ havana.usembassy.gov.

CUBAN CONSULATES AND EMBASSIES ABROAD

For all Cuban consulate and embassy websites see Ⓦ cubadiplomatica.cu.
Australia Embassy, 1 Gerogery Place, O'Malley ACT 2606, Canberra ☎ 6290 2151.
Canada Embassy, 388 Main St, Ottawa, ON K1S 1E3 ☎ 613 563 0141; Consulate-General in Montréal, 4542–4546 Decarie Blvd, Montréal, QC H4A 3P2 ☎ 514 843 8897; Consulate-General in Toronto, Suite 401–402, 5353 Dundas St West, Kipling Square, Toronto, ON M9B 6H8 ☎ 416 234 8181.
Ireland Embassy, 32B Westland Square, Pearse Street, Dublin 2 ☎ 353 1 671 8300.
New Zealand Embassy, 76 Messines Road, Karori, Wellington 6012 ☎ 4 464 2210.
South Africa Embassy, 45 Mackenzie St, Brooklyn 0181, Pretoria ☎ 12 346 2215.
UK Embassy and Consulate, 167 High Holborn, London WC1 ☎ 020 7240 2488; 24hr visa and information service ☎ 0891 880 820.

US Embassy, 2630 16th St NW, Washington DC 20009 ☎ 202 797 8518. Consulate Office, 2639 16th St NW, Washington DC 20009 ☎ 202 797 8609.

Insurance

Travel insurance covering medical expenses is mandatory when visiting Cuba. Immigration authorities have been known to do spot-checks when you are entering the country. Those without insurance are required to take out an insurance policy with Asistur before they are granted entrance. A typical travel insurance policy usually provides medical cover, as well as coverage for the loss of baggage, tickets and – up to a certain limit – cash or cheques, as well as cancellation or curtailment of your journey. Most of them exclude so-called dangerous sports unless an extra premium is paid. If you do take medical coverage, ascertain whether benefits will be paid as treatment proceeds or only after return home, and whether there is a 24-hour medical emergency number. If you need to make a claim, you should keep **receipts** for medicines and medical treatment, and in the event you have anything stolen, you must obtain an official statement from the police.

For all **insurance issues within Cuba**, including the purchase of policies, contact Asistur (☎ 7 866 5560, Ⓔ asistur@asistur.cu), the tourist-assistance agency. It has branches in most provincial capitals (listed throughout the Guide). Asistur may be the logical place to buy a policy for many **US citizens** as US insurance providers generally don't cover Cuba.

Internet

Getting **internet access** in Cuba is still not particularly easy but it took a huge leap forward in 2015 when

ROUGH GUIDES TRAVEL INSURANCE

Rough Guides has teamed up with WorldNomads.com to offer great **travel insurance** deals. Policies are available to residents of over 150 countries, though not to US citizens travelling to Cuba. A wide range of **adventure sports** are covered, as is 24hr emergency assistance, high levels of medical and evacuation cover and a stream of **travel safety** information. Roughguides.com users outside the US can take advantage of their policies online 24/7, from anywhere in the world – even if already travelling. And since plans often change when you're on the road, you can extend your policy and even claim online. Roughguides.com users who buy travel insurance with WorldNomads.com can also leave a positive footprint and donate to a community development project. For more information go to Ⓦ **www.roughguides.com/ travel-insurance**.

public **wi-fi** zones were established in all the major towns and cities. There are currently around 500 public wi-fi zones throughout the country; a full list is available on the website of the country's sole internet provider, ETECSA (Ⓦ etecsa.cu). To get online you'll need to buy a Nauta scratch card, available from ETECSA centres and some hotels, though stock regularly runs out. Once you have finished your session, make sure you log off to preserve any remaining minutes for next time. Wi-fi, also available in some hotels and in one or two sophisticated *casas particulares*, is the best way to access the internet on your mobile phone, although Cuba also launched its first 3G network in late 2018.

There are also cybercafés in all the major Cuban cities and resorts but usually just one or two, and in many towns there are none at all. The upmarket **hotels** offer the fastest and most robust connections. ETECSA, which also runs the national telephone network, operates **Telepunto centres** where you can get online.

Laundry

There are few public laundry services in Cuba. Most foreign visitors do their own or rely on the hotel service, although if you are staying in a *casa particular* your hosts are likely to offer to do yours for you for a few pesos.

Mail

There's a good chance you'll get back home from Cuba before your postcards do. Don't expect **airmail** to reach Europe or North America in less than two weeks, though it's more common for letters and postcards to arrive a month or more after they have been sent. **Theft** is so widespread within the postal system that if you send anything other than a letter there's a significant chance that it won't arrive at all. You should also be aware that letters and packages

coming into Cuba are sometimes opened as a matter of government policy. **Stamps** are sold at post offices, white-and-blue post office kiosks (marked Correos de Cuba) and in many hotels.

All large towns and cities have a **post office**, normally open Monday to Saturday from 8am to 6pm. Most provincial capitals and major tourist resorts have a branch with DHL (Ⓦ dhl.com) and EMS (Ⓦ ems. post) **courier services**. Some of the larger hotels offer a full range of postal services, including DHL, EMS and the Cuban equivalent Cubanacán Express (Ⓦ cubanacan-express.cu), usually at the desk marked Telecorreos.

If you're sending **packages** overseas, stick to DHL, by far the safest and most reliable option.

Maps

In general, Cuban maps are infrequently updated, a little unreliable and hard to find. The exception is the national road map book, the *Guía de Carreteras*, which covers the whole country and also carries basic street maps for many of the major cities – invaluable if you plan to make any long-distance car or bike journeys around the island. You can buy it in bookshops, tourist gift shops and some branches of Infotur. However, some minor roads are not marked on this or any other map and there is still a gap in the market for a fully comprehensive national road map or street atlas. Geographical and orienteering maps are non-existent.

Opening hours and public holidays

Opening hours in Cuba are far from an exact science and should generally be taken with a generous pinch of salt. **Office** hours are normally 8.30am to 5pm, Monday to Friday, with one-hour lunchtime closures common, anytime between noon and 2pm. Standard opening hours for **state restaurants** and **paladars** are from noon to 11pm. but it's not unusual for places to close early, depending on the level of business. **Museums** are usually open Tuesday to Saturday from 9am to 6pm, and many also close for an hour at lunch. Those open on Sunday generally close in the afternoon. Expect museums, especially in Havana, to keep longer opening hours in July and August and sometimes in January, February and March too. **Shops** are generally open 9am to 6pm Monday to Saturday, a minority closing for lunch, while the shopping malls and department stores in Havana and Varadero stay open as late as 8pm. Sunday trading is increasingly common, with most places open until noon or 1pm, longer in the major resorts. Hotel shops stay open all day. **Banks** generally operate Monday to Friday 8am to 3pm, but this varies. There is no culture of siesta in Cuba.

Phones

The chances are that it will be cheaper to use your mobile phone than a payphone to **ring abroad from Cuba**, though US travellers may encounter added complications. However, if you are making a call to a Cuban number then it's usually much more economical to use a **payphone**.

Mobile phones

Cubacel, part of national telecommunications company ETECSA (◍etecsa.cu), is the sole **mobile phone service provider** in Cuba. If you intend to bring your own handset to Cuba you should check first whether or not your service provider has a roaming agreement with Cubacel, either by contacting your own provider or consulting the "Roaming" list on the ETECSA website. Most of the major British, Australasian and Canadian operators now have such agreements and, as of September 2015, Verizon became the first US-based mobile phone company to offer roaming in Cuba to its customers – currently only available as a pay-as-you-go international service.

There are significant parts of the country, such as much of Pinar del Río province, where you are unlikely to get any mobile phone network coverage at all, rendering your phone useless for calls and texts in these parts.

Payphones

There are various kinds of **payphone** in Cuba, and several distinct ways that you can make and pay for calls.

Prepaid phone cards

Prepaid cards, known as **Chip cards**, can be bought from post offices, hotels, travel agents, some banks, Telepuntos (see page 58) and large walk-in phone

(see page 58)

NATIONAL HOLIDAYS

Jan 1 Liberation Day. Anniversary of the triumph of the Revolution.
May 1 International Workers' Day.
July 25–27 Celebration of the day of national rebellion.
Oct 10 Anniversary of the start of the Wars of Independence.
Dec 25 Christmas Day.

---

booths known as Minipuntos. They only work in Chip card phones, most of which are coloured blue and found in hotels, Telepuntos, Minipuntos and other tourist establishments. They are straightforward phone cards which, once the credit has expired, are useless and can be thrown away.

Propia cards are rechargeable, reusable and valid for six months, effectively phone credit accounts. They are compatible with all phones besides the Chip card phones. Rather than inserting the card in a phone, when calling you enter the unique account code found on the card.

Coin-operated phones

The new generation of **coin-operated phones**, grey in colour and with a digital display, are an easy and cheap way to make a local call – international calls aren't permitted. Coin-operated phones can be hard to find and tend to be located outside in the street and rarely in call centres. There are also still some rusty old analogue payphones, especially in small towns, which only accept 5 centavo coins, have no digital display and have a slim chance of working at all.

Making calls

To **make a call** within the same province but to a different municipality you may need an **exit code** (*código de salida*) for the place from where you are making the call. Exit codes are available from the operator. If you are calling from a prepaid card phone simply dial ❶0 followed by the area code and number and this will put you through directly.

Some interprovincial calls are only possible through the operator. If you're consistently failing to get through on a direct line, dial ❶00 or ❶110.

You may see Cuban telephone numbers written as, for example, "48 7711 al 18", meaning that when dialling the final two digits you may have to try all the numbers in between and including 11 and 18 before you get through.

Making an overseas phone call from a private phone in a house has its own special procedure and

USEFUL NUMBERS AND CODES

Police Department ☎ 106.

Fire Department ☎ 105.

Directory enquiries ☎ 113.

National operator ☎ 00 from most places, including major towns, cities and resort areas. The most common alternatives are ☎ 011 and ☎ 110.

International operator The number for the international operator, which you'll need for reverse charge calls or if you are having problems connecting directly to a number outside Cuba, is either ☎ 012 (from Havana) or ☎ 180 (from outside Havana). A call connected via the international operator from a payphone incurs a higher call rate than normal.

International call prefix ☎ 119. This code must precede the country code when making any international call.

Interprovincial area codes These codes are provided with all phone numbers throughout this guide though many are technically now part of the number itself since a phasing out of separate area codes began in 2015. When dialling, each code is preceded by the appropriate national grid prefix (*prefijo de teleselección nacional*), which is either ☎ 0 or ☎ 01 depending on where in the country the call is made from. The codes are printed in the telephone directories available in all Telepunto and Minipunto call centres.

Mobile phone codes Cuban mobile phone numbers begin with a 5. When calling a mobile phone from a fixed phone, including payphones, the 5 is preceded by 0 (when calling from Havana) or 01 (when calling from outside Havana).

International dialling code for calls to Cuba ☎ 53.

---

can be quite confusing, not to mention very costly – use a payphone if at all possible.

Time

Cuba is on **Eastern Standard Time** in winter and **Eastern Daylight Time** in summer. It is five hours behind London, fifteen hours behind Sydney and on the same time as New York.

Tourist information

The national tourist information network is **Infotur** (🌐 infotur.cu), and has desks in many hotels and at the larger airports and branches in most major cities and resorts, though many are rudimentary affairs. The friendly staff are generally willing to help with all sorts of queries, though they do try to steer visitors towards the state-run tourist apparatus. They carry a few basic guides and maps but are generally low on free literature and printed information. You can, however, book hotel rooms, rental cars, organized excursions and long-distance bus tickets through them. Officially they do not supply information on paladars or *casas particulares*, though the staff are often willing to help with their own recommendations.

The three principal national **travel agents**, Cubanacán, Cubatur and Havanatur, have offices in most major cities and resorts and effectively double up as information offices, particularly in those places where there is no Infotur office. Though their principal aim is to sell you their own packages and organized excursions, the staff are accustomed to supplying any kind of tourist information. These agencies can also book hotel rooms and are usually the most convenient place to book Víazul bus tickets. Be aware that all information outlets and travel agents in Cuba, including Cuban websites, are run by the state and are unlikely to offer impartial advice on, for example, accommodation deals or places to eat.

With very little printed tourist literature it's well worth checking the internet for tourist information. The official Cuban sites, 🌐 cubaweb.cu and 🌐 dtcuba.com, are worthwhile, but foreign sites tend to be more reliable. Among the best is 🌐 cuba-junky.com.

An international network of tourist information offices is run by the **Cuban Tourist Board**. There are branches in several Latin American and European countries, including the UK, as well as in Canada and China.

CUBAN TOURIST BOARD OFFICES ABROAD

Canada 1200 Bay Street, Suite 305, Toronto, ON M5R 2A5 ☎ 416 362 0700.

Mexico Darwin 68, piso 1, Colonia Anzures, Delegación Miguel Hidalgo, Mexico City 06100.

UK 154 Shaftesbury Avenue, London WC2H 8JT ☎ 020 7240 6655, 🌐 travel2cuba.co.uk.

Working and studying in Cuba

Working in Cuba as a foreign national is more complicated than in most countries, and anyone thinking of picking up a casual job on the island can pretty much forget it. All wages in Cuba are paid by the state, so if the bureaucracy doesn't stop you the hourly rates probably will. The majority of foreign workers here are either diplomats or in big business, and the only realistic chance most people have of working is to join one of the voluntary brigades. **Studying** here is easier, as Spanish classes are offered at universities, by tour operators and also represent a significant niche in the private enterprise market.

If you plan to study or work in Cuba then you must have the relevant **visas** organized before you arrive. Students must have a **student visa** entitling them to stay in the country for longer than a month; these can be arranged through the Cuban consulate, though sometimes language schools can assist you with this.

Work

Working holidays in Cuba are organized in the US by the Venceremos Brigade (Ⓦvb4cuba.com), in Canada by the Canadian Network on Cuba (Ⓦcanadiannetworkoncuba.ca) and in the UK by the Cuba Solidarity Campaign (Ⓦcuba-solidarity.org.uk). Known as brigades, these organized volunteer groups usually spend two or three weeks working alongside Cubans on agricultural projects, living on purpose-built camps. There is a strong pro-government slant to the experience – which also involves visits to schools, hospitals and trade unions -- but the opportunity to witness working conditions and gain a sense of the Revolution in action is nevertheless unique.

Study

There is an array of organizations that send people to Cuba to **study**, mostly to learn Spanish. You can, however, take Spanish classes independently without too much hassle. The most obvious place to go is the University of Havana, where the Faculty of Modern Languages has been running courses aimed specifically at foreign students and visitors for many years. The most basic **Spanish course** is an intensive one-week affair, with two-week, three-week and month-long options. You can also combine Spanish studies with courses in dance or Cuban culture, or even just study Cuban culture on its own. The university provides full-board on-campus accommodation for two weeks, including the cost of lessons. Courses start throughout the year on the first Monday of every month except August. For more details, contact the Oficina de Servicios Académicos Internacionales, Ⓔserviciosacademicos@rect.uh.cu. Similar courses are run at just about every principal university in the country, most of them found in the provincial capital cities.

Aside from the universities, the best way to arrange a proper course of Spanish classes in Cuba is through professional organizations based outside the country, like Cactus Language (Ⓦcactuslanguage.com).

Havana

PLAZA VIEJA

1 Havana

Havana pulsates with life and hums with vitality, but not in the city-never-sleeps sense you'll encounter elsewhere in Latin America. There's a definite end to the night here, but when habaneros get up and out the next day, they do it together – and people's lives in this captivating city unfold unselfconsciously and in plain view. Some of them make it no further than the doorstep but, especially in the central neighbourhoods, almost nothing is private. Front doors are left open, washing is hung out on balconies, conversations are shouted between buildings and families watch TV with passers-by in exposed street-side living rooms. Infectious informality pervades, punctuated here and there by the earnest straight faces of a bureaucratic and authoritarian state. Domino players sit at tables on the kerb, policemen on military service flirt with waitresses, women dressed in white from head to toe sit on walls and smoke cigars and taxi drivers in cowboy hats lean proudly against their 1950s Buicks and Chevrolets.

Having celebrated its 500th anniversary in 2019, the story of the city's and the country's past, with its dramatic twists and turns, is told through the striking diversity of Havana's architecture and the stark differences between its neighbourhoods. Sixteenth-century Spanish forts, eighteenth-century Baroque churches and mansions, early twentieth-century Art Deco theatres and Soviet-era Brutalist office blocks all mark distinct periods in the history of Havana and Cuba. In the centre especially, almost every street seems to have an intriguing story to tell, whether one of colonial grandeur, bygone glamour, economic hardship or revolutionary change – and sometimes all of these, wrapped up in just one block. What was once contained within the seventeenth-century city walls now forms harbourside **Habana Vieja**, the old city, and the capital's tourist centre. Soldered on to Habana Vieja is gritty, lively **Centro Habana**, often bypassed by tourists on their way to more visitor-friendly parts of town but home to the most striking and idiosyncratic section of Havana's oceanfront promenade, the **Malecón**. Sharing the Malecón with Centro Habana is **Vedado**, heart of the city borough of Plaza, where the city expanded in the nineteenth and early twentieth centuries, spreading out into attractive, leafy, open-plan neighbourhoods. Today Vedado is blessed with most of the city's abundant theatres, cabarets, nightclubs and cinemas. From here you could walk the couple of kilometres to the vast and famous **Plaza de la Revolución**, with giant monuments to three icons of the Cuban struggle for independence, Che Guevara, Camilo Cienfuegos and José Martí. Beyond Vedado to the west, on the other side of the Río Almendares, **Miramar** ushers in another change in the urban landscape. Modelled on mid-twentieth-century Miami, this part of the city comes into its own at night, with some of Havana's most sophisticated restaurants and best music venues scattered around the leafy streets.

Though muggings are undoubtedly on the increase, Havana remains one of the safest capital cities in Latin America. Even so, some foreign visitors are still surprised by what can seem like an onslaught of touts peddling anything from cigars and taxi rides to a place to stay and a young woman to stay with, though this kind of hassle is hardly ever aggressive.

Brief history

Havana's success and riches were founded on the strength and position of its **harbour** – the largest natural port in the Caribbean. However, the original **San Cristóbal de la**

Highlights

❶ Plaza Vieja This has become the most animated and alluring square in Old Havana, alive with the chatter and clatter of a great set of cafés and restaurants. See page 81

❷ Museo Nacional de Bellas Artes The best and largest art collection in Cuba, split between a lovely, bright Art Deco building and an austere Neoclassical one. See page 87

❸ Parque Morro-Cabaña Explore the nooks and crannies of this easily overlooked fortress complex. See page 90

❹ The Malecón Havana's sociable seafront promenade comes alive in the evening. See page 95

❺ Hotel Nacional This luxurious twin-towered hotel still embodies 1930s Havana glamour. A perfect setting for a mojito. See page 98

❻ Fábrica de Arte Cubano Nowhere quite symbolizes the direction in which Havana's contemporary arts and culture is moving like this immense art centre and nightclub. See page 108

❼ El Cocinero With a new-wave Cuban menu assembled with flair, *El Cocinero* is redefining eating out in Havana. See page 124

❽ Gran Teatro Enjoy the world-renowned Cuban National Ballet in this stunningly restored cultural cathedral. See page 131

HIGHLIGHTS ARE MARKED ON THE MAP ON PAGE 68

1

Habana settlement, established on July 25, 1515, St Christopher's Day, was actually founded at modern-day Batabanó, on the south coast of what is now Mayabeque province. It wasn't until November 25, 1519, that the city was relocated to the banks of the large bay known as the **Bahía de la Habana**.

Port, bridge and gateway

The early settlement began to ripple out into what is now Habana Vieja, with the first streets established down on the waterfront between the present-day Plaza de Armas and Plaza de San Francisco. However, it was with the discovery of a deep, navigable channel through the treacherous shallow waters between Cuba and the Bahamas that Havana really took off as a major city, becoming a bridge between Spain and the New World thanks to its strategic location on the newly established **trade routes**.

As the Spanish conquistadors plundered the treasures of the Americas, Havana became the meeting point for the **Spanish fleet** on its way back across the Atlantic. For several months of the year, ships returning from all over the Americas laden with precious cargoes would slowly gather at the port until a force strong enough to deter possible **pirate attacks** in the Caribbean had been assembled. An infrastructure of brothels, inns and gambling houses sprang up to cater for the seamen, and the port itself became a target for frequent attacks by buccaneers.

Fortification and free trade

In 1558, after consolidating shipping operations by making Havana the only Cuban port authorized to engage in commerce, Spain started a long period of fortification with the construction of the first stone fort in the Americas, the impressive **Castillo de la Real Fuerza**. Work started on the **Castillo de San Salvador de la Punta** and the formidable **Castillo de los Tres Reyes del Morro** in 1589 and was finally completed in

1

1630. Three years later a protective wall began to be built around the city, and was completed in 1740.

Assaults on the city persisted, however, and in 1762 Havana fell to the **British**. The free trade that the port enjoyed during its brief eleven months of occupation – the British swapped Havana for Florida – kick-started the island's **sugar trade**; previously restricted to supplying Spain, it was now open to the rest of the world. Spain wisely kept British trade policies intact and the consequential influx of wealthy Spanish sugar families propelled Havana into a new age of affluence.

The building booms

The **nineteenth century** was a period of growth, when some of the most beautiful buildings around Habana Vieja were constructed and the city enjoyed a new-found elegance. At the same time, crime and political corruption were reaching new heights, causing many of the new bourgeoisie to abandon the old city to the poor and to start colonizing what is now Vedado. By the 1860s the framework of the new suburbs stretching west and south was in place.

In 1902, after the **Wars of Independence**, North American influence and money flowed into the city, and the first half of the twentieth century saw tower blocks, hotels and glorious Art Deco palaces like the Edificio Bacardí built as the tourist industry boomed. Gambling flourished, run by American gangsters like Meyer Lansky, who turned Havana into something of a Caribbean Las Vegas.

Equality, decay and rebirth

The **Revolution** put an abrupt end to all this decadence, and throughout the 1960s the new regime cleaned the streets of crime and sex work, laying the basis for a socialist capital. Fine houses, abandoned by owners fleeing to the US, were left in the hands of servants, and previously exclusive neighbourhoods changed face overnight. With the emphasis on improving conditions in the countryside, city development was haphazard and the **post-Revolution years** saw many fine buildings crumble while residential overcrowding increased, prompting Fidel Castro to take action. Happily, since the 1990s there have been steady improvements, with redevelopment work recapturing some of the former glory, especially in the worst-affected areas of Habana Vieja. The reconstruction was given added impetus by the 500th anniversary of the city in 2019, with hotel, housing and restoration projects all over Havana timed for completion that year.

Today the growing **prosperity** in the capital is evident from fancy restaurants full of locals, increasingly well-appointed houses, and new cars on the roads. Many of its citizens, however, still live on minimal resources, and the city's increasing inequalities remain one of the biggest challenges for twenty-first century Havana.

Habana Vieja

Remarkably unmarred by modernity but famously ravaged by time and climate, **Habana Vieja** (Old Havana), despite all the redevelopment, remains a true vision of the past. Cobbled plazas, shadowy streets, colonial mansions, leafy courtyards, sixteenth-century fortresses and, at its core, hardly any motorized traffic, make it a real living museum. But though its central streets are heaving with visitors, Habana Vieja is no sanitized tourist attraction, and the area buzzes with a frenetic sense of life. Neighbours chat through wrought-iron window grills while school lessons are delivered in open-window classrooms, a metre from the road, and school kids take their breaks and play sport in the street. For every recently restored building, there are five more packed to the rafters with residents – and tenement buildings are cobbled together from the decaying mansions of imperial counts.

1

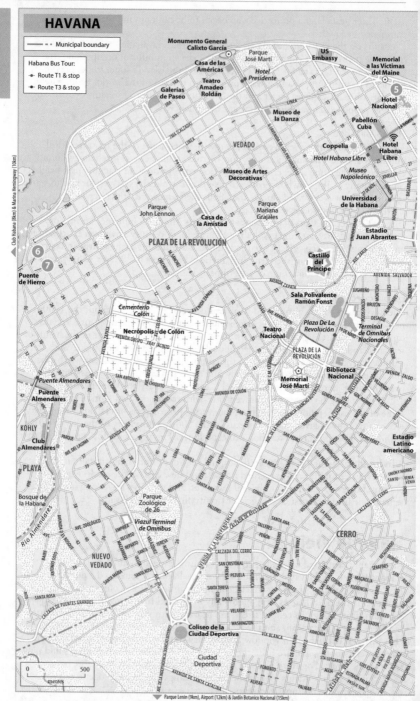

HAVANA

- — - - Municipal boundary

Habana Bus Tour:
- Route T1 & stop
- Route T3 & stop

Monumento General
Calixto García

Casa de las
Américas

Parque
José Martí

US
Embassy

Memorial
a las Víctimas
del Maine

Teatro
Amadeo
Roldán

Hotel
Presidente

Hotel
Nacional

Galerías
de Paseo

Museo de
la Danza

Pabellón
Cuba

VEDADO

Coppelia

Hotel Habana Libre

Hotel
Habana
Libre

Museo de Artes
Decorativas

Museo
Napoleónico

Parque
John Lennon

Casa de
la Amistad

Parque
Mariana
Grajales

Universidad
de la Habana

PLAZA DE LA REVOLUCIÓN

Estadio
Juan Abrantes

Castillo
del
Príncipe

AVENIDA SALVADOR

Puente
de Hierro

Sala Polivalente
Ramón Fonst

Cementerio
Colón

AVENIDA ZAPATA

Plaza De La
Revolución

Terminal
de Omnibus
Nacionales

Necrópolis de Colón

Teatro
Nacional

PLAZA DE LA
REVOLUCIÓN

Biblioteca
Nacional

AVENIDA ZALDO

Puente Almendares

SAN ANTONIO

Memorial
José Martí

Puente
Almendares

KOHLY

Club
Almendares

AVENIDA DE COLÓN

Estadio
Latino-
americano

PLAYA

Bosque de
la Habana

UNIÓN Y MORRO

Parque
Zoológico
de 26

LA ROSA

CERRO

Viazul Terminal
de Omnibus

TALLERES

SANTA ANA

NUEVO
VEDADO

CALZADA DEL CERRO

SAN CRISTÓBAL

SANTA TERESA

Coliseo de la
Ciudad Deportiva

VÍA BLANCA

WASHINGTON

Ciudad
Deportiva

AVENIDA DE SANTA CATALINA

PALMAR

0   500
metres

Club Habana (8km) & Marina Hemingway (10km)

Río Almendares

Parque Lenin (9km), Airport (12km) & Jardín Botánico Nacional (15km)

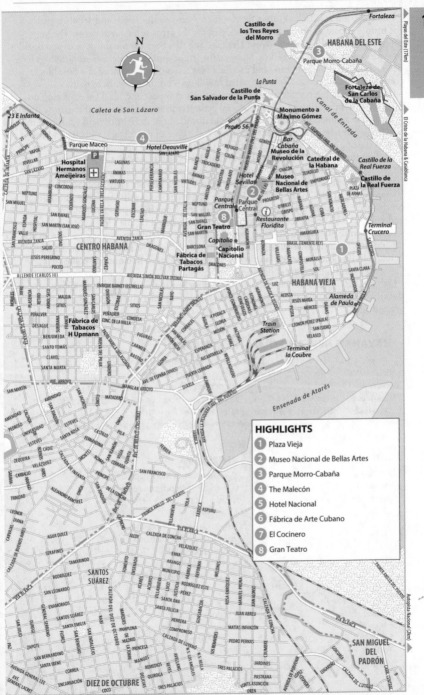

HIGHLIGHTS

1. Plaza Vieja
2. Museo Nacional de Bellas Artes
3. Parque Morro-Cabaña
4. The Malecón
5. Hotel Nacional
6. Fábrica de Arte Cubano
7. El Cocinero
8. Gran Teatro

1

Ironically, the very lack of urban development between the 1960s and 1990s, which left the historical core so untouched, also allowed for the area's subsequent decay. The huge project to restore this Unesco World Heritage Site that began some thirty years ago is still in evidence all over Habana Vieja. Some of the largest and most prestigious buildings have been renovated in recent years, and there are now a significant number of whole blocks completely lined by beautifully renovated buildings – but much work remains.

Habana Vieja's main sightseeing area is relatively compact and ideal for exploring **on foot**, with an increasing amount of official pedestrianization. Although the narrow streets and eclectic architecture lend a sense of wild disorder, the straightforward grid system is very easy to navigate. The **Plaza de Armas** is the core of the historic old city and the logical starting point for touring the district, with numerous options in all directions, including the prestigious **Plaza de la Catedral** three blocks away to the north and the larger, more enjoyably workaday but equally historic **Plaza Vieja** five blocks to the south.

For the other unmissable sights head from the Plaza de Armas up **Obispo**, Habana Vieja's busiest street, to the **Parque Central**. The wide boulevards and grand buildings on this western edge of Habana Vieja differ in feel from the rest of the old town, and belong to an era of reconstruction heavily influenced by the United States, most strikingly in the **Capitolio** building, which has more recently undergone its own major reparations, including a stunning face-lift. Some of the most impressive museums are here, including the **Museo de la Revolución** and the **Museo Nacional de Bellas Artes**, Cuba's best and biggest art collection.

Habana Vieja is not only a magnet for *jineteros* but is also the **bag-snatching** centre of the city, with a significant number of petty thieves working the streets, so take the usual precautions.

HAVANA'S NEW AND OLD STREET NAMES

Some streets in Havana have both a post-Revolution and a pre-Revolution name. Locals normally refer to the older, pre-Revolution names, street signs give the new ones and maps, just to add to the confusion, do a bit of both. Below are the most important of these distinctions – in the Guide we provide the new name except where the old name is so widely used that the new name is all but redundant, as is the case with the Avenida Antonio Maceo, which is always referred to as the Malecón. Where both names are used equally, we provide the old name in brackets.

OLD NAME	NEW NAME
Avenida del Puerto	Avenida Carlos Manuel de Céspedes
Avenida de Rancho Boyeros	Avenida de la Independencia
Belascoaín	Padre Varela
Cárcel	Capdevila
Carlos III	Avenida Salvador Allende
Egido	Avenida de Bélgica (southern half)
Galiano	Avenida de Italia
Malecón	Avenida Antonio Maceo
Monserrate	Avenida de Bélgica (northern half)
Monte	Máximo Gómez
Paseo del Prado	Paseo de Martí
Paula	Leonor Pérez
Reina	Avenida Simón Bolívar
San José	San Martín
Teniente Rey	Brasil
Vives	Avenida de España
Zulueta	Agramonte

Plaza de Armas

The oldest of Habana Vieja's squares, the **Plaza de Armas** is where Havana established itself as a city in the second half of the sixteenth century, and for most of the eighteenth and nineteenth centuries it was the seat of government in Havana. It still boasts some distinguished colonial buildings, several of which now house museums, most notably the **Museo de la Ciudad**. The three brick streets that form the edges of the plaza and, uniquely, its single wooden one, enclose the square's bushy central gardens. Often seething with tourists, and bathed in live music wafting over from the restaurant in one corner, this is the visitor capital of the old town.

El Templete

Baratillo e/ Nico López y O'Reilly, Plaza de Armas • Tues–Sat 9.30am–5pm, Sun 9am–1pm • Charge

In the northeastern corner of Plaza de Armas, the incongruous classical Greek architecture of **El Templete**, a curious, scaled-down version of the Parthenon in Athens, marks the exact spot of the foundation of Havana and the city's first Mass in 1519. The building itself was established in 1828; the large ceiba tree which now stands within its small gated grounds is the last survivor of the three that were planted here on that inaugural date. Inside the tiny interior, two large **paintings** depict these two historic ceremonies, both originals by nineteenth-century French artist Jean Baptiste Vermay, whose work can also be seen inside the Catedral de la Habana.

Museo de la Ciudad

Tacón no.1 e/ Obispo y O'Reilly, Plaza de Armas • Tues–Sun 9am–5pm • Charge • ☎ 7861 5779

The robust yet refined Palacio de los Capitanes Generales on the western side of Plaza de Armas was the seat of the Spanish government from the time of its inauguration in 1791 to the end of the Spanish–American War in 1898. It's now occupied by one of Havana's best museums, the **Museo de la Ciudad**, which celebrates the original building itself as well as the city's colonial heritage in general. Highlights on the ground floor include a fantastic nineteenth-century **fire engine** and a collection of **horse-drawn carriages**. Upstairs, among rooms that have been restored to their original splendour, is the magnificent **Salón de los Espejos** (Hall of Mirrors), lined with glorious gilt-looking mirrors, ornate candlestick holders and three huge, ostentatious crystal chandeliers. Next door is the slightly less striking **Salón Verde**, also known as the Salón Dorado (Golden Hall), where the governor would receive guests amid golden furniture and precious porcelain. Completing the triumvirate of the building's most impressive rooms is the sumptuous **Salón del Trono** (Throne Room) which, with its dark-red, satin-lined walls, was intended for royal visits, though no Spanish king or queen ever visited colonial Cuba.

Palacio del Segundo Cabo

O'Reilly esq. Tacón, Plaza de Armas • Tues–Sat 9.30am–5pm, Sat 9.30am–1pm • Charge • ☎ 7801 7176

The construction of the elegant, stern-faced **Palacio del Segundo Cabo** began in 1770; its Baroque architecture is typical of Cuban buildings of that era. Along with the adjacent Palacio de los Capitanes Generales, it formed part of the remodelling of the Plaza de Armas ordered under the governorship of the Marqués de la Torre. Originally the Royal Post Office, it didn't become the residence of the Segundo Cabo, the second-highest ranking official on the island, until 1854. It has since been used by a host of institutions, including the Tax Inspectorate, the Supreme Court of Justice, the Cuban Geographical Society and the Cuban Book Institute, before spending most of the last half-decade undergoing Unesco and European Union-funded renovations. Its latest role is as a "Center for the Interpretation of Cultural Relations between Cuba and Europe", a purpose given no more clarity when it was defined by the City Historian, Eusebio Leal, at its opening in May 2017 as "something totally different from a museum or a cultural centre". Across ten rooms, including a small theatre and a library, audiovisual

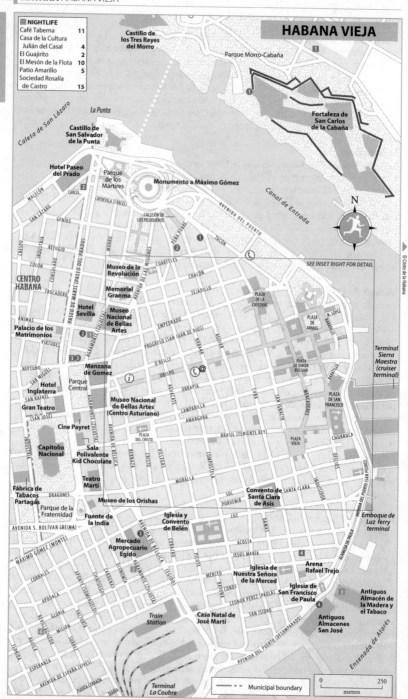

HABANA VIEJA

NIGHTLIFE
Café Taberna	11
Casa de la Cultura Julián del Casal	4
El Guajirito	2
El Mesón de la Flota	10
Patio Amarillo	5
Sociedad Rosalía de Castro	15

Castillo de los Tres Reyes del Morro

Parque Morro-Cabaña

Fortaleza de San Carlos de la Cabaña

La Punta

Caleta de San Lázaro

Castillo de San Salvador de la Punta

Canal de Entrada

N

Hotel Paseo del Prado

Parque de los Mártires

Monumento a Máximo Gómez

AVENIDA DEL PUERTO

MALECÓN

SAN LÁZARO

CÁRCEL

CAPDEVILA (CÁRCEL)

GENIOS

CALLEJÓN DE LOS PELUQUEROS

REFUGIO

PEÑA POBRE

TACÓN

El Cristo de la Habana

CRESPO

INDUSTRIA

CONSULADO

COLÓN

CUARTELES

SEE INSET RIGHT FOR DETAIL

TROCADERO

Museo de la Revolución

CHACON

PLAZA DE LA CATEDRAL

N. LÓPEZ

CENTRO HABANA

Memorial Granma

TEJADILLO

PLAZA DE ARMAS

JUSTIZ

ANIMAS

Hotel Sevilla

Museo Nacional de Bellas Artes

EMPEDRADO

AGUIAR

HABANA

BARATILLO

Palacio de los Matrimonios

VIRTUDES

PROGRESO (SAN JUAN DE DIOS)

PLAZA DE SIMÓN BOLÍVAR

Terminal Sierra Maestra (cruiser terminal)

NEPTUNO

Manzana de Gomez

D'REILLY

OBISPO

CUBA

SAN IGNACIO

MERCADERES

PLAZA DE SAN FRANCISCO

SAN MIGUEL

Hotel Inglaterra

Parque Central

OBRAPÍA

AGUACATE

SAN RAFAEL

Gran Teatro

(SAN JOSÉ)

Museo Nacional de Bellas Artes (Centro Asturiano)

LAMPARILLA

AMARGURA

OFICIOS

CHURRUCA

Cine Payret

BRASIL (TENIENTE REY)

PLAZA VIEJA

Capitolio Nacional

Sala Polivalente Kid Chocolate

PLAZA DEL CRISTO

BERNAZA

CRISTO

VILLEGAS

COMPOSTELA

Fábrica de Tabacos Partagás

Teatro Martí

MURALLA

Convento de Santa Clara de Asís

SANTA CLARA

INQUISIDOR

DRAGONES

Museo de los Orishas

SOL

Parque de la Fraternidad

Fuente de la India

PORVENIR

AVENIDA DEL PUERTO (SAN PEDRO)

Emboque de Luz ferry terminal

AVENIDA S. BOLÍVAR (REINA)

AVENIDA DE BÉLGICA (EGIDO)

Iglesia y Convento de Belén

LUZ

DAMAS

MÁXIMO GÓMEZ (MONTE)

Mercado Agropecuario Egido

CIENFUEGOS

ECONOMÍA

ACOSTA

JESÚS MARÍA

Arena Rafael Trejo

CORRALES

APODACA

GLORIA

MISIÓN

CÁRDENAS

FACTORÍA

SUÁREZ

MERCED

CONDE

Iglesia de Nuestra Señora de la Merced

BAYONA

Iglesia de San Francisco de Paula

Antiguos Almacén de la Madera y el Tabaco

REVILLAGIGEDO

LEONOR PÉREZ (PAULA)

Antiguos Almacenes San José

Train Station

Casa Natal de José Martí

SAN ISIDRO

Ensenada de Atarés

AGUILA

FLORIDA

ESPERANZA

AVENIDA DE ESPAÑA (VIVES)

PUERTA CERRADA

DIARIA

AVENIDA DEL PUERTO (DESAMPARADO)

Terminal La Coubre

--- Municipal boundary

0 ————— 250
metres

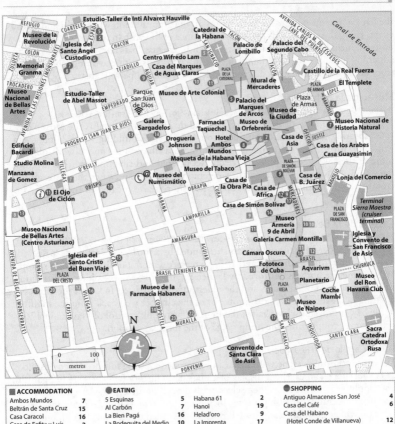

■ ACCOMMODATION			● EATING				● SHOPPING	
Ambos Mundos	7		5 Esquinas	5	Habana 61	2	Antiguo Almacenes San José	4
Beltrán de Santa Cruz	15		Al Carbón	7	Hanoi	19	Casa del Café	6
Casa Caracol	16		La Bien Pagá	16	Helad'oro	9	Casa del Habano	
Casa de Fefita y Luís	2		La Bodeguita del Medio	10	La Imprenta	17	(Hotel Conde de Villanueva)	12
Casa de Pablo y Lidia	14		Café del Angel	4	Ivan Chefs Justo	8	Casa del Ron y del Tabaco Cubano	13
Casa Vitrales	5		Café Bohemia	21	Más Habana	13	Clandestina	16
Conde de Villanueva	9		Café Taberna	18	Oasis Nelva	22	Ediciones Boloña	14
Florida	8		El Chanchullero	20	O'Reilly 304	14	Experimental Gallery	15
Los Frailes	12		La Divina Pastora	1	Osteria	12	Feria de Arte Obispo	10
Greenhouse	4		Lo de Monik	6	El Pórtico	3	Feria de Publicaciones	
Havana Casablanca	1		El Del Frente	15	El Shamuskia'o	23	y Curiosidades	7
Hostal Chez Nous	13		Doña Eutimia	11			Habana 1791	9
El Mesón de la Flota	10						Librería Venecia	11
Parque Central	3		■ DRINKING				Memorias	2
Raquel	11		Antiguo Almacén de la		El Floridita	8	Mercado Egido	3
Santa Isabel	6		Madera y el Tabaco	3	Plaza de Armas	6	Piscolabis	5
			El Dandy	12	La Reliquia	9	Puchito's Shop	17
			Don Eduardo Alegre	14	Sloppy Joe's	1	Quitrín	8
			Factoría Plaza Vieja	13	Tabarish	7	La Vega	1

displays and interactive materials promote the historical and cultural links between Cuba and Europe, demonstrating how European countries have helped to shape Cuba past and present, including influences on music, dance, literature and architecture.

Museo Nacional de Historia Natural

Obispo no.61 esq. Oficios, Plaza de Armas • Tues–Sun 10am–5pm • Charge • ☎ 7863 9361

The **Museo Nacional de Historia Natural** is, on an international scale, an unremarkable and rather diminutive natural history museum. Nevertheless, it is one of the biggest and best of its kind in Cuba, and one of the only museums in Habana Vieja suitable for children. Housed in what was the US Embassy building in the 1930s, mammals of

1

the five continents occupy the back rooms on the ground floor, where light and sound effects bring the cluttered displays to a semblance of life. **Cuban species** are displayed upstairs, including the prehistoric *manjuarí* fish, iguanas, bats and various birds. In an adjoining building, the **sala infantil** offers a space for kids with crayoning tables, games, story books and a somewhat macabre stuffed-baby-animal petting area.

Museo de la Orfebrería

Obispo no.113 e/ Oficios y Mercaderes, Plaza de Armas • Mon–Sat 9.30am–5pm, Sun 9.30am–1pm • Free • ☎ 7863 9861

A few doors along from the Museo Nacional de Historia Natural is the **Museo de la Orfebrería**, worth a twenty-minute scoot round. This building was a colonial-era workshop for the city's prominent goldsmiths and silversmiths and now displays some of their work, alongside an eclectic set of **gold** and **silver** pieces from around the world. As well as pocket watches, ceremonial swords and vases there are some fantastic, ostentatious old clocks. A jewellery shop is also located in the same building.

Castillo de la Real Fuerza

O'Reilly e/ Avenida del Puerto y Tacón, Plaza de Armas • Tues–Sun 9.30am–5pm • Charge, under-12s free • ☎ 7864 4488

A heavy-set sixteenth-century fortress surrounded by a moat, the **Castillo de la Real Fuerza** was built between 1558 and 1577 to replace a more primitive fort that stood on the same site but was destroyed by French pirates in 1555. The oldest construction still standing in Havana today, and the oldest surviving fortress in Cuba, the impressive building never fulfilled its role as protector of the city. Set well back from the mouth of the bay, it proved useless against the English, who took control of Havana in 1762 without ever coming into the firing range of the fortress's cannon.

Museo Castillo de la Real Fuerza

The castle's 6m-thick stone walls make an atmospheric setting for the **Museo Castillo de la Real Fuerza**, an excellent display of Cuba's naval history (all labels are in Spanish). The emphasis is on the **ships** themselves, with models of fifteenth-, sixteenth- and seventeenth-century Spanish galleons, including the *Santa María*, *La Pinta* and *La Niña* on which Columbus and his fellow explorers sailed to the New World, but predominantly the models are of ships that were built in Cuba itself. Most spectacular is the huge scale model of the *Santísima Trinidad*, the largest boat of its era, built in 1768 in Havana, complete with four decks and 140 cannon. Reconstructed in fantastic detail, a cutaway section reveals the trappings and complexities of the hull, manned by model sailors busy at work. Accompanying the models throughout the museum are displays of original artefacts used on the boats and **treasure** culled from Spanish colonies – gold and silver coins, jewellery and the like – some of it retrieved from the sea bed over the last few decades.

In the castle's upper level there are more model boats but the real draw is the rooftop view over the eastern bay. Atop the **bell tower**, complete with the original bell used to warn Habaneros of approaching pirates, is a replica of **La Giraldilla**, one of the historic emblems of the city. This bronze statue of a woman is also a city symbol of Seville and was named after the Giralda tower there. The original is now in the Palacio de los Capitanes Generales, following its deposition in the 1926 hurricane.

Oficios

The oldest street in the city, **Oficios** heads south from the Plaza de Armas through the Plaza de San Francisco and down to the port road on the southern side of Habana Vieja. Flanked by colonial residences, the three blocks between the two plazas make up its most travelled section and are lined with several small **museums**, a few shops, a couple of restaurants and a hotel.

Casa de los Árabes
Oficios no.16 e/ Obispo y Obrapía • Tues–Sat 9.30am–5pm, Sun 9am–1pm • Free or donation • ☎ 7861 5868

A former religious school, the **Casa de los Árabes** building was constructed in the seventeenth century, and is one of the most striking single examples of the Moorish influence on Spanish – and therefore Cuban – architectural styles. It tends to outshine the sketchy collection of Arabian furniture and costumes found in its corridor-room, which is set up like a Marrakesh market and features fabrics and rugs hanging from the walls and ceilings.

Plaza de San Francisco
Three blocks from the Plaza de Armas, Oficios opens out onto the **Plaza de San Francisco**, opposite the faded **Terminal Sierra Maestra**. Formerly underused, the dock has become busier now a number of major cruise-ship companies have added Cuba to their Caribbean itineraries. With the main port road running the length of its west side and two of its main buildings given over to offices – including, on the north side, the theatrical five-storey **Lonja del Comercio**, built in 1909 – the square is the most open and functional of Habana Vieja's main plazas, and the one you're least likely to linger in.

Iglesia y Convento de San Francisco de Asís
Oficios e/ Churruca y Amargura, Plaza de San Francisco • Tues–Sat 9am–4.30pm, Sun 9am–12pm • ☎ 7862 3467

Taking up the entire southern side of Plaza de San Francisco is the **Iglesia y Convento de San Francisco de Asís**, built in 1739 on the site of an older structure, which from 1579 was one of the most prestigious religious centres in Havana, a kind of missionary school for Franciscan friars who set off from here for destinations throughout Spanish America.

Museo de Arte Sacro
Iglesia y Convento de San Francisco de Asís • Mon–Sat 9.30am–5pm, Sun 9am–1pm • Charge • ☎ 7862 9683

Wonderfully restored in the early 1990s, the San Francisco de Asís monastery now contains the neatly condensed **Museo de Arte Sacro**, featuring religious art and silverware, church furniture and pottery found on the site, as well as the cope and shoes worn by the first Auxiliary Bishop of Cuba, Dionisio Rezino y Ormachea (1645–1711). However, the real pleasure here comes from wandering around the beautifully simple **interior**, admiring the solid curves of the north cloister, and climbing the wooden staircase up the 46m bell tower for magnificent **views** across the bay and over most of Habana Vieja.

Galería Carmen Montilla
Oficios no.162 e/ Brasil (Teniente Rey) y Amargura • Tues–Sat 9.30am–5pm, Sun 9.30am–1pm • Free • ☎ 7866 8768

Opposite the entrance to the Iglesia de San Francisco is the **Galería Carmen Montilla**, a delightful colonial townhouse restored in the mid-1990s from scratch by Carmen Montilla Tinoco, a Venezuelan artist and friend of Fidel Castro. Used for exhibitions of Cuban and overseas artists alike, Tinoco's own surreal and sometimes morbid paintings hang on the interior balcony.

Coche Mambí
Churruca e/ Oficios y Avenida del Puerto (San Pedro) • Tues–Sat 9.30am–5.30pm, Sun 9.30am–1pm • Charge

Squeezed down a short street called Churruca, just beyond the Iglesia y Convento de San Francisco de Asís is a perfectly restored train coach from 1900, the **Coche Mambí**, presenting an unexpected, captivating and brief diversion. One of just three that were built in the US, and formerly the property of the American-owned Cuban Railroad Company, its exclusive interior, which includes a reception room with foldaway beds and a dark-wood dining room, all on view to visitors, was befitting of its illustrious travelling occupants, the presidents of Cuba in the early decades of the twentieth century.

Museo del Ron Havana Club

Avenida del Puerto (San Pedro) no.262 esq. Sol • Mon–Fri 9am–4pm • Charge • ⓦ havana-club.com/en-gb/museum

A couple of blocks south of the Plaza de San Francisco on the port road is one of Havana's more engaging museums, the **Museo del Ron Havana Club**, a showpiece for the country's sizeable rum industry. Tracing the history and production methods behind this 400–year-old liquor, the lively **tour** (with guides who speak English, French, German and Italian) offers one of the city's slicker museum experiences. Passing through darkened atmospheric rooms, the tour is designed to follow the rum-making process in sequential order, charting the transformation of sugar cane into Cuba's national drink. On the walk round you will see historical and contemporary rum-making machinery, and a captivating model of a sugar mill, and smell the odours from bubbling tanks full of fermenting molasses. You finish up in a fully functioning replica of a 1930s **bar**, where you're given a sip of the brew itself. There is also a shop selling the full range of Havana Club rums.

Sacra Catedral Ortodoxa Rusa

Avenida del Puerto (San Pedro) esq. Santa Clara • Daily 9am–3.30pm • Free

One of the most unexpected sights in Habana Vieja, on the Avenida del Puerto, is the neo-Byzantine **Sacra Catedral Ortodoxa Rusa Nuestra Señora de Kazán**, to give it its full name. With its bright white hemispherical domes and cylindrical base it looks like a whimsical fairytale fortress but is actually Cuba's only Russian Orthodox cathedral, inaugurated on October 19, 2008. There are thought to be between five and ten thousand Russians in Havana, most of whom moved here during the 1960s and 1970s, a time of enthusiastic economic and cultural exchange between Cuba and the Soviet Union.

In contrast to its striking exterior, the interior is memorable mostly for its simplicity. The starkness of the white-walled, white marble-floored **nave**, accessed via the pleasant little courtyard up the steps at the rear, is punctuated by three golden chandeliers and a gleaming gold altar, full of painted saints and angels, but otherwise there is very little to avert your gaze.

The bay front

Rescued from the clutches of decay, the unspectacular but pleasant **bay front** between the Terminal Sierra Maestra and the Avenida de Bélgica is disturbed slightly by one of the busier roads in Habana Vieja but one of the few places on this side of the bay from where you can take in the city's impressive natural harbour, much of it blighted by industry. The waterfront promenade here has been brought back to life and old industrial warehouses have been converted into decent places to eat, drink and shop, the latter in the shape of the largest arts and crafts market in the country (see page 132). This is all part of a more ambitious long-term plan to completely transform Havana's harbour, whose waters for now remain badly polluted and whose vistas to the south are dominated by cranes, smokestacks and large cargo ships.

You can catch ferries to the eastern side of the bay from the small Emboque de Luz ferry terminal here. The **Antiguo Almacén de la Madera y el Tabaco**, an old wood and tobacco warehouse, is one of the few spots you can get a drink and bite to eat right on the bay itself. Built in 1908 by the Havana Central Railroad Company, it extends out over the water along a concrete jetty, opposite the southern end of the Alameda de Paula.

Alameda de Paula and the waterfront promenade

Trapped between the two lanes of the port road but raised above it and now beautifully restored to its colonial-era prestige, the tree-lined balustraded promenade known as the **Alameda de Paula**, running parallel to its waterfront counterpart, officially known as the **Paseo Marítimo de Paula**, was originally completed in 1777. No more than several blocks in length, either of these two walkways provide a pleasant route along the bay front to the church, waterside restaurant and market which sit at their southern end.

Iglesia de San Francisco de Paula

Avenida del Puerto, southern end of Alameda de Paula • Mon–Sat 9am–5pm • Free • ☎ 7 860 4210

A mishmash of arches, alcoves, porticoes and columns and an unusual squat shape make the **Iglesia de San Francisco de Paula** look somewhat cobbled together but also one of the quirkier churches in the city. Its lack of uniformity reflects its chequered history. The church was once the chapel of a hospital for poor and homeless women, first established in 1664 but then completely rebuilt after being damaged by a hurricane in 1730. In 1946, having passed into private ownership, the hospital was demolished, leaving the apparently designless structure left standing today. Nowadays it's used for classical and orchestral **concerts**, but you can pop in during the day to appreciate the simple, compact and delicately restored grey-stone interior, where a few splashes of colour are provided by modern paintings of biblical scenes and an almost abstract stained-glass window.

Plaza de la Catedral and around

The **Plaza de la Catedral**, just a couple of blocks northwest of the Plaza de Armas, is one of the most historically and architecturally consistent squares in the old city. Perfectly restored and pleasantly compact, it's enclosed on three sides by a set of symmetrical eighteenth-century aristocratic residences. The first houses were built on the site – which was swampland when the Spanish found it – around the turn of the sixteenth century. It wasn't until 1788 that the Plaza de la Ciénaga (Swamp Square), as it was then known, was given its current moniker, after the Jesuit church on its north face was consecrated as a cathedral.

Catedral de la Habana

Empedrado no.156 e/ San Ignacio y Mercaderes, Plaza de la Catedral • Mon–Sat 9am–5pm, Sun 9am–2pm • **Bell tower** Mon–Fri 9am–4.30pm, Sat 9–11.30am • Charge • ☎ 7 861 7771 • Dress appropriately (no short shorts)

The striking yet surprisingly small **Catedral de la Habana**, hailed as the consummate example of the Cuban Baroque style, dominates the Plaza de la Catedral with its swirling detail, curved edges and cluster of columns. Curiously, however, the perfect symmetry of the detailed exterior was abandoned in the design of the two **towers**, the right one noticeably and unaccountably wider than the left. The **interior** features a set of grandiose framed portraits by French painter Jean Baptiste Vermay (copies of originals by artists such as Rubens and Murillo), commissioned by Bishop José Díaz de Espada in the early nineteenth century to replace those works he considered to be in bad taste. One of the cathedral's principal heirlooms, a funeral monument to Christopher Columbus said to have contained his ashes, now stands in the cathedral in Seville, where it was taken when the Spanish were expelled from Cuba in 1898. A spiral stone staircase leads to the top of the **bell tower**, where the views take in the Capitolio and the other side of the bay.

Museo de Arte Colonial

San Ignacio no.61 esq. Plaza de la Catedral • Tues–Fri 9.30am–4.30pm, Sat & Sun 10am–3.30pm • Charge • ☎ 7862 6440

Opposite the cathedral, the Casa de los Condes de Casa Bayona, a gorgeous colonnaded patio-centred mansion built in 1720, houses the **Museo de Arte Colonial**,

1

a comprehensive collection of mostly nineteenth-century furniture and ornaments. The predominantly European-made artefacts include elaborately engraved mahogany dressers and a clavichord. One room is full of colourful **vajillas**, plates engraved with the family coats of arms of counts and marquises from Cuba. It was customary in colonial aristocratic circles to give one of these *vajillas* to your hosts whenever visiting the house of fellow nobility.

Casa del Marques de Aguas Claras

San Ignacio no.54 esq. Empedrado, Plaza de la Catedral • Restaurant noon–midnight; café 24hr • Free • ☎ 7867 1034

Sharing the northwestern corner of the Plaza de la Catedral with the cathedral, and host to the *El Patio* restaurant and café, is the **Casa del Marques de Aguas Claras**, which scrapes first prize for most arresting colonial interior on the plaza. You'll have to eat at the overpriced restaurant to get a proper look inside, where a serene fountain-centred courtyard is encompassed by pillar-propped arcs and coloured-glass portals.

Palacio de Lombillo

Empedrado no.151 esq. Mercaderes, Plaza de la Catedral • Mon–Fri 9am–5pm & Sat 9am–1pm • Free

The **Palacio de Lombillo** dates from 1741 and was originally home and office to a sugar-factory owner. Much of it is closed to the public, as it now functions as an administrative building for the Office of the City Historian, but you can take a peek inside via the door on Empedrado. There is usually a small but interesting exhibition of the latest plans for the old city's restoration.

Palacio del Marqués de Arcos

Mercaderes no.16 e/ Empedrado y O'Reilly, Plaza de la Catedral • Mon–Fri 9am–5pm & Sat 9am–1pm • Free

The **Palacio del Marqués de Arcos**, constructed alongside the Palacio de Lombillo on the east side of the square in 1741, was reopened in 2016 after years of closure and restoration. It's easy to see why this is considered one of the most prestigious examples of colonial-era domestic architecture in the city, its striking sweep of Doric columns supporting 28 arches encasing the central patio. Visitors can access a café and digital art library.

Taller Experimental de Gráfica

Callejón del Chorro no.62, Plaza de la Catedral • Mon–Fri 9am–4pm • Free • ☎ 7862 0979

At the end of Callejón del Chorro, a short cul-de-sac on the southwestern corner of the plaza, is the low-key **Taller Experimental de Gráfica**, an artists' workshop, gallery and market. The specialism here is etching and engraving, and the lithographs and stencil art displayed (and on sale) are more innovative and original than much of what you'll see in the arts and crafts shops around Habana Vieja. You can chat to the artists themselves, who are either busy at work in the open workshop or standing by their displays trying to make sales.

Centro de Arte Contemporáneo Wifredo Lam

San Ignacio esq. Empedrado • Tues–Sat 10am–5pm • Free • ⊕ wlam.cult.cu

In the shadow of the cathedral, the **Centro de Arte Contemporáneo Wifredo Lam** has two floors of galleries with temporary exhibitions, sometimes of quite off-centre contemporary art, including photography, painting and sculpture.

Mercaderes

Bookended by the Plaza de la Catedral and the Plaza Vieja is **Mercaderes**, the most heavily trodden and interesting route between these two old squares, full of small museums and simple but pleasing distractions. Along with Oficios, this is one of the oldest streets in Havana and one of the most historically evocative in Habana Vieja, and almost every building on its six blocks has now been restored or renovated. The most densely packed sightseeing section is south of Obispo, where a museum, gallery, hotel or café occupies almost every building. Halfway along, the cafés gathered around the diminutive **Plaza de Simón Bolívar** are ideally located for a drink in the shade as you tour the area.

The Mural de Mercaderes

Mercaderes e/ Empedrado y O'Reilly

Within a block of the Plaza de la Catedral on Mercaderes is the giant **Mural de Mercaderes**, portraying 67 figures from Cuban arts and politics. Pictured as a group standing outside and on the balconies of a classic colonial Cuban building, they include Carlos Manuel de Céspedes (nineteenth-century revolutionary), José de la Luz y Caballero (nineteenth-century philosopher), Jean Baptiste Vermay (French painter whose work appears in the cathedral and in El Templete on the Plaza de Armas) and José Antonio Echeverría (1950s student leader and revolutionary).

Maqueta de la Habana Vieja

Mercaderes no.114 e/ Obispo y Obrapía • Mon–Sat 9am–6pm • Charge • ☎ 7866 4425

The **Maqueta de la Habana Vieja** is an enthrallingly detailed model of the old city, including the bay and Habana del Este. Made up of some 3500 miniature buildings, the cityscape took three years to construct and occupies the larger part of the single room you can visit here. You should be able to pinpoint a few hotels, the main squares and the largest buildings, like the Capitolio. Each scheduled viewing is meant to replicate a day in the life of Habana Vieja and comes complete with the sounds of birdsong and car horns.

Museo del Tabaco

Mercaderes no.120 e/ Obispo y Obrapía • Mon–Sat 10am–5pm • Free • ☎ 7861 5795

Given Cuba's heritage in this industry, the **Museo del Tabaco** presents a surprisingly small collection of smoking memorabilia. Stretched over five rooms are modest collections of ashtrays, pipes and snuff boxes as well as a slightly more substantial set of twentieth-century lighters in all kinds of shapes and designs, from miniature telephones to a dinky piano and a machine gun. There's also an interesting collection of smoking paraphernalia from archaelogical excavations, and a cigar shop next door.

Casa de Asia

Mercaderes no.111 e/ Obispo y Obrapía • Tues–Sat 10am–6pm, Sun 9am–1pm • Free • ☎ 7810 1749

Another of the small museums on Mercaderes, the long narrow rooms of the **Casa de Asia** hold a hotchpotch of items from numerous Asian countries. The diversity of what's on display means that most visitors will find at least one thing to catch their eye, whether it's the samurai-style sword from tenth-century Laos, the model boats from Bangladesh or the metal statuette of the Hindu deity Shiva Nataraja.

Plaza de Simón Bolívar and around

One block from Obispo on Mercaderes, a mixed group of museums and galleries huddles around the **Plaza de Simón Bolívar**, a delightful and cosy little square consisting of exuberant gardens squeezed up against the surrounding buildings and crisscrossed by pathways. A **statue** of Simón Bolívar looks down from a plinth, and at the back of the square are the tables of a café based over the other side of Obrapía, the street hugging the square's northern border and dissecting Mercaderes.

Casa de Benito Juárez

Obrapía esq. Mercaderes • Tues–Sun 9am–12.30pm • Free • ☎ 7861 8166

1

SIMÓN BOLÍVAR AND LATIN AMERICAN INDEPENDENCE

One of the few people in history to have had a country named after him, the man who put Bolivia on the map is also one of the most enduring and highly regarded icons of Latin America. **Simón Bolívar** was lauded for his prominent role in the independence struggles of the early nineteenth century, not least by Hugo Chávez, whose Bolivarian Revolution was inspired by the man who is remembered as the "Liberator of the Americas".

Born into an aristocratic family on July 24, 1783, in Caracas, Venezuela, Bolívar had lost both his parents by the age of nine. Sent to Europe for the final years of his formal education, he returned to Venezuela in 1802 a married man. His wife, the daughter of a Spanish nobleman, died of yellow fever within a year of the wedding and, grief-stricken, he returned to Europe and immersed himself in the writings of Montesquieu, Jean Jacques Rousseau and other European philosophers. It was under such influences in Paris and Rome that Bolívar developed a passion for the idea of American independence.

He returned once again to Venezuela in 1807, just as the Spanish Crown was forced into a loosening of its grip on the American colonies, following the Napoleonic invasion of Spain. Bolívar was to be the single most influential man during the ensuing **Spanish–American wars of independence**, as state by state South and Central America broke free of their colonial shackles. Involved personally in the liberation of five of these countries, including Venezuela, perhaps the most important and heroic of all the military campaigns he waged was the taking of **New Granada** (modern-day Colombia). Against all the odds he led an army of some 2500 men through the Andes, enduring icy winds and assailing the seemingly non-negotiable pass of Pisba. When Bolívar and his men descended into New Granada the colonial army was completely unprepared, and on August 10, 1819, after victory at the battle of Boyacá, they marched triumphantly into Bogotá.

On September 7, 1821, **Gran Colombia** (a state covering much of modern-day Colombia, Panama, Venezuela, Ecuador, northern Peru and northwest Brazil) was created, with Bolívar as president. Though his goal of creating a federation of South American nations along the lines of the USA ultimately failed, tarnishing his contemporary reputation before he died in 1830, Bolívar's legacy was already cemented in history. By 1833 the Spanish–American wars of independence, in which he had played such a prominent role, concluded with every mainland Spanish American country from Argentina to Mexico free of colonial rule, leaving Spain clinging onto just the Philippines, Puerto Rico and Cuba.

Facing the plaza from the Obrapía side is the occasionally worthwhile **Casa de Benito Juárez**, also known as the **Casa de México**. The two rooms set aside for temporary exhibitions of Mexican photography, painting or craftwork tend to be the more interesting sections, but are not always in use.

Casa Guayasimín

Obrapía no.111 e/ Mercaderes y Oficios • Tues–Sun 9.30am–2.30pm • Free • ☎ 7861 3843

The sparse interior of the **Fundación Guayasimín** displays paintings by the Ecuadorean artist and friend of Fidel Castro, Oswaldo Guayasimín (1919–99). The works on display include a portrait of Fidel Castro, which the painter presented to him on his seventieth birthday. The house was originally set up as a studio and apartment for Guayasimín himself, and the bedroom and dining room are still intact.

Casa de Simón Bolívar

Mercaderes no.156 e/ Obrapía y Lamparilla • Tues–Sun 9am–5pm • Free • ☎ 7861 3988

The **Casa de Simón Bolívar** details the life and times of the Venezuelan known as "El Libertador de las Américas". Significant or symbolic events in Bolívar's life – such as his birth, baptism and even his first sexual experience – are rendered via a series of often comically cartoonish clay models. Display screens in a separate room go into more depth, with useful written explanations in English, and there are also prints of some great paintings from the period that provide a lively visual context, plus an art gallery upstairs.

Casa de Africa

Obrapía no.157 e/ Mercaderes y San Ignacio • Tues–Sat 10.15–5.45pm, Sun 9.15am–12.15pm • Free • ☎ 7861 5798

Just a few paces away from the Plaza de Simón Bolívar is the standout museum in the vicinity, the **Casa de Africa**, a three-storey showcase for African and African-Cuban arts, crafts and culture. Many of the tribal artefacts, traditional artworks, sculptures and statues here once belonged to Fidel Castro, most of them given to him by leaders of the African countries he visited. Among the most arresting exhibits are two fantastic life-size wooden sculptures of large birds from the Ivory Coast and a marvellous sculpted depiction of a royal procession from Benin, featuring a pipe-smoking chieftain being carried on a hammock.

Casa de la Obra Pía

Obrapía esq. Mercaderes • Tues–Sat 9am–4.30pm, Sun 9.30am–12.30pm • Charge • ☎ 7861 3097

Opposite the Casa de Africa, and distinguished by its ornately framed front entrance, is the eclectic **Casa de la Obra Pía**. An expansive seventeenth-century mansion with a spacious central patio, it's now a somewhat underused museum space. The interior architecture and original features of the house are the real draws, though they are well complemented by the substantial set of exhibits **upstairs**. Many of the rooms are impressively complete: the master bedroom, for example, is full of Rococo and Renaissance-style furniture, including a grand bed and a cot designed to resemble an old boat. The threadbare displays **downstairs**, in the two rooms devoted to Alejo Carpentier (1904–80), Cuba's most famous novelist, are too limited to hold broad appeal.

Museo Armería 9 de Abril

Mercaderes e/ Obrapía y Lamparilla • Mon–Sat 9.30am–5pm, Sun 9.30am–1pm • Free • ☎ 7861 8080

As the original 1950s sign outside indicates, **Museo 9 de Abril** was once an *armería*, or gun store, but is now a one-room museum with display cabinets full of pistols, machetes, rifles, knives and various other weapons. It is more renowned, though, as a monument to what happened here on **April 9, 1958**, when, following calls for a general strike led by Fidel Castro, four rebels were killed trying to raid the store. There are photos of those who died as well as a few documents and newspaper articles from the time.

Plaza Vieja

Animated and chock-a-bloc with visitors, **Plaza Vieja**, at the southern end of Mercaderes, more than any of the other old town squares, hums with the energy not just of a tourist attraction but as somewhere to come for a drink, a meal or to while away some time, for Cubans as well as foreign tourists, though certainly there are more of the latter. To a lesser but significant extent the square still reflects its original purpose as a focus for the community, with some of the buildings around its colourful borders still home to local residents and others occupied by educational and cultural institutions. This has been one of the most redeveloped spots in Habana Vieja over the last few decades, distinguished with a central fountain, a museum, a planetarium, a photography gallery, an arts centre and primary school, a rooftop camera obscura and some decent shops, restaurants and several excellent cafés. Located in the southeastern corner, the freshly restored Art Nouveau Palacio Cueto was built between 1906 and 1908 and functioned as a stunning hotel in the 1920s. After a long period of neglect, it's now, once again, a hotel.

Despite its name, this is not the oldest square in Havana, having been established at the end of the sixteenth century after the creation of the Plaza de Armas. It became the "Old Square" when the nearby Plaza del Cristo was built around 1640, by which time Plaza Vieja had firmly established itself as a centre for urban activity, variously used as a marketplace and festival site. Most of its beautifully restored, porticoed buildings, however, were built in the eighteenth and nineteenth centuries, long after its foundation.

Cámara Oscura

Brasil (Teniente Rey) esq. Mercaderes, Plaza Vieja • Mon–Sat 9.30am–5pm • Charge • ☎ 7862 1801

In the northeastern corner of Plaza Vieja, where Mercaderes crosses Brasil, is the **Cámara Oscura**, a captivating ten-minute tour of Habana Vieja and the bay through a 360-degree-rotating telescopic lens. At the top of the seven-storey Gómez Vila building, built in 1933 and one of only two post-colonial edifices on the square, this impressive piece of kit can pick out sights and scenes from all over the old city in close detail.

Fototeca de Cuba

Mercaderes no.307 e/ Brasil (Teniente Rey) y Muralla, Plaza Vieja • Tues–Sat 10am–4pm • Free • ☎ 7862 2530

On the same side of the square as the Cámara Oscura, the **Fototeca de Cuba** is an underused and often understocked photography gallery with two rooms of temporary exhibitions. Both Cuban and international themes, subjects and photographers feature, and past exhibitions have ranged from portraits of Fidel Castro to showcases of *National Geographic* photography.

Planetario

Mercaderes e/ Brasil (Teniente Rey) y Muralla, Plaza Vieja • Wed–Sat 9.30am–5pm, Sun 9.30am–12pm • Charge • ☎ 7865 9544

The Havana **planetarium**, a project largely funded by the Japanese government, is on a smaller scale than versions in many cities around the world but is still one of the more impressive things to go and see in Habana Vieja, especially for kids. The 45-minute guided tours walk you through four floors of rooms, charting a journey through the cosmos, from the Big Bang (represented by a light and sound display) onwards. In the main hall is a three-dimensional representation of the **solar system**. Other highlights include the **Space Theatre**, providing projections of stars, constellations and meteor showers and, on the fourth level, an observatory.

Museo de Naipes

Muralla esq. Inquisidor, Plaza Vieja • Tues–Sun 9.30am–6pm • Free • ☎ 7860 1534

Occupying the oldest building on Plaza Vieja, the **Museo de Naipes** takes a cursory but colourful look at the evolution and culture of **playing cards**. Decks of cards from around the world and down the years are neatly laid out in display cases, grouped into loose themes such as commerce and culture, and accompanied by related paraphernalia. Many are from Spain – not surprisingly, since most of the collection was donated by the Fundación Diego de Sagredo, a Madrid-based cultural and architectural institution which part-funded the museum's creation.

Museo de la Farmacia Habanera

Brasil (Teniente Rey) e/ Compostela y Habana • Daily 9am–5pm • Free • ☎ 7866 7556

In between Plaza Vieja and the residential Plaza del Cristo is the **Museo de la Farmacia Habanera**, housed in the old Farmacia La Reunión, a huge pharmacy established in 1853 that stayed in business until the Revolution in 1959. Restored to the impressive splendour of its heyday, it features an extravagantly adorned ceiling and walls lined with finely carved wooden cabinets brimming with hundreds of porcelain jars, which would once have contained the medicinal mixtures sold here. Some of the nineteenth-century laboratory apparatus used to make these mixtures, including a bizarre contraption once used to treat skin inflammations, is exhibited to the rear of the building.

There are still concoctions for sale here, including natural medicines, some herbs and spices, and more prosaic products like toothpaste and Alka-Seltzer.

Obispo and around

Linking the Plaza de Armas with Parque Central to the west is **Obispo**, Habana Vieja's busiest, most hectic street and home to its thickest concentration of **shops** and **bars**. Redeveloped in its entirety since the mid-1990s, this narrow, pedestrianized thoroughfare is almost always crowded with a lively, sometimes intense mix of street vendors, bar touts, Cuban shoppers and foreign visitors. An endless stream of people pour in and out of the open-fronted bars, clothes and homeware shops, neighbourhood hairdressers, hotels, restaurants and front-room galleries, or browse the secondhand bookstalls, haggle with the CD bootleggers and queue at the banks and phone centre.

Hotel Ambos Mundos

Obispo no.153 esq. Mercaderes • Room 511 open Mon–Fri 10am–5pm • Charge • ⓦ hotelambosmundoshabana.com

A Havana classic built between 1923 and 1925, the *Hotel Ambos Mundos* is most famous as Ernest Hemingway's Cuban base for ten years from 1932, from where he allegedly wrote *Death in the Afternoon* and embarked on *For Whom the Bell Tolls*. The hotel's rooftop-garden restaurant and bar is a good place for a drink with a view and is open to non-guests. On the way up in the original 1920s cage-elevator, stop off on the fifth floor and visit Room 511, where Hemingway stayed. The original furniture and even his typewriter have been preserved, and there's usually a guide on hand to answer any questions.

Farmacia Taquechel

Obispo no.155 e/ San Ignacio y Mercaderes • Daily 9am–7pm • Free • ☎ 7862 9286

Founded in 1898, **Farmacia Taquechel** is one of Habana Vieja's triumvirate of prestigious nineteenth-century pharmacies, along with the Droguería Johnson (see below) and La Reunión (see page 82). The fully functioning but clearly tourist-focused pharmacy specializes in natural medicines and displays admirable attention to period detail: from the shelves of porcelain medicine jars down to the cash register, there isn't a piece out of place.

Droguería Johnson

Obispo no.260 esq. Aguiar • Daily 9am–5pm • Free • ☎ 7862 0311

Founded in 1886, the **Droguería Johnson** moved from O'Reilly, a block to the north, to this more commercially lucrative location on Obispo in 1914. Completely renovated after a fire in 2006 closed it down for the rest of the decade, it now has a mixture of original features and brand-new elements modelled on the original design. The striking fifty-foot dark wood counter runs the length of the marble-floored building, while hundreds of elegant porcelain medicine jars line the floor-to-ceiling display cases.

Museo del Numismático

Obispo no.305 e/ Habana y Aguiar • Daily 9.15am–5.45pm • Charge • ☎ 7861 5811

Halfway along Obispo, in a grandiose, pillar-fronted building, is the **Museo del Numismático**, whose collection of coins, medals and banknotes over two floors is more interesting than you might think, acting as a window on events and personalities in Cuban history. For example, the medals for the highest order of merit under both the pre- and post-Revolution regimes, displayed here, are emblazoned with the face of José Martí, testament to his wide political appeal.

1

Edificio Bacardí
Avenida de Bélgica (Monserrate) no.261 e/ Empedrado y San Juan de Dios

Undoubtedly one of the finest Art Deco buildings in Cuba is the **Edificio Bacardí**, two blocks north of the end of Obispo. Twelve storeys high and finished in shiny red granite and enamelled terracotta, its construction was completed in 1930. It stood as a symbol of the wealth and influence of the Bacardí empire (see page 380), founded by the famous rum family from Santiago. A statue of the familiar bat logo crowns the central tower but the company no longer operates in Cuba and today it is predominantly an office building. Unofficially, tipping the security guard may allow you to take the lift to the top and enjoy the knockout views.

Parque Central

Just beyond the western end of Obispo is the grandest square in Habana Vieja. The **Parque Central** sits at the halfway point of the Paseo del Prado, running along the border between Habana Vieja and Centro Habana. In the late nineteenth and early twentieth centuries this area saw many colonial buildings demolished and replaced with flamboyant palaces, imposing Neoclassical blocks and some of the finest hotels ever built in the city, many of them still standing today around the square's borders. Mostly shrouded in shade, the square lies within shouting distance of one of Havana's most unforgettable landmarks, the **Capitolio Nacional**. Though the traffic humming past on all sides is a minus, the grandeur of the surrounding buildings lends the square a stateliness quite distinct from the residential feel which pervades elsewhere in Habana Vieja.

When it opened as a five-star hotel in 2017, the grandiose, Neoclassical **Manzana de Gómez** building transformed the eastern side of the square, bringing back to life an imposing edifice which has stood largely derelict and decrepit for much of the last decade. Street-level commercial galleries, cutting diagonally through the building's belly, house luxury brands such as Versace, Armani and Lacoste.

Gran Teatro de la Habana 'Alicia Alonso'
Paseo del Prado e/ San Rafael y San Martín, Parque Central • Tues–Sat 9am–5pm, Sun 9am–1pm • Charge • ☏ 7861 7391

The attention-grabber on the Parque Central is undoubtedly the Gran Teatro, one of Havana's most magnificently ornate buildings, an explosion of balustraded balconies, colonnaded cornices and sculpted stone figures striking classical poses. Home to the Cuban National Ballet, it was closed for several years for a meticulous restoration. The theatre reopened in 2016, when performances returned to its stage once again and the grande dame of Cuban ballet Alicia Alonso's name was added to the building's title. It's particularly awe-inspiring at night when its shining regal exterior, which has been cleaned so thoroughly you'd think it had only just been built, is captivatingly lit.

Hotel Inglaterra
Paseo del Prado no.416 esq. San Rafael, Parque Central • ☏ 7860 8593

In the thick of the commotion on the Parque Central is the oldest hotel in the country, the **Inglaterra**, opened in 1856; past guests include Antonio Maceo, who lodged here in 1890 during a five-month stay in Havana. The pavement café out front is one of the few places around the park where you can sit and take it all in, though don't expect peace.

Capitolio Nacional
Paseo del Prado e/ San Martín y Dragones • Thurs–Sat 10.30am–10pm, Sun 10.30am–1pm • Charge, children under 12 free

Visible from the Parque Central, and from points all over the city, looming above the surrounding buildings and dominating this part of Havana, is the familiar-looking

Neoclassical dome of the **Capitolio Nacional**. Bearing a striking resemblance to the Capitol Building in Washington, DC, this was the seat of the House of Representatives and the Senate prior to the Revolution. Built in just three years by several thousand workers, it was opened in 1929 amid huge celebrations. From 1960, following the Revolution, it became the headquarters of the Ministry for Science, Technology and the Environment. Following decade-long refurbishment, its exterior is now gleaming, having been painstakingly cleaned and repaired from top to bottom. Finally open to the public again, at least for now, by guided visit only, tours (in English or Spanish) of its stunning interior take in the 17.5m bronze *Estatua de la República*, said to be one of the world's tallest indoor statues, and the two resplendent debating chambers with their breathtaking gold-and-bronze Rococo detail. Buy tickets from the kiosks hidden down the side of the grandiose steps up to the entrance.

Paseo del Prado

Cutting through the Parque Central's western edge and marking the border between Habana Vieja and Centro Habana is the **Paseo del Prado**, one of the old town's prettiest main streets. Also known as the Paseo de Martí, but more often simply as **El Prado**, its reputation comes from the boulevard section north of the park, beginning at the *Hotel Parque Central* and marching down to the seafront. A wide walkway lined with trees and stone benches bisects the road, while on either side are the hundreds of columns, arches and balconies of the mostly residential neo-colonial buildings, painted in a whole host of colours. Encouragingly, despite its position in the city's touristic centre, El Prado still belongs to the locals and is usually overrun with newspaper sellers and children playing ball games, while most weekends it is host to an art market.

Parque de la Fraternidad

The network of lawns dissected by paths and roads immediately to the south of the Capitolio is the **Parque de la Fraternidad**, the biggest expanse of open land in Habana Vieja and the city's largest transport hub. Alive with buses, taxis and people, only a few of them stopping to sit on the park's benches, the sense of commotion here overrides all else. With so much traffic and so many roads to cross, few visitors spend much time in the park itself, though there are some points of interest, including the fascinating **Museo do los Orishas**. Until May 2022, the eastern side was dominated by the magnificent **Hotel Saratoga**, when a gas explosion razed it to the ground, tragically killing over forty people just days before it was due to reopen post-pandemic.

Constructed as part of the sixth Pan-American Conference that took place in Havana, the park took its current form and name in 1928. This was when the centrepiece – a huge, encaged ceiba tree, the **Arbol de la Fraternidad Americana** – was planted, using soil brought from every country that attended the conference. In addition, busts of some of the continent's most revered leaders were installed, including Abraham Lincoln, Simón Bolívar and Benito Juárez, the first Indigenous president of Mexico.

The Fuente de la India
Parque de la Fraternidad

Stranded on what has effectively become a traffic island, on the Prado side of the Parque de la Fraternidad, a monument known as the **Fuente de la India** has become one of the symbols of the city. Erected in 1837, a Native American woman in a feather headdress sits atop this marble monument holding the city's coat of arms, flanked by four fierce-looking fish. The woman is **La Noble Habana**, who, according to popular legend, greeted the Spanish colonialists who first arrived at the port in 1509 with a gesture that appeared to refer to the bay and uttered the word "habana" – thus spawning the name of the city.

1

SANTERÍA AND CATHOLICISM

Walking the streets of Havana, you may notice people dressed head-to-foot in white, a bead necklace providing the only colour in their costume. These are practitioners of **Santería**, the most popular of African-Cuban religions, and the beads represent their appointed **orisha**, the gods and goddesses at the heart of their worship.

With its roots in the religious beliefs of the Yoruba people of West Africa, Santería spread in Cuba with the enforced importation of enslaved people from that region. Forbidden by the Spanish to practise their faith, the enslaved found ways of hiding images of their gods behind those of the Catholic saints to whom they were forced to pay homage. From this developed the **syncretism** of African *orishas* with their Catholic counterparts – thus, for example, the Virgen de la Caridad del Cobre, the patron saint of Cuba, embodies the *orisha* known as Oshún, the goddess of femininity, in part because both are believed to provide protection during birth. Similarly, Yemayá, goddess of water and queen of the sea – considered the mother of all *orishas* – is the equivalent of the Virgen de Regla, whom Spanish Catholics believed protected sailors. Other pairings include San Lázaro, patron saint of the sick, with Babalu-Ayé, Santa Bárbara with Changó, and San Cristóbal with Aggayú. There are some four hundred African-Cuban *orishas* in all.

Museo de los Orishas

Paseo del Prado e/ Máximo Gómez (Monte) y Dragones, Parque de la Fraternidad • Tues–Sun • Charge • ☏ 7863 5953

At the southern end of El Prado, housed within the Asociación Cultural Yoruba de Cuba headquarters (a focal point and meeting place for the capital's Santería community) is the **Museo de los Orishas** or "Museum of the Gods". It's populated with full-size terracotta statues of the best-known African-Cuban deities, each one full of personality and set in its own representative scene. With the assistance of the on-hand English-speaking guide, this offers a straightforward and fascinating insight into the main deities, as well as some of the practices that form the basis of this earthy, colourful faith. There are also activities here open to the public, including dance performances; details can be found on the notice board in the entrance hall. A restaurant-cum-cafeteria on site serves African-Cuban food.

Southern Habana Vieja

South of the Parque de la Fraternidad and Plaza Vieja, the tourist attractions almost instantly die out, reappearing again on the port road and the bay front, site of the city's largest artisan craft market, the Antiguo Almacenes San José. In between, Habana Vieja takes on a more workaday character, dotted with churches, food markets, *casas particulares* and a couple of old convents among all the tumbledown apartment buildings. Ambling around these ramshackle, vibrant streets offers a stimulating, undiluted taste of life in Old Havana, served up through its open doorways, pavement living rooms and curbside socializing.

Casa Natal de José Martí

Paula no.314 e/ Picota y Avenida de Bélgica • Tues–Sat 9am–5pm, Sun 9.30am–1pm • Charge • ☏ 7861 3778

Two blocks east of the Parque de la Fraternidad is the Avenida de Bélgica, a main road leading down to the most tangible and best-kept tourist attraction in this part of town, the **Casa Natal de José Martí**. This modest two-storey house was the birthplace of Cuba's most widely revered freedom fighter and intellectual, though he only lived here for the first three years of his life. Dotted with the odd bit of original furniture, the rooms of this perfectly preserved blue-and-yellow house don't strive to re-create domestic tableaux, but instead exhibit photographs, documents, some of Martí's personal effects and other items relating to his tumultuous life. The eclectic set of memorabilia includes a plait of his hair, his bureau and a watch chain given to him by pupils of a Guatemalan school where he taught. There are images of his arrest, imprisonment and exile on the Isla de Pinos (now the Isla de la Juventud), and details of his trips to New York, Caracas and around Spain.

Museo Nacional de Bellas Artes

Tues–Sat 9am–5pm, Sun 10am–2pm • Charge • ⓦ bellasartescuba.co.cu

Set along the broad avenues that fill the relatively open spaces on the western edge of Habana Vieja, the **Museo Nacional de Bellas Artes** is the most impressive and spectacular of Havana's museums and by far the largest art collection in the country, with its collection divided between two completely separate buildings, two blocks apart. The museum stands head and shoulders above the vast majority of its city rivals, smartly presented and properly curated, with no unnecessary clutter. The large Art Deco **Palacio de Bellas Artes** showcases a history of exclusively Cuban painting and sculpture, including everything from portraits by Spanish colonists to Revolution-inspired work – though pre-Columbian art is notably absent. Artists from the rest of the world are represented in the **Centro Asturiano**, with an impressive breadth of different kinds of art, including Roman ceramics and nineteenth-century Japanese paintings.

No English translations have been provided for any of the titles in either building, which can be a hindrance to fully appreciating some of the works on display – particularly in the ancient art section, where it's not always clear what you are looking at. Both buildings have **bookshops** where you can buy good-quality Spanish guides to their collections – invaluable if you have an interest in the context and background of the paintings.

Palacio de Bellas Artes

Trocadero e/ Agramonte (Zulueta) y Avenida de las Misiones (Monserrate)

No other collection of **Cuban art**, of any sort, comes close to the range and volume of works on display in the beautifully lit, air-conditioned **Palacio de Bellas Artes**, a two-minute walk north along Agramonte from the Parque Central. The collection spans five centuries but has a far higher proportion of twentieth-century art.

To tackle the three floors chronologically, take the lifts up to the top floor and walk around clockwise. From a set of relatively ordinary colonial-era portraits and landscapes there is an abrupt leap into the twentieth century, not only the most substantial but also the most engaging part of the collection. *Gitana Tropical* (*Tropical Gypsy*) by **Victor Manuel García** (1897–1969), one of the first Cuban exponents of modern art, is his evocative yet simplistic portrait of a young Native American woman and a widely reproduced national treasure. Paintings by other Cuban greats such as **Wifredo Lam** (1902–82) and **Fidelo Ponce de León** (1895–1949) are succeeded by art from the 1950s through to the 1970s, and then finally a section dedicated to works produced since 1979. This includes installation art, sculptures and, in the work of **Raúl Martínez** (1927–95), an example of a very Cuban take on pop art.

To see anything from this century, check the single room on the top floor by the lifts, where temporary exhibitions are hung, or visit the bookshop (the best in the city for books on Cuban art, with a decent selection of posters too) on the ground floor, where you'll also find a simple café and the pleasant open courtyard, dotted with a few modern sculptures. Before leaving, check the notice board in the entrance hall for upcoming **events** in the museum, often in its 248-seat theatre.

Centro Asturiano

San Rafael e/ Agramonte (Zulueta) y Avenida de las Misiones (Monserrate)

In contrast to the simplicity of the Palacio de Bellas Artes, the interior of the stately **Centro Asturiano**, on the east border of the Parque Central, is a marvel to look at in

1

ARTIST STUDIOS AND COMMERICAL GALLERIES

All over Havana, and especially in Habana Vieja, there are increasing numbers of individual **artist studios**, workshops and galleries, most of them with at least some commercial element, providing a welcome alternative to the blandly repetitive arts and crafts that appear around the city's tourist-focused markets and shops. This relatively new phenomenon allows not only a broader, more interesting range of paintings, prints and sculptures to choose from for buyers but reveals sides to **contemporary Cuban art** that were previously relatively difficult to discover. These small gallery-workshops usually allow visitors to make direct contact with the painters, photographers and sculptors themselves, many of whom work on the premises. Some galleries have names but others do not and are known simply by the name of the artist. Here are some of the most interesting and engaging:

Estudo-Taller de Abel Massot Empedrado 406 e/ Compostela y Aguacate ☎ 5254 3964

Abel Massot, painter, photographer and sculptor, displays his most recent work here at his small gallery. Over the last few years his work has consisted most notably of intense and disturbed faces and figures, not unlike some of the work of Oswaldo Guayasamín.

Estudio-Taller de Inti Alvarez Hauville Cuarteles 118 e/ Ave. de las Misiones y Habana ⓦ cuban-artist. com. Painter and sculptor Inti Alvarez has exhibited internationally and you can get a taste of his distinctive, slightly haunting painted figures here.

El Ojo del Ciclón: Estudio Taller Leo D'Lázaro

O'Reilly 501 esq. Villegas ☎ 7 861 5359 or ☎ 5 258 1300. Works with wood and exhibiting since the 1980s. Born in 1965. Collage, sculpture, photography, abstract paintings.

Studio Molina Villegas no.114B e/ O'Reilly y San Juan de Dios ☎ 7801 4124

Young artist Marcel Molina Martínez works with his brother and wife to produce bleak and powerful black and white pictures themed on the sugar industry. Some of his large-scale wood etchings are displayed in this, one of the most professionally run and presented studio-workshops, with the familiarly sparse feel of modern art galleries.

itself. Housing the international collections of the Museo de Bellas Artes, this grandiose building is plastered with balcony-supported columns and punctuated with carved stone detail. The entrance hall with its wide marble staircase is captivating, punctuated by thick pillars and, looming above, spacious balustraded balconies from which you can admire the stunning stained-glass ceiling.

The exhibits are divided up by **country of origin**, with the largest collections by Italian, French and Spanish artists, on the fifth, fourth and third floors respectively. There are one or two standouts among the more mundane British, German, Dutch and Flemish collections, all on the **fifth floor**, such as *Kermesse* by Jan Brueghel (the younger), one of the only internationally famous artists in this section. The painting depicts a poorer scene with all sorts of debauchery going on, a focus typical of his work.

Elsewhere you can see **ancient art** from Rome, Egypt, Greece and Etruria, including vases, busts, and most notably the coffin from a 3000-year-old tomb; a small room of nineteenth-century Japanese paintings; and, sketchiest of all, a haphazard set of Latin American and North American paintings.

Museo de la Revolución

Refugio no.1 e/ Agramonte (Zulueta) y Avenida de las Misiones (Monserrate) • Daily 9am–5pm (last entry 4pm) • Charge • ☎ 7862 4091

Next to a small piece of the old city wall is Havana's most famous museum, the **Museo de la Revolución**. Triumphantly housed in the sumptuous presidential palace of the 1950s dictator General Fulgencio Batista, the museum manages to be both unmissable and overrated at the same time. The events leading up to the triumph of the Revolution in 1959 are covered in unparalleled detail, but a clear narrative of what happened is lost in the sometimes disjointed displays, and your attention span is unlikely to last the full three storeys. Visitors work their way down from the top floor, which is the densest part of the museum. Rooms are grouped chronologically into historical stages, or **etapas**, from Etapa Colonial to Etapa de la Revolución, though the layout is a bit higgledy-piggledy in places, making it unclear what point in the timeline you have reached.

The Revolutionary War and the urban insurgency movements during the 1950s were surprisingly well documented photographically and it's at this stage of the story that the exhibits are most engaging. Among them are the classic photos of the campaign waged by Castro and his followers in the Sierra Maestra and the sensationalist **Memorial Camilo-Che**, a life-sized wax model of revolutionary heroes Camilo Cienfuegos and Che Guevara. However, even serious students of Cuban history may overdose on models of battles and weapons exhibits also found in this section.

Much of the second floor is given over to exhaustive depictions of battle plans and the "construction of Socialism", bringing the story up to the present. It's the **interior of the building** itself, built between 1913 and 1917 during the much-maligned "pseudo-republic" era, that is most captivating on this floor. There's the gold-encrusted Salón Dorado; the lavish dining room of the old palace when it was occupied by General Batista; the dignified furnishings of the Presidential Office (used by all the presidents of Cuba from 1920 to 1965); and the wonderfully colourful **mural** on the ceiling of the Salón de los Espejos.

Granma Memorial

To the rear of the Museo de la Revolución building, in the palace gardens, is the **Granma Memorial**, where the boat which took Castro and his merry men from Mexico to Cuba to begin the Revolution is preserved in its entirety within a giant glass case. Also here are military vehicles (whole or in bits, depending on which side they belonged to) used during the 1961 Bay of Pigs invasion, and a poignant pink marble monument to those who died in the revolutionary struggle.

Castillo de San Salvador de la Punta and around
Avenida del Puerto esq. Paseo del Prado

Hogging most of La Punta, the paved corner of land at the entrance to the bay, the sixteenth-century fortress of **Castillo de San Salvador de la Punta** is one of the oldest military fortifications in the city, yet little visited compared to its counterparts. Construction began in 1589 at the same time as that of El Morro, and together these two forts formed the city's first and most important line of defence. Today it houses a modest museum (see below).

La Punta itself caps one end of the official border between Habana Vieja and Centro Habana. Despite its prosaic position right next to the busy junction where the Malecón meets the Avenida del Puerto, it still attracts large groups of chattering locals and youngsters, who gather to throw themselves off the Malecón into the rocky pools that jut out from the sea wall here. The mega luxury *Hotel Paseo del Prado* now looms over La Punta.

Museo de San Salvador de la Punta
Castillo de San Salvador de la Punta • Weds–Sat 10am–4.30pm, Sun 10am–1pm • Charge

Most of the rooms at the fort are empty or closed to the public but two of them house the exhibits of the understocked **Museo de San Salvador de la Punta**, tracing the curious history of a sixteenth and seventeenth-century family of Italian military engineers and architects and their work. The Antonellis, in the service of the Spanish Crown, built forts all over the territories of the Spanish Empire, including this one and two others in Cuba. In what was the munitions storeroom there are models of some of the forts and storyboards, in Spanish, Italian and English, breaking down the history in considerable detail.

You can ascend to the ramparts which are lined with cannon and afford modest views along the Malecón, over to El Morro and down into the harbour.

1

Monumento a Máximo Gómez

On a giant traffic island between La Punta and the rest of Habana Vieja is the Neoclassical **Monumento a Máximo Gómez**, one of the grandest memorials in Havana. Dedicated to the venerated leader of the Liberation Army in the nineteenth-century Cuban Wars of Independence, the statue has the general sitting on a horse held aloft by marble figures representing the People.

Parque de los Mártires

Over the road from the *Monumento a Máximo Gómez* is the pretty little **Parque de los Mártires**, marking the spot where the notorious prison, the **Cárcel de Tacón**, built in 1838, once held such political prisoners as José Martí. It was mostly demolished in 1939, and all that remains are two of the cells and the chapel in what is little more than a large concrete box.

Parque Morro-Cabaña

Carretera de la Cabaña, Habana del Este • Daily 10am–10pm • Charge • Transport options include the ferry (see below), a taxi, or the Habana Bus Tour from the Parque Central; get off at the first stop after the tunnel on the route to the Playas del Este • ☎ 7862 4095 & 4097

While many visitors don't make it to the **Parque Morro-Cabaña**, across the bay from Habana Vieja, those who do are rewarded by the uncrowded sights of an impressive, sprawling complex of fortifications that, along with the two fortresses in Habana Vieja, comprised the city's colonial defence system. A stalwart part of both the Havana skyline and timeline, the two fortresses here dominate the view across the channel into the harbour, and mark key events and periods in the city's history. Beyond the forts, further into the bay, a gargantuan statue of Christ, **El Cristo de La Habana**, was one of the last public works completed before Cuba was taken over by Fidel Castro and his revolutionary – and subsequently atheist – government.

There are several **restaurants** and **bars** in and around this military park, and *La Divina Pastora* makes a delightful spot for lunch or dinner with bay views (see page 125).

Castillo de los Tres Reyes Magos del Morro

Parque Morro-Cabaña • Daily 10am–7pm • Charge • ☎ 7861 9727

Crowning the low cliffs of the rocky headland that marks the entrance to the Bahía de la Habana is the imposing **Castillo de los Tres Reyes Magos del Morro**, more commonly known as **El Morro**. This castle was built between 1589 and 1630 to form an impeding crossfire with the Castillo de San Salvador de la Punta on the opposite side of the bay, a ploy that failed spectacularly when the English invaded overland in 1762 and occupied the city for six months.

CROSS-BAY FERRIES

Used very little by tourists, the rudimentary **cross-bay ferry services** that link Habana Vieja with Casablanca and Regla on the eastern side of the bay represent a cheap and pleasant (but slow) way of getting to the Parque Morro-Cabaña. Ferries leave from the small Emboque de Luz ferry terminal opposite the *Hotel Armadores de Santander* on San Pedro in Habana Vieja, two minutes' walk from the Plaza de San Francisco and the main Sierra Maestra Terminal. Bikes are not permitted. The ferry runs daily between 6am and 11pm.

Habana Vieja to: Casablanca (every 30min; 10min); Regla (every 30min; 20min).
Casablanca to: Habana Vieja (every 30min; 10min).
Regla to: Habana Vieja (every 30min; 20min).

THE HERSHEY TRAIN FROM HAVANA

Aside from the *Cristo de La Habana* statue, the only other diversion in Casablanca is the terminus of the **Hershey train**, one end of Cuba's only electric train service (the other is in the provincial capital of Matanzas). Regularly used by Cubans travelling to stations in Mayabeque and Matanzas, the line is not an official tourist attraction, but the loveable little trains, built in the 1940s, are a great way to take a slow, relaxing ride through picturesque landscape to Canasí, Jibacoa or all the way to the city of Matanzas, which takes about three hours.

Once you get beyond the bar, shop and the exhibition room laid out with scale models of Cuban forts just off the central courtyard, the castle has an eerie, just-abandoned feel. The cavernous billet rooms and cannon stores are empty but in near-perfect condition, while the easy-to-follow layout and peaceful, uncluttered spaces lend themselves to wandering around at your own pace. Particularly fine are the broad castle **ramparts** studded with rusted cannon and offering splendid views on all sides. There are even better views from the summit of the **lighthouse** (extra charge) built on the cliff edge in 1844, over two centuries after the rest of the fortress had been completed.

Fortaleza de San Carlos de la Cabaña

Parque Morro-Cabaña • Daily 10am–10pm • Charge

Situated roughly 500m further into the Bahía de la Habana from El Morro, the **Fortaleza de San Carlos de la Cabaña** needs a half-day to do it justice. Despite containing a much larger number of things to see and do within its grounds, its wide-open spaces, benches and trees, along with a garden area, make it the more relaxing of the two forts. Built to be the most complex and expensive defence system in the Americas, the fortress was started in 1763 as soon as the Spanish traded the city back from the English. However, its defensive worth has never been proved, as takeover attempts by other European powers had largely died down by the time it was finished in 1774.

You can see why it took so long to finish after touring the extensive grounds, akin to a small village complete with a chapel, spacious lawns, several more recently installed cafés and restaurants, and impeccable cobbled streets lined with houses where soldiers and officers were originally billeted – now a miscellany of workshops, touristy arts-and-crafts stores and a number of small **museums**. Among these one- and two-room museums is a weaponry and armoury collection, a set of colonial-era furniture once in practical use at the fortress and a commemoration of the 1961 Bay of Pigs invasion and the 1962 Cuban Missile Crisis, featuring some dramatic photographs from the time. It's worth sticking around for the **Ceremonia del Cañonazo**, in which soldiers in nineteenth-century uniforms fire the cannon at 9pm every evening, and whose familiar boom, known popularly simply as **El Cañonazo**, has Havana residents checking their clocks whenever they hear it.

El Cristo de La Habana

Daily 9am–6pm • Free if you show a ticket for Parque Morro-Cabaña • The best way to get here from Habana Vieja is the cross-harbour ferry, which docks close by

On the hill above the picturesque village of Casablanca, 1km southeast from the entrance to the Fortaleza San Carlos de la Cabaña, is **El Cristo de La Habana**, a17m-high Christ figure commissioned by Marta Batista, wife of the dictator, and sculpted from Italian marble by Jilma Madera in 1958. Although impressive close-up, where you can

1

ponder the massive scale of the sandaled feet and the perfectly sculpted hands, said to weigh a tonne each, there's precious little to do on the hillside other than admire the **views** over Havana. The best perspective of the statue itself is from Habana Vieja, especially in the evening, when you can gaze across the bay and enjoy its floodlit grandeur.

Centro Habana

For many visitors the crumbling buildings and bustling streets of **Centro Habana**, crammed between the hotel districts of Habana Vieja and Vedado, are glimpsed only through a taxi window en route to the city's more tourist-friendly areas. Yet this no-frills quarter has a character all of its own, as illuminating and fascinating as anywhere in the capital. Its late eighteenth- and nineteenth-century neighbourhoods throb with life, particularly around San Rafael and Avenida de Italia, famous shopping streets where many of the most glamorous department stores were located before the Revolution, when the Avenida de Italia was known as Galiano, the name most locals still use. Near the southern end of Galiano is **El Barrio Chino**, Havana's Chinatown, small by international standards but still a busy focal point for the area.

For the most part, Centro Habana is not that attractive on the surface. Full of broken sewage systems, potholed roads and piles of rubbish, it hasn't yet enjoyed the degree of investment and rejuvenation lavished on Habana Vieja. However, the famous **Malecón** seafront promenade is regaining its former glory, with many of its buildings given face-lifts in recent years, and there's nowhere in the city that feels more alive. Centro Habana's streets buzz with people and nonstop noise, ringing with an orchestra of street vendors shouting their wares, *bicitaxis* blasting their sound systems, schoolchildren's screams and doorstep politics.

STORE DETECTIVE

During the 1950s, Havana's most prestigious shopping destination was the Centro Habana intersection where San Rafael and Neptuno converged with Galiano. At its heart, on the corner of San Rafael and Galiano, stood **El Encanto**, the most renowned of the department stores, occupying an entire block and boasting the patronage of Hollywood stars like Lana Turner, John Wayne and Errol Flynn. In 1961 the store, which by this time had been nationalized, was burned to the ground, the result of a bomb attack in the tumultuous early years of the Revolution.

Five decades later and general neglect coupled with the on-going effects of the US trade blockade has left the area sorely dilapidated. Rather than unearthing great retail finds, the real pleasure here is spotting the vestiges of a glamorous past in the old shop signs, marble pavements, faded interiors and elaborate tiled frontages that dazzle amid the ruins. In particular, look out for the **Hotpoint mosaic** on San Rafael esq. Industria; the stylish flourish of lettering spelling out **Fin de Siglo** along the building on the corner of Aguila and San Rafael, once a fancy five-storey department store featuring a hair salon decorated with floor-to-ceiling mirrors; and the **Flogar** logo imprinted on the dusty glass frontage of the large, half-empty store at Galiano no.42, where mannequins once displayed the latest fashions in the Macy's-style window displays.

The only department store to have been fully redeveloped since the Revolution is **La Epoca**, reborn a little less than half a century after it first moved into its home on the corner of Galiano and Neptuno in 1954, becoming the third largest department store in Havana at the time, employing over four hundred staff. Locals flock here today to buy clothes, electrical goods and homewares, though the current design of its five floors owes more to modern supermarkets than the chic interiors of yesteryear.

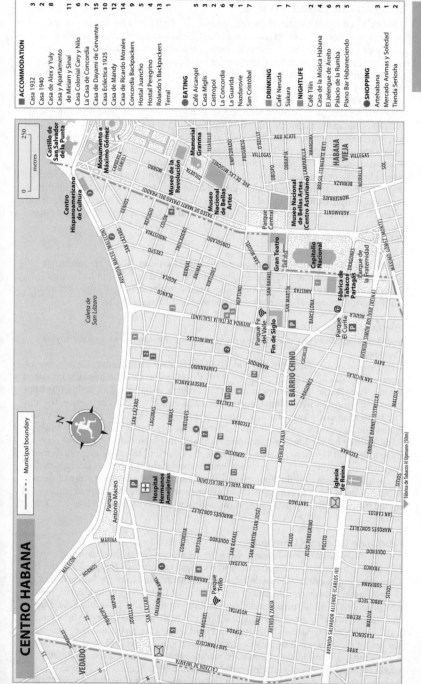

1

El Barrio Chino and around

About a block inside Centro Habana from Habana Vieja's western border, the grand entrance to **El Barrio Chino**, Havana's version of Chinatown, is likely to confuse most visitors, as it's placed three blocks from any visibly ethnic change in the neighbourhood. The **entrance**, a rectangular concrete arch with a pagoda-inspired roof, is south of the Capitolio Nacional, on the intersection of Amistad and Dragones, and marks the beginning of the ten or so square blocks which, at the start of the twentieth century, were home to some ten thousand Chinese immigrants. Today only a tiny proportion of El Barrio Chino is discernibly any more Chinese than the rest of Havana, principally the small triangle of busy streets comprising Cuchillo, Zanja and San Nicolás – collectively known as the **Cuchillo de Zanja** – three blocks west of the arched entrance. Indeed, the first thing you are likely to notice about El Barrio Chino is a distinct absence of Chinese people, the once significant immigrant population having long since dissolved into the racial melting pot. The Cuchillo de Zanja itself does, however, feature its own tightly packed little backstreet food market, composed mostly of simple fruit and vegetable stalls. It's lined with eccentric-looking restaurants, where the curious and unique mixture of tastes and styles is as much Cuban as Asian.

Fábrica de Tabacos Partagás

Industria no.50 e/ Dragones y Barcelona

Behind the Capitolio stands the **Fábrica de Tabacos Partagás**, one of the country's oldest factories, and now a reputable cigar shop. Founded in 1845, in its heyday, the factory employed some 750 workers producing twelve brands of cigar, including Cohiba, Monte Cristo, Romeo y Julieta, Bolívar and Partagás itself.

Iglesia de Reina

Avenida Simón Bolívar (Reina) no.461–463 e/ Padre Varela (Belascoaín) y Gervasio • Daily 8am–noon & 3–5pm • Mass daily 8am & 4.30pm • Free

Well away from any tourist traffic, a block from the Avenida Salvador Allende, one of Centro Habana's broadest thoroughfares, sits the magnificent church locally known as the **Iglesia de Reina**. The tallest church in the country, with a spire rocketing out from a block of worn-out neo-colonial apartment buildings, it was built between 1914 and 1923 and is officially known as the Parroquia del Sagrado del Corazón de Jesús y San Ignacio de Loyola. Its unlikely location in the grime of Centro Habana, with heavy traffic passing by outside, contrasts effectively with its Neo-Gothic splendour. The church's **interior** is infinitely more impressive than that of Habana Vieja's much more heavily visited cathedral: the cavernous vaulted roof of the three naves is supported by colossal columns and the huge central altar incorporates a dazzling array of detail. Wherever you look, something catches the eye, from the skilfully sculpted scenes etched into the central pillars to the stained-glass windows at different levels on the outer walls.

Fábrica de Tabacos H Upmann

Padre Varela (Belascoaín) no.852 e/ Peñalver y Desagüe • Mon–Fri 9am–1pm; shop Mon–Sat 9am–5pm • Charge for tours

Commonly referred to as the Romeo y Julieta cigar factory, this is technically the H Upmann factory, or the **Fábrica de Tabacos H Upmann**, but Romeo y Julieta cigars, and those of other brands, are also made here. Like most Cuban cigar brands, H Upmann, first produced in 1844, predates the Revolution, but since all Cuban brands are now state owned most factories, like this one, produce multiple brands under the same roof. The impressive factory, with its grand marble staircase just inside the entrance, has one of the largest rolling galleries in the country, with over 200 workers employed here in total. The fascinating tours walk you through the several floors of the building, where you see how the tobacco leaves are selected, rolled, branded and boxed. Though you can take your chances and just turn up, you may find that by doing so you are restricted to the excellent shop – the only way to guarantee a tour is by booking one in advance through *buros de turismo* in hotels. As well as H Upmann and Romeo y Julieta, Partagas, some Montecristos and Cohiba cigars are made here too. No photography is permitted.

The Malecón and around

The most picturesque way to reach Vedado from Centro Habana or Habana Vieja is to stroll down the famous **Malecón** sea wall, which snakes west along the coastline from La Punta for about 4km. It's the city's defining image, and ambling along its length, drinking in the panoramic views, is an essential part of the Havana experience. But don't expect to stroll in solitude: the Malecón is the capital's front room and you won't be on it for long before someone strikes up a conversation. People head here for free entertainment, particularly at night when it fills up with guitar-strumming musicians, vendors offering cones of fresh-roasted nuts, and star-gazing couples, young and old alike. At weekends and in the daytime it's crowded with children hurling themselves into the churning Atlantic, while wide-eyed tourists and anglers climb down onto the rocks below.

The Centro Habana section, referred to on street signs as the **Malecón tradicional**, has been undergoing tortoise-paced renovations for over two decades now. Lined with colourful neo-colonial buildings but potholed and sea-beaten, it's the oldest, most distinct section in the city. Construction began in 1901, after nearly a decade of planning, and each decade saw another chunk of wall erected until, in 1950, it finally reached the Río Almendares. Today there are a few places worth stopping in for eating and drinking with enjoyable sea views (see page 125).

Centro Hispanoamericano de Cultura
Malecón no.17 e/ Paseo del Prado y Capdevila (Cárcel) • Mon–Sat 9.30am–5pm • ☎ 7860 6282

A seafront arts centre in a wonderful Neoclassical building, the **Centro Hispanoamericano de Cultura** stages art exhibitions, book and poetry readings and, on Saturday afternoons, live music performances. There's also a library and a small cinema but it's worth just taking a quick wander around the beautifully restored building, one of the few open to the public on the Malecón that isn't a hotel, restaurant or bar.

Parque Antonio Maceo
On the western edge of Centro Habana, a few blocks from Vedado, the Malecón passes in front of the **Parque Antonio Maceo**, known simply as the Parque Maceo, an attractive, open concrete park. Overlooked by the best hospital in the country, the towering Hospital Hermanos Ameijeiras, the park is marked in the centre by a statue of Antonio Maceo, the Cuban general and hero of the Wars of Independence. The only other monument is the **Torreon de San Lázaro**, a solitary little turret in the northwest corner, once part of the city's defence system and dating back to 1665, making it 250

HAVANA FROM A HEIGHT

With its architecturally distinct neighbourhoods dating from separate eras, Havana looks stunning from above, but since the city is laid out on relatively flat land, you have to go to the southern outskirts or over to the eastern side of the bay for hills high enough to afford a decent **view**. There are, however, numerous tall buildings open to the public dotted around the city proper, with fabulous vistas across the boroughs. The best of these are **Café Laurent**, the **Cámara Oscura**, **Edificio FOCSA**, **Habana Libre**, **Iglesia de San Francisco de Asís**, **Memorial José Martí** and the swanky **Torre del Oro Roof Garden**, atop the *Hotel Sevilla*, where the views far exceed the quality of the food.

1

years older than the park itself. There's a small playground here and the park attracts scores of kids and chattering adults every evening, which is the best time to visit.

Callejón de Hamel

Four blocks west from the Parque Maceo on San Lázaro, a wide alleyway known as the **Callejón de Hamel** has been converted into an intriguing and cultish monument to African-Cuban culture. Often featured in Cuban music videos, this bizarre backstreet is full of **shrines**, cut into the walls and erected along the sides, brimming with colour and a mishmash of decorative and symbolic images. The backdrop is an abstract **mural** painted by Salvador González in 1990, when it was decided that it was high time for a public space dedicated to African-Cuba. A few chairs and tables make up a tiny café at one end and the alley also features a small studio workshop selling smaller pieces of art done by González. On Sundays from around 11am, Callejón de Hamel becomes a venue for **Santería ceremonies**, mini street festivals in which participants dance passionately to the rhythm of rumba in a frenetic atmosphere, accentuated by chants invoking the spirits of the *orishas*. The alley becomes overrun with visitors – not to mention *jineteros* – and the event has unfortunately become slightly contrived, though it's still a very accessible way to experience one of the most engaging expressions of Santería.

Vedado

The heart of contemporary culture in the city, graceful **Vedado** draws the crowds with its palatial hotels, art galleries, exciting (and sometimes incomprehensible) theatre productions and live music concerts, not to mention its glut of restaurants, bars and nightspots. Loosely defined as the area running west of Calzada de Infanta up to the Río Almendares, Vedado is less ramshackle than other parts of the city. Tall 1950s buildings and battered Cadillacs parked outside glass-fronted stores lend the downtown area a strongly North American air, contrasted with the classical ambience of nineteenth-century mansions; the general impression is of an incompletely sealed time capsule, where the decades and centuries all run together.

Vedado is fairly easy to negotiate, laid out on a grid system divided by four main thoroughfares: the broad and handsome boulevards Avenida de los Presidentes (also called Calle G) and Paseo, running north to south, and the more prosaic Linea and Calle 23 running east to west. The most prominent sector is modern **La Rampa** – the name given to a busy section of Calle 23 immediately west from the Malecón, as well as the streets just to the north and south. Presenting a rather bland uniformity that's absent from the rest of Vedado, it's a relatively small space, trailing along the eastern part of the Malecón and spanning just a couple of streets inland. A little to the south of La Rampa proper is the elegant **Universidad de La Habana**, attended by orderly students who personify the virtues of post-Revolution education.

Southwest of the university is the **Plaza de la Revolución**, with its immense monuments to Cuban heroes José Martí, Ernesto "Che" Guevara and, more recently added, Camilo Cienfuegos. Although generally considered part of Vedado, Plaza de la Revolución (also known just as Plaza) is actually the municipality to which the Vedado neighbourhood belongs, and with its huge utilitarian buildings has a flavour quite distinct from the other parts of Vedado. The uncompromisingly urban landscape of the plaza itself – a huge sweep of concrete – is a complete contrast to the area's other key attraction, the atmospheric **Necrópolis de Colón**, a truly massive cemetery.

In the part of Vedado north of Calle 23 up to the Malecón, west to the Río Almendares and east roughly as far as the Avenida de los Presidentes, the backstreets are narrow and avenues are overhung with leaves. Many of the magnificent late- and post-colonial buildings here – built in a mad medley of Rococo, Baroque and Neoclassical

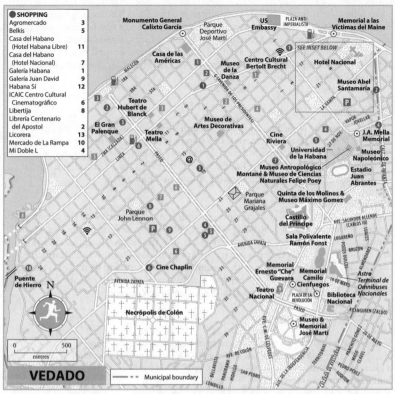

VEDADO

SHOPPING

Agromercado	3
Belkis	5
Casa del Habano (Hotel Habana Libre)	11
Casa del Habano (Hotel Nacional)	7
Galería Habana	1
Galería Juan David	9
Habana Sí	12
ICAIC Centro Cultural Cinematográfico	6
Libertija	8
Librería Centenario del Apostol	2
Licorera	13
Mercado de La Rampa	10
Mi Doble L	4

– – – Municipal boundary

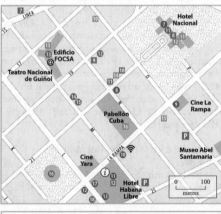

EATING

Los Amigos	14	Coppelia	16
Atelier	3	Decameron	6
El Biky	4	Ideas	1
Café Laurent	15	Plan B	9
Café Presidente	7	Q Bolá	5
Cafetería La Rampa	17	La Torre	13
California Café	12	Unión Francesa	8
Camino al Sol	2	La Veranda	11
El Cocinero	10	Waoo!	18

NIGHTLIFE

Cabaret Parisién	12	Club Jardines de 1830	8
Café Cantante Mi Habana	9	Delirio Habanero Piano Bar	9
Café Teatro Bertolt Brecht	1	El Gato Tuerto	10
Casa de la Amistad	6	Hurón Azul UNEAC	4
Casa de la Cultura de Plaza	5	Pabellón	16
		Salón Rojo	14
		La Zorra y El Cuervo	15

DRINKING

Bar Galería	11	La Esencia	3
Café Bar Madrigal	7	La Fuente	2
El Emperador	13		

ACCOMMODATION

Casa de Aurora Ampudia	7	Hostal Peregrino	2
Casa Aide	10	Hostal Silvia	5
Casa de Leydiana Navarro Cardoso	9	Nacional	8
Casa de Magda	4	NH Capri	11
Casa de Mélida Jordán	6	Presidente	1
Habana Libre	12	Riviera	3

1

styles – have been converted into state offices and museums. Particularly noteworthy is the **Museo de Artes Decorativas**, an exhausting collection of fine furniture and *objets d'art*. Further west from the Malecón, dotted around Linea, Paseo and the Avenida de los Presidentes, are several excellent galleries and cultural centres. Not to be missed is the **Casa de las Américas**, a slim and stylish Art Deco building that was set up to celebrate Pan-Americanism.

La Rampa

Halfway along the Malecón's length an artificial waterfall, at the foot of the *Hotel Nacional* precipice, marks the start of **La Rampa** (The Slope), the road into the centre of Vedado. Once the seedy pre-revolutionary home of Chinese theatres, casinos and pay-by-the-hour knocking shops, La Rampa is now lined with airline offices and official headquarters, its seedy side long gone (or at least well hidden).

Hotel Nacional

Set on a bluff above the Taganana cave and with a magnificent view of the ocean, the landmark **Hotel Nacional** is home to a princely tiled lobby, and an elegant colonnaded veranda looking out to sea across an expanse of well-tended lawn commandeered by tame guinea fowl. The perfect cinematic backdrop for a *mojito*, it was built in 1930 and quickly became a favourite with visiting luminaries – among them Ava Gardner, Winston Churchill, Josephine Baker and John Wayne – and more recently has added the likes of Naomi Campbell and Jack Nicholson to its clientele.

Edificio FOCSA
Calle M esq. 17

Considered variously as a feat of engineering or a monolithic eyesore, the giant Y-shaped luxury apartment block **Edificio FOCSA** looms over the heart of Vedado like a giant chunk of honeycomb. When built in 1956 this was the second-tallest concrete building in the world; it exemplified modern living with a cinema, supermarket, shops and even a television studio within. According to Alfredo José Estrada in his book *Havana: Autobiography of a City*, by the 1960s the building was known as "*edificio coño*" (roughly equivalent to the "Oh my God!" building) because of the stunned reaction of visiting country bumpkins. Following the Revolution, it housed Soviet personnel whose lack of respect, according to locals, resulted in widespread disrepair. By the early 1990s vultures nested in crumbling eyries, a snapped cable in the deteriorated elevator resulted in a fatal accident in 2000, and the state stepped in with a repair programme that has restored much of the building's former glory. Today FOCSA has one of Vedado's better shopping complexes at ground level, while *La Torre* restaurant on the 33rd of the building's 35 floors boasts panoramic views over the Malecón and beyond.

Memorial a las víctimas del Maine
Malecón y Linea

Just to the north of the *Hotel Nacional* stands the striking **Memorial a las víctimas del Maine**, erected in memory of 260 crew members of the US battleship *The Maine*, which was blown up in Havana harbour on February 15, 1898 (and so is studiously ignored by Cuban maps and guidebooks).

Following the Revolution, crowds attacked the monument, toppling and destroying the heavy iron eagle that once perched on the top (the wings are displayed in the Museo de la Ciudad, while the head is reputedly in the US Embassy canteen). The present government has stamped its presence with the terse inscription: "To the victims of *The Maine*, who were sacrificed by imperialist voraciousness in its zeal to seize the island of Cuba from February 1898 to 15 February 1961".

SQUARING UP

Deliberately built to obscure as much as possible of the US Embassy in its former incarnation as the US Interest Section building, of which it sits directly in front, the Plaza Anti-Imperialista is a huge, sweeping space under a series of metal suspension arches like the ribs of a giant carcass. Many of the supports are covered in plaques bearing the names and quotes of Cubans and non-Cubans who have supported the country's struggle for self-determination and independence over the last century or so.

Also known as Plaza de la Dignidad, the Plaza Anti-Imperialista open-air auditorium was hurriedly constructed in 2000 as a forum for Fidel Castro's protestations and invective during the furore surrounding the flight to the US (and eventual return) of schoolboy **Elián Gonzáles**. In January 2006, North American diplomats began displaying messages about human rights via an electronic **ticker-tape** on the side of the building facing the plaza; the US termed this as an attempt to break Cuba's "information blockade"; Fidel Castro denounced it as a "gross provocation". Later that year the Cuban authorities retorted by erecting **138 black flags** facing the ticker tape, each decorated with a white star and said to symbolize Cubans who have died as a result of violent acts against the country by unsympathetic regimes since the Revolution began in 1959. US diplomats subsequently announced in 2009 they would desist from displaying inflammatory messages; in return the numerous flag poles are now generally left bereft of flags. Today the plaza is as often used for free music concerts as it is for speeches.

US Embassy

Calzada e/ L y M • ☎ 7839 4100, ⊛ havana.usint.gov

Straddling the entire block formed by Calzada, L, M and the Malecón is the **US Embassy**. The somewhat monolithic modernist building was built as the US Embassy by architect firm Harrison and Abramovitz in 1953. Between 1961 and 2015 it became the US Interest Section, which acted in lieu of a US Embassy when diplomatic relations ceased to exist between Cuba and the US, severed by US President Eisenhower. The space in front of the embassy is dominated by the Plaza Anti-Imperialista (see page 99).

Museo Abel Santamaría

Calle 25 no.164 e/ O e Infanta • Mon–Sat 9am–5pm • Free • ☎ 7835 0891

Tucked away in an unassumingly residential corner just east of La Rampa is one of Havana's smallest museums, the **Museo Abel Santamaría**. It was here in 1952 that Abel Santamaría, his sister Haydee Santamaría, Fidel Castro and others planned the attack on the Moncada barracks (see page 382). Following the unsuccessful attack, Abel was captured and tortured to death on Batista's orders. In tribute to him, his simply decorated apartment has been preserved as it was on his final days living there.

Coppelia

Calle 23 esq. L • Tues–Sun 11am–8pm • ☎ 7831 9908

In the middle of an attractive park dotted with weeping figs and rubber trees is Havana's mighty ice-cream emporium, **Coppelia**, the flagship branch of this national chain. Looking like a giant space pod, with a circular white chamber atop a podium, the multi-chamber restaurant was designed by Mario Girona in 1966 as an eating place with prices within the reach of every Cuban. It was named *Coppelia* by Celia Sánchez (see page 405) after her favourite ballet of the same name. Serving over a thousand customers a day, it's a city institution, hugely popular with locals, who regularly wait in line for over an hour. Cuban film buffs will recognize the park from the opening scenes of Tomás Gutiérrez Alea's seminal 1993 film, *Fresa y Chocolate*. To appreciate the space-age architecture fully, go up to *La Torre* restaurant for a panoramic view.

1

Universidad de La Habana
San Lázaro y L

Regal and magnificent, the **Universidad de La Habana** sits on the brow of the Loma Aróstegui Hill, three blocks or so south of La Rampa, overlooking Centro Habana. Founded in 1728 by Dominican monks, the university originally educated Havana's white elite; Black people, Jews, Muslims and mixed-race peoples were all banned, though by an oversight surprising for the time, women weren't, and by 1899 one-seventh of its students were female. It counts among its **alumni** many of the country's famous political figures, including Cuban liberator José Martí, independence fighter Ignacio Agramonte, and Fidel Castro, who studied law here in 1945. Originally based in a convent in Habana Vieja, it was secularized in 1842 but did not move to its present site, a former Spanish army barracks, until 1902, spreading out across the grounds over the next forty years. Today, the university is an awesome collection of buildings and home to some of the city's most unusual **museums**.

The scene of countless student protests, including one led by Julio Antonio Mella in 1922 (see page 439), the university was long seen as a hotbed of youthful **radicalism**. Guns were stashed here during the Batista administration, when it was the only site where political meetings could take place unhindered. The present administration, however, keeps the university on a firm rein and firebrand protests are no more, though its politicized past is evoked in some quirky details scattered throughout the grounds. These include the original American **tank** captured during the civil war in 1958 and placed here by the Union of Young Communists as a tribute to youth lost during the struggle, and, opposite, an "**owl of wisdom**" made of bits of shrapnel gleaned from various battle sites. Still a respected seat of learning, the university today has a rather serious air: earnest students sit on the lawn and steps in front of faculty buildings locked in quiet discussion, while inside a library-like hush reigns. At the top of the stairs, beyond the lofty entrance chamber, and lavishly fêted with Corinthian columns lies the Ignacio Agramonte courtyard, with a central lawn scattered with marble benches and bordered on four sides by grandiose faculty buildings.

Memorial a Julio Antonio Mella

The rubbly pile of oversized grey and whitewashed concrete blocks, near the foot of a sweeping stone staircase capped by twin observation points, is the **Memorial a Julio Antonio Mella**, a modern tribute to this former student, political agitator and founder of the Communist Party, thought to have been murdered for his beliefs. Off to one side, a bust captures his likeness while the words on the main column are his: "To fight for social revolution in the Americas is not a utopia for fanatics and madmen. It is the next step in the advance of history."

Museo de Ciencias Naturales Felipe Poey
Felipe Poey building, Patio de los Laureles · Mon–Fri 9am–noon & 1–4pm · Free · ☎ 7879 3488

To the left of the university's main entrance is the **Museo de Ciencias Naturales Felipe Poey**, the most bewitching of all the campus buildings, with a beautiful central atrium from which rises a towering palm twisted with vines. Named after an eminent nineteenth-century naturalist, and with the musty atmosphere of a zoologist's laboratory, the dimly lit room holds an assortment of stuffed, preserved and pickled animals. The highlight is the collection of **Polymita snails' shells**, delicately ringed in bands of egg-yolk yellow, black and white; while other notables are a (deceased) whistling duck, the gargantuan jaw bone of a sperm whale and Felipe Poey's death mask, incongruously presented along with some of his personal papers. If you have young children, you might want to check out the kids' corner, where you can pet the stuffed duck, squirrel and iguana.

Museo Antropológico Montané

Felipe Poey building, Patio de los Laureles • Mon–Fri 9am–4.00pm • Free • ☎ 7879 3488

Those unmoved by the charms of taxidermy can press on from the Museo de Ciencias Naturales up the right-hand staircase along the cloistered balcony to the **Museo Antropológico Montané**, home to an extensive collection of pre-Columbian pottery and idols from Cuba and elsewhere. Though padded out with apparently indiscriminately selected pieces of earthenware bowls, the collection contains some beautifully preserved artefacts, like the macabre shrunken heads of vanquished chiefs of the Shoal people of Ecuador and Peru and the fierce stone figurine of the Maya god Quetzalcoatl, the plumed serpent, tightly wrapped in a distinctive clay coil design. Star attractions include a **Taíno tobacco idol** from Maisí in Guantánamo; roughly 60cm tall, the elongated, grimacing, drum-shaped idol with shell eyes is believed to have been a ceremonial mortar used to pulverize tobacco leaves. Also fascinating is the delicate reproduction of a Haitian two-pronged **wooden inhaler** carved with the face of a bird, which the Taíno high priest would use to snort hallucinogenic powder in the Cohoba ceremony, a religious ritual for communicating with the dead. Finally, check out the stone **axe** found in Banes, Holguín, engraved with the stylized figure of Guabancex, a female deity governing the uncontrollable forces of nature, her long, twisted arms wrapped around a small child.

Museo Napoleónico

San Miguel no.1159 esq. Ronda • Tues–Sat 9.30am–5pm, Sun 9.30am–12.30pm • Charge, extra for guided tours in English, Spanish or French • ☎ 7879 1412

Just behind the university, the **Museo Napoleónico**, the only Napoleonic museum in Latin America, boasts an eclectic array of ephemera on the French emperor, spread over four storeys of a handsome nineteenth-century house. The collection was gathered at auction by Orestes Ferrara, an Italian ex-anarchist who became a colonel in the rebel army of 1898 and subsequently a politician in Cuba. Ranging from state portraits, *objets d'art* and exquisite furniture to military paraphernalia, sculpture and one of Napoleon's molars, it should appeal to anyone with even a passing interest in the era. The renovated museum was reopened in 2012 with great pomp and ceremony by Alix, Princess Napoleon, a descendant of the man himself.

Central Vedado

West of the university grounds lies **Central Vedado**, quieter than the boisterous La Rampa area and more scenic than Plaza de la Revolución. To walk through these silent, suburban streets, once the exclusive reserve of the wealthy, is one of the richest pleasures Havana holds, the air scented with sweet mint bush and jasmine. At night, the stars, untainted by street lamps, form an eerie ceiling above the swirl of ruined balconies and inky trees. No less attractive in the daytime, with few hustlers, it is also one of the safest areas to stroll, and the added attraction of several museums will give extra purpose to a visit.

Museo de Artes Decorativas

Calle 17 no.502 e/ E y D • Tues–Sat 9.30am–4pm • Charge • ☎ 7830 9848

A fifteen-minute walk west from the university, the beautifully maintained **Museo de Artes Decorativas** contains one of the most dazzling collections of pre-revolutionary decorative arts in Cuba. The mansion in which it's set was built towards the end of 1920s as the private estate of the Count and Countess of Revilla de Camargo, who fled Cuba in 1961, whereupon it was appropriated by the state as the ideal showcase for the nation's cultural treasures. With its regal marble staircase, glittering mirrors and high ceilings, it is a perfect backdrop for the sumptuous, if overwrought, collection of Meissen and Sèvres china, *objets d'art* and fine furniture – a tantalizing glimpse of

1

Vedado's past grandeur. The nine rooms are **themed** according to period, style and function, with some significantly more distinct and coherent than others, particularly those that most faithfully replicate their original purpose, when the house was lived in, such as the largely unaltered bathroom. **Guides** are knowledgeable and friendly but tend to bombard you with information, and with such a massive collection in so small a space you may feel more comfortable setting your own agenda and seeing the rooms unattended.

To the left of the grand entrance hall, the **Salón Principal** (Main Room), richly panelled in gold and cream, is full of lavish Rococo ornaments, like the pair of stylishly ugly eighteenth-century German dog-lions, while the **Chinese Room** next door is dominated by large, intricately screen-printed wooden panels. Upstairs, the rooms are gathered around a majestic balconied hall, among them a fabulous **bathroom** with a marble bathtub inset in the wall. Don't miss the fascinating framed **photographs** hanging in the upstairs hallways depicting over-the-top banquets and high-society social functions that took place in the house itself in the 1940s and 1950s, alongside pictures of the treasures stashed by the owners in the basement.

Parque John Lennon

For an ambling detour, head further up Calle 17 until you reach Calle 6 and **Parque John Lennon**, so named for the sculpture, created in 2000 by José Villa Soberón, of the eponymous musician seated on one of the park benches. It's a pretty good likeness and more or less life-sized. Although Lennon never came to Cuba, the Beatles have always been wildly popular here, so much so that it's not uncommon to hear people claiming to have learnt English through listening to their songs. Perhaps proving his popularity, Lennon's trademark circular glasses have been prised off by thieving souvenir hunters several times, and now the sculpture is protected at night by an armed guard.

Museo de la Danza

Linea no.251 esq. G • Tues–Sat 10am–6.30pm • Charge • ☎ 7831 2198

A few blocks away north of the Museo de Artes Decorativas, the **Museo de la Danza** charts the history of the ballet in Cuba and elsewhere via an immense number of exhibits crammed into a small colonial house. Though the displays struggle to maintain a clear focus, the common thread is **Alicia Alonso**, Cuba's most famous prima ballerina, and every effort has been made to relate exhibits to her. That said, twentieth-century Russian ballet, and particularly **Anna Pavlova**, is given its own spotlight, with an embroidered cape worn by Pavlova, photos of her and a poster from a 1917 production of *El Gallo de Oro* (*Le Coq d'Or*) in which she starred. Some of the best exhibits are found in the museum's back room, where original preliminary sketches for costumes and stage sets are exhibited. The final and largest rooms are devoted entirely to Alonso and the **Ballet Nacional de Cuba**, founded by Alonso herself, her husband Fernando and his brother Alberto in 1948, widely recognized as one of the top ballet companies in the world.

Galería Habana

Linea e/ E y F • Mon–Fri 9am–5pm • Free • ☎ 7832 7101

A short detour west from the Museo de la Danza brings you to the unprepossessing doorway (at the base of an apartment block) of one of Havana's longest-standing and most respected art spaces: **Galería Habana**. Established in 1962 to showcase Cuban talent, several of the country's most celebrated artists are represented here. With white walls and marble floor, the airy and minimal gallery perfectly frames the work of masters like the late **Wifredo Lam**'s African-Cuban Surrealism and **Pedro Pablo Oliva**'s dreamy mysticism. Younger contemporary artists include the collective **Los Carpinteros**, whose architectural installations mix sly humour and social commentary. Exhibitions change every three months, with many pieces offered for sale.

Casa de las Américas

Avenida de los Presidentes, esq. Calle 3ra • Mon–Fri 10am–4.30pm • Free • ⓦ casadelasamericas.org

The **Casa de las Américas** is housed in a dove-grey Art Deco building inlaid with panes of deep blue glass. Previously a private university, it was established as a cultural institute in 1959 – with its own publishing house, one of the first in the country – by the revolutionary heroine Haydee Santamaría to promote the arts, history and politics of the Americas. Since then, its promotion and funding of visual artists, authors, playwrights and musicians has been successful enough to command respect throughout the continent and to attract endorsement from such international literary figures as Gabriel García Márquez.

Today it hosts regular conferences, musical performances and talks, many of which are open to the general public and a few of which take place outside of the building's regular opening hours. The monthly programme of events is published on the website and is also available from the reception hall or the Librería Cayuela, the building's small bookshop. It's worth ringing in advance before you visit, as attendance at some events is by prior arrangement only. Outside of these events, visitors are restricted either to the bookshop, the ground-floor reception area that sometimes hosts small art exhibitions or, most worthwhile of all, the lovely little **Galería Latinoamericana** on the first floor.

Galería Latinoamericana

Mon–Fri 10am–4.30pm • Free • ☎ 7838 2706

This understated **Galería Latinoamericana** stages high-quality bimonthly exhibitions, showcasing anything from painting and sculpture to photography and film-poster art from other Latin American countries.

Galería Mariano

Calle 15 no.607 e/ B y C • Mon–Fri 10am–4.30pm • Charge • ☎ 7838 2702

Ten blocks away from the main building, the Casa de las Américas operates another gallery, the **Mariano**, where exhibitions tend to be of ornamental arts and handicrafts from all over Latin America and the Caribbean.

Monumento General Calixto García

Within view of Casa de las Américas on the Malecón is the aristocratic **Monumento General Calixto García**. Set in a walled podium, it's an elaborate tribute to the War of

---

AVENIDA DE LOS PRESIDENTES' STATUES

On a white plinth near the northern end of Avenida de los Presidentes are the remnants of a statue of Cuba's first president, **Tomás Estrada Palma**, one of the two presidents after whom the avenue is named. Torn down in a wave of anti-American feeling in 1959 as a response to his role in signing the Cuban–American Treaty that leased Guantánamo Bay to the US government in 1903, all that remains of the statue are his feet.

Further along, the tributes become more international. Among non-Cubans honoured are Chile's socialist president and friend of Fidel Castro, **Salvador Allende**, and Mexican president and national hero **Benito Juárez**. Perhaps less expected is the statue of US president **Abraham Lincoln**, in the grounds of the Abraham Lincoln School on the west side of the avenue between calles 17 and 19.

The second of the avenue's original presidents is at the southern end of the boulevard. Framed by several metres of impressive curved marble colonnade adorned with Neoclassical figures, the statue of **José Miguel Gómez** is redolent of bombastic pomp and self-glorification. Cuba's second president, whose term was dogged by accusations of corruption, he was also removed from his plinth in the early 1960s, though was mysteriously returned to it in 1999.

1

Independence general who led the campaign in Oriente, and shows him dynamically reining in his horse surrounded by friezes depicting his greatest escapades, which would warrant closer inspection were it not widely used as a public toilet.

Avenida de los Presidentes

Bisecting Vedado from northwest to southeast, the **Avenida de los Presidentes** (aka Calle G) is one of the suburb's main arteries, connecting the Malecón area to the southern side of Municipio Plaza. The avenue is at its most beautiful between the sea and Calle 27, a wide boulevard lined with lawns, benches and trimmed topiary bushes, and statuesque houses rising amid the trees on either side. Sculptures, statues and tributes to an assortment of presidents are interspersed along its length. At the southeastern foot of the Loma Aróstegui hill, Avenida de los Presidentes intersects with Avenida Salvador Allende (also known as Carlos III), which heads east towards Centro Habana. Set back from this traffic-clogged avenue are the romantic remains of the **Quinta de los Molinos** tobacco mill estate.

Castillo del Príncipe

Avenida de los Presidentes

At the foot of the José Miguel Gómez memorial the wide pedestrian-friendly boulevard comes to an abrupt halt; to explore further, those on foot must negotiate the narrow, dusty track that runs alongside the busy flow of traffic heading over the brow of the Loma Aróstegui hill. Almost completely obscured by trees and shrubs lining the sharp banks of the hill to the right is the **Castillo del Príncipe** (used as a military building and closed to visitors). Something of a curiosity, if only because of its notable absence from official tourist literature and maps, the castle was built between 1767 and 1779 by the Spanish military engineer Don Silvestre Abarca, who also designed the Fortaleza de San Carlos de la Cabaña.

Quinta de los Molinas

Av Carlos III e/ Av de la Independencia y 10 de Octubre • Open to the public for guided tours only, Mon–Fri 7am–7pm, & Sat 8am–8pm • Charge • ☎ 7873 1611

The former residence of Independence War general Máximo Gómez, the **Quinta de los Molinos** have operated as botanical gardens since 1839. Forming an idyllic retreat from the surrounding city, glossy palms and ceiba trees tower above benches and a small pagoda while walkways lined with hot pink, yellow and orange flowers weave through the 1.5-square-kilometre expanse. Tour guides point out the various animals, such as tortoises, cockerels and multicoloured snails. Set back towards the rear of the site, a butterfly house is home to some 20 indigenous species, including the striking black and white Zebra Longwing, all of which flutter among specially selected plants.

Plaza de la Revolución

At the southwest corner of the Quinta de los Molinos grounds, the Avenida de los Presidentes becomes Avenida de Ranchos Boyeros and continues south for about 1km to the **Plaza de la Revolución**. For much of the time the plaza comes as a bit of a letdown, revealing itself to be just a prosaic expanse of concrete bordered by government buildings and the headquarters of the Cuban Communist Party. You'll find a more animated scene if you coincide your visit with May Day or other annual parade days, when legions of loyal Cubans, ferried in on state-organized buses from the *reparto* apartment blocks on the city outskirts, come to wave flags and listen to speeches at the foot of the José Martí memorial. Tourists still flock here throughout the year to see the plaza's threefold attractions: the **Memorial Ernesto "Che" Guevara**, **Memorial José Martí** and the **Memorial Camilo Cienfuegos**.

JOSÉ MARTÍ

Almost every Cuban town, large or small, has a bust or a statue of **José Martí** somewhere, and if they don't already know, it doesn't take long for most people who spend any time touring round Cuba to start wondering who he is. Born José Julián Martí y Pérez to Spanish parents on January 28, 1853, this diminutive man, with his bushy moustache and trademark black bow tie and suit, came to embody the Cuban desire for self-rule and was a figurehead for justice and independence, particularly from the extending arm of the US, throughout Latin America.

EARLY PROTEST

An outstanding pupil at the San Anacleto and San Pablo schools in Havana, and then at the Instituto de Segunda Enseñaza de la Habana, Martí was equally a man of action, who didn't take long to become directly involved in the **separatist struggle** against colonial Spain. Still a schoolboy when the first Cuban War of Independence broke out in 1868, by the start of the following year he had founded his first newspaper, **Patria Libre**, contesting Spanish rule of Cuba. His damning editorials swiftly had him pegged as a dissident, and he was arrested a few months later on the trivial charge of having written a letter to a friend denouncing him for joining the Cuerpo de Voluntarios, the Spanish volunteer corps. Only 16 years old, Martí was sentenced to six years' hard labour in the San Lázaro stone quarry in Havana. Thanks to the influence of his father, a Habaneran policeman, the sentence was mitigated and the now-ailing teenager was **exiled** to the Isla de la Juventud, then known as the Isla de Pinos, and finally to Spain in 1871.

Martí wasted no time in Spain, studying law and philosophy at the universities in Madrid and Zaragoza, all the while honing his literary skills and writing **poetry**, his prolific output evidenced today in the countless compendiums and reprints available in bookshops around Cuba. One of his poems, taken from the collection Versos Sencillos (Simple Verses), was adapted and became the official lyrics of the song Guantanamera, a Cuban anthem.

FORMING IDEAS

By 1875 he was back on the other side of the Atlantic and reunited with his family in **Mexico**. Settling down, however, was never an option for the tireless Martí, who rarely rested from his writing or his agitation for an independent Cuba and social justice throughout Latin America. Returning to Havana briefly in 1877 under a false name, he then moved to **Guatemala** where he worked as a teacher and continued his writing. Among his students was the daughter of Guatemalan president Miguel García Granados, who fell in love with Martí but whose love went unrequited. Martí returned again to Cuba in 1878 and during another brief stay he married Carmen Zayas Bazán, with whom he had a son that same year. By 1881 he was living in **New York**, where he managed to stay for the best part of a decade. His years in New York were to prove pivotal. Initially swept away by what he perceived to be the true spirit of freedom and democracy, he soon came to regard the US with intense suspicion, seeing it as a threat to the independence of all Latin American countries.

CHARGING TO BATTLE

The final phase of Martí's life began with his founding of the **Cuban Revolutionary Party** in 1892. He spent the following three years drumming up support for Cuban **independence** from around Latin America, raising money, training for combat, gathering together an arsenal of weapons and planning a military campaign to defeat the Spanish. In April 1895, with the appointed general of the revolutionary army, Máximo Gómez, and just four other freedom fighters, he landed at Playitas on Cuba's south coast. Disappearing into the mountains of the Sierra Maestra, just as Fidel Castro and his rebels were to do almost sixty years later, they were soon joined by hundreds of supporters. On May 19, 1895, Martí went into **battle** for the first time and was shot dead almost immediately. Perhaps the strongest testament to José Martí's legacy is the esteem in which he is held by Cubans on both sides of the Florida Straits, his ideas authenticating their vision of a free Cuba and his dedication to the cause an inspiration to all.

1

Memorial José Martí

Plaza de la Revolución • Mon–Sat 9.30am–4pm • Charge for museum and lookout

Although widely seen as a symbol of the Revolution, the star-shaped **Memorial José Martí** had been in the pipeline since 1926 and was completed a year before the Revolution began. Its 139m marble super-steeple is even more impressive when you glance up to the seemingly tiny crown-like turret, often circled by a dark swirl of birds. Near the base sits a 17m **sculpture** of Martí, the eloquent journalist, poet and independence fighter who missed his chance to be Cuba's first populist president by dying in his first ever battle against the Spanish on April 11, 1895. Carved from elephantine cubes of white marble, the immense monument captures Martí hunched forward in reflective pose.

Behind the statue of José Martí, the stately ground floor of the memorial tower houses an exhaustive **museum**, which charts Martí's career mainly through letters and photographs. The lavish entrance hall, its walls bedecked with Venetian mosaic tiles interspersed with Martí's most evocative quotes, certainly befits a national hero and is the most impressive aspect of a museum that tends to stray off the point at times. The most eye-catching exhibit is close to the entrance to the first room: a replica of Simón Bolívar's diamond-studded **sword**, which was given to Fidel Castro by Venezuelan president Hugo Chávez in 2000. The second room holds **photographs** of Martí in Spain, Mexico and North America along with an assortment of **artillery**, most notably Martí's six-shooter Colt revolver engraved with his name, and the Winchester he took with him into his only battle.

When you've finished in the museum, take the lift to the top floor and the highest **lookout point** in Havana. The room is divided into segments corresponding to the five spines of its star shape, so you can move around to take in five separate views including the far reaches of Miramar in the west.

Memorial Ernesto "Che" Guevara

Plaza de la Revolución

On the opposite side of the square to the north, the ultimate Cuban photo opportunity is presented by the **Memorial Ernesto "Che" Guevara**, a stylized steel-frieze replica of Alberto "Korda" Gutiérrez's famous photo of Guevara, titled *Guerrillero Heroico* – the most widely recognized image of him. The sculpture that you see now on the wall of the Ministry of Interior building, where Guevara himself once worked, was forged in 1993 from steel donated by the French government. Taken on March 5, 1960, during a memorial service for victims of the *La Coubre* freighter explosion on Calle 23, Korda's photograph, with Guevara's messianic gaze fixed on some distant horizon and hair flowing out from beneath his army beret, embodies the unwavering, zealous spirit of the Revolution. It was only in 1967, after his capture and execution in Bolivia (see page 249), that the photo passed into iconography, printed on T-shirts and posters throughout the 1970s as an enduring symbol of rebellion.

Korda, who died in 2001, famously received no royalties from the image, and even gave its wide dissemination his blessing. As a lifelong supporter of the Revolution and Guevara's ideals, he believed that spreading the image would allow Guevara's ideals to spread alongside it, which neatly allows for the image's commercial use in Cuba itself.

Memorial Camilo Cienfuegos

Plaza de la Revolución

Erected in 2009 on the front of the Ministry of Informatics and Communications on the east side of the square is Enrique Ávila's 100-tonne steel sculpture of **Camilo Cienfuegos**, in a similar style to the Che image, including the words "*Vas bien Fidel*". This somewhat obsequious tagline is a reference to a reply Cienfuegos gave to Fidel Castro at the victory rally on January 8, 1959: "How am I doing?" asked Castro. "You're doing fine, Fidel," came the reply.

Necrópolis de Colón

Avenida Zapata • Mon–Fri 8am–5pm • Charge

Five blocks northwest from Plaza de la Revolución along tree-lined Paseo, there's a worthwhile detour to the left at the Zapata junction: the **Necrópolis de Colón**, one of the largest cemeteries in the Americas. With moribund foresight the necropolis was designed in 1868 to have space for well over a hundred years' worth of corpses, and its neatly numbered "streets", lined with grandiose tombstones and mausoleums and shaded by large trees, stretch out over five square kilometres. A tranquil refuge from the noise of the city, it is a fascinating place to visit – you can spend hours here seeking out the graves of the famous, including the parents of José Martí (he is buried in Santiago), celebrated novelist Alejo Carpentier, photographer Alberto "Korda" Gutiérrez and a host of revolutionary martyrs.

The main avenue sweeps into the cemetery past tall Italian-marble tombstones, including a copy of Michelangelo's *Pietà*. Particularly noteworthy is the **mausoleum**, just behind the main avenue on Calle 1 y Calle D; draped with marble maidens depicting Justice and Innocence, it holds the remains of a group of medical students executed in 1871 on the charge of desecrating the tomb of a Spanish journalist.

CAMILO CIENFUEGOS – HERO OF THE REVOLUTION

Good looking, personable and a formidable soldier, **Camilo Cienfuegos** was one of the most significant rebels in the revolutionary struggle. Born in Havana to Spanish anarchists, Cienfuegos did not share the wealthy middle-class background of other key rebels and accounts of his early life are characterized by financial struggles. He enrolled in the Escuela Nacional de Bellas Artes in 1940 but lack of money forced him to leave and work as an apprentice in the El Arte fashion store in Havana.

EARLY ACTIVISM

Cienfuegos became active in the underground student movement against Fulgencio Batista and was wounded during a protest in 1955. Shortly afterwards, sick of the police harassment that identification as a student rebel warranted, he left Cuba for the US and then Mexico.

It was in **Mexico** that he met Fidel Castro and decided to join forces with his revolutionary expedition. An apocryphal tale has it that the *Granma* boat, ready to set sail from Mexico to the motherland, was already overloaded with would-be rebels, and Cienfuegos was only granted last-minute passage because he was deemed so thin that the extra weight would be of no consequence.

MILITARY BRILLIANCE

Surviving the rebels' initial catastrophic battle, Cienfuegos went on to be one of the rebel army's most successful generals, attaining the rank of **comandante** in 1957. His most significant victory was in winning the key **Battle of Yaguajay** in Santa Clara province in December 1958, which impelled Batista's forces to surrender a crucial garrison helping cement the revolutionary success.

FATAL DISAPPEARANCE

Following the revolution, Cienfuegos continued in a military role, quashing anti-Castro uprisings. Whether he would have played a more political role in the new Cuban order is open to speculation. Within a year of victory, on October 28, 1959, his **plane disappeared** over the ocean during a night flight from Camagüey to Havana, and after a search failed to reveal any trace of the remains, he was declared dead. Cienfuegos was feted as one of the heroes of the Revolution, and even today schoolchildren throw flowers into the seas and Cuban rivers in his honour on the anniversary of his disappearance.

1

In the southern half of the cemetery, marked by large plots of as yet unused land, veterans of the Revolution, including luminary figures Celia Sánchez, July 26 Movement leader and companion to Fidel Castro, and poet Nicolás Guillén, lie in an extensive and faintly austere **pantheon house** just off the main avenue.

Octagonal chapel
In the centre of the necropolis is the Romanesque **octagonal chapel**, opened in 1886. Masses are held every day at 8am but the chapel is also open at various times during the day. You should seize the chance to peek inside and admire the luminous German stained-glass windows and, towering above the altar, Cuban artist Miguel Melero's fresco *The Last Judgement*.

The tomb of Amelia Goyri de la Hoz
Close to the octagonal chapel at Calle 1 e/ F y G and always engulfed by a cornucopia of flowers and guarded by an attendant, the tomb of **Amelia Goyri de la Hoz** and her child is an arresting sight. A Habaneran society woman, Goyri de la Hoz died in childbirth on May 3, 1901, and was buried with her child, who survived her by only a few minutes, placed at her feet. During a routine exhumation the following year, she was supposedly found to be cradling the child in her arms. The story spread immediately. Goyri de la Hoz was dubbed **La Milagrosa** (The Miracle Worker) and the event was attributed to the power of a mother's love working beyond the grave. Soon La Milagrosa was attributed with universal healing powers, and to this day supplicants queue round the block to have their wishes granted.

Fábrica de Arte Cubano
Calle 26 esq. 11 • Thurs–Sun 8pm–2am • ☎ 7838 2260
Few venue openings have caused the stir that this avant-garde arts-centre-cum-club has, with profiles in international papers including *The New York Times* and *The Guardian*. Housed in an old peanut oil factory in the far reaches of Vedado, and decked out with sleek lines, minimal shades and multiple rooms, **Fábrica de Arte Cubano (FAC)** follows the tried and tested route of counter-culture colonization of industrial spaces that has transformed Shoreditch, Berlin and New York's Meatpacking District. Yet despite the cosmopolitan air, from the contemporary art displayed in the gallery space upstairs to bands playing in the rooms downstairs, FAC is quintessentially Cuban.

Opened by X Alfonso, a Cuban musician and artist, what's particularly surprising is that FAC is classified as a community project rather than being either a private enterprise or a state-run facility. As such, it enjoys a cultural autonomy evident in the sometimes politically challenging artwork, eclectic clientele and mix of performance

CASA DE LAS TEJAS VERDES

If you are arriving onto Quinta Avenida via the tunnel from Vedado, keep an eye out for the Casa de las Tejas Verdes (the House with the Green Tiles), that looms up on the right-hand side of the road. As incongruous as a gingerbread cottage amid the bougainvillea bushes, this fairytale apparition is one of the few examples in Cuba of American Queen Anne-style architecture. Designed by architect, civil engineer and pre-Revolution politician Jorge Luis Echarte y Mazorra, it was built in 1926, complete with moss green walls, wraparound porch and sharply pitched green-tiled roof. The building fell into disrepair after the Revolution and its subsequent dilapidated state gained it a reputation for mystery and hauntings. Following extensive restoration in the 2000s it won the 2010 National Prize for Restoration and is now part of the offices for modern and contemporary architecture, town planning and interior design.

artists. A night here might involve sipping cocktails on the moonlit patio, watching a local theatre company, listening to classical music – or the latest Cuban hip-hop artists – or letting loose at a weekend club night. Whichever side of FAC you see, you can't miss the fact that you're watching Havana's arts and cultural scene being forged.

Miramar and the western suburbs

Home to the city's flashiest neighbourhoods, **Miramar and the western suburbs** comprise Havana's alter ego, replete with sleek Miami-style residences, swish new business developments and brash five-star hotels. Among the last sections of the city to be developed before the Revolution, this is where the wealth was then concentrated, and it's slowly trickling back through a growing clique of international investors and well-heeled foreign residents. The area still has its share of broken sewage systems, unlit streets and overcrowded buses, but a gentler pace of life exists throughout the western suburbs, calmed by the broad avenues and abundance of large drooping trees.

Though there is an **aquarium**, one or two small **museums** and plenty of wonderful houses and embassies to gawp at, most visitors to this part of the city come here for the **nightlife** and **entertainment**, particularly the famous **Tropicana** cabaret, as well as for the area's swanky international **restaurants** and its upmarket **paladars**, which between them offer the most diverse and sophisticated eating options in Havana. You'll have to go all the way to the western extremities to find the only proper beach, at **Club Habana** and, just beyond that, **Marina Hemingway**, where boat trips and diving expeditions are the main draw.

The whole area west of the **Río Almendares** is occasionally mistakenly referred to as Miramar, but this is in fact the name only of the oceanfront neighbourhood closest to Vedado, the two linked together by a tunnel under the river. Most of this western section of the city, including Miramar and its even leafier neighbour **Kohly**, belongs to the sprawling borough of **Playa**, stretching out for some 15km along the coast.

Museo del Ministerio del Interior

Calle 14 e/ 3ra y 5ta • Tues–Fri 9am–5pm, Sat 9am–3.30pm • Charge • ☎ 7202 1240

About 1km from the mouth of the tunnel to Vedado is the **Museo del Ministerio del Interior**, the museum of the Cuban secret services. Housed in two airy Miramar mansions, the displays are mainly devoted to charting the conflict between the secret services and alleged US attempts to undermine the Revolution. Many of the exhibits comprise billboards written in Spanish, which non-Spanish speakers will find considerably less interesting, though there is still enough here – not least the first ever Cuban police dog stuffed and mounted – to warrant a quick spin around should you be in the area.

Acuario Nacional de Cuba

Avenida 3ra esq. 62 • Tues–Sun 10am–6pm; dolphin shows 11am, 3pm & 5pm; sea lion shows noon & 4pm • Charge • ⓦ acuarionacional.cu

A good bet for some family fun is the **Acuario Nacional de Cuba**, 1.5km west of the Maqueta de la Habana, an outdoor marine park where mammals, reptiles, birds and fish are showcased in wildly varying degrees of animation. There are twenty-minute dolphin shows and regular sea lion shows, or you can stop here for lunch at the on-site **restaurant**, *El Gran Azul*, where, usually at 1.30pm, you can watch an underwater dolphin show from your table, viewed through a huge window set below the surface of the water. You may want to read up on the welfare of marine mammals kept in captivity in Cuba before you go, though (see page 54).

Much of the rest of the park can seem a bit lifeless after one of these shows. Away from the larger enclosures, where turtles, pelicans and sea lions usually attract the most

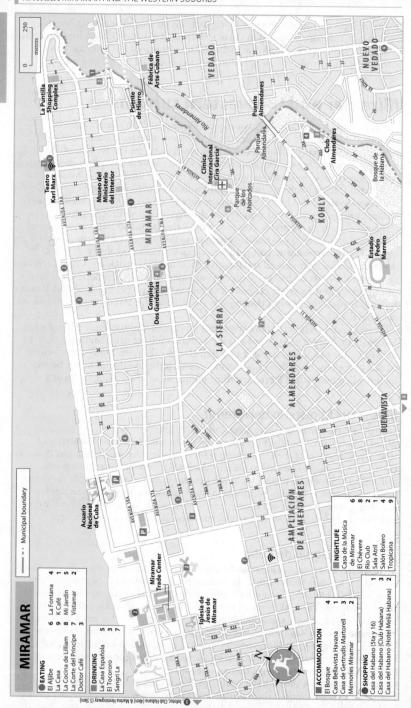

MIRAMAR

EATING
El Aljibe   6
La Casa   9
La Cocina de Lilliam   8
La Corte del Príncipe   7
Doctor Café   3
La Fontana   4
K Café   1
Mi Jardín   5
Vistamar   2

DRINKING
La Casa Española   5
El Tocororo   3
Sangrí La   7

ACCOMMODATION
El Bosque   4
Casa Bellavista Havana   1
Casa de Gertrudis Martorell   3
Memories Miramar   2

NIGHTLIFE
Casa de la Música
  de Miramar   6
El Chévere   8
Río Club   2
Sala Atril   4
Salón Bolero   1
Tropicana   9

SHOPPING
Casa del Habano (5ta y 16)   1
Casa del Habano (Club Habana)   3
Casa del Habano (Hotel Meliá Habana) 2

- - · Municipal boundary

attention, there are dozens of uninspiring fish tanks and this section of the park by itself is not really worth the entrance fee.

Parque Almendares and around

South of Miramar, in the green and hilly suburb of **Kohly** and alongside an attractive and open stretch of the Río Almendares, the **Parque Almendares** is the only decent-sized city park in Havana. Running for about 400m along the river, its tangle of palms, giant weeping figs and pine trees coats much of the park in dense woodland, filling it with dappled light and an almost eerie enchantment, especially at dusk. This moody charm is enhanced by wishing wells, twisting pathways and iron benches but is tempered by scuffed lawns and abandoned buildings, along with other signs of neglect. At weekends and during holidays it's a popular spot frequented by local families, with salsa reverberating through the park from speakers arrayed around the parking lot.

The park is the landscaped section of a much larger forested area known as the **Bosque de la Habana**, extending over 2km along the river, most of it quite wild with no obvious paths. Plans to develop the woodlands and make them more visitor-friendly are slowly getting underway, but for now the woods and parkland offer a slice of the countryside right in the heart of the city.

Club Habana

Avenida 5ta, 8km from western edge of Vedado, in the neighbourhood of Flores • Daily 9am–7pm (restaurant noon–11pm) • Charge, children under 12 free • ☎ 7275 0100

Several kilometres west of Miramar is **Club Habana**, an upmarket leisure and business complex based in and around an enormous stately mansion. Most significantly, it is also the site of Havana's only proper city **beach**, as well as some of the best sports facilities in the city. Prior to the Revolution, this was the Havana Biltmore Yacht and Country Club, whose members were drawn predominantly from the Cuban aristocratic classes and the wealthy US business community, and it maintains an air of exclusivity today, with membership costs prohibitively high for most Cubans.

The palm-lined 200m sandy **beach** is a real treat compared to anything else this close to the city centre, and given the entrance cost, it's usually pretty deserted. With several half-decent eateries on site and three **swimming pools**, this is the best place in Havana to spend a whole day of pure undisturbed escapism. There's also a gym, tennis court and a cigar shop and lounge. The palatial clubhouse is dominated by business facilities but does feature a wall of intriguing photographs depicting the club and its members pre-1959.

ARRIVAL AND DEPARTURE   **HAVANA**

BY PLANE

JOSÉ MARTÍ INTERNATIONAL AIRPORT
All international flights land at José Martí International

Airport (information ☎ 7266 4133 or ☎ 7649 5666; switchboard ☎ 7 275 1200 or ☎ 7 266 4644), about 16km south of the city centre.

Airlines There are two main clusters of airline offices, in

PARQUE ALMENDARES ACTIVITIES

As well as providing a welcome expanse of greenery, Parque Almendares has several **activities** to choose from. This is an ideal place for a picnic, particularly as the park's sole café, situated in the centre (Tues–Sun 10am–5pm), is somewhat sparsely stocked. The river, though dirty, makes a good venue for **rowing boats** (Tues–Sun 10am–6pm), while a **crazy golf course** (Tues–Sun 10am–5pm), pony rides (no fixed times), a playground and an aviary make the park one of the better attractions in Havana for children.

1

Vedado at Calle 23 e/ Infanta y P, where you'll find, among others, Aerocaribbean (☎7 879 7524), Air Canada (☎7836 3226), Cubana (☎7649 0410) and Jet Blue (☎800 5258); and in Miramar at the Miramar Trade Center, 5ta Avenida e/ 70 y 80, where you'll find, among others, Aeroflot (☎7204 3200), Air Europa (☎7204 6904), Air France (☎7206 4444), American Airlines (☎7214 4847), Iberia (☎7204 3460), KLM (☎7206 4444), LTU (☎7833 3524) and Virgin Atlantic (☎7204 0747). Aerogaviota ☎7 203 0686 or ☎7 203 0668) is at Avenida 47 no.2814, e/ 28 y 34, Kohly, Playa.

Facilities The vast majority of international passengers are deposited at Terminal 3 (☎7649 0410), where most airport services are concentrated, including a few shops, a restaurant, bureaux de change and, upstairs on the departures level a set of ATMs – these latter two for most people represent the first chance to actually get hold of any Cuban money, given that it cannot be exchanged outside of Cuba, and it's worth getting some cash out while the opportunity presents itself (ATMs are relatively scarce even in the capital). There are car rental desks in each of the three terminals.

Getting to Havana Since there is no public transport linking the rest of Havana directly with the airport, you'll almost certainly have to take a taxi into town; the standard fare for the half-hour journey into Havana is the equivalent of US $25.

BY BUS

VÍAZUL BUSES

Essentials The national interprovincial bus service drops its passengers at the Víazul terminal (☎7 881 1413 ext 101 or ☎7 881 5652), on Avenida 26 across from the city zoo.

Tickets It's best to book Víazul bus tickets in advance online (🖰viazul.wetransp.com) but you need to book a week in advance. You can also make reservations in advance at the Víazul terminal itself; there are sometimes last-minute tickets available an hour before departure times but leaving it until then is a gamble. In the terminal car park there are always long-distance taxis offering journeys to all the Víazul destinations, and usually claiming, at least initially, that they will charge the same as the respective Víazul fare. The truth of this will depend on how many other passengers they can round up.

Destinations Bayamo (3 daily; 13hr); Camagüey (5 daily; 8hr 15min); Ciego de Ávila (4 daily; 7hr); Cienfuegos (2 daily; 4hr 20min); Holguín (3 daily; 12hr); Las Terrazas (1 daily; 1hr 30min); Las Tunas (5 daily; 11hr); Matanzas (4 daily; 2hr 10min); Pinar del Río (3 daily; 3hr); Playa Girón (2 daily; 3hr 15min); Sancti Spíritus (3 daily; 5hr 30min); Santa Clara (5 daily; 4hr 30min); Santiago de Cuba (3 daily; 15hr 30min); Trinidad (2 daily; 6hr); Varadero (4 daily; 3hr 10min); Viñales (3 daily; 3hr 40min).

CONECTANDO CUBA

Essentials This service picks up and drops off passengers from designated hotels in Habana Vieja, Vedado and Miramar. To buy tickets go to any Cubanacán travel agent, such as the one in the *Hotel Plaza* on the Parque Central, at least a day in advance of travel but for Santiago, Camagüey, Ciego de Avila and Holguín three days' notice is advised.

CITY TOURS WITH CITIZENS

In 2010, privately run travel agents and tour companies were permitted by Cuban law for the first time. In the years since, city tours offered by locals have proliferated. Though compared to their state-run equivalents the guides are not always as well qualified in the city's history and cultural heritage, they tend to offer **greater flexibility** and a more **personal touch**, while the best of them still offer a very professional, reliable service and some do have very well informed guides. Most of them conduct tours in **classic American cars**. Easily found online, you are unlikely to come across them by chance in Havana itself, their presence still very much hidden from view as they are usually based in houses and apartments in residential neighbourhoods – though there's a good chance you'll be offered a tour just by walking around Habana Vieja. Below we list three of the best.

Havana Journeys 🖰havanajourneys.com. Friendly, well-informed guides, some of whom worked previously for the state as guides, make this one of the most highly regarded private tour companies. The tour of Havana includes a walking tour of Habana Vieja and a car ride around Centro Habana and Vedado. Tours to Trinidad, Viñales and other destinations are also offered.

Havana Super Tours Campanario no.63 e/ San Lázaro y Lagunas, Centro Habana 🖰campanario63. com. Themed tours, all in gleaming vintage convertible

American cars, include Art Deco Tour and the Mob Tour, tracing the history of the Mafia in pre-revolutionary Havana. Run by the irrepressible Luis Miguel and his team.

Havana Vintage Car Tours Ave. 43 no.8418 e/ 84a y 86, Marianao 🖰havanavintagecartours.com. Family-owned and -run business based in Marianao, in western Havana, who conduct their tours in a beautifully maintained 1955 Oldsmobile convertible. There are several three-hour tour packages, but you can request a bespoke tour at the same rate.

Destinations Camagüey (1 daily; 10hr); Ciego de Avila (1 daily; 8hr); Cienfuegos (1 daily; 5hr); Holguín (1 daily; 13hr); Pinar del Río (1 daily; 3hr 30min); Santiago de Cuba (1 daily; 15hr); Trinidad (1 daily; 7hr); Varadero (1 daily; 3hr); Viñales (1 daily; 4hr 30min).

EMPRESA AND TERMINAL DE OMNIBUS NACIONALES

Essentials The main long-distance bus station is the Terminal de Omnibus Nacionales (switchboard ☎7870 940), at Avenida Independencia esq. 19 de Mayo, near the Plaza de la Revolución. The vast majority of arrivals here are Empresa Omnibus Nacionales (EON) buses, reserved exclusively for Cubans, but foreign travellers do very occasionally arrive and depart here. The bus for the ferry terminal serving the Isla de la Juventud leaves from here. The centre of Vedado is a twenty-minute walk away, the #P12 and #P16 buses stop nearby on their way into the centre.

BY TRAIN

ESTACIÓN CENTRAL DE FERROCARRILES

Essentials The main terminal, the Estación Central de Ferrocarriles (☎7860 9448 or ☎7862 1920) in southern Habana Vieja is currently closed for renovation. Until it reopens most trains arrive and depart from Terminal La Coubre (☎7864 6041 or ☎7862 1006), 200m down the road from the main terminal on Avenida del Puerto. The Parque Central is about 1km from here. Several local buses (see below) stop close to the main station, including the #P4 and #P5, but hauling a lot of luggage onto a crowded Havana bus isn't much fun. There are often private cabs outside the station and the occasional tourist taxi, though you're more likely to find a *bicitaxi*.

Tickets You'll need to get to Terminal La Coubre by 8.30am

a whole five days before your date of travel, and expect to join a large queue.

Schedules and routes Long-distance services are patchy at best, with trains running every two to three days; check at the station to find out the current situation. There is also a very limited suburban train network that reaches out to the outskirts of rural Havana and into Mayabeque and Artemisa provinces.

Destinations Bayamo (2 weekly; 15hr); Camagüey (4 weekly; 9–14hr); Ciego de Ávila (4 weekly; 7–12hr); Guantánamo (2 weekly; 18hr); Jaruco in Mayabeque (4 daily; 2hr); Matanzas (4 weekly; 2hr); Pinar del Río (every other day; 6hr); Sancti Spíritus (3 weekly; 11hr); Santa Clara (4 weekly; 5–7hr); Santiago de Cuba (2 weekly; 18hr).

TERMINAL CASABLANCA AND THE HERSHEY TRAIN

Essentials The other train terminal in the city is at one end of the Hershey line, the only electric train service in Cuba. It connects Havana to the city of Matanzas, the terminal at the other end of this line. The station, the Terminal Casablanca (☎7862 4888), is in the small suburb of Casablanca, on the eastern side of the harbour, near the Parque Morro-Cabaña. There are dozens of tiny stations along the route but trains only stop sporadically at most of them though a regular stop is at Camilo Cienfuegos, formerly the town of Hershey itself. Destinations Canasí (4 daily; 2hr 20min); Guanabo (4 daily; 40min); Hershey (4 daily; 1hr); Jibacoa (4 daily; 2hr); Matanzas (4 daily; 3hr); San Antonio (4 daily; 2hr 45min).

BY BOAT

Terminal Sierra Maestra An increasing number of cruise ships dock in Havana, at the Terminal Sierra Maestra (☎7866 6524 or ☎7862 1925), facing the Plaza de San Francisco in Habana Vieja.

GETTING AROUND

Havana has a poor **public transport** system, with no metro, a skeletal municipal train network and an overcrowded bus service. You will almost certainly find yourself having to use a **taxi** at least once, though this is not such a bad thing when the car is a 1955 Chevrolet.

BY BUS

HABANA BUS TOUR

Essentials Though this service is ostensibly for tours of the city, it actually offers a decent alternative to the public bus system, and with a timetabled schedule, route maps at bus stops and guaranteed seats, it offers a lot that the regular municipal system doesn't – albeit for a greater cost. There are two routes: the #T1 runs between the Terminal de Cruceros and the western end of Miramar via the Parque

Central and the Plaza de la Revolución; the #T3 runs between the Parque Central and the Playas del Este. (#T2 was joined with #T1 but they didn't renumber.)

Tickets and schedules Tickets are sold on board (under-6s ride free) and are valid for unlimited journeys all day. Though there are designated bus stops, you can often, though unofficially, flag buses down anywhere on their routes. In theory the service runs daily from 9am to 9pm at half-hourly intervals, but in reality this varies; you may sometimes wait an hour or more, while last buses set off as early as 7pm.

PUBLIC BUSES

Essentials The public bus system, divided between the Metrobús and Omnibus Metropolitanos networks, is how the majority of residents (but only a tiny minority of foreign

1

METROBÚS ROUTES

ROUTE NUMBER		ROUTE
P1	(for Miramar)	San Miguel del Padrón–Playa
P2	(for Museo Ernest Hemingway)	Cotorro–Vedado
P3	(for Guanabacoa)	Habana del Este–Vedado
P4	(for Kohly)	Playa–Terminal de Trenes (Habana Vieja)
P5	(for Miramar)	Playa–Terminal de Trenes (Habana Vieja)
P6		Vedado–Arroyo Naranjo
P7	(for Museo Ernest Hemingway)	Parque de la Fraternidad (Habana Vieja)–Cotorro
P8	(for Parque Morro-Cabaña)	Habana del Este–Arroyo Naranjo
P9	(for Tropicana and Kohly)	Marianao–Diez de Octubre
P10		Diez de Octubre–Playa
P11	(for Parque Morro-Cabaña)	Habana del Este–Vedado
P12	(for Santiago de las Vegas)	Santiago de las Vegas–Parque de la Fraternidad
P13		Santiago de las Vegas–Diez de Octubre
P14	(for La Lisa)	Playa–Parque de la Fraternidad (Habana Vieja)
P15	(for Guanabacoa)	Habana del Este–Parque de la Fraternidad (H.V.)
P16	(for Santiago de las Vegas)	Santiago de las Vegas–Vedado
PC	(for Parque Lenin)	Habana del Este–Playa

visitors) get around Havana. Though both networks are still characterized by overcrowding and long waits, the Metrobús service is more regular and the easier of the two to use. Its buses – most of them Chinese-made bendy buses – are distinguishable by their route numbers, all preceded by "P". The front of the vehicle will tell you its final destination, but for any more detail you'll need to consult the route map posted inside – you'll be lucky to get a bus number at a bus stop, let alone a route itinerary or map.

Network hubs The major bus hubs are the Parque de la Fraternidad in Habana Vieja, the network of roads between the Parque Maceo and the Hospital Hermanos Ameijeiras in Centro Habana, and *Coppelia* in Vedado.

BY TAXI

STATE TAXIS

There are plenty of official metered state taxis. It shouldn't take long to flag one down in the main hotel districts and particularly along the Malecón. For a 24-hour pick-up service, ring Cubataxi (☎ 7855 5555 or ☎ 7877 5762). Rates are usually by negotiation.

Taxi ranks There are taxi ranks on the Paseo del Prado at the Parque Central in Habana Vieja, and outside the hotels *Habana Libre* on Calle L and *Nacional* on Calle O in Vedado.

PRIVATE TAXIS AND COLECTIVOS

As with the rest of Cuba, Havana is full of privately owned taxis, mostly huge, 1950s American cars operating as *taxis colectivos* (aka *almendrones*; see page 30). The main routes are along Neptuno in Centro Habana, and Calle L,

Calle 23 and Linea in Vedado. You should be able to flag one down anywhere along these roads.

Taxi ranks Between the Parque de la Fraternidad, Parque El Curita and opposite the face of the Capitolio building, *colectivos* form a huge, jumbled taxi rank, some of them transporting passengers to the city limits and beyond.

The only state-run taxi using classic American cars is Gran Car (☎ 7837 1602), though their cars are used more for ad-hoc tours than conventional taxi rides. These taxis congregate at the Parque Central and on Tacón near the cathedral in Habana Vieja and outside the *Hotel Nacional* in Vedado, though you can call for one and even request your preferred model – they are generally in outstanding condition.

Fares Fares are higher than normal taxis but you won't have to share with anyone else and you can also rent a car and chauffeur for tours around the city.

BICITAXIS AND COCOTAXIS

Bicitaxis Three-wheeled, two-seater bicycle cabs, *bicitaxis* are found all over Havana but are not necessarily any cheaper than cars.

Cocotaxis Swelling Havana's taxi ranks even further are *cocotaxis*, three-wheeled motorscooters encased in large yellow spheres, usually found waiting outside the *Hotel Inglaterra* and the *Hotel Nacional*. You pay no extra for their novelty value.

BY CAR

Though expensive, with many of the city's day-trip destinations poorly connected by public transport, renting a car can save you a lot of time and hassle. The car-rental agencies have desks in the lobbies of most of the four- and five-star hotels; be warned, though, that booking a car in advance is often difficult as demand frequently outweighs supply.

CAR RENTAL

Habana Vieja Cubacar (☎7 835 0000) and REX (☎7 835 6830) both have offices in the Galería de Tiendas Parque Central on Agramonte (Zulueta) e/ Virtudes y Animas and at the Terminal Sierra Maestra opposite the Plaza de San Francisco.

Miramar Go to Cubacar at Avenida 3ra y 28 in Miramar (☎7 204 3356).

Vedado You can find Cubacar at Paseo esq. 3ra in Vedado (☎7 833 2164) and REX at Linea esq. O, just off the Malecón (☎7 836 7788 or ☎7 835 6830).

CAR PARKS

There are official state-run car parks at Avenida de Italia (Galiano) esq. Avenida Simón Bolívar (Reina; daily 8am–8pm), near the Habana Vieja border in Centro Habana, and at Calle O e/ 23 y 25 (daily 24hr) in Vedado.

BY SCOOTER

There are very few scooter rental outlets in the city and most are located within hotel complexes either in the western suburbs or right outside the city at the Playas del Este. There is a Cubanacán Motoclub branch at the Dos Gardenias commercial complex, at Avenida 7ma esq. 26 in Miramar, and further west at the *Hotel Comodoro*, at Avenida 3era esq. 84.

BY BICYCLE

Given the poor public transport and the relatively low levels of traffic, travelling by bicycle is a fantastic way to see the city. Away from the main thoroughfares many streets seem to be pedestrianized, though outside of Habana Vieja very few of them actually are. There are now, finally, multiple places you can rent a bike and many of the private rental firms offer city tours too. You'll usually need a passport when you rent a bike

HA'BICI

In 2018 the city launched its first public bike rental scheme, Ha'Bici. It currently consists of just 60 bicycles and the several bike stations are all in Habana Vieja, the main one at the Emboque de Luz ferry terminal on the port road, near the cruise ship terminal, though there are plans to widen the scheme to nine bike stations and 350 bikes. Velo Cuba (🌐veloencuba.com), a privately-bike shop, is also taking part in the scheme and you can pick up bikes from their workshops at Obrapía no.360 e/ Habana y Compostela or Vedado, Calle Montero Sánchez, No. 34 e/ 21 y 23. You'll need ID.

PRIVATE BIKE RENTAL

Habana Vieja Roma Rent Bike at Compostela no.255 e/ O'Reilly y Obispo in Habana Vieja (daily 9am–5pm; Ciclo Cuba at San Pedro no.258 e/ Sol y Muralla (Mon–Fri 9am–5pm; 🌐ciclocuba.com, ☎7866 2559), over the road from the cruise ship terminal, rent out high-spec hybrid bikes and all kinds of equipment, like luggage trailers and panniers.

Vedado CubaRuta Bikes at Calle 16 no.152 esq. 13 (Mon–Sat 8am–5pm; 🌐rutabikes.com, ☎5247 6633) offer day rentals and city tours. In between Vedado and Centro Habana, and very close to both, is Bike Rental & Tours Havana at Ave. Salvador Allende (Carlos III) no.1115 e/ Luaces y Montoro (daily 9am–1pm & 2–6pm; 🌐bikerentalhavana.com, ☎5463 7103). They have a great selection of good quality bikes.

BY HORSE AND CARRIAGE

You can pick up a horse and carriage at the Plaza de San Francisco in Habana Vieja, on the corner of San Ignacio and Chacón near the cathedral or opposite the *Hotel Parque Central* on the Parque Central.

INFORMATION

Tourist information Infotur (🌐infotur.cu), the national tourist information network, operates several information centres in Havana. The three principal offices are at Obispo no.521 e/ Bernaza y Villegas in Habana Vieja (daily 9.30am–1pm & 2–5.30pm; ☎7866 3333 or ☎7863 6884); Calle 23 e/ L y M in the same building as the *Hotel Habana Libre* (☎7832 926 or ☎7832 9288) in Vedado (Mon–Sat 8.30am–5pm); and in Miramar at Avenida 5ta y 112 (daily 9am–6pm; ☎7204 7036). They also have a *buro de turismo* desk in the *Habana Libre* hotel (daily 8.30am–6pm; ☎7832 9288).

Maps Maps are pretty scarce, but the best place to find them is either Infotur or one of Havana's bookshops.

Listings For a brief rundown of what's on, look for the occasional listings publications and printouts at Infotur offices. In Habana Vieja, look out also for the "Programa Cultural" noticeboards installed in the plazas, which carry details of upcoming concerts, exhibitions, workshops and the like.

Websites The only comprehensive music, theatre, festival and arts listings for Havana are online. One of the best official sites is Habana Cultural (🌐habanacultural.ohc.cu). Try also the "Cartelera" section of La Jiribilla (🌐lajiribilla. cu/cartelera).

ACCOMMODATION

Accommodation in Havana is abundant and, as in the rest of Cuba, splits into two distinct categories, hotels and *casas particulares* (private houses). From sumptuous houses with large gardens or patios to small apartment rooms in buildings with no elevators, the city boasts a fantastically broad range of **casas particulares** which, broadly speaking, grow more luxurious the further west you venture. All areas, however, possess a significant number of *casas* that are far classier than the cheapest hotels, and it's a mistake to assume that a stay in a house means a compromise in comfort. Some *casas particulares* offer five or six rooms and are more like boutique hotels themselves. *Casas particulares* have practically cornered the budget market, though a rapidly increasing number of hostels, a relatively new concept in Cuba, are now popping up around the city, particularly in Centro Habana.

BOOKINGS, RATES AND AVAILABILITY

Though new *casas* open every month and there are around a dozen state hotels currently under construction, demand currently often outstrips supply and you are highly advised to make a reservation whether you are staying in a hotel or a *casa particular*, especially in high season (in Havana, unlike the beach resorts, this is usually Nov–April). Similarly, it's always worth making a reservation in a *casa particular*. Prices are sometimes negotiable if you are making a longer stay and there may be some flexibility around meals. The majority of places will provide breakfast on request, and other services including minibar, laundry and cocktails. Many *casas particulares* will have a menu of services and prices. If not, you should agree the price for extras at the beginning of your stay. All state hotel prices include breakfast unless otherwise stated.

HABANA VIEJA   SEE MAP PAGE 72

The most visited part of the city, Habana Vieja is bursting with accommodation options. *Casas particulares* here are almost exclusively in apartments rather than houses, and while they're decidedly less spacious than those further west, their proximity to most of the key sights and huge numbers of restaurants and bars makes them an excellent choice. Though many of the hotels are small boutique affairs, with ten to twenty rooms in charismatic colonial-era properties, the old town is undergoing a spate of luxury hotel building, adding five new imposing palaces to its portfolio, all along or near the Paseo del Prado: the *Gran Hotel Manzana Kempinski*, *Packard* and *Paseo del Prado* are already open. Until recently, all of the boutique hotels were operated by **Habaguanex**, a commercial arm of the City Historian's Office, and though they are still branded with that name they are now part of the national **Gaviota** chain (ⓦ gaviotahotels.com and ⓦ gaviota-grupo.com) – unless otherwise stated the hotels below have wi-fi and are found online at the Gaviota websites.

HOTELS

Ambos Mundos Obispo no.153 esq. Mercaderes ☎ 7860 95329. This stylishly artistic 1920s hotel, where Ernest Hemingway stayed between 1932 and 1939, is bang in the middle of the most visited part of Habana Vieja. It features an original metal cage lift and a fantastic rooftop terrace that hosts live music. $$$$

Beltrán de Santa Cruz San Ignacio no.411 e/ Muralla y Sol ☎ 7860 8330. Located in the thick of the old city but just off the main tourist circuit, this handsomely converted family townhouse – with balconied hallways, wide stone staircase and courtyard – has a relaxed vibe. $$$

★ **Conde de Villanueva** Mercaderes esq. Lamparilla ☎ 7801 1294. Also known as the *Hostal del Habano*, this is a cigar smoker's paradise with its own cigar shop, an attic-like smokers' lounge and the freedom to puff away throughout the premises. Despite its relatively small size, this place packs in several other charming communal spaces, including a courtyard heaving with plants and a fantastic cellar-style restaurant. $$$$

Florida Obispo no.252 esq. Cuba ☎ 7801 3127. The restoration of this aristocratic and splendid building has been impressively detailed and complete. There's a perfect blend of modern luxury and colonial elegance with marble floors, iron chandeliers, birds singing in the airy stone-columned central patio and potted plants throughout. Incorporates the adjoining *Hotel Marqués de Prado Ameno*. There are no single rooms here. $$$$

Los Frailes Brasil (Teniente Rey) no.8 e/ Mercaderes y Oficios ☎ 7801 2510. Unique in character, this moody little place is themed on a monastery, with staff dressed as monks. The low-ceiling staircase, narrow central patio and dim lighting work well together to create a serene and restful atmosphere, while the rooms are very comfortable. $$$

El Mesón de la Flota Mercaderes e/ Amargura y Brasil (Teniente Rey) ☎ 7801 1838. Similar in size and character to a traditional inn, this well-priced *hostal* has just five spacious rooms, all with simple but attractive stained-wood furnishings. The whole ground floor is occupied by a rustic and noisy Spanish restaurant. $$$

★ **Parque Central** Neptuno e/ Paseo del Prado y Agramonte (Zulueta), Parque Central ☎ 7860 6001, ⓦ iberostar.com. This luxury five-star hotel attracts business travellers and holidaymakers alike with its justified reputation for good service, while its elegant interior – particularly the wonderful leafy lobby – is a real knockout. Rooms are sumptuously comfortable, there are two classy restaurants, a gym and a marvellous roof terrace featuring a café and swimming pool. $$$$

Raquel Amargura esq. San Ignacio ☎ 7860 8280. Handsome and sleek with Art Deco touches, this is an unexpectedly upmarket hotel given its low-key side-street location. A cage lift, metal chandeliers and a glass ceiling revealing the first floor contribute to the sophisticated finish. $$$$

MOB HOTELS

Many of Havana's most glorious hotels, especially those in Vedado, were built in the 1950s with a casino attached and the funds for their construction put up by members of the American **Mafia**, who were busy building an empire in the Cuban capital. With a booming tourist economy, a shortage of top-class hotel rooms and American mobsters queuing up to take advantage of lax Cuban gambling laws, Cuban President Fulgencio Batista, in cahoots with the Mob, passed Hotel Law 2074 in 1955. This provided tax exemptions to any hotel providing tourist accommodation and guaranteed government financing and a gaming licence to anyone willing to invest $1 million or more in hotel construction, or $200,000 for the building of a nightclub. An unprecedented boom in hotel and casino construction followed as the Havana Mob expanded its portfolio, which already included the *Hotel Nacional*, the *Sevilla Biltmore* and the *Hotel Comodoro*, establishing landmark hotels like the *Habana Hilton*, the largest hotel in Havana when it opened in 1958, renamed the *Habana Libre* after the Revolution; the seafront *Hotel Deauville*, built in 1957 by Santo Trafficante, the Florida crime boss and long-time investor in Cuba; the luxurious *Hotel Riviera*, inaugurated in late 1957, conceived and funded by Meyer Lansky, the Don of the Havana-based mob; and the *Capri*, which also opened in 1957 and where the Mob installed the Hollywood tough-guy actor George Raft as a meeter-and-greeter, the personification of the hotel and casino industry in 1950s Havana, with its mixture of celebrity glamour and gangster backing.

Santa Isabel Baratillo no.9 e/ Obispo y Narcisco López, Plaza de Armas ☎ 7801 1201. One of the most exclusive of Habana Vieja's hotels, this impressively restored eighteenth-century building features colonial-style furnishings in all the rooms, and a fountain in the idyllic arched courtyard. $̄$$$$

CASAS PARTICULARES

Casa Caracol Cristo no.40, 2do piso e/ Brasil (Teniente Rey) y Muralla ☎ 7864 3085, ✉ caracol.cubano@outlook.es. This down-to-earth, compact second-floor apartment with three simple rooms, a mixture of doubles and quadruples, is light and airy, with bright white walls and shells dotted about the place giving it its name. Managed by likeable, youthful Julio Hernández and his family, this is a friendly place to stay, with great breakfasts. $̄$

Casa de Fefita y Luís Paseo del Prado no.20, apto. B, 5to piso e/ San Lázaro y Capdevila (Cárcel) ☎ 7867 6433, ✉ fefita_luis@yahoo.com. Situated on the fifth floor of a superbly located apartment block, the comfort standards here are fairly basic but the two simple en-suite rooms for rent have great views across the bay. Similarly, the views from the windowed terrace balcony make it perfect for long breakfasts. Wi-fi. $̄$

Casa de Pablo y Lidia Compostela no.532 e/ Brasil (Teniente Rey) y Muralla ☎ 7861 2111, ✉ compostela532@gmail.com. A spacious upstairs colonial-era apartment with a huge two-part lounge leading into a colourful patio corridor off which the two bedrooms are located. There's also a very spacious roof terrace suitable for sunbathing. Pablo (who speaks English) and Lidia are an older, very welcoming and friendly couple.

★ **Casa Vitrales** Habana no.106 e/ Cuarteles y Chacón ⊛ cvitrales.com. Highly impressive, beautiful *casa particular*, closer to a boutique hotel than a homestay, with six understated, arty rooms, two of them suites, spread across two levels around a lovely interior balcony and just below a handsome roof terrace with a bar where breakfasts are served, one of several communal areas. A little impersonal compared to some *casas* and certainly pricier but great value and as stylish as they come. $̄$

★ **Greenhouse** San Ignacio no.656 e/ Jesús María y Merced ☎ 7862 9877, ✉ fabio.quintana@infomed.sld.cu. Deep in southern Habana Vieja, this large and exceptional apartment is spotlessly clean and brimming over with precious furniture and curios. A sensational roof-terrace garden is a terrific spot for lounging, and the six luxurious double bedrooms are exquisitely and ornately furnished with antiques. $̄$

★ **Havana Casablanca** Complejo Morro Cabaña, Casa 29, Habana del Este ⊛ havanacasablanca.com. This nineteenth-century *villa* set within the Parque Morro-Cabaña on the other side of the bay is one of Havana's most luxurious *casas particulares*. The elegant space has two double rooms (one with an extra single bed), en-suite bathrooms with power showers, dining and seating area and kitchen. Outside, a wraparound porch features an alfresco dining area, loungers and hammocks beside the suntrap garden. A regal breakfast is included and English is spoken. Whole house $̄$$$

★ **Hostal Chez Nous** Brasil (Teniente Rey) no.115 e/ Cuba y San Ignacio ⊛ cheznoushabana.com. Outstanding *casa particular* with a majestic exterior and

1

an impressive interior, dignified by perfectly preserved nineteenth-century furnishings. Two superb balconied rooms are on the first floor, while from the central patio a spiral staircase leads up to the fabulous roof terrace where there's another very comfortable, contrastingly modern room with en-suite bathroom and its own porch. A separate dazzling Art Deco three-bedroom apartment is available in its entirety or room by room. Rooms $\bar{\mathsf{S}}$; whole apartment $\bar{\mathsf{S}}\bar{\mathsf{S}}$

CENTRO HABANA SEE MAP PAGE 93

Adjacent to Habana Vieja, some of the houses in Centro Habana are so close to the old town that you can consider them as good as in it. There really is very little point in staying in any of the very few and mostly poor hotels in this district unless you want oceanfront luxury, in which case there's the *Hotel Terral*. If you're absolutely desperate for a pool or want ocean views on more of a budget go to the still-overpriced *Deauville* on the corner of the Malecón and Avenida de Italia but otherwise you're far better off at a *casa particular*, the best of which are very comfortable and oozing with historic character. There are now at least half a dozen dorm-style hostels in Centro Habana, making it the best district for rock-bottom budgets.

HOTEL

Terral Malecón esq. Lealtad ⓦgaviota-grupo.com. This sleek, modernist affair is a great place to stay. Of the fourteen comfortable rooms, twelve have sea-facing balconies with fabulous views, and all are furnished and decorated with a touch of 1980s minimalism, heavy on the blacks and whites; there's also a rooftop terrace. $\bar{\mathsf{S}}\bar{\mathsf{S}}\bar{\mathsf{S}}\bar{\mathsf{S}}$

HOSTELS

Concordia Backpackers Concordia no.476 e/ Gervasio y Padre Varela (Belascoaín) ☎7861 0471, ⓔconcordiabackpackerhostel@gmail.com. Four plain rooms with two bunks in each on the first floor of a typical Centro Habana apartment building, with high ceilings and a large communal front room with a balcony overlooking the lively street below. This is budget accommodation at its most basic, but you can't beat the price and there are some fantastic paladars within a block. $\bar{\mathsf{S}}$

Rolando's Backpackers San Miguel no.567 e/ Gervasio y Padre Varela (Belascoaín) ☎7 879 9045, ⓔrolancesar@yahoo.es. First-floor apartment hostel, with three well-maintained bunk-bed dorms. Each dorm has its own bathroom, a/c and fans, lockable closets and a capacity of four to six guests. $\bar{\mathsf{S}}$

CASAS PARTICULARES

★ **Casa 1932** Campanario no.63 (bajos) e/ San Lázaro y Lagunas ⓦcasa1932.com. The Jazz Age is still alive and well inside this remarkable, tightly packed ground-floor apartment brimming with pre-Revolution photos,

advertising signs, furniture and other paraphernalia. The treasure-trove of interwar antiques includes a 1930s cash register, a gramophone and the dark-coloured hardwood beds, wardrobes and chests in the three excellent bedrooms. En-suite bathrooms, TV, fridge, tea-making facilities, a/c and a complementary laundry service provide the modern comforts. Fabulous, huge breakfasts too. $\bar{\mathsf{S}}$

Casa 1940 San Lázaro no.409 e/ Manrique y Campanario ☎7 863 7437, ⓔcasahabana@gmail.com. You can rent the whole of this clean and uncluttered apartment, one block from the Malecón, or just one of the two simple but stylish double rooms. Some nice touches – like the photos of 1950s Havana, a collection of vintage snuff boxes and some attractive old furniture – provide splashes of character. A good option for families. $\bar{\mathsf{S}}$

Casa de Alex y Yuly Neptuno no.905, apto. 3 e/ Soledad y Aramburo ☎7 878 1146, ⓔiyuli@nauta.cu. A whole second-floor apartment on the Vedado side of Centro Habana, well suited to long stays. A small kitchen, large bedroom with a/c, TV and two beds, a telephone and a lounge/diner are crowned by a roof terrace, which enjoys lovely evening breezes and views across the rooftops. $\bar{\mathsf{S}}$

★ **Casa y Apartamento de Miriam y Sinaí** Neptuno no.521 e/ Campanario y Lealtad ☎7 878 4456, ⓔsinaisole@yahoo.es. Fantastic, capacious, smartly furnished first-floor apartment run by one of the friendliest, hardest-working landladies in the city and her sociable, helpful English-, Italian- and German-speaking daughter. There's an enchanting central patio filled with rocking chairs, plants and a fountain and three comfortable double bedrooms, one with a balcony and all with hotel-standard bathrooms. There's a separate, very smart independent apartment next door too if you want complete privacy. $\bar{\mathsf{S}}$

Casa Colonial Cary y Nilo Gervasio no.216 e/ Concordia y Virtudes ☎7 862 7109, ⓔcaridadgf45@yahoo.es. An elegant but – thanks to its likeable elderly owners – unpretentious and very spruce ground-floor apartment where three guest rooms, with en-suite bathrooms and antique furniture, help to fill the considerable space. $\bar{\mathsf{S}}$

★ **La Casa de Concordia** Concordia no.421 e/ Escobar y Gervasio ☎7 862 5330. An exceptional house, dating from 1790, whose two large doubles and two impressive suites combine high-spec comfort, such as silent a/c units, and spacious pristine bathrooms, with flawless antique furniture. Artistic touches and authentic colonial trappings include Cuban paintings and photography, the restored details of an original mural in the front room and the colourful stained-glass *vitrales* between the patio and the back of the house. $\bar{\mathsf{S}}\bar{\mathsf{S}}$

Casa de Dayami de Cervantes San Martín no.618, e/ Escobar y Gervasio ☎7 873 3640, ⓔlchavao@infomed. sld.cu. Homely two-level apartment where guests are given the run of the upstairs floor, which features a roof terrace at either end and two neat and cosy bedrooms. Run by a friendly family, one of whom speaks English. $

Casa Ecléctica 1925 Neptuno no.619 e/ Gervasio y Escobar ⓦ casaeclectica1925.com. José, the proud owner of this airy, blemishless second-floor apartment spent over a decade restoring it in painstaking detail to its original 1925 splendour, with no detail overlooked, all the way down to the window locks. Colourfully painted, there's a lovely balcony terrace scattered with plants and nice light rooms with excellent bathrooms. $

Casa de Mandy Neptuno no.519, apto. 3 e/ Campanario y Lealtad ☎ 7867 9899. Two large and lovely rooms with a/c, fridge and TV, and one with a street-side balcony in an impeccably well-maintained second-floor flat. $

Casa de Ricardo Morales Campanario no.363, apto. 3 e/ San Miguel y San Rafael ☎ 7 866 8363, ✉ moralesfundora@yahoo.es, ⓦ casaricardo.info. Ideal for anyone looking for privacy and security, this thoughtfully decorated first-floor apartment (fitted with an alarm) is rented out in its entirety. There's a spacious, well-equipped kitchen, two comfy double bedrooms with connecting bathroom and a homely lounge-diner with a TV, large sofa, balcony and decorative items from Mexico. $

★ **Hostal Juancho** Concordia no.863 e/ San Francisco y Espada ⓦ hostaljuanchocuba.com. As impressively managed, equipped and presented *casa particular* as you will find in Centro Habana. Unparalleled characteristics include a reception area with a bar, both top notch, and six rooms, all of them minimalist yet high spec. Rooms line up along an airy ground-floor corridor and a balcony above, and communal spaces are beautifully decked out in house plants, antique furniture and lots and lots of plates – the walls are covered in them and the effect is very memorable. Worth the above-average cost, which includes breakfast. $$

★ **Hostal Peregrino** Consulado no.152 e/ Colón y Trocadero ☎ 7860 1257, ✉ info@hostalperegrino.com. A first-floor flat with tonnes of character and five smart yet homely rooms, two of which have split levels and four of which have balconies. The flat is artistically plastered in evocative old photos of Havana, interesting prints and wall hangings and though very professionally run there is a lovely sense that you are sharing Elsa and Julio's home with them – though they actually own several other *casas* besides this one. $

VEDADO   SEE MAP PAGE 97

Quiet, leafy Vedado is a more relaxed place to stay than further east in the city, although you'll need transport to visit Habana Vieja regularly. One-time playground of North America's rich and famous, the best of the hotels here date from the pre-Revolution era, and while some of their rooms could do with a refurb, the restaurants, pools and lounging areas give a real sense of the insouciance of yesteryear. Vedado *casas particulares*, among them some of the city's most elegant nineteenth- and early twentieth-century

residences, tend to be spacious and quiet, often with gardens and patios.

HOTELS

Habana Libre Calle L e/ 23 y 25 ⓦ meliacuba.com. This stylish Vedado landmark, with stunning atrium and exterior mosaic by celebrated 1950s artist Amelia Pelaez has three restaurants, a terrace pool, a business centre and good-quality rooms with all mod cons. A stylish choice, even if some amenities have seen better days. $$$$

★ **Nacional** Calle O esq. 21 ⓦ hotelnacional-decuba.com. One of Havana's best-looking hotels, with the air of an Arabian palace particularly evident in the main lobby where Moorish tiles and beamed ceiling create a splendid backdrop. The rooms are sensitively decorated with reproduction furnishings while the swimming pools, health and fitness facilities, cabaret and open-air garden-terrace make this a fine choice. There are also three decent restaurants and cafés on site. $$$$

NH Capri Calle 21 e/ N y O ⓦ nh-hotels.com. This one-time stylish pre-Revolution, well-located downtown option is well appointed and in good nick, but now somewhat anodyne. Services include shops, hairdresser, gym, wi-fi and best of all a small rooftop swimming pool with stunning ocean views. $$$

Presidente Calzada no.110 esq. Ave. de los Presidentes ☎ 7838 1801. Vedado's most charismatic hotel, retaining many original features from its 1928 inauguration. The small lobby is a delight, with marble flooring and enormous teardrop chandeliers, while the rooms complement the general feel with antique furniture, views over the city and marble bathrooms. $$$$

Riviera Paseo y Malecón ☎ 7 836 4051, ⓦ hotelhavanariviera.com. Built by the Mafia in the 1950s as a casino hotel, the *Riviera* retains much of that era's style. Many original features – like its long, sculpture-filled lobby, rooms boasting original furniture and *Copa Room* cabaret – capture the retro vibe. Regular online offers can work out at a quarter of the rack rate price here. $$$$

CASAS PARTICULARES

★ **Casa de Aurora Ampudia** Calle 15 no.58 (altos) e/ M y N ☎ 7832 1843, ✉ olmarostegui@gmail.com. One self-contained first-floor apartment with its own huge bedroom, living room, kitchen and bathroom, in a beautiful colonial house within a stone's throw of the Malecón. An expansive balcony decked with wrought-iron rocking chairs make it the perfect lounging spot. Aurora and her family are among the friendliest and most helpful owners in the city. $

Casa Aide Calle 21 no.55 (bajos) e/ M y N, ☎ 7 831 8062, ✉ aide.cuellar@nauta.cu. Four rooms in a fantastic location within view of the *NH Capri* and *Nacional*. Two have their own kitchen and bathroom while a further two share a bathroom between them. An enclosed terrace with a marble floor and plants completes the offering. The apartment upstairs has four rooms. $\overline{\varsigma}$

Casa de Leydiana Navarro Cardoso Calle N, no.203 (bajos) e/ 19 y 21 ☎ 7835 4030, ✉ casaleydiana@gmail. com. Every effort has been made to equal hotel service and mod cons in the two rooms here, with fridges stocked with minibar treats, television, fan and faux colonial furniture. Breakfast is served on a large terrace overlooking the Edificio FOCSA. $\overline{\varsigma}$

Casa de Magda Calle K, no.508 (bajos) e/ 25 y 27 ☎ 7832 3269, ✉ milagrotrev@infomed.sld.cu. The elaborate Baroque furniture, chandeliers and china leopards adorning this house are worthy of a decorative arts museum. The two rooms both have a/c and en-suite bathrooms; one is particularly splendid, with a king-sized mahogany bed and matching wardrobe. A wide porch out front is perfect for people-watching. Some English is spoken. Mark reservation emails for the attention of Armando, who checks emails for Magda. $\overline{\varsigma}$

★ **Casa de Mélida Jordán** Calle 25 no.1102 e/ 6 y 8 ☎ 7836 1136, ✉ melida.jordan@gmail.com. A big, stylish house set back from the road beside a garden filled with roses and ferns. Both of the rooms are beautifully furnished and have a private bathroom. The largest has twin beds and the other has a double, although an extra bed can be added. English is spoken and there are various extra services available. A superb choice. $\overline{\varsigma}$

Hostal Peregrino Calle 9na no.406, apto. 12 (bajos) e/ G y F ☎ hostalperegrino.com. High spec, very clean, airy ground-floor apartment with four harmoniously styled rooms for rent, two of them very large. There are small decorative touches, down to the magnets on the fridge, and more significant features, especially the front room, plant-filled conservatory and the back patio, that make this more a holiday home than a B&B. $\overline{\varsigma}$

★ **Hostal Silvia** Paseo no.602 e/ 25 y 27 ☎ hostalsilvia. com. An ornate stained-glass window, marble staircase and mahogany period furniture make this one of the city's most regal *casas particulares*. The four double rooms, one with an extra bed for a child, each has its own bathroom and a/c. The lush garden and conservatory are an added bonus. $\overline{\varsigma}$

MIRAMAR AND THE WESTERN SUBURBS
SEE MAP PAGE 110

Replete with Western-style luxury, Miramar's slick, towering hotels represent the best the city has to offer, and though not very convenient for sightseeing, they all operate a regular shuttle service to Habana Vieja. Miramar's *casas particulares* are also in a league of their own, with several offering independent apartments complete with dining areas, living space and, in some cases, swimming pools – and an increased price tag to match.

HOTELS

El Bosque Ave. 28A e/ 49A y 49C, Reparto Kohly, Playa ⓦ gaviotahotels.com. In a leafy suburb overlooking the eponymous Bosque de la Habana wood, this is the perfect retreat from the city. Some of the basic but well-maintained rooms have views over the wood itself. Amenities include a pool. $\overline{\varsigma}\overline{\varsigma}\overline{\varsigma}$

Memories Miramar Ave. 5ta e/ 72 y 76 Miramar, Playa ⓦ memoriesresort.com. Despite its uninspiring facade, the sleek interior and smooth, professional service make this an excellent choice. Facilities include a business centre, a top-class gym, squash and tennis courts and huge pool. Rooms have all mod-cons including wi-fi, and there's a choice of three restaurants. $\overline{\varsigma}\overline{\varsigma}\overline{\varsigma}$

CASAS PARTICULARES

★ **Casa de Gertrudis Martorell** Ave. 7ma no.6610 e/ 66 y 70, Miramar, Playa ☎ 7202 6563. A perfect marriage of high-class comfort and facilities, with restrained, subtle decoration and furnishings, this *casa particular* knocks the socks off most hotels for sheer luxury. Complete with a huge terrace, the whole top floor is rented in its entirely, and features three bedrooms with king-size beds and original paintings by renowned Cuban artists. Whole apartment $\overline{\varsigma}\overline{\varsigma}\overline{\varsigma}\overline{\varsigma}$

Casa Bellavista Havana Calle A no.312 apto. 9 e/ 3ra y 5ta, Miramar, Playa ☎ 7 203 7581, ✉ masexto@ infomed.sld.cu. One of the major selling points of this stylish retro penthouse apartment, owned by a very friendly English-speaking owner, is its view over the ocean and Havana. One of the spacious rooms has its own bathroom, while the other two share. $\overline{\varsigma}$

EATING

Eating out in Havana has been transformed in the last decade.Though you will still see the same clutch of traditional Cuban dishes time and time again, what really elevates the capital's food scene above that of the rest of the country is the increasing number of establishments abandoning the old formulas. Creative spins on Cuban classics and cuisine previously untried in Cuba, from Indian to Swedish and even vegan, have raised the bar and the choice of food is wider than ever before, with imported

ingredients and international flavours slowly proliferating. The new breed of paladars have also elevated their look and feel, from yesteryear's norm of a few tables laid out in the spare room of someone's home to today's entirely remodelled houses, eye-catching interiors and a trained and professional staff. Vedado and Miramar remain the homes of the city's finest dining but you can eat great food all over the city. The capital's **cafés** are often indistinguishable from restaurants, serving meals as much as drinks, and there are

VEGAN AND VEGETARIAN HAVANA

Pescatarians do okay, but Havana has never been a great city for eating out if you're vegetarian. There are now, however, a clutch of quality, bona fide vegetarian restaurants offering a decent number of vegan dishes, and a growing number of places recognizing that it pays to provide vegetarian options. Below are our top choices.

★ **Camino al Sol** Call 3ra no.363 e/ Paseo y 2, Vedado ☎7832 1861; see map page 97. A vegetarian deli-restaurant with vegan options and a lean towards Italian cuisine. There are several simple but delectable pastas with sauces such as spinach and blue cheese, and a nice variety of smaller bites and starters. The gazpacho, chickpea falafel with tomato sauce and veggie calzone are all worth ordering. Excellent freshly made soups and juices are also highlights. The place itself is light and laidback. ⑤⑤

El Shamuskia'o Muralla no.308A e/ Habana y Compostela ☎7863 9150; see map page 72. Though they do serve some meat dishes at this cosy little kerbside paladar, the emphasis is on vegetarian and vegan food. The varied menu includes vegan burgers and sandwiches, vegetable tempura, vegetable kebabs, tacos and aubergine lasagne, but despite spreading their net wide they handle most of these successfully. There are also one or two more distinctively and enjoyably Cuban takes on plant-based eating, like malanga fritters, fried plantain and the black bean and vegetable stew. ⑤

Lo de Monik Chacon esq Compostela, ⓦfacebook. com/lodemonik; see map page 72. Though meat and seafood are served here, this cute, cosy restaurant offers lots of tasty vegan and vegetarian dishes, with seasonal produce top of their priorities. Expect inventive sandwiches, salads and tacos, with heartier fare available too. The coffee and cocktails are also pretty great. ⑤⑤

also a few places more akin to coffeeshops, worth searching out if you are looking for a relaxing, hassle-free snack or drink.

HABANA VIEJA AND PARQUE MORRO-CABAÑA   SEE MAP PAGE 72

CAFÉS
Café Bohemia Plaza Vieja, ⓦhavanabohemia.com. Largely hidden from view from the plaza, sunk back inside a delightful colonial building, you can sip your cocktails and munch on your sandwiches and tapas here in relative comfort and serenity. The salads are excellent. ⑤⑤

Helad'oro Aguiar no.206 e/ Empedrado y Tejadillo ☎5305 9131. The best ice cream in Habana Vieja and the most Cuban of flavours are found at this straightforward ice-cream parlour. *Mojito*, guava, soursop, mamey and *turrón de maní* flavours, among others. ⑤

★ **Oasis Nelva** Habana esq. Muralla ☎7864 6842. Creatively designed and soothingly relaxed, Oasis Nelva constitutes a small room open to the street and a hidden balcony level overlooking a house-plant shop, part of the same business. Seats are made from tyres and girders, lamps from tin cans and picture frames from crates. Food and drink are excellent quality and value too: sweet and savoury crêpes, baguettes served with the fillings on the side, Greek salads and addictive fresh fruit juices. You can get breakfasts here too. ⑤⑤

STATE RESTAURANTS
La Bodeguita del Medio Empedrado e/ San Ignacio y Cuba ☎7867 1374. The city's most famous restaurant – and its busiest tourist trap – still has some appeal. Beyond the often impossibly crowded bar, a former haunt of Hemingway, is an enthralling labyrinth of rooms, the walls caked in scribbled messages and photos of celebrity customers. The food isn't bad for such a touristy place, mostly classic national dishes like *ropa vieja* or roasted pork. ⑤⑤⑤

La Imprenta Mercaderes no.208 e/ Lamparilla y Amargura ☎7864 9581. A mixture of excellent-value tapas – stuffed potatoes, tortilla or fish fritters– and carefully cooked, attractively presented mains such as salted shrimp and slices of beef served in a handsome, airy building full of earthy tones and decorative nods to its previous incarnation as a nineteenth-century printing house. ⑤⑤

PALADARS
★ **5 Esquinas** Habana no.104 esq. Cuarteles ☎7860 6295. Billing itself as a trattoria, *5 Esquinas* has a wood-fired oven dishing out a pleasing variety of pizzas. Offers some particularly delicious filled pastas, risottos packed with ingredients, salads, seafood and meat dishes. The set lunches and dinners are particularly good value. Tables along pedestrianized Callejón de Espada make a great evening spot but the harshly lit interior doesn't. ⑤⑤

Al Carbón Chacón esq. Aguacate ☎5 343 8540. The slightly pricey menu here, of mostly mouthwatering meat dishes, can look deceivingly familiar but in fact the cuts of meat, most of it cooked on the charcoal grill that gives the place its name and the quality of preparation are in general way above average. Something similar can be said for the place itself, a wonderfully engaging jamboree of old clocks, statues, portraits, film posters, birdcages and countless other individual touches. **$$$**

★ **El Chanchullero** Brasil (Teniente Rey) e/ Bernaza y Cristo, Plaza del Cristo ⓦ el-chanchullero.com. Determined to avoid Cuban clichés, this laidback little place on the old town's only untouristy square was a pioneer among Havana's new breed of paladars and continues to trailblaze, its nonconformist vibe the perfect antidote to the staid formality in so many state restaurants. The mixed, casual crowd here, enjoying a music policy of reggae, jazz and blues rather than salsa and reggaeton, are brought earthenware bowls full of juicy, herby sausages or chicken, tuna, lamb or pork, accompanied not by the usual rice and beans, but bread and salad instead. **$$**

El Del Frente O'Reilly e/ Habana y Aguiar ⓦ facebook.com/EldelFrente303. Marked by a voguish, stripped-down, international chic, this is the hangout for sophisticated locals and trendy foreigners. Delight at moreish starters like fried octopus or artisan bread with hummus and house pâté, then savour mains like the rich, mouthwatering Tony Soprano Meat Ball Spaghetti or the lobster risotto. An intimate roof terrace bar looks down on the slightly older sister restaurant, *O'Reilly 304*, hence the name "The one opposite". **$$**

★ **Doña Eutimia** Callejón del Chorro no.60c, Plaza de la Catedral ☎ 7861 1332. One of the best paladars around the Plaza de la Catedral. There's nothing unusual on the menu but national culinary trademarks like roast chicken and fish *enchilado* are cooked to an excellent standard, as are starters like malanga fritters and croquettes, and all excellent value, too. Tables sit snugly together in the artistically decorated and very sociable interior. Reservations recommended. **$$**

Habana 61 Habana no.61 e/ Cuarteles y Peña Pobre ☎ 7861 9433. The menu presents diners with a choice of well-prepared "traditional" and refreshingly "modern" Cuban dishes, big on contrasting flavours. There's red snapper with caper butter or sirloin cooked with pepper, mustard, oregano and parmesan, for example. The decent salads are a bonus. Feels a bit like a hotel bar with its black, white and chrome furnishings and glass-topped tables. **$$$**

Ivan Chefs Justo Aguacate no.9 esq. Chacón ⓦ ivanchef.com. Also referred to by its address, Aguacate no.9, as there is no sign outside, this place gets away with the lack of advertising thanks to its deserved reputation for high-quality food, the fame of its founding chefs, one of whom, Justo Pérez, cooked for Fidel Castro for 35 years, and the beautiful, intimate, split-level interior. The tacos and the tenderized suckling pig are among the most lauded dishes here but you can't go too far wrong with any of the seafood or grilled meat mains. Reservations recommended. **$$$**

Más Habana Habana no.308 e/ San Juan de Dios y O'Reilly ☎ 7864 3227. Starters like cheese balls with papaya sauce and coconut shrimp tempura plus mains like pork ribs with guava and excellent tacos and fajitas put this trendy but low key restaurant-café firmly among Havana's

---

BREAKFAST VENUES

There aren't many cafés or restaurants offering decent **breakfasts** in Havana, and though it's usually best to stick to your hotels or *casa particular*, there are some places worth getting up and out for before lunchtime. Some of the best are listed below and also worth a shot are *Oasis Nelva, Café Bohemia, Papa Ernesto* and *California Café.*

★ **Café Arcangel** Concordia no.57 e/ Aguila y Ave. de Italia (Galiano) ⓦ cafearcangel.com, see map page 93. Diners squeeze into the fabulous little curbside room here for great value American breakfasts, or the house breakfast of fruit, toast, ham, eggs, jam and juice, plus croissants and good coffee. There's a read-the-paper vibe, with jazzy, soulful, easy-listening tunes playing at a relaxingly low volume and a vintage theme, which includes silent movies playing on a discreet screen behind an old movie projector. **$**

Cafetería La Rampa Hotel Habana Libre, Calle 23 esq. L, Vedado ☎ 7834 6100; see map page 97. A good choice of breakfast platters in this US-style diner, from traditional Cuban featuring pork and rice to the full American, all served round the clock on a daily basis. **$$**

Café del Angel Compostela esq. Cuarteles ⓦ jacquelinefumero.com; see map page 72. This westernized coffeeshop, sharing space with the designer-owner's tacky artisanal boutique, serves good-quality crêpes, American and continental breakfasts. Get away from the sense of eating in a shop by sitting on the outside tables in the shadow of a church. **$$**

El Pórtico Hotel Parque Central, Paseo del Prado esq. Neptuno, Habana Vieja ☎ 7860 6627; see map page 72. The marvellous lobby café at this five-star hotel, full of classic colonial charm, serves top-notch continental breakfasts of cakes, croissants, toast and fruit, with the option to add smoked salmon, eggs, bacon, ham, chorizo, cheese, milk and yoghurt. **$$**

La Veranda Hotel Nacional, Calle O esq. 21, Vedado ☎ 7836 3564; see map page 97. The buffet breakfast in the basement of this fabulous hotel is unbeatable for sheer scale and choice, with everything you would hope to see in a classic English or American spread, plus loads of extras including cereal, fresh fruit, sweets and bread. **$$**

CHEAP EATS

Decent restaurants in Havana may be plentiful but add in a few drinks, an entrée and a flan and the restaurant tab starts to shoot skywards. Options that are light on the pocket are not always immediately apparent. The list below details places in which you can eat **for under $200CUP**. In addition to these, numerous small street food stalls sell tasty and filling snacks like *papas rellenas* (potato balls stuffed with mince) and slabs of home-made cake.

La Bien Pagá Aguacate no.259 e/ Obispo y Obrapía, Habana Vieja ☎ 7866 1972; see map page 72. The habitual scrum at the takeaway counter here attests to the popularity of the chunky sandwiches on which this place has made its name. The fruit milkshakes are well worth queuing for, too. ⑤

Hanoi Brasil (Teniente Rey) esq. Bernaza, Habana Vieja ☎ 7867 1029; see map page 72. This rustic place, with its small rooms and tightly packed trellis-roof courtyard, is one of the cheapest state restaurants in old Havana, with basic beef, chicken and pork meals and a great-value vegetarian set meal. ⑤

Ideas Linea no.110 (altos) e/ L y M ☎ 7830 8900; see map page 97. This pleasant spot has a first-floor balcony overlooking the street and serves a good-value *comida criolla* lunch menu. There's a great cocktail menu here too. ⑤

Plan B Calle 6 no.511 e/ 23 y 21 Vedado ☎ 7832 1824; see map page 97. Clean and friendly snack joint with bar seating opening onto a tranquil residential street. The menu offers simple breakfasts, tasty toasted sandwiches, and more substantial meals like pork chops with a side of rice go. ⑤

Q Bolá Calle J no.558 e/ 25 y 27 Vedado; see map page 97. Expect pocket-pleasing home-made pizzas, pulled pork rolls, juices and hot dogs at this open-air café. There are a couple of other cheap places to eat on the same block. ⑤

new breed. A stripped back interior with a nice mezzanine balcony and modern artwork on the walls make for an enjoyably informal lunch or boozy evening meal. ⑤⑤⑤

★ **O'Reilly 304** O'Reilly 304 e/ Habana y Aguiar ☎ 5264 4725. A very cool tapas restaurant and bar and deservedly one of the hits of the last few years in Habana Vieja. The tapas are excellent, among them authentic tacos and flavourful Cuban pastries, *empanadillas*, while there are more substantial meat and seafood meals too. Two tightly packed floors, with tables downstairs huddled around a small bar counter, provide a convivial intimacy and original, modern artworks and photography on the walls top off this innovative place. ⑤⑤⑤

Osteria Empedrado no.509 e/ Villegas y Ave. de las Misiones (Monserrate) ☎ 5291 5538. Italian owned and run, this is as authentic as Italian food gets in Habana Vieja – and, hands down, it's the best. Pastas are full of intense flavours and ingredients rarely seen in Cuban restaurants, such as spicy sausage, gorgonzola and plain old broccoli. The meat and seafood mains are equally lip-smacking while the restaurant itself is happily simple – it's the food that does the talking here. ⑤⑤

CENTRO HABANA   SEE MAP PAGE 93

PALADARS

★ **Casa Miglis** Lealtad no.120 e/ Animas y Lagunas ☎ 7 864 1486. This stylish Swedish place right in the thick of run-down Centro Habana is one of the most surprising and welcome additions to the city's eating-out scene. The menu, which includes nods to Cuban, Greek and Mexican cooking, does nevertheless provide the city's only opportunity to eat *skagen* (Sweden's take on prawns on toast) or meatballs with mashed potato and lingonberries, both authentic and flavourful. The problem is sourcing the ingredients – expect a few shakes of the head when you place your order. ⑤⑤⑤

La Concordia Concordia no.453 e/ Gervasio y Padre Varela (Belascoaín), ⌨ facebook.com/laconcordiacuba. A charcoal grill sends the mouthwatering smell of kebab meat up the stairs to the enchanting roof terrace where many diners choose to sit, though there is a terrific dining room in a large and comfy loft space below. There's plenty more besides kebabs, almost all of it top notch, like Cuban jerked beef, coconut shrimp and grilled octopus. A classy but relaxed place with excellent cocktails. ⑤⑤⑤

★ **La Guarida** Concordia no.418 e/ Gervasio y Escobar, ⌨ laguarida.com. The city's most renowned paladar has long been an obligatory stop-off for visiting celebrities, from Queen Sofía of Spain to Jay Z, and is worth every penny of its higher-than-average prices. The meat and fish menu breaks with all the national norms, and the dishes – like rabbit lasagne, salmon in a spring onion sauce with bacon, and sugar cane tuna glazed with coconut – brim with flavour and originality. Set in the aged apartment building where the acclaimed *Fresa y Chocolate* was filmed, the decor is eye-catchingly eclectic and the moody ambience in the three rooms perfect for a long-drawn-out meal. Reservations are essential. ⑤⑤⑤⑤

★ **San Cristóbal** San Rafael no.469 e/ Lealtad y Campanario ☎ 7 867 9109 or ☎ 7 860 1705. Perfectly presented juicy and saucy Creole cuisine, including full-flavoured "country-style pork slices", lots of hearty beef

1

dishes and some chicken options. The knockout interior consists of a lovely, leafy narrow terrace and three captivating dining rooms, two heaving with pictures. A feast for the eyes and stomach. $\overline{\$\$\$}$

VEDADO   SEE MAP PAGE 97

CAFÉS

California Café Calle 19 e/ N y O ⓦ californiacafehabana. com. More an urban beach shack than a café, this hipsterish little neighbourhood joint features homemade rustic furniture and a menu with veggie options, fish tacos and more substantial meals. There's music nightly and DJs all day on Wednesdays and Fridays. Breakfasts too. $\overline{\$}$

Coppelia Calle 23 esq. L ☎ 7 832 6184. Havana's massive and famous ice-cream emporium contains several cafés and an open-air area serving rich sundaes in exotic flavours like coconut, mango and guava. $\overline{\$}$

STATE RESTAURANTS

La Torre Edificio FOCSA, piso 33, Calle 17 no.55 esq. M ☎ 7 838 3088. Mesmerizing views from atop the city's second-tallest building plus an extensive cocktail menu and decent food mean this is well worth a visit. $\overline{\$\$}$

Unión Francesa Calle 17, no.861 e/ 4 y 6 ☎ 7 832 4493. Set in a nineteenth-century mansion, this culinary complex includes a bakery and café on the ground floor. There are three floors to choose from, with alfresco tables overlooking Parque Lennon and a patio at the top lined with antique cabinets and a floral canopy. Friendly and attentive staff serve creative dishes like chicken with glazed pineapple or an orange sauce. $\overline{\$\$}$

PALADARS

Los Amigos Calle M no.253 e/ 19 y 21 ☎ 7 830 0880. Tasty lunchtime choices include rice and beans or *ajiaco* stew and possibly the best home-made chips in Havana. It's always busy so reservations are recommended (though you can wait on the patio outside if you prefer). They also do a takeaway service – you supply the container. $\overline{\$}$

★ **Atelier** Calle 5ta no.511 (altos) e/ Paseo y 2 ☎ 7 8362025. Cuban food made with a touch of panache in a shabby-chic first floor paladar with artsy touches peppered throughout. The elegantly presented mains like candied duck, rabbit in wine, and churrasco steak are made with top-quality ingredients and preparation is unrushed. A stack of transistor radios, old cash registers and pendulum clocks are some of the vintage items decorating the classy dining room and the two terraces. $\overline{\$\$\$}$

★ **El Biky** Infanta esq. San Lazar ⓦ elbiky.com. Slick and shiny eatery with captivating black-and-white photos of yesteryear Havana. There's a somewhat Spanish-cum-*comida criolla* vibe to the food with peppers stuffed with tuna, chickpea stew and Galician chicken on offer. A soda

fountain, range of coffee and generous cocktails make this a good daytime hangout too. $\overline{\$\$\$}$

★ **Café Laurent** Calle M no.257 e/ 19 y 21 ☎ 7 831 2090. This airy penthouse papered with 1950s magazines and filled with white furniture is one of the best of Havana's new wave of restaurants. Mains like slow roast lamb or fish in salsa verde are beautifully presented and taste as good as they look, while starters are delicate and inventive and desserts are worth saving room for. Eat out on the balcony and enjoy the stunning views over Vedado and the ocean. Reservations recommended. $\overline{\$\$\$}$

Café Presidente Calle G esq. 25 ☎ 7 832 3091. This bar-restaurant is a chic enclosed terrace curved around the front of a statuesque apartment block. Sandwiches and burgers are great value, as are the *comida criolla* mains. Given it feels like a sultry hotel bar it's best for people watching over a cool drink. $\overline{\$\$}$

★ **El Cocinero** Calle 26 e/ 11 y 13 ⓦ elcocinerocuba. com. Housed in an old peanut oil factory adjoining Fábrica de Arte Cubano, if any restaurant can claim to match standards of international excellence, it's *El Cocinero*. Decor (Panton chairs, wooden floored terrace, contemporary Cuban artwork, abundance of greenery), attentive service, chic clientele and the well-thought-through menu are all on point. Duck confit blinis, goats' cheese and papaya salad and an excellent lobster bisque are just some of the delights on offer. There's also a great dessert menu too. The first floor bar is is open all day. $\overline{\$\$\$}$

★ **Decameron** Linea, no.753 e/ Paseo y 2 ☎ 7 832 2444. The decor and ambience here are inspired and low-key, with pendulum clocks lining the walls, soft lighting and cane-backed chairs. A mix of Italian, Cuban and European food contributes to the cosmopolitan air. The *ropa vieja* is one of the city's best; shrimp in coconut and ginger is delicious and beautifully presented. For the quality, the prices are reasonable too. Strong and sweet *mojitos*, plus attentive service, round things off nicely. $\overline{\$\$\$}$

Waoo! Calle L no.414 e/ 23 y 25 ☎ 7830 5264. A cheerful airy spot overlooking the *Habana Libre*. Competently assembled goats' cheese salad, octopus carpaccio and Serrano ham, sliced from the bone in front of you, elevate this above the other mid-range restaurants. A set lunch menu adds to the great value. $\overline{\$\$\$}$

MIRAMAR AND THE WESTERN SUBURBS
SEE MAP PAGE 110

CAFÉS

K Café Teatro Karl Marx, Ave. 1ra e/ 8 y 10, Miramar, Playa ☎ 7203 0801. One of the area's most popular spots with locals and tourists alike, this large and lively café in the lobby of a huge theatre serves coffees and cocktails as well as sandwiches and pizzas. Child seats (and portions) are an added bonus for parents. $\overline{\$\$}$

OCEANFRONT EATING AND DRINKING

Given the Malecón's starring role as the soul of the city's nightlife, not to mention its 4km length, it's surprising how few restaurants, bars and cafés line up along it, though several new establishments have opened on the oceanfront promenade in recent years. In Miramar, beyond the Malecón, the rocky shore also has a steadily increasing smattering of venues from where you can contemplate the Florida Straits; while the Parque Morro-Cabaña, on the eastern side of the channel leading to the bay, houses some good waterfront venues with great views of the city.

Café Neruda Malecón no.355 e/ San Nicolás y Manrique ☎7864 4159; see map page 93. In a gap between ocean-view apartment buildings is this pleasant outdoor café, one of the most pleasant drinking spots on the Malecón. Features a lawn, park benches and tables protected from the wind by panes of glass sealing the place off from the street. Hot and cold drinks plus light snacks and main meals – lobster features large. $$$

Castropol Malecón no.107 e/ Genio y Crespo ☎7861 4864; see map page 93. Run by an Asturian emigrant society, the upstairs balcony of this restaurant on the Malecón is a great place to eat with views along the Havana coastline. As well as the usual, perfectly decent Cuban meat and seafood offerings are some worthwhile departures from the norm, especially among the starters, like smoked salmon and lobster ceviche. Downstairs, in the cheaper *taberna*, you can order pizza, pasta and grilled food. $$

Club Jardines de 1830 Malecón no.1252 esq. 20 ☎7838 3090; see map page 97. Eat elsewhere to avoid the mediocre offerings but head to this fabulously faded colonial house to drink on the terrace overlooking the sea and to dance into the early hours with the salsa set. This is one of the liveliest dance venues in the city and definitely the most scenic. $$

La Divina Pastora Parque Morro-Cabaña ☎7860 8341; see map page 72. Occupying a fabulous waterside terrace right on the edge of the most attractive stretch of the bay, this restaurant works equally well by day or by night, though after dark, when you can combine a visit with a trip to *El Cañonazo*, the lights of Habana Vieja on the opposite shore provide a particularly romantic backdrop. The standout dishes here include paella and a delicately prepared octopus dressed in olive oil and rosemary. $$$

Nazdarovie Malecón no.25, 3er piso e/ Paseo del Prado y Capdevila (Cárcel) ☎7860 2947, ⓦfacebook.com/NazdarovieCUBA; see map page 93. The closest oceanfront restaurant to Habana Vieja, with views along the Malecón from its balcony, was opened in 2015 by sons and daughters of immigrants from the former USSR who married Cubans. They do a good job with the Russian and Eastern European cuisine here; the Ukrainian-style ravioli filled with mashed potatoes and sautéed onions is succulent, the shashlik kebabs good quality and the stroganoff and chicken Kiev authentic. A choice of twelve different vodkas and engaging Soviet artwork tops off one of the more novel dining experiences in the city. $$$

Vistamar Ave. 1ra no.2206 e/ 22 y 24, Miramar, Playa ⓦrestaurantevistamar.com; see map page 110. Beautiful shorefront paladar with mesmerizing sea views from its first-floor dining room. House specialities include a Caribbean chicken curry, red snapper with pesto and teriyaki chicken beautifully presented. Equally good are the crisp and well-dressed salads. $$$

STATE RESTAURANT

El Aljibe Ave. 7ma e/ 24 y 26, Miramar, Playa ☎7204 1584. *El Aljibe* offers a touch of luxury, with a rustic, open-air setting and a fabulous wine cellar that make it a top choice for diners in the mood for pushing the boat out. House specialities include the beef *brocheta* and the renowned chicken marinated with bitter orange, and there's plenty of it. $$$

PALADARS

La Casa Calle 30 no.865 e/ 26 y 41, Nuevo Vedado ☎7881 7000. There's a '70s Bond movie vibe in this long-established venue with rough stone walls, black tablecloths and deep-green marble floors. The *comida criolla* menu is safe but done well with a couple of welcome wild cards such as ceviche fish and mushroom risotto. $$$

★ **La Cocina de Lilliam** Calle 48 no.1311 e/ 13 y 15, Miramar, Playa ☎7209 6514, ⓦlacocinadelilliam.com. Expats and ex-presidents (check out Jimmy Carter's thank-you letter in the menu) patronize this discreet and luxurious restaurant, with tables set in a beautiful garden. Though the menu is perennial the food is very good, with the aubergine and parmesan, the black rice and octopus and the flan particular standouts. $$$$

★ **La Corte del Príncipe** Calle 9na esq. a 74 Playa ☎5255 9091. Run by Italian expat Sergio and overlooking an expansive park, Havana's most authentic Italian restaurant is an absolute gem. Sun-dappled terrace tables

1

are spread with fresh baked bread, home-made tagliatelli with shrimp and courgette, spaghetti carbonara and paper-thin Parma ham. A credible wine list adds to the gastronomic delight. $\overline{\$\$\$}$

★ **Doctor Café** Calle 28 no.111 e/ 1ra y 3ra, Miramar, Playa ☎ 7203 4718. Little touches like warm home-made bread, plus the big flavours in the exquisitely cooked seafood and meat dishes on a constantly changing menu, reflect the owners' insistence on the freshest ingredients. The professionalism extends to the friendly and attentive service, and the setting is pleasant, split between a convivial garden patio and a small stone-floor dining room. $\overline{\$\$\$}$

La Fontana Calle 46 no.305 esq. 3ra, Miramar, Playa

ⓦ lafontanahavana.info. A lively restaurant specializing in barbecued and grilled platters, equally popular with the Cuban bohemian set and foreigners. The food is almost as good as the atmosphere, with large portions of lobster , pork chops and ribs on the menu. $\overline{\$\$\$}$

Mi Jardín Calle 66, no.517 esq. 5ta B, Playa ☎ 7203 4627. This atmospheric Mexican–Italian paladar serves mains such as *topotos con frijole* (refried beans with cheese, hot pepper sauce and tacos) and *pollo en mole* (chicken in a savoury chocolate sauce), which are perfectly presented and rich with complex flavours. Seating is out in the pretty garden patio or in a dining room with marble floor and Mexican artwork. Reservations recommended. $\overline{\$\$}$

DRINKING

Havana is at last developing what you could realistically call a drinking scene away from the tourist traps that had dominated it for years. There are still surprisingly few straight-up bars in Havana. Most **drinking venues** are part bar, part café or restaurant, offering coffee and cocktails, food and drink in equal measure (some drinking venues are listed with restaurants above). Finding "the buzz" can be hard work, as there are virtually no streets or squares lined with bars. Your best bet for a lively, multi-venue night is usually Habana Vieja where, in a relatively small area, a plethora of privately owned cafés and bars have recently sprung up. There are concentrations of restaurant-bars around Plaza Vieja, on and around O'Reilly, and on the Callejón de los Peluqueros, a single block of the street Aguiar now given over almost entirely to eating and drinking venues. Touristy, packed **Obispo** retains the biggest concentration of drinking spots – and of *jineteros* – while the nearby **Plaza de la Catedral** and its immediate vicinity are also quite animated at night. In **Vedado**, the *Habana Libre* hotel is the best starting point for evening drinking, and the *Riviera* hotel is another good option, while the **La Rampa** area has a good clutch of bars and clubs that heat up after 11pm. It's also worth checking out theatre bars and gardens in Vedado for atmospheric and discerning tipples, even if you haven't attended a performance. However, for sheer *joie de vivre* you can't beat taking some beers or a bottle of rum down to the **Malecón** and mingling with the crowds beneath the stars.

HABANA VIEJA   **SEE MAP PAGE 72**

Antiguo Almacén de la Madera y el Tabaco Avenida del Puerto, opposite southern end of Alameda de Paula ☎ 7 864 7780. Extending out over the water along a concrete jetty is an early twentieth-century wood and tobacco warehouse whose gaping interior affords enough space for a brewery alongside a bar, café-restaurant and dancefloor. The best thing on offer here is the draught beer brewed in the vats visible on a stroll round the building, and served either in pint glasses or towering dispensers for

sharing.

★ **El Dandy** Brasil (Teniente Rey) esq. Villegas, Plaza del Cristo ⓦ bareldandy.com. A welcoming sense of jumbled yet stylish disorder make this lovable dinky café-bar a very casual, hard-to-get-up-once-you-sit-down kind of place, where you could happily lose an afternoon. A crate of vinyl, a hotchpotch of pictures, books and vintage bric-a-brac lying around the place might well be contrived but who cares? It's like drinking in the living room of a trendy, disorganized friend – who happens to keep a quality set of hot, cold and alcoholic drinks in stock at all times. Top tapas, too.

Don Eduardo Alegre Muralla e/ Inquisidor y San Ignacio, Plaza Vieja ☎ 7 861 0327. To the right of the Museo de Naipes, stairs sunk back in a smart colonial mansion lead up to this very loungey, minimalist tapas bar, characterized by clean lines, muted colours and a large splash of magenta. Drinks are on the expensive side, though the menu is extensive and there is a good selection of food. Sit at the square bar, in the main room lined with couches and dotted with comfy chairs, or on stools on the balcony overlooking the busy plaza below.

Factoría Plaza Vieja San Ignacio esq. Muralla, Plaza Vieja ☎ 7 866 4453. Not only is this one of the few places in Havana where you can get a beer on tap, but the deliciously smooth house tipple is brewed on the premises, served by the glass or in communal five-glass dispensers. No wonder this corner of the square is always buzzing. You can order food too, like pork, fish and lobster.

El Floridita Monserrate esq. Obispo ☎ 7 867 1300. Home of the Cuban daiquiri, this was one of Hemingway's favourite hangouts and, for some, a necessary box to tick on a visit to Habana Vieja. The comfy chairs, flowery wallpaper and velvet curtains make it feel like a posh living room, albeit one crammed with tourists sampling an expensive range of fifty-odd cocktails, including fifteen types of daiquiri. Meals here, however, are unjustifiably expensive.

Plaza de Armas Hotel Ambos Mundos, Obispo no.153 esq. Mercaderes ☎ 7 860 9530. One of the best places in Habana Vieja for a drink with a view, this rooftop patio-bar (also a restaurant) has a great perspective on the Plaza de Armas, the surrounding neighbourhood and the fortifications on the other side of the bay.

La Reliquia San Ignacio no.260 esq. Amargura ☎ 7 862 3513. A successful combination of the old with the new and the sleek with the rustic, although you're more likely to hear Jack Johnson or the Red Hot Chilli Peppers pumping out here than the Buena Vista Social Club. Stone arches curve over comfortable white leather couches on the enticing hideaway mezzanine level and brick walls surround the sociable, back-lit bar downstairs.

Sloppy Joe's Ánimas esq. Agramonte (Zulueta) ☎ 7 866 7157. Once a favourite among American prohibition-era visitors to the island, this legendary saloon bar, having closed in 1965, was reborn in 2013, authentically replicating the famously long dark mahogany bar but not the speakeasy atmosphere - this new version is more like a *Hard Rock Café*, with overpriced cocktails and TVs blaring music videos.

Tabarish O'Reilly no.465 e/ Villegas y Aguacate ☎ 7801 4009. Popular and lively Soviet-themed, Russian-owned bar and restaurant where all the usual Cuban cocktails sit on the drinks menu alongside a slew of vodka cocktails, including the Caipiroska, a vodka-based caipriña. The glass-topped bar counter is an ice breaker, housing as it does cabinets full of Soviet curios, from caviar spoons, old cameras, watches and badges to a Soviet version of a Beatles single on vinyl.

CENTRO HABANA   SEE MAP PAGE 93

★ **Siakara** Barcelona e/ Industria y Amistad ☎ 7867

4084. Distinctly new-school Havana, this shabby chic, loungey bar, where the walls and shelves are lined with a jamboree of artefacts and quirky decorations, like a collection of suit ties, serves competitively priced cocktails, fifteen different rums as well as beer and ten different whiskies. Cool music, soft lighting, an easy-going, dress-down vibe, an inviting alcove lined with comfy seats and a cosy little mezzanine snug make this somewhere to get installed for the evening.

VEDADO   SEE MAP PAGE 97

Bar Galería Hotel Nacional, Calle O esq. 21 ☎ 7836 3564. Seasoned visitors swear a cooling daily *mojito* on the palatial terrace bar of this hotel is the way to beat the languid afternoon heat. The *Salón de la Fama* bar just inside is a bit tackier, but intriguing for all the photos of the hotel's famous guests.

★ **Café Bar Madrigal** Calle 17 no.809 (altos) e/ 2 y 4 ☎ 7831 2433. This bar is redolent of hipster trysts and late-night cool: a cocktail on the curved balcony may just be the highlight of your day. Raw brick walls are hung with film posters, old box brownie cameras and Cuban artwork, while the bar is well stocked with local and international favourites. Tapas is served and bands regularly play.

El Emperador Edificio FOCSA, Calle 17 e/ M y N ☎ 7 832 4998. This classy little 1950s bar hidden at the foot of the Edificio FOCSA succeeds where so many others fail, with sultry lighting, hushed tones and a long marble bar serving perfect cocktails to a discreet clientele. Throw in the live piano music and this becomes one to return to again and again.

★ **La Esencia** Calle B no.153 e/ Calzada y Linea T 7836

LOBBY GROUP

Habana Vieja and Vedado have some fantastically elegant hotels, and the most arresting feature in many of them is the **lobby**. The enchanting cafés and bars that occupy many of these lobbies are ideal spots for escaping the humidity and hassle of the city streets, relaxing, sipping drinks, snacking or simply enjoying the magnificent setting. Below are six of the best, all of them open to non-guests.

Ambos Mundos (see page 116). The epicentre of the most visited part of Habana Vieja, and perfectly located for a rest as you tour the old city. The lobby is often filled with the sounds of bolero and chachacha coming from the grand piano in the corner, and there's a sociable buzz, with people constantly milling around and drinking cocktails and coffees.

Los Frailes (see page 116). A small, narrow and very simple lobby with a bar at one end and an almost sombre vibe, with the lights permanently on an evening setting, several low-slung couches and a resident clarinet quartet playing soothing tunes. Great place for a sneaky snooze or a coffee.

Parque Central (see page 116). Protected from the cacophony of the Parque Central, the delightful, leafy *El Pórtico* café is the perfect spot to recharge or wind down. Tea, coffee and alcoholic drinks are on offer alongside sandwiches, salads, tapas and sweets.

Sevilla Trocadero no.55 e/ Paseo del Prado y Agramonte (aka Zulueta) ☎ 7 860 8560. The lobby in this classic Havana hotel blends into the pretty *Patio Sevillano* café and though it's a little worn around the edges, this increases the sense of pre-Revolution authenticity. Full of slouch-inducing chairs and dotted with photos from its mafia-owned heyday, relaxing here with a cocktail comes with a dose of history.

3031. Lively weekend spot with a mix of Cubans and ages, all up for a good night out. The high-ceilinged colonial house with tiled floors and pre-Revolution posters has bags of atmosphere and a great cocktail menu.

La Fuente Calle 13 e/ F y G. The crowd is mostly Cuban at this open-air café/bar. Tables clustered around a water feature and musicians plucking out impromptu tunes add to the relaxed vibe.

MIRAMAR   SEE MAP PAGE 110

La Casa Española Ave. 7ma esq. 26, Miramar, Playa

NIGHTLIFE

Havana's **nightlife** doesn't jump out at you, but instead works its magic from isolated corners all over the city, in secluded clubs, hidden courtyards, theatre basements and on hotel rooftops. Spontaneous nights out are difficult as there's no single area with much of a buzz and venues are widely dispersed. Clubs and music halls are generally open later and are livelier for longer in Vedado and Miramar than in Habana Vieja where nightspots are far fewer and noise pollution is a bigger issue given the density of the housing. To find out what's going on at night it's a good idea to keep your eye out for fliers in bars and paladars, at Infotur offices and in hotel lobbies, or to ask around as online listings sites are generally fairly poor (you can try ⊕lapapeleta.cult.cu).

CLUBS, CABARETS AND LIVE MUSIC

Many of the biggest and brashest clubs and cabarets are found in the mansions and hotels of Vedado and Miramar; outside its restaurants, Habana Vieja is surprisingly low

☎7206 9644. There's a café, bar and rooftop views to enjoy, spread around the five floors of this mock fortress complete with suits of armour and mock-medieval paraphernalia inside. Tasty Spanish dishes such as paella are served alongside Cuban-style lobster, pork and prawns.

Sangri La Calle 42 esq. Calle 21. Hip little basement hangout with white banquette seating and an expanse of dark flecked marble. Strong cocktails and understated background tunes attract a well-heeled international crowd.

on clubs and music venues. Whatever the venue, a night out almost always involves some form of live music, with numerous small concert venues and plenty of places where you can enjoy a meal with a performance. Modern salsa, timba and reggaeton dominate the city's music scene and though styles such as trova, bolero and son are regularly performed at bars, cafés and restaurants, they are less common in concert venues and nightclubs.

HABANA VIEJA   SEE MAP PAGE 72

Casa de la Cultura Julián del Casal Revillagigedo no.162 e/ Gloria y Misión ☎7 863 4860. Well off the beaten track and aimed primarily at locals, the programme of daytime and evening events at this cultural community centre includes live music – rumba features heavily, but there's also a monthly trova ranging from bolero and tango to rumba and reggaeton. Visit the building to get the weekly programme.

THE TROPICANA

Not for nothing were the female dancers of the **Tropicana** described in their heyday as Las Diosas de Carne (Goddesses of the Flesh). Evolving to cater to the North American tourist trade, **Cuban cabaret** really started when nightclub owner Victor de Correa cut a deal with casino operators Rafael Mascaro and Luis Bular and relocated the dance troupe and musicians from his successful nightclub, *Edén Concert*, to the rented grounds of Guillermina Pérez Chaumont's stately villa in Havana's Marianao. The new business partners renamed the cabaret *Tropicana* in reference to the lush vegetation that would characterize their outdoor cabaret; and with a winning combination of dazzling musical shows and high-stakes casino, the club went from strength to strength.

Its heyday was in the 1950s, when the famous Arcos de Cristal glass-walled stage opened. The 1950s also saw cabaret-casinos open in various venues across Havana including at the *Hilton*, the *Riviera* and the *Nacional* hotels – all of which still operate cabarets to this day. Following the Revolution all cabarets were nationalized and the Mob, which had grown to have a large commercial interest in the cabarets, were expelled from the country.

Today the standard of both house band and dancers at the *Tropicana* is phenomenal, with the troupe often including several dancers who narrowly failed to make the grade at the Cuban national ballet. While some might find the sexist nature of scanty costumes and provocative dances somewhat hard to swallow, there's no denying that this spectacle is a quintessential Cuban experience.

El Guajirito Zulueta no.658 e/ Apodaca y Gloria ⓦ legendariosdelguajirito.com. The Legendarios del Guajirito show draws its prestigious changing line up from the ex-membership of the African-Cuban All Stars, Buena Vista Social Club and the like, so high levels of musicianship are guaranteed. This great show, performed daily from 8pm, is aimed firmly at the tourist market but no worse for it – but the food is pretty bad.

Patio Amarillo San Ignacio no.22 e/ Empedrado y Tejadillo ☎ 7864 2426. Traditional Cuban music is performed nightly on the miniature stage of this small tables-and-chairs venue just off the Plaza de la Catedral. More subdued than its equivalents on raucous Obispo.

Sociedad Rosalía de Castro Ave. de Bélgica (Egido) no.504 e/ Máximo Gómez (Monte) y Dragones ☎ 5270 5271. The two-hour nightly show here is called the Tradicionales de los 50 and will appeal to fans of the Buena Vista Social Club, and anyone into the golden era of Cuban music.

CENTRO HABANA SEE MAP PAGE 93

Café Tilín Ave. de Italia (Galiano) no.119 e/ Animas y Trocadero ⓦ cafetilin.com. A small stage at the end of a bar in this modern establishment set over two levels hosts nightly performances by a wide variety of musicians. The weekly schedule has included "saxophone nights" and "fusion nights" while mainstream Cuban music features regularly too. They're very proud of their coffee here, of which there is a wide range, but full meals and drinks of all kinds are also served.

Casa de la Música Habana Ave. de Italia (Galiano) no.155 e/ Neptuno y Concordia ☎ 7860 8297 or ☎ 7 862 4165. One of the top live music and club venues in Havana, with large and raucous queues forming outside every weekend and often during the week as well. All the biggest and most-talked-about names in Cuban salsa, reggaeton and cubaton play here.

El Jelengue de Areito San Miguel no.410 e/ Campanario y Lealtad, Centro Habana ☎ 7862 0673. Also known as the Patio Areito or the Patio EGREM, this relatively new, small but authentic music venue is attached to the inauspicious recording studios of the country's most renowned record label, EGREM. A patio bar leads into a rather plain performance room where a different band or soloist play every evening. Expect anything from trova and son to rumba and hip-hop. Top-quality live music in the backstreets.

Palacio de la Rumba San Miguel no.860 e/ Hospital y Aramburu ☎ 7873 0990. A neighbourhood venue attracting a solidly Cuban crowd who let loose to timba, salsa, sometimes hip-hop and r'n'b and of course rumba, in what used to be a cinema. Live bands play regularly here and more subdued, traditional music features too, often for the matinee sessions. Real local flavour.

Piano Bar Habaneciendo Neptuno e/ Ave. de Italia (Galiano) y Aguila ☎ 7862 4165. A tables-and-chairs affair, where punters can eat, drink and enjoy all types of Cuban music, both traditional and popular. Above the *Casa de la Música Habana* and under the same management, thus guaranteeing that big names perform here.

VEDADO SEE MAP PAGE 97

Café Cantante Mi Habana Teatro Nacional de Cuba, Paseo y 39, Plaza de la Revolución ☎ 7878 4273. One of the top clubs for Havana's salsa, timba and merengue enthusiasts. Top artists like Paulito FG and Los Van Van sometimes headline here, while other genres like hip-hop and rock put an appearance in too – prices depend on who's playing. Arrive before 11pm at weekends, when the small basement gets jam-packed and the queue can be enormous.

Café Teatro Bertolt Brecht Calle 13 no.259 esq. Calle I ☎ 7832 9359. The dark sultry basement of this theatre houses one of the hippest music venues in the city, with performances by the likes of Interactivo, Qba Libre, Raul Paz and Síntesis. Opening hours are informal so it's worth calling ahead to check

Casa de la Amistad Paseo no.406 esq. 17 ☎ 7830 3114. Resident troubadour groups perform well-executed salsa, son and bolero in the majestic grounds of a Rococo building that was once a private house. Saturdays are livelier with old-school salsa while Sunday is old-school rock.

Casa de la Cultura de Plaza Calzada 909 esq. 8 ☎ 7831 2023. There is no end to the activities at this off-the-beaten-track culture house, from theatre and poetry readings to every type of music Havana offers. Every week there's a choice of bolero, hip-hop, rumba and feelin'. With flamenco evenings and dance or art classes also available, this is a wonderful venue for those looking to immerse themselves in community-based culture.

Delirio Habanero Piano Bar Teatro Nacional de Cuba, Paseo y 39, Plaza de la Revolución ☎ 7878 4273. This sultry and atmospheric late-night jazz hangout is popular with Cuban sophisticates and visitors alike, with low-key piano music, live bands nightly (10.30pm–1am) and rumba on Sundays. Limited table space makes reservations essential at weekends.

★ **Hurón Azul UNEAC** Calle 17 no.351 esq. H ☎ 7832 4152. It's always worth checking out the programme posted outside this beautiful Vedado mansion, home to the Writers' and Artists' Union. Regular events include bolero (Sat 9pm–2am), nueva trova alternated with rumba (Wed from 5pm) and son or rumba (Sun from 5pm). In addition, there are various art exhibitions, fashion shows and festivals on the grounds throughout the week.

Pabellón La Rampa esq. N. Head to this sprawling brutalist arts centre in the middle of downtown Calle 23 for impromptu salsa and jazz concerts in the open-air

1

auditorium. There's generally jazz on Thursdays though information is a bit haphazard.

★ **Salón Rojo** Calle 21 esq. N ☎ 7834 6560. One of Havana's hottest nightspots, with seating sloping down towards the stage and a dancefloor from which people spill over to dance in the aisles. It's often host to big-hitting Cuban acts like Charanga Habanera and Havana D´ Primera. An atmospheric venue though single men may find themselves besieged by *jineteras* somewhat.

La Zorra y El Cuervo Calle 23 no.155 e/ N y O ☎ 7833 2402. A cool and stylish basement venue, with contemporary decor and a European feel, which puts on superior live jazz shows each night. It doesn't heat up until the band starts at 11pm.

MIRAMAR AND THE WESTERN SUBURBS SEE MAP PAGE 110

Casa de la Música de Miramar Calle 20 esq. 35, Miramar, Playa ☎ 7202 6147. One of the most animated nightspots in Havana, this *casa de la música* is worth the trip out to Miramar. The mansion in which it's set is beautiful, and regular bands have included Bamboleo, Adalberto Alvarez and Paulo FG – however, it's a popular pick-up spot for hopeful *jineteros* and *jineteras*. If you want a table it's advisable to book in advance.

★ **El Chévere** Club Almendares, Calle 49C esq. 28A, Kohly, Playa. A favourite venue for many of the city's salsa schools, this friendly, open-air salsa club has a large dancefloor and stage under a high roof. Cubans and foreigners mix amicably, with *jineterismo* frowned upon and

a strict door policy. Cuban dance enthusiasts and learners should make a beeline here.

Río Club Calle A e/ Ave. 3ra y Ave. 3ra, Miramar, Playa ☎ 7206 4219. Popularly known as *El Johnny*, this large split-level club currently attracts a boisterous college-age crowd with a soundtrack of international dance music and contemporary Cuban sounds.

★ **Sala Atril** Teatro Karl Marx, Ave. 1ra e/ 8 y 10, Miramar, Playa ☎ 7206 7596. A great venue for easy access to some of Havana's less well-represented music scenes in a relatively intimate stage venue attracting a diverse, trendy crowd. The programme of events represents an interesting cross-section of mostly modern and alternative Cuban music. The layout includes private booths and an outdoor terrace.

Salón Bolero Complejo Dos Gardenias, Ave. 7ma esq. 26, Miramar, Playa ☎ 7204 2353. Upstairs in a restaurant and bar complex, the *Salón Bolero* is a saloon bar where exponents of bolero entertain subdued crowds seven nights a week. For a laidback and intimate evening of music, enjoyed from tables gathered around a small stage, this is a good option.

Tropicana Calle 72 no.504 Marianao ☎ 7267 1717. Possibly the oldest and most lavish cabaret in the world, Cuba's unmissable, much-hyped open-air venue hosts a pricey extravaganza in which class acts and a ceaseless flow of dancers, clad in sequins, feathers and frills, regularly pull in a full house. Starts at 8.30pm with the show at 10–11pm, followed by dancing. You can arrange all-inclusive bus trips from most hotels. Booking is essential.

EAT TO THE BEAT: TOP FIVE PLACES FOR LIVE MUSIC AND A MEAL

It's actually quite hard to avoid live music when eating out in Havana, but there are some restaurants that offer more than just the ubiquitous – and often very good – guitar-strumming, maraca-shaking trio. Here are some of our favourites:

Cabaret Parisién Hotel Nacional, Calle O esq. 21 ☎ 7836 3663; see map page 97. The city's most renowned cabaret after *Tropicana*, staged in a custom-built cabaret theatre with a long history. Productions are usually well attended and contain all the extravagant costumes and musical styles you would hope for, and last for about two hours with a dance class after.

Café Taberna Mercaderes esq. Brasil (Teniente Rey) ☎ 7861 1637; see map page 72. The food at this restaurant is nothing to shout about but the music is excellent and performed nightly. One of the resident bands is billed as the Buena Vista Social Club, and though you won't recognize anyone from the world-famous album bearing that name, the music is in exactly the same vein.

El Gato Tuerto Calle O e/ 17 y 19 ☎ 7 838 2696; see map page 97. This pre-Revolution, beatnik jazz bar,

whose name translates as the "one-eyed cat", has kept its cool edge despite a complete renovation. There's live music in the bar on weekday nights and there are three jazz or salsa shows on Fridays and Saturdays, two on weekdays. There's also a mediocre restaurant upstairs.

El Mesón de la Flota Mercaderes e/ Amargura y Brasil (Teniente Rey) ☎ 7863 3838; see map page 72. Nightly flamenco music and dance performances on a central stage in a tavern-type restaurant serving cheap tapas and mostly seafood main dishes. Also a hotel.

★ **El Tocororo** Calle 18 esq. Ave. 5ta, Miramar, Playa ☎ 7204 2209; see map page 110. This alluring bar, separate to the dining area, is where musicians often play until late, entertaining drinkers having a post-meal *mojito*. One of the few proper bars in Miramar – non-diners are welcome.

ENTERTAINMENT

BALLET AND FOLKLÓRICO DANCE

Ballet Cuba also has one of the world's finest ballet companies, the Ballet Nacional de Cuba (w balletcuba.cult.cu), founded in 1948 by prima ballerina and Cuban heroine Alicia Alonso. Performances might be slightly shabbier round the edges than aficionados are accustomed to, but are still an enriching cultural experience.

Folklórico dance From open-air street performances (particularly around Habana Vieja) to minutely choreographed shows in theatres, the city also has plenty of *folklórico* dance, which celebrates African-Cuban culture. Many of the major theatres have regular performances by companies like the state-funded Conjunto Folklórico Nacional de Cuba (w facebook.com/ConjuntoFolkloricoNacionalCuba) and excellent contemporary dance company Danza Contemporánea de Cuba (w facebook.com/DCCuba), which worked with Carlos Acosta on his internationally acclaimed Tocororo show.

CINEMA

Cinema is very popular in Havana, and there are plenty of atmospheric venues dotted around the city. They may be run-down – air-conditioning often breaks and the smell of the toilets can be an unwelcome distraction – but a refreshing lack of anonymous multiplexes makes for an idiosyncratic experience. Most screen a selection of Cuban, North American and European films, with the English-speaking ones generally subtitled in Spanish or, if you're unlucky, badly dubbed. Programmes can change daily, and there are cinema listings daily in the *Granma* newspaper.

Cine Chaplin Calle 23 e/ 10 y 12, Vedado ☎ 7831 1101. The Chaplin may be small but it's one of Havana's most important cinemas, showing classic and modern Cuban films.

Cine La Rampa Calle 23 esq. O, Vedado ☎ 7878 6146. Although the auditorium is a bit run-down, the entrance and atrium in brass and marble is rather stunning. Mostly North American and European films on show.

Cine Riviera Calle 23 e/ G y H, Vedado ☎ 7830 9564. A stylish cinema, painted cobalt blue, that shows a range of Cuban and international films.

Cine Yara Calle L esq. 23, Vedado ☎ 7832 9430. A large, old-fashioned auditorium showing the latest Spanish and Cuban releases, with a small video room showing special-interest films.

THEATRE, CLASSICAL MUSIC AND DANCE VENUES

Supported and overseen by the state since the Revolution, **theatre** and **dance** have flourished in Havana, and as affordable arts became a national tenet under Castro, ticket prices are low. Performances are of a very high standard,

and contrary to expectations, political opinions are often fairly freely expressed. Though a good level of Spanish is needed to get the most out of theatre performances, it's nevertheless worth checking out at least one show on your trip. Companies like Teatro Buendía (☎ 7881 6689) and Teatro de la Luna (☎ 7879 6011) have attracted international acclaim for their work.

Callejón de Hamel e/ Hospital y Aramburu, Centro Habana. The best-known African-Cuban dance location in the city (see page 96) now has a slightly offputting staged feel, attracting more *jineteros* than dancers, but the rumba ceremonies that take place here every Sunday are still a sight to behold.

Centro Cultural Bertolt Brecht Calle 13 no.259 e/ J y I, Vedado ☎ 7832 9359. Two auditoria which feature theatre including musicals and farces and a Sunday matinee as well as performances for kids and comedy.

El Gran Palenque Calle 4 no.103 e/ Calzada y 5ta, Vedado ☎ 7833 4560. Home to the Conjunto Folklórico Nacional de Cuba, which puts on rumba and other African-Cuban dance performances on the patio on Saturday afternoons. The regular Peña de la Rumba is a highly charged, energetic affair with group and individual dancers plus audience participation.

Gran Teatro Paseo del Prado esq. San Rafael, Habana Vieja ☎ 7861 3096. This outstandingly ornate building on the Parque Central is the home of the Cuban national ballet but also hosts operas and contemporary dance pieces. The biannual Festival Internacional de Ballet de la Habana takes place here in late October, and there's a season of Spanish ballet each August.

★ Teatro Nacional de Guiñol Calle M e/ 17 y 19, Vedado ☎ 7832 6262. Resourceful and inventive puppet theatre, aimed at children but magical enough to be enjoyed by all. Renowned local writers and actors are often part of the production team.

Iglesia de San Francisco de Asís Oficios e/ Churruca y Amargura ☎ 7862 3467. A prestigious and popular venue for classical music concerts where the excellent acoustics and precious, historic surroundings always add to the sense of occasion. Some of the country's best chamber ensembles, pianists and orchestras have played here. Check the programme at the church in the day.

Teatro Karl Marx Calle 1ra e/ 8 y 10, Miramar ☎ 7209 1991. Distinctive 1960s building hosting all kinds of music and dramatic arts events, including international rock concerts and classical theatre. Definitely worth checking what's on.

Teatro Martí Agramonte (Zulueta) esq. Dragones, Habana Vieja w facebook.com/TeatroMarti. Fabulously renovated, late nineteenth-century theatre brought back from ruins and now as good as anywhere in the city

1

for classical concerts and operas while excellent dance productions and other kinds of musical performances are staged here too. Box office Tues–Fri 10am–noon & 1–4pm. On performance days you can also buy tickets up until 30min before performance times, which are usually 5pm or 8.30pm.

Teatro Mella Linea no 657, e/ A y B, Vedado ☎7833 5651. This large theatre puts on many performances by the

Conjunto Folklórico Nacional de Cuba as well as comedy, theatre and variety shows.

Teatro Nacional de Cuba Paseo y 39, Plaza de la Revolución ☎7878 0769. Havana's biggest theatre puts on some of the city's best events all year round, from ballet to guitar and jazz. Spanish-speakers should check out the avant-garde drama, especially during the February theatre festival.

SHOPPING

Havana stands out, refreshingly for some, as a capital city whose centre is not dominated by a **shopping district** – Obispo, in Habana Vieja, is as close as it gets. Elsewhere, although new malls and boutiques are mushrooming steadily around the city, the general standard of merchandise is quite low, with rum, cigars, coffee and crafts

the exceptions. For everything else the large hotels and the Artex and Caracol state chain stores have some of the best-quality products. Standard opening hours are Monday to Saturday 9am to 6pm; only a tiny minority of shops stay open after 7pm. Some shops are open all Sunday but most either don't open or close at lunchtime.

VINTAGE SHOPPING IN HAVANA

In the early days of the Revolution, wealthy Havana families buried their prized possessions in cellars before fleeing the country, hoping to return when the revolutionary government had been ousted. Others stayed, clinging onto their valuables in what became the land that consumer culture forgot. Recent economic liberalization has allowed the owners of these treasures to come out from behind the once closed doors of their sumptuous Vedado mansions, or set up stalls in Centro Habana markets, and become legitimate **antique** and **vintage furniture** and **art** dealers. Serious collectors will be knocked out by the Art Deco furniture and huge chandeliers on sale; easier to fit in your suitcase are collectable glasses, drinks trays or cocktail stirrers from the famous 1950s cabarets and casinos; or, more widely available are cigar-box artwork, film posters and mid-century black-and-white postcards or photographs. Many items are in remarkably good condition, but don't expect a bargain – most antique dealers know the value of their stock. The list below represents some of the best places to find vintage goods in Havana.

Belkis Calle 2 no.607 e/ 25 y 27, Vedado ☎7830 4124;see map page 97. An entire Vedado mansion turned over to antique dealing with an overwhelming selection of pre-revolutionary glassware, colonial-era ceramics, crockery and art, a varied collection of furniture and small collectable items like compact mirrors, costume jewellery and brooches.

★**Feria de Publicaciones y Curiosidades** Baratillo esq. Justiz, Habana Vieja; see map page 72. Havana's largest book market, which for many years dominated the Plaza de Armas, has relocated around the corner. Among the revolutionary pamphlets, Che Guevara tomes and the occasional novels you can find vintage Cuban and US tourist brochures, postcards and lifestyle magazines, some reflecting life before Castro, plus copies of rare books and all sorts of other collectors' items like revolutionary posters and Cuban film art. Starting prices are high – be prepared to haggle.

Librería Venecia Obispo no.502 e/ Villegas y Bernaza; ☎7862 6620; see map page 72. A hoard

of striking revolutionary propaganda posters, film posters, some vintage photography and lots of books, both vintage and contemporary. A great place for a root around, with shelves and tables heaving with messily displayed stock.

★**Memorias** Animas no.57 e/ Paseo del Prado y Agramonte (Zulueta), Habana Vieja ☎7862 5153; see map page 72. This is a real diamond. Though many of the vintage posters and photographs here are reproductions, they are excellent quality and you'll struggle to find the same copies anywhere else. There are tonnes of originals too and the little shop is heaving with pre-revolutionary memorabilia including Cuban beer and cigar adverts, chocolate box covers, Cuban and American 1950s magazines, postcards from around the world and old photos of Havana.

Mi Doble L Calle 25 no.956 (bajos) e/ Paseo y 2, Vedado ☎7833 8502; see map page 97. A brilliant array of lamps from the 50s, 60s and 70s including ceiling roses, bronze wall lamps, milk-glass table lamps and some splendid crystal chandeliers.

1

THE VINYL FRONTIER

Havana is no record-buyer's paradise, but its isolation from Western markets for so many decades and the absence of a significant record-buying public since the advent of CDs meant that old vinyl collections, most of them leaning heavily towards Cuban and Latin American music, were left unwanted and unbought. Though the odd record pops up in arts and crafts markets, most often in the Feria de Publicaciones y Curiosidades (see page 132) record shopping is otherwise restricted, for the timebeing, to just two shops – but wherever vinyl appears it's almost certain to be collectible and usually dates from the 60s, 70s or 80s.

Puchito's Shop San Ignacio no.410 e/ Sol y Muralla, Habana Vieja ☏5347 1136; see map page 72. Opened in 2016, this is very much a response to the vinyl revival of the last decade and there's a hip feel to this cool stockist of LPs, 12-inch singles and 45s. Not only are there rare-as-hen's-teeth Cuban albums, but also Cuban imprints of music from elsewhere in the world, so pop, rock and various other bits and pieces appear between the salsa, son and trova.

Tienda Seriosha Neptuno no.408 e/ San Nicolás y Manrique, Centro Habana ☏7862 2385; see map page 93. A long-standing little crate-digger's paradise for collectors of Cuban, Latin and easy-listening music on vinyl, nestling at the back of a kind of indoor hardware market.

ARTS, CRAFTS AND CLOTHING   SEE MAPS PAGES 72 AND 97

Havana's street markets tend to overstock with Che Guevara-themed memorabilia, paintings of old American cars, black coral jewellery and wooden sculptures. However, if you're prepared to put in the hours you can find the occasional sculpture, piece of jewellery or handmade item of clothing that stands out from the rest. Alternatively, check out the new breed of shops providing an antidote to the design-by-numbers monotony of the markets. Markets tend to close on a Sunday or a Monday (rarely both), and generally trade between 9am and 6pm. See also the Books, music and films listings for places to get hold of the distinctive Cuban film-art posters.

Antiguo Almacenes San José Ave. del Puerto, Habana Vieja. In a huge nineteenth-century warehouse right on the harbourfront, this is the largest arts and crafts market in the city. There is strikingly little that stands out, but for the sheer volume of paintings, jewellery, Che hats, leather bags, T-shirts, posters, instruments and handicrafts it can't be beat. There are several cafés and a *casa de cambio*.

Clandestina Villegas no.403 e/ Brasil (Teniente Rey) y Muralla, Habana Vieja, ⊛ clandestina.co. Opened in 2015 and among the avant garde of hipster Havana, this design and fashion shop has an eclectic stock but everything is made exclusively for the store by hand. Best known for their screen print T-shirts, emblazoned with their trademark "99% diseño cubano" motif, among others, there are also phone covers, baseball caps, towels, posters and more.

Experimental Gallery Amargura no.321 esq. Aguacate, Habana Vieja ☏58384124. A wide range of quirky posters, some humourous, others just odd – but all uniquely Cuban. The Rolling Stones concert in Havana and Obama's visit are both commemorated, the latter inscribed

with "Yes We Came", whilst ironic takes on state propaganda and figures superimposed over Havana street scenes are common themes.

Feria de Arte Obispo Obispo e/ Compostela y Aguacate, Habana Vieja. Around fifteen stalls in the ruins of an old building on the main shopping street in the old town, selling ornamental gifts, clothing, jewellery and ceramics.

Galería Habana Linea no.460 e/ E y F, Vedado ☏7 832 7101. One of Havana's most internationally respected galleries always has an impressive collection of contemporary art on display and for sale.

Habana 1791 Mercaderes no.156 e/ Obrapia y Lamparilla, Habana Vieja ☏7861 3525. This unique shop sells perfumes like those used during the eighteenth and nineteenth centuries in Cuba, handmade from flowers and plant oils.

Libertija Calle 21 esq. N, Vedado ☏7832 3260. A relatively unusual shop for Cuba, selling handmade objects, many from recycled materials. A marked alternative to the kind of merchandise you find in the touristy markets, you'll find lots of one-offs here which could be anything from clothing, cushions or tote bags to screen prints, drawings and ornamental items of various kinds.

Mercado de La Rampa La Rampa e/ M y N, Vedado. The miscellaneous merchandise at this small craft market includes wooden carvings, handmade leather items, imported clothes and enough gold chains to sink a ship.

★ **Piscolabis** San Ignacio no.75 e/ Plaza de la Catedral y O'Reilly, Habana Vieja ⊛ piscolabishabana.com. This upmarket, trendy little shop is full of handcrafted and locally manufactured items, and a great place to find unique, if expensive, souvenirs or keepsakes. The selection is eclectic but sways towards modern designs, a little less folksy than much of what you'll find elsewhere, and includes anything

1

TOP FIVE CIGAR LOUNGES AND SMOKING ROOMS

Even if you don't smoke, there is an allure to the world of **Cuban cigars**, with its kudos-bearing brand names such as Montecristo and Cohiba, its world-famous patrons from Winston Churchill to Jack Nicholson, and all its stylish trappings, like the artistic cigar labels and the smart box designs. There is no better place to immerse yourself in this world than in Havana's **cigar lounges** and **smoking rooms**, mostly attached to cigar shops. With dignified furnishings, a subdued atmosphere and neat little bars, they provide the perfect setting for the slow consumption of a Churchill or Double Corona. Whether you're testing a cigar before a purchase or enjoying the smokes you've just bought, you'll have to light up to sit down in one, but you don't have to be an aficionado to enjoy these smoking dens. Five of the best are listed below.

★ **Casa del Habano (5ta y 16)** Ave. 5ta. no.1407 esq. Calle 16, Miramar; see map page 110. An array of smoking spaces, including a "private sales" room with tiled floor and high-backed chairs, a bar with wicker furniture and a cigar-friendly restaurant make this one of the best places to sit down and test your smokes in the city.

Casa del Habano (Hotel Conde de Villanueva) Mercaderes no.202 esq. Lamparilla, Habana Vieja ☎ 7862 9293; see map page 72. The inconspicuous mezzanine-level entrance, low ceilings and dimmed lights make you feel like you're in on a secret here. At one end of the slender shop is an easy-chair lounge, at the other a very cool bar – you won't find a more atmospheric place to smoke a cigar in all of Havana. The shop is run by one of Cuba's foremost *torcedors* (master cigar rollers), Reynaldo Jiménez.

Casa del Habano (Club Habana) Ave. 5ta e/ 188 y 192, Flores, Playa ☎ 7204 5700; see map page 110. The spacious wood-panelled back room at this sports and social club has artwork on the walls, a bar and comfortable leather furniture.

Casa del Habano (Hotel Nacional) Calle 0 esq. 21, Habana Vieja ☎ 7836 3564; see map page 97. At the back on the basement level of this two-storey shop is the *salón de fumadores*, with two wicker three-piece suites and a bar.

Casa del Habano (Hotel Meliá Habana) Ave. 3ra e/ 76 y 80, Miramar, Playa ☎ 7204 8500; see map page 110. There are large, comfortable leather sofas in the centre of this cigar shop, next to an eye-catching curved bar with a great selection of Scotch, plus an open-air seating area and a quiet smoking room off in the back.

from cushions, lamps and framed pictures to wooden bowls and clothing. The cosy café serves great coffee, snacks and juices.

Quitrín Obispo esq. San Ignacio. This Cuban clothing brand has its own outlet in the heart of the old town where *guayabera shirts* and traditional Cuban dresses are for sale.

BOOKS, MUSIC AND FILM
SEE MAP PAGES 72, 93 AND 97

With one or two exceptions Havana no longer has any music stores per se, with small stocks of CDs located, instead, in bookshops and tourist giftshops. But as stock tends to consist only of music recorded on the island by Cuban labels, you'll find obscure gems in almost all genres, from salsa, son, and bolero to Cuban hip-hop, rock and reggaeton albums, many of which you're unlikely to come across anywhere else in the world. The same shops are also the primary suppliers of DVDs and collectible Cuban film-art posters. Bootleg sellers of CDs and DVDs and equally makeshift secondhand bookstalls are dotted all over the city, mostly in markets, on kerbs, doorsteps and in streetside hallways and front rooms – there are quite a few on Obispo in Habana Vieja.

Artehabana San Rafael esq. Industria ☎ 7860 8414.

This *plaza cultural*, or "cultural shopping centre", stocks a better choice of CDs than anywhere else in Centro Habana or Habana Vieja, which isn't saying much. Nevertheless, if you want to avoid bootlegs and favour a choice not just of reggaeton and salsa but of jazz and traditional Cuban genres too, this is currently the best there is. There are books and posters here too.

Ediciones Boloña Amargura no.66 e/ Mercaderes y San Ignacio, Habana Vieja. The larger of the two bookshops run by the publishing arm of the Oficina del Historiador de la Ciudad carries an interesting selection of books, magazines and pamphlets on Havana. There is contemporary Cuban fiction too and various other bits and pieces including posters and postcards.

Galería Juan David Cine Yara, Calle L esq. 23, Vedado. Tiny outlet but one of the better places to buy film-poster art and prints of Cuban paintings and photography.

Habana Sí Calle L esq. 23, Vedado ☎ 7838 3162. One of the few official CD stockists left in Vedado, although the selection of music here is slowly dwindling and shelves are filling instead with souvenirs, mugs, coffee sets, baseball hats and some books and DVDs.

★ **ICAIC Centro Cultural Cinematográfico** Calle 23

no.1155 e/ 10 y 12, Vedado ☎7830 4579. An excellent source of cool screen-printed film posters, plus cult films on video (including many by Tomás Gutiérrez Alea), and some specialist film publications, mainly in Spanish.

Librería Centenario del Apostol Calle 25 no.164 e/ Infanta y O, Vedado ☎7835 0805. Stuffed full of stock, this is the kind of bookshop you move round slowly and is a fun place to browse. There are some pre-Revolution publications, back issues of post-revolutionary magazines and shelves choc-a-bloc with Cuban literature, political writing, history and culture.

CIGARS, RUM AND COFFEE   SEE MAP PAGES 72 AND 97

The Casa del Habano chain accounts for most of the cigars sold in Cuba and is well represented all over Havana. Many of the top-class hotels have their own cigar shops; among the best are the *Conde de Villanueva* and *Parque Central* in Habana Vieja and the *Meliá Cohiba*, *Habana Libre* and the *Hotel Nacional* in Vedado. The cigar lounges and smoking rooms listed in the box above are all, also, great places to buy smokes. Many cigar shops also sell rum and coffee and though specialist rum or coffee shops are much less common, you can usually pick up bottles and packets in hotel gift shops, almost all supermarkets and grocery shops, all over the city, usually at very cheap prices.

Casa del Café Obispo esq. Baratillo, Plaza de Armas, Habana Vieja ☎7866 8061. Specialist coffeeshop, though there are cigars and rum for sale here too.

Casa del Habano Hotel Habana Libre Calle L e/ 23 y 25, Vedado. The largest cigar store in Cuba, with an extensive range of *habanos*, an open smoker's lounge and a bar.

Casa del Ron y del Tabaco Cubano Obispo e/ Bernaza y Ave. de Bélgica, Habana Vieja ☎7866 8911. One of the best selections of rum under one roof in the whole of Havana, and a decent range of *habanos* too.

Licorera Hotel Habana Libre, Calle 25 esq. L, ☎7834 6139. There's a decent selection of rum in this hotel liquor shop found on the little parade of shops outside on L. Prices are reasonable.

La Vega Palacio de la Artesanía, Cuba no.64 e/ Cuarteles y Peña Pobre, Habana Vieja ☎7866 8072. A good place for purchasing cigars in affordable quantities, with, for example, Romeo y Julietas, Cohibas, Partagas and Robainas all sold in singles and for the cheaper, machine-made, Guantanamera brand.

FOOD MARKETS   SEE MAP PAGES 72, 93 AND 97

Farmers who have supplied their government quota are allowed to sell their surplus produce in *agromercados* (farmers' markets), where everything is fresh and you generally find more variety than you do in hotels and restaurants. In addition, everything is fantastically cheap, and most of the larger food markets have a *casa de cambio* on hand. Bring a bag for your goodies, as these are rarely provided.

Agromercado Calle 19 esq. B, Vedado. The prettiest of Havana's *agros*, this picturesque market sells meat, flowers, honey and dry goods like rice and beans alongside heaps of fresh fruit and vegetables.

Mercado Animas y Soledad Animas e/ Soledad y Arambura, Centro Habana. One of the largest *agromercados* in Centro Habana.

DANCE SCHOOLS

Havana is the spiritual home for salsa in general but particularly for **casino**, the Cuban brand of salsa, and its spin-off, *rueda de casino*, a group dance sometimes referred to simply as *rueda* – and as good a city as any in the world to learn the steps. Classes are still relatively cheap and increasing numbers of schools are appearing since the enterprise was included on the list of permissible private sector businesses in 2010. Most schools also offer evenings out in salsa clubs, sometimes with the tutors, so you can try out your moves for real. Classes at the schools below can be booked from abroad or on spec once in Cuba.

La Casa del Son Empedrado 411 e/ Compostela y Aguacate, Habana Vieja ⓦlacasonadelson.com. An efficiently run school, with half a dozen dance rooms and a bar. As the main sponsor of the ambitious Ritmo Cuba salsa festival, this school is one of the movers and shakers on the salsa school circuit. If you just want a taster you can book a one or two-hour class. For a proper course the main package is five days of classes, with a minimum of two hours of tuition per day. There are also rumba, chachacha, son, danzón, bachata, tango and percussion classes available.

Salsabor Neptuno 558, 1er piso e/ Lealtad y Escobar, Centro Habana ⓦsalsaborcuba.com. A staircase direct from a busy street leads up to the first-floor premises of this professional, reliable outfit who offer salsa, *rueda de casino*, rumba, bachata, merengue and various other Cuban and Latino dance classes in their five dance rooms and even on their 60-square-metre rooftop. Group classes, singing, percussion and piano classes are also offered. Book online or in person – if they can accommodate you on the same day, they will.

1

Mercado Egido Ave. de Bélgica, e/ Corrales y Apodaca, Habana Vieja. This is the daddy of food markets – a huge indoor space selling fruit and vegetables, spices, honey, rice, beans and meat, as well as a few household goods like soap and razor blades.

SPORTS, DANCE AND OUTDOOR ACTIVITIES

You only need to spend a few hours wandering the streets of any part of the capital to appreciate the prominent role that **sport** plays in the lives of Habaneros. Fierce arguments strike off every evening on basketball courts all over the city, and you'll rarely see an open space not hosting a game of baseball or football. On a professional level, Havana is the finest place for live sport in Cuba, with teams in all the national leagues and a number of large stadia. Booking in advance is unnecessary and rarely possible.

BASEBALL

Estadio Latinoamericano The city's national-league baseball team, Industriales, traditionally the most successful team in Cuba, plays at the 55,000-capacity Estadio Latinoamericano (☎7 870 8175) at Pedro Pérez no.302 e/ Patria y Sarabia in Cerro, the city borough south of Centro Habana and Vedado.

Essentials To catch a game all you need do is turn up and pay at the gate. The big crowds usually only come out for the most important confrontations, and especially when they play their arch rivals Santiago de Cuba. The most reliable and detailed source for game schedules is the website ⓦ baseballdecuba.com.

BASKETBALL

Essentials The local basketball team, Capitalinos, spends the winter months (usually Jan–April) in weekly combat with the other seven teams in the Liga Superior de Baloncesto (LSB), the national league. Advance information on games is hard to find, a situation not helped by the irregular timing of the league from season to season. Your best bet is either to ask around or to contact one of the relevant arenas (see box below). Over the years, games have been played variously at the Sala Polivalente Ramón Fonst, the Ciudad Deportiva and the Sala Polivalente Kid Chocolate. Games usually begin around 6pm.

FOOTBALL

Essentials The home of football in Havana is the Estadio Pedro Marrero (☎7209 5428) at Avenida 41 no.4409 e/ 44 y 46 in Marianao in the western suburbs, where the more popular and successful of the city's two league teams – Ciudad de la Habana – and the national team play most of their matches. Games tend to kick off between 3pm and 5pm but match schedules have been highly irregular in recent seasons, with games taking place on any day of the week.

GOLF

The Club de Golf Habana (daily 8am–9pm; ☎7649 8918) runs the only golf course in the city. Located on the Carretera de Vento just off the airport road, the Avenida de Rancho Boyeros, this basic nine-hole course covers an area of less than one square kilometre. Golf lessons also offered. The complex also features a tennis court, bowling alley, pool and restaurant.

MULTISPORT SPECTATOR VENUES

Havana has a number of **multisport arenas** and **stadiums**, with baseball the only sport enjoying the luxury of its own exclusive stadium. As event information is so hard to get hold of and individual team websites all but nonexistent, one of the best ways to stay informed is to contact the venues themselves.

Coliseo de la Ciudad Deportiva Vía Blanca y Ave. de Rancho Boyeros, Cerro ☎7648 5000. This 15,000-capacity arena, built in 1957, is part of a huge sports complex of the same name. Volleyball is most frequently played here, though gymnastics, martial arts, boxing and occasionally basketball also take place.

Estadio Panamericano Vía Monumental Km 4 1/2, Habana del Este. The huge Complejo Panamericano sports complex, not all of it open to the public, was originally built to host the 1991 Pan American Games. The centrepiece Estadio Panamericano (☎7795 4140) athletics stadium has also staged football matches in recent years.

Sala Polivalente Kid Chocolate Paseo del Prado e/ Brasil (Teniente Rey) y San Martín, Habana Vieja ☎7862 8634. Opposite the Capitolio Nacional, this rickety old sports hall is best known for staging boxing matches, but also hosts basketball, five-a-side football and other sports. Event programmes are posted on a notice board at the entrance.

Sala Polivalente Ramón Fonst Ave. de Rancho Boyeros e/ Bruzón y 19 de Mayo, Plaza de la Revolución ☎7881 4296. Used predominantly for basketball, this arena has also hosted volleyball, handball, gymnastics and fencing.

TOP FOUR SWIMMING POOLS

There's only one proper beach in Havana itself, so if you want to swim or sunbathe without travelling the 15km to the Playas del Este, you'll need to find yourself a **swimming pool**. The city has a few municipal public pools, but these are often not filled and are so unreliable that you're almost always better off aiming for one of the hotel or tourist-complex pools listed below. Non-guests have to pay to use hotel pools, but the cost usually includes a *consumo*, which you can use to buy food and drink; you may also be asked to show a passport.

Club Almendares Calle 49B, Kohly. Some 200m from Parque Almendares, this is a fairly small but very sociable pool with various eating and recreation facilities.

Hotel Nacional Calle O esq. 21, Vedado. This hotel has two pools, a small, rectangular one used by swimmers, and a more classic freeform hotel pool used by splashers and paddlers.

Hotel Memories Miramar Ave. 5ta e/ 72 y 76 Miramar, Playa. One of the largest pools in Miramar.

Hotel Riviera Paseo y Malecón, Vedado. The only hotel pool with diving boards, this is also the most evocative of the pre-Revolution era, barely changed since it opened in the late 1950s.

Fishing Both marinas offer deep-sea fishing (*pesca de altura*); trips that include all equipment and bait, a fishing instructor and crew plus some on-board drinks. Bottom-fishing (*pesca a fondo*) trips are also available.

DIVING AND FISHING

Marinas Havana has two marinas, the Marina Hemingway at Avenida 5ta y Calle 248 (☎ 7204 1689) in the far western suburbs of Santa Fe in Playa (you'll need your passport for any trip from here, as it's an international port of entry), and Marina Tarará at Vía Blanca Km 18 in Habana del Este (☎ 7796 0242). Most of the fishing, diving and sailing in the waters around Havana is arranged through one of these two, offering a very similar set of packages and the same prices.

Diving Visit the Marina Hemingway to ask about diving with the Hemingway Dive Center. Twenty or so sites line the Playa coastline, including a couple of shipwrecks, coral walls and small caves. Blue Scuba Dive Club (Avenida 1ra, ☎ 7209 3660) also come recommended.

DIRECTORY

ATMs Clusters of Banco Metropolitano 24hr ATMs accepting Visa and MasterCard have been installed around Havana in recent years, making access to cash easier than ever before. You can find them in sets of four to six at Obispo no.257 e/ Aguiar y Cuba in Habana Vieja; on San Rafael e/ Industria y Amistad in Centro Habana; and at Linea no.705 e/ Paseo y A in Vedado. There's also a set of ATMs hidden from the street in a small room on La Rampa at Calle 23 e/ P y Malecón.

Embassies The vast majority of embassies and consulates are based in Miramar.

Health There is no single emergency number for ringing an ambulance, but you can call ☎ 105 or ☎ 7838 1185 or ☎ 7 2185 to get one. You can also contact Asistur, the tourist assistance agency, on its emergency number (☎ 7866 8339). One of the best hospitals, run predominantly for foreigners, is the Clínica Internacional Cira García in Miramar at Calle 20 no.4101 esq. Avenida 41 (☎ 7204 4300 to 4309). Among the best stocked pharmacies are the Farmacia Internacional in the Galería de Tiendas at the *Hotel Habana Libre* (☎ 7834 6187; entrance on Calle 25); the Farmacia Internacional at Avenida 41 no.1814 esq. 20, in Miramar (☎ 7214 4744; Mon–Fri 9am–6pm, Sat 9am–noon); and at the Clínica Internacional Cira García (see above), also in Miramar.

Money and exchange There are CADECA *casas de cambio*

at Baratillo esq. Oficios on the Plaza de San Francisco (Mon–Sat 8.30am–12.30pm, 1–8pm & Sun 9am–5pm) in Habana Vieja; at Calle 23 e/ L y K in Vedado (Mon–Sat 9am–4.30pm & Sun 9–11.30am); and at Avenida 5ta e/ 40 y 42 (Mon–Sat 9am–4.30pm & Sun 9am–noon) in Miramar. Not all banks can handle currency exchange; opt for the Banco Metropolitano at Obispo no.257 e/ Aguiar y Cuba (Mon–Sat 8.30am–7.30pm, Sun 8.30am–3.30pm); branches of the Banco Financiero Internacional and the Banco de Crédito y Comercio; and the bank located at Avenida 1ra e/ 0 y 2 (Mon–Fri 8am–3pm) in Miramar.

Police There are police stations at Dragones esq. Agramonte in Habana Vieja, and at Dragones e/ Lealtad y Escobar (☎ 7862 4412) in Centro Habana. In an emergency ring ☎ 106.

Post offices and stamps Post offices are at Oficios esq. Lamparilla in Habana Vieja (Mon–Fri 8am–6pm); Calzada de Infanta esq. Concordia, Centro Habana (Mon–Fri 8am–6pm), just a few metres from Vedado; and Calle 23 esq. C in Vedado itself (Mon–Fri 8am–6pm & Sat 8am–noon). You can also buy stamps at the store on Obispo e/ Villegas y Bernaza, Habana Vieja (Mon–Sat 9am–5pm).

Telephones To buy a mobile phone, and for and banks of public telephones, go to an ETECSA Telepunto centre (see box, page 138).

1

WI-FI ZONES IN AND AROUND HAVANA

As with the rest of Cuba, in 2015 designated public wi-fi zones were established all over the city, opening up internet access to unprecedented levels. There are now over eighty such zones across Havana, as well as the wi-fi provided in many but not all hotels.

PUBLIC ZONES

Habana Vieja currently has just two public zones, at the Plaza del Cristo and the Parque de San Juan de Dios. **Centro Habana** has over half a dozen including at the Parque Fe del Valle (at San Rafael esq. Avenida de Italia) and the Parque Trillo. **Vedado**'s biggest wi-fi zone is on La Rampa; there are other zones at Parque Linea y L, Parque 15 y 14 and elsewhere. In Miramar go to the Teatro Karl Marx or Parque Coyula. The full list of wi-fi spots can be found on the ETECSA website at ⓦetecsa.cu.

NAUTA INTERNET CARDS

You need a Nauta internet card (*tarjeta de internet*) to use wi-fi. You can buy them at some hotels but primarily at ETECSA branches, known as Telepuntos, Minipuntos and Centros Multiservicios. They are scattered across the city but three of the largest branches are the Telepuntos at Obispo no.351 esq. Habana in Habana Vieja (daily 8.30am–7pm), at Aguila no.565 esq. Dragones in Centro Habana (daily 8.30am–7pm) and in the FOCSA building at Calle M e/ 17 y 19 in Vedado (daily 8.30am–7pm).

Visas and tourist cards To renew and extend tourist cards and visas go to the office at Factor esq. Final in Nuevo Vedado (Mon–Fri 8.30am–3pm). Arrive early and expect a wait.

Internet/computer terminals There are *salas de navegación* where you can use Nauta wi-fi cards on computer terminals in the city's Telepuntos (see box above) and Centro Multiservicios at Calle 17 e/ B y C in Vedado. Among the least inefficient internet services are in the cybercafés and business centres of the hotels *Inglaterra* at Paseo del Prado esq. San Rafael and *Parque Central* in Habana Vieja, and the *Habana Libre* and *Nacional* hotels in Vedado. For public wi-fi zones, see box above.

Around Havana

Havana's **suburbs** stretch out for miles, and though they are technically within the city's political boundaries, they feel far removed – a sense that's reinforced by the extremely poor public transport links. The best beaches, notably the top-notch **Playas del Este**, are to the east, past the uncomplicated towns of **Cojímar** and **Guanabacoa**. The neatly packaged **Museo Ernest Hemingway**, the writer's long-time Cuban residence, lies **south** of Havana, as do the picturesque landscaped expanses of **Parque Lenin** and the impressive **Jardín Botánico Nacional**.

GETTING AROUND

By public transport, car or taxi The tourist bus service, the Habana Bus Tour (see page 113), is the best way of getting to the Playas del Este and the rest of Habana del Este. For the rest of the outlying boroughs you'll either need your own transport, be prepared to pay for a taxi or tackle the Metrobús system.

East of Havana

Taking the tunnel in Habana Vieja under the bay and heading east on the Vía Monumental, past El Morro and parallel to the coast, leads you straight to **Cojímar**, a fishing village famed for its Hemingway connection. Past here the road dips inland to become the Vía Blanca and passes Villa Panamericana, the village built to support the 1991 Pan American Games, and runs south towards **Guanabacoa**, a quiet provincial town with numerous attractive churches and a fascinating religious history. For many, the big attraction east of Havana will be the boisterous **Playas del Este**, the nearest beaches to the city, where clean sands and a lively scene draw in the crowds.

With the exception of the route to the beach, scarcity and unreliability of **public transport** becomes even more pronounced once outside the city proper, and you'll need a car to see many of these sights.

Cojímar

Just 6km east of Havana, the tiny fishing village of **COJÍMAR** is a world apart from the bustling city. Its sole claim to fame revolves around one of its late residents, **Gregorio Fuentes**, the first mate of Ernest Hemingway's boat *The Pilar*, who also claimed to be the old man upon whom Hemingway based Santiago, the protagonist of his Pulitzer- and Nobel Prize-winning novel *The Old Man and the Sea*. Up until the late 1990s Fuentes could be seen sitting outside his house or in *La Terraza de Cojímar* restaurant, charging US$10 for a consultation with fans eager for Hemingway stories. When Fuentes died in 2002, aged 104, it marked the end of an era. There's not a whole lot to do here, though a half-day trip is tailor-made for enjoying such simple pleasures as watching fishing boats bob about in the calm, hoop-shaped bay, or wandering the tidy, bougainvillea-fringed streets.

ARRIVAL AND DEPARTURE   COJÍMAR

By bus Cojímar is served by the #58 bus which leaves from Prado, by the mouth of the tunnel in Habana Vieja.

By taxi A taxi from Havana will cost around $350 CUP one way.

Guanabacoa

Less than 2km inland from the Vía Monumental turn-off to Cojímar is **GUANABACOA**, a little town officially within the city limits but with a distinctly provincial feel. The site of a pre-Columbian community and later one of the island's first Spanish settlements, it is historically important, and home to a disproportionately large number of churches. Most notable is the **Iglesia Parroquial Mayor** on Parque Martí, which has a magnificent, though age-worn, gilded altar and a strong tradition of African-Cuban religion, a result of its position as an important centre for the slave trade. The latter is displayed to impressive effect at the Museo Histórico de Guanabacoa on Martí (Tues– Fri 9am–5.30pm; ☎7 797 9117).

TOURS IN AND AROUND HAVANA

Organized excursions are by far the easiest – though not the cheapest – way of getting to attractions on the city outskirts such as the Museo Ernest Hemingway and the Jardín Botánico Nacional, which are difficult to reach by public transport. All the travel agents listed below also offer day-long **city tours**, while there are all sorts of **themed tours**, such as visits to all of Ernest Hemingway's old haunts, or trips hinged on architecture or African-Cuban culture. Most agents have desks in hotel lobbies but they also have their own offices open to the public. Unique to Habana Vieja is the San Cristóbal agency, the official travel agency of the organization overseeing the restoration of the old city, the Oficina del Historiador de la Ciudad de La Habana. They offer specialized history and culture-oriented tours of the old town. See also the box on page 112.

Cubanacán Calle 68 no.503 e/ Ave. 5ta y 5ta A, Miramar ☎7 204 1658 and in hotels Plaza, Deauville, St John, Cohiba and Meliá Habana among others, ⓦ viajescubanacan.cu.

Cubatur Calle 23 e/ M y L, Vedado ☎7 835 4155, ⓦ cubatur.cu.

Gaviota Tours Ave. 49 no.3620 e/ 36 y 49a, Kohly ☎7 204 7683, ⓦ gaviota-grupo.com.

Havanatur Calle 23 esq. M, Vedado ☎7 835 3720, ⓦ havanatur.cu.

Paradiso Calle 19 no.560 esq. C, Vedado ⓦ facebook. com/paradiso.cuba.

San Cristóbal O'Reilly esq. Tacón, Habana Vieja ☎7801 1135, ⓦ viajessancristobal.cu.

1

ARRIVAL AND DEPARTURE   GUANABACOA

By bus The #P15 bus from the Parque de la Fraternidad in   Habana Vieja cuts right through the centre of town.

Playas del Este

Fifteen kilometres east of Cojímar, the Vía Blanca reaches Havana's nearest beaches – Playa Santa María del Mar, Playa Boca Ciega and Playa Guanabo, collectively known as the **Playas del Este**. Hugging the Atlantic coast, these three swathes of fine sand form a long, twisting ochre ribbon that vanishes in the summer beneath the crush of weekending Habaneros and tourists. There's not a whole lot to distinguish between the beaches, geographically, although as a general rule the sand is better towards the western end.

If you're based in Havana, the excellent self-catering and hotel **accommodation** here makes this area a good choice for a mini-break. Those craving creature comforts should head for the big hotels in Santa María, while budget travellers will find the best value in the inexpensive hotels and *casas particulares* in Guanabo. Although a number of restaurants serve cheap meals, these all tend to be much the same, and your best bet is to eat at one of the two paladars in Guanabo; otherwise, see if one of the *casas particulares* can recommend somewhere.

ARRIVAL AND DEPARTURE   PLAYAS DEL ESTE

By bus The excellent Habana Bus Tour company's #T3 runs a regular service that picks up and drops off at several hotels along the Santa María strip roughly every 40–60 minutes from 9am to 6pm. It's worth bearing in mind that the route gets extremely busy in summer, particularly on the last Havana-bound buses of the day.
By taxi A metered taxi from the centre of Havana as far as Guanabo will cost around $350 CUP.

Playa Santa María del Mar

Because of its proximity to Havana, **Playa Santa María del Mar**, usually just called Santa María, is the busiest and trendiest of the eastern beaches, with boombox reggaeton, watersports and beautiful bodies on sunloungers. It extends for about 4km from the foot of Santa María Loma, a hill to the south of the Río Itabo, with the bulk of hotels dotted around the main Avenida de las Terrazas, just behind the beach. Arguably the most attractive of the three beaches, with golden sands backed by grassland and a few palm trees, it's also the most touristy and can feel a bit artificial.

The beach has plenty of sunloungers for rent and is patrolled by eager beach masseurs, and there are various **activities** on offer – though sadly you'll see more empty beer cans than fish if you go snorkelling.

ACCOMMODATION			
Casa de Bernardo y Adelina	4	Casa de Raisa García Güell	2
Casa Eydis y Harol	6	Casa de René y Esperanza	3
Casa de Mileydis y Julito	5	Terrazas Atlántico	1

A recent addition to the beach activities is kitesurfing, which is helmed by the HKC Kite and Surf Club (⊕havanakite.com) and responsible for a sudden surge of interest in the sport. The club offers kitesurfing courses, plus surfing and stand-up paddleboarding lessons. They also hire out equipment. Boat safaris, catamaran trips and jeep excursions are available, too. Additionally, they have a surf-and-stay kitesurf school, Kite Village Cuba at Marina Tarará nearby.

ACCOMMODATION
PLAYA SANTA MARÍA DEL MAR; SEE MAP PAGE 140

Terrazas Atlántico Ave. de las Terrazas e/ 11 y 13 ⊕islazulhotels.com. Spacious and airy apartments in a complex, some with views over the beach. Each room has a TV and fridge, and there are two pools in the grounds. Good value for groups. $\overline{\$\$}$

EATING AND DRINKING
SEE MAP PAGE 140

With thatch-hut **beach bars** at intervals along the sand and roving vendors selling rum-laced coconuts, there's no shortage of refreshments. A big shop on Avenida de las Terrazas sells the makings of a **picnic**, although the prices are higher than for goods in Havana, so you'd do well to bring what you need with you. A nest of snack bars near Avenida de las Terrazas create a shady spot for a drink.

Don Pepe Ave. de las Terrazas ☎7976 0700. This open-sided restaurant makes an airy retreat from the midday sun. *Comida criolla* and pizzas are served slowly, though with a smile. Rather incongruously, you may be approached by a magician. $\overline{\$}$

Mégano Santa María beach ☎7797 1670. At the western end of the beach, this is the best of the few cafés dotted around and is generally well stocked with drinks, ice cream, and very reasonable pork and rice dinners. $\overline{\$}$

Playa Boca Ciega
A bridge across the Río Itabo connects Santa María to **Playa Boca Ciega**, also known as Playa Mi Cayito. A paucity of public facilities makes this the least user-friendly of all the beaches. However, the beautiful sherbet-yellow beach is open to all, and the waters around the estuary mouth are usually quite busy and cheerful, with kids and adults paddling and wading in the river currents. Further west, towards Santa María, the beach is popular with the LGBTQ+ community.

Playa Guanabo
Far more pleasant than Playa Boca Ciega is laidback **Playa Guanabo**, roughly 2.5km to the east, where the sun-faded wooden houses and jaunty seaside atmosphere go a long way to compensate for the slightly poor brownish-sand beach. With fewer crowds and no big hotels, it feels much more authentic than Santa María, especially towards the east end of town where tourism has hardly penetrated at all. While not idyllic, it still has its charms: palm trees offer welcome shade, and if you're not

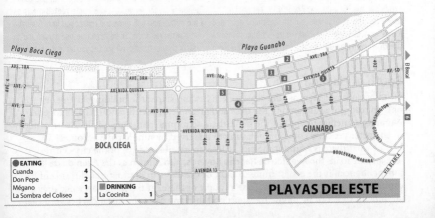

● EATING	
Cuanda	4
Don Pepe	2
Mégano	1
La Sombra del Coliseo	3

■ DRINKING	
La Cocinita	1

PLAYAS DEL ESTE

1

bothered about the odd bit of seaweed, this is a refreshingly unaffected spot to hang out.

As most tourists stay on the better beaches further west, Guanabo is pretty much left to the Cubans, with many residents commuting daily from here to Havana. Avenida 5ta, the appealing main street, has a clutch of cafés and shops, while around the side streets and near the beach are a couple of excellent paladars. For general information head to Infotur on Avenida 5ta e/ 468 y 470 (☎7 69 6868; Mon–Sat 8.15am–1pm & 1.30–4.15pm). The Banco Metropolitano on Avenida 5ta has a cash machine.

ACCOMMODATION   PLAYA GUANABO; SEE MAP PAGE 140

Casa de Bernardo y Adelina Calle 478 no.306 e/ 3ra y 5ta ☎7796 3609, ✉bernaguanabo@gmail.com. The whole place is for rent here, with two a/c rooms each with a private bathroom, an adjoining sitting room, a dining area and a kitchen with a fridge. The balcony with a sea view is a bonus. $$

Casa de Mileydis y Julito Calle 468 no.512 e/ 5ta y 7ma ☎7796 0100, ✉antuanmuriel@nauta.cu. Two beautiful a/c rooms, one with disabled access in a *casa particular*, close to the beach. Has a pretty garden and a porch where

you can relax, plus extremely hospitable owners. $

Casa de Raisa García Güell Ave. 3ra no.47801 e/ 478 y 480 Guanabo ☎7796 2878, ✉raisa2510@nauta.cu. This beautiful house has a sun-dappled patio filled with plants and two massive en-suite rooms. It's close to the beach, and there's space for parking too. $

Casa de René y Esperanza Ave. 3ra no.47607 e/ 476 y 478 ☎7796 3867, ✉jcparra@infomed.sld.cu. The double room, with its own kitchen, boasts a wide terrace with a sea view. $

EATING AND DRINKING   SEE MAP PAGE 140

La Cocinita Calle 5ta e/ 178 y 180. This open-sided bar is the liveliest spot in town, with a live band most nights. It's safe enough but can feel a little edgy at times due to the groups of raucous men who patronize it. $

Cuanda Calle 472 esq. 5ta D. A basic restaurant dishing up reasonable meals on the pork, salad, rice and beans

theme. $

La Sombra del Coliseo 5ta Ave. no.48011 e/ 480 y 482. This pleasant pizzeria is set back from the busy main road with a marble-floor terrace. Delicious and authentic margarita and salad with attentive service make it a great spot. $

Brisas del Mar

Some 4km east of Guanabo is the virtually deserted **Brisas del Mar**. Were it not for the lovely *casa particular* practically built on the strand, this appealing stretch of clean brown sand would make for an awkward day-trip. However, it's well worth making an overnight stay to experience the near solitude so rare in Playas del Este and to enjoy the hospitality of one of the best *casas* in the area.

ACCOMMODATION   BRISAS DEL MAR; SEE MAP PAGE 140

★ **Casa Eydis y Harol** Calle F no.4 e/ 24 y Lindero, Brisas del Mar, Guanabo ☎7796 5119, ✉hanoi9402@ nauta.cu. The two simple but thoughtfully decorated rooms in a building that backs onto an almost-private stretch of beach make for the perfect coastal idyll. One room

has its own lounge and both have their own bathroom. The lovely owner serves delicious home-cooked meals on a sun terrace and will come and collect you from Guanabo centre when you arrive. There's a picturesque garden and an outdoor shower to wash off sand as you leave the beach. $

South of Havana

Heading south of Havana, the city fades in fits and starts, the buildings dying out only to reappear again among the trees and green fields which bind this area together. Numerous satellite towns dot the semiurban, semirural landscape, distinctly provincial in character yet close enough to Havana to be served by municipal bus routes. The best of what there is south of the city is all within a 30km drive of the city centre. The airport road, the **Avenida de Rancho Boyeros**, also known as the **Avenida de la Independencia**, is the easiest route to most of the day-trip destinations this side of the capital. It makes sense to visit at least a couple of these on the same day, since they are all difficult to get to by public transport and in many cases the distances between them are short. A near-perfect preservation of the great writer's home in Havana, the **Museo Ernest Hemingway**, is the most concrete option and one of the few that stands up well by itself. The relative proximity of **Parque Lenin** – an immense park – to the **Parque Zoológico Nacional** and the sprawling **Jardín Botánico Nacional**, over the road from **ExpoCuba**, makes any of these a convenient and worthwhile combination.

Museo Ernest Hemingway

San Francisco, 11km southeast of Habana Vieja • Mon–Sat 10am–4pm • Charge • ☎ 7891 0809 • Take Metrobús #P7 from the Parque de la Fraternidad in Habana Vieja or the #P2 from the junction between Calle 23 and Avenida de los Presidentes in Vedado; it's a 10min walk from the bus stop in San Francisco de Paula

Out in the suburb of San Francisco de Paula is **Finca La Vigía**, an attractive little estate centred on the whitewashed, late nineteenth-century villa where Ernest Hemingway lived for twenty years until 1960. Now the **Museo Ernest Hemingway**, it makes a simple but enjoyable excursion from the city, and is also visitable on an organized tour.

On top of a hill and with splendid views over Havana, this single-storey colonial residence, where Hemingway wrote a number of his most famous novels, has been preserved almost exactly as he left it – with drinks and magazines strewn about the place and the dining-room table set for guests. Brimming with character, it's a remarkable insight into the writer's lifestyle and personality, from the numerous stuffed animal heads on the walls and the bullfighting posters to the bottles of liquor and the thousands of books lining the shelves in most of the rooms, including the bathroom. The small room where his typewriter is still stationed was where Hemingway did much of his work, often in the mornings and usually standing up. Frustratingly, you can't walk into the rooms, but must view everything through the open windows and doors; by walking around the encircling veranda, however, you can get good views of most rooms. In the well-kept **gardens**, which you can walk round, surrounded by bamboo, Hemingway's fishing boat is suspended inside a wooden pavilion; the graves of four of his dogs are next to the empty swimming pool. You can also scale the **lookout tower** and take in the fantastic 360-degree vistas from its roof terrace.

Note that the museum closes when it rains, to protect the interior and grounds, so try to visit on sunny days.

Parque Lenin

Avenida San Francisco (Calle 100) • June–Sept Wed–Sun 9am–5pm; July & Aug Tues–Sun 9am–5pm • Free • Information ☎ 7 643 1165, switchboard ☎ 7644 3026 • Metrobús routes #P13 and #PC pass closest to the park, but do not stop at the park itself; to drive there, follow signs from Avenida de Rancho Boyeros

Roughly a twenty-minute drive south of the city, about 3km east of the José Martí International Airport, are the wide-open grounds of **Parque Lenin**, a cross between a landscaped urban park and a rolling tract of untouched wooded countryside. Founded in 1972, this was once a popular escape for city residents who came here to picnic, ride around on horseback or on the park's own steam train, and enjoy the other facilities, including restaurants and cafeterías, swimming pools, a small art gallery, boats and fairground rides. The deterioration in public transport in the 1990s led to a sharp drop in visitors, and today a pervasive air of abandon blows around the park, with many of the facilities, including the train and pools, now closed and in disrepair. Nonetheless, its sheer size (almost eight square kilometres) and scenic landscape make Parque Lenin a great place for a picnic, a wander or just a breath of fresh air, and there are still a couple of basic restaurants here. The park's attractions are spread quite sparsely, so it can be a tiring place to explore on foot; roads around the park allow you to explore by car.

South of the park's central reservoir, the Presa Paso Sequito, is the **Galería Amelia Peláez** (Tues–Sun 9am–5pm; free), a small art gallery that stages temporary exhibitions; nearby is the semi-abandoned and quite surreal **aquarium** where, in over sixty small tanks, you can see all sorts of fish, crabs, turtles and even a couple of crocodiles; and the park's most famous monument, the 9m-high **marble bust of Lenin**.

Parque Zoológico Nacional

Avenida Varona Km 3.5, Capdevila, Boyeros • Wed–Fri 10am–3.30pm, Sat & Sun 10am–4.30pm • Charge • Bus tours every 30min • ☎ 7643 0490

A perpetually half-finished safari park in between Avenida Rancho Boyeros and Parque Lenin, the **Parque Zoológico Nacional** features a small lake and two completed enclosures. Herbivores of the African savannah, including elephants, rhinos, giraffes and zebras, roam about in the **Pradera Africana** enclosure, while the park's twenty or so lions are in the **Foso de Leones**, a huge grass- and tree-lined pit. Both enclosures usually allow excitingly close contact with the animals. However, the majority of the various species here, mostly big cats and apes, are kept in cramped conditions.

Jardín Botánico Nacional

Carretera del Rocío, 4km south of the entrance to Parque Lenin, Calabazar • Weds–Sun 9am–4pm • Charge • Tractor-bus tours (roughly 2hr) leave every hour or so from just inside the main entrance, near the information office • ⓦ jardinbotanico.co.cu

A sweeping expanse of parkland showcasing a massive variety of plants and trees, the **Jardín Botánico Nacional** is the prettiest, most pleasant and most worthwhile of the attractions on Havana's southern outskirts of the city. Laid out as a savannah rather than a forest, the grounds are split into sections according to continent. Highlights include the collection of 162 surprisingly varied species of palm, the cacti in the **Pabellones de Exposiciones** greenhouse-style buildings and the meticulously landscaped **Japanese Garden**, donated by the Japanese government on the thirtieth anniversary of the Revolution in 1989. The restaurant near the Japanese Garden is also the best place to stop for lunch.

Though you can explore the park yourself, a lack of printed literature and plaques means you'll learn far more by booking an organized excursion from the city or taking the **guided tour**. There's usually at least one English-speaking guide available, but the tours do not necessarily cover the whole park.

ExpoCuba

Carretera del Rocío • Wed–Sun 9am–5pm, closed Sept–Dec, except for special events • Charges for rollercoaster and boats

On the other side of the Carretera del Rocío, directly opposite the Jardín Botánico Nacional, what looks like a well-kept industrial estate is in fact **ExpoCuba**, a permanent exhibition of the island's endeavours in industry, science, technology and commerce since the Revolution. Despite its impressive scope, displays are a little dry and the hordes of children here on school trips tend to be more interested in riding on the mini rollercoaster and boating on the small lake. There are various cafeterías and a restaurant with great views. The place is at its liveliest when it hosts the **Feria Internacional de la Habana**, an international trade fair that usually takes place the first week in November.

ACTIVITIES IN PARQUE LENIN

A horseback ride is a great way to explore the park's large spaces; you can hire horses from the **Centro Ecuestre**, signposted at the first right-hand turn as you enter from the city side, though there are also locals offering rides on their own horses nearby – be prepared to haggle. It's in this northern half of the park that you'll find the **Parque Mariposa**, a Chinese-designed amusement park built in 2007. Though unspectacular, this is nonetheless one of Havana's best attractions for young children, with over twenty different rides including bumper cars, a swinging pirate ship, a water slide, a rollercoaster and a 42m-high Ferris wheel.

EL DÍA DE SAN LÁZARO

On December 17, the road between Santiago de las Vegas and El Rincón closes as hordes of people from all over Cuba come to ask favours of **San Lázaro** in exchange for a sacrifice, or to keep promises they have already made to the saint. Some have walked for days, timing their **pilgrimage** so that they arrive on the 17th, but the common starting point is Santiago de las Vegas, 2km down the road. The most fervent of believers make their journey as arduous as possible, determined that in order to earn the favour they have asked for they must first prove their willingness to suffer. In the past people have tied rocks to their limbs and dragged themselves along the concrete road to the church; others have walked barefoot from much further afield; while others bring material sacrifices, often money, as their part of the bargain.

Santiago de las Vegas

Metrobús #P12 runs from Parque de la Fraternidad in Habana Vieja

With a history dating back to the late seventeenth century and a population of around 35,000, **SANTIAGO DE LAS VEGAS**, 2km south of José Martí airport, is one of Havana's more noteworthy satellite towns. That said, there are few specific sights beyond the attractive central square and the modest national hockey stadium, both just off the main street, but if you're on your way to the church and pilgrimage point in El Rincón (see below) you may want to stop here for a bite to eat or a stroll to get a feel for Cuba beyond the big city.

The Santuario de San Lázaro

El Rincón, 2km south of Santiago de las Vegas on the main road, the Carretera Santiago de las Vegas • Daily 7am–6pm • Free

Ten kilometres south of central Havana, the **Santuario de San Lázaro**, on the edge of the tiny village of **El Rincón**, is the final destination of a **pilgrimage** made by thousands of Cubans every December. Amid scenes of intense religious fervour, pilgrims come to this gleaming, lovingly maintained church to ask favours of San Lázaro, whose image appears inside, in exchange for sacrifices (see box). Throughout the year, though, people come here to cut deals with the saint and lay down flowers or make a donation, and the road through the village is always lined with people selling flowers and statuettes. Sitting peacefully in the grounds of an old hospital, the church itself is striking only for its immaculate simplicity, though there are several fine altars inside.

Artemisa and Pinar del Río

FARMERS IN THE VIÑALES VALLEY

2

Artemisa and Pinar del Río

Despite their relative proximity to Havana, the provinces of Pinar del Río and Artemisa (the latter created in 2010) are a far cry from the noise, pollution and hustle of the capital. This is a distinctly rural region, where the laidback towns and even Pinar's regional capital of Pinar del Río are characterized by a provincial feel. The major attractions are well away from the population centres, the majority situated in and around the green slopes of the Cordillera de Guaniguanico, the low mountain range that runs like a backbone down the length of the landscape. Famous for producing the world's finest tobacco (that most time-consuming of crops), Pinar del Río is stereotyped as a province populated by backward country folk, and is the butt of a string of national jokes. Life here unfolds at a subdued pace, and its hillside and seaside resorts are well suited to unfettered escapism. That sense of escapism escalates around the Península de Guanahacabibes, a remote destination that's especially rewarding for divers and birdwatchers.

Hidden within the **Sierra del Rosario**, the relatively compact eastern section of the cordillera, the peaceful, self-contained ecotourism centres of **Las Terrazas** and **Soroa** provide perfect opportunities to explore the tree-clad hillsides and valleys. Heading west along the *autopista*, which runs parallel with the mountain range along the length of the province, there are a few low-key attractions to the north. It's unlikely you'll want to make much more than a fleeting visit to any one of them, unless you're in search of the healing qualities of the spa at **San Diego de los Baños**, a small village straddling the border between the Sierra del Rosario and the western section of the cordillera, the **Sierra de los Organos**. Although the area is host to a large park and a set of caves of both geological and historical interest, their considerable potential is mostly untapped through neglect and isolation.

Most visitors instead head straight for Pinar del Río's undoubted highlight, the **Viñales valley**, where the flat-topped mountains, or *mogotes*, give the landscape a unique, prehistoric look and feel. While heavily visited, Viñales remains unspoilt – with no big tourist developments and very low level of hassle from touts – and the village at its centre, full of simple houses with rooms to rent out to tourists, has an uncontrived air about it. Easily visited out on a day-trip from Havana, there's also enough to see away from Viñales' official sights for a longer, more adventurous stay. Conveniently close to the valley is the secluded little beach on serene **Cayo Jutías**, while on the same northern coastline is the more substantial but even more remote **Cayo Levisa**, better suited for a longer visit and for diving.

You'll need to be pretty determined to get to the country's westernmost locations, which are beyond Pinar del Río's provincial capital, where the *autopista* ends, and more or less out of reach unless you rent a car or book an official excursion. If you make it, you'll find the serene and scenic patchwork landscape of the Vuelta Abajo region, said to produce the finest tobacco leaves in the world and home to some internationally renowned tobacco plantations, including the **Alejandro Robaina**, which is one of the few you can easily visit. The modest beaches of **Playa Bailén** and **Boca de Galafre** and the small tourist site at **Laguna Grande** provide quick detours if you want to break up the journey to **María La Gorda**, whose fine sandy shores, crystal-clear waters, outstanding scuba diving and fantastic sense of out-of-reach tranquillity are the real justification for coming all this way.

BAÑOS DE SAN JUAN

Highlights

❶ Baños de San Juan Perfect for picnics or a midday bathe, this delightful river haven above Las Terrazas also has a unique set of treehouses on stilts where you can stay the night. See page 154

❷ Hiking at Las Terrazas Guided hikes from here are the best way to delve into the stunning sierra. See page 155

❸ Viñales The unique humpbacked *mogote* hills, prehistoric caves and friendly vibe in the village all make this an unmissable stop-off. See page 164

❹ Finca Agroecológica El Paraíso Home-grown and -reared food, panoramic views and attentive owners make this eco-farm the best dining experience for miles. See page 170

❺ Cayo Jutías The popularity of this virtually untouched islet is growing, so catch it at its natural best while you can. See page 173

❻ Gran Caverna de Santo Tomás The most complex cave system in Cuba, plunging into a hillside on eight different levels and surprisingly easy to visit. See page 174

❼ Península de Guanahacabibes Boasting a bird-rich Unesco Biosphere Reserve and top-notch diving, this remote region is well worth heading out west to. See page 175

HIGHLIGHTS ARE MARKED ON THE MAP ON PAGE 150

ARTEMISA AND PINAR DEL RÍO

HIGHLIGHTS

1. Baños de San Juan
2. Hiking at Las Terrazas
3. Viñales
4. Finca Agroecologica El Paraiso
5. Cayo Jutías
6. Gran Caverna de Santo Tomás
7. Peninsula de Guanahacabibes

Gulf of Mexico

HAVANA

Cojimar
San Felipe
Surgidero de Batabanó
Güira de Melena
Alquízar
Ceiba Nueva
Guanajay
Habana Libre
Mariel
Agusto César
Sandino
Cabañas
Quiebra
Hacha
Cafetal
Buenavista
ARTEMISA
Artemisa
Las Cañas
Las Mangas
Las Terrazas
Soroa
Hacienda Unión
Baños de Bayate
Candelaria
San Cristóbal
Guanímar

Bahía Honda
Las Pozas
SIERRA DEL ROSARIO
Cueva de los Portales
San Diego de los Baños
Pata Real de San Diego
Los Palacios
Maspotón
Golfo de Batabanó

Palma Rubia
Cayo Levisa
La Palma
Puerto Esperanza
SIERRA DE LOS ÓRGANOS
San Andrés
Entronque de Herradura
Consolación del Sur
La Juventud Reservoir
AUTOPISTA NACIONAL
PINAR DEL RÍO
Pinar del Río
CARRETERA CENTRAL

ISLA DE LA JUVENTUD
Nueva Gerona
Isla de la Juventud

Cayo Jutías
Santa Lucía
Minas de Matahambre
Pons
Viñales
Gran Caverna de Santo Tomás
Sumidero
Alejandro Robaina tobacco plantation
San Luis
La Coloma
Los Canos

San Juan y Martínez
Boca de Galafre
Playa Bailén
Ensenada de Cortés
Guane
Isabel Rubio
Sábalo
Manuel Lazo
La Fe
Laguna Grande
CARRETERA CENTRAL
PINAR DEL RÍO
Mantua

Sandino
Golfo de Guanahacabibes
Cabo de San Antonio
Las Tumbas
Faro Roncalli
La Bajada
María la Gorda
Bahía de Corrientes

N

0   20

Gulf of Mexico

GETTING AROUND **ARTEMISA AND PINAR DEL RÍO**

As with much of Cuba, relying on **public transport** in Artemisa and Pinar del Río is a hazardous, patience-testing business. Much of these two provinces are quite simply out of range of any of the public services, which, where they do exist, are more often than not extremely unreliable.

By bus Víazul provides a daily bus service from Havana to Pinar del Río city and then north to Viñales (2 daily; 3hr).

By colectivo Unofficial tourist taxis leave from the Víazul terminal in Havana throughout the day, waiting until they are full.

By train Very few visitors ever take the train from Havana into Pinar del Río (3–4 weekly; 6hr), as it's notoriously slow and doesn't make any useful stops except for the city itself; the other towns which it stops in are at least a few kilometres from anywhere worth visiting.

By car For any kind of independent travel in and around the Sierra del Rosario or the eastern half of the Sierra de los Organos, you'll need your own car, which you will have to rent in Havana, Viñales or Pinar del Río city. Most drivers speed their way through the province on the four-lane *autopista nacional* (marked on most road maps as A4), which comes to an end at the city of Pinar del Río. You can pick it up around 5km south of Avenida 5ta in Miramar, Havana. Running roughly parallel is the Carretera Central, a slower option which begins its route in La Lisa, the western suburb south of Playa, and takes you closer to the mountains and gives better views of the surrounding landscape. The most scenic, slowest and least travelled route of all is along the northern coastline. Once past Pinar del Río city, the Carretera Central is the only major road.

Eastern Artemisa

With its verdant fields, expansive reservoirs and lush plantations all glistening in the sunlight, it's no surprise to learn that **Eastern Artemisa** is known as the **Jardín de Cuba** (Garden of Cuba), an area of great fertility where bananas, sugar cane, citrus fruits and tobacco flourish in the rich red ferric soil. It's a somnolent area, with a couple of passing attractions like the photogenic town of **San Antonio de los Baños** and the poetic decay of **Antiguo Cafetal Angerona**. The area had a brief moment of infamy thanks to Mariel on the northern coast. The nearest port to the US, it was from here that some 125,000 Cubans left the island in 1980 in what was known as the **Mariel Boatlift** (see page 445).

San Antonio de los Baños

Of all the small towns in Artemisa, **SAN ANTONIO DE LOS BAÑOS**, about 20km south of Havana's western suburbs and a 45-minute drive from Habana Vieja, is the only one that merits more than a fleeting visit. A riverside hotel with good opportunities for swimming and boating, an engaging museum and a countryside park provide at least a day's worth of laidback activity. The town itself has the undisturbed, nonchalant feel that characterizes so much of Cuba's interior, with an archetypal shady square and residential streets largely free of traffic.

Museo de Humor

Calle 60 esq 43 • Tues–Sat 10am–8pm, Sun open when there are activities • Charge • ☎ 47 38 2817

Based in a colonial house, the entertaining **Museo de Humor** has a small permanent exhibition charting the history of graphic humour in Cuba – the caricatures of national and international figures are particularly engaging. The best time to visit, however, is when the museum hosts several national and international **competitions** of comic art, when the best entries are displayed. The two most prestigious competitions, the **Salón de Humorismo y Sátira** and the **Bienal Internacional del Humorismo Gráfico**, take place in alternate years starting in March or April and lasting as late as August. If you're coming all this way specifically for the museum, it's worth ringing in advance, as it sometimes closes for days at a time to mount exhibitions.

Museo de Historia

Calle 66 e/ 41 y 45 • Tues–Sat 10am–6pm, Sun 9am–1pm • Charge • ☎ 47 38 2539

Situated on a quiet street, the **Museo de Historia** has a relatively diverse collection that comprises five rooms housing a permanent collection of cartoons, examples of graphic design and programmes from past comedic and theatre shows. A temporary exhibition space is given over to local contemporary artists. Even if you can't understand the Spanish punchlines, the imagery alone gives an amusing insight into Cuban humour past and present. Keep an eye out for the monthly tango club and movie nights.

ARRIVAL AND DEPARTURE   SAN ANTONIO DE LOS BAÑOS

By car The simplest route from Havana is to follow the Avenida de Rancho Boyeros to the first major junction heading south from the city, then turn west onto the Pinar del Río road, the *autopista nacional*. Head west for 9km to reach another major junction, for the *autopista del mediodía* which heads south for the 17km to San Antonio de los Baños.

ACTIVITIES

Boating You can rent rowing boats, motorboats, and pedalos from a café (daily 9am–4pm) on a terrace on the banks of the Río Ariguanabo; from the grounds of *Las Yagrumas* hotel, head down to a bend in the river where you'll see the freestanding building.

ACCOMMODATION

Las Yagrumas On the outskirts of town, a block east of Río Ariguanabo ☎ 47 38 4460, ✉ gerencia@yagrumas.co.cu. A family-oriented hotel catering predominantly to Cubans. It's rather rundown, though the large pool set amid the palm-fringed grounds to a bend in the Río Ariguanabo makes a picturesque backdrop. $

Antiguo Cafetal Angerona

Before crossing the provincial border into Pinar del Río, it's worth taking a detour to the **Antiguo Cafetal Angerona**, a nineteenth-century coffee plantation 6km west of the town of Artemisa. Here, where 750,000 coffee plants once grew, you'll find the derelict ruins of the Neoclassical mansion where the owner – a German named Cornelio Souchay – resided, as well as the enslaved people quarters and a 10m-high watchtower, all of it now in the grip of advancing vegetation. Legend has it that Souchay used the seclusion of the plantation to engage in a clandestine interracial affair with a Black Haitian woman named Ursula Lambert, away from the gossip and prejudice of the city. Nowadays, tour groups occasionally visit the site, but you're more likely to be the only visitor wandering about.

Sierra del Rosario

Heading west on the *autopista nacional*, the first attractions you'll come to, just inside the provincial border, are Artemisa's star attractions, the isolated mountain valley resorts at Las Terrazas and Soroa. These are by far the best bases from which to explore the densely packed forest slopes of the protected **Sierra del Rosario**, but only **Las Terrazas** can uphold the claim popularized in tourist literature of connecting tourism with conservation and the local community. Considerably smaller but no less popular than Las Terrazas, **Soroa**'s compact layout makes it more accessible to day-trippers from Havana.

The sierra was declared a Biosphere Reserve by Unesco in 1985, acknowledgement in part for the success of the reforestation project of the 1970s, and visitors are encouraged to explore their surroundings using official **hiking routes**. There's a comprehensive programme of guided hikes at Las Terrazas and some gentler but still rewarding walks around Soroa. Though sometimes referred to as such, the peaks of the Sierra del Rosario don't quite qualify for mountain status, the highest point reaching just under 700m, but there is some fantastic scenery.

THE SIERRA DEL ROSARIO'S BIRDS

A mixture of semitropical rainforest and evergreen forest, the Sierra del Rosario is home to a rich variety of **bird species**, fifty percent of which are endemic to this region. Among the more notable of the seventy-or-so species here are the white-and-red Cuban trogon or *tocororo*, Cuba's national bird, the Cuban grassquit, known in Spanish as the *tomeguín del Pinar*, and the Cuban tody.

Las Terrazas

Daily 9am–5pm • Charge • ⓦ www.lasterrazas.cu

A wonderfully harmonious resort and small working community, **LAS TERRAZAS**, 74km southwest of Havana, is one of the most important ecotourism sites in the country. About 2km beyond the tollbooth on the main access road, where you pay your entry fee unless you're staying at the resort's solitary hotel, there are right- and left-hand side-roads in quick succession. The right turn leads to the Rancho Curujey visitor centre, while the left turn leads several hundred metres down to the **village**, a well-spaced complex of red-roofed bungalows and apartment blocks, beautifully woven into the grassy slopes of a valley, at the foot of which is a man-made **lake**. Below the housing, you can see the compact Las Terrazas village buildings dotted around the lake. Though the cabins look as if they're meant for visitors, they belong to the resident population of around a thousand.

The final stretch of the main road leads up to the other tollbooth (where you won't get charged if you already paid at the Havana end) on the western border of the resort, immediately after which a left turn will take you on the road to Soroa and back to the *autopista*.

Brief history

The Las Terrazas community was founded in 1971, with its residents encouraged to play an active role in the preservation and care of the local environment. They formed the backbone of the workforce, whose first task was a massive government-funded **reforestation project** covering some fifty square kilometres of the Sierra del Rosario. As well as building the village itself, this project entailed planting trees along terraces dug into the hillside, thus guarding against erosion and giving the place its name. This was all part of a grander scheme by the government to promote self-sufficiency and education in rural areas, one of the promises of the Revolution. Today a large proportion of the community works in tourism, some as employees at the hotel and others as owners of the small businesses that have been set up in response to the growing numbers of visitors.

Las Terrazas village workshops

Several sets of steps lead from the *Hotel Moka* back down the slopes into the Las Terrazas village, where small, low-key **workshops** have been set up inside some of the apartment-block buildings. Local artists produce pottery, silkscreen prints, paintings and other crafts and artwork, which you can buy or simply watch being made; though a tad contrived, the latter is still quite engaging.

LAS TERRAZAS & SOROA

■ ACCOMMODATION		● EATING	
Hospedaje Estudio de Arte	5	El Bambú	5
Hotel Moka	1	Café de María	4
Hotel Moka cabins	3	Casa del Campesino	2
Villa Soroa	4	Fonda de Mercedes	3
Villas Moka	2	El Romero	1

2

ACTIVITIES IN LAS TERRAZAS

As well as hiking and birdwatching, there are several other activities on offer in Las Terrazas. Most thrilling is an aerial **canopy tour** of the village on one-man seats suspended from steel cables 25m above the ground. It starts from a platform in the woodlands around the hotel and extends for 800m all the way down to the boating house, the Casa de Botes, on the edge of the lake, stopping at several other platforms along the way. Bookings are taken at the *Hotel Moka* or the Casa de Botes.

More sedate options include **horseriding**, booked at the *Hotel Moka*. The various set rides include 2hr excursions to the *Casa del Campesino* and the Baños de San Juan, a 3hr ride to the Cafetal Buenavista and a couple of 2hr rides, including one that scales the nearby Loma de Taburete. If you want an even more subdued pastime, you can rent **rowing boats** on the lake. The Casa de Botes, where boats are moored, is easy to find just off the main road through the village.

Plaza Comunal

On one side of the gaping trench that separates the two halves of the Las Terrazas village, the **Plaza Comunal** boasts benches, trees and modest views of the lake and valley. It's a focal point for local residents, and gets quite sociable in the evenings.

Peña de Las Terrazas Polo Montañez

Daily 9am–5pm • Charge

Down on the edge of the lake, a signposted right-hand turn from the road into the village leads to the small **Peña de Las Terrazas Polo Montañez** museum. Indistinguishable to all the others from the outside, this cabin was where one of Cuba's most heralded musicians, **Polo Montañez**, lived and gave impromptu concerts before he was killed in a car accident in 2002. The simple little four-room museum exhibits some of Montañez's personal belongings, including his guitars; his bedroom has been left as it was when he lived here.

Cafetal Buenavista

Daily 9am–4pm • Free

A turning next to the Las Terrazas tollbooth at the Havana end of the resort leads to the **Cafetal Buenavista**, an excellent restoration of a nineteenth-century coffee plantation and the final destination for some of the official hikes in the area. French immigrants who had fled Haiti following the 1791 revolution established over fifty coffee plantations across the sierra, but this is the only one to be almost fully reconstructed. The superbly restored stone house, with its high-beamed ceilings, now holds a restaurant, with the food cooked in the original kitchen building behind. The terraces on which the coffee was dried have also been accurately restored, and the remains of the enslaved workers' quarters are complete enough to give you an idea of the incredibly cramped sleeping conditions they experienced.

Baños de San Juan

Daily dawn–dusk • Charge, free if you show a receipt from the Las Terrazas checkpoint

From the south side of Las Terrazas village, at the junction where the road to the hotel begins, another road leads off in the opposite direction for the **Baños de San Juan**. This is a delightful spot featuring natural pools, riverside picnic tables, a simple restaurant and some even simpler cabins providing rudimentary accommodation. From here it's a hop and a skip down to the river, where a footbridge takes you over the water to the paths zigzagging both ways along the river's edge. These mingle with tiny tributaries branching off from the main river, creating a network of walkways punctuated by paved clearings where you can stop and sit under matted roofs. Following the route downstream leads to the focal point here, a small set of clear, natural **pools** fed by dinky waterfalls – ideal for a bit of midday bathing.

Hacienda Unión
Set back from the banks of Río San Juan about 2km west from the Las Terrazas checkpoint, is the neighbouring **Hacienda Unión**, one of the area's partly reconstructed nineteenth-century coffee plantations. A stone path leads down the slope and onto the right-hand fork of the same dirt track that branches off from the main road. There is nothing to restrict you from wandering down and taking a look around the

2

RANCHO CURUJEY AND HIKING AT LAS TERRAZAS

There is no better or more accessible way to experience the diversity and beauty of the Sierra del Rosario than the official **hiking routes** and **nature trails** around Las Terrazas. Of varying lengths and difficulty, each one is characterized by a different destination of historical or ecological interest, and collectively they offer the most comprehensive insight available into the region's topography, history, flora and fauna. All hiking here must be arranged through the Oficinas de Reservaciones y Coordinación at **Rancho Curujey** (☎48 57 8555).

To reach Rancho Curujey from Havana and the west, take the signposted right-hand turnoff from the main through-road just before the left turn that leads to the village and hotel. The centre can supply you with a guide – without which you are not permitted to follow any of the trails through this protected area – and tailor a programme or just a day of walking to your requirements. For groups of six people or more, expect to pay around around $300CUP per person on a pre-booked excursion, though prices vary depending on the size of the group and your specific needs, and can reach $800–1000CUP. You may be able to join another visiting group if you call a day in advance, or if you arrive before 9am. The *Hotel Moka* works closely with Rancho Curujey and can arrange hiking packages for guests.

HIKING ROUTES AND NATURE TRAILS
Cascada del San Claudio (20km) The longest hike offered here lasts a whole day, or around eight to ten hours, and is a gruelling affair, scaling the hills looming over to the northwest of the complex and down the other side to the San Claudio River. But it's well worth it for the reward of pushing through the indigenous flora clinging to the hillsides and the stunning vistas.

El Contento (8km) This pleasant, easy-going hike descends into the valley between two of the local peaks and joins the Río San Juan. It passes the La Victoria ruins, another of the area's old coffee plantations, as well as fresh and sulphurous water springs, and reaches its limit at the Baños de San Juan, a beautiful little set of pools and cascades where you can bathe.

Loma del Taburete (7km) One of the tougher hikes, this route climbs some relatively steep inclines on the way up a 453m-high hill (from the peak of which there are views all the way over to the coast) then slopes down to the Baños de San Juan on the other side, where the hike concludes.

Sendero Las Delicias (3km) This trail finishes up at the Cafetal Buenavista and takes in a viewpoint at the summit of the Loma Las Delicias, from where there are some magnificent panoramic views.

Sendero La Serafina (4km) A nature trail ideal for birdwatching, leading uphill through rich and varied forest. Guides can point out some of the 73 bird species that inhabit the sierra, such as the endemic Cuban tody (catacuba) and the enchanting Cuban nightingale.

Valle del Bayate (7km) On the road to Soroa, 6km from Las Terrazas, a dirt track next to the bridge over the Río Bayate follows the river into the dense forest. Passing first the dilapidated San Pedro coffee plantation, this undemanding trail arrives at the Santa Catalina plantation ruins, a peaceful spot where you can take a dip in the natural pools.

broken stone walls of the plantation, which has at least kept enough of its structure to be recognizable as what it was two centuries ago. The circular grinding mill, with its cone-shaped roof and stone base, is the most intact section and the easiest to spot. The majority of the space here has been given over to the cultivation of various flowers and plants, divided up into small, rock-lined plots forming an attractively laid out, if somewhat rudimentary, **garden**.

Baños de Bayate

On the main through-road for Las Terrazas, 3km past the turning for the *Casa del Campesino* restaurant, another dirt track, this one more of a bone-rattler than the last, winds down about 1km to a section of forest-shrouded river known as the **Baños de Bayate**. The depth and clearness of the water at this lovely spot provides a perfect opportunity to cool off from the jungle's humidity, although its tranquillity is sometimes broken by the screams and shouts of young swimmers leaping into the river.

ARRIVAL AND INFORMATION
LAS TERRAZAS

By bus The Havana-Viñales Víazul route serves Las Terrazas and three buses stop at The Rancho Curujey visitor and information centre a day.

By car Las Terrazas is reached by a signposted 8km turnoff at Km 51 of the *autopista nacional*. Once through a thickly wooded landscape, you continue up to a junction where, a few metres after a left turn, you'll reach a tollbooth marking the beginning of the main through-road to the resort.

Tourist information The Rancho Curujey visitor and information centre (☎ 48 57 8555) has maps of the resort, and can help to book activities around Las Terrazas.

ACCOMMODATION
SEE MAP PAGE 153

★ **Hotel Moka** Comunidad Las Terrazas, 1km northwest of the checkpoint ☎ 48 57 8600. This peaceful hillside hideaway is well worth a visit even if you're not staying, as non-guests can make use of the restaurant and the pool. The graceful main building hugs the surrounding trees, which in some places actually grow through the structure itself. There's an adjoining bar and moderately priced restaurant serving typical Cuban food, while the swimming pool and tennis courts are set further back. Reserving well ahead is advisable. $$$
Hotel Moka cabins Baños de San Juan ☎ 48 57 8600. Set back from the river, at the foot of some grassy slopes

breaking up the woodlands here, are five rooms (known as *cabañas rusticas*) for rent via *Hotel Moka*. They're no more than roof-covered platforms on stilts, aimed squarely at the backpacker set, with no furniture and just about enough space to lay a couple of sleeping bags down. $
Villas Moka Hotel Moka, Comunidad Las Terrazas ☎ 48 57 8600. If you prefer to be among the locals and don't mind having to walk a bit further to use the *Hotel Moka's* facilities, you can stay in one of the five *villas comunitarias* down by the lake. These are effectively *casas particulares* run by the hotel, and are the only way you can stay in a family home here. $$$

EATING AND DRINKING
SEE MAP PAGE 153

El Bambú Baños de San Juan ☎ 48 57 8555. On the riverbank looking over the waterfalls, this rustic café serves simple Cuban food including fried pork and fish with sides of rice and beans. $$
Café de María Las Terrazas village. ☎ 48 57 8527. The freshly ground, locally grown coffee here is splendid whether you have it straight up or go for one of the numerous fancier options like frozen liquor *café*. $
Casa del Campesino Las Terrazas village ☎ 48 52 25 5516. Just beyond the left-hand turn for the hotel and village off the main through-road, a sign indicates the short dirt track to this secluded little woodland ranch housing a restaurant. You can just have a drink or choose from the simple *comida criolla* menu, though you may have to wait a little while for the latter, especially if you arrive before

1pm. You'll need bug repellent to combat the rapacious mosquitoes. $$
Fonda de Mercedes Las Terrazas village ☎ 48 57 8647. A few buildings along from *El Romero*, this open-air restaurant-cum-paladar on a roof-covered balcony platform serves top-notch Cuban cuisine with a real home-cooked flavour. The fried chicken is simple but perfectly executed, while the corn stew and pork fricassee are also prepared with imagination and taste. $$
★ **El Romero** Edificio 5, Las Terrazas village ☎ 48 57 8555. In an apartment building near the steps leading down from the hotel, with a unique menu of organic vegetarian dishes such as a savoury pumpkin pie, vegetable fritters, bean-filled crêpes and chickpea balls marinated in onion and garlic. Small tapas-style portions also available. $$

Soroa

Sixteen kilometres southwest of Las Terrazas, the tiny village of **SOROA** nestles in a long narrow valley. Although a cosy spot, access into the hills is limited and the list of attractions brief, meaning the resort is best suited to a shorter break than a prolonged visit.

El Salto

Daily dawn–dusk • Charge

Most of what you'll want to see is within ten minutes' walk of Soroa, but if you've driven up from the *autopista*, the first place you'll get to, 100m or so from the *Villa Soroa* hotel, is the car park for **El Salto**, a 20m-high waterfall. Though a relatively modest cascade compared to others, a dip in the refreshing waters is a fitting reward for the half-hour walk through the woods to reach it; take the dirt track from the car park.

El Mirador de Soroa

Horses can be arranged at *Villa Soroa*

Signposted from the El Salto car park, the scenic viewpoint of **El Mirador de Soroa** is the more challenging of the two hills in the area, and you may well feel like a massage (see below) after the thirty-minute hike up along an increasingly steep and narrow (though shady) dirt track. While there are a number of possible wrong turns on the way up, you can avoid getting lost by simply following the track with the horse dung – many people choose to ride up on horseback. At the summit you'll find vultures circling the rocky, uneven platform and impressive views over the undulating peaks of palm-smothered hills.

Baños Romanos

Daily 9am–4pm • ☎ 48 52 3534

On the way up to El Mirador de Soroa, a sign points over a small bridge towards the **Baños Romanos**, located in an unassuming stone cabin; massages, cold sulphurous baths and other treatments including acupuncture can be arranged here through the *Villa Soroa* hotel.

El Castillo de las Nubes

El Castillo de las Nubes is the more developed of Soroa's two hilltop viewpoints and the only one you can drive to. The road up to its summit, which you'll have to follow even if you're walking up as there are no obvious trails through the woods, starts from between the car park for El Salto and the hotel. On foot, it shouldn't take more than twenty minutes to reach the hilltop, where there is a perfect lookout spot from the deserted stone house at the end of the road – from here you can see all the way to the province's southern coastline.

Jardín Botánico Orquideario de Soroa

Daily 8.30am–4.30pm • Charge • ☎ 48 57 2558

At the foot of the road up from the El Salto car park to the Soroa summit, the **Jardín Botánico Orquideario de Soroa** is a well-maintained botanical garden specializing in orchids and spreading across 35,000 square metres. Currently used by the University of Pinar del Río, it was constructed in 1943 by Tomás Felipe Camacho, a wealthy lawyer and botanist from the Canary Islands. Until his death in 1960, Camacho dedicated his time to the expansion and glorification of the *orquideario*, travelling the world in search of different species. The obligatory tours are a little rushed, but you get to see flowers, plants, shrubs and trees from around the globe, including some seven hundred species of orchid, in grounds radiating out from a central *villa* where Camacho lived.

ARRIVAL AND DEPARTURE

SOROA

By car The turning from the *autopista* is marked by the first petrol station en route to Pinar del Río from Havana, but you can also get there direct from Las Terrazas along the linking road without returning to the motorway.

ACCOMMODATION

SEE MAP PAGE 153

Hospedaje Estudio de Arte Carretera a Soroa, Km 8.5 ☎ 48 59 8116, ✉ infosoroa@hvs.co.cu. On the right some 500m past *Villa Soroa*, this *casa particular* is a comparable alternative to the hotel. Located in a pleasant household owned by local artist Jesús Gastell Soto and his wife Aliuska, the one a/c room has its own bathroom. ⑤

Villa Soroa Carretera a Soroa, Km 8 ☎ 48 52 3534, ✉ recepcion@hvs.tur.cu. The best place to stay in Soroa, this is a well-kept complex encircling a swimming pool, with comfortable, modern-looking cabins. Three- to six-hour guided treks into the surrounding hillside are available. ⑤

San Diego de los Baños and around

West of Soroa along the *autopista* lie a number of relatively entertaining detours, all within a forty-minute drive of the main road. If you are driving – which is the best option, given no bus routes currently operate to this area from Havana or Pinar del Río city – it's easy to cover them all in a single day. The place you're most likely to spend a night, or at least stop for a meal, is the sleepy town of **San Diego de los Baños**, famous for its health spa, which is said to be the best in the country, though there are now several more modern, upmarket hotel-spas on the island offering better facilities (minus the same range of therapies).

The box-like exterior of the spa contrasts strikingly with the flourishing forests on the other side of the river. When you've had your fill of the waters, you might want to rent bikes and motorbikes at the hotel, or arrange hiking and fishing trips into the hundred square kilometres of protected **woodlands** just a leisurely stroll away. You could also wander around the village to the leafy little square, with its creaking seesaws and swings and church; or spend a few hours in the **cinema**, next door to the *Hotel Mirador*.

From here it's only a short drive to the area's other main attraction: towards the north, the **Cueva de los Portales**, a modestly impressive cave that cuts a dramatic hole straight through the Loma de los Arcos, and which was once the military headquarters of Che Guevara and his army.

Balneario San Diego

Mon–Sat 8am–5pm, Sun 8am–noon • Charges for bathing and treatments • ☎ 48 54 8880

Perched above the river that cuts along the edge of San Diego de los Baños, the **Balneario San Diego**'s reputation for medicinal powers dates back to 1632, when an enslaved worker, forced into isolation because of ill health, took an afternoon dip in the natural springs here and was supposedly instantly cured. Word rapidly spread and the country's infirm began to flock here to be healed. By 1844 a town had been established to provide for the visitors, and eventually a rather utilitarian health spa was built to house the waters, though this didn't take its current shape until after the Revolution.

Nowadays most visitors are tourists, or Cubans on a prescribed course of treatment, as well as for beauty therapy, though you can just take a wallow in the waters. Popular treatments include acupuncture, medicinal mud and apitherapy (the therapeutic use of bee products), a field in which Cuba is reportedly a pioneer.

ARRIVAL AND DEPARTURE

SAN DIEGO DE LOS BAÑOS

By car San Diego de los Baños is 40km west of Soroa on the *autopista*: at Km 100, take the right-hand turning, follow this to its conclusion and then take the right turn (signposted to San Cristóbal); some 12km along, you'll reach the Balneario San Diego.

ACCOMMODATION AND EATING

Hotel Mirador Calle 23 final ☎48 77 8338, ✉ carpeteros@mirador.sandiego.tur.cu. Beautifully set in small-scale landscaped gardens, the pleasantly furnished rooms and overall tranquillity make this the perfect place to stay while visiting the spa; in fact, many of its guests are here on a treatment-plus-accommodation package deal.

Qualified medical specialists work with staff across the road and can arrange consultations and courses of treatment. $\overline{5}\overline{5}$

Restaurante Terraza Hotel Mirador ☎48 77 8338. The hotel restaurant is the only place you can rely on for a meal, offering a selection of fish, meat and basic spaghetti dishes. $\overline{5}\overline{5}$

Cueva de los Portales

There is no public transport and no tours which come here so your only option is to drive. Take the heavily potholed road north of Parque La Güira for 10km before turning at the sign to the now-abandoned *Cabaña Los Pinos* • Daily 8am–5pm • Charge

The gaping hillside corridor known as **Cueva de los Portales** was the suitably remote **former headquarters** of Che Guevara and his army during the Cuban Missile Crisis of October 1962. It was declared a national monument in 1987, and it is its historical rather than geographic significance that will impress. Anyone can drive up and wander in free of charge, and, when you're in the area, it's well worth thirty minutes of your time. If you're lucky, there'll be a guide about to offer a tour of the complex.

The solitary road from Parque La Güira leads all the way to the turning for the cave, a right turn as you are heading north from the park. Then, from a clearing in the woods a stone path leads into and through a wide-open tunnel, the full length of which is visible from outside the high arching entrance. Through the arch, running parallel with the path, is the **Río Caiguanabo**, a tributary of the Río San Diego, which swirls into a natural pool perfect for a post-inspection dip. Off to the side is the headquarters cave itself, a giant chamber adorned with imposing stalactites and stalagmites. Inside are some intriguing remnants of Guevara's occupation – the stone table where he worked and played chess, an unfinished little breeze-block hut that acted as his office and some stone staircases and paths hewn out of the rock.

ACCOMMODATION   CUEVA DE LOS PORTALES

Campismo Los Portales ☎48 49 7347. Though the eleven clean and basic cabins are primarily for Cubans, they are sometimes rented out to tourists, providing there's space. All are equipped with only the bare minimum of

comfort requirements, but everything is in good nick. Among the fittingly simple facilities are a four-table restaurant and a games room with a ping pong table. $\overline{5}$

Pinar del Río city

Stranded out on the far side of the westernmost province in Cuba at the end of the *autopista*, **PINAR DEL RÍO** is, quite simply, a backwater of a city. Close to some more alluring destinations – particularly Viñales, just 25km to the north, but also María La Gorda and the beaches Boca de Galafre and Playa Bailén to the south – the city works best as a base for exploring this half of the province. Despite its 125,000-strong population, Pinar del Río has the feel of a much smaller place, its central streets more reminiscent of a residential neighbourhood than a town centre.

Although it's the capital of the province, Pinar del Río is comparatively undeveloped for tourism: none of the international or upmarket hotel chains is represented here, nightlife is limited and the museums could do with a rethink. On the other hand, countless *casas particulares* are spread all over the city. You'll need no more than a couple of days to get to know the place inside out, and in fact very few visitors spend even that long here. The highlight is the **Fábrica de Tabacos Francisco Donatién**, a diminutive cigar factory offering illuminating tours, while the *Cabaret Rumayor* offers a taste of classic Cuban entertainment whose extravagance feels somewhat out of place in this less-than-cosmopolitan town. If you do find yourself here for any length of time you're probably best spent seeking out a paladar or *casa particular* to suit your taste and retreating to one of these, or lounging around the pool and grounds of the *Hotel Pinar del Río*, away from the attentions of the *jineteros*. To see Pinar del Río in a more favourable light, time your visit to coincide with the November Nosotros music and culture festival when musicians perform for free at stages set up around the central streets. Contact Infotur (see page 162) for dates.

2 Fábrica de Tabacos Francisco Donatién

Antonio Maceo no.157 • Mon–Fri 9am–noon & 1–4pm, Sat 9am–noon • Charge; buy tickets from Casa del Habano • ☎ 48 77 3069

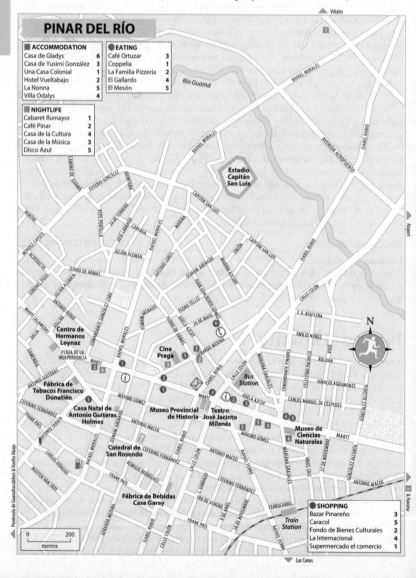

PINAR DEL RÍO

ACCOMMODATION		EATING	
Casa de Gladys	6	Café Ortuzar	3
Casa de Yusimi González	3	Coppelia	1
Una Casa Colonial	1	La Familia Pizzeria	2
Hotel Vueltabajo	2	El Gallardo	4
La Nonna	5	El Mesón	5
Villa Odalys	4		

NIGHTLIFE	
Cabaret Rumayor	1
Café Pinar	2
Casa de la Cultura	4
Casa de la Música	3
Disco Azul	5

SHOPPING	
Bazar Pinareño	3
Caracol	5
Fondo de Bienes Culturales	2
La Internacional	4
Supermercado el comercio	1

Two blocks southeast of the road-bound Plaza de la Independencia, the **Fábrica de Tabacos Francisco Donatién** is the city's premier attraction and home of Vegueros cigars, a lesser-known brand but one that's well respected among connoisseurs. Compared to the Fábrica de Tabacos H Upmann in Havana, however, this place is tiny and the brief guided tour (available in English or French) much less illuminating, though the intimate non-mechanized workshop offers a genuine insight into the care and skill involved in producing some of the world's finest cigars. A small selection of cigar brands is sold in the Fábrica de Tabacos Francisco Donatién shop.

Casa de Tabaco

Antonio Maceo no.162 • Mon–Sat 9am–5pm, Sun 9am–noon • ☎ 48 77 2244

There's a wider choice of cigars in the excellent **Casa de Tabaco**, over the road from the factory. All the best Cuban brands are on sale, and there's a smart little smokers' lounge as well as a café out the back.

Fábrica de Bebidas Casa Garay

Isabel Rubio • Mon–Fri 9am–5pm, Sat 9am–1pm, Sun 8am–noon (shop only) • Charge • ☎ 48 75 2966

Four blocks south of Martí is the **Fábrica de Bebidas Casa Garay** rum factory, founded in 1891 and where the popular Guayabita del Pinar brand is produced. The entrance charge includes a ten-minute guided tour of the three rooms and courtyard that make up the compact factory, beginning in the back room (where barrels of fermenting molasses create a potent smell) and finishing in the claustrophobic bottling and labelling room. Unsurprisingly, bottles of Guayabita are on sale, and you get a free sample of both the dry and sweet versions to help you make your decision.

Museo Provincial de Historia

Martí e/ Isabel Rubio y Colón • Mon noon–4pm, Tues–Sat 8am–10pm, Sun 8am–noon • Charge • ☎ 48 75 4300

The more central of the two museums along Martí is the **Museo Provincial de Historia**. It contains some interesting bits and pieces – including pre-Columbian tools and bones, and displays on the history of tobacco, coffee and slavery in the province – but overall is too disparate to present any kind of coherent narrative about the region. As with all history museums in Cuba, the Revolution is emphasized.

Museo de Ciencias Naturales

Martí esq. Comandante Pinare • Mon–Sat 9am–5pm, Sun 9am–1pm • Charge • ☎ 48 77 9483

Down at the quiet eastern end of Martí, the Palacio de Guach contains the **Museo de Ciencias Naturales**. This eclectic building is the most architecturally striking in the city, its arches mottled with dragons and other monstrous figures and the whole place riddled with elaborate chiselled detail. Inside, each room has a specific theme, and although the ocean and plant rooms seem to be made up of whatever the museum could get its hands on, like bottled fruits and some miscellaneous dried leaves, there are more complete collections of butterflies, moths, exotic insects, shells and birds. Kids will enjoy the convincing giant stone tyrannosaurus and stegosaurus in the courtyard, where there's also a mural depicting other prehistoric creatures.

ARRIVAL AND DEPARTURE   **PINAR DEL RÍO**

By car Arriving in Pinar del Río by car is a breeze, as the *autopista* leads straight into the middle of town. You should be particularly mindful of your speed when entering the city, as one or two of the waiting touts who line the main road are sometimes willing to stand in the middle of the street and flag you down with false urgency; drive on by, as they rarely have anything useful to tell you.

By bus Arriving by bus, whether Astro or Víazul, you'll

be dropped at the Terminal de Omnibus on Adela Azcuy (☎ 48 75 2572), one block from Martí. The station is within walking distance of most of the hotels and a good number of *casas particulares*; although there are usually plenty of private taxis outside the station, they are usually looking to fill their cars for long-distance journeys.

Destinations Havana (2 daily; 3hr); Trinidad (1 daily; 9hr);

Viñales (2 daily; 40min).

By train In the unlikely event that you arrive by train, be prepared for a walk from the small station (☎ 48 75 2272), four blocks south of Martí, as there are rarely any taxis.

Destinations Boca de Galafre (1 daily; 1hr 30min); Havana (1 daily; 5hr); Playa Bailén (1 daily; 1hr 45min); San Cristóbal (1 daily; 3hr).

GETTING AROUND

On foot The city centre is manageable on foot and it's unlikely you'll stray more than three or four blocks either side of Martí.

By car or scooter Most of the city's car rental agencies operate from the *Pinar del Río* hotel at the end of Martí, just before the *autopista*. Cubacar has a desk here (24 hours;

☎ 48 77 8278) and at *Hotel Vueltabajo*, Martí no.103, esq. Rafael Morales (8am–6pm; ☎ 48 77 70 50). Havanautos (daily 8am–6pm; ☎ 48 77 8015) rents scooters and has an office in the car park of the hotel.

By taxi The only taxi rank in town is outside the *Pinar del Río* hotel; otherwise call Turistaxi ☎ 48 75 8080.

INFORMATION AND TOURS

Infotur The most useful and most central information office, based at *Hotel Vueltabajo*, Martí (Mon–Sat 8am–6pm; ☎ 48 72 8616), offering general information about the region as well as hotel reservations, car rental, guided city tours and excursions to many of the province's highlights.

Cubanacán Also on Martí no.115 (Mon–Sat 8am–noon & 1–5pm; ☎ 48 75 0178) and offering hotel reservations, car

rental, guided city tours and excursions.

Cubatur Less than a block from the main street on Martí no.51 esq. Rosario (Mon–Fri 8am–5pm, Sat 8am–noon; ☎ 48 77 8405), can take tour bookings.

Havanatur At Martí esq. Colón (Mon–Sun 8am–6pm; ☎ 48 77 8494); services include hotel reservations, plane tickets sales, guided city tours and excursions.

ACCOMMODATION

SEE MAP PAGE 160

HOTEL

★ **Hotel Vueltabajo** Martí no.103, esq. Rafael Morales ⓦ islazulhotels.com. This delightful little place is easily the prettiest and most comfortable option in the centre. The stylish colonial facade, with its dinky balustraded, canopy-covered balconies, is complemented by a handsome, simple interior full of polished wood, shining floors and reasonably well-appointed rooms. $\overline{\underline{\text{$\$$}}}$

CASAS PARTICULARES

★ **Casa de Gladys** Ave. Comandante Pinares no.15 e/ Martí y Máximo Gómez ☎ 48 77 9698, ⓔ alexdj@nauta. cu. Both the rooms for rent in this huge house next to the Museo de Ciencias Naturales have double beds and en-suite bathroom, and there are some memorable furnishings, like the matching colonial-style wardrobe, bed and dresser in one room. Secure parking for two cars and a fantastic backyard complete with a fountain. $\overline{\underline{\text{$\$$}}}$

Casa de Yusimi González Martí no.164 e/ Ave. Cmdte Pinares y Calle Nueva ☎ 48 75 2818. A complete apartment with two a/c rooms, a kitchen with hob, and a pleasant living room with a balcony overlooking a lively

road complete with passing horse-drawn carriages. $\overline{\underline{\text{$\$$}}}$

Una Casa Colonial Gerardo Medina no.67 e/ Isidro de Armas y Adela Azcuy ☎ 48 75 3173, ⓔ popiro1952@ nauta.cu. The nearest thing to a privately-run hotel in Pinar del Río. The rooms, many with en-suite bathrooms, are gathered around a lovely patio garden where there's a tiny restaurant area and an impressive outdoor jacuzzi. There's space for three cars in the garage. Its success is such that there are several imitators using the same name elsewhere in the city so make sure you confirm your booking with the details provided here. $\overline{\underline{\text{$\$$}}}$

La Nonna Máximo Gómez no.161 e/ Rafael Ferro y Ciprian Valdés ☎ 48 77 0777, ⓔ karla104@nauta.cu. There are three rooms available in this lavishly appointed house. Two of the rooms have two double beds apiece, while one has one double bed. All have a/c and a private bathroom. Breakfast is served on a pretty plant-filled terrace. $\overline{\underline{\text{$\$$}}}$

Villa Odalys Martí no.158 e/ Ave. Comandante Pinares y Calle Nueva ☎ 48 75 5212. Two rooms each with its own bathroom and kitchen in a friendly house. One room has the added virtue of a sunny terrace. $\overline{\underline{\text{$\$$}}}$

EATING

SEE MAP PAGE 160

A clutch of new paladars have given Pinar del Río's lacklustre eating scene something of a boost and you can now dine,

if not exactly in high style, with ample satisfaction in a number of well-tended and personable paladars all within

ORGANIZED EXCURSIONS FROM PINAR DEL RÍO

One of the best reasons to stay in Pinar del Río is to use it as a base for **excursions** into the nearby countryside. The national travel agents Havanatur, Cubanacán and Cubatur offer a number of day-trips, along with some one- and two-night stays, to the province's main tourist spots as well as a selection of hard-to-get-to attractions. Discover Vinales also offer an extensive range of private, group, and personalised tours. As public transport is particularly poor within Pinar del Río province, an organized excursion is often the only (and certainly the easiest) way to get to these destinations if you don't have your own vehicle. Even if you do have a car, the poor roads, lack of maps and road signs, and basic remoteness involved in many journeys here mean the various excursions detailed below are all the more useful. What follows is a list of a small selection of tours currently offered.

Birdwatching tours of Viñales Discover Viñales also offer an expert-guided birdwatching trip to key sites in Viñales National Park. Expect to see the Cuban trogon, the Cuban solitaire, the Cuban bullfinch, the Cuban grassquit, the tawny-shouldered blackbird, the summer tanager, the red-legged honeycreeper, and multiple flycatchers, woodpeckers and kingbirds.

Cayo Levisa One of the area's most popular day-trips is to the small resort on this offshore cay. Cubanacán offers various packages.

Gran Caverna de Santo Tomás Both Havanatur and Cubanacán offer tours of the extensive cave systems near Viñales valley.

Tobacco Tour A day-trip to the Vuelta Abajo region (see page 175) with Discover Vinales (w discover-vinales.com) takes in a tobacco farm, a UBPC (farming cooperative) and cigar factory .

Viñales See all the main sights in the Viñales valley, such as the Mural de la Prehistoria, the Cueva del Indio, El Jardín de Caridad, Mirador Los Jazmines, and an ecological farm, with Discover Vinales.

---

a few minutes' walk of the centre.

Café Ortuzar Martí no.127 w cafeortuzarcuba.com. This picturesque marble patio, sequestered behind low balustrades and iron railings, is one of the best places for a quiet drink or coffee away from the madding crowds. Sweet and creamy flan and other short eats make it a good place to linger. It's also great for dinner, with a range of vegetarian options and an extensive wine list. $\overline{\underline{\$\$}}$

Coppelia Gerardo Medina e/ Antonio Rubio y Isidro de Armas. Good-value ice cream: standard flavours are chocolate or strawberry, and more exotic options like chocolate ripple and guava are available intermittently. $\overline{\underline{\$}}$

La Familia Pizzeria Martí no.117. The crowd spilling onto the pavement stands testament to the quality of these bumper-value, classic thick-crust Cuban pizzas. $\overline{\underline{\$}}$

El Gallardo Martí no.207 (frente al Museo de Ciencias Naturales) w facebook.com/El-Gallardo. A canopied restaurant area with rustic wooden-and-hide furniture that serves simple and inexpensive *comida criolla* including grilled pork, prawns cooked in rum, fried chicken and rice and beans $\overline{\underline{\$\$}}$

★ **El Mesón** Martí e/ Pinares y Pacheco w facebook. com/elmeson1995. You'll find Pinar's best *comida criolla* in this beautifully maintained colonial house. The roast chicken and breaded pork steak with sides of fried malanga, green bananas along with rice and beans are particularly good, all served with a flourish. $\overline{\underline{\$\$}}$

NIGHTLIFE AND ENTERTAINMENT

Don't expect much **nightlife** until the weekend, when Pinar del Río's main streets buzz with young people. That said, there is a reasonable spread of **live music venues** open during the week, and if you're here over a weekend, it's worth investigating the programme at the **theatre**; although in Spanish, performances here offer an authentic insight into Cuban culture.

LIVE MUSIC VENUES   SEE MAP PAGE 160

★ **Cabaret Rumayor** Carretera Viñales Km 1 ☎ 48 76 3051. Like most cabarets in Cuba, the show here is drenched in gaudy 1970s-style glamour, and the open-air setting adds to the drama of a seemingly endless sequence of song-and-dance routines from tearful ballads to button-busting showtime numbers. It's not all glitzy throwbacks, though; the venue also has a wide-ranging roster of modern-day Cuban crooners, salsa bands and comedians. Food also available.

Café Pinar Gerardo Medina e/ Antonio Rubio y Isidro de Armas. The one place in town that can generally be relied upon to deliver a buzz, though the music here – often played live – doesn't get going until 11pm or so, by which time the place is typically bumping with dressed-up locals.

Casa de la Cultura Martí no.65 e/ Rafael Morales y Rosario ☎ 48 75 2324. There are regular bolero and danzón nights here as well as a *peña campesina*, a traditional rural

Cuban song and dance. Entrance is free.

Casa de la Música Gerardo Medina ☎48 75 4794. Staged in an open-air courtyard, the pleasantly entertaining unpretentious son, bolero and salsa shows here cater to an undemanding audience.

CLUB SEE MAP PAGE 160

Disco Azul Hotel Pinar del Río, Martí ☎48 75 5070. Just before the *autopista*, this is the only real nightclub in town, with slick decor and a playlist that mixes reggaeton, salsa and pop.

THEATRES

Teatro José Jacinto Milanés Martí no.60 e/ Recreo y Colón ☎48 75 3871. This elegant nineteenth-century venue has a regular programme of theatre and comedy as well as international and national dance shows. Highlights include local slapstick comedians and inventive contemporary theatre productions, often with quasi-political themes.

SHOPPING SEE MAP PAGE 160

Bazar Pinareño Martí no.28 e/ Gerardo Medina y Isabel Rubio. A small but worthy collection of Cuban music CDs is complemented by some screen-printed film and propaganda posters.

Caracol Maceo esq. Antonio Tarafa. You'll find a good selection of Cuban music CDs here.

Fondo de Bienes Culturales Martí esq. Gerardo Medina. This market has quite a good range of nut and seed jewellery, plus ugly leather sandals and clay figurines.

La Internacional Martí esq. Colón. A small selection of books that may be of interest to foreign visitors, including some specialist guidebooks, coffee-table photography and some English–Spanish dictionaries.

Supermercado el comercio Martí Oeste y Arenado. The best of the several supermarkets on Martí, this one sells groceries, toiletries and cheap clothing.

DIRECTORY

Baseball The 14,000-capacity Estadio Capitán San Luis (☎48 75 4290), near the road to Viñales Pinar del Río, has one of the most successful baseball teams in the national league, with games usually played Tues–Thurs & Sat from 7.30pm start, and Sun from 4pm.

Health Hospital Abel Santamaría, Carretera Central Km 3 ☎48 76 2068. Ring ☎104 for an emergency ambulance. The only pharmacy for tourists is in the *Pinar del Río* hotel.

Money and exchange The best bank for foreign currency transactions and credit-card withdrawals is the Banco Financiero Internacional at Gerardo Medina no.46 e/ Isidro de Armas y Martí (Mon–Fri 8am–3pm). Banco de Crédito y Comercio has branches at Martí no.32 e/ Isabel Rubio y Gerardo Medina (Mon–Fri 8am–noon & 1.30–3pm, Sat 8–11am) and Martí e/ Rosario (Ormani Arenado) y Rafael Morales (same hours). The latter has a 24hr cashpoint outside. The CADECA *casas de cambio* are on Gerardo Medina e/ Antonio Rubio y Isidro de Armas and Martí no.46 e/ Isabel Rubio y Gerardo Medina (both Mon–Sat 8.30am–5.30pm, Sun 8.30am–12.30pm).

Police Dial ☎48 75 2525, or ☎106 in case of emergency.

Post office The main branch is at Martí esq. Isabel Rubio, where you can make photocopies.

Swimming pools The pool at the *Hotel Pinar del Río*, at the end of Martí just before the *autopista* is your best bet for poolside lounging within the town. Non-guests can also use the pool at the *Aguas Claras* hotel, 7.5km from Pinar del Río at Carretera de Viñales (☎48 77 8426).

Wi-fi The local ETECSA Telepunto at Gerardo Medina no.127 esq. Juan Gualberto Gómez (daily 8.30am–6.30pm) has several internet terminals. You can also buy wi-fi access cards here. Pinar's two main wi-fi hotspots are Parque Independencia and Parque Roberto Amarán.

The Viñales valley

An official **national park** and by far the most visited location in Pinar del Río, the jewel in the province's crown is the valley of **VIÑALES**, with its fantastically located accommodation, striking landscapes and an atmosphere of complete serenity. Though only 25km north of Pinar del Río city, the valley feels very remote, with a lost-world quality that's mainly due to the unique *mogotes*, the boulder-like hills that look as if they've dropped from the sky onto the valley floor. These bizarre hillocks were formed by erosion during the Jurassic period, some 160 million years ago. Rainfall slowly ate away at the dissolvable limestone and flattened much of the landscape, leaving a few survivors behind, their lumpy surface today coated in a bushy layer of vegetation. Easily the most photographed examples are the **Mogote Dos Hermanas** or "twin sisters", two huge cliffy mounds hulking next to one another on the west side of the valley, with

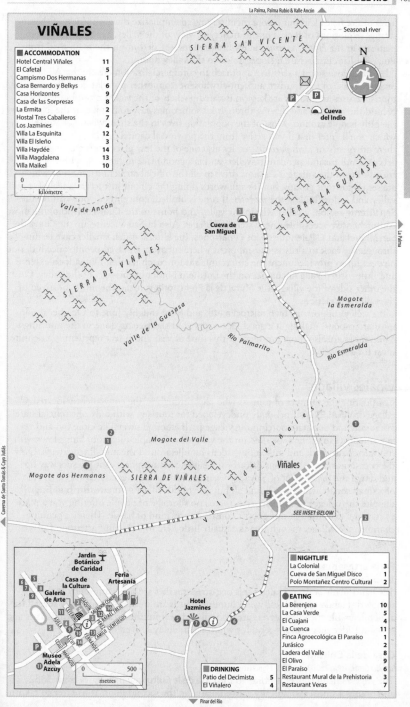

La Palma, Palma Rubio & Valle Ancón

VIÑALES

SIERRA SAN VICENTE

N

--- Seasonal river

2

ACCOMMODATION

Hotel Central Viñales	11
El Cafetal	5
Campismo Dos Hermanas	1
Casa Bernardo y Belkys	6
Casa Horizontes	9
Casa de las Sorpresas	8
La Ermita	2
Hostal Tres Caballeros	7
Los Jazmines	4
Villa La Esquinita	12
Villa El Isleño	3
Villa Haydée	14
Villa Magdalena	13
Villa Maikel	10

Cueva del Indio

0   1
kilometre

Valle de Ancón

SIERRA LA GUASASA

Cueva de San Miguel

La Palma

SIERRA DE VIÑALES

Mogote la Esmeralda

Valle de la Guesasa

Río Palmarito

Río Esmeralda

Caverna de Santo Tomás & Cayo Judás

Mogote del Valle

Viñales

Mogote dos Hermanas

SIERRA DE VIÑALES

SEE INSET BELOW

CARRETERA A MONCADA

Valle de Viñales

Jardín Botánico de Caridad

Feria Artesanía

Casa de la Cultura

Galería de Arte

Hotel Jazmines

NIGHTLIFE
La Colonial	3
Cueva de San Miguel Disco	1
Polo Montañez Centro Cultural	2

Museo Adela Azcuy

0   500
metres

EATING
La Berenjena	10
La Casa Verde	5
El Cuajani	4
La Cuenca	11
Finca Agroecológica El Paraíso	1
Jurásico	2
Ladera del Valle	8
El Olivo	9
El Paraíso	6
Restaurant Mural de la Prehistoria	3
Restaurant Veras	7

DRINKING
Patio del Decimista	5
El Viñalero	4

Pinar del Río

acres of flat fields laid out before them serving to emphasize the abruptness of these strange explosions of rock. For the archetypal **view** of the valley, head for the viewing platform at the *Hotel Jazmines*, a few hundred metres' detour off the main road from Pinar del Río, just before it slopes down to the valley floor.

Laidback locals and a sensitive approach to commercialization ensure that Viñales retains a sense of pre-tourism authenticity absent from other popular destinations. The tourist centres and hotels are kept in isolated pockets of the valley, often hidden away behind the *mogotes*, and driving through it's sometimes easy to think that the locals are the only people around. Most of the population lives in the small **village** of Viñales, which you'll enter first if you arrive from the provincial capital or Havana, and where there are plenty of *casas particulares*. It's also one of the few places in the country that acts as a hub for independent travellers and is a good place to hook up with travel friends. From the village it's a short drive to all the official attractions, most of which are set up for tour groups, but it's still worth doing the circuit just to get a feel of the valley and a close look at the *mogotes*. If time is limited, concentrate your visit on the **San Vicente** region, a valley within the valley and home to the **Cueva del Indio**, the most comprehensive accessible cave system in Viñales. Also in San Vicente are the **Cueva de San Miguel** and **El Palenque de los Cimarrones**, the latter a much smaller cave leading through the rock to a rustic encampment where runaway enslaved people once hid, but now set up to provide lunchtime entertainment for coach parties. Difficult-to-explore and little-visited **Valle Ancón** lies on the northern border of this part of the valley. On the other side of the village, the **Mural de la Prehistoria** is by far the most contrived of the valley's attractions.

The valley supports its own **microclimate**, and from roughly June to October it rains most afternoons, making it a good idea to get your sightseeing done in the mornings. Mosquitoes are also more prevalent at this time of year and insect repellent is a definite must for any visit.

Viñales village

Considering the number of tourists who pass through it, the conveniently located village of **VIÑALES** is surprisingly undeveloped for tourism, with only one official state restaurant and one state hotel in the village itself (though several lie close by) and very few amenities in general. Nestled on the valley floor, simple tiled-roof bungalows with sunburnt paintwork and unkempt gardens huddle around the pine-lined streets. Only the occasional car or tour bus disturbs the laidback atmosphere as it plies its way up and down the main street of Salvador Cisnero, which slopes gently down either side of a small square where you'll find all but one of the village's noteworthy buildings. Despite the village's diminutive size, there's no shortage of people offering you a place to stay or a taxi, though this doesn't constitute any kind of hassle. There's a genuine charm to the village, though there's actually little here to hold your attention for very long.

Feria artesanía
Salvador Cisnero • Daily 9am–7pm

The hand-made crafts on sale at this one-street market are of an unusually high standard. Hand-carved, local-wood hummingbirds are small enough to buy several for a mobile, while the salad servers are smooth and well finished. Elsewhere straw hats and cartoon fridge magnets are good for whimsical holiday souvenirs.

Casa de la Cultura
Salvador Cisnero • Daily 7am–3pm & 3.30–11pm • Free

The village's main square is home to the **Casa de la Cultura**, which dates from 1832 and houses a small, sporadically active theatre on the second floor. You're free to take

ACTIVITIES AROUND VIÑALES

Paradiso (see page 168) can arrange **dance classes** and **percussion lessons** as well as **horseriding** around the valley, as do Havanatur (see page 168) and the hotels. There are also plenty of local residents who, for a fee, can fix you up with an unofficial tour through the valley by horse – you won't have to ask around for long before someone obliges, assuming the price is right.

Though **rock climbing** has become increasingly popular in Viñales over the last ten years, it is still not state-approved and there are no official guides or routes. The US website ⓦcubaclimbing.com has some good information on tried-and-tested routes in the region, though it's not updated regularly. There are long-standing plans to establish official climbing routes, so check with the Centro de Visitantes (see page 168) for the latest information.

2

a quick peek upstairs, where there's still some old colonial-style furniture and a partial view of the hills.

Galería de Arte
Salvador Cisnero • Daily 8am–11pm • Free

Next door to the Casa de la Cultura, the diminutive **Galería de Arte** displays small collections of paintings by local artists. Most are somewhat mawkish acrylic landscapes of the Viñales valley, though there's a handful of more original abstracts thrown in for good measure.

Jardín Botánico de Caridad
C.P. Esperanza • Daily 8am–5pm • Free

A five-minute walk north from the plaza just beyond the end of Salvador Cisnero, the most intriguing of the village's attractions is the densely packed garden referred to as the **Jardín Botánico de Caridad**. A gate adorned with pieces of real fruit marks the easily missable entrance of these almost fairy-tale grounds. The compact, shady garden is a botanist's dream, squeezing in all kinds of trees, shrubs and plants – papaya, begonias, orchids, mango and starfruit trees and many others. A guide is usually around to help you pick your way through, explaining and identifying all the plants and noting many of their medicinal qualities, making it clear that there is order among this seeming chaos.

Museo Adela Azcuy
Salvador Cisnero no.115 • Tues–Sat 8am–8pm, Sun 1–4pm • Charge

Heading west down Salvador Cisnero from the plaza is the lightweight though relatively engaging municipal museum, the **Museo Adela Azcuy**. Its four small rooms present an eclectic picture of local history, geology and culture, as well as bits and pieces of tourist information. Exhibits include a mock-up of the wall of a *mogote* and a short corridor dressed up to resemble a cave chamber, complete with stalactites. There is also a scant set of objects relating to the one-time occupant of the house, **Adela Azcuy** herself, one of the few women to fight in armed combat and be hailed in Cuba as a heroine of the nineteenth-century Wars of Independence.

ARRIVAL AND DEPARTURE VIÑALES VILLAGE

By bus All buses pull up opposite the main square, outside the Víazul ticket office (ⓣ48 79 3112) at Salvador Cisnero no.63a. From here all the *casas particulares* in the village are within walking distance, but to get to any of the hotels you'll need to catch a taxi or the local tourist bus.

Destinations Cienfuegos (2 daily; 9.5hr); Havana (2 daily; 4hr 30min); Pinar del Río (2 daily; 40min); Trinidad (2 daily; 8hr).

By minibus transfer An appealingly hassle-free way to get to the capital and beyond, minibus transfers can be booked through any of the travel agents in the village, or through the Víazul ticket office on Salvador Cisnero. As there are often more prospective passengers than seats on the Havana-bound services, it's wise to book your onward journey several days prior to travel, particularly in peak seasons.

By taxi You can take a *colectivo* taxi to Havana by arrangement with Cubataxi (☎52 94 5047 or ☎53 10 1227) which shares an office with Víazul at Salvador Cisnero no.63a. Taxis leave sporadically throughout the day, and only if they are full, so it's best to arrive early to guarantee departure. Havana is the most regular destination, though Cienfuegos and Trinidad are also served. Taxis will drop you at your door in your destination city. Touts for unlicensed taxis also hang around outside the office.

GETTING AROUND

By car Car rental is available from Havanautos (☎48 79 6330) at the petrol station on Salvador Cisnero on the northeastern edge of town. There's also Cubacar (☎48 79 6060), in the Cubanacán office on Salvador Cisnero opposite the square.

By tourist bus The easiest way of getting around is on the hop-on, hop-off Viñales Bus Tour, an extremely convenient minibus service with stops at all the tourist attractions in the area and hotels. It runs daily from 9am to 6pm and begins at the bus stop just outside the main square on Salvador Cisnero. Tickets can be bought on the bus itself and are valid for a whole day.

By scooter The best place for scooter rental is Palmares Motoclub, opposite the *Casa de Don Tomás* restaurant on Salvador Cisnero. You can also try Havanautos at the petrol station on Salvador Cisnero, or Cubanacán at Salvador Cisnero no.63c. A third option is at the Centro de Visitantes (see below) for a comparable price.

By bike Cubanacán, Salvador Cisnero no.63c, rents out bikes. You can also rent mountain bikes from Palmares.

By taxi Transtur (☎48 76 80 78).

INFORMATION AND TOURS

Information Centro de Visitantes Viñales' visitor centre at Carretera a Viñales Km 23 (daily 9am–6pm; ☎48 79 6144, ✉reservas@pnvinales.co.cu), on the road into the village from Pinar del Río, has a permanent exhibition dedicated to the geography and political history of the area and a panoramic viewing platform overlooking the valley. It also offers various activities, including hiking and horseriding.

Infotur The office at Salvador Cisnero no.63b (Mon–Sat 8.30–4.45pm; ☎48 79 6263) offers local information from helpful staff, some tours and good-quality maps.

Cubanacán At Salvador Cisnero no.63c (daily 8.30am–12.30pm & 1.30–9pm, usually closes early Sept–Oct and April–May; ☎48 79 6393) and with a similar set of services to Havanatur.

Havanatur The biggest national travel agent, at Salvador Cisnero no.84 (daily 8am–10pm, usually closes early Sept–Oct and April–May; ☎48 79 6262), offering one-day visits to locations around Viñales and beyond and a useful long-distance minibus service.

Paradiso Various cultural activities and excursions, as well as horseriding trips, walking tours, mountain biking and dance classes are available to book from the office-cum-bookshop at Salvador Cisnero no.65 (daily 8.30am–8pm; ☎48 79 6258).

ACCOMMODATION

SEE MAP PAGE 165

There's an even spread of good **places to stay** in the Viñales valley, with options to suit all tastes and budgets, from two of the best-situated and most attractive **hotels** in Cuba to a surprising abundance of **casas particulares**, many of which have views of the *mogotes*. Finding the latter shouldn't be a problem, as most have signs outside and buses dropping tourists in Viñales village are usually met by a crowd of locals equipped with business cards; but note that despite the large number of rooms, demand often far outweighs supply and the whole village is sometimes full to capacity by 7pm – make sure you book *casas particulares* during the day. Mosquito repellent is a necessity if you're going to stay in one of the places on the valley floor, otherwise you'll be plagued throughout the night.

HOTELS

Hotel Central Viñales Salvador Cisnero Street Esq. Ceferino Fernández ☎48 69 5815. Viñales' only town hotel is graceful, airy and well-located, on the edge of the plaza within easy walking distance of all the main attractions. The 23 rooms are spacious and well appointed, with a/c and a minibar. Inside, there's a restaurant and snack bar while outside a wrap-around verandah makes a good spot for a cooling drink at sundown. While there's no pool, guests are able to use the ones at La Ermita and Los Jazmines free of charge. $$

★ **La Ermita** Carretera de Ermita Km 2, ⓦhotelescubanacan.com. Gorgeous open-plan hotel in immaculate grounds high above the valley floor, with panoramic views of the San Vicente valley and out beyond the *mogotes*. The tidy complex features three dignified apartment blocks with columned balconies, a central pool, a tennis court, a wonderful balcony restaurant and a comprehensive programme of optional activities

ORGANIZED EXCURSIONS FROM VIÑALES

All the travel agents in the village offer very similar and similarly priced excursions, day-trips and transfers around Viñales and the rest of the province. Here are a few suggested tours, with the average prices you can expect to pay. Contact Discover Viñales (ⓦ discover-vinales.com) for more tour options in the region; they're also open to organizing personalized trips.

ORGANIZED TOURS

Cayo Jutías This subdued offshore cay is actually so easy to get to that you're better off visiting independently if you have your own car. $400CUP.

Cayo Levisa This daily excursion is an uncomplicated way of getting over to the more developed but less accessible of the two visitor-friendly cays in the province. The cheapest option covers transportation only; lunch is included for the more expensive choice. $1000–1200CUP.

Pinar del Río A day-trip to the provincial capital, including a visit to the cigar factory. $1500CUP.

Recorrido por Viñales A tour of the valley that takes in all the major attractions, with lunch included. It's particularly worthwhile if you fancy eating outside the village or hotels, as many of the restaurants around the valley tailor their meal times to suit visiting tour groups. $1000CUP.

Ruta del Tabaco This day-trip is like a day in the life of a cigar, taking you from its inception as a seedling on a tobacco farm, through the crop fields and then onto the drying houses and finally the cigar factory. Various farms are visited including Alejandro Robaino. $1600CUP including lunch.

Sendero por el valle This three-hour hike from the village into the valley is a great way to explore beyond the roads that most visitors stick to, visiting a tobacco plantation along the way. $250CUP.

WALKING TOURS AND HIKES

The staff at the Museo Adela Azcuy (see page 167) organize walking tours in the valley setting off daily at 9am and 3pm (1–4hr; $200CUP per person). The **Centro de Visitantes** (see page 168) offers various hikes around the valley with an ecological slant, including trips to a tobacco plant and a traditionally run farm, excursions through areas of endemic wildlife and a walk through the centre of a *mogote* called Cueva Silencio. Treks start at 9am and 2pm from the centre, last between two and a half and three hours, and typically cost $150CUP.

---

and excursions including horseriding, trekking and birdwatching. Rooms are tasteful and reasonably well equipped. $\overline{\underline{\$\$}}$

Los Jazmines Carretera a Viñales Km 25 ⓦ hotelescubanacan.com. There are stunning views of the most photographed section of the valley from virtually every part of the hotel complex, including the elegant colonial-style main building and its balconied restaurant. While the rooms themselves (some in a separate, more modern block and a few in red-roofed cabins) could do with a makeover, the dinner buffet isn't bad, there's a pool, and it's all about the views here. $\overline{\underline{\$\$}}$

CASAS PARTICULARES

★ **El Cafetal** Adela Azcuy Norte final ☎ 53 31 1752, ✉ elcafetalvinales@nauta.cu. Nestled in the lee of the mountains with a beautiful view of the countryside, this idyllic spot has two rooms, each with two beds and en-suite bathrooms. The garden, complete with mango trees and coffee plants, is bedecked with hammocks from which to soak up the atmosphere. The owners can organize rock climbing, walking and horseriding tours. $\overline{\underline{\$}}$

Casa Bernardo y Belkys Adela Azcuy Norte no.36 ☎ 53 74 6729 or ☎ 48 69 5669, ✉ bernardoybelkyscasa@ nauta.cu. Two well-appointed rooms in a quiet house each with a sparkling bathroom. An attractive breakfast area has views over the mountains. $\overline{\underline{\$}}$

Casa Horizontes Sergio Dopico Norte no.40A ☎ 48 695182, ✉ fnodarse@nauta.cu. The upper floor of this sugar-pink house offers two double rooms and their own bathrooms. The terrace has fantastic views over the *mogotes*. $\overline{\underline{\$}}$

Casa de las Sorpresas Adela Azcuy Norte no.47A ☎ 48 69 5675. This beautifully maintained property has two

2

double rooms each with twin double beds and a kitchen. There are two further double rooms in the next-door property which is owned by extended family. A sun terrace overlooks tobacco fields and the mountains. The owners offer excursions and an occasional surprise (hence the name) for guests. $

Hostal Tres Caballeros Sergio Dopico Norte no.20 ☎ 48 79 6166, ✉ chostaltrescaballeros@nauta.cu. Two a/c rooms, each with en-suite bathroom, in a lovely house on one of the roads that leads out of the village into the countryside. A terrace overlooks the *mogotes* while there are also front and back verandas. $

Villa La Esquinita Rafael Trejo no.18 e/ Mariana Grajales y Joaquín Pérez ☎ 48 79 6303. One of the a/c rooms for rent in this spruced-up house has three beds – two double and one single – while the other has two beds and is en suite, with a fridge. Outside is a bountiful fruit and vegetable plot, and a menagerie of animals. $

★ **Villa El Isleño** Carretera a Pinar del Río ☎ 48 79 3107, ✉ lauren.gonzales91@yahoo.es. Right on the edge of the village and one of the first houses you'll come to if you've driven from the provincial capital, this handsome place offers three excellent double rooms in a separate

block out the back with its own terrace. There's also a self-contained rustic cabin, and a patio to dine on, surrounded by tropical plants and covered by a thatched roof. The backyard shares a border with a tobacco field and there are views of the Mogote Dos Hermanas. $

★ **Villa Haydée** Chiroles Rafael Trejo no.139 ⓦ casahaydee.blogspot.com. Centrally located on the road behind the main drag, this airy and spacious house has six rooms each with private bathroom. An ample sun terrace makes an ideal spot from which to view the *mogotes*. Owner Aylen works at Infotur so is very well informed and can also organize tours, excursions and salsa lessons. $

Villa Magdalena Rafael Trejo no.41 esq. Ceferino Fernández ☎ 48 79 6029. One of the only colonial houses in the village backstreets, with a grand-looking, pillar-lined porch. Both double rooms have a/c and en-suite bathrooms, and one has a walk-in closet. A large, friendly family lives here. $

Villa Maikel Rafael Trejo no.14B ☎ 48 69 6700, ✉ leamay@nauta.cu. Pleasant five-room house close to the centre with helpful owners. One room has three beds, suitable for a family. Excursions, minibar and various extras are also on offer. $

EATING
SEE MAP PAGE 165

Even those with jaded palates, bored of rice and beans, should find something to delight in Viñales. The village streets are peppered with interesting places to eat throughout the day and evening – there's even a couple of **vegetarian options**. Many of the out-of-town hillside options serve banquet buffet set menus; the quantity of food served to one is often enough for two hungry people. In response to the competition, *casas particulares* have upped their game too, so if you decide to dine where you're staying you'll generally be assured an excellent meal – and prices are often lower than at paladars, too.

La Berenjena Mariana Grajales No 1 e/Salvador Cisneros ☎ 48 69 6733. Though you'll find several meat options at this purportedly vegetarian restaurant, it's the vegetable options that shine through. Aubergine sliced with pumpkin in sauce and refried beans are good options. The juices also come in interesting combinations like guava, mint and cumin. $$

★ **La Casa Verde** 50m from Hotel Los Jazmines ☎ 48 69 5776. Genial proprietors, a great location in a tropical garden overlooking the mountains and an abundance of well-prepared food make this one of the most popular paladars in the area. A wide array of *comida criolla* is served, with the perfectly cooked fresh fish particularly good. Sides include sweet potato chips and rice and beans. Home-grown coffee and rum are often included on the house, too. $$

El Cuajani El Carretera Moncada km 2.2 Dos Hermanas ☎ 588 28 925. The *comida criolla* served in this scenic

clapperboard house at the foot of the *mogote* goes one step further than most. The food is beautifully presented and the daily menu is created from what's been harvested in the owner's surrounding garden. Expect mains such as white-bean hummus and pumpkin risotto. $$

La Cuenca Salvador Cisnero no.97 ☎ 48 69 6968. Striking black and white design make this arguably the most stylish restaurant on the strip. The food stands up well too with a range of decent pastas like carbonara and lasagne along with some *comida criolla* including roast rabbit and lamb, and more ambitious plates like duck in orange and mango sauce. Friendly staff and excellent cocktails add to the allure. $$

★ **Finca Agroecológica El Paraíso** Carretera Al Cementerio Km 1.5 Wilfredo Garcia Correa ☎ 581 88 581. Much of the abundant and delicious banquet served at this hillside organic farm has been grown or raised there. The *comida criolla* meal includes succulent lamb, BBQ chicken, pork, tuna fish, shrimp, all served with a range of sides including shredded cabbage, pickled cucumber, avocado and stuffed *tostones*. The panoramic views over the surrounding vegetable garden and countryside beyond complete the excellent dining experience. Reservations essential. $$$

Ladera del Valle Los Jazmines, Carretera a Viñales Km 23 ☎ 58 18 8998. Within sight of the Centro de Visitantes, this paladar in an atmospheric clapboard house with a thatched roof serves solid and dependable *comida criolla*. Dishes include barbecued pork and chicken roasted to a turn on an open grill, as well as lobster. $$

2

El Olivo Salvador Cisnero no.89 ✆ 48 69 6654. Combines ambience, attentive service and an interesting menu. The plates are largely Spanish and Italian, with choices like Andalucian pork skewers, roast lamb with vegetables and chicken in white wine sauce all reasonably well executed. Vegetarians are catered for too with a number of interesting small plates including fresh cheese with dressing, mixed grilled vegetables and *gazpacho*. $$

El Paraíso Los Jazmines (100m before the CITMA office) ✆ 52 23 8905, ✉ marlen.cordero@nauta.cu. Not to be confused with the Finca Agroecológica El Paraíso above, this is a smorgasbord of locally grown food served in the ambient surrounds of farmland and fields set back from the road leading down from the Centro de Visitantes. There is a little pond a short way from the restaurant itself; the owners are happy to serve you waterside drinks while you wait for your food. Reservations recommended. $$

Restaurant Veras 40m from Los Jazmines ✆ 52 44 6467. Set in an open-sided thatched balcony overlooking a leafy glade. A buffet banquet of *comida criolla* with lamb, marinated and BBQ pork and a range of sides including green banana fritters, *tostones* and many more. $$

DRINKING AND NIGHTLIFE
SEE MAP PAGE 165

La Colonial Centro Nocturo no.61 Salvador Cisnero ✆ 48 79 3281. This bar and free entry live music venue is an animated spot popular with locals and tourists, who line the tables on the sidewalk outside early on and then pile inside to dance once the music heats up after 10pm. Everything from local son crooners to disco, salsa and reggaeton gets played.

Cueva de San Miguel Disco Km 32 Carretera a Puerto Esperanza ✆ 48 79 3203. For nightlife on the valley floor, some 4km north of Viñales village, your only real option is this cheesy disco, which has a quieter bar attached. Lack of demand, especially in low season, means it's worth checking in advance before you go; ring or enquire with one of the travel agents for details.

Patio del Decimista Salvador Cisneros no.102 ✆ 48 79 6014. Streetside bar where musicians sit strumming on the patio. Though nothing glamorous, it's a pleasant spot with a laidback vibe. Free-to-enter live stage shows take place inside nightly at 9pm.

Polo Montañez Centro Cultural Salvador Cisneros esq. Joaquín Pérez. The village's biggest and best spot for live music is this semi-covered outdoor venue tucked away in a corner of the central square. Nightly shows of mostly traditional Cuban music begin at 9pm and are followed by recorded salsa and disco until the place closes down, usually no later than 2am and often earlier.

El Viñalero Salvador Cisnero. The strains of the house guitar band can often be heard throughout the day on this amiable spot a block from the main square. Occasional live traditional music in the larger patio at the rear once they stop serving food in the evening.

DIRECTORY

Cigars Las Vegueros tobacco and rum shop, Salvador Cisnero no.51 (Mon–Sat 10am–6pm, Sun noon–5pm), sells a good selection of Robaina, Monte Cristo, Romeo y Julieta and others, alongside a selection of rums and traditional clothing.

Money and exchange In Viñales village, Banco de Crédito y Comercio, at Salvador Cisnero no.58 (Mon–Fri 8am–noon & 1.30–3pm, Sat 8–11am), can handle credit card transactions and cash travellers' cheques, as can the *casa de cambio* at Salvador Cisnero no.92 (Mon–Sat 8.30am–4pm, Sun 8.30–11.30am), where you can also purchase pesos.

There are also two cash point machines here.

Police station Salvador Cisnero no.69.

Post office Ceferino Fernández e/ Salvador Cisnero y Rafael Trejo (Mon–Sat 8am–6pm).

Swimming pool The pool at *La Ermita* is open to the public for a charge.

Wi-fi ETECSA office, Ceferino Fernández no.3 e/ Salvador Cisnero y Rafael Trejo, Viñales village. You can access the internet on site here. You can also buy wi-fi cards though you'd do well to buy them out of town before you arrive as demand outstrips supply.

Mural de la Prehistoria
Mogote Dos Hermanas • Daily 8am–7pm • Charge

Less than 1km to the west of Viñales village, the valley floor's flat surface is abruptly interrupted by the magnificent hulking mass of the Mogote Dos Hermanas. It plays host to the somewhat misleadingly named **Mural de la Prehistoria**, hidden away from the main road down a narrow side turning. Rather than the prehistoric cave paintings you might be expecting, the huge painted mural, measuring 120m by 180m and desecrating the face of one side of the *mogote*, is in fact a modern depiction of evolution on the island, from molluscs to man. It's impressive only for its size, with garish colours and lifeless images completely out of tune with this otherwise humble yet captivating valley. The mural was commissioned by Fidel Castro and painted in the early 1960s.

ACCOMMODATION AND EATING · MURAL DE LA PREHISTORIA; SEE MAP PAGE 165

Campismo Dos Hermanas ☎ 48 79 3223. Hidden away within the jagged borders of the surrounding *mogotes*, on the road to the Mural de la Prehistoria, this picturesque *campismo* is better equipped than most, despite having no a/c or fans in its neat, well-kept white cabins. On the spacious site are a TV room, games room, bar and restaurant, swimming pool and a regional museum, as well as a nightly disco. The cheapest of the state-run options, this is the place to come if you want to share your stay with Cuban holiday-makers, but be prepared for the constant blare of music in peak season. $

Jurásico Campismo Dos Hermanas ☎ 48 79 3223. Decent

comida criolla, including a tasty roast chicken special, served in the intimate white-walled dining room of a pleasant tile-roof lodge, with a dinky patio out front where you can also eat. $$

Restaurant Mural de la Prehistoria ☎ 48 79 6260. The bar, restaurant and souvenir shop just off to the side of the mural do nothing to alleviate the place's contrived nature, although it's not an unpleasant spot to have a drink and a bite to eat. The speciality pork cooked "Viñales style", roasted and charcoal-smoked is the highlight on an otherwise limited menu. $$

Cueva de San Miguel
6km northwest of Viñales · Daily 9am–4pm · Charge

By taking the left-hand fork at the petrol station at the northeastern end of the village, you can head out of Viñales through the heavily cultivated landscape to the narrower, arena-like San Vicente valley, around 2km away. Just beyond the *mogotes* that stand sentry-like at the entrance to the valley is the **Cueva de San Miguel**, also called the Cueva de Viñales. The cave's dramatic, gaping mouth is unmissable from the road, though the bar blaring loud music just inside the entrance somewhat detracts from its eerie promise.

El Palenque de los Cimarrones
Cueva de San Miguel · Daily 9am–4pm · Price included in the entrance price to Cueva de San Miguel.

You can pay extra to investigate past Cueva de San Miguel's bar and venture down a corridor that disappears into the rock, emerging after just 50m or so at **El Palenque de los Cimarrones**. This reconstruction of a runaway slave (*cimarron*) settlement provides limited insight into the living conditions of the enslaved people who, having escaped from the plantations, would have sought refuge in a hideout (*palenque*) such as the one on display here. There's little more than some cooking implements and a few contraptions made of sticks and stones, though there are some original pieces used by enslaved workers. You're left to guess what each one was used for and, although there is a small plaque declaring its authenticity, it's not even made clear whether this was actually the site of an original *palenque*.

EATING · EL PALENQUE DE LOS CIMARRONES

Restaurante El Palenque de los Cimarrones Valle de San Vicente ☎ 48 79 6290. This large restaurant, set under round *bohío* roofs, caters predominantly to lunchtime tour groups, but the food is better than you might expect.

Traditional Cuban roast chicken and pork dishes are cooked in appetizing seasonings. The guava cocktail is worth a try too. $$

Cueva del Indio
6km north of Viñales village · Daily 9am–5pm · Charge

From the Cueva de San Miguel it's a two-minute drive or a twenty-minute walk north to San Vicente's most captivating attraction, the **Cueva del Indio**. Rediscovered in 1920, this network of caves is believed to have been used by the Guanahatabey Native Americans, both as a temporary refuge from the Spanish colonists and – judging by the human remains found here – as a burial site. Well-lit enough not to seem ominous, the cool caves nevertheless inspire a sense of escape from the humid and bright world outside. There are no visible signs of Native American occupation: instead of paintings, the cave walls are marked with natural wave patterns, testimony to the flooding that took place during their formation millions of years ago. Only the first 300m of the large jagged tunnel's damp interior can be explored on foot before a slippery set of steps leads down to a subterranean river.

It's well worth taking the **boat ride** here, where a guide steers you for ten minutes through the remaining 400m of explorable cave. The boat drops you off out in the open, next to some souvenir stalls and a car park around the corner from where you started.

EATING
CUEVA DEL INDIO

Restaurante Cueva del Indio Cueva del Indio ☎ 48 79 6280. Canteen on the path leading up to the caves' entrance, bearing close resemblance to a school dining hall and with a slight Indo-Cuban slant to the Creole cooking on offer, which includes *tortas de yuca* (a cassava bread) and *ajiaco* (a traditional Cuban stew) alongside the usual roast chicken and fried pork. $$

Valle Ancón

A few hundred metres up the road from the Cueva del Indio, just past an isolated post office, is the *Rancho San Vicente* cabin complex. About 500m further, a left turn leads to the last stop in Viñales, the **Valle Ancón**. Mostly untouched by tourism, this least-visited and unspoilt of the valleys in Viñales is also the most complicated to explore and can become uncomfortably muddy in the rain. There's a small village of the same name, plenty of coffee plantations and a number of hard-to-find caves and rivers, but the rewards are usually outweighed by the effort needed to get there.

ACCOMMODATION
VALLE ANCÓN

Rancho San Vicente ☎ 48 79 6201, ✉ reserva@vinales. hor.tur.cu. Opposite the abandoned *Hotel Ranchón*, on the way out of San Vicente towards the Valle Ancón, with twenty attractive though somewhat run-down a/c cabins spread out around the site's gentle, wooded slopes. There's a swimming pool, large terrace and a bathhouse offering massage and mud therapy. $$$

Cayo Jutías and Cayo Levisa

The nearest beaches to Viñales are the two cays, **Jutías** and **Levisa**, that lie off the northern coast of Pinar del Río province. Both are easily accessible by car, and sometimes served by excursion from Viñales. They are both relatively undeveloped, so if you're looking for white-sand beaches without the contrived air that's part and parcel of the all-inclusive resorts elsewhere in the country, the cays are ideal.

Cayo Jutías

Just off the north coast of this part of Pinar del Río province (a 60km drive north and west from Viñales) is **Cayo Jutías**, a secluded island hideout that's relatively untouched compared to most of the other tourist magnets in the region. Besides the road ploughing through the middle of the low-lying thicket that covers most of the cay, the only signs of construction are a wooden restaurant at the start of the 3km of **beach** on the north side, and an old metal lighthouse built in 1902. The beach itself is admittedly a little scrappy in places and rarely more than 3m wide, but this does nothing to spoil the place's edge-of-the-world appeal – this may well be the best spot in Cuba to lie back and do absolutely nothing.

ARRIVAL AND DEPARTURE
CAYO JUTÍAS

By car Driving to the cay from Viñales is surprisingly easy, as the route is well marked. Follow the signposted road out of Viñales village to the Mogote Dos Hermanas until you reach the tiny village of Pons, where you take the signposted right-hand turn. The road surface deteriorates as you zigzag to Minas de Matahambre village, from where you head for Santa Lucía, following the signs to Cayo Jutías all the way, until you reach the causeway linking the cay to the mainland.

By organized tour Havanatur (☎ 48 79 6262) runs trips from Viñales.

ACTIVITIES

Watersports A hut by the beach restaurant rents out fairly shabby snorkelling equipment and small kayaks as well as sun loungers and sunshades. You can also explore the local coral reef on an outboard motorboat.

Beach sports The watersports hut also offers volleyball or football on sandy beachside pitches.

ACCOMMODATION AND EATING

Camping The only way to spend a night on the cay (though very rarely does anyone do this) is to camp – be sure to bring plenty of insect repellent, as the mosquitoes come out in force in the evening.

Beach restaurant A wooden restaurant at the start of the beach does simple mains of seafood and chicken. $\bar{\underline{\underline{\S}}}$

Cayo Levisa

On the same stretch of north coast as Cayo Jutías, 50km northeast of Viñales, the lonely military outpost of Palma Rubia is the jumping-off point for **Cayo Levisa**, more developed for tourism than Cayo Jutías but still relatively unspoilt. This 3km-wide, densely wooded islet boasts some of the finest white sands and clearest waters in Pinar del Río, and unless you take advantage of its **diving centre**, there's blissfully little to do here.

The boat moors on a rickety wooden jetty, a two-minute walk from the only accommodation on the island, *Hotel Cayo Levisa,* sprawled untidily along the gleaming white beach. Behind the beach, thick woodland reaches across the island to the opposite shore, forming a natural screen that encourages a sense of escape and privacy.

There are no ATMs on the cay so you'll need to bring all the cash with you that you intend to spend.

ARRIVAL AND DEPARTURE
CAYO LEVISA

By boat The only regular boat to the island leaves at around 10am every day from Palma Rubia, where you can

---

GRAN CAVERNA DE SANTO TOMÁS

An impressive and complicated set of caves set in the limestone rock of a hulking *mogote*, the magnificent **Gran Caverna de Santo Tomás** (daily 8.30am–3pm; charge for a 1hr tour with lamp and helmet) makes a good day-trip from the Viñales valley. The most extensive cave system in Cuba, with 46km of tunnels, it attracts serious speleologists and small tour groups alike, but happily it has not yet become overrun with visitors. You can book a visit to the caves through Havanatur, Cubanacán or Paradiso (see page 168).

Seventeen kilometres along the road west from Viñales village is the clearly marked turn-off for **El Moncada**, a scattering of houses that shares a sheltered valley with the caves. From the turn-off, a pine-lined road leads down into the valley and the first right-hand turn off this leads through El Moncada village and up to a specialist school, the Escuela Nacional de Espeleología Antonio Núñez (daily 8.30am–5pm), which doubles as a visitor centre with a tiny museum (free) and provides basic **accommodation** in a four-room, cement-walled bungalow with breakfast and dinner included. Most people, unless they are experienced spelunkers, are taken into either level six or seven of the **eight levels**, the mouths of which are semi-hidden up a rocky, forested slope from where there are fabulous views of the valley. Highlights of the walk – which covers 1km of chambers – include surprising cave winds, bats flying about and underground pools. The knowledgeable guides point out easy-to-miss plants, deposits of guano and, on level six, a replica of a **mural**. The mural is part of the evidence, as is the 3400-year-old skeleton found here, that these caves were once the refuge of the Guanahatabeys, the original inhabitants of Cuba.

safely leave your car. If you're staying at one of the cabins on the island there's no charge for the 30min crossing, otherwise expect to pay around $900CUP return, which includes lunch at the island's restaurant. The return journey is at 5pm, but check before leaving the rickety wooden jetty, which is a 2min walk from the forty grey-brick and newer wooden cabins.

Getting to Palma Rubia From Viñales, take the valley road north, past the turning for the Valle Ancón, and follow it to the small town of La Palma, just under 30km from Viñales village. From La Palma take the road heading roughly north, towards the coast, and stay on it for 17km until you reach a left turn which heads directly to Palma Rubia.

ACTIVITIES

Diving and snorkelling A dive centre within the small hotel complex rents out snorkels and diving gear, and offers courses and dives around the nearby coral reef, a short boat-trip away. Diving courses are also offered, from a basic two-immersion course, to a full course lasting for a week or more.

Fishing trips The dive centre also offers fishing trips and a day-trip to nearby Cayo Paraíso, a similarly unspoilt islet once favoured by Ernest Hemingway, where you can dive or snorkel.

Watersports The hotel has kayaks and catamarans for rent.

ACCOMMODATION AND EATING

Hotel Cayo Levisa ☉ 48 75 65 01. The grey-brick and newer wooden cabins right on the beach are well equipped, with spacious interiors and large porches. Loungers and hammocks hung under wooden shades line a beachfront dotted with *uva caleta* trees in front of the hotel. An attractive open-sided hotel restaurant serves average meals of fresh fish, shellfish and pasta. As the phone line to the cay can be unreliable you should contact the Cubanacán head office (see page 34) if you're booking a room here from Havana. $\underline{\$\$\$}$

Southwestern Pinar del Río

Heading southwest from Pinar del Río city on the Carretera Central, the only main road through this part of the region, the tourist centres become less developed and the towns more isolated, snoozy but likeable little places that hold scant reward for even the most enthusiastic explorer – twenty minutes in any one of them should suffice for the whole lot. The one place that demands a longer visit between Pinar del Río city and the **Península de Guanahacabibes** is the **Alejandro Robaina tobacco plantation**, just under 25km from the centre of the provincial capital. Of the numerous *vegas* (tobacco farms) in the area, this is the one best prepared for visitors and the most renowned.

After the small town of **Isabel Rubio**, 60km from the provincial capital, the landscape becomes increasingly monotonous and doesn't improve until the dense forest and crystalline waters of the peninsula move into view, well beyond the end of the Carretera Central at the fishing village of **La Fe**. On Cuba's virtually untouched western tip, **María La Gorda** is one of the best scuba-diving locations in the country.

GETTING AROUND

SOUTHWESTERN PINAR DEL RÍO

By public transport Getting around by public transport can be a real problem, though the unreliable and very slow train service and the occasional bus from the provincial capital do at least provide the possibility of getting to some of the beaches.

By car Even with a car the going can be tough, as the Carretera Central features very few signs, becomes increasingly potholed and hands over to minor roads just before the Península de Guanahacabibes, the highlight of this area.

Alejandro Robaina tobacco plantation

To get there by car, take a left turn, marked by a small collection of huts and a solitary bungalow, off the Carretera Central 18km from Pinar del Río. Follow this almost ruler-straight side road for 4km until you reach another left turn, just before a concrete roadside plaque that reads "CCS Viet-Nam Heróico". This dusty track leads to the plantation • Daily 9am–5pm, but calling in advance is recommended • 40min tours • Charge • ☉ 48 79 7470

2

BEACHES AROUND LA FE

There are a couple of **beaches** in the La Fe vicinity, around the wide-open bay of Ensenada de Cortés, although the appeal lies more in their proximity to the provincial capital and their popularity with locals than in their negligible beauty. Around 15km beyond San Juan y Martínez on the Carretera Central there's a clearly signposted turn-off for **Boca de Galafre**. Five kilometres past the turning for Boca de Galafre, a side road leads down 8km to a more substantial beach, **Playa Bailén**, the most popular seaside resort along the southern coastline.

As the Carretera Central heads southwest from the provincial capital, it cuts through the famed **Vuelta Abajo** region, one of the most fertile areas in the country and the source of the finest **tobacco** in the world. There are countless *vegas* (tobacco plantations) in this zone, but one, the **Alejandro Robaina**, has an edge over the rest. While most plantations produce tobacco for one or more of the state-owned cigar brands, such as Cohiba, Monte Cristo and so on, this is the only one to farm the crop exclusively for its own brand, named after the grandson of the original founder, who bought the plantation in 1845. The brand was established in 1997, then only the third brand to have been created since the Revolution in 1959. The owners have gone further than any other *vega* in their efforts to attract tourists, offering engaging guided tours of the plantation, product sampling opportunities and even the chance to meet members of the Robaina family, though Alejandro himself died in April 2010, aged 91. You can visit on an excursion from Viñales, though it is the enterprising owners, not the state, running the short tours. Though this adds to the sense of authenticity, it also means the plantation is difficult to find, for independent visitors, with no road signs pointing the way nor any mention of the place on maps.

The best time of year to visit is between October and January during the tobacco growing season. The **tours** (which are conducted variously in English, French and Italian) take in the various stages of tobacco production, starting with a visit to plots of land covered by cheesecloth under which the seeds are planted. Next you're taken to one of the *casas de secado*, the drying barns, where the leaves are strung up in bundles and the fermentation process takes place. There's a table here where cigar rolling is demonstrated, although no cigars are actually produced for sale on the farm.

A pleasant on-site restaurant, for which you need to book in advance, serves set meals of *comida criolla* ($$$) with a choice of mains (daily noon–2pm).

Península de Guanahacabibes

Though a challenge to reach independently, the forest-covered **Península de Guanahacabibes** has become a popular destination for organized excursions and in this respect is easier than ever to get to. The journey is certainly not without its rewards, especially for scuba divers, who can enjoy some of the best **dive sites** in Cuba. One of the largest national forest-parks in the country, the **Parque Nacional Guanahacabibes** covers most of the peninsula, the whole of which was declared a Unesco Biosphere Reserve in 1987. Some of Cuba's most beautiful and unspoilt coastline can be found here around the **Bahía de Corrientes**, the bay nestling inside this hook of land. It was on the peninsula that the Cuban Native Americans sought their last refuge, having been driven from the rest of the island by the Spanish colonists. Guanahacabibes is still relatively untouched by tourism and the only two hotel resorts are the low-key **María La Gorda** and **Villa Cabo San Antonio**.

This is also an important area for wildlife. May to September is the best time for seeing turtles, and birdlife is particularly rich between November and March, during the migration season when the peninsula becomes a corridor for around 50 migrant species. That said, the area will reward birdwatchers year-round. The bee hummingbird, the blue-headed quail dove, the giant kingbird, Gundlach's hawk, and the restricted-range yellow-headed warbler and red-shouldered blackbird are among the area's avian highlights.

Make sure you bring enough cash to cover all your costs on a trip to this area, as you cannot withdraw money or use credit cards for accommodation or restaurants. The only way into the peninsula is along a potholed road through a thick forest that begins where the Carretera Central ends, at the tiny fishing village of **La Fe**, 15km beyond the turning for Laguna Grande.

2

La Bajada meteorological station
Daily 9am–4pm • Charge • ☎ 48 75 1007

From La Fe, the road twists and turns south and then west through the dense vegetation of the national park for some 30km until it reaches the broad, open bay, the Bahía de Corrientes, around which most of the peninsula's main attractions are based. The first of these, **La Bajada**, is a scrappy clearing on the edge of the forest just a

---

TOURS AND TRAILS AROUND PARQUE NACIONAL GUANAHACABIBES

Among the small cluster of buildings at La Bajada is the **Estación Ecológica Guanahacabibes** (☎ 48 75 0366, ✉ aylen04@yahoo.es), a small lodge over the road from the meteorological station where you can arrange various trips around the peninsula. Access to the trails and indeed to any part of the peninsula beyond the road and resorts is forbidden without a guide, so if you want to explore you'll have to go on a tour. The centre employs six guides, two of whom speak English and all of whom are experts on the local flora and fauna. With no fixed days or times for excursions (the guides work on an ad hoc basis) it's vital to **ring in advance** to make arrangements. To get the most out of any of the three excursions, the staff at the centre generally advise start times of between 8.30am and 10am, when you are likely to see more birdlife and the day is not at its hottest.

There are currently three **organized tours** on offer, two hikes along the official Cueva Las Perlas and Del Bosque al Mar trails, and one that takes in the entire area by car or jeep. The centre is happy to tailor day-trips to your own specifications and can make them as long or short as you like. You'll need to present your passport or some form of ID before you can embark on any of the excursions here. Long sleeves and insect repellent are always a good idea, particularly in May and June when the mosquitoes are out in force.

THE TOURS

Del Bosque al Mar This is the shortest trail (around 2hr) and takes in both coastline and forested areas, beginning about 1500m from the Estación Ecológica. The route skirts small lagoons harbouring aquatic birds, while the floral highlight is orchids.

Cueva Las Perlas This 1.5km-, 3hr-long trek through the semi-deciduous forest offers the chance to observe local birdlife such as the Cuban tody, the bee hummingbird and the red-legged thrush. At the end of the trail is the Cueva Las Perlas itself, an explorable cave sinking back over half a kilometre with various galleries and chambers, and shafts of light pouring through holes in the roof.

Safari tour The most expensive and comprehensive tour, this 50km-, 5hr-long excursion includes the Cabo de San Antonio at the far western reaches of the peninsula. You will need your own vehicle, as the centre has no transport of its own; you can rent jeeps (though not cars, as the going is tough) from Vía in María La Gorda (see above). The tour follows the coast, with stops to observe wildlife and the changes in the landscape – from rocky-floored, semi-deciduous forest to marshy jungle and palm-fringed beaches, to jagged seaside cliffs. Animals you might see include iguanas, deer, jutias and boars.

few metres before the road hits the bay. The biggest and most obvious landmark is the 23m-high sphere-topped tower of the **meteorological station**, which holds scant appeal for visitors, though for a small fee you can scale the tower's metal spiral staircase and enjoy 360-degree **views** across the treetops and over to the bay.

María La Gorda

Charge for non-guests to enter the *Villa María La Gorda* resort and use its beach • ☎ 48 77 8131 ✉ comercial@mlagorda.co.cu

Turn left after La Bajada to get to the Península de Guanahacabibes' most popular spot, **María La Gorda**, where there is an international dive centre and a small hotel complex on a fine white-sand beach. The relaxing drive here follows the shoreline of the bay, with dense forest on one side and an open expanse of brilliant, placid blue-green water on the other. Along the way are a few slightly scrappy but likeable little beaches, which you can make your own if you want complete privacy, but there's usually plenty of room on the much larger beach belonging to the resort at the end of the road. The white-sand **beach** is expansive enough for guests and non-guests to spread out without feeling too crowded. The sense of idyll is marred only slightly by the presence of a hard frill of rock which fringes the sand at the water's edge; and the fact that as the beach is rarely swept, a small amount of debris usually accumulates.

You should bring enough cash to cover all your costs here, as there are no banks, ATMs or places to change money, and the restaurants don't accept credit cards (though the little shop does).

ARRIVAL AND DEPARTURE   MARÍA LA GORDA

By prebooked transfer The easiest way to visit María La Gorda is to book a transfer with one of the national travel agents based in Pinar del Río city or Viñales village. Havanatur, for example, charges around $500CUP for a return trip from its office in Pinar del Río (☎ 48 79 8494) and $650CUP for the trip from the Viñales branch (☎ 48 79 6262).

GETTING AROUND

By car or scooter Cars, scooters and jeeps can be rented from the Vía office (☎ 48 75 7693) near the dive centre.

ACTIVITIES

Watersports Snorkelling masks, snorkels and fins are available to rent at the dive centre.

DIVING AND BOAT TRIPS AT MARÍA LA GORDA

The pristine waters around María La Gorda are widely regarded as among the best for **diving** in the whole of Cuba, protected by the bay and spectacularly calm and clear, averaging 25m in depth. Diving here is enhanced by a quick drop in water depth, with a large number of the fifty-odd dive sites only ten to twenty minutes by boat from the shore, while the spectacular variety of fish life here includes barracuda, moray eels, several species of ray, lobsters, whale sharks and more. Among the specific **dive sites** of note are Ancla del Pirata, featuring a two-tonne eighteenth-century anchor covered in coral; colourful Paraíso Perdito, which reaches depths of 33m and is particularly abundant in coral and fish life; and Yemayá, a 2m-high cave at 32m deep, which ascends almost 20m through a long, gently curving, mysterious tunnel.

The two yachts belonging to the resort's diving club, **Centro Internacional de Buceo María La Gorda** (daily 8.30am–5.30pm; ring *Villa María La Gorda* on ☎ 48 77 8131, 44 12261, ask for the Centro de Buceo), depart for the dive sites twice a day. You need to be at the club at least thirty minutes before departure time to arrange equipment and pay for your diving. A single dive costs around $1000CUP, but ask about their packages.

You will need to add an extra for equipment rental, unless you bring your own. The club caters to both first-timers and advanced divers, with a short **initiation course** involving some theory and a single immersion. Also on offer are four- to five-day ACUC Open Water courses.

Ball games There's a small soccer pitch and a sandy volleyball court which you can use for free; there's a small charge for renting a ball.

ACCOMMODATION AND EATING

As the **food** at the hotel buffet is poor and parts of the menu at *El Carajuelo* subject to availability, it's worth bringing some of your own **supplies** if you intend to stay longer than one night – there is only a tiny grocery store here, and the nearest supermarket is at least 50km away.

El Carajuelo ☎ 48 77 8131. With a wooden-walled interior and shady front porch, this also serves as the *Villa María La Gorda* bar. You can get decent pizzas and pricier chicken; when available, fresh fish simply served with lemon is the best option. $\overline{\underline{\$\$}}$

Villa María La Gorda María La Gorda ⓦ villamarialagorda.com. Used as a base for divers as much as a beach hotel, and pleasant enough if somewhat basic for the price, with two distinct sets of accommodation. Along the top of the beach, close to the water's edge, the most attractive options are the wood-panelled bungalows and two-storey concrete apartment blocks; a sea view costs extra a night but is definitely worth considering. Hidden away from the beach in their own little wooden gangway-linked complex on the edge of the forest, the newer log cabins can be quite dark inside and are prey to legions of insects, so bring repellent. A mediocre buffet breakfast is included, and you can add a buffet dinner for a bit extra. $\overline{\underline{\$\$}}$

Cabo de San Antonio

From La Bajada, the right-hand turn-off from the main road through the peninsula (away from María La Gorda) is the fairly potholed road to the **Cabo de San Antonio**, the cape at the westernmost tip of the peninsula. There are several pleasant little beaches along the way, and at the extreme tip of the cape is a lighthouse, the **Faro Roncali**, built in 1849 (closed to visitors). Several kilometres beyond the lighthouse, past some more beautifully secluded beaches, are the last two stops on this 60km-stretch of coastal road, the picturesque and isolated white-sand beaches of **Las Tumbas** and neighbouring **Los Morros de Piedra**.

ACCOMMODATION AND EATING   CABO DE SAN ANTONIO

Marina cafeteria The modest but well-kept cafeteria facing the marina is the only source of food hereabouts, with a small selection of sandwiches, soft drinks and ice cream. For a proper meal you'll have to travel the 77km to María La Gorda. $\overline{\$}$

Villa Cabo de San Antonio Los Morros de Piedra ☎ 48 75 7655. This eight-cabin, sixteen-room resort, with a simple, reconstructed marina, has been built with complete respect for the local environment. Located about 80m from the shore, the eight neat and comfortable wooden cabins, each with two rooms, have solar-powered a/c, and nothing has been built above the height of the trees. $\overline{\underline{\$\$}}$

Varadero, Matanzas and Maya- beque

Varadero, Matanzas and Mayabeque

Varadero, with almost 25km of beach, most of it lined with hotels, is Cuba's largest tourist resort. It occupies the Península de Hicacos, a slender finger of land pointing into the warm currents of the western Atlantic from the northern coastline of the province of Matanzas. That stunning esplanade of fine white sand certainly makes Varadero a world-class beach. While increasing numbers of luxury hotels provide optimum accommodation, this remains the best major beach resort in Cuba for independent or budget travellers as it's one of the few with a wide spread of low-priced accommodation options and a decent, ever-improving choice of restaurants outside the hotels.

3

Roughly 30km west along the coastline from the peninsula is the provincial capital, also named **Matanzas**, while to the east, and somewhat closer, is the bayside town of **Cárdenas**. These once grand colonial towns now live largely in Varadero's shadow, relegated to day-trip destinations for holidaymakers. Many of their historic buildings are in considerable disrepair but they do still make a refreshing contrast to their more cultureless and one-dimensional neighbour. What's more, the Matanzas city surrounds hold three of the most captivating natural phenomena in the province: the subterranean cave network of the **Cuevas de Bellamar**; the broad, slinking **Río Canímar**, host to some great boat trips; and the enchanting tropical landscapes of the **Yumurí valley**. The valley nudges into the neighbouring province of **Mayabeque**, bypassed by most tourists on the journey between Havana and Varadero but whose pretty stretch of uncrowded coastline at the resort of **Playa Jibacoa** is easier to get to from Matanzas than any other town or city. The hills of the **Escaleras de Jaruco**, also in Mayabeque, offer somewhere interesting and attractive to head for if you want to get well off the beaten track. Back in Matanzas province, another little-visited but charming spot is the once wealthy village of **San Miguel de los Baños**, now a slightly surreal but intriguing testament to a bygone era. The village is just a few kilometres from the Carretera Central, the road that cuts a scenic route through the centre of the province, much of it covered in endless sugar cane fields and huge citrus orchards, bisecting workaday towns like Colón and Jovellanos.

On the southern side of the province, the **Península de Zapata**'s sweeping tracts of coastal marshlands and wooded interior can be explored with guides, who help protect this encouragingly unspoiled national park and biosphere reserve. There are a couple of very modest beaches here but the area is better suited to hiking, birdwatching and scuba diving than sunbathing. It is also the site of one of the most infamous acts in Cuban–US history – the Bay of Pigs invasion.

Varadero

Expectations of **VARADERO** vary wildly: some people anticipate a picture-perfect seaside paradise; some hope for a hedonistic party resort; while others dismiss it altogether, assuming it to be a synthetic, characterless place devoid of Cubans. In reality it is none of these extremes, though it is *the* package-holiday resort in Cuba. What most stands out about the place is the sheer length of its brilliant white-sand **beach**, a highway of sand running virtually the entire length of an almost ruler-straight 25km peninsula shooting out from the mainland. The blues and greens of the calm waters create a

RÍO CANÍMAR BOAT TRIP

Highlights

❶ Varadero beach Walk or run for miles on the golden sands of Cuba's most famous beach, then cool down in the shallow turquoise water. See page 182

❷ Mansión Xanadú Sleep, eat or drink in opulent style at one of Varadero's most alluring addresses. See page 187

❸ Learn to kitesurf in Varadero One of the best places in Cuba to learn to kitesurf is at the Varadero Kitesurf School. See page 197

❹ Hershey train It may be slow and unreliable, but this dinky electric train passes through some beautiful scenery. See page 208

❺ Cuevas de Bellamar Descend over 50m underground into these awesome underground caves and along 750m of atmospheric passageways. See page 211

❻ Río Canímar boat trip Enjoy the Cuban countryside on a fun-packed cruise up this broad, tree-lined river. See page 212

❼ Loma de Jacán Climb the hillside staircase outside San Miguel de los Baños to admire the forgotten village and valley below. See page 215

❽ Get back to nature at the Península de Zapata This one of the best birding areas in the Caribbean, with flooded caves and coral reefs providing the province's dive sites. See page 223

HIGHLIGHTS ARE MARKED ON THE MAP ON PAGE 184

HIGHLIGHTS

1 Varadero beach

2 Mansión Xanadú

3 Learn to kitesurf in Varadero

4 Hershey train

5 Cuevas de Bellamar

6 Río Canímar boat trip

7 Loma de Jacán

8 Get back to nature at the Península de Zapata

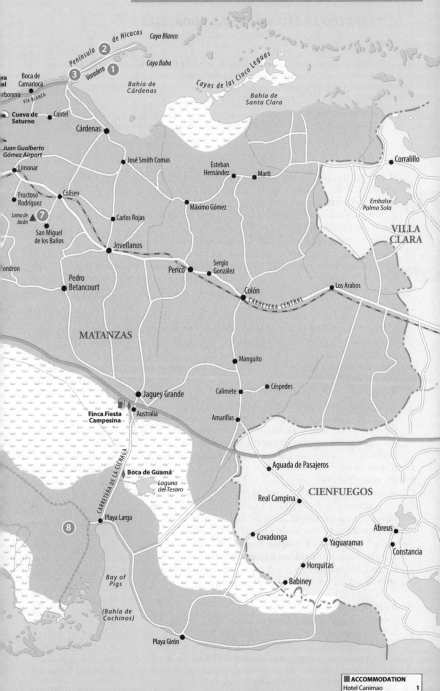

VARADERO, MATANZAS & MAYABEQUE

Cayo Blanco

Península de Hicacos

②

③ Varadero ①

Cayo Buba

Cayos de las Cinco Leguas

va
al

Boca de
Camarioca

rbonera

VIA BLANCA

Cueva de
Saturno

Cantel

Bahía de
Cárdenas

Bahía de
Santa Clara

Juan Gualberto
Gómez Airport

Cárdenas

José Smith Comas

Esteban
Hernández

Martí

Corralillo

Limonar

Fructoso
Rodríguez

Coliseo

Máximo Gómez

Embalse
Palma Sola

VILLA
CLARA

Loma de
Jacán ▲ ⑦

San Miguel
de los Baños

Carlos Rojas

ondron

Pedro
Betancourt

Jovellanos

Perico

Sergio
González

Colón

Los Arabos

CARRETERA CENTRAL

MATANZAS

Manguito

Jaguey Grande

Finca Fiesta
Campesina

Australia

Calimete

Céspedes

Amarillas

Boca de Guamá

Laguna
del Tesoro

Aguada de Pasajeros

CIENFUEGOS

Real Campina

⑧

Playa Larga

Covadonga

Abreus

Yaguaramas

Constancia

Horquitas

Bay of
Pigs

Babiney

(Bahía de
Cochinos)

Playa Girón

■ ACCOMMODATION	
Hotel Canimao	1

> ## VARADERO'S ROAD NAMES AND ADDRESSES
>
> The principal street in Varadero town, and the only one running its entire 5km length, is **Avenida Primera**, shown on street signs and in addresses as Avenida 1ra. This street runs into Reparto Kawama, where it is also known as **Avenida Kawama**. Connecting to the other end of Avenida Primera is the **Avenida de las Américas**, linking a dozen or so hotels and also referred to as the **Carretera Las Américas**. Running along almost the entire southern shore of the peninsula is the **Autopista del Sur**, also known (particularly at its eastern end) as the **Carretera de las Morlas**. Most addresses in the eastern half of the peninsula are expressed as the distance along the Autopista del Sur from the mainland, though these distances are frequently inaccurate.

stunning turquoise barrier between the land and the Florida Straits and, to cap it all off, because the peninsula rarely exceeds half a kilometre in width, the beach is rarely more than a five-minute walk away.

Though Varadero is not the place to come for an authentic taste of Cuban culture, this is no faceless shrine to consumerism – the town area houses some ten thousand residents, most of them in faded homes surrounded by scraps of grassland and unlit streets, a reminder of which side of the Florida Straits you are on. None of this detracts from the beach, the town section of which attracts as many holidaying Cubans as foreigners in July and August. Numerous **boat trips** leave from the three marinas on the peninsula, while diving clubs provide access to over thirty rewarding **dive sites**.

Unlike some of Cuba's high-profile beach resorts, there are *casas particulares* in Varadero, providing plenty of relatively cheap **accommodation**, alongside the expensive all-inclusive mega-complexes. However, with shops and restaurants spread thinly across the peninsula, and nightlife and entertainment confined mostly to the big hotels, there is a distinct lack of buzz – visit in the low season and it can seem quite deserted. But the level of hassle from *jineteros* here is lower than you might expect, especially in comparison to Havana, and on the whole tourists blend into the local surroundings with greater ease than in most of the rest of Cuba.

The peninsula is divided into three distinct **sections**, though all are united by the same stretch of beach on the northern coastline. The bridge from the mainland joins Varadero at the western end of the **town area** (Maps A and B), where all the Cubans live, and the eastern end of the **Reparto Kawama** (Map A), the narrowest, least-visited section of the peninsula and home to about half a dozen hotels. The **eastern** half of the resort (Map C) is relatively secluded and wandering about is not really an option, as the landscape is dominated by the newest and largest luxury hotels and there are no pavements or footpaths. It's worth catching the tourist bus or a taxi out this way, however, as a number of the local highlights are here, including the magnificent **Mansión Xanadú**, the Varadero golf course, a dolphinarium, and the misleadingly named **Varahicacos Ecological Reserve**. On the hook of land at the eastern extreme of the peninsula is the **Marina Gaviota Varadero**, which became one of the largest marinas in the Caribbean when it was expanded beyond recognition in 2015, now centred around a commercial and leisure complex.

Brief history

Varadero began life as a town as late as 1887, founded by a group of wealthy families from nearby Cárdenas intent on establishing a permanent base for their summer holidays. The archetypal old Varadero residence, built in the early decades of the twentieth century, was one modelled on the kinds of houses then typical of the southern US: two- or three-storey wooden constructions surrounded by broad verandas, with sloping terracotta-tile roofs.

By the time of the Revolution at the end of the 1950s, Varadero had become one of the most renowned **beach resorts** in the Caribbean, attracting wealthy Americans and considered to be a thoroughly modern and hedonistic vacationland. Standards slipped, however, after power was seized by Fidel Castro and his rebels, who tended to frown on tourism. It wasn't until the government's attitude on this issue came full circle in the early 1990s that serious investment began to pour back into Varadero. Since then, over twenty new hotels have been built, most of them all-inclusive **mega-resorts** occupying the previously undeveloped land in the eastern section of the peninsula.

La Casa de Al

Avenida Kawama • Daily 10am–10pm • Free • ☎ 45 66 8018

The only notable sight outside the hotels in Reparto Kawama is the grand **Casa de Al**, the former holiday home of Al Capone. Now a restaurant, this attractive, sprawling grey-stone *villa* with its broad arches, wooden balconies and terracotta-tile roof is one of the most distinct remaining hallmarks of Varadero's pre-1959 exclusivity. Have a meal or a drink here and you can take a look at the photos, spread around the interior, of some of the notorious gangsters who lived and did business in Cuba prior to the Revolution.

Parque Josone

Avenida 1ra e/ 56 y 60 • Daily 10am–11pm, pool closes 5pm • Free; charges to hire rowing boats and pedal boats • ☎ 45 66 7738

The underused **Parque Josone**, sometimes referred to as Retiro Josone, is the most tranquil and picturesque spot in central Varadero. The landscaping is simple, with no intricately designed gardens – just sweeping, well-kept lawns dotted with trees and a small lake. There are rowing boats and pedal boats for hire, a couple of outdoor cafés, four restaurants (see page 194), an intermittently operational crazy-golf course and, at the southern edge of the park, where it borders the Autopista del Sur, an unspectacular swimming pool which attracts a few locals.

Mansión Xanadú

Autopista del Sur Km 8 • ☎ 45 66 7388

The first tangible visitor attraction east of town, about 2km from central Varadero, is the **Mansión Xanadú**, a hotel, restaurant, bar and one of the few buildings on the peninsula you could call a historic landmark. Sometimes referred to as the Mansión Dupont, it was built between 1926 and 1929 by the American millionaire Irenée Dupont at a cost of over US$600,000, a vast sum for that era. At the same time, Dupont bought up large tracts of land on the peninsula for hotel development and effectively kick-started Varadero as a major holiday destination. The mansion has hardly changed since the Dupont family fled the island in 1959, and stands testament to the wealth and decadence of the pre-revolutionary years in Varadero. These days, to appreciate the splendidly furnished four-storey interior, its large rooms full of marble and mahogany, you either have to be a hotel guest, eat at the *Las Américas* restaurant or sip a cocktail and admire the views of the coast and golf course from the dignified top-floor bar.

Dolphinarium

Autopista del Sur Km 12 • Daily 9am–5pm • Shows 11am & 3.30pm • Swim with dolphins 9.30am, 11.30am, 2.30pm & 4pm • Charge • ☎ 45 668031

This outdoor **Dolphinarium** puts on two shows daily. The verdant setting of the Laguna Los Taínos – a small natural pool surrounded by trees and bushes a few metres from

3

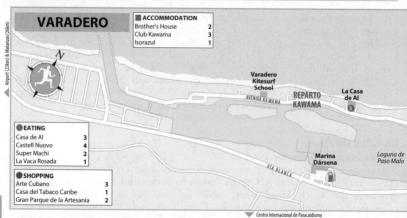

VARADERO

ACCOMMODATION
Brother's House	2
Club Kawama	3
Isorazul	1

EATING
Casa de Al	3
Castell Nuovo	4
Super Machi	2
La Vaca Rosada	1

SHOPPING
Arte Cubano	3
Casa del Tabaco Caribe	1
Gran Parque de la Artesanía	2

CONTINUED ON MAP A

ACCOMMODATION
Beny's House	9
Casa de Leila y Alina	5
Casa Mary y Angel	7
Casa de Rafael Guada Morffi	10
Casa de Rosa	11
Cuatro Palmas	6
Dos Mares	8
Los Delfines	4
Norma's B&B	12

EATING
La Barbacoa	9	Nonna Tina	6
La Bodeguita del Medio	5	El Rápido	7
La Campana	15	El Retiro	13
Casa del Chocolate	10	Salsa Suárez	12
Don Alex	11	Varadero 60	17
Esquina Cuba	8	Waco's Club	16
Mesón del Quijote	14		

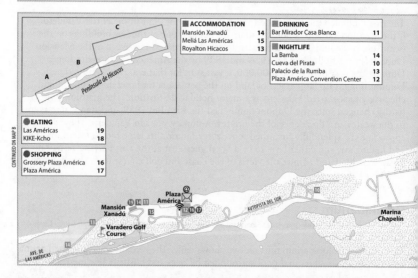

CONTINUED ON MAP B

ACCOMMODATION
Mansión Xanadú	14
Meliá Las Américas	15
Royalton Hicacos	13

DRINKING
Bar Mirador Casa Blanca	11

NIGHTLIFE
La Bamba	14
Cueva del Pirata	10
Palacio de la Rumba	13
Plaza América Convention Center	12

EATING
Las Américas	19
KIKE-Kcho	18

SHOPPING
Grossery Plaza América	16
Plaza América	17

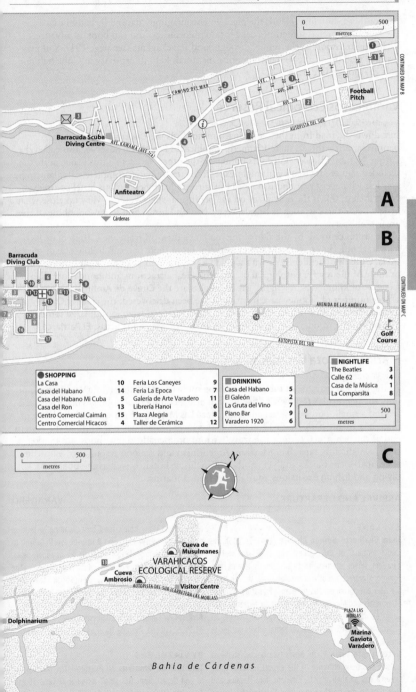

A

Barracuda Scuba
Diving Centre

Football
Pitch

Anfiteatro

Cárdenas

CONTINUED ON MAP B

3

B

Barracuda
Diving Club

AVENIDA DE LAS AMÉRICAS

AUTOPISTA DEL SUR

Golf
Course

CONTINUED ON MAP C

●SHOPPING			
La Casa		Feria Los Caneyes	9
Casa del Habano	14	Feria La Epoca	7
Casa del Habano Mi Cuba	5	Galería de Arte Varadero	11
Casa del Ron	13	Librería Hanoi	6
Centro Comercial Caimán	15	Plaza Alegria	8
Centro Comercial Hicacos	4	Taller de Cerámica	12

■DRINKING	
Casa del Habano	5
El Galeón	2
La Gruta del Vino	7
Piano Bar	9
Varadero 1920	6

■NIGHTLIFE	
The Beatles	3
Calle 62	4
Casa de la Música	1
La Comparsita	8

C

N

Cueva de
Musulmanes

VARAHICACOS
ECOLOGICAL RESERVE

Cueva
Ambrosio

AUTOPISTA DEL SUR (CARRETERA LAS MORLAS)

Visitor Centre

Dolphinarium

PLAZA LAS
MORLAS

Marina
Gaviota
Varadero

Bahia de Cárdenas

the southern shoreline – lends the place an encouragingly natural feel and beats the fabricated arenas sometimes used for dolphin shows. You can book in advance, including transport to the venue, through local travel agents (see page 191). You may want to read up on the welfare of marine mammals kept in captivity in Cuba before you go, though (see page 54).

Varahicacos Ecological Reserve

Autopista del Sur Km 17 • Visitor centre daily 8am–5pm • Charge • ☎ 45 613594

Just down the road from the Dolphinarium, towards the eastern extreme of the peninsula, is the three-square-kilometre **Varahicacos Ecological Reserve**, also called the Parque Natural Hicacos. Given its billing as "the other Varadero", this is not quite the secluded nature sanctuary you might expect; the undramatic, completely flat landscape gets less wild every year and is now all but surrounded by enormous hotel complexes. Nevertheless, this is the only place on the peninsula where you can view up close what little wildlife there is, such as lizards, crabs, bats and birds, and learn something of the area's prehistory.

The **visitor centre** is by the side of the road, at a turn-off from the Carretera de las Morlas about 1km past the Marina Chapelín. From there you can follow one of several **trails**, either independently or with a guide if you book in advance, each featuring one or more of the reserve's ecological or archaeological attractions and none more than a couple of kilometres in length. The highlights are the **Cueva de Ambrosio**, where a large number of Siboney cave paintings have been discovered; the smaller **Cueva de Musulmanes**, where human bones over 2500 years old were found; large **termite mounds** in the woods; and an impressively huge 500-year-old cactus, **El Patriarca**.

Marina Gaviota Varadero

End of Autopista del Sur • ☎ 45 664115

At the furthest extreme of the peninsula, the sprawling **Marina Gaviota Varadero** is not only the peninsula's top nautical facility but also a commercial holiday village, centred around a small, outdoor, waterside mall, **Plaza Las Morlas**, which wouldn't look out of place in a theme park. With 1200 berths, this huge project has transformed the eastern end of the peninsula, adding a short waterfront promenade, a few shops and market stalls, a nightclub, tapas bar, Mexican, Argentinian and seafood restaurants, a bowling alley, apartment blocks and yet another all-inclusive hotel, as well as the **boat trips**, **diving** and **fishing excursions** you'd expect from a marina.

ARRIVAL AND DEPARTURE

VARADERO

BY PLANE

Juan Gualberto Gómez Airport (☎ 45 247015) The single terminal of this modest airport, 25km west of Varadero, serves international flights, mostly to and from Toronto, Montreal and other Canadian cities, though there are also direct connections to Miami, Frankfurt, Munich, Manchester and Mexico City, plus domestic flights to Cayo Largo (1 daily; 45min). It has a bureau de change, an information centre and several car rental offices outside in the car park.

Getting into town Víazul buses (see below) stop just outside the main entrance to the airport terminal three times a day on their way to Varadero from Havana, and four times a day on their way from Varadero to Havana

and Viñales. Many hotels have buses waiting to pick up guests with reservations, and it may be worth talking to the driver or tour guide to see if there are any spare seats. There are always plenty of taxis, which will take you to the centre of Varadero. Alternatively, you can book a taxi online in advance with the WijinCuba agency (☎ 5 263 6854, ⟳ wijincuba.com).

Airlines Air Canada, Juan Gualberto Gómez Airport (☎ 45 61 3016); Cubana, Avenida 1ra e/ 54 y 55 (☎ 45 61 1823).

BY VÍAZUL BUS

Terminal de Omnibus All interprovincial buses arrive at and depart from this small terminal at Calle 36 esq. Autopista del Sur (☎ 45 61 4886), 150m from Avenida 1ra and with several hotels and *casas particulares* within a few blocks; there are often taxis waiting out front – if not, call Taxi OK (☎ 45 61 4444).

Bus tickets To book tickets go to the Víazul ticket office at the bus station (daily 7am–9.30pm) at least a day in advance.

Destinations Bayamo (1 daily; 13hr); Camagüey (1 daily; 8hr 30min); Cárdenas (1 daily; 25min); Ciego de Ávila (1 daily; 6hr 30min); Cienfuegos (2 daily; 4hr); Havana (4 daily; 3hr); Holguín (1 daily; 12hr); Juan Gualberto Gómez Airport (4 daily; 30min); Las Tunas (1 daily; 10hr); Matanzas (4 daily; 50min); Pinar del Río (1 daily; 6hr 30min); Playa Girón (1 daily; 2hr 30min); Playa Larga (1 daily; 2hr); Sancti Spíritus (1 daily; 5hr 20min); Santa Clara (2 daily; 3hr 25min); Santiago de Cuba (1 daily; 16hr); Trinidad (2 daily; 5hr–6hr 30min); Viñales (1 daily; 7hr 20min).

BY CAR

The road to Varadero, either from the airport or Havana, is the Vía Blanca, which leads right to the bridge providing the only road link between the peninsula and the mainland. There's a tollgate a few kilometres before the bridge. Arriving from the east you'll connect first with Cárdenas (see page 200) and reach the bridge on the only road between there and Varadero.

GETTING AROUND

3

BY TOURIST BUS

Varadero Beach Tour This hop-on, hop-off double-decker bus service is the cheapest way of getting around the peninsula, going as far as the Marina Gaviota and stopping at many of the hotels in eastern Varadero. It operates between 9am and 8pm, starting its last lap around 7pm. There are 45 officially designated stops, and at most of these a timetable is posted, though it shouldn't be taken too literally – buses can be infrequent, with waits of up to an hour in low season. Though the Transgaviota buses marked Panoramic Bus Tour may appear to be a separate service,

they are not – tickets are valid on both types of bus.

Matanzas Bus Tour Operating between Varadero and Matanzas when there's sufficient demand in peak season (Jan–March & July–Aug), it usually runs between 9am and 7pm, with the last bus leaving Varadero at 3.30pm.

Turitren This theme-park-style transport is only sporadically in use. It makes frequent stops along Avenida Primera between the *Superclubs Puntarena* hotel in Reparto Kawama and the Plaza América shopping mall east of the town; it also makes regular stops at and around Parque Josone.

TOURS AND EXCURSIONS FROM VARADERO

Public transport from Varadero to the rest of Matanzas is limited, and unless you rent a car, **organized excursions** provide the only convenient way of visiting some of the most memorable landscapes and natural spectacles in the province. This is especially true of the **Yumurí valley**, which is bypassed by both local buses and long-distance coaches; the Jeep Safari Yumurí tour (see page 211) costs $1800–2000CUP). An organized excursion is also an excellent way to visit the **Cuevas de Bellamar**, from around $800CUP; **Río Canímar**, from around $1400CUP; the **Península de Zapata**, from around $1500CUP; and **Matanzas city**, from around $800CUP. Excursions to all of these places can be booked for very similar if not identical prices through any of the **national travel agents** operating in Varadero, from the agents' *buros de turismo*, found in the larger hotel lobbies, and through Infotur information offices (see above). Of the agencies below, Cubatur tends to be the most reliable as far as opening hours go. There are also, now, a number of **privately-run agencies**, most of which offer a set of fixed excursions around the province and beyond as well as the option to tailor a trip to your preferences. None of these have public offices – bookings are made online or by phone.

Contact the agents for activities within Varadero too.

STATE TRAVEL AGENTS
Cubanacán Calle 24 y playa ☎ 45 667061.
Cubatur Ave. 1ra esq. 33 ☎ 45 614405, ext 224.
Ecotur Ave. 1ra esq. 15 ☎ 45 614405.
Gaviota Tours Calle 13 e/ 2da y 4ta ☎ 45 667864.
Havanatur Ave. 3ra e/ 33 y 34 ☎ 45 667027.

Paradiso Ave. 1ra esq. 36 ☎ 45 614758.

PRIVATE TRAVEL AGENTS
Varadero Tour Taxi ⓦ varaderotourtaxi.com.
WijinCuba ⓦ wijincuba.com.

3

BY TAXI

Regular taxis There's a constant stream of taxis along Avenida Primera, as well as a rank outside the *Cuatro Palmas* hotel between Calle 60 and Calle 62. Alternatively, ring Cubataxi (☎ 45 614444 or ☎ 41 610555).

Scooter-taxis Two-seater scooter-taxis encased in yellow spheres, *cocotaxis* cost more or less the same as a normal taxi. There are ranks at Calle 15 esq. Avenida 1ra and outside the *Cuatro Palmas* hotel at Avenida 1ra e/ 60 y 64.

Gran Car For a ride in a classic American car, contact Gran Car (☎ 45 614768, ☎ 614444 or ☎ 611718) or pick one up at Calle 16 next to the craft market there.

HORSE-DRAWN TRANSPORT

Horse-drawn carriages For a tour of the town or beyond you can pick up a horse and carriage outside Parque Josone, among other places.

Coches Hicacos Less touristy, and frequently used by locals, Coches Hicacos are horse-drawn carts closer to a local bus service than a taxi. They operate up and down Avenida Primera and congregate at Avenida 1ra esq. 54 but you should be able to hail one anywhere you see them.

BY CAR, SCOOTER OR BICYCLE

Car rental As well as the car-rental desks in many hotels, Cubacar and Havanautos (ⓦ transturvaradero.com) have branches around the peninsula, including at Avenida 1ra esq. 31 (☎ 45 668196; 8am–8pm) and at Calle 20 e/ Avenida 1ra y Avenida 2da (☎ 45 611808; 8am–5pm); there's also Rex at Calle 36, opposite the bus station (☎ 45 662121).

Scooter rental There are rental points up and down the peninsula at various hotels and at Cubacar, Avenida 1ra esq. 21 (daily 9am–6pm).

Bike rental Bikes can be rented from *Solymar* hotel on the Avenida de las Américas, roughly opposite the *Mesón del Quijote* restaurant, and from Happy Bikes at Avenida 4ta esq. 18 (☎ 5352 5949, ⓦ happybikecuba.com; daily 8am–8pm) where they rent out a variety of bicycles.

INFORMATION

Tourist office Infotur, at Avenida 1ra esq. 13 (daily 8.30am–4.30pm; ☎ 45 662961), can supply maps, book accommodation, bus tickets and organized excursions, and advise on public transport and almost anything you need to know about visiting the area.

ACCOMMODATION

SEE MAP PAGE 188

The proliferation of **casas particulares** in Varadero has rendered the budget hotel market here pretty much redundant, with many of the *casas* offering a far higher standard of accommodation, food and service. All the *casas* and cheaper hotels are located in the town area. As Cuba's tourism capital, there is no shortage of luxury **hotels** here either, most of them in the east of the peninsula, beyond the town, where all the newest hotels and mega-complexes are also found. The prices quoted below are for **high season** – in low season, you can get lucky and secure a room in a *casa* for the equivalent of $25 USD. Booking ahead is strongly recommended for the all-inclusives, preferably via a discount website or package holiday operator, since the rack rates appearing in this guide for these places can be four or five times higher than pre-booked prices. There is no **camping** on the peninsula.

HOTELS

REPARTO KAWAMA

Club Kawama Ave. 1ra y Calle 0 ⓦ gran-caribe.cu. Large, landscaped all-inclusive complex, bordered by 300m of beach, which loses some character away from the main building, a stylish neo-colonial terraced structure built in 1930 as a gentlemen's club. Choose from private or shared houses, or apartments, though they could all do with some sprucing up. There's a fantastically chic restaurant and cosy basement cabaret. **$$$**

FISHING AROUND VARADERO

There are plenty of better locations around Cuba to go **saltwater fishing** than off the coast of Varadero, but this is one of the easiest places to charter a boat, and sailing out to the surrounding cays is a great way for the casual enthusiast to combine a spot of fishing with a relaxing day-trip. You have to get well away from the beach to have even a chance of a half-decent catch, which could be wahoo, barracuda, grouper, snapper or tuna among others, and some fishing trips actually take place on the other side of the province, off the Península de Zapata. Tailor-made excursions and fishing packages are available at the three **marinas** (see page 195), which will supply any necessary fishing equipment; the *buros de turismo* in most hotel lobbies can also usually also help with arrangements.

THE TOWN

Cuatro Palmas Ave. 1ra e/ 60 y 64 ⓦ starfishresorts. com. An artistically designed complex at the eastern end of the town, featuring a variety of accommodation buildings, some for all-inclusive guests, others for bed and breakfast guests, and a completely separate block over the road neighbouring Parque Josone. There's a good choice of restaurants, a nice pool and watersports facilities. $$$$

Dos Mares Calle 53 esq. Ave. 1ra ⓦ islazulhotels.com. Atypically for Varadero, this agreeable little hotel feels more like those found in provincial colonial towns. What it lacks in facilities it makes up for with plenty of character and a pleasant intimacy, especially in the sunken bar. Rooms are quite small and simple. $$

Los Delfines Ave. 1ra e/ 38 y 39 ⓦ islazulhotels.com. This is the most tasteful and attractive of the cheaper-than-average landscaped-garden hotels in this part of town, incorporating several accommodation blocks, linked together by outdoor corridors cutting across grassy lawns and a pool right down to the beach. $$

EASTERN VARADERO

Mansión Xanadú Autopista del Sur Km 7 ⓦ varaderogolfclub.com. Housed in the splendidly opulent Dupont Mansion, this hotel is unique in Varadero. The eight refined rooms, six of which face the sea, have been individually furnished – two with colonial American originals. Restoration of the house to its 1930s glory has been on-going for some time, but disruption is kept to a minimum. Aimed at golfers, room prices include golfing packages for the Varadero Golf Course, whose clubhouse is next door. Breakfast and dinner included in price. $$$$

Meliá Las Américas Autopista del Sur Km 7 ⓦ meliacuba.com. One of the most imaginatively designed hotels on the peninsula, with paths weaving down from the huge circular main building through intricately landscaped gardens to the beach – even the pool drops down a level while it twists itself around the pathways and pond. Rooms are tastefully furnished, and there are five restaurants, plus special deals for golfers who want to use the course over the road. Over-18s only. $$$$

★ **Royalton Hicacos** Carretera de las Morlas Km 15 ⓦ royaltonresorts.com. The fabulous rooms here, all of them suites, have split-level designs, living-room areas, king-size beds and all the amenities you could want. Highlights include a two-man cave built into the side of the stunning pool, a fully equipped spa, a squash court and some great drinking and dining areas with waterways woven around them. Over-18s only. $$$$

CASAS PARTICULARES

THE TOWN

★ **Beny's House** Calle 55 no.124 e/ Ave. 1ra y Ave. 2da

ⓣ 45 61 1700. Sitting 100m from the beach, this superb, pristine house with a neatly landscaped garden full of cacti and little rockeries also has a fabulous patio equipped with sun-loungers which Beny and his friendly family are happy for you to take to the beach. The two high-spec guest rooms come with TV, DVD, a/c and minibar, and are cleaned daily. The food here is also excellent and the generous breakfast spreads are included in the cost of the room – though you can opt out and knock a few pesos off the price. $

★ **Brother's House** Calle 22 no.504 e/ Ave. 3ra y Ave. 4ta ⓦ facebook.com/brotherhouse.cu. This porch-fronted house surrounded by greenery sits at the end of a short cul-de-sac, and offers four pastel-painted, neatly finished rooms, one a bedroom-kitchen suite, all with a/c, shiny tiled floors and simple, good-quality furnishings. Rooms are spread around an attractive, plant-filled patio area which links up to the gorgeous shrub-lined garden where you can lounge on the lawn under the branches of a beautiful weeping bottlebrush tree. The couple who own the place, Adriana and Tito, are very personable. $

Casa de Leila y Alina Calle 57 no.6 e/ Ave. 1ra y playa ⓣ 45 66 9241. One of the best located casas in Varadero, on the grass-lined path to the museum and beach and a stone's throw from Parque Josone. Guests rent a separate, spacious and well-equipped apartment building around the back of a handsome bungalow, both of which share a garden patio area featuring an inviting outdoor lounge. $

Casa Mary y Angel Calle 43 no.4309 e/ Ave. 1ra y Ave. 2da, ⓦ casamaryyangel.com. Up a drive, raised above a street in the heart of the town is the yellow, green and burgundy painted patio that provides the focal point and one of several outdoor spaces for guests. There are three spacious, well-kept, simple but comfortable rooms with a/c. Mary and Ángel are warm, professional and speak good English. $

Casa de Rafael Guada Morffi Calle 36 no.117 (alto) e/ Ave. 1ra y Autopista del Sur, ⓣ 45 61 2925, ⓔ rafaelguada7@gmail.com. A small but inviting first-floor apartment within a compact two-storey house near the bus station, consisting of a spruce kitchen-diner and a tightly packed little bedroom with a bunk bed and a single bed, plus a safety deposit box and internet access. $

Casa de Rosa Calle 36 no.119 e/ Ave. 1ra y Autopista del Sur ⓣ 45 61 2016, ⓔ ochi.diaz@nauta.cu. The most conveniently located casa for anyone arriving by bus, this bungalow with a garden and a patio wrapped around three of its sides is less than 100m from the bus station. The pleasant landlady rents out one plain, large twin-bed room with a/c, TV, fridge and a large bathroom. $

Isorazul Calle 27 no.105 e/ Ave. 1ra y Ave. 2da ⓣ 45 61 3629, ⓔ isorazulvaradero@gmail.com. Two decent, en-suite rooms, one on the ground level with a pantry, the other upstairs with its own cosy terrace at the back of the house, both with a/c, TV, hairdryer, safe and fridge. Isora,

3

CHEAP EATS AND FAST FOOD

Eating out is not that expensive in Varadero — being a town as well as a beach resort ensures there's a selection of cheap places to grab a meal. They are mostly takeaway, roadside affairs, though there are one or two dirt-cheap restaurants as well. Here are a few options.

Castell Nuovo Ave. 1ra no.503 esq. Calle 11 ☎45 66 7786; see map page 188. Its low prices make this Italian restaurant popular despite being low on charm. You can get seafood here too. $

El Rápido Calle 47 e/ Ave. 1ra y Ave. Playa ☎45 61 3326; see map page 188. A large branch of the

national fast-food chain where pizzas, sandwiches and hot dogs are served with no sense of urgency. $

Super Machi Calle 15; see map page 188. Open-air takeaway grill knocking out pork, chicken and fish meals accompanied with rice, salad and one additional side. $$

---

the friendly landlady, is very helpful and hospitable. $

★ **Norma's B&B** Calle 59 no.21 e/ 2da y 3ra ☎45 61 3763, ✉normasbedandbreakfast@gmail.com. Tucked away on a quiet street behind Parque Josone, this is a very relaxing place to stay. Rooms are clustered around a lovely garden patio, with picnic bench and garden furniture,

surrounded by shrubs and trees. The three double, en-suite, a/c rooms are perfectly comfortable, one with its own kitchen, and are in a guest block with its own separate access and therefore completely independent. You can rent bikes here too. Room rates are the same year-round. $

EATING

SEE MAP PAGE 188

Eating-out options have taken a leap forward over the last few years with the proliferation of **paladars**, and there's now a broader selection of places offering good-quality Cuban cuisine. That said, there's still very little variety for such a large resort, with the few "international cuisine" options mostly rehashing Cuban staples and raising questions about their chef's geography. If you're staying at an upmarket all-inclusive, you'll almost certainly eat better non-Cuban food there than outside; non-guests can buy a **day-pass** to some of these hotels, which covers use of their facilities and restaurants. But for Cuban cuisine, the paladars are your best bet. To check out a few places before making your choice, head for Parque Josone, or the few blocks between there and the top of town.

PALADARS

Don Alex Calle 31 no.106 e/ Ave. 1ra y Ave. 3ra ☎45 61 3207. Popular for its excellent-value thin-crust pizzas, they also serve pastas and hearty Cuban food. On the whole, the kitchen knows what it's doing and will happily personalise your pizzas. Tables are spread around the front-of-house porch which is surrounded by a nice-looking, neatly planted garden. $$

Nonna Tina Calle 38 no.5 e/ Ave. 1ra y Ave. Playa ☎45 612450, ✉paladar-nonnatina.it. This Italian paladar is a pizza and pasta specialist; the thin-crust pizzas are satisfyingly authentic, and the pasta dishes are generally stuffed full of ingredients and make for very hearty and enjoyable meals. $

★ **Salsa Suárez** Calle 31 no.103 e/ Ave. 1ra y Ave. 3ra ☎45 614194. They spread their culinary net wide here but, unusually for restaurants that don't specialize, they get away with it. Tacos, sushi, pizza, pasta and *comida criolla*

all feature but very little is served up that is not worthy of the slightly above average prices. For ambience it's among the best in Varadero, the choice seats on a veranda hidden behind a wall of matted trees, the music at just the right volume and the lighting subdued. The good service and the uniformed staff, who look like air hostesses, complete the enjoyable experience – just stay out of the a/c interior room where the attractive fish tank doesn't do enough to dispel the more sterile atmosphere. $$$

La Vaca Rosada Calle 21 e/ Ave. 1ra y 2da ☎45 612307. Rooftop-terrace paladar flanked by palm trees and best after dark, when it's nicely lit and becomes a good place for a romantic meal – perhaps a lobster and shrimp kebab, one of their square pizzas or, that most romantic of dishes, a massive slab of pork in breadcrumbs. Leave room for dessert. $$$

★ **Varadero 60** Calle 60 esq. Ave. 3ra ☎45 613986. The most impressive paladar in Varadero, where the owner Luis's collection of 1960s memorabilia, most notably a wonderful set of old posters and adverts, creates a memorable setting, as do the patio dining area and the shiny '58 Buick parked on the drive. Try the usually excellent lobster, or mix it up by choosing the Tesoros del Mar, a shrimp, fish and lobster medley. $$$

Waco's Club Ave. 3ra no.212 e/ 58 y 59 ☎45 613728. One of the priciest paladars in Varadero goes some way to justifying the prices of its lobster and signature surf 'n' turf and shrimp dishes with the quality and freshness of the food, generous portions, excellent service and the lovely setting. The roof terrace has views of the Bay of Cárdenas and there's an inviting little covered patio for diners too, all in a hidden corner of a pretty neighbourhood nestling next to the Parque Josone. $$$

STATE RESTAURANTS

Las Américas Mansión Xanadú, Autopista del Sur Km 7 ☎ 45 667750. A classily-run restaurant, with a setting to match. There's seating in the library, down in the wine cellar or out on the terrace overlooking the garden perched above the waves – you can wander down for a post-meal drink or up to the rooftop bar (see below). The house speciality is lobster is usually good quality, with French dishes also well represented on the menu. $$$

La Barbacoa Ave. 1ra esq. 64 ☎ 45 667795. A steakhouse and barbecue grill tucked into the top corner of town, shielded from the road by a screen of trees. Topping the menu are the usually good-quality Chateaubriand steaks but there are plenty of other cuts plus good lobster and some chicken, pork and fish options. $$$

La Bodeguita del Medio Ave. Playa e/ 40 y 41 ☎ 45 667784. Spin-off of the famous Havana restaurant where, like the original, diners can add their scribble to the thousands that already adorn the walls. The food is typical Cuban fare – think juicy shredded beef or fried pork chunks. Very touristy but generally not in a bad way, with live music from a local band. $$

La Campana Parque Josone ☎ 45 667224. The tasty *ropa vieja*, or shredded beef, is available with or without jerk seasoning, and the pork slices are also good at this cosy stone-and-wood hunting lodge with a large fireplace and animal heads adorning the walls. You can opt for these dishes and others as part of the good value three-course set meal deal. There's also outdoor dining on the veranda. $$

Casa de Al Ave. Kawama, 1.5km west of the Varadero bridge ◍ lacasadeal.com. The gangster-themed menu – Langosta 'Al Capone' or Don Camarón, for example – is just a gimmicky version of the usual Cuban staples, but the setting, in a refined two-storey stone mansion, once a holiday home of Al Capone, is one of the best on the peninsula, with views up the beach and tables on a cool, tiled terrace surrounded by low arches. $$$

Casa del Chocolate Ave. 1ra e/ 61 y 62 ☎ 45 667746. A gimmicky but interesting and unusual restaurant and chocolatier, where cuts of meat are served with bitter or sweet chocolate sauces and everything is cooked in cocoa butter instead of cooking oil. There's a bar as well and you can buy bon bons, made on the premises, from the sweet-shop counter. The chocolate rum shake comes highly recommended. $$

Esquina Cuba Ave. 1ra y 36 ☎ 45 614019. Tasty, great value tomato shrimp, smoked pork and fish dishes are served on a wide-open veranda under a thatched roof, where the bordering plants do just enough to separate the place from a sense of the road. A white-and-pink Oldsmobile makes up the bulk of the interior decoration. $

KIKE-Kcho Marina Gaviota Varadero, Autopista del Sur y final ☎ 45 667330. With a reputation for excellent lobster, which you can pick direct from submerged cages, this bright and airy seafood restaurant, housed in a large blue and white, open-sided wooden ranch-style building hovering over the sea, is a great place for a drawn-out meal, with views out across the marina. $$$

Mesón del Quijote Ave. de las Américas ☎ 45 667796. The speciality here is paella, with four different versions, but the lobster is more reliable and the food in general presented with minimal garnish, relying instead on simple

3

BOAT TRIPS AND THE MARINAS

With entertainment options a little thin on the ground in Varadero, it's no surprise that **boat trips** to the islets and reefs around the peninsula are so numerous and popular. The family of cays beyond the eastern tip of the peninsula – cayos Blanco, Piedras and Romero, among others – make up most of the stopping-off points; they're bordered by small coral reefs and offer the best opportunities for **snorkelling**.

Most of the trips can be **booked** through any of the principal travel agents (see page 191) or at the marinas themselves; book at least a day in advance, or earlier during times of high demand. Most trips include the transfer from your hotel to the point of departure; children under 12 are usually charged half-price rates.

Marina Chapelín (aka Marina Marlin) Autopista del Sur Km 12 ☎ 45 667550 or ☎ 45 667565. This marina – home to Aquaworld – has its own information kiosk at Avenida 1ra y 59 (daily 8am–5pm) where you can book the popular Seafari Cayo Blanco or, unique to this marina, the 2hr Boat Adventure, an excursion on ski-bikes or speedboats to a cay where you can see crocodiles, iguanas and other creatures.

Marina Dársena 1km from the Varadero bridge at Vía Blanca ☎ 45 66 8060 ext 661. Predominantly a docking station rather than a boat-trip departure point, with 112 berths, though it does organize fishing and boat trips.

Marina Gaviota Varadero Eastern end of Autopista del Sur ☎ 45 664115. Now the second largest marina in the Caribbean, offering a wide choice of catamaran excursions to Cayo Blanco; most include snorkelling, lunch and some beach time, while one option, the Crucero del Sol (daily 9am–4.30pm), includes swimming with dolphins.

flavours. Perched atop a small hill, the dining experience is better before dark, when the views from inside make up for the bare interior of dark benches and tables, wine racks and wall-to-wall windows lined with wax-covered bottles. $\overline{\text{555}}$
El Retiro Parque Josone ☎ 45 667738 ext 102. This

lobster specialist is Parque Josone's one option for fine dining, with decor that's restrained rather than refined. Other options besides lobster include the seafood platter, and there are less expensive fish, shrimp and chicken dishes. $\overline{\text{555}}$

DRINKING AND NIGHTLIFE

SEE MAP PAGE 188

Nightlife in Varadero falls way short of the standards you might expect for such a large resort, partly because so many of the hotels provide their own entertainment programmes, though almost all of it is corny variety entertainment. You'll struggle to find a straight-up **bar** and should be ready for drinks with karaoke or live music. There are one or two decent venues for **live music** but there is no area with a buzz and you can't easily bar- or club-hop your way through the night, with most places in isolated pockets around the town. Note that some **clubs** and **cabarets** do not allow shorts or sleeveless tops to be worn. For drinking in the day there are a few **cafés**, most of which serve food too.

BARS AND CAFÉS

★ **Bar Mirador Casa Blanca** Mansión Xanadú, Autopista del Sur Km 7 ☎ 45 667388. A sophisticated place with an ornate wooden ceiling supported by black pillars. The location at the top of this splendid mansion affords fabulous views along the coastline.
Casa del Habano Ave. 1ra e/ 63 y 64 ☎ 45 667843. The dinky, stylish, balconied café upstairs from an excellent cigar shop makes a good place for a quiet drink.
El Galeón Hotel Dos Mares, Calle 53 esq. Ave. 1ra ☎ 45 612702. One of the few proper bars in the town, just a straight-up, laidback place to get a drink, set just below street level with a stylish varnished-wood finish and a slight Mediterranean feel.
La Gruta del Vino Parque Josone ☎ 45 667224. This novel little bar and eatery, sinking back into a tiny cave on the far side of the lake in Parque Josone, has a wide selection of wine and a patio out front where you can sip your drinks near the water's edge.
Piano Bar Centro Cultural Artex, Calle 60 e/ Ave. 2da y Ave. 3ra ☎ 45 667415. Next door to *La Comparsita* (see

below) and part of the same complex, this slightly cheesy bar, which sometimes hosts karaoke, can be fun in a group and is the clubbiest bar in the town.
Varadero 1920 Parque Josone ☎ 45 667224. An open-air café propped above the banks of the park lake, and one of the most laidback spots for a drink in Varadero.

CLUBS

Most hotels offer something more akin to a school disco than a nightclub, and a karaoke night is never far away, but there are a few hotel nightclubs that have become destinations in their own right. In the Cuban tradition, the music at these venues is sometimes performed by live bands, thus blurring the lines between club nights and live music shows, but they will almost always feature a DJ at some stage in proceedings and often for the whole night. Expect the same mix of reggaeton, salsa, Latin pop and commercial electronic dance music at all of them.
La Bamba Hotel Tuxpán, 800m from the eastern end of Ave. de las Américas ☎ 45 667560. One of the largest and best-known hotel nightclubs, it can get pretty crowded here and the music tends to be provided by DJs rather than live bands. Expect Latin and generic dance music.
Palacio de la Rumba End of Ave. de las Américas ☎ 45 668210. Often referred to simply as *La Rumba*, this is one of the area's biggest and best-designed venues. It's just beyond the *Bella Costa* hotel.

DANCE SHOWS AND CABARETS

The most popular alternative to clubs are the cabarets, with their displays of kitsch glamour, over-sentimental crooners and semi-naked dancers. The most famous Cuban cabaret, the *Tropicana*, has a branch just a short drive away in Matanzas, near the Río Canímar, which knocks the socks

---

VARADERO BAILA

Every year, usually in the second week of July, Varadero hosts an **International Festival of Salsa**, also known as **Varadero Baila**, a week-long programme of concerts, dance shows and classes organized by the national "cultural tourism" agency Paradiso (🌐 paradiso.cu) and the Academia Baile en Cuba (🌐 bailaencuba.com). Dancers of all abilities as well as complete beginners can enrol on the festival's five-day dance courses, while the programme of concerts and events are spread around a half-dozen or so venues including the local branch of the Academia Baile en Cuba and a number of the nightclubs. To make enquiries in person go to the Paradiso office at Calle 26 e/ Avenida 1ra y Avenida 2da (☎ 45 614758). In recent years the festival has been held jointly in Varadero and Havana.

DANCE CLASSES AT THE ACADEMIA BAILE EN CUBA

Many of Varadero's larger hotels provide **salsa classes** as part of their entertainment package, but, regardless of where you're staying, you can also take classes covering all Cuban dance styles at the excellent **Academia Baile en Cuba**, Avenida 1ra e/ 34 y 35 (daily 8am–6pm; ⓦ varaderobaila.com), where they offer anything from a two-hour class to week-long courses tailored to your preferences. You book through the local branch of Paradiso (Calle 26 e/ Avenida 1ra y Avenida 2da; ❶ 45 614758, 614759 and 612506), the national cultural tourism agency that runs the centre.

off anything on the peninsula for sheer scale and spectacle.

La Comparsita Centro Cultural Artex, Calle 60 e/ Ave. 2da y Ave. 3ra ❶ 45 667415. This open-air club and concert set-up is one of the larger, slicker stage venues attracting a lively mix of locals and tourists. There's a weekly programme of audio-visual DJ nights, live salsa and reggaeton concerts, cabarets and various other music and dance performances. The programme is posted outside during the day.

Cueva del Pirata Autopista del Sur Km 8 ❶ 45 667751. The show and the disco that follows take place in a cave next to the entrance to *Allegro Varadero*, which makes for a different atmosphere. The performers dress as pirates for a slight twist on the usual dress code.

LIVE MUSIC VENUES

The Beatles Ave. 1ra e/ 58 y 59 ❶ 45 667329. Most nights, the large streetside patio of this novelty restaurant is the stage for tribute bands playing homage not just to the Beatles but other rock and pop gods from Led Zeppelin and Pink Floyd to AC/DC and Guns N' Roses. The musicians are pretty accomplished and there's usually an enthusiastic crowd. Show times are usually around 10pm.

Calle 62 Calle 62 esq. Ave. 1ra. This open-sided 'snack bar' might not look like much in the day but when there's a live band playing on the stage at night the place packs out and is as lively as it gets in the town area. At its best it feels more like a street party.

★ **Casa de la Música** Ave. Playa no.4206 e/ 42 y 43 ❶ 45 667568 ext 111. Varadero's top venue for reliably high-quality live music, this converted cinema usually has comedy shows earlier in the week and, from Thurs to Sun, concerts covering a broad variety of mostly Cuban styles, from traditional son and bolero to modern salsa and jazz. It's advisable to book advance tickets in July & Aug (box office Tues–Sun 8.30am–12.30pm). Over-18s only.

★ **Plaza América Convention Center** Autopista del Sur Km 7 ❶ 45 668181. The best live music show in Varadero features various incarnations of the Buena Vista Social Club performing in the Salón Plenario of the convention centre adjoining Varadero's largest shopping mall on Wednesdays and Fridays. Shows usually feature a selection of some of the best-known songs from the world-famous albums that reignited a global appetite for traditional Cuban music.

SPORTS AND RECREATION

LEISURE COMPLEXES

Complejo Recreativo Record Ave. Playa esq. 46 ❶ 45 614880. Features a pool hall, ping pong tables, a snack bar and a bowling alley.

Marina Gaviota Varadero Bolera Autopista del Sur y final ❶ 45 664115. An eight-lane bowling alley in the small commercial complex at the largest marina in Varadero. There are four pool tables here too.

Todo en Uno Calle 54 esq. Autopista del Sur ❶ 45 668290. A small amusement park, more popular with Cubans than foreign tourists, featuring bumper cars, a carousel and a diminutive roller coaster as well as pool tables, fast-food outlets, a couple of shops and a four-lane bowling alley.

WATERSPORTS

Essentials For watersports equipment you're largely dependent on the hotels, many of which have their own watersports clubs. Snorkelling is barely worth bothering with near the beach as there's little to see, but there are plenty of boat trips with snorkelling at the nearby cays. You can also go scuba diving or fishing. Varadero is one of the best spots in Cuba for kitesurfing and a couple of kitesurfing schools were established here just a few years ago. The best conditions tend to be at the western end of the peninsula.

Barracuda Scuba Diving Centre Ave. Kawama esq. Calle 4 and Ave. 1ra e/ 58 y 59 ❶ 45 667072. This watersports club rents out aqua bikes, catamarans, kayaks and other bits and pieces of equipment plus sun chairs and parasols.

★ **Cubakiters** Varadero Kitesurf School, Casa 12, Club Karey, Ave. Kawma ⓦ cubakiters.com. A great place for first-timers offering various kitesurfing courses with enthusiastic and patient instructors, from an initiation class to an 8hr beginners' course, plus plenty of other options. Based just off the beach among the roadside villas of the

3

SCUBA DIVING IN VARADERO

There are far superior dive sites around Cuba than the ones off the Varadero coast, but with several **diving clubs** on the peninsula this is one of the best-served areas for diving. The clubs below can offer diving equipment and instruction, and can arrange excursions to elsewhere in the province, commonly to the Península de Zapata in southern Matanzas. Most of the local dive sites are on the coral reefs around the offshore cays to the east of Varadero, such as **Cayo Blanco** and **Cayo Piedras**, where there are various wrecks, and also at **Playa Coral**, with a coral reef just 30m from the shore along the coast towards Matanzas. As well as the standard coral reef visits, clubs usually offer night- and cave-dives, the latter often in the **Cueva de Saturno** to the west of Varadero, not far off the Vía Blanca (see page 202).

DIVING CLUBS

Barracuda Scuba Diving Centre Ave. Kawama esq. Calle 4 and Ave. 1ra e/ 58 y 59 ☏45 667072. Operating in partnership with the Marina Chapelín, this club offers a comprehensive programme of diving including ACUC and SSI courses for advanced divers and instructors. It's also the best organized for first-time divers, with beginners' classes including a theory class, a lesson in the club's own swimming pool and then a sea dive.

Centro Internacional de Buceo Gaviota Marina Gaviota Varadero, Autopista del Sur y final ☏45 664121. A very professionally run dive club at the peninsula's best-equipped marina offering single dives through to open-water, week-long ACUC courses.

Hotel Club Karey, though not part of the hotel itself.

GOLF

Varadero Golf Club Austopista del Sur Km 7 ⓦvaraderogolfclub.com. One of only two courses in Cuba, with eighteen holes in a narrow 3.5km strip alongside the Autopista del Sur; the caddy house and golf shop are right next to the *Mansión Xanadú* hotel. Prices are advertised in US dollars, with packages from one Green Fee (18 Holes) of golf with reserved tee time, shared golf cart and club storage for $120 USD per golfer, through to $400 USD for seven Green Fees. The Golf Academy of three qualified instructors offer one-to-one and group sessions for beginners through to experienced golfers, with a maximum of four people per instructor for group options. Contact the club (✉info@varaderogolfclub.com) for details and costs.

SHOPPING

Aside from the half-dozen or so arts and crafts markets along Avenida Primera, and the cigar shops in the town and the hotels, Varadero's **shops** are generally worth a quick browse only if you're passing. Note that market opening times vary and in low season sometimes close an hour or two earlier than stated below. Self-caterers have their work cut out, with no big **supermarkets** in the town or any fresh food markets on the entire peninsula. There are a few small convenience stores along Avenida Primera and in some of the hotels, but the pickings are slim and you're better off buying food before you arrive.

TENNIS

La Raqueta Dorada Ave. 1ra e/ 37 y 38. An outdoor synthetic-surface court that's free to use, though you need your own racquet and balls.

SKYDIVING

Centro Internacional de Paracaidismo Just under 2.5km from the Varadero bridge along Vía Blanca ☏45 662828, ⓦskydivingvaradero.com. This centre offers skydiving over Varadero from around $220 USD, which includes the transfer from your hotel, a class and the drop itself, in tandem with the instructor. Flights are in old Russian Antonov An-2 biplanes or helicopters. Bookings are taken directly or through Cubanacán or Cubatur (see page 191). To get here, take the turning off the Vía Blanca opposite the Marina Dársena; at the T-junction turn right and after 350m turn left down the ruler-straight driveway to the centre.

SEE MAP APGE 188

SUPERMARKETS

Grossery Plaza América Autopista del Sur Km 7 ☏45 667869. Inside the Plaza América mall, this is Varadero's largest and best supermarket, with a fresh meat counter and lots of packet food but very little fresh vegetables or fruit.

ARTS AND CRAFTS

Feria Los Caneyes Ave. 1ra e/ 51 y 52. Around thirty stalls with a good selection of jewellery and hand-carved wooden ornaments, plus all the other usual Cuban commercial arts and crafts.

Feria La Epoca Ave. 1ra esq. 47. This smallish market is one of the better places in town for a broad range of handmade products, from jewellery to ornamental drums and painted wall plaques.

Galería de Arte Varadero Ave. 1ra e/ 59 y 60 ☎ 45 668260. A more highbrow option than most arts and crafts vendors, with framed paintings, lithographs, jewellery and screen prints.

Gran Parque de la Artesanía Ave. 1ra e/ 15 y 16. Varadero's best and biggest craft market, with over a hundred stalls around a little roadside square selling all the trademark Cuban crafts, textiles and gift items: wooden statuettes, lace shawls, coral necklaces, cigar boxes and Che T-shirts as well as bags and ceramics.

Plaza Alegria Ave. 1ra e/ 47 y 48. This indoor market with over thirty stalls is one of Varadero's best places to buy handmade jewellery. You'll also find plenty of paintings as well as the usual selection of carved wooden figures and statuettes, T-shirts and leather goods.

Taller de Cerámica Ave. 1ra e/ esq. 60 ☎ 45 667829. You can watch pottery being made in the busy workshop here, then buy a piece in the little shop where everything for sale is a good-quality original and not the usual tourist tat.

CIGARS AND RUM

Casa del Habano Ave. 1ra e/ 63 y 64 ☎ 45 667843. Varadero's outstanding cigar store, with an impressive selection of all the major brands as well as all sorts of smoking paraphernalia, a smokers' lounge, a separate section selling rum and coffee, and an upstairs bar.

Casa del Habano Mi Cuba Ave. 1ra esq. 39 ☎ 45 614719. The choice of cigars here is only average but the options for where you smoke them are a cut above: choose between the upstairs smokers' lounge, the leather three-piece suite downstairs or a bar with a leafy outdoor terrace.

★ **Casa del Ron** Ave. 1ra e/ 62 y 63 ☎ 45 668393. As well as stocking the best selection of rum in Varadero, this is one of the peninsula's most novel shops. A captivating model of an early twentieth-century Cuban rum factory

occupies almost the whole front room, while in the back there's a 1920s-era bar set up solely for try-before-you-buy purposes.

Casa del Tabaco Caribe Ave. 1ra esq. 27 ☎ 45 667872. A small *tabaquería* where you can buy a number of the best-known brands and also sometimes watch cigars being made on a table out the front.

BOOKS AND MUSIC

Arte Cubano Ave. 1ra esq. 12 ☎ 45 668172. A packed gift shop with one of the better selections of CDs in Varadero and as good as anywhere for picking up salsa and reggaeton albums or more traditional styles like son and bolero.

La Casa Ave. 1ra esq. 59 ☎ 45 614584. A two-storey ranch-style building with too much space for its selection of books, mostly on revolutionary and political themes, Cuban wildlife and photography. Also stocks CDs, Cuban film posters and other pictures.

Librería Hanoi Ave. 1ra esq. 44 ☎ 45 612694. The cramped premises house a limited selection of mostly Cuban political literature and fiction which nevertheless constitute the biggest selection of new books in Varadero. An above-average stock of CDs too.

SHOPPING CENTRES AND MALLS

Centro Comercial Caimán Ave. 1ra e/ 61 y 62 ☎ 45 668214. Half a dozen shops gathered around a pleasant outdoor space selling toys, clothes, shoes, rum, perfume and groceries.

Centro Comercial Hicacos Parque de las 8000 Taquillas, Ave. 1ra e/ 44 y 46 ☎ 45 614837. The largest shopping complex in the town area, with around a dozen fairly basic shops, though there is a decent cigar place and one of the few photography shops around.

Plaza América Autopista del Sur Km 9 ☎ 45 668570. The slickest shopping centre in Varadero, with restaurants, clothing and jewellery boutiques, arts, crafts, T-shirts and souvenirs, a large cigar shop, a small bookshop, the area's best CD retailer and the largest supermarket on the peninsula.

DIRECTORY

Consulates Canadian Consulate, Calle 13 no.422 e/ Camino del Mar y Avenida 1ra (☎ 45 667395 & 612078). All other consulates and embassies are in Havana (see page 137).

Health Clínica Internacional de Varadero at Avenida 1ra y 61 (☎ 45 667710), which includes the best-stocked pharmacy in Varadero, is open 24hr. At the other end of town is another reasonable pharmacy at Avenida Kawama e/ 2 y 3 (daily 9am–7pm). The nearest major hospital is in Matanzas (see page 210). For an ambulance call ☎ 45 612950.

Immigration and visas The immigration office, for visa extensions and passport matters, is at Calle 39 esq. Avenida

1ra (Mon–Fri 9am–4pm; ☎ 45 613494). Tourist cards can also be extended through some hotels and information centres.

Left luggage Terminal de Omnibus, Calle 36 esq. Autopista del Sur.

Library Biblioteca José Smith Comas, Calle 33 e/ Avenida 1ra y Avenida 3ra ☎ 45 612358 (Mon–Fri 8am–7pm, Sat 9am–5pm). Has a selection of English literature, including a surprisingly good stock of Penguins.

Money and exchange Banks are scarce but include Banco Financiero Internacional, Avenida 1ra e/ 32 y 33, entrance on Avenida Playa (Mon–Fri 9am–7pm), and Avenida 2da esq.

62 (Mon–Fri 9am–12.30pm & 1.30–3pm); and Banco de Crédito y Comercio, Avenida 1ra esq. 36 (Mon–Fri 8.30am–5.30pm & Sat 9–11am). The CADECA *casas de cambio* are at the Centro Comercial Hicacos (daily 9am–7pm) and Avenida 1ra esq. 59 (Mon–Sat 8am–5pm, Sun 8am–noon). There are ATMs at the Banco de Crédito y Comercio and at Plaza América. For financial emergencies, including loss of credit cards or insurance matters, go to Asistur, Edificio Marbella, apto.6, Avenida 1ra no.4201 e/ 42 y 43 (☎ 45 667277).

Police ☎ 106. Police station at Calle 39 esq. Avenida 1ra.

Post office Plaza América shopping mall (Mon–Sat 8am–6pm). Many hotels have their own post office service.

Wi-fi The public wi-fi zones are at the Todo en Uno leisure complex at Calle 54 esq. Autopista del Sur; the Centro Comercial Hicacos at Ave. 1ra e/ 44 y 46; the Plaza América shopping mall; the Casa de la Música at Avenida Playa e/ 42 y 43; and Plaza Las Morlas at Marina Gaviota Varadero. Most of the upmarket hotels also have wi-fi, though you usually have to buy a card – available at hotels, and the ETECSA centres at Avenida 1ra y 30 (8.30am–7pm) and Plaza América (daily 8.30am–7pm), which both also have telephones and computer terminals where you can get online with a card.

Cárdenas

Ten kilometres southeast of Varadero and home to much of the peninsula's workforce, **CÁRDENAS** offers a taste of Cuban life away from the tourist spotlight, with a much stronger sense of history and a town centre dotted with crumbling colonial and neo-colonial buildings. Though it's on the coast, Cárdenas doesn't feel like a seaside town since most of its shoreline, hugging the **Bay of Cárdenas**, is an industrial zone. Few visitors are tempted to spend more than a day here, and the town is quite run down, its battered roads full of potholes, but there are one or two excellent *casas particulares* that help to make an overnight stay a little more worthwhile. The **Catedral de la Inmaculada Concepción** is Cárdenas' most distinguished historic building; its creditable museums, including the **Museo a la Batalla de Ideas**, with its fantastic views of the town, are on or right next to the Parque José Antonio Echeverría, the most inviting square in the city, though far less lively than **Plaza Malacoff**, the bustling market square.

Brief history

Founded in 1828 and known as the **Ciudad Bandera** (Flag City), it was here in 1850 that what became the national flag was first raised by the Venezuelan General Narcisco López and his troops, who had disembarked at Cárdenas in a US-backed attempt to spark a revolt against Spanish rule and clear the way for annexation. The attempt failed, but the flag's design was later adopted by the independence movement.

In 1878 José Arechabala, an immigrant from the Basque Country who'd moved to Cárdenas from Havana, founded what was then known as La Vizcaya, a rum distillery. It was at this distillery that Havana Club, Cuba's most famous rum, was born, distilled for the first time in 1934. The factory, located in the portside industrial zone, still exists to this day; nationalized after the Revolution, it's now known as the **José Antonio Echeverría Distillery**.

The town's more recent claim to fame is as the birthplace of **Elian González**, the young boy who came to symbolize the ideological conflict between the US and Cuba during a 1999 custody battle of unusual geopolitical significance. The government wasted no time in setting up a **museum** here to commemorate their perceived triumph when Elian was returned to his home town.

> ## ORIENTATION IN CÁRDENAS
>
> Cárdenas revolves around **Avenida Céspedes**, running right down the centre of town towards the dilapidated port. Anything running parallel with it is also an avenida, while the calles run perpendicular to it, with **Calle 13** crossing Avenida Céspedes bang in the centre of town. However, locals refer to the old street names that the numbers replaced.

Parque Colón

Avenida Céspedes e/ 8 y 9

Cárdenas's main square, run-down **Parque Colón** is bisected by the city's main street and is conducive to neither a sit-down nor a stroll around. The only reason to stop here is to gawp at the noble but withered **Catedral de la Inmaculada Concepción**, the grandest building in the city, dating from 1846. Resembling twin lighthouses, two stone towers flank the body of the building and a dome pokes its head above the treetops.

Unfortunately, the cathedral is almost always closed. In front of it is an elevated **statue** of a romantic-looking Columbus with a globe at his feet. Sculpted in 1862, it's said to be the oldest statue of him in the whole of the Americas.

Parque José Antonio Echeverría

Two blocks from Avenida Céspedes, southeast along Calle 12, is plain but tranquil **Parque José Antonio Echeverría**, the archetypal town square that Parque Colón fails to be, dotted with trees and benches and enclosed by buildings on all sides. The real reason to visit, though, is for the three surrounding museums.

Museo Oscar María de Rojas

Calle 13 e/ Avenida 4 y Avenida 6 • Tues & Fri 9am–6pm, Wed, Thurs & Sat 8am–5pm, Sun 9am–1pm • Charge • ☎ 45 52 2417

Founded in 1900 and one of the oldest museums in the country, the **Museo Oscar María de Rojas**, occupying the entire southwestern side of Parque José Antonio Echeverría, brings together a jamboree of coins, medals, bugs, butterflies and weapons along with other seemingly random collections across its thirteen rooms. By far the most engaging and substantial sections are the two rooms of pre-Columbian Cuban and Latin American artefacts. Among the archaeological finds displayed are human skeletal remains found on the island, dating back almost 5800 years, a bizarre shrunken head from southern Ecuador, examples of Mayan art and some stone idols from Mexico.

Museo José Antonio Echeverría

Avenida 4 e/ 12 y 13 • Tues–Sat 9am–noon & 1–5pm, Sun 9am–noon • Charge • ☎ 45 52 4145

The Cuban Revolution was not orchestrated by Fidel Castro and Che Guevara alone and on the northwestern side of Parque José Antonio Echeverría, in the **Museo José Antonio Echeverría**, the life of one of the many other protagonists is illuminated. Echeverría, the 1950s anti-Batista student leader and activist, a statue of whom stands casually, hand in pocket, in the square outside, was born in this house. Echeverría and several of his comrades were shot and killed by Batista's police during an attack on the Presidential Palace in Havana on March 13, 1957, and joined a long list of revolutionary martyrs whose memories are kept alive in the names of countless buildings, streets and institutions all around the country. The museum charts his life growing up in Cárdenas and his protest years in Havana, as well as examining the wider role of the Federation of University Students (FEU) in Cuba, of which Echeverría became president in 1954. You can see his parents' pink 1954 Chrysler Windsor Deluxe parked in the courtyard.

Museo a la Batalla de Ideas

Avenida 6 esq. 12 • Tues–Sat 9am–noon & 1–5pm, Sun 8am–noon • Charges for entry, guided tour and rooftop viewing platform • ☎ 45 52 3990

Touching the corner of the Parque José Antonio Echeverría, the propagandist **Museo a la Batalla de Ideas** is set in a cheery yellow fortress of a building which is actually a nineteenth-century fire station. As much a symbol of victory as a museum, it was opened in June 2001 to mark the triumph claimed by the Cuban government over the

3

CUEVA DE SATURNO

Just by the road connecting Juan Gualberto Gómez Airport to the Vía Blanca, a few hundred metres south from the Vía Blanca itself, is the **Cueva de Saturno** (daily 8am–6pm), a flooded cave where you can **snorkel** and **scuba dive**. Modest in comparison to the Cuevas de Bellamar nearer Matanzas, the cave isn't worth going out of your way for unless you intend to dive, but it does make a good stop-off between Varadero and Matanzas. You can walk down through the impressive gaping mouth of the cave to the pool at the bottom and take a swim or have a snorkel. A snack bar has been built near the steps down into the cave, mostly to serve the organized visits that regularly come here from Matanzas and Varadero. You can prebook visits with one of Varadero's various dive clubs or travel agents.

US when **Elian González**, the 6-year-old boy who came to personify the political and theoretical conflict between the US and Cuba, was repatriated from Florida. The whole Elian episode is charted in photographs with poster boards decrying US interference in Cuban affairs. There are also insights into the national education system, like the Cuban classroom motto "*Seremos como el Che*" ("We will be like Che"). Be sure to venture upstairs to the rooftop **viewing platform** looking over the whole city and beyond – well worth the extra charge. A member of staff is often on hand to point out the various sights, including an otherwise rarely seen perspective, on the distant horizon, of the Varadero peninsula.

Plaza Malacoff

Calle 12 e/ Avenida 3 y 5

Since its foundation in 1859, curious-looking **Plaza Malacoff** has hosted the stalls and booths that make up the city's main **food market**. The centre of this old market square is occupied by a 15m-high, cross-shaped building consisting of four two-storey hallways and a large iron-and-zinc dome in the centre, which gives it the appearance of a run-down Islamic temple. While the square has seen better days, it is still full of life and perhaps the best place in Cárdenas to find some genuine local flavour.

ARRIVAL AND DEPARTURE   CÁRDENAS

By train Trains from Colón (2 daily; 1hr 30min) and Jovellanos (run according to availability of fuel; 1hr) pull in at the station on Avenida 8 y Calle 5 (☎ 45 52 1362), a few blocks from the city centre.

By bus The interprovincial bus terminal (☎ 45 52 1214) is at Avenida Céspedes esq. Calle 22 and serves mainly Astro buses. The cheapest way to get here from Varadero is to catch the Víazul coach destined for the east, which passes through Cárdenas, and stops either at the terminal or drops off passengers on Avenida Céspedes, though it generally doesn't pick up passengers going either way. To move on from Cárdenas by public transport your best bet is usually

to make your way first to Varadero. Local buses navigating this part of the province operate from the smaller terminal on Calle 13 esq. Avenida 13 (☎ 45 52 4958). There is a steady stream of workers' buses between Cárdenas and Varadero, and though these don't officially seat tourists most drivers will let you on board for a small charge. They leave from Calle 13 between Avenida 1 and 3, a block away from Avenida Céspedes.

By car or scooter Arriving by car or scooter couldn't be easier as the main road from Varadero cuts directly into the centre of town.

ACCOMMODATION

Hostal Angelo's Ave. 14 no.656 e/ 14 y 15 ⓦ hostalangelos.com. The impressive and extensive outdoor space here provides an oasis of leafy luxury amid the grime of central Cárdenas. Not only is there a small bathing pool but also a separate jacuzzi, a lovely tree- and

shrub-lined dining area and a simple concrete bar. Extrovert owner Angelo, with 25 years of experience in Varadero hotels, provides three neat rooms, one with a theatrical, ornate bathroom. $\overline{\underline{\$}}$

Hostal Ida Calle 13 e/ Ave. 13 y Ave. 15 ☎ 45 52 1559.

There's a faded glamour about the two bedrooms for rent at this upstairs apartment seven blocks towards Varadero from the main street. In the "master suite" there are two small double beds, with satin sheets and pillows, united by an enormous, gold-rimmed headboard. Throughout the apartment are fancy lamps and decorative ceiling trims and mouldings. There's comfort too with a nice modern bathroom and good a/c. 55

EATING AND NIGHTLIFE

★ **Don Qko** Ave. Céspedes no.1001 esq. 21 ☎45 52 4572. This is an impressive paladar, with large, leafy outdoor eating areas in addition to the indoor dining room, as well as a pool and a stage for the regular live music shows. The food, mostly traditional Cuban with roast pork and seafood specialities, is beautifully presented and they don't skimp on the portions either. For a night out in a town like Cárdenas this place has got the whole evening covered. 55

Las Palmas Ave. Céspedes no.528 esq. Calle 16 ☎45 52 3762. The city's standout nightlife venue (usually open Wednesday to Sunday) is the large courtyard of this pseudo-oriental Spanish villa, packed out at the weekends with a young crowd here to see popular music and dance routines performed by local talent.

★ **Studio 55** Parque José Antonio Echeverría, Calle 12 e/ Ave. 4 y Ave. 6 ☎45 52 2172. This arty, chic café, bar and restaurant with a nice garden courtyard – where a great semi-circular concrete couch provides the best seat in the house – is one of the most pleasant and the most innovative eating and drinking environments in the city. Serves inexpensive, quality *comida criolla*.

Matanzas

Just 25km west along the coast from the beach resorts, **MATANZAS** is one of the closest and easiest day-trip destinations from Varadero. Christened the Athens of Cuba some 150 years ago on account of its abundance of poets and rich cultural life, this is the biggest and most interesting city in the eponymous province. Clustered on the hillsides around a large bay and endowed with two rivers and several of its own beaches, the city's setting is perhaps its greatest asset. That said, huge investment in renovating historic buildings, and hosting the 2019 Biennial de la Habana (⊕biennialhavana. org), Cuba's largest festival, has seen the city itself re-energised, with plans afoot for the Biennial to return. It's also a convenient base for the caves on its outskirts, the nearby Yumurí valley and Río Canímar.

The best place to get your bearings is the more central of Matanzas' two main plazas, the **Parque de la Libertad**, home to the fantastically well-preserved **Museo Farmacéutico Matanzas**. Though the other main square, the **Plaza de la Vigía**, is less inviting, it's worth visiting for the **Museo Provincial** and the stately, still-functioning **Teatro Sauto**. Surrounding the plazas and the main street, **Calle 85** (known to locals as Medio), is a slightly claustrophobic city centre which quickly becomes a series of similar-looking streets plagued by drainage problems, until you get to one of the two rivers. The Río San Juan and Río Yumurí are spanned by five bridges in total, earning the city another of its monikers, Ciudad de los Puentes (City of Bridges). Beyond the rivers tangible focal points are few and far between until you reach **Monserrate** on the edge of town, and the lovely views of the bay and city it provides.

Parque de la Libertad

A traditional Spanish-style plaza, the **Parque de la Libertad** is a welcome open space amid the city's claustrophobic streets. The mostly restored, mostly colonial and neo-

---

STREET NAMES IN MATANZAS

As is the case elsewhere in Cuba, streets in Matanzas are known by both **names** and **numbers**. Most Cuban maps and the signs on the streets themselves use the numbers but almost all locals refer to the older names. In this guide we show the old names in brackets.

3

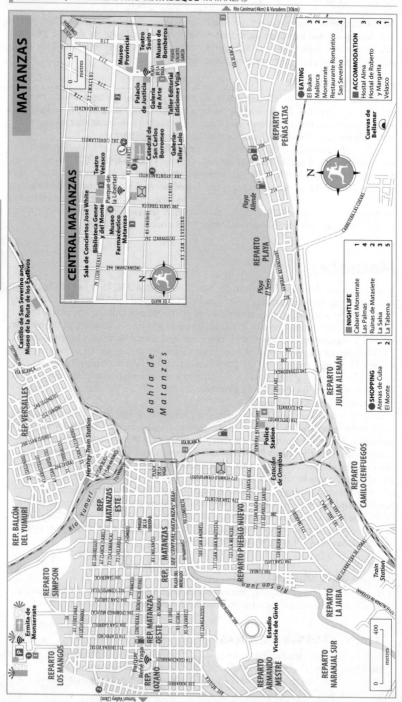

MATANZAS

CENTRAL MATANZAS

Sala de Conciertos José White
Biblioteca Gener y del Monte
Teatro Velasco
Museo Farmacéutico Matanzas
Catedral de San Carlos Borromeo
Galería-Taller Lolo
Palacio de Justicia
Galería de Arte
Taller Editorial Ediciones Vigía
Museo Provincial
Teatro Sauto
Museo de Bomberos

Bahía de Matanzas

Río Yumurí

Río San Juan

REP. BALCÓN DEL YUMURÍ
REP. VERSALLES
REPARTO SIMPSON
REPARTO LOS MANGOS
Ermita de Monserrate
Parque René Fraga
REPARTO ARMANDO MESTRE
REP. MATANZAS OESTE
REP. LOZANO
REPARTO NARANJAL SUR
Estadio Victoria de Girón
REPARTO LA JAIBA
Train Station
REPARTO PUEBLO NUEVO
REPARTO CAMILO CIENFUEGOS
REPARTO JULIAN ALEMÁN
REPARTO PLAYA
REPARTO PEÑAS ALTAS
REP. MATANZAS ESTE
Hershey Train Station
Plaza del Mercado
Estación de Omnibus
Police Station
SEE CENTRAL MATANZAS MAP

Playa El Tenis
Playa Allende
Cuevas de Bellamar

Castillo de San Severino and Museo de la Ruta de los Esclavos

Río Canimar (4km) & Varadero (30km)

Yumurí Valley (2km)

● EATING
El Bukan — 3
Mallorca — 2
Monserrate — 1
Restaurante Romántico — 4
San Severino

▮ ACCOMMODATION
Hostal Alma — 3
Hostal de Roberto y Margarita — 2
Velasco — 1

▮ NIGHTLIFE
Cabaret Monserrate — 1
Las Palmas — 4
Ruinas de Matasiete — 3
La Salsa — 2
La Taberna — 5

● SHOPPING
Atenas de Cuba — 1
El Monte — 2

0 ___ 400 metres
0 ___ 50 metres

colonial buildings around the square, provide an attractive backdrop, including the provincial government headquarters from 1853, which occupies the entire east side, and the old *casino* building, a traditional Spanish social club, built in 1835 and now housing a library.

Museo Farmacéutico Matanzas

Calle 83 (Milanés) e/ 288 (Ayuntamiento) y 290 (Santa Teresa) • Mon–Sat 10am–5pm, Sun 10am–4pm • Charge • ☎ 45 24 3179

The **Museo Farmacéutico Matanzas** was founded in 1882 by two doctors, Juan Fermín de Figueroa and Ernesto Triolet, and functioned as a **pharmacy** right up until May 1964, when it was converted into a museum. The hundreds of French porcelain jars lining the shelves and cabinets, along with the many medicine bottles (and even the medicines still inside them) are originals, making it hard to believe business ever stopped. Many of the concoctions were made in the laboratory at the back of the building, using formulae listed in one of the 55 recipe books kept in the compact but comprehensive **library**. The fabulous old cash till looks as though it should have been driven by a steam engine.

3

Sala de Conciertos José White

Calle 79 (Contreras) e/ 288 (Ayuntamiento) y 290 (Santa Teresa) • ☎ 45 26 7032

Restorations completed in 2015 have brought the **Sala de Conciertos José White**, a wonderful old concert hall in a beautiful yellow-and-white Neoclassical building, back to life. If you're not here for a concert by the resident Matanzas Symphony Orchestra you can still enjoy its bright, elegant interior by visiting the bar (9am–11pm; closed Mon), photo gallery and, in the lovely central patio, taking a look at a version of the sheet music, forged in bronze, for *Las Alturas de Simpson*, the first ever danzón, a traditional Cuban musical style which premiered here in this building in 1879, when it was the Club Matanzas.

Catedral de San Carlos Borromeo

Calle 282 (Jovellanos) e/ 83 (Milanés) y 85 (Medio)

A block east towards the bay from Parque de la Libertad is the renovated **Catedral de San Carlos Borromeo**, whose heavy frame, with its detailed Neoclassical exterior, is squeezed in between the two busiest streets in the city centre. One of the first buildings in Matanzas, it was founded in 1693 and originally made of wood which, unsurprisingly, didn't last. Rebuilt in 1755, it did not survive the last two and a half centuries intact and a painstaking restoration began in 2008. Re-inaugurated in 2016, the gleaming, smooth-walled, white and mellow yellow interior has given the cathedral a distinctly modern makeover. There is still much left of historic and artistic value however, including the original altar.

Plaza de la Vigía

Two blocks from Catedral de San Carlos Borromeo and right next to the river, humble **Plaza de la Vigía** struggles for space with the heavy traffic running along one side. Little more than a road junction, the plaza features a swashbuckling statue of a rebel from the Wars of Independence on a concrete island in the centre.

Museo de Bomberos

Plaza de la Vigía • Mon–Fri 9am–noon & 1–4pm, Sat 9am–noon • Free • ☎ 45 24 3685

Flanking the bay side of Plaza de la Vigía is an ornate but austere Neoclassical fire station, which also houses the simple **Museo de Bomberos**. It's worth popping inside to see the old fire engines, including one from 1888, still in perfect working order, alongside displays of uniforms and photographs.

Taller Editorial Ediciones Vigía

Plaza de la Vigía (corner nearest the river) • Mon–Sat 8.30am–4pm • Free • ☎ 45 24 4845

The **Taller Editorial Ediciones Vigía** may not look like much at first sight, but its humble interior belies its unique purpose. The home of a publishing cooperative founded in 1985, this intriguing little workshop produces books as works of art and craft. Dotted about the two floors are small cases containing the finished articles, each a one-off and most of them heavily illustrated. Upstairs are paintings and drawings and, most strikingly, a huge **mural** of Matanzas made entirely of paper. Though the books are for sale (prices by negotiation) there is little sense of commercialism here, and the friendly staff, atmosphere of creativity and the books themselves make for a memorable visit.

Teatro Sauto

Plaza de la Vigía • ☎ 45 24 2721

Facing the ceremonious-looking pink Palacio de Justicia, the august **Teatro Sauto** is one of the city's best-preserved historic monuments and its most prestigious cultural institution. You can tour the theatre outside performance times, normally by joining an organized excursion from Varadero, but it's worth asking inside for an impromptu tour if you can find a member of staff in the reception area. Grand but lacking in decorative detail, the dignified Neoclassical exterior belies the more elaborate **interior**, whose main hall features a painted ceiling depicting the muses of Greek mythology, which leads into an Italianate three-tier auditorium.

Museo Provincial

Calle 83 (Milanés) esq. 272 (Magdalena) • Tues–Sat 9am–noon & 1–5pm, Sun 9am–noon • Charge • ☎ 45 24 3195

Just north of the Teatro Sauto, the orderly collection at the **Museo Provincial** charts the political and social history of the province. Providing a succinct overview of the last two hundred years in Matanzas, there are early plans and pictures of the city, including a fantastic, large-scale drawing dating from 1848. Other displays depict the living and

---

SUGAR AND SLAVERY

The **sugar industry** in Cuba, and indeed all over the Caribbean, was up until the end of the nineteenth century inextricably linked to the slave trade and **slavery** itself. It's been estimated that at least a third of enslaved people in Cuba during the nineteenth century worked on sugar plantations, playing a vital role in Cuba's biggest industry and accounting for the largest single investment made by most plantation owners. **Working conditions** for enslaved people were even worse on the massive sugar estates than on the smaller tobacco or coffee plantations. Death from overwork was not uncommon as, unlike tobacco and coffee, levels of production were directly linked to the intensity of the labour, and plantation owners demanded the maximum possible output from their workforce. The six months of harvest were by far the most gruelling period of the year, when the plantation workforce often slept for no more than four hours a day, rising as early as 2am. They were divided into gangs and those sent to cut cane in the fields might be working there for sixteen hours before they could take a significant break. A small proportion would work in the mill, grinding the cane and boiling the sugar cane juice. **Accidents** in the mills were frequent and **punishments** were harsh; the enslaved were sometimes left in the stocks – which took various forms but usually involved the head, hands and feet locked into the same flat wooden board – for days at a time.

The enslaved workforce was typically housed in communal **barrack buildings**, which replaced the collections of huts used in the eighteenth century, subdivided into cramped cells, with the men, who made up about two-thirds of the workforce, separated from the women. This was considered a more effective method of containment as there were fewer doors through which it was possible to escape.

working conditions of enslaved people on the sugar plantations and in the mills (see box, page 206) and include a large wooden *cepo* and the leg clamps employed in the punishment of enslaved workers.

Galería-Taller Lolo

Calle 97 (Narvaez) no.27 e/ 282 (Jovellanos) y 280 (Matanzas) • No fixed opening times • Free • ⓦ osmanybetancourt.com

In the **Galería-Taller Lolo**, on a street by the Río San Juan, you'll find some of the most striking sights in Matanzas: the **sculptures** of award-winning artist Osmany Betancourt Falcon, also known as Lolo, who shares this large gallery-workshop with other artists. All his work is very expressive, often darkly so, with many of his ceramic, bronze and mixed-media figures wearing strained, pained or melancholy expressions – though there are lighter, more upbeat pieces as well, plus some more decorative ceramics and artworks for sale.

Monserrate

Perched just above and beyond the residential neighbourhood in the northwestern corner of the city is **Monserrate**, a small hilltop plateau where you can enjoy some of the best views in town, with the city and bay on one side and a fantastic perspective on the magnificent Yumurí valley on the other. It's a peaceful spot, centred on a renovated church, the **Ermita de Monserrate**, built between 1872 and 1875 by colonists from Catalonia and the Balearic Islands, and restored in 2006.

Set back from the church are several snack bars and cliff-edge cafés, with great views of the valley, and the more down-at-heel *Restaurante Monserrate* and *Cabaret Monserrate*.

The beaches

With one of the best beaches in Cuba just 25km up the road, few visitors bother with the rag-tag beaches in Matanzas. Some of them, however, do offer the chance of some secluded sunbathing, and if you're staying in the city for a couple of days you could do worse than to seek one of them out. By far the largest and most popular is **Playa El Tenis**, hemmed in by a busy viaduct and complemented by a bar and restaurant. Much smaller and more private is **Playa Allende**, hidden away below a steep slope just off General Betancourt. With overhanging trees and a sense of enclosure there is a more attractive look and feel here than at Playa El Tenis but there are no amenities and a lot less sand.

Versalles

About three blocks north from the Plaza de la Vigía, over the Puente de la Concordia, which spans the Río Yumurí, is the almost exclusively residential **Versalles** district. Few visitors to the city choose to explore this area and those who do are usually heading for the **Hershey train terminal** (see box, page 208) or, in an industrial zone on the north face of the bay, the **Castillo de San Severino** fort.

Castillo de San Severino

50m from the bayfront, 500m west of the port • Tues–Sat 9am–noon & 1–4pm, Sun 9am–noon • Charge • ☎ 45 28 3259

Constructed in 1734, the **Castillo de San Severino** fort is based around a wide, open central square and surrounded by a now-empty moat. With imposing, thick stone walls and broad ramparts, where three cannon still stand, this was the principal structure in the local colonial defence system, once guarding Matanzas from pirates intent on plundering the substantial wealth of the city. It functioned as a prison in the latter part of the nineteenth century but stood derelict thereafter, though unconfirmed hearsay has

3

3

THE HERSHEY TRAIN

In 1916 **Milton Hershey**, founder of US chocolate manufacturer Hersheys, established a sugar mill halfway between Matanzas and Havana. Built to process sugar cane for the company's chocolate factory in Pennsylvania, the renowned businessman and philanthropist also commissioned 135km of railway line to transport workers and goods to and from the mill and the workers' village he erected around it. Today the **Hershey train line** transports the only **electric trains** left in Cuba, which pass through the Yumurí valley and within sight of the Atlantic coastline on their three-hour journey between the two terminals, Casablanca in Havana and the Matanzas station in Versalles.

Calling at dozens of stations along the way, including the one in Camilo Cienfuegos (the post-1959 name for the tiny town of Hershey), a **ride on the Hershey train** is to experience Cuban public transport at its most idiosyncratic. Services are scheduled to leave three times a day, but there is never any guarantee of this, with reasons for delays and cancellations ranging from power failures to cattle on the line. The current tram-like interurban train cars were imported from Spain in the 1990s, though they date back to the 1940s. Rarely exceeding speeds of 40km/hr, the journey unfolds at the perfect speed for taking in the marvellous landscapes along the way, the best of them in the **Yumurí valley** with its mosaic of cultivated fields, open countryside, patchwork forests and snaking rivers. Stations are more like bus stops, and some platforms are little more than a metre or two long, leaving some passengers having to literally jump off the train. To buy a **ticket** for one of the three daily services to Havana, arrive at the station in Versalles (see above) an hour before the scheduled departure time. Full timetables are given in Chapter 1 (see page 113).

it that right up until the late 1970s political prisoners of the revolutionary regime were locked up inside. It now houses the **Museo de la Ruta de los Esclavos**. The limited displays on slavery and the slave trade reflect the fort's one-time use as a storage unit for enslaved people unloaded from boats on the coast below, many of them destined for nearby sugar plantations.

ARRIVAL AND DEPARTURE   MATANZAS

BY TRAIN

Mainline trains National network trains pull in at the nondescript station (☎45 29 2409) on the southern outskirts of the city, from where nothing of any convenience is within walking distance. Arrivals usually attract a few private taxis, but *bicitaxis* and horse-drawn carriages are more likely to be waiting. Trains in Cuba are notoriously unreliable and timetables are only guidelines.

Destinations Havana (1 daily; 1hr 30min); Sancti Spíritus (3 weekly; 6hr); Santa Clara (5 weekly; 2hr 30min); Santiago (3 weekly; 12hr).

Hershey Line The other train service into the city is on the picturesque but leisurely Hershey line (see box), running between Matanzas and Havana. The station (☎45 24 4805) is in the Versalles neighbourhood at Calle 73 e/ Carretera a Yumurí y Calle 67, north of the Río Yumurí; arriving here, you will most likely have to walk to the centre, which should take around 15min.

Key destinations Havana Casablanca (3 daily; 4hr); Hershey/Camilo Cienfuegos (3 daily; 1hr 50min); Mena, Yumurí Valley (3 daily; 10min).

BY BUS

Víazul buses Interprovincial buses arrive at the Estación de Omnibus (☎45 29 1473), at the junction between Calle 272 (Cienfuegos), Calle 171 (Calzada de Esteban) and General Betancourt.

Getting into town There are usually private taxis and *bicitaxis* waiting in the car park. If you have more patience and less money you could wait for the #12 bus to pass (roughly every 45min), which will take you to the Parque de la Libertad. Walking isn't out of the question either – you should be able to get to the Parque de la Libertad within 20min.

Destinations Havana (4 daily; 2hr); Varadero (4 daily; 45min); Varadero airport (3 daily; 25min).

BY TAXI COLECTIVO

Be prepared to negotiate with the driver for *taxis colectivos* (see page 30) to Varadero. Cars gather at the bus station; the junction where Calle 282 (Jovellanos) and Calle 83 (Mílanés) cross, outside the cathedral; and the junction just over the train tracks where the road from the Plaza de la Vigía meets the Vía Blanca.

BY CAR

If you drive to Matanzas from Varadero, be ready for the charge at the Matanzas–Varadero tollgate on the Vía Blanca. Parking in the city can be difficult, with no official car parks, though there are designated spaces at Plaza de la Vigía, where there's usually an unofficial attendant who will watch over the vehicle for a tip. This is also the best place to leave your car overnight, though if you're staying in a *casa particular* the chances are your hosts will make sure a safe spot is found for it.

GETTING AROUND AND INFORMATION

By local bus Omnibus Yumurí runs a small number of buses in and around the city. By far the most useful is the #12, which leaves from outside the Museo Farmacéutico on the Parque de la Libertad roughly every 45min, between 9am and 8pm daily, linking the city centre with the Cuevas de Bellamar and Monserrate via the bus station and the Plaza del Mercado. The main central hub for local buses, including the #16 to the Río Canímar and the *Tropicana* cabaret, is on Calle 83 outside the cathedral.

By tourist bus Operating between Varadero and Matanzas, the Matanzas Bus Tour is a useful option, though it's unreliable during low season (April–June & Sept–Dec), when it sometimes stops running altogether. In high season (Jan–March & July–Aug) it usually passes through the Parque de la Libertad four times a day on the way up to Monserrate, and also heads over the Río Canímar to and from Varadero. Tickets are bought on the bus itself and are valid for the whole day, allowing you to hop on and off, and go all the way to Varadero and back.

By taxi Try Cubataxi (☎ 45 24 4350), though they are only sporadically available.

Tourist information Since the Infotur branch shut down there has been no official source of tourist information in Matanzas – *casa particular* owners or hotel staff are your best bet.

ACCOMMODATION

SEE MAP PAGE 204

Hostal Alma Calle 83 (Milanés) no.29008 (altos) e/ 290 (Santa Teresa) y 292 (Zaragoza) ☎45 29 0857, ✉ hostalalma63@gmail.com. Artistically decorated with vases, paintings, plants and other adornments, this house, half a block from the main square, has plenty going for it, including a large and attractive central terracotta terrace where you can sit or sunbathe, as well as a roof terrace with marvellous views across the city. Accommodation is in two excellent rooms, one a quadruple. $\overline{\underline{S}}$

Hostal de Roberto y Margarita Calle 79 (Contreras) no.27608 e/ 280 (Matanzas) y 272 ☎45 24 2577, ✉ roberto.margarita2000@gmail.com. One of the largest houses renting rooms in the centre of the city, this nineteenth-century residence has five rooms, including two airy triples, and a garage. Almost everything here seems to be on a big scale, including the bedroom furniture and the open-air central patio. $\overline{\underline{S}}$

Velasco Contreras e/ 288 (Ayuntamiento) y 290 (Santa Teresa), Parque de la Libertad ⓦ hotelescubanacan. com. Dating from 1902, this is the only hotel in Matanzas for non-Cubans, and one of the city's most stylish buildings thanks to lengthy restorations. It's saturated in early twentieth-century elegance, from the refined, breezy lobby and its saloon bar to the pillared interior balcony hallways looking down on the central patio restaurant. Some of the standard rooms are a bit pokey and lack natural light – book a suite or ask to view a room before checking in. $\overline{\underline{SS}}$

EATING

SEE MAP PAGE 204

El Bukan Calle 210 esq. 127 y 129 ☎45 28 9999. The speciality of the house here is the swordfish but actually you'd do as well to order one of the simple roast pork or chicken offerings, and there is a wide variety of inexpensive alternatives. The smart dining room is a floor-and-a-half up from the street and some tables have views of the bay. $\overline{\underline{SS}}$

★**Mallorca** Calle 334 no.7705 e/ 77 (Maceo) y 79 (Contreras) ☎45 28 3282. Among the best and most ambitious of the city's paladars. The extensive menu does feature the usual Cuban suspects but also tries to break the mould with tasty starters such as stuffed piquillo peppers and mains like chicken breast filled with spinach. The backstreet venue, in the west of the city, and the moody night-time lighting add to the sense of exclusivity. $\overline{\underline{SS}}$

Monserrate End of Calle 306 (Domingo Mujica), Monserrate ☎45 24 4222. Standard Creole cooking in the best-located restaurant in the city, in an open-sided building with great views of the bay. $\overline{\underline{SS}}$

Restaurante Romántico San Severino Calle 290 (Santa Teresita) no.7903 e/ 79 (Contreras) y 83 (Milanés), Parque de la Libertad ☎52 28 1573. Upstairs in a carefully renovated house dating from 1860, right on the Parque de la Libertad, the best seats in this relatively dignified paladar are out on the narrow balcony looking down on the square. Best for Cuban classics like shrimp and lobster. $\overline{\underline{SS}}$

NIGHTLIFE

SEE MAP PAGE 204

The city centre is remarkably lifeless at night, especially midweek, though locals come out every evening to shoot the breeze at Parque de la Libertad. Just a short bus or taxi ride beyond the city limits, however, the **Tropicana cabaret** (see page 213) is the most spectacular night-time venue in the province.

Cabaret Monserrate End of Calle 306 (Domingo Mujica), Monserrate ☎45 24 2620. Open Thursday–Sunday, it can sometimes get a bit rowdy at this outdoor hilltop, nightclub and live music venue, but it is undoubtedly the most memorably located nightspot in Matanzas, with great views down into the city.

Las Palmas Calle 254 (Levante) e/ General Betancourt y Calle 137 (Pilar) ☎45 25 3255. Live and recorded music of all sorts and midweek comedy shows performed under the stars, in the palm-studded, weather-beaten courtyard of a large mansion. The music-and-light shows put on most weekends are among the city's most popular locals' night out. No shorts or sleeveless tops.

Ruinas de Matasiete Vía Blanca ☎45 25 3387. The ruins of a colonial sugar warehouse have been half-heartedly converted into this open-air restaurant, bar and music venue, stranded out by the main road to Varadero but still one of the more reliable spots for Saturday-night live music and dancing shows.

La Salsa Vía Blanca ☎45 25 3330. One of the most popular venues among young Matanceros, this semi-outdoor, slightly ramshackle *discoteca* between a busy road and the rocky shore hosts nights of pop, reggaeton and salsa from Friday through to Sunday. The best way to get here is by car, but there's a bus stop about half a kilometre away served by the #16 and #17.

La Taberna Plaza de la Vigía. Cheesy but fun, this basement bar and nightclub has a weekly programme which includes live comedy, karaoke and small-scale live music performances.

ENTERTAINMENT

THEATRE AND CLASSICAL MUSIC

Sala de Conciertos José White Calle 79 (Contreras) e/ 288 (Ayuntamiento) y 290 (Santa Teresa) ⓦfacebook.com/SaladeConciertosJoseWhite. This splendidly renovated old concert hall is the home of the Matanzas Symphony Orchestra. Both they and other classical and traditional Cuban musical ensembles play to audiences of up to two hundred here – there are a limited number of seats reserved for foreigners.

Teatro Sauto Plaza de la Vigía ☎45 24 2721. A reminder of Matanzas' past glory in the arts, the centrepiece of the city's contemporary cultural life stages dance, live music and comedy acts. National theatre groups and ballet companies sometimes grace the stage, though local productions are just as prevalent. Monthly programmes are sometimes posted at the entrance.

SPECTATOR SPORTS

Baseball Estadio Victoria de Girón, at the southern end of San Carlos (☎45 24 3881), has weekly national-league baseball games from October to April. It's a 20min walk from Parque de la Libertad.

SHOPPING
SEE MAP PAGE 204

Self-caterers would do well to visit the **Plaza del Mercado** next to the river at the Puente Sánchez Figueras. As well as a source of fruit, vegetables and meat, it's a good place for cheap snacks; Saturdays are particularly lively.

Atenas de Cuba Calle 286 esq. 83 (Milanés) ☎45 28 4778. This department store right in the centre of town has one of the better-stocked supermarkets, though stock is still very limited and this is somewhere simply to pick up a few basics.

El Monte Calle 85 (Medio) e/ 282 (Jovellanos) y 288 (Ayuntamiento) ☎45 28 7427. The city's best outlet for books and CDs, and though the range is limited there are at least titles here unavailable outside of the country; there's some craftwork here too, including ceramics.

DIRECTORY

Health The well-equipped hospital Comandante Faustino Pérez Hernández is located on the Carretera Central, 1km from the city (☎52 25 3426 or ☎52 25 3427, ⓔhospital@atenas.inf.cu).

Left luggage At the interprovincial bus station.

Money and exchange For foreign currency and credit card transactions, go to Banco Financiero Internacional at Calle 85 (Medio) esq. 2 de Mayo (Mon–Fri 8.30am–4.30pm) or Banco de Crédito y Comercio Calle 85 (Medio) e/ 288 (Ayuntamiento) y 282 (Jovellanos) (Mon–Fri 8am–4.30pm); the latter has an ATM. The CADECA *casa de cambio* is at Calle 85 (Medio) e/ 280 (Matanzas) y 282 (Jovellanos).

Post office The main branch is at Calle 85 (Medio) e/ 288 (Ayuntamiento) y 290 (Santa Teresita).

Wi-fi There are two dozen public wi-fi zones around Matanzas including at Parque de la Libertad, Plaza de la Vigía, Parque René Fraga and Monserrate. You can buy wi-fi cards at the ETECSA Telepunto at Calle 282 (Jovellanos) esq. 83 (Milanés; daily 8.30am–7pm), where there are computer terminals and several phone cabins.

Around Matanzas

Highlights around the city include the **Cuevas de Bellamar**, also a popular day-trip from Varadero, while the **Yumurí valley** offers a fantastic showcase of Cuban plant life in a sublime and peaceful landscape. The **Río Canímar** offers some excellent boat trips and organized excursions, and the hotel here is home to the prodigious **Tropicana** cabaret.

Local buses and the Matanzas Bus Tour (see page 191) will get you to all these places except the Yumurí valley, which you can visit by catching the Hershey train (see page 208) or by taking a taxi or rental car.

Cuevas de Bellamar

Around 4km southeast of the city centre • Guided tours (45min–1hr; minimum ten people) daily at 9.30am, 10.30am, 11.30am, 12.30pm, 1.15pm, 2.15pm, 3.15pm & 4.15pm • Charge • ☎ 45 25 3538 • The #12 bus from the Parque de la Libertad in Matanzas goes right to the caves. Alternatively, Varadero travel agents offer tours.

Just beyond the southeastern outskirts of Matanzas, the **Cuevas de Bellamar** is the most awe-inspiring natural wonder in the province. The cave system attracts coachloads of tourists and is very visitor friendly, allowing anyone who can scale a few sets of steps to descend 50m under the ground along 750m of underground corridors and caverns. The entrance is located within a small complex called Finca La Alcancía, hosting shops, two restaurants and a children's playground.

The caves were first happened upon in 1861 – although there's some dispute over whether credit should go to an enslaved labourer working in a limestone pit or a more parable-sounding shepherd looking for his lost sheep. **Tours** are conducted in various languages, including English, and start with a bang as a large staircase leads down into the first, huge gallery, where a gargantuan stalactite known as *El Manto de Colón* takes centre stage. From here the damp, occasionally muddy and moodily lit trail undulates gently through the rock, passing along narrow passageways. Every so often the cave widens out into larger but still tightly enclosed galleries and chambers lined with lichen and crystal formations.

The Yumurí valley

Hidden behind the hills that skirt the northern edges of Matanzas, the **Yumurí valley** is the provincial capital's giant back garden, stretching westwards from the city into Mayabeque province. Out of sight until you reach the edge of the valley itself, it's the most beautiful landscape in the province, and it comes as quite a surprise to find it so close to the grimy city streets. There's a new vista around every corner, as rolling pastures merge into fields of palm trees, and small forests are interrupted by plots of banana, maize, tobacco and other crops.

The valley has remained relatively untouched by tourism, with its tiny villages few and far between, and though it draws much of its appeal from being so unspoilt, this also means that there's no obvious way to explore it independently. Several minor roads allow you to cut through its centre, but the best way to get here on public transport is to catch the Hershey train from Matanzas and get off at Mena, the first stop on the line and just ten minutes from the city. From the station you can wander in any direction and you'll soon chance upon an idyllic scene.

For a more structured approach, book the Jeep Safari Yumurí (see page 191), an organized excursion from Varadero to **Rancho Gaviota**, the only tourist-oriented stop in the valley, where you can eat a hearty Cuban meal and go horseriding. For the most breathtaking views of the valley, however, make your way by road to the **Puente Bacunayagua**, 20km northwest along the Vía Blanca from the centre of Matanzas. At 112m high, this is the tallest bridge in Cuba, spanning the border between Havana and

---

RÍO CANÍMAR CRUISES AND TOURS

Two of the most popular excursions from Varadero involve a **Río Canímar river cruise**. Cruises leave from the Centro Turístico Canímar (☎45 26 1516), a visitor centre at the foot of the Puente Antonio Guiteras, the bridge that carries the Vía Blanca road over the river. The centre features a snack bar and rents out rowing boats, pedal boats and kayaks. Depending on demand, the cruise boat leaves daily at 12.30pm and travels 12km upstream to a wooded grove. Most visitors are on **organized excursions** from Varadero, booked through the travel agents on the peninsula. Exclusive to visitors arriving via the Varadero travel agents are the fun-packed **jeep safaris** that include the river in a larger tour of the area. Tours can be booked through any agent in Varadero.

Matanzas province. Up the hill from here is the viewpoint, **Mirador de Bacunayagua**, where a snack bar looks out to the coastline and from where a trail leads down to the sea, a thirty-minute walk away by the side of a river.

ARRIVAL AND DEPARTURE   THE YUMURÍ VALLEY

By train From the station in Matanzas, the Hershey has three daily services to Mena (10min).

By car If you're driving from Matanzas, head for the Parque René Fraga, from where the road heading west out of town will take you directly into the valley.

Río Canímar

Snaking its way around fields and woodlands on its journey to the coast, the **Río Canímar** meets the Bay of Matanzas 4km east of the city. With thick, jungle-like vegetation clasping its banks and swaying bends twisting out of sight, a trip up the Canímar is an easily accessible way to delve a little deeper inland and is one of the most rewarding ways of experiencing the Cuban countryside around these parts. A short stay at the basic but cheap *Hotel Canimao*, which overlooks the river, combines well with one of the **boat trips** that leave from below the Puente Antonio Guiteras, the impressive bridge spanning the river near its mouth and the focal point for the area. Next to the hotel is the **Tropicana**, sister venue of the internationally renowned Havana cabaret and one of the most prestigious entertainment centres in the country, while the Museo El Morrillo by the mouth of the river offers a rather more sedate diversion.

Museo El Morrillo

1km north of the Puente Antonio Guiteras • Daily 9am–3pm • Charge • ☎45 28 6675

Directly opposite the turning for the *Hotel Canimao*, a road slopes down to an isolated, simple two-storey building known as the **Castillo del Morrillo**, an eighteenth-century Spanish fortification near the mouth of the river and alongside a scrappy little beach. With its terracotta-tiled roof, beige paintwork and wooden shuttered windows, the so-called fort looks more like a large and very plain house, and only the two cannons facing out to sea suggest that it was once used to defend Matanzas from pirates and other invaders. Nowadays it's the home of the **Museo El Morrillo**, currently only partially open (and temporarily free) as it undergoes renovations with no known reopening date. The interest here is in the connection the building has to **Antonio Guiteras Holmes**, a political activist in 1930s Cuba. With his companion Carlos Aponte and a small group of revolutionaries, Guiteras plotted to overthrow the Mendieta regime, and chose the Castillo del Morrillo as a hideout from where they would depart by boat to Mexico to plan their insurrection, exactly as Fidel Castro did twenty years later. Intercepted by military troops before they could leave, they were shot down on May 8, 1935, at this very spot. Among the bits and pieces commemorating Holmes's life and death are usually the rowing boat that transported the corpses of Guiteras and Aponte, as well as the tomb containing their remains.

ARRIVAL AND DEPARTURE

RÍO CANÍMAR

By bus Buses #16 and #17 run daily between the city and the Puente Antonio Guiteras every hour or so. You can pick up either bus outside the cathedral on Calle 83 (Milanés); get off at the end of the route just over the bridge.

By car To drive here, simply follow the Vía Blanca from either Varadero or Matanzas and take the turn-off next to the bridge.

By organized tour There are plenty of organized excursions to the river from Varadero (see page 191).

ACCOMMODATION AND EATING

Hotel Canimao ⓦislazulhotels.com, see map pge 184. This cheap hotel sits high above Río Canímar, which coils itself halfway around the foot of the steep, tree-lined slopes dropping down from the borders of the grounds, which feature a swimming pool and afford views of the river. Rooms are somewhat less picturesque, with only basic facilities, and this place works best as a base for a river trip

rather than somewhere to spend time inside – that goes for the ropey restaurant too. $\overline{\underline{\underline{\mathsf{5}}}}$

El Marino ⓣ45 26 1483. At the entrance to the road leading up to *Hotel Canimao*, this place is less sophisticated than its bow-tied waiters would suggest, but still offers a good choice of food, with a menu of paella, fish, shrimp and lobster. $\overline{\underline{\underline{\mathsf{55}}}}$

NIGHTLIFE AND ENTERTAINMENT

Sala de Fiesta La Cumbre ⓣ45 25 3387. Right next to the *Tropicana* and part of the same complex, this unsophisticated nightclub, where karaoke and music videos are part of the entertainment, is incredibly popular with young locals at weekends.

Tropicana ⓣ45 26 5555. Set in a spectacular outdoor auditorium, the 1.5hr shows here are everything you'd expect from such a renowned outfit, with lasers shot into the night sky, troops of glittering dancers and a stream of

histrionic singers working through back-to-back sets of ballads, ear-busters and routines covering classic Cuban musical styles, from romantic bolero to energetic salsa and the more traditional son. There's also an after-show disco. Ticket prices depend on whether you have a meal (for which you have to book in advance), how close your table is to the stage, and whether you opt for transfers to and from your hotel; only one complimentary drink is included in the cheapest entrance price.

Mayabeque

Sandwiched in between Havana and Matanzas, **Mayabeque** is one of the two new provinces created in 2010 and previously one half of the province known as La Habana. A predominantly rural province, dotted with small uneventful towns, its main draws are the relatively secluded beach resorts of **Jibacoa** and low-key **Canasí**, along the northern coast, easily reachable from Matanzas if you have your own transport but really quite tricky to get to if you don't. Marooned inland and nearer to Havana than Matanzas, the **Escaleras de Jaruco** are even harder to reach, though this isolation is part of the charm of these beautiful forested hills.

Canasí

Around 25km west of Matanzas city along the Vía Blanca, high upon a cliff-like precipice overlooking the narrow Arroyo Bermejo estuary, the tiny hamlet of **CANASÍ** doubles as the informal weekend campsite for a hippie-chic crowd of young Habaneros. In the summer, scores of revellers descend every Friday to pitch tents in the tranquil woodland around the cliff's edge, spending the weekend swimming and snorkelling in the clear Atlantic waters, exploring the woods and nearby caves, singing folk songs and generally communing with nature. It's a refreshingly uncontrived experience with a peace-festival kind of atmosphere. There are no facilities, so you'll have to bring everything with you (most importantly fresh water), but don't worry too much if you don't have a tent, as the summer nights are warm enough to bed down beneath the stars.

ARRIVAL AND DEPARTURE

CANASÍ

By train The Hershey train (see page 208) sporadically connects Canasí to Havana and Matanzas. The road from the train station down to the water's edge is badly signposted – look for a left turn off the Vía Blanca (a 5min walk from the station) and take the dirt track to the estuary mouth, where the fishermen who live in the waterside cottages will row you across the shallow waters to the site, though the hardy can wade.

Playa Jibacoa

Eight kilometres west of Canasí, tucked behind a barricade of white cliffs, is **Playa Jibacoa**, a stretch of coastline basking in relative anonymity, and hard to reach by public transport. Approaching from Matanzas on the Vía Blanca road, the first turning before the bridge over the Río Jibacoa leads down onto the coastal road that runs the length of this laidback resort area. Predominantly the domain of Cuban holidaymakers, the beach is unspectacular but pleasantly protected by swathes of twisting trees and bushes, with an appealing sense of privacy. There are modest coral reefs offshore and basic snorkelling equipment can be rented at the *campismo* (see below).

ARRIVAL AND DEPARTURE   PLAYA JIBACOA

By train The Hershey train (see above) connects Havana and Matanzas to Jibacoa, but there's no public transport from the station to the beach, which is 5km away.

ACCOMMODATION

Memories Jibacoa On the beach ⓦmemoriesresorts. com. With a good pool and 250 rooms, this adults-only resort is the only international-standard hotel in these parts, though it caters almost exclusively to tourists on pre-booked packages. Also offers jeep trips into the countryside and short boat trips. $\overline{\underline{\$\$\$}}$

Villa Los Cocos Just up from the beach; reservations through Cubamar in Havana at Calle 3ra e/ 12 y Malecón ⓣ7831 2891, ⓦcubamarviajes.cu. This excellent-

value *campismo* has a pool, video room, small library and restaurant serving no-frills food. The concrete chalets, with rudimentary showers and only the most basic of facilities, are on the grassy slopes leading down to the beach. $\overline{\underline{\$}}$

Villas Tropico On the beach ⓦgran-caribe.cu. Spread around an attractive site, this hotel has simple rooms, sweeping lawns, two restaurants, tennis courts, several modest bars and a pool, all on a great stretch of beach. $\overline{\underline{\$\$}}$

Escaleras de Jaruco

Around 25km east of Havana, 20km inland from the Playas del Este, the **Escaleras de Jaruco**, a small crop of scenic hills, make a stimulating detour on the way to or from the beaches in Mayabeque or Matanzas. The hills are around a kilometre west of **Jaruco**, the nearest town of any significant size, and a trip here is only really realistic if you have your own transport. Covered in a kind of subtropical rainforest, this steep-sided mini-mountain range erupts from the surrounding flatlands. The Carretera Tapaste cuts through the area like a mountain pass, leading past the fantastically located *El Arabe* restaurant (see page 215) which, despite its erratic opening hours, provides a focus of sorts for the area. It's one of several places where you can stop and take in the **view** across the lush, forested hillsides and over the palm-spotted flatlands to the Florida Straits.

ARRIVAL AND DEPARTURE   ESCALERAS DE JARUCO

By train If you're prepared to do a bit of walking, you can catch the Hershey train (see page 208) and jump off at Jaruco station then walk the kilometre or so to the start of the hills.

By car The best way to find the Escaleras de Jaruco is to first head for Jaruco, roughly 25km from the Vía Blanca. There are lonely roads inland from any of the beach resorts east of Havana, but the most straightforward route is to leave the

Vía Blanca at the small coastal town of Santa Cruz del Norte, which the Vía Blanca passes through around 30km east of the Playas del Este. From Santa Cruz del Norte, the only road leading inland will take you through several small towns en route: first La Sierra, then Camilo Cienfuegos and San Antonio de Río Blanco, each only several kilometres apart, before arriving at the sloping roads of Jaruco.

EATING

El Arabe 5km west of Jaruco along the Carretera Tapaste ☏ 47 87 3828. In its pre-Revolution heyday, this was undoubtedly a classic, with its splendid Arabic-style interior, balcony terrace with views to the coastline and domed tower, but it's now as low on food as it is on staff, and there's no guarantee it will even be open when you turn up; call ahead to check. $$

San Miguel de los Baños

The provincial interior of Matanzas, wedged between the two touristic poles of Varadero and the Península de Zapata, is dominated by agriculture, with islands of banana and vegetable crops dotting the seas of sugar cane fields. There are a few small towns in this sparsely populated territory – a couple of the larger ones, **Colón** and **Jovellanos**, are on the Carretera Central, the main road bisecting the northern half of the province. Away from the highway the smaller, more picturesque hamlet of **SAN MIGUEL DE LOS BAÑOS** is one of the province's lesser-known treats, off the official tourist track and accessible only by car, hidden away in its own cosy valley 25km southwest of Cárdenas. A cross between an alpine village and a Wild West ghost town, this once opulent settlement has lost most of its wealth, with the wood-panelled ranch-style houses and villas on the hillside among the few reminders of what this outpost once was. These faded signs of success are part of the enchantment of a place that made its fortune during the first half of the twentieth century through the popularity of its health spa and hotel, the **Balneario San Miguel de los Baños**, still one of the focal points for visits here, along with the **Loma de Jacán**, though don't miss the magnificently perched outdoor public **swimming pool** either, five minutes' walk from the old hotel through the centre of the village – often empty but with lovely views of the enclosing, fir-covered, palm-dotted hills.

Balneario San Miguel de los Baños

Located near the centre of the village, the turreted, mansion-like **Balneario San Miguel de los Baños** had its heyday in the 1930s but is now completely derelict, though you can still wander through its entrancingly overgrown gardens. At the rear of the building and spread around the garden, the red-brick wells and Romanesque baths built to accommodate the sulphurous springs that were discovered here in the mid-nineteenth century are still more or less intact, though the pools of water slushing around in them are no longer fit for human consumption. The three **wells** are themselves only about 3m deep; each was supplied from a different source and the supposed healing properties of the waters differed accordingly. With the stone benches encircling the centre of the garden and the wall of shade provided by the old trees, this is a pleasant spot for a picnic, the silence broken only by the sound of running water.

Loma de Jacán

From the swimming pool in San Miguel de los Baños village you should be able to see the route to the foot of the **Loma de Jacán**, the highest peak among the small set of hills in the north of Matanzas province. It's also one of the easiest to climb, thanks to a large set of concrete steps leading up it: a short drive from the northern edge of town up a steep and potholed road takes you to the bottom of this giant staircase. The 448 steps up to the peak are marked by murals depicting the **Stations of the Cross**, and at the top is a shrine, whose concrete dome houses a spooky representation of the Crucifixion, the untouched overgrowth and the airy atmosphere contributing to the mood of contemplation. For years the shrine has attracted local pilgrims who leave flowers and

A HISTORY OF SUGAR IN CUBA

Matanzas has traditionally been at the heart of the country's historically important sugar industry but while it has been said in Cuba that "*sin azúcar no hay país*" ("without sugar there's no country"), the crop is not actually native to the island, having been introduced by colonial pioneer Diego Velázquez in 1511. Initially produced almost entirely for local consumption, decades of declining population in Cuba meant the market for sugar was initially very small. In 1595, King Philip II of Spain authorized the construction of sugar refineries on the island, but for the next century and a half, the industry remained relatively stagnant. Impeded by the **Spanish** failure to take notice of new techniques in sugar production, the lack of a substantial and regular supply of enslaved people, and by stifling regulations imposed by the Spanish Crown forcing Cuba to trade sugar only with Spain, sugar production on the island initially developed slowly.

THE ENGLISH INVADE

In 1762, however, the **English** took control of Havana and during their short occupation opened up trade channels with the rest of the world, simultaneously introducing the industry to the technological advances Spain had failed to embrace. The number of people brought to Cuba as enslaved labourers almost doubled in the last two decades of the eighteenth century. In 1791 a slave-led revolution in Santo Domingo, the dominant force in world sugar at that time, all but wiped out its sugar industry, causing prices and the demand for Cuban sugar to rise, just as the global demand was also rising. By the end of the eighteenth-century Cuba had become one of the world's three biggest sugar producers.

SLAVERY AND THE WARS OF INDEPENDENCE

Technological advances throughout the nineteenth century, including the mechanization of the refining process and the establishment of railways, saw Cuba's share of the world market more than double and the crop become the primary focus of the economy. With hundreds of thousands of **enslaved people** being shipped into Cuba during this period, the island's racial mix came to resemble something like it is today. Equally significant, the economic and structural imbalances between east and west, which were to influence the outbreak of the Ten Years' War in 1868 and its successor in 1895, emerged as a result of the concentration of more and larger sugar mills in the west, closer to Havana. These **Wars of Independence** (see page 437) weakened the Cuban sugar industry to the point of vulnerability, thus clearing the way for a foreign takeover.

THE TWENTIETH CENTURY

Cuba began the twentieth century under indirect US control, and the **Americans** built huge factories known as *centrales*, able to process cane for a large number of different plantations. By 1959 there were 161 mills on the island, over half of them under foreign ownership, a fact that had not escaped the notice of Fidel Castro and his nationalist revolutionary followers. It was no surprise then that one of the first acts of the revolutionary government was, in 1960, to **nationalize** the entire sugar industry. Over the following decades Cuban economic policy fluctuated between attempts at diversification and greater dependency than ever on the *zafra* – the sugar harvest, influenced by artificially high prices paid by the Soviet Union for Cuban sugar. This dependency reached a disastrous peak when, in 1970, Castro zealously declared a target of ten million tonnes for the national annual sugar harvest, which has never been met.

THE INDUSTRY TODAY

Since the mid-1990s there has been a sharp decline in the productivity of sugar. In 2002 a government plan to make production more efficient meant almost half of Cuba's sugar mills were closed while the output of those that remained would, in theory, increase. In 2012, the Brazilian firm Odebrecht, of Operation Car Wash notoriety, became the first foreign company to administer a Cuban sugar mill since the Revolution. But the decline continues, with sugar production only reaching 52% of the planned yield for 2021–2022. .

coins at its base, though the real attraction here is the all-encompassing **view** of the valley and beyond.

By car San Miguel de los Baños is easy to miss. To drive here, head east on the Carretera Central from Matanzas and take a right turn just before entering the small town of Coliseo; the village is 8km from the turn-off.

Península de Zapata

The whole southern section of Matanzas province is taken up by the **Península de Zapata**, also known as the Ciénaga de Zapata, a large, flat national park and Unesco-declared biosphere reserve covered by vast tracts of open swampland and contrastingly dense forests. The largest but least populated of all Cuba's municipalities, the peninsula is predominantly wild, unspoilt and a rich habitat for Cuban **animal life**. It's also one of the best **birdwatching** areas in the Caribbean region. Despite its 30km of accessible Caribbean coastline, the Península de Zapata's modest beaches and mostly rocky shores make it unsuitable for sun-and-sand holidays, regardless of what the brochures claim, but it is an excellent area for **diving**, with crystal-clear waters, coral reefs within swimming distance of the shore and a small network of flooded caves known as *cenotes*.

As one of the most popular day-trips from Havana and Varadero, the peninsula has built up a set of conveniently packaged diversions, though these are best combined

with the more active business of birdwatching, fishing, diving or trekking, for which you'll need to hire a **guide** and, in some cases, rent a car – entrance is restricted to most of the protected wildlife zones, which are spread over a wide area and not accessible on foot. Of the ready-made attractions, the **Finca Fiesta Campesina**, just off the Autopista Nacional, is a somewhat contrived but nonetheless likeable cross between a farm and a tiny zoo. Further in, about halfway down to the coast, **Boca de Guamá** draws the largest number of bus parties with its **crocodile farm**, restaurants and pottery workshop. This is also the point of departure for the boat trip to **Guamá**, a convincingly reconstructed **Taíno Indian village** on the edge of a huge lake. Further south on the **Bay of Pigs**, scene of the infamous 1961 **invasion**, the beaches of **Playa Girón** and **Playa Larga** are nowhere near as spectacular as their northern counterpart, but offer far superior scuba diving to the offerings near Varadero. The invasion itself is commemorated in a museum at Playa Girón and along the roadside in a series of grave-like **monuments**, each representing a Cuban casualty of the conflict.

3

ARRIVAL AND GETTING AROUND   PENÍNSULA DE ZAPATA

BY BUS

Víazul buses Víazul buses make timetabled stops at Playa Larga and Playa Girón on the Varadero–Trinidad and Havana–Trinidad routes, and refreshment stops at *La Finquita* at the Entronque de Jagüey.

Destinations (times from Playa Girón) Cienfuegos (2 daily; 1hr 15min); Havana (2 daily; 3hr 30min); Trinidad (3 daily; 3hr); Varadero (1 daily; 3hr 15min).

Shuttle buses Most of the peninsula is covered by the unreliable Guamá Bus Tour, a hop-on, hop-off tourist bus service that, in theory, travels between Boca de Guamá and Playa Girón twice daily in both directions. The morning service leaves the *Hotel Playa Girón* at 9am, arrives at Boca de Guamá at 10am and heads back the other way at 10.30am. In the afternoon it's 2pm from the *Hotel Playa Girón*, turning back at Boca de Guamá at 3.30pm.

BY CAR, SCOOTER OR BIKE

Driving to the peninsula If arriving by car from Havana or elsewhere in Matanzas province, your point of entry is the

Entronque de Jagüey, the main entry to the park at a junction on the southern outskirts of the small town of Jagüey Grande. This is where the Autopista Nacional, which runs more or less along the entire northern border of the peninsula, meets the Carretera de la Ciénaga, the only reliable road leading south into the park. This junction is marked by the *La Finquita* snack bar and information centre (see page 219). Travelling from Cienfuegos, you'll arrive at Playa Girón.

Driving around the peninsula The Carretera de la Ciénaga offers very few opportunities for wrong turns, cutting more or less straight down from the Autopista Nacional to the top of the Bay of Pigs. Almost all the land west of this road (well over half the peninsula) is officially protected territory and open only to those with a guide in tow.

Car, scooter and bike rental There's a Cubacar/ Havanautos car and scooter rental office (daily 8am–5pm; ☎ 45 98 4126) at Playa Girón, opposite the museum. You can also hire bicycles at Playa Girón. Both of the beachfront hotels also rent out scooters.

PLOTS TO KILL CASTRO

Even before the dramatic failure of the military offensive at the Bay of Pigs, the US had been planning less overt methods for **removing Fidel Castro** from power. Fabián Escalante, the former head of Cuban State Security, claims that between 1959 and 1963 over six hundred **plots** were hatched to kill the Cuban president, which became more devious and ludicrous as the US grew increasingly desperate to take out the communist leader. In 1960, during a visit which Castro was making to the UN, it was planned that he be given a **cigar** which would explode in his face; while back in Cuba, in 1963, Rolando Cubela, who had been a commander in the rebel army, was given a **syringe** disguised as a pen to be used in an assassination attempt. The Mafia also took a stab at killing Castro with their **poison pill plot**, but got no further than their CIA counterparts. Some of the more outlandish schemes included poisoning a diving suit, poisoning a cigar, leaving an explosive shell on a beach frequented by Castro and spraying LSD in a television studio in the hope of inducing an attack of uncontrollable and presumably fatal laughter.

INFORMATION

Tourist information The best source of information is *La Finquita* (daily 8am–8pm; ☎45 91 3224, ✉dcomercial@peninsula.co.cu), a snack bar/information centre by the side of the *autopista* at the junction with the main road into Zapata. It's run by Cubanacán (✉cubanacan.cu), the travel agent and tour operator responsible for all the hotels and organized excursions on the peninsula, which also has *buros de turismo* in the lobbies of the *Playa Larga* (☎45 98 7294)

and *Playa Girón* (☎45 98 4110) hotels.

Park information For information and arrangements relating to trekking, birdwatching or fishing, your first point of contact should be Cubanacán, though you can also make enquiries at the office of the Parque Nacional Ciénaga de Zapata (daily, daylight hours; ☎45 98 7249), located in a signposted bungalow just before the fork in the main road at Playa Larga.

Finca Fiesta Campesina

Carretera de la Ciénaga • Daily 9am–5pm • Charge

The pretty little **Finca Fiesta Campesina** is a kind of showcase of the Cuban countryside, presenting an idealized picture of rural life and serving as a superficial introduction to traditional food, drink, crafts and native animals. You can watch cigars being made by hand, sample a Cuban coffee or raw-tasting *guarapo* (pure sugar cane juice), or play spin-the-guinea-pig, a cruel gambling game. Dotted around the landscaped gardens are small cages and enclosures containing various species of **local wildlife**, all of which can be found living wild on the peninsula, including a crocodile. Some of the most fascinating creatures are the *manjuarí*, eerie-looking stick-like fish, survivors of the Jurassic period. You can also ride horses, and there's an on-site restaurant.

ACCOMMODATION
FINCA FIESTA CAMPESINA; SEE MAP PAGE 217

★ **Hotel Batey Don Pedro** Next door to Finca Fiesta Campesina ☎45 91 2825, ✉carpeta@donpedro.co.cu. This immaculately kept little cabin complex is the peninsula's best bargain, consisting of ten spacious wooden cabins, simply and thoughtfully furnished and connected by stone pathways running through cropped lawns. There are ceiling fans instead of a/c, but this is in keeping with the overall homespun appeal of this rural retreat. $$

Australia

Less than 1km south of the Finca Fiesta Campesina is the pocket-sized village of **AUSTRALIA**, where a right turn onto the Carretera de la Ciénaga takes you into the peninsula proper. Continuing straight on about 100m past the turning, however, brings you to **Central Australia**. This is not, as you might expect, the heart of the village, but a sugar refinery used by Fidel Castro in 1961 as a base of operations during the Bay of Pigs invasion. Despite its name, the **Museo de la Comandancia** (when open Mon–Sat 8am–5pm, Sun 8am–noon; charge; ☎45 91 2504), in the building which Castro and his men occupied, is less a tribute to its purpose in the famous Cuban victory over the US and more a survey of the whole area's broader history.

EATING
AUSTRALIA; SEE MAP PAGE 217

Pío Cuá Carretera de la Ciénaga, 1.5km south of Australia. Set up for tour groups but anyone can stop by at this somewhat isolated, thatched-roof, roadside dining hall on the way into the peninsula for the good-value buffet based on the meat, rice and beans formula with a modest selection of extras. $

Boca de Guamá

Eighteen kilometres down the Carretera de la Ciénaga from the Autopista Nacional, **Boca de Guamá**, or Boca, as it's referred to locally, is a firm favourite with tour groups and geared up predominantly for the busloads of day-trippers arriving here regularly from Varadero, Havana and beyond, though it also accommodates independent visitors easily. No more than a few buildings gathered around a car park, sandwiched between the road and a canal, its headline attraction is a **crocodile farm**, but there is also a pottery workshop, a couple of restaurants and some souvenir shops. Though a little artificial, it's relatively slick and a good spot to stop for lunch. For an extended, more engaging visit catch a boat on the canal to Guamá (see page 220), site of a re-created Taíno village.

Criadero de Cocodrilos

Daily 9.30am–5pm • Charge, under-5s free • ☎ 45 91 5666

Boca is most famous for the **Criadero de Cocodrilos**, a crocodile-breeding farm and show pen. Established in 1962, the farm was set up as a conservation project in the interests of saving the then-endangered Cuban crocodile (*cocodrilo rhombifer*) and American crocodile (*cocodrilo acutus*) from extinction – the success of the project is perhaps best, or worst, measured by the fact that you can now dine on crocodile at the on-site restaurants. The biggest beasts are in the **show pen**, which forms the centrepiece of the complex – a walk around the twisting paths that snake around the small swamp where the crocs live is pleasant, but sometimes you may have trouble spotting one as they often lie motionless in the water. The most dramatic encounters are during one of the twice-weekly **feeding sessions**, for which there is unfortunately no timetable.

Over the road is the **farm** itself which now competes for visitors with the show pen; and though the grounds are less attractive it's actually the more engaging and less staged of the two options. Here, 4500 of the critters lie piled up in several dozen uninspired concrete and wire enclosures. You're guided round the farm, though usually in Spanish, and shown the animals at various stages of their development.

Taller de Cerámica Celia Sánchez

Mon–Sat 9am–5pm • Free, but tip welcome

Set in an open-fronted building, the mildly engaging **Taller de Cerámica Celia Sánchez** is a pottery workshop and warehouse-cum-production-line where you can witness the ceramics production process, which includes setting the moulds and baking them in the large furnaces behind the stocks of finished pottery stored around the building. As well as the tacky ornamental pieces, there are replicas of Taíno cooking pots and the like, most of which get distributed to craft shops around the country.

EATING	BOCA DE GUAMÁ; SEE MAP PAGE 217

El Colibri You can dine on crocodile meat here or opt for the alternatives, a reasonable choice of more familiar, moderately priced Cuban dishes. If you arrive after 5pm, food can sometimes still be ordered from the bar. $$

Guamá

Boca is the departure point for boats travelling to **GUAMÁ**, a replica Taíno village and hotel set on a network of small islands on the far side of the **Laguna de Tesoro**, the largest natural lake in Cuba. Boats depart several times daily along the perfectly straight, tree-lined canal connecting to the lake, into which the Taíno people, hundreds of years ago, threw its treasure to prevent the Spanish seizing it – hence its name, **Treasure Lagoon**. The complex, complete with lesser-known Taíno constructions like a disco and swimming pool, may be a little contrived but it is no worse for it, captivatingly linked together by a series of bridges and pathways. The first of the neatly spaced islets, where you'll be dropped off, is occupied by life-sized statues of Native Americans in photogenic poses, each representing an aspect of Taíno culture. Cross the footbridge to reach the diminutive **museum** detailing Taíno life and featuring a few genuine artefacts. If the hour or so allotted here for tours isn't enough, you could stay the night at *Villa Guamá* (see page 222).

ARRIVAL AND DEPARTURE	GUAMÁ

By boat Boats from Boca to the village leave 9am–5pm according to demand, and take a minimum of four passengers.

WILDLIFE ON THE PENÍNSULA DE ZAPATA

The Zapata Peninsula is Cuba's best birdwatching region. On the migratory routes between the Americas, the area is home to all but four of Cuba's endemic species. So, while you won't see the Cuban kite, Cuban gnatcatcher, Cuban solitaire and orient warbler here, you can expect sightings of endemic bee hummingbirds, blue-headed quail-doves, Cuban pygmy owls, yellow-headed warblers and Zapata wrens. If you manage to see the critically endangered Zapata rail, you'll be in rare company. Almost flightless as a result of its short wings, it was thought to be extinct for forty years until a fleeting 2014 sighting raised hopes.

The Zapata region is also home to the Cuban Crocodile, the American Crocodile, the endemic Cuban ground lizard and two subspecies of the Cuban giant anole. The endemic Cuban racer snake and huge Cuban boa are found here too, along with three species of hutia, wiry-furred rodents that spend most of their time in trees.

Besides managing most of the attractions on the peninsula, Cubanacán (wcubanacan. cu) organizes less touristy trips into the heart of the **Parque Nacional Ciénaga de Zapata nature reserve**. They can supply specialist guides, some of whom speak English, for **diving**, **fishing** and **birdwatching**. The marshes and rivers of Zapata are great areas for **fly-fishing**; however, very little equipment is available locally and you should bring your own kit (plus your passport, needed to obtain a fishing licence).

There are around ten excursions and trails around the peninsula, all of which can only be visited with a guide. Charting routes through and past swamps, rivers, lagoons, sinkholes, brush and woodland, the trips can be anywhere between 4km and 60km in length, some just trekking on foot, others involving some driving. You can **arrange a trip** at *La Finquita*, at the entrance to the peninsula (see page 219), or through the *buros de turismo* in the hotels. Alternatively, go directly to the office of the Parque Nacional Ciénaga de Zapata (☎45 98 7249), where the guides are based. You will need your own car for these excursions, as Cubanacán cannot always supply transport. Havanautos and Cubacar have a rental office at Playa Girón. The three excursions described below are in the western, Unesco-protected parts of the peninsula.

THE RÍO HATIGUANICO

Hidden away in the woods on the northwestern edge of Zapata is the base camp for trips in small motor boats on the peninsula's widest river, the **Hatiguanico**. A tree-lined canal connects the camp to the river, and the whole route is abundant in birdlife, including Zapata sparrows and Cuban green woodpeckers. Before reaching the widest part of the river, the canal flows into a narrow, twisting corridor of water. After, the river opens out into an Amazonian-style waterscape and curves gracefully through the densely packed woodland.

SANTO TOMÁS

Thirty kilometres west from the small village just before Playa Larga, along a dirt road through dense forest, **Santo Tomás** sits at the heart of the reserve. Beyond the scattered huts which make up the tiny community here is a small, 2m-wide tributary of the Hatiguanico. In winter it's dry enough to walk but during the wet season groups of four to six are punted quietly a few hundred metres down the hidden little waterway, brushing past the overhanging reeds. This is real swampland and will suit the dedicated birdwatcher who doesn't mind getting dirty.

LAS SALINAS

In stark contrast to the dense woodlands of Santo Tomás, the open saltwater wetlands around **Las Salinas** are the best place on the peninsula for observing migratory and aquatic birds. From observation towers dotted along a track that cuts through the shallow waters you can see huge flocks of flamingos in the distance and solitary blue herons gliding over the shallow water, while blue-wing duck and many other species pop in and out of view from behind the scattered islets. Las Salinas is also a great fly-fishing spot, home to bonefish, permit and barracuda among others. Since this is a protected area, no more than six anglers per week are permitted to fish here.

Horizontes Villa Guamá Laguna del Tesoro Ⓦ hotelescubanacan.com. Aiming to recreate the appearance of Taíno dwellings, this attractive complex comprises 44 thatched wooden cabins equipped with TVs, air-conditioning and showers. Dotted around a network of islets on the edge of the lagoon, with balconies right over the water, the location is enchanting and ideal for birdwatchers. $\overline{\underline{SS}}$

Bay of Pigs

The Carretera de la Ciénaga splits at the point where it reaches the **Bay of Pigs**, the Bahía de Cochinos. The main road leads down the east side of the bay where virtually all the worthwhile distractions are along the seafront, including the hotel and beach resorts of **Playa Larga** and **Playa Girón**, based around the only sandy sections of the otherwise rocky shore. On the western side of the bay, in the protected **nature reserve** that occupies the most untouched part of this national park (and which you can only visit with a guide), are **Las Salinas** and **Santo Tomás**, two of the peninsula's best areas for birdwatching (see page 221).

Playa Larga

Taking the main coastal road southeast from the junction at the top of the Bay of Pigs will bring you almost immediately to **Playa Larga**, a resort area right on the beach with little to offer other than the facilities of the hotel complex itself. The beach is about 100m long, with traces of seaweed on the shore and the grass encroaching onto the sand from behind. Nearby **diving** points can be explored by arrangement with the *Hotel Playa Larga*'s own Club Octopus diving centre, on a jut of land at the opposite end of the beach, beyond the large car park just before the hotel.

La Casa del Buzo Caletón ☎ 45 98 7396, ✉ yaquelin. roque@nauta.cu. This large house with three guest rooms is one of the best places to stay on the peninsula if you're here for the diving. Owner Osnedy, a qualified diving instructor, can rent out diving equipment at below-average prices and take you out on dives. A taxi service is offered here too. $\overline{S}$

★ **Casa Frank** Calle 3ra no.8 e/ 2da y 4ta, Entronque de Playa Larga ☎ 45 98 7189, ✉ frankvegascz@gmail. com. A small network of staircases, terraces and balconies characterize this large house, with two of the four well-kept guest rooms on the huge mid-level terrace where meals are served. A level up from here there are views over to the bay and a rooftop swimming pool. The owners offer a taxi service and can arrange horseriding. $\overline{S}$

Casa de Josefa Pita Caletón ☎ 45 98 7133, ✉ neyi. torres@nauta.cu. Backing onto the seafront, this is one of the more presentable houses among a grouping of shacks off an inlet at the top of the bay. One of the two bedrooms, both doubles with en-suite bathroom and a/c, looks out onto the water, just 5m away, and you're usually given the run of the house as the owners like to stay out of the way, though they are happy to help arrange diving and walks around the peninsula. $\overline{S}$

Hotel Playa Larga Ⓦ hotelescubanacan.com. With the look and feel of a sprawling 1970s holiday camp, this tired-out old place is nevertheless on the best swathe of beach on the peninsula and is reasonably well equipped. Stretching for a few hundred metres along the coastline, it has a swimming pool, tennis court and even a small soccer pitch, but the restaurant is poor. $\overline{\underline{SS}}$

Villa Morena Barrio Mario López ✉ casaameryfelix@ gmail.com. Two pleasant a/c rooms – one with capacity for five people, the other for four – in a house full of sculpted wooden furniture at a backstreet location. Driving down to the bay on the Carretera de la Ciénaga, 50m beyond the sign announcing Playa Larga, a right-hand turn leads down to a dirt track where another right turn leads up to the house. $\overline{S}$

Fernando Pálpite ☎ 5 225 8023 or ☎ 5 821 1799. Backyard patio paladar in Pálpite, a village 4km inland on the Carretera de la Ciénaga, where the owner-chefs offer platters of seafood and succulent meat, from pork and venison to lobster and crocodile, along with the side orders of your choosing, allowing you to feast until full. $\overline{\underline{SS}}$

Cueva de los Peces

Around 16km south of Playa Larga and 16km north of Playa Girón • Daily 9am–6pm • Free

The **Cueva de los Peces**, also known as **El Cenote**, is a flooded cave full of tropical fish and one of the most serene spots on the peninsula (though do bring mosquito spray). At the bottom of a short track leading down from the road, the glassy-smooth natural **saltwater pool** emerges, oasis-like, against the backdrop of almost impenetrable woodlands. Enclosed by the scrub and about the size of a municipal swimming pool, it's the kind of place you'd want to keep secret if it hadn't already been discovered. Despite the pool's proximity to the road it's perfectly tranquil and you're free to dive in and swim with the numerous species of fish, many of which were introduced after the natural population died out. The pool leads to a flooded **cave system** of mostly unexplored underwater halls and corridors, more than 70m deep and ideal for scuba diving, which can be arranged through any of the dive centres in the area (see box), including the one at the entrance here.

EATING
CUEVA DE LOS PECES; SEE MAP PAGE 217

Cueva de los Peces restaurant Right on the edge of the pool in thick woodland, this simple, rustic restaurant is one of the best in the area, serving set meals. Choose between squid, shrimp, fish, pork, chicken, crocodile or lobster, with all side orders included. $$

Punta Perdíz
Around 22km south of Playa Larga and 10km north of Playa Girón • Daily 9am–6pm, restaurant daily 10.30am–4.30pm • Entrance fee includes open bar and buffet restaurant

Southeast along the coast road, **Punta Perdíz** is a slice of sun-baked rocky coastline packaged up for visitors, where the entrance fee includes a buffet lunch, an open bar, use of the sun loungers and wooden sun shelters and, of course, access to the sea, where you can go snorkelling and diving. There is no beach here, just a large scrap of grassy land jutting out into the sea along a craggy shore, but it's a pleasant spot and features a recently built **watersports** and **dive club** building, where you can rent equipment and arrange diving packages. It's a short swim from the shore to a reef wall that drops down as far as 300m in places.

Playa Girón
Following the coastal road southeast, it's roughly 10km from Punta Perdíz to **Playa Girón**, the place most synonymous with the Bay of Pigs invasion in April 1961 – Cubans

---

SCUBA DIVING AND SNORKELLING OFF THE PENÍNSULA DE ZAPATA

The Península de Zapata is one of the top spots in Cuba for **scuba diving** and **snorkelling**, with waters here generally calmer than those around Varadero, coral reefs close to the shore, some fantastic 30–40m coral walls and in-shore flooded caves. Scorpion fish, moray eels, groupers and barracuda are resident here, while the coral life is extremely healthy, with an abundance of brightly coloured sponges, some giant gorgonians and a proliferation of sea fans. At least ten good **dive sites** are spread along the eastern coast of the bay and beyond, right down to the more exposed waters around *Hotel Playa Girón*. Most of the coral walls are no more than 40m offshore, so to get to them you just swim from the shore. The principal **cave dive** on the peninsula is at El Cenote, known in tourist literature as the Cueva de los Peces, a limestone sinkhole linked to the sea through an underground channel and home to numerous tropical fish. There are a number of other flooded sinkholes around the peninsula and more excellent snorkelling and diving at Caleta Buena and Punta Perdíz.

The dive clubs in Varadero (see page 198) organize some of the diving that goes on around these waters, but on the peninsula itself you should report to either **Club Octopus** (☎45 98 3224) at Playa Larga or the **International Diving Center** (☎45 98 4118) at Playa Girón. There are also small diving and snorkelling clubs at Caleta Buena, Punta Perdíz and Cuevas de los Peces.

actually refer to the invasion attempt as Girón. The **beach** here is more exposed than Playa Larga, and though it's blessed with the same transparent green waters, there is an unsightly 300m-long concrete wave breaker that creates a huge pool of calm seawater but ruins the view out to sea. Although the hotel complex hogs the seafront here, non-guests are free to use the facilities as well as wander down through the grounds to the beach.

Museo Girón

By the beach, next door to *Hotel Playa Girón* · Daily 8am–5pm · Charge · ☎ 45 98 4122

Besides the beach, the other reason for stopping here is the **Museo Girón**, a two-room museum documenting the events prior to and during the US-backed invasion. Outside the building is a British-made Hawker Sea Fury, one of the fighter planes used to attack the advancing American ships, alongside two tanks. Inside, the era is successfully evoked through depictions of pre-Revolution life, along with dramatic photographs of US sabotage and terrorism in Cuba leading up to the Bay of Pigs invasion. The second room goes on to document the battle itself, with papers outlining Castro's instructions and some incredible photography taken in the heat of battle.

ACCOMMODATION PLAYA GIRÓN; SEE MAP PAGE 217

Hostal Aida y Miguel On the junction where the hotel road meets the village ☎45 98 4251, ✉ aidamiguel.2013@yahoo.es. They've squeezed six bedrooms out of this house, just a few hundred metres from

---

THE BAY OF PIGS

The triumph of the Cuban Revolution was initially treated with caution rather than hostility by the US government, but tensions between the two countries developed quickly. As Castro's reforms became more radical, the US tried harder to thwart the process and in particular refused to accept the terms of the **agrarian reform law**, which dispossessed a number of American landowners. Castro attacked the US in his speeches, became increasingly friendly with the Soviet Union and in the latter half of 1960 expropriated all US property in Cuba. The Americans responded by cancelling Cuba's **sugar quota** and secretly authorizing the CIA to organize the training of Cuban exiles, who had fled the country following the rebel triumph, for a future invasion of the island.

On April 15, 1961, US planes disguised with Cuban markings and piloted by exiles bombed Cuban airfields but caused more panic than actual damage, although seven people were killed. The intention had been to incapacitate the small Cuban air force so that the invading troops would be free from aerial bombardment, but Castro had cannily moved most of the Cuban bombers away from the airfields and camouflaged them. Two days later **Brigade 2506**, as the exile invasion force was known, landed at Playa Girón, in the **Bay of Pigs**. The brigade had been led to believe that the air attacks had been successful and were not prepared for what was in store. As soon as Castro learned the precise location of the invasion he moved his base of operations to the sugar refinery of Central Australia (see page 219) and ordered both his air force and land militias to repel the advancing invaders.

The unexpected **aerial attacks** caused much damage and confusion; two freighters were destroyed and the rest of the fleet fled, leaving 1300 troops trapped on Playa Larga and Playa Girón. During the night of April 17–18 the Cuban government forces, which had been reinforced with armoured cars and tanks, renewed attacks on the brigade. The battle continued into the next day as the brigade became increasingly outnumbered by the advancing revolutionary army. Several B-26 bombers, two manned by US pilots, flew over to the Bay of Pigs from Nicaragua the next morning in an attempt to weaken the Cuban army and clear the way for the landing of supplies needed by the stranded brigade. Most of the bombers were shot down and the supplies never arrived. Castro's army was victorious, having captured 1180 prisoners who were eventually traded for medical and other supplies from the US. Other ways would have to be found to topple the Cuban leader.

the beach, all with en-suite bathroom and minibar. Owners Aida and Miguel, who both worked in the local hotel restaurant, rent out mountain bikes and diving equipment to guests and there's internet access here too. $

Hotel Playa Girón On the beach ⓦ hotelescubanacan. With its family-sized bungalows spread out over a large site right on the beach, the rooms in this hotel complex have been redecorated. There's a pool and tennis court, but it works best as a base for diving, as it's the closest of any hotel on the peninsula to the area's dive sites, and has its own diving club. The location also makes it popular with birdwatchers. $$

K.S. Abella Carretera a Cienfuegos ☏ 45 98 4383, ⓔ ricardoabellamercy@yahoo.es. Ricardo, the English-speaking chef who owns this neatly kept house in the Playa Girón village, offers great breakfasts and seafood dinners. Two guest rooms and a suite, just off a lovely little backyard patio, have a connecting lounge and bathroom, making this a great option for groups or a family. $

DIRECTORY

Car rental You'll find a Cubacar/Havanautos car and scooter rental office (daily 8am–5pm; ☏ 45 98 4126) opposite the Museo Girón.

Money and exchange There's a CADECA *casa de cambio* (Mon–Fri 8.30–noon & 12.30–3.30pm, Sat 8.30–11am) opposite the Museo Girón.

Caleta Buena
8km southeast of Playa Girón • Daily 10am–6pm • Charge; includes drinks and buffet lunch

Further down the coastal road from Playa Girón, the last stop along this side of the bay is **Caleta Buena**, a pay-to-enter coastal park on a rocky but very picturesque stretch of coastline and one of the best places on the peninsula for snorkelling. Based around the calm waters of a large sheltered inlet with flat rocky platforms jutting out into the sea but no beach as such, the unspoilt serenity here befits this most secluded of Zapata's coastal havens. It's a perfect place for lazing about on the waterfront, with red-tile-roof shelters on wooden stilts providing protection from the midday sun. The best way to spend time here is to go snorkelling or diving and take advantage of the fact that you needn't go more than 150m out from the shore to enjoy a coral-coated sea bed. The site is equipped with its own **diving centre** and diving initiation courses are available, though these should be arranged in advance through Cubanacán. There is also a **volleyball** net and **rowing boats** for rent.

Cienfuegos and Villa Clara

CHE GUEVARA MONUMENT, SANTA CLARA

Cienfuegos and Villa Clara

For a combination of city, sand and sierra, the provinces of Cienfuegos and Villa Clara are as good as anywhere in the western half of Cuba. Their attractive capitals, Cienfuegos and Santa Clara, make convenient bases for day trips to decent beaches, especially on the northern cays of Villa Clara, and a significant stretch of Cuba's gentle but wonderfully scenic central mountain range, the Sierra del Escambray. Though far from cosmopolitan metropolises, and a little lacking in the nightlife and eating-out stakes, they are nevertheless both culturally respectable cities, endowed with significant universities, nationally renowned theatres and large and lively central squares. They're also blessed with some top-notch places to stay, making either city a good place to enjoy a slice of modern Cuba.

Of the two provinces **Cienfuegos** has the inferior beaches, but its main attractions, including some memorable **botanical gardens**, the **Castillo de Jagua** and the beaches themselves, at the small-scale coastal resort of **Rancho Luna**, are huddled closer together, many of them on or within 15km of the Bahía de Jagua, a huge bay in the south of the province. The calm waters of the almost completely enclosed bay, and the mountainous backdrop far off to the east, provide **Cienfuegos city**, nestling on its eastern shores, with one of the prettiest, most serene settings of any provincial capital in Cuba. Jarring with this serenity are the clusters of heavy industry in this part of the province, though they are largely out of sight except when travelling between places. The most heavily trodden route through the province is the road to Trinidad, the **Circuito Sur**, much of it running along the corridor of land between the province's picturesque Caribbean coastline and the **Sierra del Escambray**. On these leafy slopes is **Parque El Nicho**, criss-crossed by hiking trails and waterfalls and a great day-trip destination.

The postcard-perfect beaches of **Villa Clara**, on its northern cays, are among the best in the country but are almost 100km from the most obvious base in the province for independent travellers, the provincial capital **Santa Clara**. This city's connections to the Che Guevara story are heavily marketed, though there is much more to the city than its numerous interesting homages to the revolutionary hero. Slightly livelier, larger and more dynamic a city than Cienfuegos, Santa Clara enjoys excellent theatrical and musical events and supports a broader spectrum of subcultures than most provincial Cuban cities, including a subversive heavy metal scene and one of Cuba's most off-beat, LGBTQ-friendly music and performance venues. Between the city and those northern cays – **Cayo Las Brujas**, **Cayo Ensenachos** and **Cayo Santa María**, where an entire package holiday resort has been created from scratch over the last two decades – lies sleepy **Remedios**, a tranquil, colourfully spruced-up, welcoming little town steeped in history. On the other side of the province, a reservoir, the **Embalse Hanabanilla**, provides straightforward access into the Sierra del Escambray, the well-situated hotel at its northern tip equipped with facilities for fishing, hiking and boat trips, open to guests and non-guests alike.

Cienfuegos city

Having celebrated its 200th anniversary in 2019, **CIENFUEGOS** is one of the more recently established major Cuban cities. It's the only city in the country – and in the whole of Latin America – founded by French settlers, many of them from Louisiana,

REMEDIOS

Highlights

❶ Finca del Mar and El Lagarto Cienfuegos has two of the best paladars outside of Havana, serving great, simple food in splendid bayside locations. See page 239

❷ Jardín Botánico de Cienfuegos Lose yourself amid bamboo cathedrals and countless varieties of palm trees. See page 241

❸ Parque El Nicho Walk to the picturesque El Nicho waterfalls and pools in the Sierra del Escambray. See page 243

❹ The Jagua ferry Enjoy the laidback pace of local life on the slow chug across the bay from Cienfuegos, taking in city views and the distant mountains. See page 243

❺ Parque Vidal The main square in Santa Clara is among the most vibrant in Cuba. See page 245

❻ El Mejunje This unusual music and arts venue in Santa Clara has an entertainingly diverse programme and a welcoming vibe. See page 254

❼ Remedios Historic Remedios is one of the best-kept small towns in Cuba, with a delightful, leafy central square and a fabulous choice of places to spend the night. See page 255

❽ The northern cays The journey to these remote, beach-blessed islets – along a 50km-long causeway skimming above clear waters – is reason enough to visit. See page 260

HIGHLIGHTS ARE MARKED ON THE MAP ON PAGE 230

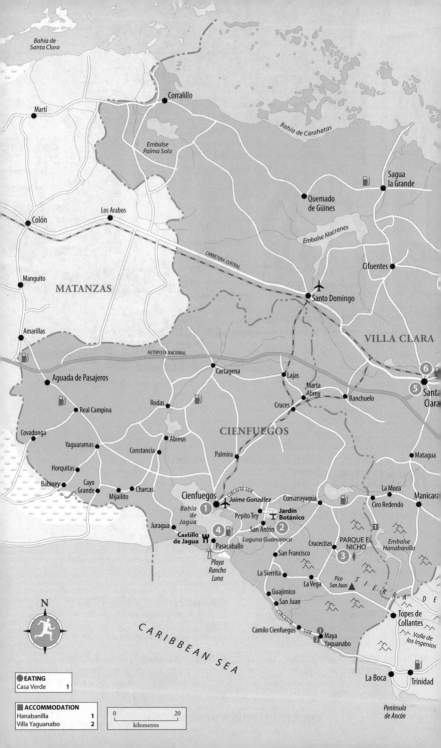

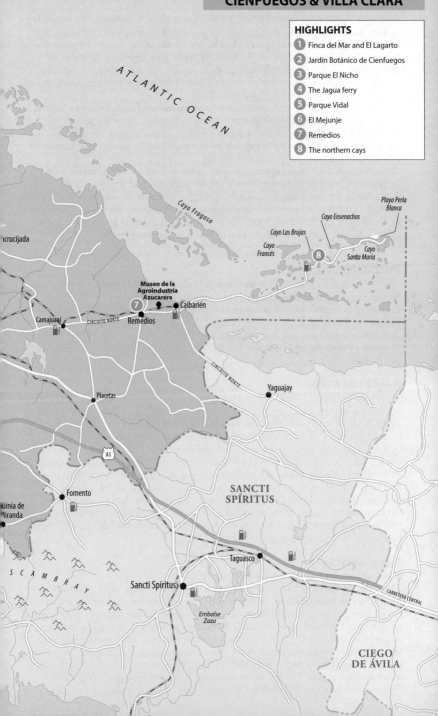

HIGHLIGHTS
1. Finca del Mar and El Lagarto
2. Jardín Botánico de Cienfuegos
3. Parque El Nicho
4. The Jagua ferry
5. Parque Vidal
6. El Mejunje
7. Remedios
8. The northern cays

ATLANTIC OCEAN

Cayo Fragoso

Playa Perla Blanca

Cayo Ensenachos

Cayo Las Brujas

Cayo Francés

Cayo Santa María

8

ncrucijada

Museo de la Agroindustria Azucarera

7

Caibarién

Camajuani

CIRCUITO NORTE

Remedios

CIRCUITO NORTE

Placetas

Yaguajay

A1

Fomento

üinia de liranda

S C A M B R A Y

SANCTI SPÍRITUS

Taguasco

CARRETERA CENTRAL

Sancti Spíritus

Embalse Zaza

CIEGO DE ÁVILA

lending it a distinctive look and feel. An easy-going place, Cienfuegos is noticeably cleaner and more spacious than the average provincial capital, with a relatively rich cultural heritage and deserving of its label as the "Pearl of the South". Its most alluring feature is its bayside location on the **Bahía de Jagua**, also known as the **Bahía de Cienfuegos**, which provides pleasant offshore breezes and some sleepy views across the usually undisturbed water – unless you find one of the perspectives that reveal the oil refinery on the mostly obscured northern shore.

As a base for seeing what the rest of the province has to offer, Cienfuegos is ideal, with several easy day-trip destinations – taking in **beaches**, **botanical gardens** and an old Spanish fortress, the **Castillo de Jagua** – within a 20km radius. The best way to get to the fortress is to take the **Jagua ferry** (see page 243), a wonderfully unhurried journey offering great perspectives of the city.

Most visitors don't stray beyond two quite distinct districts, the relatively built-up northern borough of **Pueblo Nuevo**, the city's cultural and shopping centre, and **Punta Gorda**, a more modern, laidback, open-plan neighbourhood where you'll find a marina, a couple of scrappy little beaches and one of the most resplendent buildings in Cienfuegos, the **Palacio de Valle**. The two are linked together by the principal city street, Calle 37, the promenade section of which is known as **Prado**.

Pueblo Nuevo

The undisputed focal point of **Pueblo Nuevo** is the **Parque José Martí**, the main square. From here, the pedestrianized section of **Avenida 54**, also known as El Boulevard, links the square to **Prado**, the liveliest street in Cienfuegos, lined with shops, a couple of bars and some cheap, fairly poor restaurants. Round the corner from El Boulevard, on Calle 29, is a daily arts and crafts **market** and, a block over on Calle 31, the diminutive **Quintero y Hermanos cigar factory**, usually open only to visitors on organized visits, but an emblem of the city.

Parque José Martí

With a statue of José Martí at the midway point of its central promenade, a traditional bandstand, its own miniature Arc de Triomphe and neatly kept little gardens nestling in the shade of royal palm trees, the **Parque José Martí** perfectly encapsulates the city's graceful character, its French heritage and its tidy and pretty appearance. Though lacking in good restaurants, this colourful and sometimes lively square is at the heart of local life, surrounded by grand buildings occupying central roles in the political, cultural and religious affairs of Cienfuegos, as well as some nice cafés and, in the northwestern corner, some inconspicuous but striking **artists' studio-galleries**. In the northeastern corner is the **Colegio San Lorenzo**, the most classically Greco-Roman structure on the square, home to a school. Opposite is the dome-topped, Neoclassical provincial government headquarters, the **Antiguo Ayuntamiento**, built in 1929 with four columns flanking its grand entrance.

Teatro Tomás Terry

Avenida 56 e/ 27 y 29, Parque José Martí • Daily 9am–6pm • Charge • ☎ 43 51 3361

The **Teatro Tomás Terry** has stood proudly on the northern edge of the Parque José Martí since its foundation in 1890. Music, dance and theatre productions are still staged here, but the glorious **interior** is a show in itself. Restored almost to its original splendour in the build-up to the city's 200th anniversary, a look inside is well worth the daytime entrance fee. In the decorative lobby, featuring the original nineteenth-century ticket booths, is a statue of the theatre's namesake – a millionaire patron of the city, whose family part-funded the building's construction. The predominantly wooden, semicircular, 950-seat **auditorium** was fashioned on a traditional Italian design, with three tiers of balconies, a dreamy Baroque-style fresco on the ceiling and a gold-framed stage sloping towards the front row to allow the audience an improved view. For details of performances, either call or check the noticeboard at the entrance; and note that guided tours aren't available if rehearsals are taking place.

Palacio Ferrer
Avenida 54 esq. 25, Parque José Martí • Tues–Sat 10am–5.30pm & Sun 9am–1pm • Charge

For the best available **views** of the square head to its southwest corner and climb the stairs of the **Palacio Ferrer**. This splendid Neoclassical mansion, built in 1918,

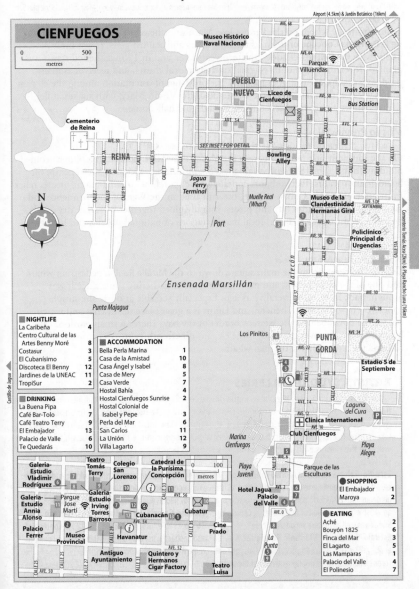

CIENFUEGOS

0 — 500 metres

Airport (4.5km) & Jardín Botánico (16km)

Museo Histórico Naval Nacional

PUEBLO NUEVO

Liceo de Cienfuegos

Train Station

Bus Station

Parque Villuendas

Cementerio de Reina

REINA

SEE INSET FOR DETAIL

Bowling Alley

Jagua Ferry Terminal

Muelle Real (Wharf)

Museo de la Clandestinidad Hermanas Giral

Policlínico Principal de Urgencias

Port

Ensenada Marsillán

Punta Majagua

Los Pinitos

PUNTA GORDA

Estadio 5 de Septiembre

Cementerio Tomás Acea (2km) & Playa Rancho Luna (16km)

Laguna del Cura

Clínica Internacional

Club Cienfuegos

Playa Alegre

Marina Cienfuegos

NIGHTLIFE
La Caribeña	4
Centro Cultural de las Artes Benny Moré	8
Costasur	3
El Cubanísimo	5
Discoteca El Benny	12
Jardines de la UNEAC	11
TropiSur	2

DRINKING
La Buena Pipa	1
Café Bar-Tolo	7
Café Teatro Terry	9
El Embajador	13
Palacio de Valle	6
Te Quedarás	10

ACCOMMODATION
Bella Perla Marina	1
Casa de la Amistad	10
Casa Ángel y Isabel	8
Casa de Mery	5
Casa Verde	7
Hostal Bahía	4
Hostal Cienfuegos Sunrise	2
Hostal Colonial de Isabel y Pepe	3
Perla del Mar	6
San Carlos	11
La Unión	12
Villa Lagarto	9

Castillo de Jagua

Teatro Tomás Terry

Colegio San Lorenzo

Catedral de la Purísima Concepción

0 — 100 metres

Galería-Estudio Vladimir Rodríguez

Galería-Estudio Annia Alonso

Parque José Martí

Galería-Estudio Irving Torres Barroso

Cubanacán

Cubatur

Palacio Ferrer

Museo Provincial

Havanatur

Cine Prado

Antiguo Ayuntamiento

Quintero y Hermanos Cigar Factory

Teatro Luisa

Playa Juvenil

Hotel Jagua Palacio del Valle

La Punta

Parque de las Esculturas

SHOPPING
El Embajador	1
Maroya	2

EATING
Aché	2
Bouyón 1825	6
Finca del Mar	3
El Lagarto	5
Las Mamparas	1
Palacio del Valle	4
El Polinesio	7

4

features a series of beautifully restored, largely empty rooms. Ceramic wall tile mosaics, Arabesque floor tiles, marble staircases and ornate cove ceilings and archway mouldings convey a sense of the original owner of this domestic palace, José Ferrer, a Spanish landowner. On the roof you can ascend the spiral staircase of the **watchtower** and snap perfectly framed photos of the square and over the rooftops to the bay.

Catedral de la Purísima Concepción

Calle 29 esq. Avenida 56, Parque José Martí • Mon–Fri 7am–3pm, Sat 7am–noon & 2–4pm, Sun 7am–noon; Mass daily 7.15am, plus Sun 10am • ☎ 43 52 5297

Across from the school on the Parque José Martí's northeastern corner is the **Catedral de la Purísima Concepción** with its fetching altars and stained glass. It was built in 1833, with the bell tower added thirteen years later, and in 1903 cathedral status was granted. It retains much of its original spirit as a local church and receives as many resident worshippers as it does tourists. The only sign of ostentation among the elegant simplicity is at the main altar where a statue of the Virgin Mary, with snakes at her feet, shelters under an ornately decorated blue-and-gold half-dome.

Museo Provincial

Avenida 54 esq. 27, Parque José Martí • Tues–Sat 9am–5pm, Sun 9am–1pm • Charge • ☎ 43 51 9722

On the southern side of the square is the **Museo Provincial**, housed in a blue balconied building founded in 1892 and originally a Spanish *casino*, a kind of social centre for Spanish immigrants. Its two floors contain a hotchpotch of colonial-era furniture, relics from pre-Columbian Cuban culture, firearms used in the Wars of Independence and all sorts of other random bits and pieces, roughly glued together by rather dry display boards recounting (in Spanish) local manifestations of national politics and history.

Muelle Real

Avenida 46, opposite southern end of Calle 29

Calle 29 descends from the main square down to the **Muelle Real**, a pedestrian wharf and one of the city's newest and most inviting social-gathering spots since it was brought back from ruin several years ago. Especially sociable at dusk, the simple concrete jetty dotted with benches and lamps is a great place to sit, chat and watch the sun go down behind the western border of the bay. There's a small outdoor café here and opposite, over the road, is the elegant nineteenth-century customs building, constructed alongside the original wharf.

ARTISTS' STUDIO-GALLERIES

The best and most accessible places in the city to see original, expressive **art**, refreshingly free of the clichéd works so prevalent in the markets and state-run arts-and-crafts shops, are the private, makeshift **studio-galleries** on the square. Here local artists exhibit and sell their work in the front rooms of handsome residential buildings, in some cases producing their work on the premises. In addition to the artists' studios listed here there are several on Calle 29 between the square and the docks. There are no formal opening hours.

Estudio-Galería de Annia Alonso Calle 25 no.5425 e/ 54 y 56 ⓦ annia.artelista.com/en/ Some of the gorgeous impressionistic paintings and engravings of an artist who has exhibited in galleries in Canada and Sweden as well as Havana are on show here.

Estudio-Galería de Vladimir Rodríguez Ave. 56 e/ 25 y 27 ⓦ vladimirodriguezvisual.blogspot.com. Three exhibition spaces display a mixture of the award-winning and recent work of this sculptor and painter with a penchant for depicting skulls and skeletons. You can buy photos and postcards of his productions.

Estudio-Galería de Irving Torres Barroso Ave. 56 no.2513 e/ 25 y 27 ☎ 43 55 1031. Conceptual and abstract artist who uses anything from oil paint to cement to create his work.

ACTIVITIES IN CIENFUEGOS

As well as the mini-theme park at Club Cienfuegos (see below), there are several other possibilities for **activities** in and around the city.

Boat tours and diving From Marina Cienfuegos (daily 8am–5pm; ☎ 43 55 1699), next to Club Cienfuegos at Calle 35 e/ Avenida 6 y Avenida 8, arrange boat tours of the bay and diving excursions.

Swimming pools The swimming pools at the *La Unión* hotel and *Hotel Jagua* are available to non-guests (daily 10am–6pm). There's also a pool at Club Cienfuegos.

Tennis Club Cienfuegos has two synthetic courts (daily 10am–6pm).

Museo Histórico Naval Nacional

Avenida 60 y Calle 21 • Tues–Sat 10am–6pm, Sun 9am–noon • Charge • ☎ 43 51 6617

A few blocks northwest of Parque José Martí, in a pleasant grassy setting on a small jut of land sticking out into the bay known as Cayo Loco, the **Museo Histórico Naval Nacional** houses a sketchy collection of items related to sea travel and naval warfare, alongside an eclectic set of displays painting a more general picture of local political, social and natural history. A whole section is devoted to the 1957 **September 5 uprising**, in which local revolutionaries instigated an insurrectionary coup at the naval barracks, now the museum's buildings and grounds. They held the city for only a few hours before the dictator General Batista sent in some two thousand soldiers and crushed the rebellion, in a battle that ended with a shoot-out at the Colegio San Lorenzo on Parque José Martí.

Punta Gorda

The southern part of the city, **Punta Gorda**, has a distinctly different flavour from the rest of Cienfuegos. Open streets and spacious bungalows – unmistakeably influenced by the United States of the 1940s and 1950s – project an image of affluence and suburban harmony. This image is perhaps more misleading today than it would have been in the 1950s, but you'll still find the most comfortable homes in Cienfuegos here, many of them with rooms for rent to visitors; there are also some gorgeous boutique hotels.

Other than the magnificent **Palacio de Valle**, Punta Gorda has no museums and few historic monuments, but does feature the **Club Cienfuegos** leisure complex and boat trips from the marina. Of the scrappy beaches, the best are **Playa Juvenil**, next to the marina, a 50m wisp of sand with a few wooden parasols and a little refreshments kiosk; and **Playa Alegre**, six blocks east along Avenida 16 from Calle 37 and three blocks south from there. Before swimming at any beach in Cienfuegos, however, bear in mind that some of the city's waste water is emptied directly into the bay.

As much as anything, Punta Gorda is the best area in the city to spend time outside, whether taking an evening stroll down Calle 37, having a drink at one of several open-air bars, sitting on the wall of the **Malecón** – the bayside promenade – and shooting the breeze, or relaxing in the pretty bayside park at La Punta.

Club Cienfuegos

Calle 37 e/ Avenida 8 y Avenida 12 • **Club** Daily 10am–10pm, Sat until 1am • **Swimming pool** Tues–Sun 10am–6pm, Mon from 2pm • Charges • ☎ 43 52 6510

Club Cienfuegos, a gleaming white, palatial three-storey mansion dating back to 1918, looks as if it might house a prestigious museum or a distinguished embassy. In fact, it's a small commercial and leisure complex featuring two restaurants, a 25m swimming pool, tennis courts and a large, first-floor terrace overlooking the marina next door (see below) that hosts a programme of night-time entertainment. There's also a shop, a few indoor games including pool tables and a very low-key **amusement park** with a minute go-kart track, bumper cars and the like.

Palacio de Valle
Calle 37 esq. Avenida 0 · Daily 10am–10pm · Free · ☎ 43 55 1003 ext 812

The most popular target for visitors to Punta Gorda is the striking **Palacio de Valle**. With its mismatched twin turrets, chiselled arches and carved windows, it looks like a cross between a medieval fortress, a Native American temple and a Moorish palace. The interior is equally majestic, with tiled mosaic floors, lavishly decorated walls and ceilings, a marble staircase, and painstakingly detailed arches and adornments scattered throughout. Built between 1913 and 1917, this spectacular building was originally a private residence whose estate occupied what are now the grounds of the *Hotel Jagua*. Designed by an Italian architect Alfredo Collí, structural contributions were made by a team of artisans, who included Frenchmen, Cubans and Arabs. Nowadays, it serves principally as a restaurant, but if you're not eating there's nothing to stop you wandering up the spiral staircase to the **rooftop bar**, a great spot for a drink.

La Punta

South of the *Palacio de Valle*, the land narrows to a 200m peninsula known as **La Punta**, home to the city's most opulent residences. Colourful wooden and concrete mansions and maisonettes, most of them now classy *casas particulares*, line the quiet road that leads down to the pretty little **park** right at the tip of the peninsula, almost completely surrounded by water. A great place to chill out during the week, the park springs into life at the weekends when the town's teenagers converge to listen to music, drink rum, flirt and cool down in the murky water.

Cementerio Tomás Acea
Avenida 5 de Septiembre · Daily 6am–5pm · Free · ☎ 43 52 5257

Some 2.5km from Calle 37, or a five-minute taxi ride from the centre, is the picturesque **Cementerio Tomás Acea**, the city's largest cemetery and the nearest thing in Cienfuegos to a landscaped metropolitan park. Completed in 1926, the grandiose Parthenon-styled entrance building, at the end of a long driveway with gardens on either side, leads into the gentle slopes of the cemetery **grounds**. Rolling, sweeping lawns are punctuated by the odd tree and from the highest point there are pleasant views of the distant bay. There are some interesting **tombs** to look out for, the monument to the Martyrs of September 5, 1957 (see page 235) the most striking.

ARRIVAL AND DEPARTURE   CIENFUEGOS

BY PLANE

Flights There are no scheduled domestic flights to or from the Jaime González Airport (☎ 43 55 1328), just over 5km from Pueblo Nuevo on the eastern outskirts of the city. There is a once-weekly direct connection to Toronto with Sunwing Airlines but no other scheduled international flights to or from this airport. Taxis provide the only transport to and from the city.

BY BUS

Víazul buses All Víazul buses pull in at the Terminal de Omnibus (☎ 43 51 5720) on Calle 49 e/ 56 y 58, from where

it's a 15min walk or a taxi ride into the town centre. For cities in the east of the country, you should go to Trinidad and catch a connecting bus there.

Destinations Havana (3 daily; 4hr); Playa Girón (3 daily; 1hr 20min); Playa Larga (3 daily; 1h 30min–2hr); Santa Clara (1 daily; 1hr 15min); Trinidad (6 daily; 1hr 30min); Varadero (2 daily; 4hr 40min).

Conectando Cuba buses This bus service (see page 28), operated by Cubanacán, runs to and from Havana (1 daily; 4hr) and Trinidad (2 daily; 1hr 30min), with several drop-off and pick-up points in the city, including outside hotels *La Unión* and *Jagua*. To buy tickets, go to the local branch of Cubanacán (see page 237) two days before the day of travel.

Local buses and camiones particulares Local intermunicipal buses are unreliable and schedules can change daily – check the chalked timetables on the blackboard on the ground floor of the Terminal de Omnibus, where they set off from. You'll also find a timetable here for *camiones particulares*, privately owned trucks converted into makeshift buses serving towns around the province as well as Pasacaballo (for the beaches), Santa Clara and Trinidad. For most visitors, the only local bus services worth considering are for Playa Rancho Luna (3 daily; 40min) and Pepito Tey (1 daily; 30min), close to the Jardín Botánico.

BY TRAIN

The train station (☎ 43 52 5495) is over the road from the bus station at Calle 49 e/ 58 y 60, though as services to or from anywhere are painfully slow, very few foreign visitors arrive or depart by train. In July 2017 the service to Havana

was reinstated after a suspension of over a year. From the station, it's a 15min walk or taxi ride into the town centre.
Destinations Havana (every third day; 10hr); Sancti Spíritus (1 daily; 6hr); Santa Clara (1 daily; 2hr 30min).

BY CAR

Arriving by car from Trinidad, you'll enter Cienfuegos on Avenida 5 de Septiembre, which connects up with the city grid four blocks east of Calle 37, the main street and the road on which you'll arrive if you've driven from Havana or Varadero. The most convenient and secure place to park is in the *La Unión* hotel car park, opposite the hotel on Calle 31.

BY FERRY

Small tugboat-like ferries to and from Castillo de Jagua (3 daily; 1hr) use the tiny ferry terminal at Avenida 46, at the foot of Calle 25, in Pueblo Nuevo, within easy walking distance of Parque José Martí.

GETTING AROUND

You can **walk** around Pueblo Nuevo, but you'll probably want to use some kind of transport if you intend to explore the 3km length of **Punta Gorda**.

By bus The #1 bus travels infrequently up and down Calle 37, with several stops in Punta Gorda and turns round at the *Palacio de Valle*. It's by far the cheapest way to get between Pueblo Nuevo and Punta Gorda.

By horse-drawn carriage Horse-drawn carriages go up and down Calle 37 all day; there are no fixed stops, you just flag them down.

By taxi Cubataxi (☎ 43 51 9145) has cars hanging around the *Jagua* hotel car park in Punta Gorda and outside the *La Unión* hotel in Pueblo Nuevo.

Car and scooter rental For car rental, Havanautos/ Cubacar are at Calle 37 e/ 16 y 18 (daily 8am–8pm; ☎ 43 55 1211); the hotel *Casa Verde* car park (Mon–Fri 8am–8pm, Sat 8am–5pm; ☎ 43 55 2014); and opposite the *Hotel Unión* at Calle 31 e/ 54 y 56 (Mon–Fri 8am–8pm, Sat 8am–5pm; ☎ 43 55 1645). Scooter rental is available from Motoclub at Avenida 18 esq. 37 (daily 9am–5pm).

INFORMATION

Tourist office The national tourist information provider Infotur has several branches in the city, at Avenida 56 no.3117 e/ 31 y 33 (Mon–Sat 9am–6pm; ☎ 43 51 4653), Avenida 54 e/ 29 y 31 (Mon–Sat 9am–6pm; ☎ 43 55 8840)

and at the bus station.
Websites The best source for film, theatre and live music listings is the state-sponsored ⊕ azurina.cult.cu.

TOURS AND TRAVEL AGENTS

The city's travel agents can organize **tours** of Cienfuegos and excursions around the province and beyond; **prices** don't vary much from one agency to another. In addition, the travel agencies listed below can book hotel rooms around the country, while cultural tours specialist Paradiso also arranges dance classes and visits to the local Quintero y Hermanos cigar factory.

TOURS

City tour Includes pick-up from hotel and takes in Parque José Martí, the Prado and Malecón, the *Palacio de Valle* and lunch. Expect to pay around $600CUP each for two people.
Paseo por la Bahía A tour of the bay by boat offering great views of the city and reaching right down to the Castillo de Jagua. You'll pay in the region of $400CUP.

Jardín Botánico A trip to the botanical gardens. Around $400CUP each for two people.
El Nicho A guided trek around Parque El Nicho in the Sierra del Escambray. $900–1000CUP.

TRAVEL AGENTS

Cubanacán Avenida 54 no.2903 e/ 29 y 31 (Mon–Sat 9am–5pm; ☎ 43 55 1680).
Cubatur Prado no.5399 e/ Avenida 54 y Avenida 56 (Mon–Fri 9am–noon & 1–5pm, Sat 9am–noon; ☎ 43 55 1242).
Havanatur Avenida 54 no.2906 e/ 29 y 31 (Mon–Sat 8am–noon & 1–4pm; ☎ 43 55 1393).
Paradiso Avenida 54 e/ 33 y 35 (Mon–Fri 9am–noon & 12.30–5pm, Sat 9am–1pm; ☎ 43 52 6673).

4

ACCOMMODATION

SEE MAP PAGE 233

Cienfuegos has a great selection of **hotels**, all run by the Spanish Meliá hotel chain. The *Hotel Jagua*, at the southern end of Punta Gorda on Calle 37, is the parent hotel of smaller, boutiquey *Casa Verde*, *Palacio Azul* and *Perla del Mar*, which form a small network, allowing guests at any of them to use the facilities at all, including the pool at the *Jagua*. There's a large number of equally impressive and much cheaper **casas particulares**, many between the bus station and Parque José Martí as well as along the length of Calle 37, with some particularly comfortable options in Punta Gorda. For the most luxurious houses, head to the tranquil surroundings of **La Punta**, the southern tip of Punta Gorda, a bit of a hike from the centre but worth it if you want a touch of exclusivity and don't mind paying a little extra.

HOTELS

★ **Casa Verde** Calle 37 e/ Ave. 0 y Ave. 2 ⓦ meliacuba. com. A fabulous conversion of a magnificent 1920s house right on the waterfront. With only eight rooms and an elegant Victorian-style interior there's both a sense of intimacy and exclusivity, and there's a restaurant, bar and natural pool on site. $$$

★ **Perla del Mar** Calle 37 e/ 0 y 2 ⓦ meliacuba.com. This nine-room boutique hotel, set in a converted 1950s bayside *villa*, has a lovely, graceful feel about it. Most of the communal spaces – including a dining and sun-lounge area and two outdoor jacuzzis on the patio – face out over the water. $$$

San Carlos Ave. 56 e/ 33 y 35 ⓦ meliacuba.com. Opened in late 2018, this is the newest and swishest hotel in the city, a couple of blocks from Parque José Martí. High-spec by local standards, it's a generically modern place whose highlight is the sixth-floor bar with the best available views of the city. Guests have access to the pool at the sister *La Unión* hotel. $$$

La Unión Calle 31 esq. 54 ☎ 43 55 1020, ⓦ meliacuba. com. This charming, stylish and comfortable hotel, occupying a Neoclassical building from 1869, has patios done in glorious Spanish tiles, a sauna, a gym, a hot tub, an art gallery and a small swimming pool. The 49 rooms are equipped with satellite TV and spotless bathrooms, and there's a roof-terrace bar overlooking the bay. $$$

CASAS PARTICULARES

★ **Bella Perla Marina** Calle 39 no.5818 esq. Ave. 60 ☎ 43 51 8991, ⓔ bellaperlamarina@yahoo.es. This large, three-storey castle of a house has three levels of open-air terraces: the lowest one is covered and features a pool table, the highest one affords views of the bay and the whole of the centre, while in between them sits a rooftop garden. There are three excellent high-spec rooms are well appointed, one with a striking Art Deco bathroom, the

largest a huge and extraordinary suite with a mezzanine level. There's also a jacuzzi. $$

★ **Casa de la Amistad** Ave. 56 no.2927 e/ 29 y 31 ☎ 43 51 6143, ⓔ casamistad@correodecuba.cu. This first-floor flat, full of colonial character, is run by a gregarious elderly couple who are as professional as they are personable. Armando will gladly talk revolutionary politics for hours while Leonor excels at playing the host, whether cooking up her house speciality of chicken in cola, or arranging excursions to the beaches and beyond. The two rooms for rent are comfortable and airy, with no a/c but good fans; a spiral staircase leads to a roof terrace with great views. $

Casa Ángel y Isabel Calle 35 no.24 e/ 0 y Litoral, La Punta ☎ 43 51 1519, ⓔ angeleisabel@yahoo.es. Magnificent neo-colonial house on the water's edge, complete with a colonnaded porch and turrets on the roof. The three well-appointed double rooms are in a separate modern block at the back, where there's also a jetty, waterside patio and roof terrace. $

Casa de Mery Ave. 6 no.3509 e/ 35 y 37 ☎ 43 51 8880, ⓔ canto@jagua.cfg.sld.cu. A top-notch, bright and orderly place run with care and attention by talkative Mery. The spacious and well-equipped guest rooms, in their own independent block out the back, are gathered around an intimate, leafy patio from where steps lead to a great little roof terrace with views of the bay. $

★ **Hostal Bahía** Ave. 20 esq. 35 no.3502 (altos) ☎ 43 52 6598, ⓔ ag.reservas@gmail.com. Guest rooms sit alongside a bay-facing first-floor balcony, in an elegant house just over a quiet road from the water's edge. Completely renovated in 2018, the fantastic location is matched by the graceful, arty and comfortable interior, and the four rooms feature a/c, safety deposit boxes, TVs and fridges bursting with drinks. Next door, under the same ownership, is *Finca del Mar*, the best paladar in the city. $

Hostal Cienfuegos Sunrise Calle 41 no.5005 e/ 50 y 52 ☎ 43 55 0247, ⓔ hostalcienfuegosunrise@gmail. com. This immaculate, capacious house, with three outdoor terraces and three guest rooms, is spread across four levels, if you include the viewing platform at the top. A handsome winding marble staircase leads from the exquisite reception up to two of the faultlessly appointed rooms on their own floor. Another spiral staircase at the back of the house connects the second-floor patio to the breakfast room on the ground floor. A holiday-brochure home. $

★ **Hostal Colonial de Isabel y Pepe** Ave. 52 no.4318 e/ 43 y 45 ☎ 43 51 8276, ⓔ hostalcolonialisapepe@ gmail.com. Within five blocks of the bus station and run by a warm and talkative couple, this *casa* is akin to a boutique hotel. Three of the five large, superbly equipped guest rooms, each with its own fridge, split a/c units and bathroom, are in a fantastically elegant neo-colonial main house and are equipped with pristine antique furniture. The other two, effectively apartments, are in an adjoining house featuring one of the city's most impressive roof terraces, lined with park benches and street lamps. Guests dine on a covered ground-level patio. $\bar{\mathbb{S}}$

★ **Villa Lagarto** Calle 35 no.4B e/ 0 y Litoral, La Punta ⓦ villalagartocuba.com. Bordering La Punta's small park, this sensational place has its own tiny pier and one of the best restaurants in the city. There are six high-standard rooms in total, three along an upstairs veranda which leads onto a wonderful treetop walkway suspended over the fantastically verdant back-garden terrace, where there's a small saltwater swimming pool. Rooms benefit from the fresh breezes blowing in across the bay. $\bar{\mathbb{S}}$

EATING

SEE MAP PAGE 233

A large proportion of the city's burgeoning number of **paladars**, at least a dozen of which are on Prado, offer value for money if you want functional food, but have little to distinguish them from each other in terms of quality or variety and suffer from bus-station lighting. Their huge menus feature a series of slight variations on traditional Cuban dishes plus a few token pizzas and pastas. For **fast food**, head for Prado or the Malecón.

STATE RESTAURANTS

Palacio de Valle Calle 37 esq. Ave. 0 ☎43 55 1003 ext.812. Offers a wide choice of seafood – from the Gran Mariscada platter with fish, shrimp and lobster to simple grilled fish – with some meat alternatives. The excellent pianist and elegant arched interior provide a sense of occasion and outshine the food, which is just above average. $\bar{\mathbb{S}}\bar{\mathbb{S}}\bar{\mathbb{S}}$

El Polinesio Calle 29 e/ Ave. 54 y Ave. 56, Parque José Martí ☎43 51 5723. One of the city's more atmospheric restaurants, dimly lit and hidden from the street in the belly of an old building, engendering an oddly clandestine feel. Expect no-frills beef, chicken and pork dishes. $\bar{\mathbb{S}}\bar{\mathbb{S}}$

PALADARS

Aché Ave. 38 no.4106 e/ 41 y 43 ☎43 52 6173. One of the city's longest-established paladars, *Aché* serves wholesome, well-prepared Cuban-style chicken, fish and pork, as well as some excellent seafood, in the roof-covered countrified backyard of a pretty bungalow surrounded by gardens. $\bar{\mathbb{S}}\bar{\mathbb{S}}$

Bouyón 1825 Calle 25 no.5605 e/ 56 y 58 ☎43 51 7376. The wall of photos of bygone Cienfuegos, an open kitchen, music videos of Cuban greats and the colonial building itself provide more atmosphere than in most comparable paladars nearby, though you'll eat better in many of the *casas particulares*. Avoid the pasta and stick to Cuban basics like smoked pork loin or grilled shrimps. $\bar{\mathbb{S}}\bar{\mathbb{S}}$

★ **Finca del Mar** Calle 35 e/ 18 y 20 ☎43 52 6598. This outstanding paladar, one of the best in the country outside Havana, busts out of provincial Cuba's culinary straightjacket. Its fantastic starters work just as well as tapas and can make a meal in themselves: the stuffed piquillo peppers are delicious, the caprese salad spot on, and the grilled sausages lip-smackingly juicy and full of flavour. Mains are more typically Cuban but are always top quality and perfectly prepared. Omar, the astute owner, works and travels tirelessly to ensure they never run out of the best ingredients and has built a marvellous open-air venue, right next to the bay, around a fountain-centred patio. $\bar{\mathbb{S}}\bar{\mathbb{S}}$

★ **El Lagarto** Calle 35 no.4B e/ Ave. 0 y Litoral, La Punta ☎43 51 9966. Knocking most of the competition out of the game thanks to its flavoursome food and atmospheric setting, this paladar is really special. Tables are spread around a backyard terrace woven into an enchanting bayside grove, filled every evening by the irresistible smell of whatever meat is slow-cooking in the outdoor charcoal oven. There are no menus, just a daily-changing choice of top-quality meat and seafood with delicious soups and sides. $\bar{\mathbb{S}}\bar{\mathbb{S}}\bar{\mathbb{S}}$

Las Mamparas Calle 37 no.4004 e/ 40 y 42 ☎43 51 8992. The best of the paladars on Prado and one of the most popular, with its menu of Cuban fish, pork and chicken offering excellent value for money. The walls are crammed with photos of past guests, Art Deco lamps hang from high ceilings and two large arches divide the nicely lit dining area. $\bar{\mathbb{S}}$

DRINKING AND NIGHTLIFE

SEE MAP PAGE 233

During the week, the city's **nightlife** is subdued, especially outside July and August, with venues often relatively empty. At the weekend, however, **Punta Gorda** really comes alive, with locals out in force – particularly around the Malecón – and reggaeton and salsa echoing through the streets. On Saturdays, from around 8pm, some brilliant local musicians grace the bandstand in the square, attracting an older but buoyant and sociable crowd.

BARS AND CAFÉS

★ **La Buena Pipa** Ave. 54 no.3721 e/ 37 y 39. A refreshing alternative to the more tourist-friendly cafés on Parque Martí is this cool, arty hangout on a residential street. As suited to a morning coffee as a late-night rum, it's popular with young locals and students. One wall is covered in vinyl records, books are suspended from the ceiling and there are other individual touches throughout.

Café Bar-Tolo Centro Cultural de las Artes Benny Moré, Ave. 56 e/ 27 y 25, Parque José Martí ☎43 55 6676. The best place on the main square for an undisturbed drink is this café retreat and small live music venue in an arts centre. In the mottled shade of a delightful mesh-covered patio, the place is as attractive as it is relaxing.

Café Teatro Terry Ave. 56 e/ 27 y 29, Parque José Martí ☎ 43 51 0770. Squeezed down the side of the theatre, this is a bijou courtyard under a roof of exuberant hanging vines and flowers where mostly traditional music genres like trova and son are performed on a cramped stage.

★ **El Embajador** Ave. 54 esq. 33 ☎ 43 55 2144. This cigar shop is ideal for a good-quality coffee or rum during the afternoon, accompanied by the aroma of tobacco. There's a stylishly simple but inviting little bar at the back and a more comfortable upstairs gallery, with easy chairs around a coffee table.

★ **Palacio de Valle** Calle 37 esq. Ave. 0 ☎ 43 55 1226. The views over the bay and the city from the rooftop bar make this hands-down the best place in Cienfuegos for a laidback drink.

Te Quedarás Ave. 54 no.3509 e/ 35 y 37 ☎ 5 826 1283. The food at this Beny Moré-themed paladar is unreliable but the bar, with its balcony drinking counter, is one of the best spots for people-watching in town. A trio plays here most nights.

CABARETS, CLUBS AND LIVE MUSIC VENUES

La Caribeña Calle 37 esq. Ave. 22. A huge concrete outdoor dancefloor and performance area set in gardens protruding into the bay from the end of the Malecón. Local salsa bands attract big crowds here.

Centro Cultural de las Artes Benny Moré Ave. 56 e/ 27 y 25, Parque José Martí ☎ 43 55 6676. There's live music here most evenings, and sometimes during the day. One night it might be a guitar trio playing trova, the next it might be a duo with a vocalist and other nights it could be a full band, but it's usually traditional styles. Check the noticeboard out front for the weekly programme. Usually free.

Costasur Ave. 40 e/ 35 y bahía ☎ 43 52 5884. One of the most popular nights out with locals of all ages, this large-scale, open-air cabaret-style music venue has a great location, with the waters of the bay literally lapping at its edges. There's rumba, salsa and techno-lite nights, among others. Loud, flamboyant and good fun.

El Cubanísimo Calle 35 e/ Ave. 16 y Ave. 18 ☎ 43 55 1255. Over the road from the edge of the bay, this atmospherically enclosed open-air venue hosts anything from comedy nights and karaoke to live singers and bands, and attracts a good mix of locals and tourists.

Discoteca El Benny Ave. 54 e/ 29 y 31 ☎ 43 55 1674. Unusually slick and polished for a Cuban nightclub, especially one in the provinces, with a music policy dominated by pop, salsa and reggaeton. Don't expect any action before 11pm.

★ **Jardines de la UNEAC** Calle 25 e/ Ave. 54 y Ave. 56, Parque José Martí ☎ 43 51 6117. One of the city's most congenial and intimate live music venues. This leafy, enchanting open-air patio has a bar and is a great place to enjoy some local bands and soloists playing Cuban musical styles such as bolero, trova and son. There are no fixed performance times but there's often something on in the afternoons and evenings; check the weekly programme posted at the gate. Usually free.

TropiSur Calle 37 e/ 46 y 48 ☎ 43 52 5488. The city's most prestigious cabaret venue, with extravagant shows in a large outdoor space and the crowds that flock here at weekends to get lively. Reggaeton concerts are sometimes staged here too. No shorts or vests.

ENTERTAINMENT

Teatro Tomás Terry Parque José Martí ⓦfacebook.com/TeatroTT. Plays, concerts, dance, kids' shows and live comedy. Performances usually start at 9pm Mon–Sat, while on Sun there's only a matinee performance, usually at 5pm. A monthly programme is posted on the noticeboards out front. Shorts and sleeveless tops are not permitted.

Cine-Teatro Luisa Prado esq. Ave. 50 ☎ 43 51 5339. Originally opened as a theatre in 1911, this classic old cinema was remodelled in the 1940s and continues to show films throughout the week. English-language films are often shown in their original version with subtitles.

SHOPPING

SEE MAP PAGE 233

For arts, crafts and souvenirs there's a daily **street market** on the pedestrianized section of Calle 29 and several shops on Avenida 54 between the main square and Prado. For more original but more expensive art visit the artists' studios on Parque Martí.

El Embajador Ave. 54 esq. 33 ☎ 43 55 2144. Cigars and

CIENFUEGOS BASEBALL

The local **baseball** team, nicknamed the **Elefantes de Cienfuegos**, currently plays in the top tier of the national league. Games (usually Tues–Sun) take place in the thirty thousand-capacity Estadio 5 de Septiembre, at Avenida 20 y 47 (☎43 51 3644). Tickets are sold on the door.

rum in an inviting shop with its own little bar at the back and an alluring lounge area upstairs where you can smoke your *habanos* and sip your Havana Club.

Maroya Ave. 54 no.2506 e/ 25 y 27, Parque José Martí

DIRECTORY

Health The best-stocked pharmacy is in the Clínica Internacional at Avenida 10 no.3705 e/ 37 y 39 (24hr; ☎ 43 55 1622) in Punta Gorda. This is also the best place for foreign nationals to come to see a nurse or doctor, or to call for an ambulance. There's also a small but well-stocked pharmacy in the *La Unión* hotel (Mon–Fri 8.30am–4.30pm, Sat 8am–noon).

Money and exchange The bank best prepared to deal with foreign currency is the Banco Financiero Internacional, at Avenida 54 esq. 29 (Mon–Fri 8.30am–3.30pm). The CADECA *casa de cambio* is at Avenida 56 no.3314 e/ 33 y 35 (Mon–Sat 8.30am–4pm, Sun 8.30am–11.30 pm). There are ATMs at Calle 33 esq. 54.

☎ 43 55 1208. The best place in the city by far for arts and crafts with a wide variety of stock, from photography and painting to sculpture and textiles.

Police Call ☎ 116.

Post office The main branch of the post office is at Calle 35 esq. Avenida 56 (Mon–Sat 8am–6pm, Sun 8am–noon). There's a DHL office, which sells stamps, at Avenida 54 e/ 35 y 37 (Mon–Fri 9am–noon, 1–5pm, Sat 9am–noon).

Visas To extend tourist visas, visit the Department of Immigration at Avenida 46 esq. 29 (Mon–Thurs 8am–3pm; ☎ 43 55 1283).

Wi-fi The city's public wi-fi zones include Parque Martí, Parque Villuendas, towards the north of the city, and the *El Rápido* fast-food restaurant opposite the Malecón. ETECSA Telepunto, Calle 31 e/ 54 y 56 (daily 8.30am–7pm), has several internet terminals and six phone booths.

Around Cienfuegos city

There are several manageable day- or half-day **excursions** from Cienfuegos city that offer some satisfyingly uncontrived but still visitor-friendly diversions. Chief among them is the exuberant **Jardín Botánico**, compact enough to tour in a couple of hours but with a sufficient variety of species to keep you there all day. A little closer to the city, towards the coast, the focus at the wilder **Laguna Guanaroca** nature reserve is birds rather than plants.

Near to the mouth of the Bahía de Jagua, **Playa Rancho Luna** has a pleasant beach and is the most obvious alternative to the city for a longer stay in the province. Further along, this coastline forms the eastern bank of the narrow channel that links the sea to the bay. On the western bank is the **Castillo de Jagua**, a plain but atmospheric eighteenth-century Spanish fortress. Though accessible from Playa Rancho Luna via a ferry across the narrow channel, it's well worth taking the boat to the fortress from Cienfuegos and enjoying the full serenity of the bay. Further afield are the forested peaks of the **Sierra del Escambray** mountains, where you can do some gentle trekking or explore the beautiful network of waterfalls at **Parque El Nicho**.

Jardín Botánico de Cienfuegos

Circuito Sur, 300m from Pepito Tey · Daily 8am–6pm, last entry at around 4.30pm · Charge · ☎ 43 54 5115 · There's a daily bus from Cienfuegos to Pepito Tey; otherwise, to drive here from Calle 37 in Cienfuegos, head east on Avenida 64 (aka Calzada de Dolores), and continue east on Circuito Sur. Organized excursions available from Cienfuegos city.

About 15km east of the Cienfuegos city limits, the gorgeous **Jardín Botánico de Cienfuegos** has one of the most complete collections of tropical plants in the country. The eleven-acre site is home to over two thousand different species, divided up into various different groups, most of them merging seamlessly into one another so that in places this feels more like a natural forest than an artificially created garden. A road runs down through the grounds to a café and a little shop selling maps of the park. This is where the only indoor areas are found, a cactus house and another greenhouse full of tropical plants.

Guides are essential if you want to know what you're looking at, but though it can be difficult to find your way around, there's a definite appeal to just wandering around on your own, following the roughly marked tracks through the varied terrain and past a series of (usually dry) pools and waterways. Highlights include the amphitheatre of **bamboo** and the vast array of **palm trees**, totalling some 325 different species.

Laguna Guanaroca

Carretera a Rancho Luna • Daily 8am–3pm • Charge • Refugio de Fauna Guanaroca-Gavilanes ☏ 43 54 8117 • Organized excursions available from Cienfuegos city

Some 12km from Cienfuegos and 5km from Playa Rancho Luna, on the way to the south coast beaches, is the **Laguna de Guanaroca**. Joined to the Bahía de Cienfuegos by a narrow channel, the lake is the site of the **Refugio de Fauna Guanaroca-Gavilanes** nature reserve; the signposted entrance is marked by a small roadside building. Guided **tours** – which you should arrange in advance through one of the travel agents in Cienfuegos – last between two and three hours and allow visitors to learn about the rich variety of **birds** that make their home here, as well as providing some insights into the plant life. **Lookout towers** have been erected to help you spot the reserve's many birds. Around 170 species nest or pass through here, including the *tocororo*, *cartacuba*, *zunzún* hummingbirds and pelicans. There's also a resident colony of over 2000 flamingos.

Playa Rancho Luna

Less than 20km south of Cienfuegos city is the province's most developed section of coastline, centred on an unspoilt but unspectacular 1km stretch of beach called **Playa Rancho Luna**. Peppered with broad-branched trees sinking into warm, slightly murky waters, the beach is flanked by craggy headlands.

A longer stretch of rocky coastline sits between the beach and the channel linking the sea to the Cienfuegos bay, and it's 6km along the coast from Playa Rancho Luna to **Pasacaballo**, the departure point for ferries to the Castillo de Jagua (see page 243) and back to the city. This coastline is also a good place for **scuba diving**, which can be arranged through either the *Rancho Luna* or *Faro Luna* hotels. There are dozens of dive sites within a couple of hundred metres of the shore, where a stretch of coral is punctuated by a number of wrecked ships. Among the sheer vertical walls and numerous caves and tunnels, you can sometimes see big fish such as nurse shark, barracuda and tarpon.

ARRIVAL AND DEPARTURE
PLAYA RANCHO LUNA

By bus The timetable changes frequently and at the time of writing the service was sporadically suspended, but buses in theory leave the main station in Cienfuegos for the beach three times a day, currently at 5.10am, 11.30am and 5.50pm. Services tend to be more frequent in July and August.

By ferry Ferries depart three times daily from both sides of the channel linking the bay to the sea; catch the ferry either from below the *Pasacaballo* hotel or just below the Castillo de Jagua.

By taxi Taxi fares from Cienfuegos are between $250CUP and $400CUP.

ACCOMMODATION

Spread out along 4km of mostly rocky, tree-lined shores that reach round to the mouth of the Jagua Bay, Rancho Luna's three **hotels** are the main focus of the area. Two of them, the *Rancho Luna* and *Faro Luna*, are part of the Gran Caribe chain and share one another's facilities, though they are 1km apart. There are also a few **casas particulares** along the coastal road between the *Faro Luna* and *Pasacaballo* hotels.

Faro Luna Carretera a Pasacaballos Km 18 ⓦ grancaribe. com. Small and quite subdued, this is Rancho Playa Luna's best hotel option for couples. The neatly kept grounds roost just above the rocky water's edge, 300m from the beach, and there's a diminutive pool and scooter rental facilities. $$
Finca Los Colorados Carretera a Pasacaballos Km 20 ☏ 43 54 8044, ✉ fincaloscolorados@nauta.cu. Over the road from a lighthouse, this attractive old ranch house has

five double rooms for rent, some featuring stylishly rustic furniture and sturdy iron beds; there's also a fabulously leafy patio garden, two swimming pools and a restaurant on site. $\overline{\underline{\$}}$

Pasacaballo Carretera a Pasacaballos Km 23 ⓦ islazulhotels.com. This 1970s hulk of a hotel looms above the channel linking the bay to the sea. Its brutalist architecture has been softened by a colourful paint job and recently refurbished rooms but it's still a little at odds with

its picturesque surroundings. There's a huge swimming pool but not a lot of beach round here. Rooms rates include all meals. $\overline{\underline{\$\$}}$

Rancho Luna Carretera a Rancho Luna Km 17.5 ⓦ grancaribe.com. This large, all-inclusive family hotel has by far the best section of beach and features a buffet and Italian restaurants, a beach grill, games room, mini-golf, tennis courts and swimming pool. $\overline{\underline{\$\$\$}}$

Castillo de Jagua

Entrance to the Bahía de Cienfuegos • Daily 8am–6pm • Charge • ☎ 43 96 5402 • Get here by ferry from Cienfuegos or by car via Pasacaballos and the smaller ferry connecting the two sides of the channel between the bay and the sea

Half the fun of a visit to the seventeenth-century Spanish fortress at the mouth of the Jagua bay, known as the **Castillo de Jagua**, is getting there. The **ferry** from Cienfuegos (see page 243) docks just below the fortress, on the opposite side of the channel to Playa Rancho Luna, from where a dusty track leads up to the cannon guarding the castle drawbridge. Inside, a small **museum** details the history of the fort, which was originally built to defend against pirate attacks, and, bizarrely, charts the history of nuclear energy in Cienfuegos – the Juraguá nuclear power plant is 5km away. There's also a couple of tables in a sunken courtyard where you can get something to eat and drink; and steps winding up to the top of the single turret from where there are modest views. It's also worth taking a peek at the cramped and dingy **prison cell** and the **chapel** on the courtyard level.

4

Parque El Nicho

5km east of the hamlet of Crucecitas, around 60km from Cienfuegos city by road • Daily 8.30am–6.30pm • Charge • Coming by car, turn off the main road at Crucecitas, from where it's 5km to the start of the trails to the waterfalls; there's no public transport here, but organized excursions from Cienfuegos city are offered by Havanatur and Cubanacán.

Near the eastern border of the province, in the lush green **Sierra del Escambray** mountains, **Parque El Nicho** is a natural park with trails cutting through it, culminating at a delightful set of waterfalls and natural pools. This is one of the five smaller hiking areas, which can only loosely be considered parks, that make up the Gran Parque Natural Topes de Collantes nature reserve, which is usually visited from Trinidad. The entrance to the park, marked by a stone gateway, leads into an official trail, the **Reino de las Aguas**, which cuts through the dense woodlands and crosses over rivers and streams, taking in numerous waterfalls, mountain vistas and

---

THE CASTILLO DE JAGUA FERRY

A rusty old vessel looking vaguely like a tugboat, the passenger **ferry** between **Cienfuegos** and the **Castillo de Jagua** chugs across the placid waters of the bay at a pace slow enough to allow a relaxed contemplation of the surroundings, including the tiny, barely inhabited cays where the ferry makes a brief call to pick up passengers. The deck is lined with benches but the metal roof is the best place to sit, allowing unobscured views in all directions.

The ferry departs Cienfuegos two to three times a day, sailing from a wharf next to the junction between Calle 25 and Avenida 46, four blocks south of Parque José Martí; departures from the city are currently 8am, 1pm and sometimes at 5.30pm; departures from the fortress to the city are at 6.30am, 10am and 3pm; the journey time is a little less than an hour.

abundant birdlife before arriving at the **El Nicho waterfalls**. More becalming and enchanting than spectacular, the waterfalls drop from over 15m at their highest, and there are several **pools** ideal for bathing, all of them fed by cascading water. There is also a restaurant within the park, lunch at which is included in organized excursions to the area.

The Circuito Sur to Trinidad

Connecting Cienfuegos city to the colonial city of Trinidad, 50km down the coast, the **Circuito Sur** is a scenic road that for much of its length hugs the coastline between the two cities. The route, which offers lovely views of the sea and mountains on either side, is used by significant numbers of touring cyclists and by the interprovincial Víazul bus service, though there are no official stops along the way (some drivers may allow you to jump off). Among the diversions en route are a number of low-key places to stop off and take a dip in the sea or a wander into the wooded countryside.

Guajimico

Tiny **Guajimico** is a scrap of a village with a roadside snack bar on the Circuito Sur, but also marks one of the two ways down (the other, 1.5km away, is marked by a large statue of a Native American man) to the fantastically remote-feeling **cabin complex**, **Villa Guajimico**, and **dive centre**, which between them provide access into the woods and waters that make this place so appealing. A day visit affords opportunities to dive and wander around the verdant cliffside running from the beach over to the open coast, occupied largely by the buildings of the cabin complex, including an outdoor café. There are paths through the woods leading to **caves** you can explore, plus the twenty offshore **dive sites** close by, including the wreck of *La Arabela*. The dive centre is ACUC-, CMAS- and ESA-certified.

Playa Yaguanabo

Around 60km from Cienfuegos city and just 25km outside of Trinidad is the tiny coastal enclave of **Playa Yaguanabo**. For food, beach and convenience this is the best stop-off between Cienfuegos and Trinidad, ideal for a few days of doing very little – though the sense of transit here makes it more a place to pause at than settle into. Its defining feature is a long bridge spanning the length of the modest but inviting beach, from which it rises on a series of concrete pillars. All the same, it's a pretty spot, tucked inside a small bay at the mouth of a river and overlooked by the low craggy cliffs of a corner of coastline. A small plateau atop the cliffs houses the *Villa Yaguanabo*, an invitingly spruce little hotel resort, and, along with the beach, the focal point for any visit here.

ACCOMMODATION AND EATING   **CIRCUITO SUR TO TRINIDAD; SEE MAP PAGE 230**

There are restaurants at both *Villa Guajimico* and *Villa Yaguanabo* but the latter is by far the better of the two for both food and accommodation. There are also one or two paladars in the local houses and a beach bar and restaurant at Playa Yaguanabo.

Casa Verde Carretera Trinidad Km 63 ☎ 52 319 632. Picturesque paladar nestling on a small hill overlooking *Villa Yaguanabo*, dishing up a good spread of typically simple Cuban meat and seafood, with goat fricassee the most unusual and jointly most expensive item on the menu alongside lobster and shrimp. $\overline{\underline{\$}}$

Villa Yaguanabo Carretera Trinidad Km 63 ⓦ islazulhotels.com. This seaside cabin complex has a fresh, well-tended appeal, with neatly trimmed lawns and 56 clean, comfortable a/c rooms, most with sea views. The best touch is a row of swinging couches, each under its own thatched roof, near the water's edge, providing a wonderfully serene spot for reading and relaxing. $\overline{\underline{\$}}$

Santa Clara

One of the largest and liveliest cities in Cuba, **SANTA CLARA**, the provincial capital of Villa Clara, landlocked near its centre, has long been a place of pilgrimage for **Che Guevara** worshippers. Home to his remains and scene of a decisive rebel victory under his command, there are two large monuments and a museum commemorating the man, his life and his part in the Cuban Revolution. Coachloads of visitors arrive every day to take all this in, but the city gets on with its own business, its large student population roaming the campus of the country's third-biggest university, cultural devotees attending performances at one of Cuba's most renowned theatres and, nearby, the offbeat music and arts complex **El Mejunje** giving expression to the swelled ranks of the local counter-cultural crowd.

Santa Clara's social life revolves around the vibrant, picture-perfect central square, **Parque Vidal**, whose diversions include the **Museo de Artes Decorativas**, a recreation of the living conditions and tastes of colonial aristocrats. Just a block away is the busy, pedestrianized main shopping street, occupying a stretch of **Independencia**, while a few blocks beyond is the **Fábrica de Tabacos Constantino Pérez Carrodegua**, the local cigar factory, whose fascinating tours are well worth booking. Further out, as well as the Che monuments, are the baseball stadium and a natural vantage point for wonderful views of the whole city, the **Loma del Capiro**.

Parque Vidal

Declared a national monument in 1996, **Parque Vidal** is the geographical, social and cultural nucleus of Santa Clara. A large, pedestrianized and vivacious town square, in the evenings it fills up with young and old alike and is particularly animated at weekends, with live music performances on the central bandstand, and on the porch of the ornate Casa de la Cultura. Traversed by shoppers, workers and tourists throughout the day, at the square's attractive core is a paved circular **promenade** laced with towering palms and shrub-peppered lawns. The park is elegantly framed by a mixture of colonial and neo-colonial buildings, the grandest of which is the Neoclassical **Palacio Provincial** on the northeastern side. Built between 1904 and 1912 and once the seat of the local government, it's now home to a library, the **Biblioteca José Martí**.

Museo de Artes Decorativas

Parque Vidal • Mon, Wed & Thurs 9am–6pm, Fri & Sat 1–10pm, Sun 6–10pm • Charge • ☎ 42 205368

On the northwest side of Parque Vidal is the **Museo de Artes Decorativas**, featuring furniture and *objets d'art* spanning four centuries of style, from Renaissance to Art Deco. Each of the eleven rooms is opulently furnished, with most of the exhibits collected from houses around Santa Clara. The **front room** has a marvellous crystal chandelier, there's a **dining room** with a fully laid table, a **bedroom** with an ostentatiously designed wardrobe and individual pieces like the stunning seventeenth-century bureau with ivory detailing.

Teatro La Caridad

Parque Vidal • Guided tours Mon–Sat 9am–4pm; charge • ☎ 42 205548

A few doors down from the Museo de Artes Decorativas, on the same northwestern side of Parque Vidal, is the **Teatro La Caridad**, with a fabulous, ornate interior that's

4

SANTA CLARA STREET NAMES

As with elsewhere in Cuba, some of Santa Clara's streets have both pre- and post-revolutionary names, the latter used on street signs, the former used by most locals; where applicable, the old names have been given in brackets in this guide.

sold short by its relatively sober exterior. It was built in 1885 with money donated by Marta Abreu Estévez, a civic-minded nineteenth-century native of Santa Clara with an inherited fortune; a bronze statue of her stands on the opposite side of the square. As part of Estévez's wider quest to help the poor and contribute to the city's civil, cultural and academic institutions, a portion of the box office receipts was set aside to improve living conditions for the impoverished, thus spawning the theatre's name ("Charity"). Renovated in 2009, it remains in fantastic condition, with a semicircular three-tiered balcony enveloping the central seating area and a stunning painted ceiling. You can get closer to it during a performance (see page 254) or the twenty-minute **guided tour** in Spanish, English or French, which takes you up into the balcony.

Galería Provincial de Arte

Máximo Gómez no.3 e/ Martha Abreu y Barreras • Tues–Thurs 9am–5pm, Fri & Sat 2–10pm, Sun 6–10pm • Free • ☎ 43 207715

Just off the Parque Vidal, round the corner from the theatre, is the **Galería Provincial de Arte**, hosting temporary exhibitions showcasing the work of predominantly Cuban artists. It's always worth a peek inside as the exhibitions vary enormously, from

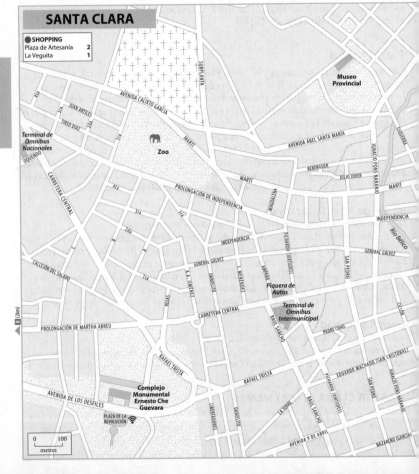

photography and painting to sculpture and installation art, and from young local artists to nationally famous painters.

Casa de la Ciudad

Boulevard esq. J.B. Zayas • Mon–Sat 8am–5pm • Charge • ☎ 43 205593

Built as a family house in the late 1840s by a wealthy Barcelona-born businessman, the **Casa de la Ciudad** retains a sense of its former glory with porticoed doorways, stained-glass windows and a colonnaded central patio. The half-dozen rooms open to the public are used for both temporary exhibitions and a fairly low-stocked permanent one, showcasing paintings of and by some of the city's most illustrious sons and daughters. Concerts are held on the patio usually several times a week.

Fábrica de Tabacos Constantino Pérez Carrodegua

Maceo esq. Berenguer • 25min pre-booked guided tours Mon–Fri 9–1pm • Charge • ☎ 42 202211

Just north of Parque Vidal, the **Fábrica de Tabacos Constantino Pérez Carrodegua** cigar factory, founded in 1961, employs around two hundred workers and produces

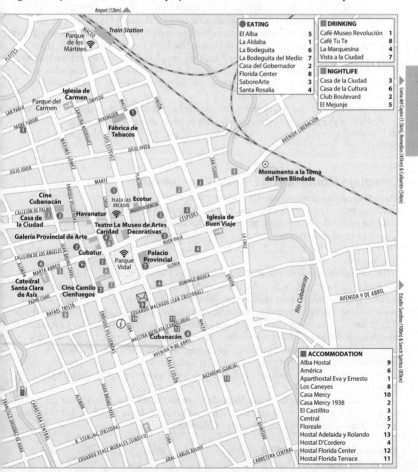

EATING

El Alba	5
La Aldaba	1
La Bodeguita	6
La Bodeguita del Medio	7
Casa del Gobernador	2
Florida Center	8
SaboreArte	3
Santa Rosalia	4

DRINKING

Café-Museo Revolución	1
Café Tu Te	8
La Marquesina	4
Vista a la Ciudad	7

NIGHTLIFE

Casa de la Ciudad	3
Casa de la Cultura	6
Club Boulevard	2
El Mejunje	5

ACCOMMODATION

Alba Hostal	9
América	6
Aparthostal Eva y Ernesto	1
Los Caneyes	8
Casa Mercy	10
Casa Mercy 1938	2
El Castillito	3
Central	5
Floreale	7
Hostal Adelaida y Rolando	13
Hostal D'Cordero	4
Hostal Florida Center	12
Hostal Florida Terrace	11

some ten thousand cigars a day for several dozen brands, including Romeo y Julieta, Partagás, Punch and Montecristo. On the **guided tours** of the factory (usually available in English) you get to see the staff at work, the most skilled assigned to the most prestigious brands, like Cohiba. Though most of the factory's rooms are closed to visitors, tours are nevertheless very engaging and take place in the main workshop where you can witness much of the production process, from rolling, measuring, sorting and quality control; to arrange a tour contact one of the local travel agents (see page 251). The finished product is on sale in La Veguita across the road, along with Cuban coffee and honey.

Monumento a la Toma del Tren Blindado

Carretera de Camajuaní • Train wagons open Mon–Sat 9am–5pm • Charge • ☎ 42 202758

A block behind the Parque Vidal, Independencia runs toward the river and the **Monumento a la Toma del Tren Blindado**, site of one of the decisive actions of the **Battle of Santa Clara**, in 1958. The battle – between the dictator Fulgencio Batista's forces and a small detachment of about three hundred rebels, led by Che Guevara – was to be one of the last military encounters of the Revolutionary War. By December 1958, over ten thousand government troops had been sent by Batista to the centre of the island to prevent the rebels from advancing further west towards Havana. An **armoured train** was despatched to reinforce this defensive line but Guevara and his men lay in wait and, using a bulldozer to raise the rails, they toppled the train from the tracks and ambushed the 408 officers and soldiers within, who soon surrendered. The train was later used by the rebels as a base for further attacks but some of the derailed wagons have lain here ever since.

This historic event and its repercussions are further evoked by the **exhibits** displayed inside four of the five wagons, including photos taken at the time, guns and uniforms, and, looking over the scene atop a large concrete star, the bulldozer that did the damage.

Complejo Monumental Ernesto Che Guevara

Rafael Tristá, around 1.5km southwest of Parque Vidal • Free • ☎ 42 205878

On the southwestern outskirts of the city, the **Complejo Monumental Ernesto Che Guevara** marks the final resting place of Che Guevara's body and pays tribute to Santa Clara's adopted son and hero, who led the Cuban rebels to victory against General Batista's dictatorship here in 1958, in one of the decisive battles of the Revolution (see box opposite).

The large thundering **monument**, inaugurated in 1988, is in classic Cuban revolutionary style: big, bold and made of concrete. Atop the grey-tiled steps of a hulking grandstand are four bulky monoliths; towering down from the tallest one is a burly looking **statue of Guevara**, on the move and dressed in his usual military garb, rifle in hand. Next to the statue is a huge, somewhat jumbled mural, with Guevara's march from the Sierra Maestra to Santa Clara and the decisive victory over Batista's troops depicted in cement. Spreading out before the monument, the **Plaza de la Revolución**, like its counterpart in Havana, is little more than an open space, though there are two huge posterboards on the far side with revolutionary slogans inspired by Che.

To the rear of the complex is the **Mausoleo Frente de Las Villas**, a memorial garden cemetery in honour of the casualties of Guevara's rebel column which he led from the Sierra Maestra to Santa Clara, known as **Column 8**.

Museo and Memorial al Che

Tues–Sun 9.30am–5pm • Free

ERNESTO "CHE" GUEVARA

No one embodies the romanticism of the Cuban Revolution more than **Ernesto "Che" Guevara**, the handsome, brave and principled guerrilla who fought alongside Fidel Castro in the Sierra Maestra during the revolutionary war of 1956–59. Referred to in Cuba today simply as "El Che", he is probably the most universally liked and respected of the Revolution's heroes, his early death allowing him to remain untarnished by the souring of attitudes over time, and his willingness to fight so energetically for his principles viewed as evidence of his indefatigable spirit.

THE EARLY YEARS

Born to middle-class, strongly left-wing parents in Rosario, Argentina, on June 14, 1928, the young Ernesto Guevara – later nicknamed "Che", a popular term of affectionate address in Argentina – became a keen soccer and rugby player while at the University of Buenos Aires, where, in 1948, he began studying medicine.

Before he graduated in 1953, finishing a six-year course in half the time, Che had taken time out from his studies and made an epic journey around South America on a motorbike. These travels, which he continued after graduation, were instrumental in the formation of Guevara's political character, instilling in him a strong sense of Latin American identity and opening his eyes to the widespread suffering and social injustice throughout the continent.

GUEVARA AND THE REVOUTION

It was in Mexico, in November 1955, that Guevara met the exiled Fidel Castro and, learning of his intentions to return to Cuba and ignite a popular revolution, decided to join Castro's small rebel army, the **M-26-7 Movement**. The Argentine was among the 82 who set sail for Cuba in the yacht *Granma* on November 24, 1956, and, following the disastrous landing, one of the few who made it safely into the Sierra Maestra. As both a guerrilla and a doctor, Guevara played a vital role for the rebels as they set about drumming up support for their cause among the local poorer people while fighting Batista's troops. His most prominent role in the conflict, however, came in 1958 when he led a rebel column west to the then province of Las Villas, where he was to cut all means of communication between the two ends of the island and thus cement Castro's control over the east. This he did in great style, exemplified in his manoeuvres during the **Battle of Santa Clara** (see page 248).

EL HOMBRE NUEVO

Guevara insisted on enduring the same harsh conditions as the other rebels and refused to grant himself any comforts that his higher status might have allowed. It was this spirit of sacrifice and brotherhood that he brought to the philosophies which he developed and instituted after the triumph of the Revolution in 1959, during his role as Minister for Industry. The cornerstone of his vision was the concept of **El Hombre Nuevo** – the New Man. Guevara believed that in order to build communism a new man must be created, and the key to this was to alter the popular consciousness. The emphasis was on motivation: new attitudes would have to be instilled in people, devoid of selfish sentiment and with a goal of moral rather than material reward, gained through the pursuit of the aims of the Revolution.

GUEVARA'S FINAL YEARS

Alongside developing abstract theories, Guevara remained at heart a man of action and, after serving four years as a roaming ambassador for Cuba to the rest of the world, he left for Africa to play a more direct role in the spread of communism, becoming involved in a revolutionary conflict in the Congo. In 1966 he travelled to Bolivia where he once again fought as a guerrilla against the Bolivian army. There, on October 8, 1967, aged 39, Guevara was captured and shot. The exact location of his burial was kept secret until 1995, when it was revealed by a Bolivian general. Two years later, in 1997, his body was exhumed and transported to Santa Clara, where it now lies in the mausoleum of the Complejo Monumental Ernesto Che Guevara.

4

Underneath the monument, accessed from the rear, the surprisingly small **Museo and Memorial al Che** occupies a single U-shaped room, and provides a succinct overview of Che's life. **Photographs** line the walls, and it's these that tend to hold the most interest, with depictions of Che from his early childhood all the way through to his life as a rebel soldier in the Sierra Maestra and a Cuban statesman in the early years of the Revolution. There are some particularly interesting exhibits relating to the earlier phase of his life, including photos taken by Che himself during his travels around Latin America. Less engaging items include the various guns that he used during his times in combat, but even if you ignore all these there is just about enough here to paint a picture of his life.

Opposite the museum entrance is the **mausoleum**, a softly lit chamber where the mood of reverence and respect is quite affecting. Resembling a kind of tomb with an eternally flickering flame, this is the resting place of Che's remains, as well as those of a number of the Peruvians, Bolivians and Cubans who died with him in Bolivia, each of whom is commemorated by a simple stone portrait set into the wall.

Loma del Capiro

Around 2km northeast of the centre • To get to the hill on foot, take the fifth right turn off the Carretera de Camajuaní after the Monumento a la Toma del Tren Blindado, at the Cupet-Cimex petrol station, onto Ana Pegudo, then the second left onto Felix Huergo from where the route is clearly signposted.

On the northeastern outskirts of Santa Clara, a good 45-minute walk from the centre, is the surprisingly inconspicuous **Loma del Capiro**, a large mound rising abruptly from the comparatively flat surroundings, providing splendid views over the city and the flatlands to the north and east. This is a peaceful, unspoilt spot for a picnic, where you're more likely to encounter a few kids flying kites than other tourists. There's a small car park near the summit from where a concrete staircase climbs gently 150m up to the top, which is capped by a steel monument commemorating the capture of the hill by Che Guevara in 1958, during the Battle of Santa Clara.

ARRIVAL AND DEPARTURE   SANTA CLARA

By plane Just off the Carretera Maleza at Km 11, Santa Clara's single-terminal airport (☎ 42 227525) handles some regular charter and scheduled flights from the US, Canada and a few charters from the UK and elsewhere in Europe. There are no regularly scheduled domestic flights. There's no public transport from the airport to the city; a taxi to the centre will cost around $400CUP.

By Víazul bus The Terminal de Omnibus Nacionales (Víazul ☎ 42 222524, general information ☎ 42 292114), where Víazul services arrive and depart, is in the western limits of the city on the corner of Carretera Central and Oquendo.

Destinations Bayamo (4 daily; 9hr 30min); Caibarién (1 daily; 1hr 15min); Camagüey (6 daily; 4hr 40min); Cayo Las Brujas (1 daily; 2hr); Cayo Santa María (1 daily; 2hr 40min); Ciego de Ávila (5 daily; 3hr); Havana (3 daily; 3hr 45min); Holguín (4 daily; 8hr); Las Tunas (6 daily; 7hr); Remedios (1 daily; 1hr 5min); Sancti Spíritus (4 daily; 1hr 30min); Santiago (4 daily; 12hr); Trinidad (2 daily; 2hr 50min); Varadero (2 daily; 3hr 20min).

By local bus Buses serving provincial destinations, including Caibarién (1 daily; 1hr 50min) and Remedios (2 daily; 1hr 30min), depart from and arrive at the Terminal de Omnibus Intermunicipal on the Carretera Central e/ Pichardo y Amparo.

By taxi colectivo As in all Cuban cities, there is never any shortage of long-distance taxi drivers at the bus station filling their cars with passengers for journeys to other provinces for the same price as a Víazul ticket. Santa Clara also has its own *almendrón* station, the Piquera de Autos, directly opposite the Terminal de Omnibus Intermunicipal, from where *colectivos* work routes within the province as well as beyond. There are usually cars heading for Remedios and Caibarién.

By train The train station (☎ 42 202895) is at Parque de los Mártires at the northern end of Luis Estévez, a 15min walk from Parque Vidal. There are usually horse-drawn carriages and taxis waiting outside. Very few train services run on daily schedules and services or whole routes are often suspended. It's advisable to book your train ticket at least a day in advance.

Destinations Bayamo (2 weekly; 12hr); Caibarién (1 daily; 2hr); Camagüey (6 weekly; 7hr); Cienfuegos (1 daily; 3hr); Havana (3 weekly; 4–6hr); Matanzas (7 weekly; 3hr 30min); Santiago (3 weekly; 12hr).

By car Arriving by car, you'll most likely enter the city on the Carretera Central; from the east, turn off the Carretera Central at Colón, and from the west at Rafael Tristá, both one-way streets which lead right to the Parque Vidal.

SANTA CLARA'S FESTIVALS

Santa Clara's busy cultural calendar, the fullest in the region, includes a seven-day **theatre festival** at El Mejunje during the last week of January; the **Festival Nacional de la Danza** in April and, in November, a five-day city-wide film festival, the **Festival de Invierno**, and the **Ciudad Metal** heavy metal event.

GETTING AROUND

Getting around the centre can be done on foot, but you may want to find some transport to the Complejo Monumental Ernesto Che Guevara and the Loma del Capiro.

By bicitaxi *Bicitaxis* congregate around the Parque Vidal, particularly on the corner of Máximo Gómez and Marta Abreu. All prices are by negotiation.

By horse-drawn carriage Horse-drawn carriages operate up and down Marta Abreu, Cuba, Colón and a number of other streets emanating out from Parque Vidal. For journeys towards the two bus stations and the Memorial

al Che, catch one on Marta Abreu; going in the opposite direction head for Rafael Tristá. Carriages on Cuba, Colón, Máximo Gómez and Luis Estévez head to and from the southeast and the northwest of the city.

By taxi Ring ☎ 42 207647.

Car and scooter rental For car rental, try Havanautos/ Cubacar at Marta Abreu e/ Alemán y J.B. Zayas (☎ 42 218177) and Rafael Tristá esq. Amparo (☎ 42 202040). Scooters can be rented at Motoclub, Marta Abreu e/ Alemán y J.B. Zayas (daily 8am–5pm; ☎ 42 218177).

INFORMATION AND TOURS

INFORMATION

Tourist office The national tourist information provider is at Cuba no.66 e/ Eduardo Machado y Maestra Nicolasa (Mon–Sat 8.30–noon & 1–5pm; ☎ 42 201352); it supplies maps and can book accommodation and excursions.

TRAVEL AGENTS AND TOURS

The travel agents listed below can organize day-trips to Embalse Hanabanilla, Remedios and the northern cays. They usually require a minimum number of customers, effectively meaning that excursions don't often run in low season (April–June & Sept–Nov). City tours are more reliable, visiting all the major attractions by minibus.

Cubanacán Colón no.101 esq. Maestra Nicolasa (Mon–Fri 8.30am–5.30pm & Sat 8.30am–12.30pm; ☎ 42 205189).

Cubatur Marta Abreu no.10 e/ Máximo Gómez y Enrique Villuendas (Mon–Fri 8.30am–5pm, Sat 8.30am–noon; ☎ 42 208980).

Ecotur Plaza Las Arcadas, Luís Esteves esq. Independencia (Mon–Fri 8am–noon & 1–5pm, alternate Saturdays 8am– noon; ☎ 42 201598).

Havanatur Máximo Gómez no.13 e/ Boulevard y Barreras (Mon–Fri 8am–noon & 1–4pm, Sat 8am–noon; ☎ 42 204001).

Paradiso Independencia no.314 e/ Plácido y Luis Estévez (Mon–Fri 8.30am–5pm, Sat 8.30am–noon; ☎ 42 20 1374).

ACCOMMODATION   SEE MAP PAGE 246

Several new hotels have opened in the city centre in the last few years, making a stay at the landmark but second-rate *Santa Clara Libre* even less worthwhile than before, despite that hotel's recent refresh. A healthy and huge variety of **casas particulares** clustered around the central streets provide all the budget options you could need. As in most major Cuban cities, tourists arriving at the bus station are met by an enthusiastic crowd of accommodation **touts**.

HOTELS

América Mujica no.9 e/ Colón y Maceo ⓦ hotelescubanacan.com. This is a simple little affair, worthy of its three stars, with small, understated but colourful rooms and perfectly pleasant communal areas. There are neat little Art Deco touches throughout, and it has wi-fi and the only city-centre swimming pool. $\overline{\$\$}$

Los Caneyes Ave. de los Eucaliptos y Circunvalación

ⓦ hotelescubanacan. Scenic holiday complex with a small pool tucked away in the low, grassy, wooded hills just beyond the city's southwestern outskirts. It features a restaurant, hot tub and Native American-styled huts, thoughtfully furnished, with good facilities. $\overline{\$\$}$

Central Parque Vidal no.3 e/ Marta Abreu y Tristá ⓦ hotelescubanacan.com. The Hotel Central actually first opened in 1929 but was turned over to housing in the final years of the last century. Recently restored after decades of decay, with its colonnaded yellow, white and clay-coloured portico, it's back among the finest buildings in the city. Dignified rooms, a delightful porch café and a central patio with a dinky, square saloon bar are among the many praiseworthy features. $\overline{\$\$}$

Floreale Rafael Tristá no.4 e/ Parque Vidal y Villuendas ⓦ hotelescubanacan.com. Opened in 2018, this bargain-priced 20-room hotel, unsurprisingly, is in tip-top condition.

4

The catering isn't up to much but the renovation is a great success, the comfortable rooms directly off the lovely central patio and on the floor above gathered around the overlooking balcony. ⑤

CASAS PARTICULARES

Alba Hostal Eduardo Machado (San Cristóbal) no.7 e/ Cuba y Colón ☎42 294108, ✉wilfredo.alba@yahoo.com. Impressive and elegant, the definite crowd-pleaser here is the splendid narrow patio spilling over with potted plants. Opening onto the patio, the two guest rooms maintain these high standards, and are decked out in colonial style, with an original eighteenth-century bed in one of them. Wi-fi. ⑤

★**Aparthostal Eva y Ernesto** J.B. Zayas no.253a e/ Berenguer (San Mateo) y Padre Tuduri ☎42 204076, ✉nestyhostal@yahoo.es. There's an air of understated sophistication about this cushy first-floor apartment, with its orderly open-plan kitchen/living room with bar stools, comfy couch and coffee table. Neat and dinky balconies back and front and a delightfully intimate terrace with park benches complete the picture. Rent the whole place (perfect for two couples), or as two separate one-bedroom apartments. ⑤

★**Casa Mercy** Eduardo Machado (San Cristóbal) no.4 e/ Cuba y Colón ☎42 216941, ✉casamercy@gmail.com. Guests have the run of the first floor where, beyond the two clean, spacious quadruple rooms with bathrooms, there are two cosy terraces. The charming and unendingly helpful hosts, who speak English, Italian and French, provide laundry and internet services and plenty of local info, as well as making an impressive list of cocktails and excellent meals (including vegetarian food). Wi-fi. ⑤

★**Casa Mercy 1938** Independencia no.253 e/ Unión y San Isidro ☎42 295555, ✉casamercy@gmail.com. An impeccably renovated house with two immaculate, spacious rooms facing a colourful central patio with an impressively decorated back wall, featuring inset arches and shelves in which two vases sit over a lovely tile mosaic. Breakfasts are generous and this is a lovely place to stay. ⑤

El Castillito Céspedes no.65A e/ Maceo y Pedro Estévez (Unión) ☎42 292671. One cosy, light and airy room with TV, DVD, safety-deposit box, fridge and a/c in a peaceful house with three terraces, one of which serves as a pleasant dining area. The man in charge, easy-going José, offers free pick-ups from the bus station if you book in advance. ⑤

Hostal Adelaida y Rolando Maceo no.355a e/ Serafín García (Nazareno) y E.P. Morales (Síndico) ☎42 206725, ✉rolandosacerio@gmail.com. Two comfortable double rooms, both with a/c and bathroom and one with its own little lounge attached, in a simple, spick-and-span house with a first-floor terrace. You'll be made to feel very welcome by the warm and friendly hosts, Adelaida and Rolando, who speak good English and have a small library of books on Cuban history. ⑤

Hostal D'Cordero Leoncio Vidal (Gloria) no.61 e/ Maceo y Pedro Estévez (Unión) ⑩hostaldecordero.com. Lavishly furnished with antiques and collectable original Cuban paintings, this museum of a house is full of eye-catching features, like the fabulous 1930 console radio, which still works, or the grand Louis XV bed. Four of the five rooms, where vintage furniture mixes with modern amenities including TV, minibar, safe and top-notch a/c, face the central patio, filled with potted ferns and shrubs gathered around a handsome fountain. ⑤

★**Hostal Florida Center** Maestra Nicolasa (Candelaria) no.56 e/ Colón y Maceo ☎42 208161, ✉angel.floridacenter@yahoo.com. Based around a fantastic, rainforest-like courtyard, this large, authentic colonial residence crammed with nineteenth-century furnishings has three superbly distinguished rooms for rent: one with a fantastic Art Deco bed and wardrobe, another with colonial-era beds. All three have TV, minibar, a/c and a spotless private bathroom. Breakfast and dinner are served on tables that nestle among the fronds and ferns. English, French and Italian are spoken. Wi-fi. ⑤

★**Hostal Florida Terrace** Maestra Nicolasa (Candelaria) no.59 e/ Colón y Maceo ☎42 291580, ✉florida.terrace@gmail.com. More impersonal than most *casas particulares*, as this is not actually someone's house, but with more individuality than most state-run hotels, there are six splendid yet understated rooms here, each with its own unique stamp, whether an Art Deco lamp, a set of old framed photographs or an Art Nouveau bed, spread across the first two floors. On the top-floor terrace is a bar and above that a viewing platform. En-suite bathrooms are top spec, communal spaces feature antique radios and precious cabinets full of vintage jugs and cafetières and the broad staircases are lined with an impressive collection of drawings by renowned Cuban artists. Wi-fi. ⑤

EATING

SEE MAP PAGE 246

Almost all the best eating-out options in Santa Clara are within easy walking distance of Parque Vidal and though there are a clutch of places where you can eat creditable Cuban food, for anything experimental, original or international the choice is poor. On the whole you're better off at one of the paladars, but if you're staying in a *casa particular*, the chances are you'll do as well (or better) to eat there.

STATE RESTAURANTS

La Bodeguita del Medio Leoncio Vidal (Gloria) no.1 e/ Parque Vidal y Maceo ☎42 203454. Though the interior decoration of the local branch of this famous national chain may feel contrived, rehashing the message-covered walls of the original, the high quality of food here is actually refreshingly out of the ordinary for somewhere so cheap. Pork ribs, *ropa vieja*, fried chicken, shrimp, fish and all other mains are served with good sides. A resident band and separate bar room cap it all off. $\overline{\underline{\$\$}}$

Casa del Gobernador Independencia esq. J.B.Zayas ☎42 202273. Doughy but generously topped pizzas or perfectly decent, inexpensive Cuban-style meat and fish dishes like smoked pork are served on the downstairs patio, the balcony above it or the formal air-conditioned dining room of this restored colonial mansion. $\overline{\underline{\$\$}}$

Santa Rosalia Máximo Gómez e/ Independencia y Parque Vidal ☎42 201438. A splendid nineteenth-century mansion that was once a school for impoverished children, with a lovely central courtyard. Offers a broad choice of good-quality meat and seafood dishes, including rabbit, lamb and pork options. $\overline{\underline{\$\$}}$

PALADARS

El Alba Rolando Pardo (Buen Viaje) no.26 esq. Maceo ☎42 203935. Top-notch, excellent-value Cuban home-cooking at this packed little paladar right in the centre. The food, though the usual meat and seafood, is cooked to an unusually high standard for a Santa Clara restaurant, and comes in huge portions. $\overline{\underline{\$}}$

La Aldaba Hostal Auténtica Pérgola, Luis Estévez no.61 e/ Boulevard y Martí ☎42 208686. On the spacious, canopy-covered, leafy rooftop terrace of a *casa particular* you can detach yourself from Santa Clara's busy shopping street, just half a block away, relax and enjoy straightforward mains like garlic shrimp, fricassee chicken and an excellent-value grilled lobster. $\overline{\underline{\$\$}}$

La Bodeguita Marta Abreu no.128 e/ Juan Bruno Zayas y Alemán ☎42 207733. Not be confused with the state-run Bodeguita del Medio, this congenial paladar is split over two sociably small rooms with pictures of singers on the wall and musical accompaniment most nights. The food is above average comida criolla. $\overline{\underline{\$\$}}$

★ **Florida Center** Maestra Nicolasa (Candelaria) no.56 e/ Colón y Maceo ☎42 208161. The jungle of plants on the central patio of one of the city's best *casas particulares* is home to its best paladar too. The straight-forward menu presents the lobster specialities of the house cooked in tomato sauce, and just a few simple but perfectly prepared classically Cuban alternatives. The house cocktail, Cuba Limón, is a refreshing treat in the heat. $\overline{\underline{\$\$\$}}$

SaboreArte Maceo no.7 e/ Independencia y Céspedes ☎42 206730. A very congenial spot for a meal, where inexpensive Cuban food like the traditional *ajiaco campesino* stew, seafood salad and grilled red snapper are served up from the open kitchen in a large, plant-strewn, partially covered patio sitting snugly between buildings and hidden away from the street. $\overline{\underline{\$\$}}$

4

DRINKING AND NIGHTLIFE

SEE MAP PAGE 246

The shopping street, Boulevard, is lined with snack bars and soulless cafés open until late, some of which have simple bar counters providing a space for quick-refill-drinkers, but most with a strictly limited selection of drinks. The best cafés and bars are in isolated little pockets within a three- or four-block radius of **Parque Vidal**. The city's **nightlife** venues, which of course include some of the bars, also emanate out from the lively central square, where there are plenty of people buzzing around until the early hours of the morning at weekends.

BARS AND CAFÉS

★ **Café-Museo Revolución** Independencia no.313 ☎52511017. A real gem of a café where an entrancing collection of vintage and revolutionary memorabilia cover the walls and surfaces leaving just enough room for a few drinkers to sip beers, cocktails and coffees. Among the treasure is a hand-written note by Che Guevara.

Café Tu Te Rafael Tristá no.113 e/ Alemán y Juan Bruno Zayas. Popular among the city's trendy young folk this low-key, hip little place steers well clear of any corny Cuban clichés. Instead, it keeps it simple with homemade furniture, bottles hanging over the tiny bar and a great coffee and tea list which includes over a dozen inexpensive coffee cocktails.

La Marquesina Parque Vidal esq. Máximo Gómez ☎42 224848. In the corner of the theatre building, serving beer, rum, soft drinks and a couple of cocktails, this is the busiest bar after dark, when there's live music almost every night – though it sometimes closes when there is a performance at the theatre.

Vista a la Ciudad Santa Clara Libre hotel, Parque Vidal ☎42 207548 ext 1100. The roof-terrace bar of the *Hotel Santa Clara Libre* has the best possible views right across the city, though they disappear behind walls once you sit down. There are a few cheap cocktails, plus beers, whiskies and soft drinks.

NIGHTCLUBS

Club Boulevard Independencia 225 e/ Maceo y Pedro Estévez (Unión) ☎42 216236. The only place in town that can call itself a true nightclub, albeit a very small one, and slightly more sophisticated and image-conscious than other spots.

LIVE MUSIC VENUES

Casa de la Ciudad Boulevard esq. J.B. Zayas. A visitor attraction by day, this is one of the city's more atmospheric live music venues, where concerts are hosted in the relative intimacy of the interior patio. A weekly programme is posted in the doorway during the day and generally features performers of traditional styles of Cuban music, from troubadours to guitar groups.

Casa de la Cultura Parque Vidal ☎ 42 217181. There is a fairly diverse monthly programme (posted in the foyer) at this cultural community centre, including local musicians performing traditional Cuban music, often trova, danzón or rumba. Entrance free. Performances often spill onto the park outside.

★ **El Mejunje** Marta Abreu no.12 e/ J.B. Zayas y Rafael

Lubián ☎ 42 282572. The city's most varied programme of live shows, dance and music, attracting a bohemian crowd and popular with both the gay community and the Santa Clara rock contingent. The main area is a rough-and-ready brick-walled open-air courtyard, but there's also an indoor performance area, a café-bar and a gallery. The entertainment ranges from live rock, rap, jazz and traditional Cuban music to drag shows, small-scale theatrical productions, and weekend discos. The week's programme is posted on a board just inside or on the door.

ENTERTAINMENT

THEATRE

Teatro La Caridad Parque Vidal ☎ 42 205548. The venue for most of the high-profile cultural events, including plays, orchestral performances and ballet. Past performers here have included Alicia Alonso and the Cuban National Ballet as well as Chucho Valdés, one of the greatest Cuban pianists of all time. Shows generally Wed, Fri & Sat from 8.30pm, Sun from 5pm.

CINEMAS

Cine Camilo Cienfuegos Santa Clara Libre hotel,

Parque Vidal no.6 e/ Rafael Tristá y Padre Chao ☎ 42 203005. As well as its own regular schedule of films, the cinema's noticeboard is a useful source of information on films showing throughout the city, at both cinemas and *salas de vídeo*.

Cine Cubanacán Boulevard no.60 e/ Villuendas y J.B. Zayas ☎ 42 205366. The home of one of the country's most renowned cinema clubs, and a good place to catch both blockbusters and independent Latin American films.

SHOPPING
SEE MAP PAGE 246

Plaza de Artesanía Enrique Villuendas e/ Marta Abreu y M. Prado. At the city-centre craft market, as well as Che Guevara-themed tat, there's gold-plated jewellery, bags, wallets, home-made cigar boxes, wall hangings, novelty

baseball bats and lots more besides.

La Veguita Maceo no.176 e/ Berenguer (San Mateo) y Julio Jover (san Vicente) ☎ 42 208952. This excellent little cigar shop sells rum, coffee and a good selection of *habanos*.

DIRECTORY

Health The Clínico Quirúrgico Arnaldo Milián Castro at Circunvalación y 26 de Julio, Reparto Escambray, in the southeast of the city, is the most comprehensively equipped hospital in the province (switchboard ☎ 42 272016, information ☎ 42 270070, ambulance ☎ 104). The best-stocked pharmacy is at Colón no.106 e/ Avenida 9 de Abril (San Miguel) y Maestra Nicolasa (Candelaria; Mon–Fri 8.30–4.30, Sat 8.30–noon).

Money and exchange Banco Financiero Internacional, Cuba e/ Rafael Tristá y Eduardo Machado (San Cristóbal; Mon–Fri 8.30am–3.30pm), and the Banco de Crédito y

Comercio, Cuba e/ Boulevard y Martí (Mon–Fri 8am–3pm), where there's an ATM. To change money, go to the CADECA *casa de cambio*, Rafael Tristá esq. Cuba on the corner of Parque Vidal (Mon–Sat 8am–8pm, Sun 9am–6pm), where there's also an ATM. There are more ATMs outside the Banco Popular de Ahorro on Luis Estévez e/ Parque Vidal y Boulevard.

Police In an emergency call ☎ 116. The central police station is at Colón no.222 e/ Serafín García (Nazareno) y E.P. Morales (Síndico; ☎ 42 212623).

Post office The main post office is at Colón no.10 e/

BASEBALL IN SANTA CLARA

The **Villa Clara Naranjas**, the local national-league **baseball** team whose distinctive orange uniform is their chief trademark, are traditionally among the top four teams in the league and have consistently qualified for the playoffs over the last decade. They play their games at the **Estadio Augusto César Sandino** (☎ 42 22 2855), a relatively intimate ballpark, founded in 1966, with a capacity of just eighteen thousand; the entrance is on Calle 2. **Games** take place Tues–Sun, usually at 1pm during the regular season (currently Nov–March); playoffs finish in May. Enquire at the travel agents in town about excursions to see a game.

> ## SANTA CLARA SWIMMING POOLS
>
> The only easy-to-access **swimming pool** in the centre of Santa Clara is at the *Hotel América*. Daytime-only visitors can use it (daily 10am–6pm), which includes a credit for food and drinks. A cheap taxi ride away on the wooded outskirts of the city is a larger pool at *Hotel Los Caneyes*, where guests can also enjoy the much leafier, loungier, more attractive surroundings.

Parque Vidal y Eduardo Machado (San Cristóbal; Mon–Sat 8am–10pm); DHL is at Cuba no.7 e/ Rafael Tristá y Eduardo Machado (San Cristóbal; Mon–Fri 8am–6pm, Sat 8–11am).

Visas To extend your tourist card go to the Department of Immigration office near the Estadio Sandino at Reparto Sandino no.9 e/ Carretera Central y Avenida Sandino (Mon & Wed 8am–7pm, Tues & Fri 8am–5pm, Thurs & Sat 8am–noon; ☎ 42 213626).

Wi-fi The city has well over 20 public wi-fi zones. They include Parque Vidal, the shopping street Boulevard, the Complejo Monumental Ernesto Che Guevara and the parkland around the baseball stadium, the Estadio Sandino. You can buy wi-fi cards at the ETECSA Telepunto, Marta Abreu no.51 esq. Enrique Villuendas (daily 8.30am–7pm) and at the *Hotel América* at Mujica no.9 e/ Colón y Maceo. Both also provide computer terminals where you can get online with the cards.

Remedios

Just over 40km northeast of Santa Clara and less than 10km from the coast, the town of **REMEDIOS** is one of the oldest and most attractive small towns in Cuba. Sitting within such perfect day-trip distance of the provincial capital and the burgeoning beach resort on the northern cays, it has enjoyed significant levels of investment in recent years, particularly in the build-up to the five-hundredth anniversary of its foundation in 2015.

Remedios now sparkles with a whole host of freshly painted buildings, several exquisite new hotels and a large, very sociable, spruced-up central garden square, **Plaza Martí**. Awash with the town's new colours, the pastel blues, pinks, oranges and yellows of the surrounding porticoed edifices, the square is unique in Cuba for containing two churches.

Despite the high number of visitors, Remedios retains an unspoilt quality, partly because the town lived on the periphery of modern Cuba until relatively recently – a fact reflected in the noticeable absence of modern constructions – but perhaps also because there really isn't very much to do here. The town's modest museums provide no more than a couple of hours of sightseeing, and you'll get the most out of the place simply by sitting at one of a number of bars and restaurants around the square and taking it easy.

This subdued place does, however, explode into life every Christmas when **Las Parrandas**, the festival for which the town is best known among Cubans, takes place (see page 258).

Brief history

Remedios is the eighth-oldest town in Cuba, founded in 1515 shortly after the establishment of the original seven *villas* (see page 432). Today's provincial capital, Santa Clara, was, in fact, founded by citizens of Remedios who, following a series of pirate attacks towards the end of the sixteenth century, transplanted the settlement further inland. The local populace was far from united in its desire to desert Remedios, however, and in an attempt to force the issue, those who wanted to leave burnt the town to the ground.

Rebuilt from the ashes, by 1696 the town had its own civic council and went on to produce not only one of Cuba's most renowned composers, Alejandro García Caturla, but also a Spanish president, Dámaso Berenguer Fuste, who governed Spain in the 1930s.

4

Iglesia de San Juan Bautista

Plaza Martí • Mon–Thurs 9am–noon & 2–5pm • Free

The most stunning sight in Remedios is the main altar of the **Iglesia de San Juan Bautista**, the town's principal church, occupying the southern face of the Plaza Martí (entry is sometimes via the back door). A church has stood on this site since the sixteenth century, but the current building dates from the late eighteenth century. Once inside, the magnificence of the illustriously detailed main **altar**, made from gilded wood, comes as quite a shock given the simple exterior. It was commissioned by Cuban millionaire **Eutimio Falla Bonet**, who funded the restoration of the church between 1944 and 1954 following his discovery that he had family roots in Remedios. Bonet's revamp, which also featured the installation of a set of golden altars lining the walls, collected from around Cuba and beyond, have transformed the place into a kind of religious trophy cabinet.

Museo de la Música Alejandro García Caturla

Camilo Cienfuegos no.5, Plaza Martí • Mon–Sat 9am–noon & 1–6pm, Sun 9am–1pm • Charge • ☎ 42 39 6851

On the eastern side of Plaza Martí is the simple **Museo de la Música Alejandro García Caturla**. A lawyer with a passion for music, especially the piano and violin, Caturla lived and worked in the building for the last twenty years of his life. He is most famous for his boundary-breaking compositions from the 1920s and 1930s which combined traditional symphonic styles with African rhythms. In December 1940, he

4

was murdered by a man he was due to prosecute the following day. Caturla's study has been preserved and there are various engaging photographs and less interesting documents. There's also a small concert room where you can sometimes catch live musical performances.

Museo de las Parrandas Remedianas

Alejandro del Río no.74 e/ Máximo Gómez y Enrique Malaret • Tues–Sat 9am–6pm, Sun 9am–1pm • Charge • ☎ 42 39 5448

The **Museo de las Parrandas Remedianas** is for most of the year the nearest you'll get to experiencing **Las Parrandas**, the annual Christmas Eve festival for which Remedios is renowned. The scene of the festival is portrayed with a scale model of the main square and two opposing floats, which form the centrepieces of the event. Photographs dating back to 1899 provide a more vivid picture of what goes on, showing some of the spectacular floats, known as **carrozas**, and the stationary **trabajos de plaza**, which have graced the event over the years. There are also examples of the torches, instruments, colourful costumes and flags that form an integral part of the raucous celebrations.

ARRIVAL AND DEPARTURE

REMEDIOS

By bus Local and interprovincial Víazul buses arrive at and depart from the Terminal de Omnibus (☎ 42 39 5290), on the western outskirts of town at Avenida Céspedes e/ Pi y Margall y Avenida de los Mártires, from where it's an eight-block walk along Pi y Margall or a five-minute *bicitaxi* ride to Plaza Martí. Moving on, services include a daily bus to the northern cays, though this is sometimes suspended (check in advance).

Local bus destinations Caibarién (3 daily; 25min); Santa Clara (3 daily; 2hr).

Víazul bus destinations Caibarién (1 daily; 10min); Cayo Las Brujas (1 daily; 45min); Cayo Santa María (1 daily; 1hr 30min); Santa Clara (1 daily; 55min); Trinidad (1 daily; 4hr).

By private taxi A taxi between Remedios and Santa Clara takes about 50min and costs around $700CUP.

INFORMATION

Tourist office Infotur, the national tourist information provider, is at Pi y Margall esq. Brigadier González (Mon–Fri 8.30am–noon, 1–5pm; ☎ 42 39 7227).

ACCOMMODATION

SEE MAP PAGE 256

There is no town of this size in Cuba that has a better choice of places to stay. There is not only a fabulous spread of **casas particulares** but also five wonderful **boutique hotels**. All are stamped with the Cubanacán chain's reliably excellent Encanto brand.

ⓦ hotelescubanacan.com. A loveable little hotel with courteous staff and a charmingly elegant yet simple, tasteful interior. Booking is advisable as there are only ten rooms, all well furnished and most of them located around an open-air balcony overlooking the delightful patio bar. $$

HOTELS

★ **Barcelona** José Antonio Peña e/ La Pastora y Antonio Maceo ⓦ hotelescubanacan.com. A meticulous restoration has converted this three-storey building from 1926 into a delightful, cheery 24-room hotel. The sunny pastels of the graceful, loungey lobby and the bright central patio make this the most restful, hard-to-leave place in town. $$

Camino del Príncipe Camilo Cienfuegos esq. Montalvan, Plaza Martí ⓦ hotelescubanacan.com. This beautiful hotel on the plaza opened in 2015 with 26 refined rooms, a broad upstairs balcony overlooking the square, a gracious dining room lobby and cheerful pastel colours outside and in. $$$

Mascotte Máximo Gómez no.114, Plaza Martí

CASAS PARTICULARES

Hostal La Casona Cueto Alejandro del Río no.72 esq. E. Morales ☎ 42 39 5350, ⓔ luisenrique@capiro.vcl.sld.cu. This cavernous, late nineteenth-century house just behind the Plaza Martí has five simple double rooms, a capacious and very leafy central courtyard and an impressive interior full of colonial antiques. $

★ **Hostal El Chalet** Brigadier González no.29 e/ Independencia y José Antonio Peña ☎ 42 39 6538, ⓔ jorgechalet@nauta.cu. This spacious 1950s house has a patio garden and parking for two cars. Bathed in a lovely natural light, the two rooms, one a triple and more like a mini apartment with its own comfortable reception area, are located up on a roof terrace, affording views over the treetops to the church on the main square and providing a

4

LAS PARRANDAS

Once a year, on the night of December 24, usually sedate Remedios erupts into organized anarchy during **Las Parrandas**, a 200-year-old tradition which originated in the town and has spread throughout the province and beyond. Since the end of the nineteenth century there have been annual *parrandas* in neighbouring towns like Camajuaní, Zulueta and Caibarién, but the one in Remedios remains the biggest and the best. In the days building up to the main event the streets around the plaza fill up with market stalls and the town becomes overrun with visitors. For the festival itself, Remedios divides into northern and southern halves, with the frontier running through the centre of Plaza Martí: north is the **San Salvador** neighbourhood, whose emblem is an eagle on a blue background, and south is the **Carmen** neighbourhood, represented by a rooster on a red background. The opposing sides mark their territory with huge static constructions (which look like floats but are in fact stationary), known as **trabajos de plaza**, whose extravagant designs change annually, each one built to be more spectacular than the last. The celebrations kick off around 4pm, when the whole town gathers in the plaza to drink, dance, shout and sing. *Artilleros*, the fireworks experts, set off hundreds of eardrum-popping **firecrackers** until the square is shrouded in an acrid pall of black smoke and people can hardly see. Following that, the revellers form huge, pulsing **congas** and traipse around the square for hours, cheering their own team and chanting insulting songs at their rivals. The neighbourhoods' avian symbols appear on a sea of waving banners, flags, staffs, placards and bandanas tied around their citizens' necks.

As night falls, the two large floats, the **carrozas**, which along with the *trabajos de plaza* form the focus of the celebrations, do a ceremonial round of the plaza. Built to represent their respective halves of Remedios, the floats are fantastical creations with multicoloured decorations and flashing lights forming intricate patterns. Constructed by the town's resident population of *parrandas* fanatics, who devote the majority of their free time throughout the year to designing and creating them, the floats are judged by the rest of the town on looks and originality. As everyone makes up their minds, a massive **fireworks display** illuminates the sky and further heightens the tension. Finally, in the early morning hours, the church bell is ceremoniously rung and the **winner** announced. The president of the winning neighbourhood is then triumphantly paraded around on his jubilant team's shoulders before everyone heads home to recover, enjoy Christmas and start planning the next year's festivities.

---

sense of privacy. 💲

Hostal La Estancia Camilo Cienfuegos no.34 e/ Ave. General Carrillo y José Antonio Peña 🌐 laestanciahostal. com. A grand old nineteenth-century residence retaining many of its original features, most strikingly in the cavernous reception room which is full of antiques, including an ornate grand piano. The three huge guest rooms, all en suite, are based around a large courtyard featuring a small pool and a jungle of plants. 💲

Hostal Haydee y Juan K José Antonio Peña no.73 e/ Maceo y La Pastora ☎ 42 39 5082, ✉ haydejk@nauta.cu. A neat and compact house, run by a friendly couple. Two of the three spruce and decorous rooms, both with a/c and en-suite bathroom, are based around a gorgeous central patio, while the spacious third is up on a lovely roof terrace. Juan loves to talk politics, so this is a good option for anyone with an interest in the Revolution. 💲

EATING
SEE MAP PAGE 256

There are several restaurants around the centre, but you're better off at the **hotel restaurants**, all of which are reliable and open to non-guests, or one of the small number of **paladars**. If you're staying in a *casa particular* the chances are you will eat as well there as anywhere.

La Paloma Balmaseda no.4 e/ Máximo Gómez y Ramiro Capablanca ☎ 42 39 5490. A meal at the paladar of this

elegant *casa particular* feels very much like eating in someone else's dining room, albeit a posh one, with guests wandering to and from their rooms and an easy-come, easy-go atmosphere. The food is excellent and always fresh – choose from the three or four seafood and meat mains that are in on the day and served with starters and sides like perfectly seasoned black bean stews, and salads full of crisp

and ripe ingredients. $$$
La Pirámide Andrés del Río no.9 e/ Enrique Malaret y Máximo Gómez ☎ 42 39 5421. A popular paladar pizzeria, which also serves good Cuban food, particularly the seafood, in a small, casual dining room on the upstairs floor of a house a couple of blocks from the square. Staff are very friendly and prices very reasonable. $$

DRINKING AND NIGHTLIFE

SEE MAP PAGE 256

Casa de la Cultura José Antonio Peña no.67 e/ La Pastora y Antonio Maceo ☎ 42 39 5581. This local community cultural centre posts a weekly programme on its porch which usually includes live and recorded music on Friday and Saturday nights at 9pm and during the day at weekends.

Driver's Bar José Antonio Peña esq. Camilo Cienfuegos ☎ 42 39 5175. A sociable mix of locals, foreigners and flies, added to the images of 1950s advertising on the wall, provide this 24-hour bar with a distinct mix of workaday and novelty character. Beer, rum, soft drinks and sandwiches.

El Guije Maceo esq. Independencia ☎ 42 36 3305. This open-air venue with a bar and dancefloor set within high walls has karaoke, live music and participatory salsa on its weekly schedule.

Las Leyendas Máximo Gómez no.124, Plaza Martí ☎ 42 39 6131. This pleasant patio comes with a bar, pizzeria and stage hosting small-scale cabarets and occasional theatrical performances plus live music too.

El Louvre Máximo Gómez no.122 e/ Independencia y Pi y Margall, Plaza Martí ☎ 42 39 5639. Right on the main square, this is the smartest, most stylish bar in Remedios and has the best choice of drinks too.

Taberna Los Siete Juanes Balmaseda esq. Máximo Gómez, Plaza Martí. Head here for good-value cocktails and other drinks in one of the square's many sensitively converted colonial buildings. Exposed original stone walls inside, a strikingly lit bar counter, and tables on the porch and on a fenced off-piece of the road outside make this an interesting and very enjoyable place to while away the time.

DIRECTORY

Internet Plaza Martí is the town's public wi-fi zone – you can buy internet cards at the *Hotel Barcelona*.
Money Exchange foreign currency at the CADECA *casa de cambio* at Máximo Gómez e/ Balmaseda y Alejandro del Río (Mon–Sat 8am–5pm, Sun 8am–noon).
Post office There's a post office at José Antonio Peña esq. Antonio Romero (Mon–Sat 8am–6pm).

Caibarién

From Remedios it's about 8km east to the huge concrete crab guarding the run-down but pleasant port of **CAIBARIÉN**, where you'll find the closest *casas particulares* to the cays – the town is a convenient base from which to explore the cays without having to pay for a package holiday or shell out for an all-inclusive.

Caibarién's streets are lined by rows of wooden sugar warehouses, painted in a faded rainbow of colours, which testify to this sleepy backwater's nineteenth-century heyday. Largely unaffected by tourism and enjoying a leisurely speed of life, Caibarién provides a marked contrast to the development on the cays. The town itself is unlikely to hold you for long, though on the far side, furthest from the mainland, there's a patchy **beach** on a small, quiet peninsula, backed at one end by an ugly, beat-up, largely abandoned old building and at the other a quirky paladar and bar plus a small hotel. There's also a quiet central square, **Parque de la Libertad**, and a seafront promenade, the Malecón. West of town, on the road to Remedios, the **Museo de la Agroindustria Azucarera Marcelo Salado** is worth a half-hour stop-off.

Museo de la Agroindustria Azucarera Marcelo Salado

On the road from Remedios, 1.5km east of Caibarién • Mon–Fri 8am–4pm, Sat 8am–noon • Charge, extra for steam train (minimum 10 people) • ☎ 42 36 3636

Dedicated to the Cuban sugar industry, the **Museo de la Agroindustria Azucarera Marcelo Salado** is set in the dilapidated grounds of the old Marcelo Salado sugar refinery, founded in 1891 and still much as it was when it finally ground to a halt in 1999, as part of a wave of closures affecting the most inefficient factories.

4

Though it's a little disjointed and the layout a bit messy, the museum's functioning steam trains and the real-life setting make it an engaging place to visit. At its core is a dormant, metal-roofed factory floor where much of the machinery used in the **sugar production** process is on display in the setting in which it was once used; there are also reconstructed scenes depicting sugar production during the age of slavery. The nearby train shed holds six fabulous working **steam trains**, built in the US between 1904 and 1920 by the famous Baldwin Locomotive Works. A seventh engine is on display with its shell removed, revealing all the working parts. In a separate, smaller building are pictures of Cuba's earliest steam engines and information on their history. It's well worth paying the higher entrance fee to ride the train to Remedios and back – but ring in advance if you want a guarantee of this, as trains sometimes only leave for pre-booked tours.

ARRIVAL AND GETTING AROUND

CAIBARIÉN

By Víazul bus Víazul buses between Trinidad and the northern cays stop at Caibarién's train station, from where it's a three-block walk to the centre.

Destinations Cayo Las Brujas (1 daily; 35min); Cayo Santa María (1 daily; 1hr 20min); Remedios (1 daily; 10min); Santa Clara (1 daily; 1hr 5min); Trinidad (1 daily; 4hr 10min).

By local bus Services from Remedios (3 daily; 25min) and Santa Clara (3 daily; 2hr) stop just outside Caibarién's train station. From here, it's a short walk along Calle 8 into town.

By taxi A taxi from Caibarién (☎42 39 5555) to the cays or Santa Clara will cost $800–1000CUP.

By car Cubacar has an office in town at Avenida 11 e/ 6 y 8 (☎42 35 1970).

INFORMATION AND TOURS

Havanatur Staff at the Havanatur office on the square (Mon–Fri 8.30am–noon & 1.30–4.30pm, Sat 8.30am–noon; ☎42 35 1171) can arrange organized excursions or provide information on transport to the cays, Remedios and Santa Clara.

ACCOMMODATION

Brisas del Mar Playa Caibarién, Reparto Mar Azul ☎42 35 1699, ✉recepcion@brisas.co.cu. Located beyond the Malecón, from where the coastal road runs along the edge of a small natural harbour full of fishing boats onto a small peninsula. The rooms face out to sea and guests have use of a pool just over the road. $̄

Hostal Calle 12 Calle 12 no.1116 e/ 11 y 13 ☎42 36 4274. Three simple double bedrooms, each with minibar, a/c and en-suite bathroom in an airy, neo-colonial house, near the main square. There's a narrow but pleasant central courtyard and the friendly owners also run a paladar in the living and dining rooms. $̄

Villa Virginia Ciudad Pesquera no.73 ☎42 36 3303, ✉virginiaspension@gmail.com. A *casa particular* 1.5km west of the centre along the seafront with a nice garden patio. The friendly hosts offer good food and three simple, slightly cramped double rooms with a/c, tiled bathrooms and shared TV and fridge. $̄

EATING

Cafetería Villa Blanca Ave. 9 esq. 18 ☎42 36 3305. Reasonably priced seafood, chicken and steaks are served in a small garden four blocks from the square. $̄$̄

En Familia Ave. 9 e/ 28 y 30 ☎42 35 1351. Around 50m from the huge concrete crab at the top of town you can eat well-cooked helpings of the real thing, the house speciality at this popular paladar. Decently priced lobster, fish and pork also rotate on the menu. $̄$̄

The northern cays

The **northern cays** form one of Cuba's newest major tourist resorts, the first hotel having opened here – on what were until then virgin islands – in 1999. Set on a network of dozens of small islets, only three of which have been built on, **Cayo Las Brujas** is the most suitable for non-package visitors; the other two, tiny **Cayo Ensenachos** and the largest and most distant **Cayo Santa María**, almost 15km in length, are largely the exclusive domain of hotel guests, though a couple of commercial "villages" have been built on Cayo Santa María in the last few years. At some of the hotels you can pay for a day-pass, which gives you access to the beach and covers all meals and unlimited drinks.

The drive down the 48km **causeway** from just outside Caibarién to the islands is quite spectacular, and is half the fun of a visit. The dark, deeper waters nearer the land give way to shallow turquoise around the cays, then become almost clear as the network of islets increases in number and complexity. The sea is dotted with mangrove colonies, while herons and cormorants swoop overhead and the occasional iguana basks in the sun on the hot tarmac. The solid rock causeway is broken up by around fifty small **bridges**, which allow the currents to flow through and provide drivers with distance markers; development on the cays begins just after bridge 36.

Cayo Las Brujas

The nearest cay to the mainland to have been developed for visitors, **Cayo Las Brujas** is home to the only marina in the area as well as the least exclusive hotel and beach, making it both more affordable and accessible than Cayo Ensenachos and Cayo Santa María.

As you arrive via the causeway, there are two left-hand turns in succession, 1km apart, and in between them the only **petrol station** on the cays. The first turning, at the pocket-sized airport terminal, cuts down to the marina and the *Villa Las Brujas* hotel, which sits at one end of the beach, **Playa La Salina**. Only guests of the hotel, or anyone paying for a day-pass can access the beach this way and will be asked to present their passport at the car park. Everyone else must take the second left-hand turn, after the airport terminal, which leads down to the slightly scrappier **eastern end** of the same beach, near the site of five new hotels, all opened in the last few years, alongside a new retail, restaurant and leisure centre. The beach itself is a sandy 2km arch, barely 5m wide in places, and slopes into usually placid waters.

Cayo Santa María

From Cayo Las Brujas, the causeway passes a dolphinarium (see box) and the next significant cay, **Cayo Ensenachos**, where the beach is the exclusive domain of guests at the *Iberostar Ensenachos*. Several bridges beyond Ensenachos, about 15km from Cayo Las Brujas, the causeway concludes at **Cayo Santa María**, home to twelve hotels at the latest count, all of them slung along a stunning 15km beach which Fidel Castro is said to have described as superior to Varadero – though he's never been spotted sun-bathing on either.

Among the few places open to non-hotel guests on Cayo Santa María are the two commercial "villages": **Pueblo Las Dunas** in the west, in between the *Meliá Cayo Santa*

INDEPENDENT TRAVEL TO THE NORTHERN CAYS

Organized excursions to the northern cays are very straightforward but for **independent travellers** there are a few extra considerations you'll need to bear in mind to prevent your trip there from unravelling. You can catch a **Víazul bus** from Trinidad, Santa Clara or Remedios directly to the cays but as this service runs just once a day and the return service leaves an hour after it arrives, a day-trip by bus is pretty pointless. Many independent day-trippers opt instead for a **private taxi** which, from Santa Clara, should cost around $1600–2000CUP return. All foreign travellers, whether drivers or passengers, must bring their **passport** to get past the police checkpoint at the start of the causeway to the cays and you should make sure you bring enough **cash** to cover your expenses as credit card transactions or cash withdrawals at *Villa Las Brujas*, the focal point for most day-trippers, are impossible.

María and the *Meliá Las Dunas* hotels; and the larger **Pueblo La Estrella**, further east, between the *Royalton Cayo Santa María* and the *Memories Paraíso Beach Resort* hotels. Unsurprisingly, they're very artificial places, both consisting of mock-colonial buildings housing shops, bars, restaurants, discos and bowling alleys.

At the far eastern end of Cayo Santa María, the splendid **Playa Perla Blanca** is one of the most untouched beaches in the whole of the northern cays, though a hotel is now being built here. It's a bit of a trek – 52km from the mainland in total – but it remains accessible to all and there are several kilometres of beach blessed with sand as fine as it gets in Cuba.

ARRIVAL, DEPARTURE AND GETTING AROUND   THE NORTHERN CAYS

By plane The small airport (☎42 35 0009) on Cayo Las Brujas is for domestic flights only and handles two flights daily to and from Havana (1hr 5min).

By Víazul bus The service to the northern cays from Trinidad via Remedios and Caibarién sometimes gets suspended, but is by far the cheapest way to get here from elsewhere in the province when it does operate. All services listed below run once a day.

Destinations (from Cayo Las Brujas and Cayo Santa María) Caibarién (35min/1hr 20min); Remedios (45min/1hr 30min); Santa Clara (3hr 40min/4hr 20min); Trinidad (4hr 55min/5hr 40min).

By tourist bus Once on the cays you can make use of the Panoramic Bus Tour, an open-top hop-on, hop-off bus

service running roughly 9am–9pm daily and calling in at all the hotels on its trip round the resort.

By car From Caibarién, a road out of town runs roughly parallel with the coastline for 4km to the bridge that leads to the 24hr checkpoint at the start of the causeway linking the mainland to the cays. To pass the checkpoint, you'll need to produce your passport.

By taxi Taxis from Caibarién to the cays (around $900CUP each way) can be organized through Transgaviota, which has an office in the town (☎42 35 1353) and another in the *Sol Cayo Santa María* hotel on Cayo Santa María.

Bike, car and scooter rental All of the all-inclusive hotels have car, scooter and bicycle rental which can be booked by non-guests.

ACCOMMODATION AND EATING

There are now more than twenty **hotels** on the cays, more than half of them built from scratch in the last decade; all but two (listed below) are **all-inclusive** package-holiday establishments unsuited to receiving guests on spec.

Las Salinas Plaza & Spa Cayo Las Brujas ⓦgaviotahotels.com. Small compared to most of the hotels on the cays, this enjoyable 67-room spot nevertheless manages to pack plenty in. As well as the spa facilities there is an infinity pool facing the beach, a bowling alley, several restaurants and bars, and a fitness centre. Bed and breakfast

options mean you can keep costs relatively low and each stay comes with a free massage. $\overline{\underline{S}}\overline{\underline{S}}\overline{\underline{S}}$

Villa Las Brujas Cayo Las Brujas ⓦgaviotahotels. com. A simple but idyllic little complex, with two lines of comfortable wooden cabins on a natural platform along the rocky shore, connected by a boardwalk. Most rooms have sea-facing balconies and all have a/c and cable TV. The restaurant, *El Farallón* (daily 7am–10pm), serves good-quality grilled fish, mixed seafood grills and the like, and can be used by non-guests who buy a day-pass. $\overline{\underline{S}}\overline{\underline{S}}$

ACTIVITIES ON THE NORTHERN CAYS

Marina Gaviota Cayo Santa María (ⓦcayosantamaria.info, daily 9am–5pm), actually on Cayo Las Brujas, next to the *Villa Las Brujas* hotel, offers **snorkelling** and a full-day snorkelling excursion with lunch. They also offer **diving**, deep-sea fishing, **catamaran cruises** and tours to **Caguanes Park**. Part of the Unesco-designated Buenavista Biosphere Reserve, this includes cays, reefs, beaches, swamps and mangroves, with over 100 species of bird nesting in the coastal and marsh areas. Boasting 35 archaeological sites, it's also of historic and cultural interest, with its caves, some of them partially submerged, displaying wall paintings.

Just off the causeway, about 800m from the southern edge of Cayo Ensenacho, is the largest **dolphinarium** (☎42 35 0013) in Latin America, consisting of six separate pools covering over three thousand square metres. Daily shows are at 11am and 3pm. You may want to read up on the welfare of marine mammals kept in captivity in Cuba before you go, though (see page 54).

EMBALSE HANABANILLA ACTIVITIES

The *Hanabanilla* hotel (☎42 20 8461, ✉carpeta@hanabanilla.co.cu) offers various tours around the surrounding countryside and on the lake and, between 7am and 3pm daily, rents out **kayaks** and **rowing boats**. **Boat trips**, which include an excursion to the **Río Negro restaurant** – an assemblage of covered platforms, perched on a forested slope and resembling an elaborate Tarzan camp – are available by speedboat (three people maximum), or a cheaper slower boat (twelve people maximum).

They also offer an excursion to the **Casa del Campesino**, a traditional rural house in a clearing in the woods, where you can sample and buy the cigars manufactured here or the locally grown coffee or honey; and a waterfall where you can bathe, following the 1.5km walk from the edge of the reservoir to get there.

The hotel also arranges **fishing excursions**, though equipment isn't supplied, so you'll need to bring your own.

Embalse Hanabanilla

Closer to Trinidad but actually easier to access from Santa Clara, 50km away, **Embalse Hanabanilla**, a 36-square-kilometre reservoir, twists, turns and stretches around the hills in a valley on the northern edges of the **Sierra del Escambray**. On arrival, views of the reservoir reveal no more than a small section as it slinks out of sight behind the steep slopes which make up most of its borders, some of them covered in thick forest and others grassy and peppered with palm trees. Along with its unforgettable setting, the Embalse Hanabanilla's claims to fame are as the only reservoir powering an electric power station in Cuba and as the host to the largest population of largemouth bass in the world, making it one of the prime locations for freshwater **fishing** in Cuba. The bass in here reach record sizes, many weighing in at over 7kg, attracting a growing number of enthusiasts from abroad. Peak season for fishing is from November until the end of March

Whether on a day-trip from Santa Clara or a longer stay, almost all visits are channelled through the *Hanabanilla* hotel (see page 263). On the whole, the banks of the reservoir are difficult to access, though the various **boat excursions** offered by the hotel offer a way round this.

4

ARRIVAL AND DEPARTURE

EMBALSE HANABANILLA

By taxi A taxi from Santa Clara will cost around $1300–1600CUP return.

By car To drive to the reservoir from Santa Clara, take a right turn at the crossroads in the centre of the small town of Manicaragua, then take the left turn marked by the faded sign for the lake about 15km beyond this.

Organized tours There is no public transport to the reservoir, though you can book an organized excursion through one of the travel agents in Santa Clara.

ACCOMMODATION

SEE MAP PAGE 230

Hanabanilla ⓦislazulhotels.com. Set in a large building right on the edge of Embalse Hanabanilla near its northern tip – the fabulous location takes the blocky edge off the hotel, just as the view from the lake-facing rooms makes up for their small size and basic furnishings. There's a pool and a restaurant. $$

Trinidad and Sancti Spíritus

ENJOYING MUSIC IN TRINIDAD

5 **Trinidad and Sancti Spíritus**

Trinidad, a thriving, colourful sixteenth-century town in Sancti Spíritus province, is one of the country's most perfectly preserved and restored colonial settlements and a Unesco World Heritage Site. Sandwiched between a nearby beach and scenic mountains, and well removed from the two main roads that scratch asphalt scars through the centre of the country and a number of its other major towns and cities, Trinidad is justifiably the single most-visited destination in central Cuba and the most touristy town on the island. More than anywhere else, Trinidad neatly encapsulates Cuba's past and future: a 500-year-old architectural showpiece whose backstreets are still traversed by farmers on horseback, and where a huge proportion of the 75,000 residents have turned their working lives over to private enterprise, mostly by catering to visitors. As a result, there are now around a thousand *casas particulares* operating there – among them some absolute diamonds – while countless paladars, cafés, arts and crafts stalls and shops, travel agents and dance schools occupy almost every house in the centre.

Less than 10km south of Trinidad is the **Península de Ancón**, site of arguably the best beach on mainland Cuba's south coast, which compared to the north coast is generally less sandy and spectacular. In the opposite direction, the mountain resort of **Topes de Collantes** makes an excellent base for hiking around the steep, lavishly forested slopes of the Sierra del Escambray. To the northeast of Trinidad, again just a few kilometres away, is the beautiful **Valle de los Ingenios**, home to the sugar estates that made Trinidad's colonial elite so wealthy. Further east, the provincial capital of **Sancti Spíritus**, though larger than its more famous neighbour, attracts far fewer visitors. For some, this is the source of the city's appeal: comparatively free of tour groups, it boasts a long history of its own and an unhurried pace of life.

Trinidad

Plenty of other Cuban towns are filled with beautiful old buildings, but there is a completeness about **TRINIDAD**'s cobbled, traffic-free centre and its jumble of pastel-coloured mansions and houses, with their red-tiled rooftops and shuttered porticoes, that puts it in a league of its own. Its pedestrianized colonial district has a distinct village feel, where people walk at a subdued pace over the uneven ground and neighbours chat from their doorsteps. With tourism continuously on the rise, however, you're as likely to see a foreign face as a local one on walks around the centre.

In general, if you're walking on cobblestones you're in the Unesco-protected part of the city, the old town, at the heart of which is beautiful **Plaza Mayor**. All of Trinidad's prominent **museums**, including the standout **Museo Romántico**, are either on the square or within a few blocks of it, so you can enjoy a full day of sightseeing without walking too far. That said, wandering around the old town's jumble of steep streets, shadowed by colonial houses and enlivened here and there by arts and crafts markets, is one of Trinidad's highlights and at least as stimulating as visiting the museums. North of the Plaza Mayor you soon reach the northern limits of the city, where some of the streets are little more than mud tracks. One of these leads to the top of the **Loma de**

Highlights

❶ **The Trinidad towers** Scale the winding wooden staircases in the towers at the Museo de la Lucha Contra Bandidos and the Museo de Historia Municipal for the best views of Trinidad, framed by coastline and mountains. See page 272

❷ **Horseriding** Take a ride to the outskirts of Trinidad, in the foothills of the Escambray mountains, and enjoy the beauty of the area from the saddle. See page 275

❸ **Casa de la Música** The standout live music venue in Trinidad, offering big-band salsa and

traditional Cuban music most nights. See page 277

❹ **Playa Ancón** One of the biggest and best beaches on the southern coast of Cuba. See page 280

❺ **Train ride to Manaca-Iznaga** Enjoy an hour-long ride from Trinidad in a charming old wooden carriage. See page 282

❻ **Trekking at Topes de Collantes** This beautiful national park in the steep, forested slopes of the Sierra del Escambray has some excellent hiking trails. See page 284

HIGHLIGHTS ARE MARKED ON THE MAP ON PAGE 268

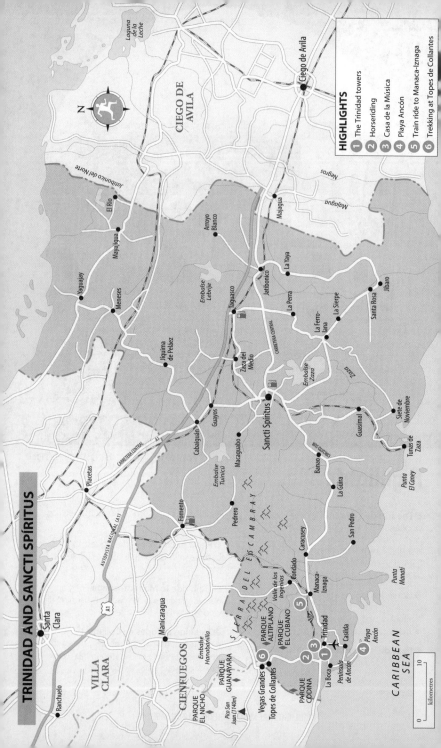

TRINIDAD AND SANCTI SPÍRITUS

HIGHLIGHTS

1. The Trinidad towers
2. Horseriding
3. Casa de la Música
4. Playa Ancón
5. Train ride to Manaca-Iznaga
6. Trekking at Topes de Collantes

CIEGO DE ÁVILA

VILLA CLARA

CIENFUEGOS

CARIBBEAN SEA

Laguna de la Leche

Ciego de Ávila

Jatibonico del Norte

El Río

Mayajigua

Taguajay

Meneses

Jiquimá de Peláez

Placetas

Santa Clara

Manicaragua

Ranchuelo

PARQUE EL NICHO

PARQUE GUANAYARA

Embalse Hanabanilla

Pico San Juan (1140m)

Vegas Grandes

Topes de Collantes

PARQUE CODINA

PARQUE ALTIPLANO

PARQUE EL CUBANO

SIERRA DEL ESCAMBRAY

La Boca

Trinidad

Casilda

Playa Ancón

Península de Ancón

Punta Manatí

San Pedro

Caracusey

Condado

Manaca-Iznaga

Valle de los Ingenios

Banao

La Güira

Pedrero

Fomento

Cabaiguán

Guayos

Macaguabo

Sancti Spíritus

Guasimal

Tunas de Zaza

Punta El Caney

Siete de Noviembre

Jíbaro

Santa Rosa

La Sierpe

La Ferrolana

La Perra

La Yaya

Jatibonico

Taguasco

Zaza del Medio

Embalse Zaza

Embalse Tuinicú

Embalse Lebrije

Arroyo Blanco

Majagua

Negros

Malagua

CIEGO DE ÁVILA

AUTOPISTA NACIONAL (A1)

CARRETERA CENTRAL

CARRETERA CENTRAL

CIRCUITO SUR

A1

Zaza

0   10
kilometres

la Vigía, an easily climbable hill overlooking Trinidad, marked at its base by a ruined church, the **Ermita de la Popa**, and one of the town's newest hotels.

Heading downhill from Plaza Mayor will lead you south, out of the historic centre towards **Parque Céspedes**, the centre of town for locals and a sociable hub of activity. Beyond this square and the historic centre there are very few specific sights; you'll get far more out of a visit if you take advantage of the nearby valley, beach and mountains.

Brief history

A Spanish settlement was first established in Trinidad in 1514, but interest in the area was short-lived. The **gold** mined in the area soon ran out and news spread of the riches to be found in Central America, contributing to a flow of emigration that left the town all but empty by the mid-1540s. It wasn't until the 1580s that the Spanish population rose again and local **agriculture** began to take off. By the 1750s the region possessed over a hundred tobacco plantations and at least as many farms and sugar mills, as well as a population of almost six thousand.

The mid-eighteenth century marked the start of the **sugar boom**, a roughly hundred-year period during which Trinidad became one of the country's most prosperous cities. Thousands of enslaved **Africans** were imported to cope with the increasing demands of the sugar industry. Trinidad's prosperity peaked when the economic tide began to turn in the 1830s and 1840s. Revolts, the exhaustion of cultivable land and the rising

TRINIDAD'S STREET NAMES

The confusion arising from old and new **street names** encountered in many Cuban towns is particularly acute in Trinidad. Most names were changed after the Revolution, but some new maps and tourist literature are reverting to the old names in the interests of the town's historical heritage, and locals usually use the old names. Many street signs now display both names, but the addresses appearing in this book are the post-Revolution versions.

OLD NAME	NEW NAME
Alameda	Jesús Menéndez
Amargura	Juan Manuel Márquez
Angarilla	Fidel Claro
Boca	Piro Guinart
Carmen	Frank País
Coco	Francisco Pettersen
Cristo	F.H. Echerrí
Desengaño	Simón Bolívar
Gloria	Gustavo Izquierdo
Gracia	Francisco Cadahía
Gutiérrez	Maceo or Antonio Maceo
Jesús María	Martí or José Martí
Las Guasimas	Julio A. Mella
Lirio Blanco	Abel Santamaría
Media Luna	Ernesto Valdés Muñoz
Olvido	Santiago Escobar
Peña	Francisco Gómez Toro
Real	Rubén Martínez Villena
Rosario	Francisco Javier Zerquera
San Antonio	Isidoro Armenteros
San Procopio	General Lino Pérez
Santa Ana	José Mendoza
Santo Domingo	Camilo Cienfuegos
Vigía	Eliope Paz

5

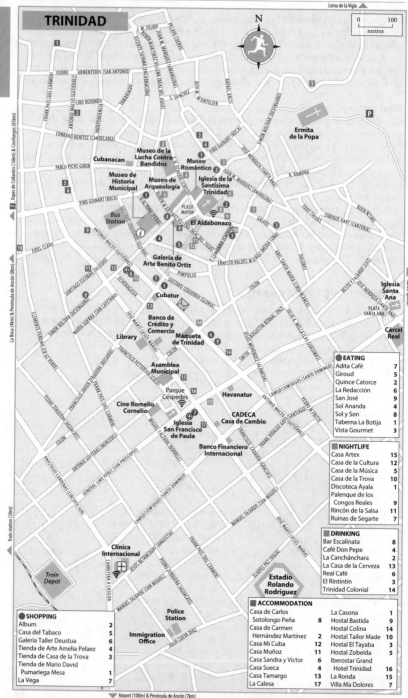

TRINIDAD

Loma de la Vigía

0   100
metres

N

Topes de Collantes (16km) & Cienfuegos (83km)

Sancti Spíritus

M. FEIJOO
PEPITO CUERVO
VICENTE SUYAMA (SAN ANTONIO)
JUAN M. MÁRQUEZ (AMARGURA)
HIBER MARTÍNEZ VILLENA (REAL DEL JIGÜE)
INDEPENDENCIA (SANTA ANA)
S. SÁNCHEZ
RITA M. MONTELIER
RAFAEL ARCIS
SIMÓN BOLÍVAR (DESENGAÑO)
PIRO GUINART (BOCA)
JOSÉ MENDOZA (SAN LUI)
N. RAMONA
JOSÉ M. MÁRQUEZ (AMARGURA)
GALDÓS
EDDY CHÁVAS
ENRIQUE HART (CANTERÍA)
BUEN RETIRO
ISIDRO
ARMENTEROS (SAN ANTONIO)
FRANK PAÍS DEL CARMEN (833km)
ANTONIO MACEO (GUTIÉRREZ)
CIRO REDONDO
YAMARINDO
PABLO PICHS GIRON
FIDEL CLARO
CONRADO BENÍTEZ (CANDELARIA)
PIRO GUINART (BOCA)
ANTONIO MACEO (GUTIÉRREZ)
CLEMENTE PEREIRA (JESÚS DEL VERDE)
SIMÓN BOLÍVAR (DESENGAÑO)
SANTIAGO ESCOBAR (OLVIDO)
ECHEMAGÜA
MARÍA GUERRA (SAN CAYETANO)
JOSÉ MARTÍ (JESÚS MARÍA)
GUSTAVO IZQUIERDO (GLORIA)
PIMPOLLO
COLÓN
ERNESTO VALDÉS MUÑOZ (MEDIA LUNA)
JESÚS MENÉNDEZ (ALAMEDA)
RECTO Y ZARAGO LUIZ
JOSÉ MENDOZA (SAN LUIS)
PLAZA SANTA ANA
JULIO A. MELLA (LAS GUÁSIMAS)
SMITH
DOLORES
ABEL SANTA MARÍA (LINO RANGO)
CAMILO CIENFUEGOS (SANTO DOMINGO)
PEDRO ZAPRIETE
ANTONIO MACEO (SANTIAGO)
FRANCISCO CADAHA (GRACIELA)
FRANK HIDALGO GATO (GUTIÉRREZ)
JESÚS AGUSTÍN BERNAL (PAZ)

Ermita de la Popa

P

Cubanacan

Museo de la Lucha Contra-Bandidos

Museo Romántico

Museo de Historia Municipal

Museo de Arqueología

Iglesia de la Santísima Trinidad

Bus Station

PLAZA MAYOR

El Aldabonazo

Galería de Arte Benito Ortiz

Cubatur

Banco de Crédito y Comercio

Library

Maqueta de Trinidad

Asamblea Municipal

Cine Romelio Cornelio

Parque Céspedes

Havanatur

CADECA Casa de Cambio

Iglesia San Francisco de Paula

Banco Financiero Internacional

Iglesia Santa Ana

Cárcel Real

Clínica Internacional

Train Depot

Estadio Rolando Rodriguez

Police Station

Immigration Office

La Boca (4km) & Península de Ancón (8km)

Train station (30m)

Airport (100m) & Península de Ancón (7km)

EATING

Adita Café	7
Giroud	5
Quince Catorce	2
La Redacción	6
San José	9
Sol Ananda	4
Sol y Son	8
Taberna La Botija	1
Vista Gourmet	3

NIGHTLIFE

Casa Artex	15
Casa de la Cultura	12
Casa de la Música	5
Casa de la Trova	10
Discoteca Ayala	
Palenque de los Congos Reales	9
Rincón de la Salsa	11
Ruinas de Segarte	7

DRINKING

Bar Escalinata	8
Café Don Pepe	4
La Canchánchara	2
La Casa de la Cerveza	13
Real Café	6
El Rintintin	3
Trinidad Colonial	14

ACCOMMODATION

Casa de Carlos Sotolongo Peña	8	La Casona	1
Casa de Carmen Hernández Martínez	2	Hostal Bastida	9
		Hostal Colina	14
Casa Mi Cuba	12	Hostal Tailor Made	10
Casa Muñoz	11	Hostal El Tayaba	3
Casa Sandra y Victor	6	Hostal Zobeida	5
Casa Sueca	4	Iberostar Grand	
Casa Tamargo	13	Hotel Trinidad	16
La Calesa	17	La Ronda	15
		Villa Ma Dolores	7

SHOPPING

Album	2
Casa del Tabaco	5
Galería Taller Deustua	6
Tienda de Arte Amelia Pelaez	4
Tienda de Casa de la Trova	3
Tienda de Mario David Pumariega Mesa	1
La Vega	7

5

challenge of European sugar beet sent the town into a downward spiral, accelerated by the **Wars of Independence**. In the early twentieth century local land fell increasingly into foreign – and especially US – hands, and unemployment shot up. Trinidad's fortunes turned again in the 1950s as tourism increased, encouraging the construction of a small airport and the *Hotel Las Cuevas*, both still standing today. This brief period of prosperity was cut short by the **revolutionary war** that ended in January 1959.

It was in the Sierra del Escambray around Trinidad that, for five years following the rebel triumph, US-backed **counter-revolutionaries** fought in a guerrilla conflict during which significant numbers of local men were killed. Celebrating its five-hundredth anniversary in 2014, Trinidad began the rise to its current prominence after its historic centre and the nearby Valle de los Ingenios were declared World Heritage Sites by Unesco in 1988.

Plaza Mayor

The beautiful **Plaza Mayor** is the heart of Trinidad's colonial old town. Comprising four simple fenced-in gardens, each with a palm tree or two and dotted with various statuettes and other ornamental touches, it's surrounded by painted colonial mansions, which are adorned with arches and balconies, and home to several museums and an art gallery.

Museo Romántico

Fernando Echerrí esq. Simón Bolívar, Plaza Mayor • Tues–Sun 9am–5pm • Charge • ☎ 41 99 4363

The fabulous **Museo Romántico** is an essential part of Trinidad's delve into the past. With one of the country's finest and most valuable collections of colonial **furniture** packed into its fourteen rooms, this 1808-built mansion, formerly owned by Count Brunet, is well worth visiting.

Iglesia de la Santísima Trinidad

Francisco Javier Zerquera no.456 esq. F.H. Echerrí, Plaza Mayor • Mon–Sat 10.30am–1pm • Free • ☎ 41 99 3668

Looking down on Plaza Mayor is the city's main church, **Iglesia de la Santísima Trinidad**, also known as the Parroquial Mayor. Though there has been a church on this site since 1620, the structure now standing was officially finished in 1892. Among the pictures and paintings inside are a disproportionate number of impressively crafted **altars**, especially the Neo-Gothic structure in the central nave, with its mass of pointed spires. Most of them were created by Amadeo Fiogere. A Dominican friar assigned to the church in 1912, he set about livening up the interior, drawing on his own personal fortune to donate many of the images on display today.

Museo de Arquitectura "El Aldabonazo"

Ripalda e/ F.H. Echerrí y Rubén Martínez Villena, Plaza Mayor • Mon, Tues & Thu–Sat 9am–5pm, plus alternate Wednesdays & Sundays • Charge • ☎ 41 99 3208

The **Museo de Arquitectura** exhibits the components that make up a typical colonial-era house in Trinidad, but the small collection of fixtures and fittings won't keep you for long. The former residence of the Sánchez-Iznaga family – local aristocrats who made their fortune from sugar – the building was constructed in 1738 and then extended to its current size in 1785. Don't leave before taking a look at the quirky looking US-made Art Nouveau shower, dating from 1912. It's in a block out the back, off a courtyard vibrantly bedecked with plants.

Galería de Arte Benito Ortiz

Rubén Martínez Villena e/ Simón Bolívar y Ripalda, Plaza Mayor • Mon–Sat 9am–4pm • Free • Shop ☎ 41 99 6626

Worth a peek even if just for the ageing building itself, it won't take long to look round the **Galería de Arte Benito Ortiz**, whose displays comprise mostly temporary exhibitions of lacework, ceramics, sculpture and paintings – often with a quite original slant – and some soulless artwork for sale. Most of the exhibitions are housed in the six rooms upstairs, where you can also catch a perfectly framed view of the plaza through the open shutters of this colonial residence, built between 1800 and 1809.

Museo de Arqueología

Simón Bolívar esq. Rubén Martínez Villena, Plaza Mayor • Mon–Sat & alternate Sundays 9am–5pm • Charge • ☎ 41 99 3420

Set in another eighteenth-century house, the **Museo de Arqueología** holds a modest collection of pre-Columbian and colonial-era artefacts which vaguely chart the development of tools and other man-made objects, from the Paleolithic era of prehistory through the Mesolithic and Neolithic eras and up to the colonial period. Among the fragments of ceramics and primitive stone tools is a 2000-year-old **skeleton**, the bits and pieces buried with it providing insights into ancient burial rituals.

Museo de Historia Municipal

Simón Bolívar no.423 e/ Francisco Gómez Toro y Gustavo Izquierdo • Mon–Sat 9am–5pm • Charge • ☎ 41 99 4460

Housed in the **Palacio Cantero**, one of Trinidad's most impressive colonial buildings, the **Museo de Historia Municipal** contains various superb examples of nineteenth-century furniture that reflect the wealth and taste of one of Trinidad's most renowned sugar families, the **Canteros**. Built between 1827 and 1830 by the sugar baron José Mariano Borrell y Padrón, the building passed into the hands of María de Monserrate Fernández de Lara y Borrell in 1841 and a year later she married Justo German Cantero, a doctor by trade. Cantero became the most significant sugar-estate owner in the area, proprietor of some of its largest estates, including the Buena Vista; his portrait, along with that of his wife, hangs here. Though the museum's collection is not as broad and complete as that of the Museo Romántico, the building does have the advantage of its own **tower** whose spiral staircase you can ascend for some great **views** at the top, including a classic snapshot of the plaza.

Museo de la Lucha Contra Bandidos

Fernando Echerrí esq. Piro Guinart • Daily 9am–5pm • Charge • ☎ 41 99 4121

A block northwest of Plaza Mayor, the building housing the **Museo de la Lucha Contra Bandidos** is also host to Trinidad's trademark dome-topped yellow-and-white-trimmed **bell tower**. The tower is part of the eighteenth-century church and convent, the Iglesia and Convento de San Francisco de Asís, which previously stood on this site. Even if the museum's contents don't appeal to you, it's well worth paying the entrance fee to climb up the rickety wooden staircase to the top of the **tower**, which has a panoramic **view** over the city and across to the hills and coastline.

The **museum displays** are mostly themed around the post-1959 fight against counter-revolutionary groups – the **bandidos**, or bandits – who fought Castro's army during the years immediately following his seizure of power. Much of the fighting took place in the nearby Sierra del Escambray. Most striking, in the central courtyard, is a military truck and a motorboat mounted with machine gun stands, examples of the hardware employed by and against the *bandidos*.

Loma de la Vigía

Looking down on the colonial centre, beyond the end of Simón Bolívar, in a more run-down part of town, stand a dilapidated church, the **Ermita de Nuestra Señora de la Candelaria de la Popa del Barco** – known locally as **La Popa** – and the perennially almost-finished *Hotel Pansea Trinidad*. This is the last line of buildings before the town dissolves into the countryside and marks the start of a rewarding, fifteen-minute walk up the **Loma de la Vigía**, the hill against which Trinidad is set. A dirt track takes you to the summit where, within the grounds of a radio station, the lush landscape of the

5

Valle de los Ingenios on the other side of the hill is revealed, as well as views back across the town and down to the coast. Back down at La Popa you can cut across to the *Las Cuevas* hotel complex on the adjoining hillside, where non-guests can use the only publicly accessible **swimming pool** in the town.

Maqueta de Trinidad
Colón esq. Maceo • Tues–Sat 9am–5pm, Sun 9am–1pm • Charge • ☎ 41 99 3613

A painstakingly detailed model of Trinidad, the **Maqueta de Trinidad**, was, when it was unveiled in 2014, the original attraction in what has become the **Centro de Interpretación de la Ciudad**, a kind of heritage centre, and remains the headline draw here. The model took over two years to construct and provides some interesting, otherwise unavailable perspectives on the town – even the trees in back gardens are said to be accurate.

Parque Céspedes

Plaza Mayor may be the city centre for sightseers, but as far as the town's population is concerned, **Parque Céspedes** is Trinidad's main square. South of the cobbled streets that define the protected part of the town, at about the mid-point of Martí, Parque Céspedes may not have Plaza Mayor's enchanting surroundings but it's got a charm of its own and is markedly livelier, particularly in the evenings. Schoolchildren run out onto the square in the afternoon, while older locals head here at the end of the day to chat on the benches lining the three walkways. In the square's centre, a distinctive dome-shaped leafy canopy provides plenty of shade, while flower-frilled bushes encase the simple gardens, which are marked in each corner by a handsome royal palm. The stately yellow-columned entrance of the **Asamblea Municipal** building, the town council headquarters, occupies the square's entire northwestern side. Set back from the southwestern edge of the square, next to the school, are a cinema and a modest tiled-roof church.

Plaza Santa Ana

To the east of Trinidad, in a neighbourhood distinctly detached from the busy centre, where visitors are more conspicuous than elsewhere, the rather neglected **Plaza Santa Ana** is surrounded by houses, the derelict shell of the Iglesia Santa Ana church and the **Cárcel Real** (daily 10am–midnight; free; ☎41 99 642), a former prison now converted into the Plaza Santa Ana tourist complex. Coach-loads of tour groups stop here for the bar, restaurant and concerts in the Cárcel Real's courtyard but, disappointingly, very little is made of its history as a military jail. From here it's a short hop to the swimming pool at the *Hotel Las Cuevas*.

ARRIVAL AND DEPARTURE   **TRINIDAD**

By plane Just a few hundred metres out of town on Paseo Agramonte is Trinidad's tiny and rarely used airport (☎41 99 6393), serving occasional chartered flights only.

By bus Víazul buses navigate slowly into Trinidad's bus station (☎41 99 4448) at Piro Guinart e/ Maceo e Izquierdo, within easy walking distance of a large number of *casas particulares*. Be ready for the scrum that usually forms as locals tout their houses to passengers descending from the bus. Conectando Cuba buses drop off and pick up at the city hotels. Given Trinidad's popularity, it's well worth booking your departure tickets at least a few days in advance, at the station itself, as services often sell out.

Víazul destinations Bayamo (1 daily; 10hr 35min); Camagüey (1 daily; 5hr); Cayo Santa María (1 daily; 5hr 40min); Ciego de Ávila (1 daily; 2hr 50min); Cienfuegos (5 daily; 1hr 40min); Havana (2 daily; 6hr); Holguín (1 daily 9hr); Las Tunas (1 daily; 7hr 45min); Playa Girón (2 daily; 3hr); Playa Larga (1 daily 3hr 30min); Remedios (1 daily; 4hr); Sancti Spíritus (1 daily; 1hr 30min); Santa Clara (2 daily; 3hr); Santiago (1 daily; 12hr 30min); Varadero (2 daily; 6hr 30min).

Conectando Cuba destinations Cienfuegos (2 daily; 1hr 30min); Havana (1 daily; 6hr); Pinar del Rio (1 daily; 7hr 30min); Viñales (1 daily; 8hr).

5

By car Arriving on the coastal road by car from Cienfuegos and the west will bring you into town on Piro Guinart, which leads directly up to the two main roads cutting through the centre of the city, Martí and Maceo. From Sancti Spíritus and points east, the Circuito Sur takes cars closer to the *Las Cuevas* hotel, but a left turn at Lino Pérez will take you into *casa particular* territory.

By train On the southwestern edge of town, at the foot of General Lino Pérez, the train station (☎ 41 99 3348) serves only local destinations, including Manaca-Iznaga (2 daily; 30min) in the Valle de los Ingenios.

GETTING AROUND

Trinidad is small enough to get around on foot or bicycle, though walking is the best way to tackle its steep, cobblestone streets. If you want to make trips to the mountains or valley, you'll need to use motorized transport. The beach is within cycling distance but most people use the Trinibús (see page 280).

By bicitaxi *Bicitaxis* are available for areas where the streets are not cobbled. They congregate outside the *Las Begonias* café at Maceo esq. Simón Bolívar.

By car or scooter You can rent a car or scooter at both Cubacar at Lino Pérez no.366 e/ Maceo y Francisco Cadahia (Mon–Fri 8.30am–12.30pm & 1.30–5.30pm, Sat 8.30am–12.30pm; ☎ 41 99 6633) and Transgaviota on Frank País no.488 e/ Simón Bolívar y Fidel Claro (☎ 41 99 6236).

By taxi There are usually plenty of private taxis waiting on Piro Guinart near the bus station. A day-trip to the mountains or the valley can be negotiated for $500–1000CUP depending on the car, the season and the driver, while a trip to the beach should cost half that. For metered state taxis, call Cubataxi (☎ 41 99 8080).

INFORMATION

Tourist office The local branch of the national tourist information provider is less than a block from the bus station at Gustavo Izquierdo e/ Piro Guinart y Simón Bolívar (☎ 41 99 8258; daily 8.30am–4.30pm). You can book excursions here, pick up maps and leaflets and get visitor advice on just about anything.

ACCOMMODATION
SEE MAP PAGE 270

Trinidad has one of the best selections of **casas particulares** in the country, with more than a thousand spread throughout the city. An excellent local **booking agency**, Trinidad Rent (ⓦ trinidadrent.com), offers a secure and reliable way to book a *casa* in advance but avoid the common pitfalls of booking *casas* in Cuba (see page 36). Now with four good hotels right in the centre, several spread around the edges of town and more in construction, accommodation choices in Trinidad are better than ever before.

HOTELS

La Calesa Martí e/ Lino Pérez y Camilo Cienfuegos ⓦ hotelescubanacan.com. Opened in 2018, this boutique hotel near the main square is a great combination of the old and the new. In tip-top condition, the vintage stylings, like the rocking chairs in the lobby, sit very neatly with the modern touches, like the hot tub-sized pool on the long narrow interior patio and the panoramic photographs of Trinidad in the excellent rooms. Bathrooms are notably high spec with plenty of space and fancy walk-in showers. $$$

★ **Iberostar Grand Hotel Trinidad** José Martí no.262 e/ Lino Pérez y Colón ⓦ iberostar.com. This fabulously plush hotel on Parque Céspedes is full of understated luxury, with just one or two ostentatious touches. There's a delightfully reposeful central patio dotted with plants and a fountain, a cushy yet dignified smokers' lounge, a large buffet restaurant and forty fantastically furnished rooms, most with either a balcony or a terrace. $$$$

La Ronda Martí no.45 e/ Lino Pérez y Colón ⓦ hotelescubanacan.com. The comfortable, tastefully furnished rooms are set around a delightful central courtyard at this marvellous boutique hotel. The nineteenth-century building has a rooftop bar, brilliant for sunset drinks, and the staff have a reputation for good service. $$$

Villa Ma Dolores Carretera de Cienfuegos Km 1.5 ⓦ hotelescubanacan.com. Outside town, on the scenic banks of the moss-green Guaurabo River and popular with tour groups, the plain cabins here come with TVs, fridges and kitchenettes. Activities include horseriding and Cuban country music evenings. There's a swimming pool, restaurant and bar. See "Around Trinidad" map (page 281) for location. $

CASAS PARTICULARES

Casa de Carlos Sotolongo Peña Rubén Martínez Villena no.33 e/ Simón Bolívar y Francisco Javier Zerquera ☎ 41 99 4169, ✉ galinkapuig@gmail.com. Built in 1825, and occupied by sixth-generation Trinitarios, it doesn't get any more central than this spacious house right on the Plaza Mayor with a large colonial-era room inside as well as a modern one in an extension at the back. Both rooms have en-suite bathrooms and look onto a large courtyard. $

Casa de Carmen Hernández Martínez Maceo no.718 e/ Conrado Benítez y Ciro Redondo ☎ 52 51 2081. There are two double a/c bedrooms at this basic bungalow, one of the cheapest places to stay in town, and the pleasant

ACTIVITIES IN TRINIDAD

Travel agents and local individuals offer **horseriding**, usually around the foothills and parkland of the Sierra del Escambray, especially in Parque El Cubano. Local man Julio Muñoz (w trinidadphoto.com) offers excursions by horseback to the Valle de los Ingenios and runs a project promoting the humane treatment of horses. You can visit him at Martí no.401 e/ Fidel Claro y Santiago Escobar, where he keeps his own horse. For experienced riders *La Casona* (see page 275) is also a good option; they offer a guided excursion to the hamlet of La Pastora.The best travel agent to consult for horseriding is Trinidad Travels (see page 279).

Salsa and other Cuban **dance lessons** are offered by state and privately run enterprises alike. Enquire at the *Rincón de la Salsa* (see page 278), *Casa de la Música* (see page 277), the Paradiso travel agency (see page 279) or Trinidad Travels (see page 279). At *Casa Artex* the Paradiso agency (see page 277) offer excellent-value **percussion classes** which you can combine with dance classes.

Local jack-of-all-trades Julio Muñoz (see above) also runs a really worthwhile set of **photography workshops** (w trinidadphoto.com) catering to beginners as well as more advanced photographers. Finally, the hillside **swimming pool** at the *Hotel Las Cuevas*, to the northeast of the town, is open to non-guests for a fee.

owners are prepared to rent out the whole house (complete with kitchen and backyard patio) if you want total self-sufficiency. It's on a bumpy track in a more run-down part of town, only a few blocks from the bus station. $

Casa Mi Cuba Simón Bolívar no.309 e/ Maceo y Martí ☎ 41 99 6686, e juliobastida@gmail.com. This lovely house has been beautifully renovated and refurbished by the astute owner who lives round the corner; you can rent the whole thing, or just one of its two bedrooms. A delightfully inviting roof terrace, a cosy little patio and a well-equipped kitchen help to make this one of the most agreeable places to stay in the city if you want complete independence. $

★ **Casa Muñoz** Martí no.401 e/ Fidel Claro y Santiago Escobar w trinidadphoto.com. There's so much to admire and appreciate at this huge house, built in 1800, and it's not just the antique cabinets, armchairs, tables and clocks. The four large, high-spec guest rooms, one an impressive two-floor suite ideal for families, feature comfortable new colonial-style mahogany beds, hair dryers in the en-suite bathrooms and have even had 220-volt, three-pin plug sockets fitted specifically for British guests. English-speaking Julio, the proprietor, runs photography workshops, horseriding excursions and has an engaging photo gallery. There are two terraces, a patio, space for parking and wi-fi. $$

Casa Sandra y Victor Maceo no.613a e/ Pablo Pichs Girón y Piro Guinart ☎ 41 99 6444. Three large bedrooms, each with two double beds and its own bathroom, in a fabulously airy and clean modern house. Two of the rooms are upstairs, which is exclusively for guests; there's a balcony at the front and an impressive walled and balustraded terrace at the back, plus two communal rooms indoors. The food is excellent. $

Casa Sueca Juan Manuel Márquez no.70a e/ Piro Guinart y Ciro Redondo ☎ 41 99 8060. Three cavernous, simply styled rooms, one with three double beds and one with two, in a beautiful, tranquil colonial-era house at the top of town. Communal areas include an intimate central split-level patio. It's run by a mother and her English-speaking daughter, both accomplished cooks, who help to create a warm family atmosphere. $

Casa Tamargo Francisco Javier Zerquerra no.266 e/ Martí y Maceo ☎ 41 99 6669, e felixmatilde@yahoo. com. A very professionally and proudly run *casa particular*. A smart dining room opens up onto one of the prettiest patios in the city, full of hanging plants and shrubs, around which the three rooms are based. There's also a lovely roof terrace with a swinging chair and sunloungers. $

★ **La Casona** Frank País no.759 y final ☎ 41 99 8692, w lacasona759trinidad.com. This stunning *casa particular* on the edge of town is most remarkable for its enormous, landscaped grounds but the six capacious rooms, presented in an uncluttered rustic chic, are only slightly less impressive. There are several patio areas, a central dusty courtyard full of trees and surrounded by pretty gardens and stables where ten horses, available to guests, are kept. Up some steps is a terraced section with a large pool and a bar framed by views of the nearby mountains. There's a price tag to match this exclusivity. $$$

★ **Hostal Bastida** Maceo no.537 e/ Simón Bolívar y Piro Guinart ☎ 41 99 6686, e juliobastida@gmail. com. Three lovely en-suite rooms, one a very spacious triple with a streetside balcony, in a house full of artistic and antique touches. It's run by a down-to-earth, personable couple and their amiable manager, Elizabeth, who speaks faultless English and can help with anything you might need, including booking transport. There are three levels of attractive roof terraces, one with outstanding views which

5

peak at sunset. $

★ **Hostal Colina** Maceo no.374 e/ Lino Pérez y Colón ☎ 41 99 2319. This highly impressive *casa particular* comes with an immaculate split-level central patio with a hotel-standard bar, and countless plants creating a park-like feel. The perfectly restored section of the house from 1820 is authentically furnished and decorated, and contrasts nicely with the rest of the otherwise modern mini-complex. All three of the fantastic pastel bedrooms are en suite. $

Hostal Tailor Made Clemente Pereira no.175 e/ Piro Guinart y Fidel Claro ✉ hostal.trinidadtailormade@ gmail.com. Yosney, the friendly proprietor, works at the Infotur tourist information office so you won't find a better informed host when it comes to local knowledge for visitors. The house is well looked after with simple ground-floor and first-floor guest rooms, the latter with a large streetside balcony in this quiet corner of the centre. Excellent breakfasts are served on a red-walled downstairs terrace. $

Hostal El Tayaba Juan Manuel Márquez no.70 e/ Piro

Guinart y Ciro Redondo ☎ 41 99 2906, ✉ irsa221188@ gmail.com. Three beautifully appointed rooms in a *casa particular par excellence*. The house is dotted with decorative colonial curios and there's an enclosed central patio perfect for leisurely breakfasts. A rooftop terrace with views over the nearby church is an added bonus, as are the helpful hosts, who are always upbeat and friendly. $

★ **Hostal Zobeida** Maceo no.619 e/ Piro Guinart y Pablo Pichs Girón ☎ 41 99 4162, ✉ zobeidarguez@ yahoo.es. One of the best-appointed, most pristine homes in the city, the comfortable, modern and thoughtfully designed interior is luxurious by Cuban standards. Two of the guest rooms are in their own independent block upstairs, where there is a lovely terrace dining area; another faces onto a little patio downstairs and there are two more in a custom-built block out the back with their own porches and roof terrace. Excellent showers, and views to the coast from the roof terrace. $

EATING

SEE MAP PAGE 270

There are said to be almost one hundred **paladars** in Trinidad now and certainly their explosion in number over the last few years has provided the city with a really good choice of worthwhile eating-out options and relegated most of the state restaurants to the second division.

★ **Adita Café** Maceo no.452B esq. Francisco Javier Zerquera ⓦ aditacafe.com. The best pizzas in Trinidad, cooked in a wood-fired oven, are best enjoyed on the balcony level at Adita Café, which gets really busy and buzzy in the evenings. The mountain-lodge interior, with ceiling fans, dark wood benches and tables, is a distinct look in Trinidad making this place, overall, a standout venue. $$

★ **Giroud** Francisco Javier Zerquerra no.403 e/ Ernesto Valdés Muñoz y Rubén Martínez Villena ☎ 41 99 3818. Casual restaurant in a kind of trendy tavern whose central location and easy-going offer of pizzas and tapas ensure a lively atmosphere, with plenty of coming and going and an enjoyable informality. Alternative dishes include the memorable Giroud Burger, which comes in fried slices of plantain instead of bread, along with one patty, ham, tomato, lettuce, mayonnaise and cheese. One of the best options for atmosphere. $$$

Quince Catorce Simón Bolívar no.515 e/ F.H. Echerrí y Juan Manuel Márquez ☎ 41 99 4255. Brimming with antique furniture and features, its tables beautifully and strikingly set with vintage china, cutlery, candelabra and cut-crystal glassware, this self-styled restaurant-museum is an unusual option. With a captivating central patio, the option of rooftop dining, a live band and dancers thrown into the mix, the food takes second place to the experience, but the lobster is fresh and well-cooked and the fish, shrimp, pork or chicken alternatives are not bad either. $$$

★ **La Redacción** Maceo no.463 e/ Simón Bolívar y

Francisco Javier Zerquerra ⓦ laredaccioncuba.com. Cuban cuisine with a twist, and the twists are not confined to the food, though they are dotted all around the excellent menu, which you fill in like a multiple-choice questionnaire and hand to the waiter. They include a vegetarian section, where stuffed peppers and tomato salad with falafels make appearances; home-cooked bread, baked in the brick ovens found under the wooden roof of the rustic central patio; and the accompaniments to the perfectly cooked Cuban mains, like the sweet potato mash and gravy that come with the slow-roasted pork belly. The newspaper *El Liberal* was first edited on these premises in 1911, the inspiration for the name ("The Editorial Team") and table mats made from pages of this week's Cuban press. $$$

San José Maceo no.382 e/ Colón y Smith ⓦ restaurantebarsanjose.com. In many of Trinidad's paladars there's a definite sense of eating in what was once, or still is, a residential building. At San José, the complete conversion has removed that feeling and turned this into very much a restaurant, and a very pleasant and professional one too. The menu ranges from the likes of bargain seafood paella and spicy croquettes, to good-value mains of rice and chicken or pork, to pricier thermidor lobster. The patches of exposed brickwork are a nice touch and the smart air-conditioned bar a bonus. $$$

Sol Ananda Rubén Martínez Villena no.45 esq. Simón Bolívar ☎ 41 99 8281. Just off the Plaza Mayor in a superbly striking building, laid out like a decorative arts museum, this is a really good go at doing something different, offering dishes from an eclectic set of countries around the world on a hit-and-miss menu. Some of it works, like the decent salad selection, vegetable tempura, and *tamboril de vegetales*; and some of it doesn't – avoid the spicy lamb and potato stew. $$

Sol y Son Simón Bolívar no.283 e/ Frank País y Martí ☎41 99 2926. A long-standing paladar where huge portions of fairly priced mains like grilled pork in rum and fish in fruit sauce are fine but unremarkable, though with over two dozen main dishes they appear to have overstretched themselves somewhat. Nonetheless the beautiful, romantically lit courtyard, brimming with plant life, is a great spot for a meal. $$$

Taberna La Botija Juan Manuel Márquez no.71B esq. Piro Guinart ⊛labotija.trinidadhostales.com. The pizzas here are among the best in Trinidad, and fanatastic value, too. There's also pasta, sandwiches and classic Cuban cooking, served in a rustic, stone-walled old house, marked by earthy tones, picnic benches and an easy-going atmosphere. $$

★**Vista Gourmet** Callejón de Galdós e/ Ernesto V Muñoz y Callejón de Gallegos ☎41 99 6700. Though the menu is made up of ubiquitous Cuban dishes, what distinguishes this popular restaurant is the careful use of flavour and spices. The sauces that come with dishes like stewed lamb with mustard and chicken with garlic, onions and orange are neatly balanced and everything looks good on the plate. Ask for a table on the roof terrace or on the perimeter of the first-floor terrace for the great views over the town. $$$

DRINKING AND NIGHTLIFE

SEE MAP PAGE 270

The uncontested heart of Trinidad nightlife is the cluster of four **live music venues** just above and beyond the Plaza Mayor, all within two blocks of one another. Parque Céspedes provides the other focal point, especially at weekends when there are often open-air discos and live music geared to the large crowd of young locals who provide the atmosphere and numbers. Most of the bars are in the live music venues, restaurants, paladars and hotels, with only a few places existing solely as a place to go for a **drink**.

BARS AND CAFÉS

Bar Escalinata At the top end of Francisco Javier Zerquera, on the steps up to the Casa de la Múisca. A very central and agreeable outdoor spot for a drink on the shady terraced area half way up the very broad flight of steps next to the church. Easy going until the live bands of the Casa de la Música start up at night, and sometimes in the day too (see below).

Café Don Pepe Piro Guinart esq. F.H.Echerrí ☎41 99 3573. Large outdoor café on a leafy split-level patio enclosed by high walls and vegetation and as good as anywhere for a drawn-out coffee stop. The house special (the Don Pepe) is coffee with Havana Club and there are over twenty other hot coffee cocktails and nine cold ones. All the usual brews feature too.

La Canchánchara Rubén Martínez Villena e/ Piro Guinart y Ciro Redondo ☎41 99 6231. One of the best bars for live music, with a band here most days and nights. A long shady courtyard, lined with squat little benches, provides a sociable and laidback environment. The house special is a cocktail of rum, honey, lemon, water and ice.

La Casa de la Cerveza Maceo e/ Francisco Javier Zerquerra y Simón Bolívar ☎41 99 8416. This outdoor beer-specialist is located in the *Ruinas del Teatro Brunet*, the ruined remains of Trinidad's first theatre, under whose arches and around whose wide-open terrace its parasol-shaded benches and tables are spread. Select from around a dozen beers, mostly lagers and many of them Dutch and one of which, the local Bucanero, is, unusually, on tap.

Real Café Real no.54 e/ Simón Bolívar y Piro Guinart ☎54 08 2321. A capacious site where the lofty open front room of a colonial residence leads through to a great set of spaces, including a very cool rustic brick bar and the delightful garden terrace. Loosely divided into several equally inviting areas the dappled light, ample elbow room and comfy seating in the garden make this one of the most reposeful retreats in the centre. Food served here too.

El Rintintin Simón Bolívar no.553 esq. Juan Manuel Márquez ☎41 99 3685. Also a below-average restaurant but it's the bar here, on a pocket-size rooftop terrace with close-by views of the symbolic Trinidad tower and beyond to the hills, that make it worth a visit and great for a sunset drink. The house special cocktail is a refreshing blend of rum, sugar, lemon and sparkling water.

Trinidad Colonial Maceo no.402 esq. Colón ☎41 99 6473. With one of the only authentic colonial-style bar counters in Trinidad, this restaurant-bar is one of the best places in town for straight-up drinking, though there is live music staged here too. A spiral staircase leads up to a roof terrace offering great views.

MUSIC VENUES

Casa Artex Lino Pérez e/ Francisco Cadahía y Martí ☎41 99 6486. One of Trinidad's less reliable music venues, in an old colonial mansion near Parque Céspedes. Puts on Cuban dance and music shows in its spacious central courtyard; when there's no live music, it functions as a bar and pumps out modern salsa and reggaeton.

Casa de la Cultura Francisco Javier Zerquerra no.406 esq. Ernesto Valdes Muñoz ☎41 99 4308. Not a live music venue as such, but it's worth dropping by to check out the weekly programme usually posted outside this community arts centre. A live trova performance or something similar usually features at some point. The free performances are as likely to be in the day as at night.

★**Casa de la Música** Francisco Javier Zerquerra no.3 ☎41 99 6622. Drawing the largest crowds in town, this is

5

Trinidad's busiest, most animated spot for big-band salsa and guaranteed dancing. Performances usually take place halfway up the broad flight of steps leading up to the venue itself, leaving the walled-in terrace at the top, officially the main concert area, comparatively underused, though it is used for daytime concerts and there is sometimes a disco here from 11.30pm. Local and national Cuban groups play most nights, starting at around 9pm and you can get drinks from the *Bar Escalinata* (see page 277).

★**Casa de la Trova** F.H. Echerrí no.29 e/ Patricio Lumumba y Jesús Menéndez, Plazuela Segarte ☎41 99 6445. Of similar renown to the Casa de la Música close by, this is a much smaller, more intimate, tightly packed place, where bands are almost shoulder to shoulder with dancers and drinkers. It's more likely to stage guitar soloists and traditional trova and son groups than the large salsa outfits that play at its neighbour. Expect to see several groups in one night.

Discoteca Ayala Loma de la Vigía ☎41 99 6133. The only nightclub in Trinidad is buried in a hillside cave network making a night here an exceptional experience – whether or not the reggaeton, house, salsa and pop floats your boat.

Quieter in low season than elsewhere in town.

Palenque de los Congos Reales F.H. Echerrí no.33 e/ Francisco Javier Zerquerra y Patricio Lumumba ☎41 99 4512. A walled-in, open-air venue under a canopy of branches where energetic rumba and other African-Cuban dance shows and musical performances are staged. There are several different shows and groups every day, the first usually starting around 2pm, the last at 11pm.

Rincón de la Salsa Rubén Martínez Villena no.15 esq. Francisco Javier Zerquerra ☎41 99 6470. A terrace tucked away behind a restaurant building and elevated above the street, with a bar and a dinky little performance area. A very pleasant spot to catch some live music. Salsa lessons take place here, too.

Ruinas de Segarte Jesús Menéndez e/ Galdos y Juan Manuel Márquez, Plazuela Segarte. Free outdoor stage venue hosting live traditional Cuban music most nights. You can sit at the bar or on the picnic benches on the cosy and atmospheric little roof-covered terrace. There's not much room for dancing but that doesn't usually stop anyone. One of the more relaxed music venues.

ENTERTAINMENT

Cine Romelio Cornelio Antonio Guiteras, Parque Céspedes ☎41 99 3458. The principal local cinema shows the widest variety of films in the city. Closed Mon.

SHOPPING
SEE MAP PAGE 270

Trinidad is a great place to buy **textiles**, with a wide selection in the street markets of the old town. There are various kinds of **arts and crafts** shops, with a particular concentration on the old-town stretch of Francisco Javier Zerquerra.

Album Halfway up the steps to the Casa de la Música, Francisco Javier Zerquerra no.3 ☎41 99 6622. One of Trinidad's best options for Cuban music, with a wide selection on CD. You can listen before you buy.

Casa del Tabaco Maceo esq. Francisco Javier Zerquerra ☎41 99 6256. The best-stocked cigar shop in the city, where you select boxes or singles of some of the most renowned Cuban brands; sells rum and coffee too.

Galería Taller Deustua Maceo no.396 e/ Colón y Smith ⓦgaleriadeustua.com. Simple but very attractive clay pots of every shape and size in lovely pastel blues, greens, yellows and white. Plates, bowls and teapots too.

Tienda de Arte Amelia Peláez Simón Bolívar esq.

Ernesto Valdés Muñoz ☎41 99 3590. Among the town's shops (as opposed to its markets), this place sells the largest selection of handmade crafts, paintings, jewellery and more touristy bits and pieces.

Tienda de Casa de la Trova F.H. Echerrí no.29 e/ Patricio Lumumba y Jesús Menéndez, Plazuela Segarte ☎41 99 6445. By local standards this is a well-stocked music shop, attached to a live music venue, selling contemporary and traditional Cuban music on CD.

Tienda de Mario David Pumariega Mesa Piro Guinart no.252 e/ Francisco Gómez Toro y Rubén Martínez Villena ☎41 99 3162. Mayito, as he is known, runs the only antique shop in town. Its small rooms are full of glassware, ceramics, clocks, paintings and all sorts of bric-a-brac.

La Vega Lino Pérez esq. Martí ☎41 99 6149. An excellent little cigar store with a good stock of rum too, facing the main square, Parque Céspedes.

DIRECTORY

Banks and exchange Banco Financiero Internacional (Mon–Fri 8.30am–3.30pm) is at Camilo Cienfuegos esq. Martí, and Banco de Crédito y Comercio (Mon–Fri 8am–3pm & Sat 8–11am) at Martí no.264 e/ Colón y Francisco Javier Zerquerra. You can change travellers' cheques and withdraw money with Visa or MasterCard at both, and the latter has two 24hr ATMs. The CADECA *casas de cambio* are at Martí no.166 e/ Lino Pérez y Camilo Cienfuegos (Mon–Sat 8.30am–8pm, Sun 1–8pm) and Maceo e/ Camilo Cienfuegos y Lino Pérez (Mon–Sat 8.30–noon & 12.30–7pm, Sun 9am–noon & 12.30–5pm).

Health Clínica Internacional at Lino Pérez no.103 esq.

5

TOURS FROM TRINIDAD

Trinidad's **state travel agents**, particularly Cubatur, are well used to offering general information and advice on sightseeing in town, but their principal purpose is to book hotel accommodation and sell organized excursions (see below); you can also use them to book a taxi or a rental car or buy Víazul bus tickets. It's a good idea to consult them before making a trip to Topes de Collantes, itself geared towards organized visits, and to a lesser extent the Valle de los Ingenios. The town also has an excellent **independent agent**, Trinidad Sightseeing. Run by locals, it offers more flexibility than the state-run outfits.

TOUR OPTIONS

The state travel agents offer more or less the same sets of tours for the same prices. The most popular organized excursions in Topes de Collantes are to **Parque Guanayara** by truck or jeep and the hike to the **Salto del Caburní.** There are several variations on trips to the **Valle de los Ingenios** but most focus on Manaca-Iznaga, San Isidro de los Destiladeros or both. An organized excursion by catamaran to **Cayo Blanco** is the only way to visit this offshore cay, around 5km south of the Península de Ancón. Ecotur is one of the best agents for organized **trekking**, including an exclusive trip to the Alturas de Banao ecological reserve, in the hills between Trinidad and the provincial capital. Most excursions include a lunch and there is normally a minimum of at least three people required.

Trinidad Sightseeing offers a range of **hiking**, **walking** and **horseback** tours and all sorts of other activities at competitive prices; get in touch for costs and to work out a tour that suits you.

TRAVEL AGENTS

Cubanacán Vicente Suyama no.13 esq. Pablo Picho Girón (daily 8am–12.30pm & 2.30–6pm; ☎41 99 6320).

Cubatur Maceo esq. Francisco Javier Zerquerra (daily 8am–8pm; ☎41 99 6314) and Simón Bolívar no.352 e/ Maceo y Izquierdo (daily 8am–8pm; ☎41 99 6368).

Havanatur Lino Pérez no.368 e/ Maceo y Francisco Cadahía (Mon–Fri 8am–noon & 1–4pm, Sat 8am–noon; ☎41 99 6317).

Paradiso Foyer of Casa Artex at Lino Pérez e/ Francisco Cadahía y Martí (Mon–Fri 8am–noon & 2–6pm, Sat & Sun 9am–noon; ☎41 99 6486).

Trinidad Sightseeing Calle Santa Ana (daily 8.30am–6pm, ⌨trinidadsightseeing.com).

Anastasio Cardenas (☎41 99 6492), which has a 24hr pharmacy, should cover most medical needs. For an ambulance call ☎41 99 2362. Serious cases may be referred to the Clínico Quirúrgico Camilo Cienfuegos (☎41 32 4017), the provincial hospital in Sancti Spíritus.

Immigration and visas For tourist cards and visa issues go to the Immigration Office (Tues & Thurs 9am–noon; ☎41 99 6650), near the police station on Julio Cuevas Díaz.

Police Call ☎106 in emergencies. The main station is at Julio Cuevas Díaz e/ Pedro Zerquerra y Anastasio Cardenas (☎41 99 6900), to the south of town.

Post office The only branch providing international services is at Maceo no.418–420 e/ Colón y Francisco Javier Zerquerra (Mon–Sat 8am–8pm).

Wi-fi The main public wi-fi spots are around the *Casa de la Música*, Parque Céspedes and the Clínica Internacional. You can buy wi-fi cards at the ETECSA Telepunto centre on Lino Pérez no.274 at Parque Céspedes (daily 8.30am–7pm) and the *Dulcinea* café at Maceo esq. Simón Bolívar (daily 7.30am–10pm), which has a bank of computers with which you can use wi-fi cards. The most reliable connection in town is at the *Iberostar Grand Hotel Trinidad* where you can also buy wi-fi cards from the hotel bar, but you are obliged to buy a drink too.

Península de Ancón

A narrow 8km finger of land curling like a twisted root out into the placid waters of the Caribbean, set against a backdrop of rugged green mountains, the **Península de Ancón** enjoys a truly fantastic and picturesque setting. Covered predominantly in low-lying scrub, the peninsula itself is unspoilt yet unfortunately unenchanting once you move away from the coastline. The real draw here is the several enticing **beaches**,

5

including Playa Ancón, and an idyllic stretch of mostly undisturbed seashore which is begging to be explored.

Much of the 7km journey from Trinidad is a glorious ride along the coast, with the turquoise blue of the Caribbean just a few metres away and the lofty mountains of the Sierra del Escambray rarely out of sight.

Playa Ancón

A gentle curve of broad beach at the far end of the peninsula, **Playa Ancón** has put the area on the tourist map and has an encouragingly natural feel, with shrubs and trees creeping down to the shoreline. As one of the largest and longest beaches on the south coast of Cuba, there's more than enough fine-grained golden sand here to keep a small army of holiday-makers happy. There's also decent **snorkelling** and **diving** in the waters and reefs around these shores. A small watersports club operating from a wooden sun shelter near the *Hotel Ancón* rents out sun-loungers, pedal boats, kayaks, and snorkelling equipment.

La Boca

Away from Playa Ancón's hotels, the signs of package tourism die out almost immediately, leaving the rest of the peninsula and the adjoining coastline largely unaffected by the nearby developments. Continuing west from Playa Ancón, the quiet coastal road runs 7km along the mostly rocky shore to **LA BOCA**, a waterfront fishing village due west of Trinidad, known simply as Boca. It has remained comparatively untouched by the hordes of international tourists settling upon Playa Ancón nearby, but is a popular holiday spot for Cubans, and around twenty *casas particulares*. Most of the shoreline in Boca is rocky but it does have its own small, patchy beach, **Playa del Río**, at the mouth of the river that gives the village its name. Though a lot of the time the beach and the village are very tranquil, they come alive at weekends and become particularly animated throughout July and August, when Boca throngs with Trinitarios, day-trippers and Cuban holiday-makers. At these times music blasts out over the seafront and the village's main drag is lined with snack stalls serving home-made pizzas, sandwiches and soda.

ARRIVAL AND GETTING AROUND   PENÍNSULA DE ANCÓN

By Trinibus The best way to get between the Península de Ancón and Trinidad is by Trinidad Bus Tour, better known as the Trinibus, the tourist double-decker bus service running between the two, usually four times a day, leaving Trinidad at 9am, 11am, 2pm and 5pm and returning at 10am, 12.30pm, 3.30pm and 6pm. In Trinidad there are several pick-up points including just outside the Cubatur office on Maceo; on the peninsula, hop on at the *Hotel Ancón*, or flag

---

DIVING, SNORKELLING AND FISHING AROUND ANCÓN

Marina Trinidad (daily 8am–5pm; ☎41 99 6205, ✉comercial@marlin.tdad.tur.cu), opposite *Hotel Ancón*, offers **diving** excursions to licensed divers. Diving courses, including beginners' classes, are also available (✉alfredo@marlin.tdad.tur.cu). **Fishing excursions** include deep-sea fishing, trolling for big game, and bottom fishing. These trips are aimed at groups of four to six anglers, but if you're prepared to pay the whole cost yourself you can go with fewer people.

Two of the most popular **snorkelling excursions** are to **Cayo Blanco**, a narrow islet 8km from the peninsula, and **Cayo Macho**, a smaller speck of land even further out also referred to as Cayo Las Iguanas. Each has its own coral reef, where the waters teem with parrotfish, trumpetfish and moray eels. Trips on catamarans last around six hours and usually include a lunch. The area is known for its easy diving with good visibility, minimal currents and an abundance of vertical coral walls. You'll need your passport for any trip leaving from the marina.

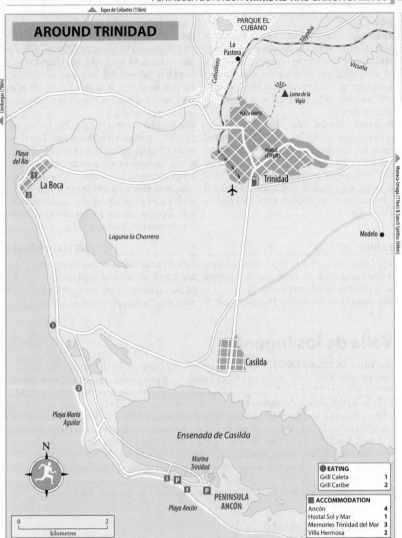

it down in Boca.

By bike or scooter You can hire bikes and scooters from Motoclub (daily 9am–4pm) at the *Brisas Trinidad del Mar* hotel in Playa Ancón (see page 282) or from *casas particulares* in Boca.

ACCOMMODATION

SEE MAP PAGE 281

There are currently only a handful of **hotels** on the peninsula, all of them family-oriented all-inclusives right on the beach, with luxury promised by the in-progress *Meliá Trinidad Península* (⊛melia.com). It's scheduled to open in 2023.

The casas particulares in Boca, many of them lined up along the main road through the village, provide great alternatives for a fraction of the price but as a base for the beach they only work if you're prepared to cycle (some *casas* rent out bikes) or use the four-times-a-day Trinibus (see above) to get there.

5

HOTELS

Ancón Playa Ancón ⊕hotelescubanacan.com. With its Soviet-influenced architecture, this is the peninsula's oldest hotel and some of the rooms are looking tired. Nevertheless, it's on the widest, most sociable section of beach and has a reasonable set of facilities – including a large swimming pool, two tennis courts, a basketball hoop, volleyball net and pool tables. $\overline{\underline{S}}\overline{\underline{S}}$

Memories Trinidad del Mar Playa Ancón ⊕memoriesresorts.com. The newest of the established hotels has unremarkable rooms and basic food but memorable outdoor areas, featuring a lookout tower with views over the peninsula, a twisting pool divided by bridges and a delightful little square, surrounded by accommodation blocks, modelled on the Plaza Mayor in Trinidad. $\overline{\underline{S}}\overline{\underline{S}}\overline{\underline{S}}$

CASAS PARTICULARES

Hostal Sol y Mar Ave. del Mar no.87, La Boca ☎41 98 4365, ✉jjpomesf6401@nauta.cu. Facing the seafront on the main drag in the village, this is one of Boca's best *casas*. Guests have their own little living room while bedrooms look onto the spacious, florid garden at the side of this pretty house. The food here is excellent and the owner, Joaquín, very personable. $\overline{\underline{S}}$

Villa Hermosa Carretera Ancón no.211, La Boca ☎53 25 5661, ✉villahermosa.trinidad@gmail.com. Just outside the village, set back from the road on its own plot of land, this bungalow with a wraparound porch is in a wonderfully peaceful spot, surrounded by the rows of garlic, onion, beans, cassava and chilli peppers growing here. The two rooms are simple but very pleasant and comfortable with a/c, en-suite bathroom and their own section of porch. There are three bikes available for rent. $\overline{\underline{S}}$

EATING

SEE MAP PAGE 281

Grill Caleta 3km south of La Boca. Simple, mid-priced seafood at an equally simple, no-frills roadside grill set back about 150m from the rocky coastline here. $\overline{\underline{S}}\overline{\underline{S}}$

Grill Caribe About 2km north of Playa Ancón ☎41 99 6241. An outdoor restaurant on a platform above a tiny strip of beach, serving freshly caught seafood like shrimp in hot sauce and lobster. Ideally, you should aim to stop by at sunset when the atmosphere is tantalizingly calm. $\overline{\underline{S}}\overline{\underline{S}}$

Valle de los Ingenios

The **VALLE DE LOS INGENIOS**, a sprawling, open valley bordered by the eastern slopes of the Sierra del Escambray, was once one of Cuba's most productive agricultural areas. In its heyday it was crammed with dozens of the sugar estates and refineries on which Trinidad built its wealth during the eighteenth and nineteenth centuries. Today just one functioning refinery remains, but the remnants and ruins of the manor houses and mills that occupied the estates remain dotted throughout the valley, the most intact example at **Manaca-Iznaga** – though **San Isidro de los Destiladeros** is a more interesting site. You can get to the former on a sporadically functioning **tourist train** from Trinidad which pulls rickety wooden carriages on an hour-long ride to the estate through rich layers of rural countryside, rattling and puffing between thick bush and small forests, then into open, lush grazing land and maize fields, with green hills and low mountains forming the backdrop.

Manaca-Iznaga estate

13km east of Trinidad • Tower daily 9am–4pm • Charge

The tiny train station at **Manaca-Iznaga** is two minutes' walk from the old house and tower, the main attractions at this former estate. Most people can't resist heading straight for the 45m **tower**, built by one of the most successful sugar planters in Cuba, Alejo María del Carmen e Iznaga. You can climb the precarious wooden staircase to one of the tower's seven levels for views of the entire valley, a patchwork of sugar cane fields, wooded countryside and farmland dotted with palm trees and the odd house. This lofty perspective over the surrounding area would have been used by plantation overseers for surveillance of their enslaved people working in the fields below. The huge bell that once hung in the tower, used to ring out the start and finish of the working day, now sits near the front of the **Casa Hacienda**, the Iznaga family's estate mansion, though they spent more of their time at their residences in Trinidad and Sancti Spíritus. The building's main function is as a gift shop, bar and **restaurant**, the latter occupying a terrace overlooking a small garden. Over the road are the scattered dwellings of the old slave barracks, now converted into family homes.

San Isidro de los Destiladeros

10km east of Trinidad • 24hr • Charge

The evocative ruins of the oldest estate house, or **Casa Hacienda**, in the valley, dating from 1838, are closer to Trinidad than the Manaca-Iznaga estate but harder to get to as the train line does not pass close by, nor any other public transport. **San Isidro de los Destiladeros**, the name of the estate and the sugar refinery that once stood here, is less contrived than Manaca-Iznaga, with no gift shop or restaurant, but more complete. Much of the surviving architecture is completely dilapidated but you can still trace the layout of the site and the structure of the buildings. The estate house itself, with its arch-lined terrace, appears largely intact but has in fact been brought back from what was just a shell twenty years ago.

Opposite is the squat three-storey bell tower and while the rest of the estate is still in ruin, the stumps of stone walls allow you to trace the ancillary buildings, including the slave quarters. The brick foundations of the boiling house, where the raw cane juice was refined, are strikingly identifiable, standing testament to the existence of the refinery itself.

ARRIVAL AND DEPARTURE

VALLE DE LOS INGENIOS

By tourist train The diesel train to Manaca-Iznaga (1hr) has now all but completely replaced the unreliable steam trains that used to ply the route, but is constantly breaking down itself – this service remains unreliable. The service leaves Trinidad at 9.30am, and returns from Manaca-Iznaga around 1.30pm. Tickets can be bought in advance from Infotur or the state travel agents in Trinidad, or at the station in Trinidad from 8.30am on the day.

By local train Though less of a novelty, commuter trains are more reliable than the tourist service, and at a fraction of the cost they are worth considering. Two daily services currently leave Trinidad in the early hours of the morning; the Manaca-Iznaga journey time is 30min. The official line on these local trains is that passenger safety cannot be guaranteed and therefore their use by tourists is frowned upon, but you are unlikely to be stopped.

By car To drive to Manaca-Iznaga, follow the main road to Sancti Spíritus, the Circuito Sur, from the east of Trinidad for around 12km and turn left; San Isidro is 2km closer to Trinidad and is a right turn.

Sierra del Escambray

Rising up to the northwest of Trinidad are the steep, pine-coated slopes of the Guamuhaya mountains, more popularly known as the **Sierra del Escambray**. This area is home to some of the most spectacular scenery in Cuba, though its highest peak – the Pico San Juan – is a modest 1140m high. A large proportion of this mountain range sits within the borders of the neighbouring provinces of Cienfuegos and Villa Clara but the heart of the visitor park and hiking area, the **Gran Parque Natural Topes de Collantes**, is in Sancti Spíritus province.

Topes de Collantes

The mountain resort of **Topes de Collantes** is a kind of hotel village, its unsubtle architecture completely out of keeping with the beauty of its surroundings – as is the road clumsily blasted down the middle of the resort. Though there are a couple of likeable museums around the village, and one or two modest venues for eating and drinking, the main reason to make the trip up here is to use the resort as a base for **hiking** along designated **trails**, which you can follow as part of an organized excursion from Trinidad or independently by first visiting the park's information centre, next to the huge **sundial** at the centre of the resort.

5

At the heart of Topes de Collantes is its founding building, the monstrous **Sanatorio Topes de Collantes**, commissioned in 1936 by Fulgencio Batista, the Cuban dictator overthrown by Fidel Castro and his rebels. Originally a huge tuberculosis clinic and once referred to as the Sanatorio General Batista, it represented Batista's Mussolini-esque

HIKING AT GRAN PARQUE NATURAL TOPES DE COLLANTES

If you want to go **hiking** around Topes de Collantes, the best way to do so is to book an **organized excursion** in Trinidad (see page 279). If you arrive **independently** you won't be permitted access to all areas of this protected park, but at the Centro de Información, the park's **information centre** (see page 285), you can get advice on the trails you can visit without a guide.

The Centro de Información is also where you pay if you want to follow any of the **official trails**, each of them located within smaller parks highlighted below. There are no clearly defined borders between these parks, which have been designated as separate entities primarily for marketing purposes (note that Parque el Nicho, over the border in the province of Cienfuegos and characterized by a network of countless waterfalls, is covered in Chapter 4). Typically, trails here are well marked and shady, cutting through dense woodlands, smothered in every kind of vegetation – from needle-straight conifers to bushy fern and grassy matted floors – opening out here and there for breathtaking views of the landscape.

There's a charge for the trails if you visit independently. The English-speaking staff at the centre can advise you on the various trails and parks, but if you want a guide to accompany you, you will need to have booked an organized excursion in advance. Several of the parks have their own restaurants, catering predominantly to groups.

As to **what to bring**, you may need sturdy hiking boots if it's pouring with rain (which it often is up here); otherwise trainers should be adequate. The air is a few degrees cooler than in the city or on the beach, so you may need more than just a T-shirt.

PARQUE ALTIPLANO

As well as being the location of all the local hotels, **Parque Altiplano** contains the area's most popular target for hikers, the fantastically situated 62m-high **Caburní waterfall**, surrounded by pines and eucalyptus trees at the end of a 2.5km trek down steep inclines and through dense forest. Independent access is at the northernmost point of Topes de Collantes. There are several other relatively easy trails within this park, including the **Vegas Grandes**, which also finishes at a waterfall.

PARQUE GUANAYARA

Fifteen kilometres north of the hotels, **Parque Guanayara** is host to one of the area's most scenic hiking routes. The gentler hike here follows the Guanayara River for a couple of kilometres up to the **Salto El Rocío**, a beautiful waterfall, and the **Poza del Venado**, a natural pool; along the way it incorporates some memorable views of Pico San Juan.

PARQUE CODINA

The focal point of **Parque Codina** is **Hacienda Codina**, an old Spanish coffee-growing ranch where you can eat and drink. From the ranch there are easily manageable walks, some no more than 1km, into the forest. Several trails lead to **La Batata**, a subterranean river at the foot of a lush green valley where you can bathe in the cool waters of the cave. You access this area independently from the southwestern corner of Topes de Collantes.

PARQUE EL CUBANO

Just 5km from Trinidad, **Parque El Cubano** is the most popular location for **horseriding**. The route here, which can also be followed on foot, takes in a *campesino* house and the remains of a colonial sugar ranch, as well as rivers, brooks and waterfalls.

desire to leave a lasting legacy, a monument to his own power and influence. It wasn't completed until 1957 and today operates as the *Kurhotel*, an anti-stress centre and hotel.

This mountainous area has its own **microclimate** and is always a couple of degrees cooler than Trinidad. It's also far more likely to rain here than down by the coast, and as the heavens open almost every afternoon for much of the year, it's a good idea to get up here early if you're visiting on a day-trip.

Museo de Arte Cubano Contemporaneo

350m southeast of the sundial • Daily 8am–8pm • Charge

During the 1980s the hotels of Topes de Collantes were filled with hundreds of artworks by Cuban artists of national renown. Scores of these are now installed in the rooms of the engaging **Museo de Arte Cubano Contemporaneo**, opened in 2008 on the main road through Topes de Collantes, 350m before the information centre on the approach from Trinidad. In all there are some sixty paintings by artists such as Rubén Torres Llorca, Zaida del Río and Tomás Sánchez, as well as some sculptures and prints. The pretty museum building, with its colourful stained-glass windows, dates from 1944, and was owned by a Cuban senator before the Revolution and its subsequent appropriation by the state.

Casa del Café

800m southwest of the sundial • Daily 7am–7pm • Free

A neatly packaged shop, café and small museum near the *Hotel Los Helechos*, the **Casa del Café** is a simple homage to coffee, which has been grown on the slopes of these mountains for centuries. Tools used in local coffee production are on display, including an industrial-size nineteenth-century grinder outside. You can buy packets of coffee in the shop, or just sip a brew on the veranda.

ARRIVAL AND DEPARTURE | TOPES DE COLLANTES

By taxi Given the lack of public transport and the dangerous roads, a taxi is the best way of getting here unless you're on an organized excursion. There are no taxis based at Topes de Collantes, but most drivers are prepared to wait for you at the resort.

By car The turn-off for the dangerously winding road into the mountains is about 3km west of Trinidad along the road to Cienfuegos; Topes de Collantes is 14km along.

INFORMATION

Information centre Next to the sundial in the centre of Topes de Collantes (daily 8am–3pm; ☎ 42 54 0117 or ☎ 42 54 0348, ✉ comercial@topescom.co.cu). Head here for information on hiking in the park independently and to pay trail fees.

ACCOMMODATION

HOTELS

Los Helechos 350m south of the sundial ⓦ gaviota-grupo.com. Rooms here have balconies and are pleasantly light and airy. There's a disco and a restaurant in a separate, marginally more run-down building, as well as a bowling alley and a large indoor pool. $$

Kurhotel 200m northeast of the sundial ⓦ gaviota-grupo.com. This striking white monolith of a building was created by Batista as a rehabilitation sanitorium, and today many of the Cubans staying here are on physical therapy programmes. Surrounded by forest, this giant of a health retreat is well located for getting back to nature. $$

Villa Caburní 400m north of the sundial ⓦ gaviota-grupo.com. The best of the Topes de Collantes hotels is at the start of the trail to the eponymous waterfall, featuring dinky bungalows, each with its own little lawn and parking space, spread around a grassy area like a model 1950s American village. Most have two double rooms, bathroom and kitchenette, and all have wonderful views of the mountains. $

CASAS PARTICULARES

El Manantial Mangos Pelones, 6km south of the Topes de Collantes hotels on the road towards Trinidad ☎ 42 54 0231, ✉ manantial@nauta.cu. A patchwork house of wood and concrete on a little ranch, 300m from the nearest house. Most of the food for meals is grown on site and cooked on a wood-burning stove. There are two simple

5

rooms with no a/c (less necessary in the cooler hills) but each with their own bathroom. $\overline{5}$

EATING

Several of the Topes de Collantes parks feature their own **restaurants**, all more geared to groups on organized excursions than impromptu visits from independent hikers. It's a good idea to ask at the information office to find out which of the restaurants are expecting visitors, as those that are not may not open at all.

Casa La Gallega Parque Guanayara. There's not normally a great deal of choice at this ranch building surrounded by lush greenery, and if no tour groups are expected there may be nothing at all, but whatever the main dish of the day is (most likely roast chicken), it'll be good, hearty Cuban country food with plenty of extras. $\overline{55}$

Mi Retiro 3km south of the Topes de Collantes resort on the road to Trinidad. The most accessible of the hiking-trail restaurants; choose from roast pork, ham steak or omelettes, all moderately priced and served on a veranda on top of a small hill in a scenic valley. $\overline{55}$

Sancti Spíritus

The provincial capital, also called **SANCTI SPÍRITUS**, sits in the dead centre of the island, 30km inland and around 70km east of Trinidad by road. There's less to do and see here than in neighbouring provincial capitals, but it nevertheless makes a good stopover if you're making the journey between Havana and Santiago – few visitors stay for more than a night or two, but as one of Cuba's original seven *villas* founded by Diego Velázquez in the early 1500s, it has plenty of historic character and holds some appeal as one of the country's least touristy original cities.

Plaza Serafín Sánchez

The logical place to begin exploring is the central square, **Plaza Serafín Sánchez**, from where all the museums, and most of the best restaurants and music venues are a short walk away. Though it's one of the more pleasant and lively spaces in the centre of town, the square lacks the laidback, sociable feel characteristic of other Cuban town squares. That said, it does attract an enthusiastic young crowd on weekend nights and though it's disturbed by the traffic passing through on all sides during the day, there are plenty of rickety metal seats around the simple bandstand for a sit-down in the shade.

On the corner of Máximo Gómez and Solano is the provincial library, the majestic **Biblioteca Provincial Rubén Martínez Villena**, built between 1927 and 1929, and resembling a colonial theatre with its balustraded balconies, Corinthian columns and arched entrance. Connecting to the southeast corner of the square is the main shopping street, the pedestrianized section of Independencia known as **Boulevard**. The square's southwestern corner is occupied by the eminently missable Museo de Historia Natural.

Museo Provincial

Máximo Gómez no.3, Plaza Serafín Sánchez • Mon–Thurs & Sat 9am–5pm, Sun 8am–noon • Charge • ☎ 41 32 7435

The **Museo Provincial** showcases a hotchpotch of historical objects dating mostly from the nineteenth and twentieth centuries. The photos of Castro and his band of merry men entering Sancti Spíritus on January 6, 1959, on their victory march to Havana, are as engaging as anything else on display.

Iglesia Parroquial Mayor

Agramonte Oeste no.58 • Daily 9am–4.30pm • Free • ☎ 41 32 4855

Sancti Spíritus's main church, and its oldest building, **Iglesia Parroquial Mayor** was built in 1680. With the dramatic exception of an unusual blue-and-gold arch spanning the top section of the nave, the interior is underwhelmingly simple, but you can scale the bell tower for the best available views of the city, and a small charge,

Museo de Arte Colonial

Plácido no.74 esq. Avenida Jesús Menéndez • Tues–Sat 9.30am–5pm, Sun 8am–noon • Charge • ☎ 41 32 5455

One block east of the river is the **Museo de Arte Colonial**, easily the best museum in Sancti Spíritus, with a collection of precious colonial furniture and household objects. The mansion in which it is housed was built for the wealthy sugar plantation Valle-Iznaga family, who spent most of their time in and around Trinidad, and the museum has been restored to resemble a typical nineteenth-century Cuban aristocratic residence. Three bedrooms, drawing and dining rooms are kitted out with baroque mirrors, eighteenth- and nineteenth-century dressers, tables, chairs, clocks and

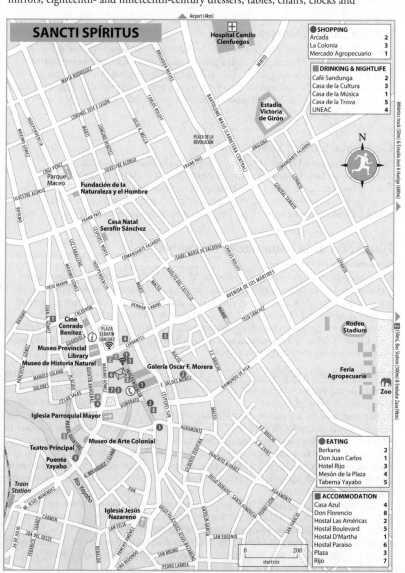

SANCTI SPÍRITUS

SHOPPING	
Arcada	2
La Colonia	3
Mercado Agropecuario	1

DRINKING & NIGHTLIFE	
Café Sandunga	2
Casa de la Cultura	3
Casa de la Música	1
Casa de la Trova	5
UNEAC	4

EATING	
Berkana	2
Don Juan Carlos	1
Hotel Rijo	3
Mesón de la Plaza	4
Taberna Yayabo	5

ACCOMMODATION	
Casa Azul	4
Don Florencio	8
Hostal Las Américas	2
Hostal Boulevard	5
Hostal D'Martha	1
Hostal Paraíso	6
Plaza	3
Rijo	7

5

ornaments. At the back of the building is the kitchen, with its built-in cooking surface, and the courtyard – the living and working area for the enslaved labourers and servants.

Puente Yayabo

On the other side of Jesús Menéndez from the Museo de Arte Colonial, an area of cobblestone streets extends down to the river. Walk down A. Rodríguez to the riverside terrace for a good view of the fairy-tale **Puente Yayabo**, the five-arch humpback stone bridge, built in 1825 and among the oldest of its kind in Cuba.

Galería Oscar F. Morera

Céspedes no.26 e/ Cervantes y E. Valdés Muñoz • Tues–Thurs 8am–5pm, Fri & Sat 9am–11pm, Sun 9am–6pm • Free • ☎ 41 32 3117

The **Galería Oscar F. Morera** showcases the work of the city's first well-known painter, who died in 1946. Morera's amateurish still-lifes and landscapes, hung around several small rooms, include various Sancti Spíritus scenes, but you'll probably find more value in the two rooms dedicated to temporary exhibitions, usually displaying the work of contemporary local artists.

Casa Natal Serafín Sánchez

Céspedes no.112 e/ Comandante Fajardo y Frank País • Tues–Sat 9am–5pm, Sun 9am–noon • Charge • ☎ 41 32 7791

The **Casa Natal Serafín Sánchez** commemorates one of the city's heroes of the two Wars of Independence, killed in combat on November 18, 1896. Consisting mostly of Sánchez's personal effects and photographs of him and his family, along with a colourful portrait of the man on his horse, it's a bit bare and not terribly interesting.

Fundación de la Naturaleza y el Hombre

Parque Antonio Maceo • Mon & Sat 9am–noon, Tues–Fri 9am–4pm • Charge

On the southern side of pretty little Parque Maceo, the **Fundación de la Naturaleza y el Hombre** is a small but captivating museum that tells the story of an expedition organized by the late Cuban writer Antonio Nuñez Jiménez. In 1987 he replicated the journey made by the first colonizers of Cuba, the Guanahatabey, by leading a team down the Amazon in five 13m-long canoes, each one carved from the trunk of a single tree. One of the monolithic canoes and some yellowing photographs of the Amazonian people are among the exhibits on display.

ARRIVAL AND DEPARTURE
SANCTI SPÍRITUS

By plane The city's tiny national airport (☎ 41 36 1590) is in the northern reaches of Sancti Spíritus.

By bus If you arrive by bus, you'll be dropped at the Terminal Provincial de Omnibus (☎ 41 32 4142), at the intersection of the Carretera Central and Circunvalación, the outer ring road. The arrival of a Víazul bus usually prompts a few private taxi drivers to come looking for business, but as there is no taxi rank as such, you may have to ring for a state taxi; try Cubataxi (☎ 41 32 2133).

Víazul destinations Camagüey (5 daily; 3hr 5min); Ciego de Ávila (5 daily; 1hr 15min); Havana (3 daily; 5hr); Holguín (3 daily; 7hr); Las Tunas (5 daily; 5hr 30min); Santa Clara (3 daily; 1hr 30min); Santiago de Cuba (5 daily; 10hr); Trinidad (1 daily; 1hr 30min); Varadero (1 daily; 3hr 30min).

By car Arriving from either the west or the east, you'll enter Sancti Spíritus on the Carretera Central, which cuts along the eastern edge of the city, becoming Bartolomé Masó as it enters Sancti Spíritus proper. To get to the centre, turn southwest off Bartolomé Masó onto Avenida de los Mártires, an attractive boulevard leading directly to the main square, the Plaza Serafín Sánchez.

By train It's a 500m walk to the central plaza from the train station (☎ 41 32 7914) on Avenida Jesús Menéndez, over the river from the city centre; if you want a taxi you'll need to call for one (see below). Train services are constantly subject to severe disruption and whole lines can be suspended for months.

Destinations Havana (2 weekly; 11hr); Matanzas (2 weekly; 9hr); Santa Clara (every other day; 3hr 30min).

GETTING AROUND

By horse-drawn carriage The city's bus system is too inefficient to be worth using; for journeys outside the centre, you're better off flagging down one of the horse-drawn carriages which operate up and down Bartolomé Masó.

Car rental Cubacar (☎ 41 32 8533) has a booth on the northern side of Plaza Serafín Sánchez and an office in the *Los Laureles* hotel, north of the centre at Careterra Central Km 383. Vía Transgaviota (☎ 41 33 6697) is opposite the Iglesia Parroquial Mayor.

Taxis Cubataxi (☎ 41 32 2133); Taxi OK (☎ 41 32 8315).

INFORMATION AND TRAVEL AGENTS

Tourist information Your best bet for information is the travel agent Cubatur at Máximo Gómez no.7 esq. Guardiola, Plaza Serafín Sánchez (Mon–Sat 9am–5pm; ☎ 41 32 8518).

Staff can sell you organized excursions and offer general visitor advice.

ACCOMMODATION
SEE MAP PAGE 287

Of the five **hotels** in Sancti Spíritus, the three in the centre are by far the most comfortable and attractive (the other two are both 4km from the centre, on the Carretera Central); all are run by the Islazul chain and the central three share one another's facilities. There are plenty of **casas particulares**, including plenty located on or within a few blocks of Plaza Serafín Sánchez.

HOTELS

Don Florencio Independencia no.63 e/ ⓦ islazulhotels. com. Elegant and lovable little hotel on the main, pedestrianized shopping street, decked out with colonial-style trappings and with a delightful courtyard featuring two jacuzzis. Rooms are comfortable and classy. $\underline{S}\underline{S}$

Plaza Independencia esq. Ave. de los Mártires, Plaza Serafín Sánchez ⓦ islazulhotels.com. Neat and compact hotel on the main square with a plain reception area and a quirky central patio café. The rooms are reasonably equipped, although slightly poky – ask for one of the four larger ones. $\underline{S}\underline{S}$

★ **Rijo** Honorato del Castillo no.12 ⓦ islazulhotels. com. Exquisite little hotel in a fine colonial mansion built in 1818, whose careful renovation highlights original features such as the terracotta-and-wood staircase. The spacious rooms, arranged around a charming patio, strike a perfect balance between comfort and stylish simplicity, with stained-wood furnishings, marble washbasins, iron-base lamps, minibar and satellite TV. $\underline{S}\underline{S}$

CASAS PARTICULARES

Casa Azul Maceo no.4 (sur) e/ Ave. de los Mártires y Doll ☎ 41 32 4336, ⓔ omaidae59@nauta.cu. Two inviting, well-equipped double rooms in a modern, homely apartment. One has a pair of fetching hand-crafted, colonial-style mahogany beds and the other (up on the roof

garden) has a double and a single bed and plenty of natural light. Both come with TV and fridge. $\underline{S}$

Hostal Las Américas Bartolomé Masó no.157 (sur) e/ Cuba y Cuartel ☎ 41 32 2984, ⓔ hostallasamericas@ yahoo.es. This 1950s house is the best option for those who like their home comforts. Each of the four cool, airy rooms has its own bathroom, TV, safety deposit box, fridge and mosquito-proof windows, plus you can feast on the bananas and mangoes that grow in the back garden. Parking is available and the bus station is a five-minute walk away. $\underline{S}$

Hostal Boulevard Independencia no.17 (altos) e/ Ave. de los Mártires y E. Valdés Muñoz ☎ 41 33 5120 or ☎ 53 80 8373. This huge and impressive first-floor establishment has three suites for rent, each of them effectively a one-bedroom apartment. All three have lounges and are smartly and comfortably furnished, but the largest also has a dining room with balcony. $\underline{S}$

Hostal D'Martha Plácido no.69 e/ Calderón y Tirso Marín ☎ 41 32 3556, ⓔ cira.ortiz@nauta.cu. Martha takes her role as host very seriously, insisting that the freshly furnished rooms are cleaned daily, offering a bilingual menu for meals and always keeping her relatively small house, with its modern interior, spick and span. There's a neat little dining area just outside two of the three rooms, and the split-level terraces on the roof, with views of the city and the Escambray mountains, provide the space missing indoors. $\underline{S}$

Hostal Paraiso Máximo Gómez sur no.11 e/ Honorato y Parque Serafín Sánchez ⓦ paraiso.trinidadhostales. com. At the heart of this elegant 1830-built residence is a lovely patio full of large potted plants; at the back are two of the four guest rooms, one of which opens onto a much smaller, cosier patio; and upstairs is a terrace where the other two rooms are located. The en-suite rooms have a/c, TV and safety deposit boxes. Wi-fi. $\underline{S}$

EATING
SEE MAP PAGE 287

Berkana Ernesto Valdez Muñoz no.113 e/ Martí y Maceo ☎ 41 32 5982. The food may not sound that special on the menu, with standard Cuban fare like grilled fish, chicken and

pork, but it's prepared here with more flare and flavour than most other places in town. The simple interior dining room enjoys an atmospherically dimmed lighting in the evening. $\underline{S}$

5

Don Juan Carlos Independencia no.9c, 2nd floor, e/ Ernesto Valdés Muñoz y Cervantes ☎ 52 47 3686. Popular with locals, the food here is well judged compared to the efforts of many of its competitors, with sensible portion sizes, well-dressed salads and quality cuts of meat. Pork and seafood feature heavily and main dishes are a snip. $

Hotel Rijo Honorato del Castillo no.12 ☎ 41 32 8588. The hotel restaurant serves decent fish and meat dishes, such as shrimp casserole and slices of pork in fruit sauce on the attractive central patio, where there's a fountain and views over to the pretty little plaza out front. $

Mesón de la Plaza Máximo Gómez no.34 ☎ 41 32 8546.

This rustic tavern-restaurant with earthenware plates, heavy wooden tables and wrought-iron lamps hanging from the ceiling rafters offers an eclectic menu that includes beef stewed with corn, *ropa vieja* with raisins and red wine, and an excellent, rich chickpea stew among the specials. Unusually, it also serves two types of sangria. $$

Taberna Yayabo Jesús Menéndez no.106 ☎ 41 83 7552. Right next to the Puente Yayabo, you can dine on chicken, pork, fish or shrimp in a picturesque provincial environment, with views of the river and bridge through open windows. Downstairs there's a nice terrace outside and a wine cellar inside. $$

DRINKING AND NIGHTLIFE   SEE MAP PAGE 287

The focal point for a lot of the city's weekend nightlife is the Plaza Serafín Sánchez, where some locals hang out all evening and others pass through on their way to the nearby **music venues**, which are also the best spots for an evening **drink**.

CLUBS AND LIVE MUSIC VENUES

Café Sandunga Cervantes e/ Máximo Gómez y Independencia, Plaza Serafín Sánchez ☎ 41 32 8051. Sometimes referred to as *Café Artex*, the discos and karaoke nights here attract the city's up-for-it young crowd and are the most raucous entertainment available in the centre.

Casa de la Cultura Cervantes esq. Máximo Gómez, Plaza Serafín Sánchez ☎ 41 32 3772. Home to occasional bolero nights, and worth checking out for other musical performances which can vary considerably, from local youth rock bands to traditional music.

Casa de la Música Padre Quintero no.32 e/ César Sala y Boquete El Guairo ☎ 41 32 4963. Hosts live salsa music and cabaret-style entertainment on Friday, Saturday and Sunday nights in an open-air setting with a stage and a terrace that overlooks the river.

Casa de la Trova Máximo Gómez sur no.26 e/ Solano y Honorato ☎ 41 32 8048. The most reliable venue for live music in the city, especially for traditional styles, with a monthly programme of bolero, trova and son nights. The patio bar is also one of the best places in town for a drink.

UNEAC Independencia no.10 e/ Plaza Serafín Sánchez y Honorato ☎ 41 32 6375. The local branch of this national artists' and writers' organization hosts small-scale live music most Saturdays, with matinee and evening concerts, and caters to all tastes, from traditional bolero to rock. There's an inviting patio and a bar. Performances are free and usually held at 4pm and 9pm.

ENTERTAINMENT

THEATRE AND CINEMAS

Cine Conrado Benítez Máximo Gómez no.13, Plaza Serafín Sánchez ☎ 41 32 5327. There are two cinemas on the main square but this one is more likely to actually be showing films. There are sometimes other cultural events here too, including comedy and musical performance, advertised on the poster board inside.

Teatro Principal Jesús Menéndez esq. Padre Quintero ☎ 41 32 5755. One of the oldest theatres in Cuba, founded in 1839, stages shows for children and infrequent music and dance performances. Check the poster board out front for

performance details.

SPECTATOR SPORTS

Baseball National-league baseball games are played at the Estadio José A. Huelga (☎ 41 32 2504), just beyond Circunvalación on Avenida de los Mártires.

Rodeo The main local event to draw in the crowds is the rodeo, held once or twice a month at the weekend, in the Feria Agropecuaria (☎ 41 32 3112) on Bartolomé Masó to the east of the centre.

SHOPPING   SEE MAP PAGE 287

Arcada Independencia no.55 e/ E. Valdés Muñoz y Agramonte ☎ 41 32 7106. This is the local branch of the Fondo Cubano de Bienes Culturales, and stocks the usual mixture of quality arts and crafts alongside made-for-tourists tat.

La Colonia Agramonte esq. Independencia ☎ 41 32

8225. The city's principal department store features one of the better supermarkets.

Mercado Agropecuario Entrances on Boulevard and Céspedes e/ Cervantes and E. Valdés Muñoz ☎ 41 32 1049. The central fresh-food market has meat, vegetables and fruit for sale.

DIRECTORY

Banks and exchange For cash, try the Banco Financiero Internacional, at Independencia no.2 e/ Plaza Serafín Sánchez y Honorato (Mon–Fri 8.30am–3.30pm). The CADECA *casa de cambio* is at Independencia no.31 e/ Plaza Serafín Sánchez y E. Valdés Muñoz (Mon–Sat 8.30am–4pm, Sun 8.30–11.30am).

Health The main hospital is the Clínico Quirúrgico Camilo Cienfuegos (☎ 41 32 4017), halfway down Bartolomé Masó. For an ambulance call ☎ 41 32 4462. The only pharmacy with a halfway decent stock of non-prescription medicines is in the *Los Laureles* hotel at Carretera Central Km 383 (☎ 41 32 7016).

Immigration and legal Consultoría Jurídica Internacional at Independencia no.39 e/ Plaza Serafín Sánchez y E. Valdés Muñoz (Mon–Fri 8.30am–12.30pm & 1.30–5.30pm; ☎ 41 32 8448).

Police Emergency number ☎ 106 or ☎ 115.

Post office Independencia no.8 e/ Plaza Serafín Sánchez y Honorato (Mon–Sat 8am–8pm, Sun 8am–noon). Also offers DHL and EMS services.

Wi-fi The most central public wi-fi zones are Parque Serafín Sánchez and along Boulevard. You can buy wi-fi cards at the Telepunto at Independencia no.14 e/ Plaza Serafín Sánchez y Honorato (daily 8.30am–7pm).

Ciego de Ávila and Camagüey

FLAMINGO, JARDINES DEL REY

Ciego de Ávila and Camagüey

Spanning the trunk of the island some 450km east of Havana, the low-lying provinces of Ciego de Ávila and Camagüey form the agricultural heart of Cuba. The westernmost of the two is sleepy Ciego de Ávila, sparsely populated and with only two medium-sized towns, Ciego de Ávila and Morón. Most independent visitors base themselves in Morón, conveniently located for trips to the province's star attraction, the Jardines del Rey, a line of cays off the north coast with flamboyant birdlife, the country's most dazzling beaches and one of the Caribbean's biggest barrier reefs, with superb offshore diving. As well as offering accommodation at a fraction of the price of the cays' all-inclusive hotels, Morón also takes you within close proximity of two alluring lakes, Laguna de la Leche and Laguna la Redonda, both well set up for fishing, boat trips and lakeside dining.

Camagüey is the country's largest province, mostly made up of low-lying farmland dappled with rural villages. Its main draws are the northern beaches and the provincial capital of **Camagüey city**, far livelier and more interesting than Ciego de Ávila's capital and one of the oldest towns in Cuba, founded in 1514. Nurtured by sugar wealth that dates to the late sixteenth century, Camagüey is a large and stalwart city by Cuban standards, with many of the architectural hallmarks of a Spanish colonial town, from plazas to churches. While the government pushes the plush northern beach resort of **Santa Lucía** as the province's chief attraction, its least spoilt beach is just west of the resort at **Cayo Sabinal**.

Ciego de Ávila city

CIEGO DE ÁVILA is more like the suburb of a larger town than an urban centre in its own right. A friendly though pedestrian place set in the plains of the province, it is young for a provincial capital – established only in 1849 – and features few tourist attractions save a couple of museums, and precious little nightlife. Often bypassed by visitors en route to Morón and the Jardines del Rey, this small city is not without charm, and an afternoon here will reveal a close-knit, slow-moving, unaffected place, its streets lined with whitewashed modern houses where families hang out on their verandas, old men relax in rocking chairs, and corn fritters and fruit juice are sold from roadside stalls. Refreshingly, Ciego de Ávila also has much less of a problem with hustlers and *jineteros* than bigger cities.

Parque Martí

At the heart of the city, bordered by the city's four main streets (including the three pedestrianized blocks of the main shopping street, Independencia), pleasant **Parque Martí** is fringed with sturdy trees and features a central 1920s bust of José Martí in a reflective pose; it's also the intermittent venue for a small **arts and crafts market**. On the park's south side stands the **cathedral**, San Eugenio de la Palma, a bland modern structure with a gigantic concrete saint tacked to the outside; next door is the stately **town hall**.

Museo de Artes Decorativas

Parque Martí • Mon–Thurs 9am–5pm, Sat 2–9pm, Sun 8am–12noon • Charge • ☎ 33 20 1661

CAYO GUILLERMO

Highlights

❶ Laguna La Redonda This idyllic lake is perfect for an afternoon of bass fishing or simply messing around in boats. See page 305

❷ Loma de Cunagua The lone high ground in an area of unremittingly flat farmland, this 364m hill is a favourite with birdwatchers. See page 305

❸ Diving the coral reefs Two of the longest coral reefs in the world can be found on opposite sides of Ciego de Ávila, at the Jardines del Rey and the Jardines de la Reina. See pages 311 and 314

❹ Playa Pilar A gorgeous beach on Cayo Guillermo's western tip, named after Ernest Hemingway's yacht. See page 312

❺ Hotel Camagüey Colón Almost a museum in itself, this beautiful 1927 hotel in the heart of Camagüey city has been artfully renovated, preserving its eclectic mix of styles. See page 321

❻ Cayo Sabinal Cayo Sabinal's isolated white sands, woodland and wildlife make for the perfect island retreat. See page 326

HIGHLIGHTS ARE MARKED ON THE MAP ON PAGE 296

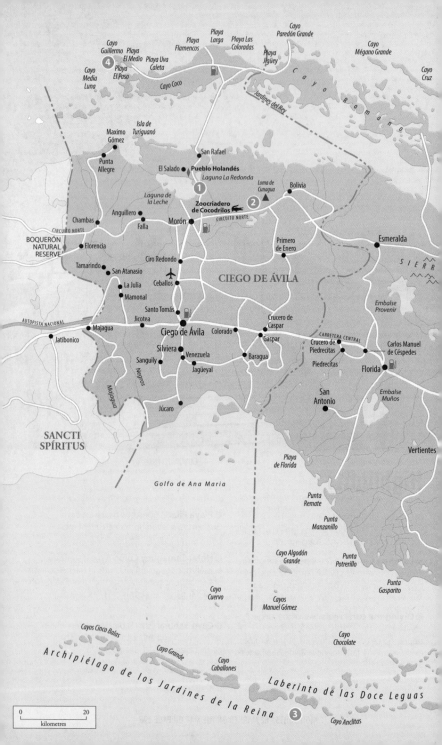

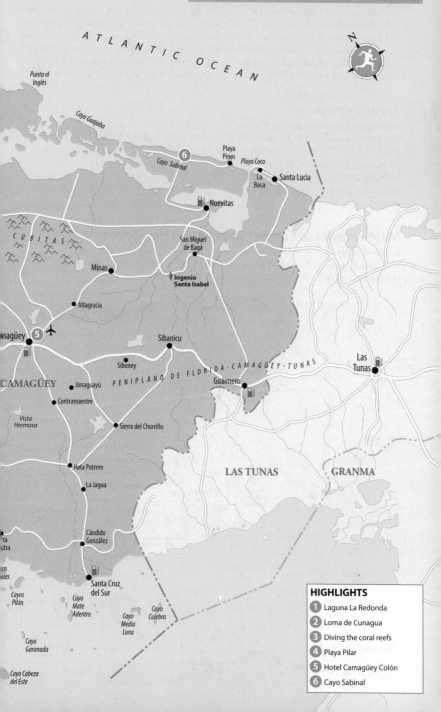

ATLANTIC OCEAN

Punta el Inglés

Cayo Guajaba

Cayo Sabinal

6

Playa Pinos

Playa Coco

La Boca

Santa Lucia

Nuevitas

CUBITAS

San Miguel de Bagá

Ingenio Santa Isabel

Minas

Altagracia

magüey

5

Sibanicu

Siboney

PENIPLANO DE FLORIDA-CAMAGÜEY-TUNAS

Las Tunas

CAMAGÜEY

Jimaguayú

Guáimero

Contramaestre

Vista Hermosa

Sierra del Chorrillo

Hata Potrero

LAS TUNAS

GRANMA

La Jagua

Cándido González

ra stra

Santa Cruz del Sur

os ies

Cayos Pilón

Cayo Mate Adentro

Cayo Media Luna

Cayo Culebra

Cayo Garanada

Cayo Cabeza del Este

HIGHLIGHTS

1 Laguna La Redonda

2 Loma de Cunagua

3 Diving the coral reefs

4 Playa Pilar

5 Hotel Camagüey Colón

6 Cayo Sabinal

Set in a beautiful 1920s colonial building on the east side of Parque Martí, the **Museo de Artes Decorativas** is the jewel in Ciego's crown. Though few of the beautiful exhibits are of Cuban origin, as a whole they provide an illuminating insight into the level of luxury enjoyed by colonial Creoles. Spanish-speaking guides are on hand to talk you through the finer pieces, which include a fabulous tall-necked Art Nouveau vase in gold and claret glass, and a nursery kitted out rather splendidly with white *pajilla* cane furniture.

Teatro Principal

Joaquín Agüero esq. Honorato del Castillo • ☎ 33 22 2086

The prettiest building in Ciego de Ávila's centre is the **Teatro Principal**, built between 1924 and 1927 by wealthy society widow Angela Hernández Viuda de Jiménez in an attempt to make the city more cosmopolitan. In an architectural fit of pique, the building manages to combine Baroque, Renaissance and Imperial exterior styles with an equally elaborate interior. There is no official tour, but you're free to enter and look around in the daytime.

Museo Provincial Coronel Simón Reyes Hernández

Honorato del Castillo esq. Máximo Gómez • Tues–Sat 8am–noon & 1–5pm, Sun 8am–noon • Charge • ☎ 33 20 4488

One block north of Parque Martí is the **Museo Provincial Coronal Simón Reyes Hernández**, attractively housed and laid out, but with a collection that's a little

underwhelming. There's a room devoted to relics from local the Taíno communities including some shards of pottery, plus some information on African-Cuban religions and a scale model of La Trocha (see page 302).

ARRIVAL AND DEPARTURE

By train The train station is on Parque Maceo, eight blocks southwest of Parque Martí. There are two terminals: the smaller Terminal Ferro-Omnibus (☎ 33 22 3076), at the western end of Parque Maceo, serves trains to and from Morón as well as buses within the province; the main station (☎ 33 22 3313), a few metres away, serves national network trains and is on the principal Havana–Santiago line. Of the five daily trains only one leaves in the morning, at 8.15am – the rest are spread through the afternoon and early evening, with the last at 7.30pm. You can buy tickets at the time of travel from the main station. There are usually *bicitaxis* waiting to ferry people into town from Parque Maceo.

Destinations Camagüey (1 daily; 2hr); Havana (3 daily; 7hr); Holguín (1 daily; 5hr); Matanzas (3 daily; 6hr); Morón (5 daily; 1hr).

By interprovincial bus All national network buses, including those operated by Víazul (☎ 33 20 3197), pull into the Terminal de Omnibus Interprovincial on the Carretera Central (☎ 33 22 5109), about 1km east of Parque Martí.

CIEGO DE ÁVILA

You can share a horse-drawn carriage into the centre for a reasonable charge, or catch a *bicitaxi*.

Destinations Camagüey (2 daily; 1hr 30min); Havana (3 daily; 6hr); Holguín (2 daily; 6hr); Las Tunas (2 daily; 4hr); Santa Clara (2 daily; 3hr).

By intermunicipal bus Bus services operating within the province run to and from the Terminal Ferro-Omnibus (☎ 33 203086) on Parque Maceo, confusingly joined to the train station there. Routes cover at least two dozen towns around the province, but non-Cubans are a rare sight on these buses, some of which are actually converted trucks. Services are slow but cheap.

Destinations Morón (9 daily; 1hr); Chambas (1 daily; 1hr 30min); Florencia (1 daily; 1hr 15min).

By taxi You can catch *almendrones* (see page 30) from opposite the train station on Parque Maceo to Morón and other destinations in and around the province; you're far more likely to find private taxi drivers offering rides beyond the province at the Terminal de Omnibus Interprovincial.

GETTING AROUND

By car Cubacar has offices at Libertad e/ Maceo y Honorato del Castillo (☎ 33 21 2570), the *Hotel Santiago-Habana*, Honorato del Castillo esq. Carretera Central (☎ 33 26 6169)

and at the *Ciego de Ávila* hotel (☎ 33 21 2050).
By taxi Taxis are available from Cubataxi (☎ 33 26 6666).

INFORMATION, TRAVEL AGENCIES AND TOURS

Tourist office The Infotur office on Parque Martí, at Honorato del Castillo esq. Libertad (Mon–Fri 9am–4pm, plus every other Sat 9am–noon; ⓦ infotur.cu), has general information on the area, and can help arrange diving excursions and day-trips to Cayo Coco.

Havanatur As well as selling maps, the office at Libertad no.54 e/ Maceo y Honorato del Castillo (Mon–Sat 8am–noon & 1–6pm; ☎ 33 26 6342) has information on trips to local sights, and to Cayo Coco and other attractions in the province.

ACCOMMODATION SEE MAP PAGE 298

The better of the three **state hotels** – all things being relative – is the *Ciego de Ávila* on the outskirts of the city, though a **casa particular** is a much better choice, and most owners will also be able to arrange transport to the cays.

HOTEL

Ciego de Ávila Carretera a Ceballos Km 1.5 ⓦ islazulhotels.com. The city's largest hotel is reasonably attractive, has friendly staff and is liveliest at weekends, when the pool is crowded with townsfolk. There's a disco and bar, though the restaurant is best avoided. It's 2km from the centre of the city – *bicitaxis* wait outside to ferry you back and forth. ⑤

CASAS PARTICULARES

Casa Margarita Independencia 28 altos e/ Marcial Gomez y Abraham Delgado ☎ 33 20 4478, ✉ villajaboncandado@gmail.com. One well-appointed room in a modern house near the centre of town. ⑤
Villa Jabón Candado Chicho Valdéz no.51 esq. Abraham Delgado ☎ 33 22 5854, ✉ marilyn@fcm.cav. sld.cu. House with two rooms for rent in a convenient location in the centre of town right on the Carretera Central. It's well worth paying the extra for the upstairs room which has its own kitchen and balcony terrace – the other is off a covered patio downstairs. Both have a/c and en-suite shower. ⑤

6

EATING

SEE MAP PAGE 298

Eating out in Ciego de Ávila won't cost you much, but the choice isn't that great either. Paladars are very widely dispersed and generally at least a 20min walk from Parque Martí. Alternatively, you can snack well at the **stalls** along and around Independencia.

La Casa Cubaquoise Julio Antonio Mella no 213 e/ Bembeta y Eduardo Marmol ☎33 20 5498, ✉diurbis. arnaiz@nauta.cu. This atmospheric restaurant-cum-nightspot dishes up *comida criolla* in an open-air courtyard. At weekends bands play, and there's a chance for audience participation with a spot of karaoke. $$

El Crucero Libertad no.366 e/ 2 y 3 ☎33 27 9405. Popular with locals and one of the city's best eating options, though the cooking is more competent than creative. *El Crucero* is also one of the quirkier, more interesting places to eat. At the top of a three-storey building with a kitsch nautical theme, there's a painting of the *Titanic* over the bar and a mural of a flamingo-populated coastline covering a set of walls. Expect reasonably priced chicken, meat, fish and shrimp dishes, and great value lobster. $$

Don Ávila Marcial Gómez no.22 esq. Libertad, Parque Martí ☎33 26 5353. An airy colonial building with several spaces for eating and drinking, including the agreeable covered patio at the back. Good-value skewered-meat kebabs for around and a modest selection of other meat and seafood deals make the food here reliable if unremarkable – a safe, convenient bet. $$

Don Pepe Independencia no.303 e/ Maceo y Simón Reyes ☎33 22 3713. An atmospheric little eatery, with walls adorned with caricatures of local characters, some of whom regularly prop up the bar. It serves good pork dishes with rice and peas, and the unique Don Pepe cocktail (a house speciality made from rum and orange with a sprig of mint). Live music and dancing most nights. Reservations advised. $$

Solaris Doce Plantas, 12th floor, Honorato del Castillo e/ Libertad y Independencia, Parque Martí ☎33 22 3424. Standard meat-based dishes for mid-range prices, served in an original setting on the top floor of Parque Martí's tallest building. A dress code – no sandals, men must wear a formal shirt – is strictly enforced. $$

NIGHTLIFE AND ENTERTAINMENT

SEE MAP PAGE 298

Ciego de Ávila has a couple of options for **live music**, and on Saturday nights the city rouses itself from its habitual torpor for the weekly **Fiesta Ávileña**, when the younger population gather near the centre to dance to booming sound systems and feast on huge joints of pork roasting on sidewalk barbecues. Some of the city's restaurants (see above) also offer live music followed by dancing later in the evening.

Casa de la Cultura Independencia no.76 e/ Maceo y Honorato del Castillo ⊕ciego.cult.cu. This rather elegant colonial building serves as a catch-all arts venue and hosts a range of bands encompassing everything from bolero to reggaeton. There's an open-air patio on the first floor which can get lively later in the evening when recorded music follows the live acts.

★ **Casa de la Trova** Libertad no.130 esq. Simón Reyes ☎33 21 5962. Ciego de Ávila's best bet for a night out – the bar serves a wide choice of cocktails, while local music groups play traditional bolero, son and guaracha to an older crowd when there's a full house.

UNEAC Libertad no.105 e/ Maceo y Simón Reyes. The pale tiled floors and high ceilings of this rather romantic building suit the regular bolero and choral concerts that are held here.

SHOPPING

SEE MAP PAGE 298

Libertad Libertad no.68 e/ Maceo y Honorato del Castillo ☎33 26 6120. For groceries, this is as good as it gets in Ciego de Ávila – your best bet if you want to stock up on a few self-catering basics.

Mercado Agropecuario Chicho Valdés y Fernando Callejas. This farmers' market, parallel to the train tracks, is the city's best place for fresh produce.

DIRECTORY

Health There is a 24-hour surgery on República no.52 esq. A. Delgado (☎33 22 2611). For an ambulance call ☎104. Farmacia La Central (☎33 22 5183; 24hr), Independencia no.163, is on the pedestrianized section of this main shopping street.

Money and exchange Banco de Crédito y Comercio, Independencia no.152 esq. Simón Reyes (Mon–Fri 8am–3pm & Sat 8–11am); Banco Financiero Internacional, Honorato del Castillo esq. Joaquín Aguero (Mon–Fri 8am–3pm, last working day of month 8am–noon). There are also a couple of out-of-hours ATMs in an alcove to the side of the grand Neoclassical building housing the Banco de Crédito y Comercio. Buy pesos at CADECA *casa de cambio*, Independencia no.118 e/ Maceo y Simón Reyes (Mon–Sat 8.30am–6pm, Sun 8.30am–12.30pm).

Police Call ☎106.

Post office Main post office is at Marcial Gómez esq. Carretera Central.

Morón

Lying 36km north of Ciego de Ávila on the road to the cays, picturesque **MORÓN** is surrounded by flat farming countryside replete with glistening palms, banks of sugar cane and citrus trees. Fanning out from a cosy downtown nucleus dotted with gaily painted colonial buildings, its proximity to the Jardines del Rey ensures its popularity with day-trippers from the cays, and it's certainly the best place to stay if you want to visit the cays but can't afford a luxury hotel. More than 24 hours in the town itself would be stretching its sights and entertainment options very thin, but even without making trips to the cays you could comfortably fill two to three days with trips into the surrounding countryside.

The town and its main street are bisected by train tracks that aren't separated from the road by any barriers – it's quite common to see trains impatiently honking horns as bicycles roll lazily over the rails. The train station is right in the middle of town, and a couple of blocks north of the station is **Plaza Martí** – north of the plaza the main street is called **Martí**, while to the south it becomes **Avenida Tarafa**.

The train station

Roughly in the centre of town, Morón's **train station** was built in the 1920s and is one of the oldest in Cuba. It remains largely unchanged and inside, amid the elegant archways and fine wrought-iron awnings, you can still buy tickets at the original booths and check destinations on a hand-painted blackboard, while high above the rows of worn wooden benches and the original stained-glass *vitrales*, birds nest under the eaves. Outside is one of the more pleasant, leafier outdoor spaces in town, the **Parque de los Ferrocarriles**.

Museo Caonabo

Martí no.374 • Tues–Sat 9am–noon & 1.30–5pm, Sun 8am–noon • Charge • ☎ 33 50 4501

From Morón's train station, a five-minute walk north along Martí will take you to the local history museum, the **Museo Caonabo**, housed in one of the town's eye-catching colonial buildings, this one fronted by simple columns and wide steps. The collection comprises an assortment of small pre-Columbian Cuban artefacts, mainly fragments of clay bowls and shards of bone necklace. By far the most impressive exhibit is the *Idolillo de Barro*, a clay idol of a fierce snarling head, found outside the city in 1947.

Galería de Arte Hugo Cortijo

Martí no.151 e/ Libertad y Narcisco López • Tues–Thurs 8am–noon & 1–5pm, Fri & Sat 2–10pm, Sun 8am–noon • Free

---

THE COCK OF MORÓN

The first thing to strike you about clean, compact Morón is the shining **bronze cockerel**, perched at the foot of a clocktower on an oval green in front of the *Hotel Morón*, just inside the southern entrance to the town. In the sixteenth century, the townsfolk of Spanish Morón found themselves the victims of a corrupt judiciary that continually levied high taxes and confiscated their land without explanation. Having suffered these oppressive conditions for several years, the people set upon and expelled the main offender, an official nicknamed **"the cock of Morón"**. The incident was quickly immortalized in an Andalucían ballad that proclaimed that "the cock of the walk has been left plucked and crowing" (a saying still used throughout Cuba today to mean that somebody has had their plans scuppered). The current statue dates from 1981.

North of the archeological museum, the **Galería de Arte** exhibits and sells an array of locally painted landscapes, colourful abstracts, lovingly executed sculptures of female nudes and mawkish religious figures. If you're planning to buy a sculpture in the area, this is the place to do it as they're a lot cheaper here than at the resorts.

ARRIVAL AND DEPARTURE
MORÓN

By train Morón's elegant train station is the most prominent building on the Parque de los Ferrocarriles, in the centre of town.
Destinations Camagüey (1 daily; 3hr); Ciego de Ávila (5 daily; 1hr); Júcaro (1 daily; 40min); Santa Clara (1 daily; 4hr).
By bus Víazul buses use the bus station (☎ 33 50 3774) at Martí no.12 e/ Felipe Poey y Carlos Manuel de Céspedes. The

only service to Morón originates in Trinidad but has been suspended at times over the last few years. Municipal buses arrive and depart from outside the train station.
Víazul destinations Trinidad (1 daily; 5hr 30min).
Municipal bus destinations Ciego de Ávila (2 daily; 1hr).
By colectivo and camion You can usually find *colectivos* and *camiones* to Ciego de Ávila and Camagüey outside the train station.

GETTING AROUND

Horse-drawn carriages There's usually a line of horse-drawn carriages waiting for fares at the Parque de los Ferrocarriles, outside the train station.
Taxis The private taxis waiting under the trees in front of

the train station are useful for forays into the countryside and to the cays. Prices are negotiable depending on how hard you're prepared to bargain. State taxis include Cubataxi (☎ 33 50 3290) on Avenida Tarafa.

INFORMATION

In the absence of an official Infotur office, Morón's closest equivalent to state-run tourist information providers are the travel agents, though they exist predominantly to book accommodation.
Cubatur Martí no.169 e/ Libertad y Agramonte (daily

8am–5pm; ☎ 33 50 5513).
Cubanacan Hotel Morón, Carretera a Ciego de Ávila (daily 8am–5pm; ☎ 33 30 1225).
Havanatur Havanautos office, Avenida Tarafa e/ 5 y 6 (daily 8am–5pm; ☎ 33 50 5866).

ACCOMMODATION

Morón's growing clutch of very reasonable **casas particulares** are your best choice for an overnight stay. They will all be able to help sort out taxis to and from the cays, and some will even provide tours and a packed picnic lunch.

HOTELS
La Casona de Morón Cristóbal Colón no.41 e/ Carretera

de Patria y Ferrocarril ☎ 33 50 4563, ⊛ islazul.cu. Set in a pretty sunshine-yellow villa with bags of personality, this friendly boutique-style hotel has just seven rooms and is across the park from the train station. It caters to the hunting and fishing crowd, offering tours of the local sporting grounds and the chance to cook your spoils yourself on an open grill by the tiny swimming pool. ⑤

LA TROCHA FORTIFICATIONS

Driving north to south on the road running from Morón to Júcaro via Ciego de Ávila, you'll pass the remnants of an old Spanish **garrison** which at one time divided the province from north to south. The tumbledown, stubby structures are the remains of a fortification line known as **La Trocha**, built between April 1871 and 1873. Increasingly worried by the Mambises (the rebel army fighting for independence) and their plans to move west through the island, the Spanish General Blas Villate de la Hera planned a 67km-long row of fortifications to block the advance. The forts were made of concrete with solid walls of stone, brick and wood and built at intervals of 3–4km. Each was manned by a single sentry, who had to enter by a removable wooden staircase, and each had two cannon. It was supposedly an impassable chain of defence, but the ineffectiveness of the whole idea was immediately apparent in 1874 when the Cuban General Manuel Suárez triumphantly breezed through with his cavalry. Most of the forts are in a poor state of repair today, though the odd one still gives an impression of its original appearance.

CASAS PARTICULARES

★ **Alojamiento Maite Valor Morales** Luz Caballero no.40B e/ Libertad y Agramonte ☎33 50 4181, ✉ alojamientomaite@gmail.com. Eight impressive, high-spec en-suite rooms to rent in a lovingly and very professionally run household. Two are on a fabulous upstairs terrace, one with three small double beds, a large four-star-hotel-standard bathroom and a wine cabinet, the rest with views over the park. Each has a/c, a fridge stuffed with drinks, TV and security box. The largest unit, a downstairs suite with space for five, has a sitting room, kitchen and terrace. There's also a small pool, a garden and parking, and a restaurant on site. The impressive host Maite speaks English and Italian and is a font of information on the area. $

★ **Alojamiento Vista al Parque** Luz Caballero no.49D (altos) e/ Libertad y Agramonte ☎33 50 4181, ✉ yio@ moron.cav.sld.cu or ✉ maite69@enet.cu. Situated opposite a children's park near the centre of town, this fantastic house has three rooms, each with a/c, private bathroom, TV and fridge. Downstairs is a large suite with two bathrooms, dining room, living room and kitchen, and capacity for four people (but all in the same bedroom). The other two rooms are upstairs and each room gets its own maid. There's a well-stocked bar and a sun terrace with views over the city. Car parking is available and Idolka, the owner, is a fabulous host and an English speaker. $

Casa Belkys Cristóbal Colón no.37 e/ Carretera de Patria y Línea del Ferrocarril ☎33 50 5763, ✉ timy63@nauta. cu. Two attractive double rooms with their own bathroom in a house with a sunny terrace and a garage, a few metres from the train station. $

Juan C. Peréz Oquendo Belgica Silva Castillo no.189 e/ San José y Serafín Sánchez ☎33 50 3823, ✉ juanclent@enet.cu. A short walk from the centre of town, with very friendly owners and two comfortable en-suite rooms, one with capacity for four people, the other for three and both with a/c. Breakfast is available for a snip. $

Onaida Ruíz Fumero Calle 5 no.46 e/ 6 y 8 ☎33 50 3409. Pleasant a/c rooms, one double and one triple, in a house on a quiet residential street. Parking and meals are available. $

EATING

Las Fuentes Martí no.169 e/ Libertad y Agramonte ☎33 50 5758. Creamy soups and pastas enliven the standard selection of chicken and pork dishes in this warm, rustic-style restaurant where you eat to the sound of water trickling down the eponymous fountains, surrounded by exuberant ferns – all drowned out after 9.30pm by salsa and such, as the restaurant morphs into a night spot. $$

★ **Maite La Qbana** Luz Caballero no.40B e/ Libertad y Agramonte ☎33 50 4181. The proprietor of the town's best *casa particular* also runs its best paladar, and the delicious and inventive home-cooked meals make this one of the best places to eat in the province. House specialities include dressed crab, fresh lobster, paella and soups. Dinner reservations recommended; it opens for lunch on request only. $$

Las Ruedas Villamil e/ Vasallo y Narciso López ☎52 81 1172. A block north of Parque Agramonte, this easy-going outdoor paladar under a traditional palm-leaf roof works well for a late-night drink or a good-value meal. Main dishes are mostly grilled, fried and breaded meats, though fajitas have also somehow found their way onto the menu. $

DRINKING AND ENTERTAINMENT

BARS AND LIVE MUSIC VENUES

Buena Vista's Club Martí no.382 e/ Dimas Daniel y Emrique José Varona ☎33 50 2045. Likeably cheesy club in the heart of town, with a small stage and a tables-and-chairs set-up where the weekly programme features a mixture of live contemporary and traditional Cuban music and usually a karaoke night at some point.

Casa de la Cultura Martí no.218 e/ Libertad y Agramonte ☎33 50 4309. The local branch of the national network of cultural centres puts on free dance classes and there's live music every week, most reliably on Saturdays.

Casa de la Trova Libertad e/ Narciso López y Martí ☎33 50 4158. A small but pleasantly unassuming local watering hole and an authentic Cuban experience, where the town's minstrels serenade drinkers with traditional *guajiras* and son.

La Cueva Laguna de la Leche ☎33 50 2239. It may be 5km north of the town at the end of a dusty road, but this simple *discoteca* gets very lively at weekends when locals flock here to dance to salsa, reggaeton and whatever else the DJs are playing.

DIRECTORY

Money and exchange Banco de Crédito y Comercio, Martí no.330 e/ Serafín Sánchez y González Arena, has ATM; CADECA *casa de cambio*, Martí no.348 esq. González Arena (Mon–Fri 8.30am–4pm, Sat 8.30–11.30am), and handles all types of foreign currency transactions.

Pharmacy At Martí no.320 esq. Serafín Sánchez (Mon–Sat 9am–6pm; ☎33 50 3344).

Post office Housed in the Colonial Española, a blue-and-white 1920s building on Plaza Martí (Mon–Sat 8am–6pm). **Wi-fi** The ETECSA telecommunications centre (daily 8am–9.45pm) on Plaza Martí, two blocks north of the train station, offers internet access and sells wi-fi cards. The town's public wi-fi zone is Plaza Martí.

Around Morón

Set in lush countryside dappled by lakes and low hills, the area surrounding Morón offers a welcome contrast to the unrelentingly flat land to the south, and holds a few surprises well worth venturing beyond the town limits to explore. Five kilometres north of town, the large **Laguna de la Leche** is fringed by reeds and woodland, while 10km northeast the tranquil **Laguna La Redonda** is an idyllic spot for drifting about in a boat. Just north of the lakes is the **Isla de Turiguanó** peninsula, home to the mock-Dutch village of **Poblado Holandés**, its faux-timbered, red-roofed houses looking completely out of place beneath tropical palms. Towards the east, rising from the plains like the shell of a tortoise, is the gently rounded **Loma de Cunagua**, its dense tangle of woodland full of bright parakeets and parrots, and a favourite spot for day-trekkers and birdwatchers. West from Morón, in an area straddled by the tiny villages of Chambas and Florencia, is the **Boquerón nature reserve**, where you can go horseriding or river-swimming and explore caves.

GETTING AROUND   AROUND MORÓN

By taxi Unless you're driving, the only efficient way to get around the Morón area is to hire a taxi driver. Taxis are available from Cubataxi (☎ 33 26 6666).

By car 3km east of the northern end of Martí in Morón is a crossroads marked by a petrol station; head north from here (a left turn from Morón) for the Jardines del Rey and Laguna La Redonda; head east (straight on from Morón) for the Loma de Cunagua and the Zoocriadero. For car rental, Cubacar/Havanautos in Morón has rental points on the Avenida Tarafa e/ 5 y 6, just west of the train station (☎ 33 50 2115) and in the *Hotel Morón*, Carretera a Ciego de Ávila (☎ 33 50 2028), where you can also rent scooters.

By horse-drawn carriage There's usually a line of horse-drawn carriages waiting for fares at Morón's Parque de los Ferrocarriles, outside the train station.

Laguna de la Leche

Driving from Morón, follow Martí northwards, passing through Parque Agramonte and staying left until the fork in the road just outside the town, where you take the right-hand fork

Accessed via its southern shore, 5km north of Morón, **Laguna de la Leche** (Milk Lake) is the largest natural lake in Cuba, with a surface area of 66 square kilometres; decked out with palm trees and a pint-sized lighthouse, it has the appearance of a miniature seafront. The opacity of its water comes from gypsum and limestone deposits beneath the surface, but despite the evocative name it looks nothing like Cleopatra's bath: rather, the lake fans out from a cloudy centre to disperse into smudgy pools of green and blue around the edges. Laguna de la Leche's wooded north and west shores, soupy with rushes and overhung branches, are great for exploring but are accessible only by **boat**. Most boat trips here are part of organized excursions from the Jardines del Rey, but rental can sometimes be arranged through the Ranchón Flora y Fauna, a roadside hut on the left of the road to the lake just before it meets the water's edge, from where the ragtag selection of boats moored and piled up at the edge of the canal opposite are administered. Swimming or bathing in the lake is not permitted.

EATING AND DRINKING   LAGUNA DE LA LECHE

La Atarraya Laguna de la Leche ☎ 33 50 5351. Perched at the end of a jetty hovering over the Laguna de la Leche, this expansive open-sided bar and restaurant, with views right across the water, serves lunch only, featuring standard Cuban meat dishes and fresh fish caught in the lake. $$

Ranchón La Boca Laguna de la Leche ☎ 33 50 4420.

Popularly known as *Pescado Frito* and marooned on the far side of the canal that runs parallel with the road to the lake, the only way over to this waterside restaurant is by a small ferry specifically for diners. The seafood is even cheaper than at *La Atarraya* and the quality not far off, while the location is equally novel and alluring. $\overline{\underline{SS}}$

Laguna La Redonda

Speedboat trips (daily 11am–3pm) and fishing excursions (daily 11am–3pm; equipment not included) set off from the Complejo Turístico La Redonda • The lake is some 400m off from the main road to the cays, its turn-off marked by an unmissable billboard sign; expect a taxi from Morón to charge around $500–650CUP for the roundtrip. Trips are readily available from resorts on the Jardines del Rey cays

Some 12km north of Morón, the **Laguna La Redonda** (Circle Lake) is the smaller of the region's two lakes, measuring 3km at its widest point, and has five mangrove canals that radiate out from the central body of water like the spokes on a bicycle wheel. All visits are funnelled through the **Complejo Turístico La Redonda**, a small complex with a restaurant, a souvenir shop and a little jetty. More intimate than Laguna de la Leche, but with better facilities for getting out on the lake – and so more popular with tour groups – it's perfect for an idle afternoon's **boating** or **trout fishing**. The delightful boat trips cross over to the far side of the lake and drift through the mangrove tunnels and canals.

EATING AND DRINKING

LAGUNA LA REDONDA

El Pescador Complejo Turístico La Redonda ☎ 33 30 2489. This serene restaurant and bar overhanging the lake serves freshly caught tilapia and carp as well as pasta, shrimp, chicken and omelettes for very reasonable prices. There are also buffet lunches, aimed at the tour groups but available to anyone. $\overline{\underline{SS}}$

Zoocriadero de Cocodrilos

Carretera a Bolivia (Circuito Norte), 11.5km east of Morón • Daily 9am–6pm • Charge

With a series of enclosed swamps full of large crocodiles, each an average length of 3.5m, the **Zoocriadero de Cocodrilos** is one of the standout things to do around these parts, though unless you have lunch here, it probably won't hold you for very long. Established in 1995 and among a number of centres around the country set up to preserve and breed Cuban and American crocodiles, the farm now holds around a thousand of the beasts, at all stages of development. The size of the enclosures means that the crocodiles are sometimes a significant distance away, but their impressive dimensions and great numbers mean that you get a good look at them. There's an iguana enclosure here, too.

Loma de Cunagua

Carretera a Bolivia (Circuito Norte), 20km east of Morón • Daily 7am–4pm, but usually no entry after midday • Charge for guides • You can get here via an organized tour from the cays

The lone high ground in an area of unremittingly flat farmland that stretches all the way to the coast, the **Loma de Cunagua** is 364m high and can be seen for miles around. Just past the foot of the hill, about 1km along a dirt track from the Circuito Norte, the main road, is a gate where, before you are permitted to pass, you will need to pick up a guide from the lodge here and negotiate a price to be taken into this protected area and up to the top; there's not much point in turning up after midday as there are rarely any guides around after that time. Note also that taxis are not allowed past the lodge, so you'll have to walk from this point on unless you have your own car.

From the gate, a gravelly road weaves its way up through the dense tangle of spindly trees clinging precariously to the steep slopes. Popular with **birdwatchers**, the hill's forests, crisscrossed by a network of trails, are home to dazzling parrots, as well as the *tojosa* (a small endemic dove), the *zunzún* (Cuban emerald hummingbird) and the *tocororo*, the country's national bird, its startling red, white and blue plumage mimicking the colour scheme of the Cuban flag. If you're lucky, you might also catch a glimpse of a cute Cuban hutia *(jutía)*. This largely tree-dwelling rodent is the island's largest native mammal. At the summit there's a restaurant and panoramic views over the surrounding countryside and out to sea. Bring mosquito spray.

Boquerón nature reserve

Veiled behind the folds of the Jatibonico sierra – the rugged tail of the Sierra de Meneses chain, which steals into the province from Sancti Spíritus to the west – the picturesque **Boquerón nature reserve** nestles a few kilometres west of the undulating farming country around the tiny towns of **Florencia** and **Chambas**, the nearest public transport links. Both sit some 40km west of Morón in landscape pocketed with dazzling green-gold sugar cane fields and tobacco meadows. Florencia's name – given for its resemblance to the Italian town – is an indication of its arcadian beauty but it's Boquerón, 5km west of Florencia, that is the best place to focus a day-trip on this side of the province. Framed by a halo of royal palms, the **Campismo Boquerón** is the entry and focal point for visits, occupying a hidden paradise of banana groves, fruit trees and flitting hummingbirds. Overnight stays here are now officially reserved for Cubans only (though foreigners sometimes slip in), but anyone can explore this beautiful spot for free. The nearby **Jatibonico River** twists through the hills and makes an excellent spot for shady swimming, while the explorable caves hollowing into the hillsides are full of stalactites, stalagmites and Aboriginal pictographs.

ARRIVAL AND DEPARTURE

BOQUERÓN NATURE RESERVE

By taxi A taxi from Morón to Boquerón will cost around $1000CUP return. Chambas and Florencia don't have any taxi firms, but you should be able to negotiate a ride to Boquerón with local drivers.

By train Chambas and Florencia are served by a train from Morón three times a week.

By organized tour Trips to the area can be arranged through Havanatur in Ciego de Ávila (☎ 33 26 6339).

Jardines del Rey

Lying 30km off Ciego de Ávila's north coast and hemmed in by 400km of coral reef, the **Jardines del Rey** (The King's Gardens) were christened by Diego Velázquez in 1514 in honour of King Ferdinand of Spain. The cays are the dazzling jewels in the province's crown, with a rich tangle of mangroves, mahogany trees and lagoons iced by sugar sands and thick with pink flamingos, and a top **diving** location with an infrastructure to match.

Despite their auspicious naming in the sixteenth century, the numerous islets spanning the coastline from Ciego de Ávila to Camagüey remained uninhabited and relatively unexplored until as recently as the late 1980s. Until then, they had only been visited by colonial-era pirates and corsairs seeking a bolthole to stash their spoils; Ernest Hemingway, who sailed around them in the 1930s and 1940s; and former dictator Fulgencio Batista, who had a secret hideaway on tiny Cayo Media Luna, a mere pinprick on the map and now a favourite haunt for sunbathers and snorkellers.

The exclusivity of the Jardines del Rey was breached in 1988 by the construction of a 29km stone **causeway** (or *pedraplén*) across the Bahía de los Perros, connecting the Isla de Turiguanó peninsula to Cayo Coco. Today, two of the islands – **Cayo Coco** and smaller **Cayo Guillermo** – have a string of all-inclusive hotels planted along their northern shores. While the causeway has had a negative environmental impact, disrupting the natural flow of water and impoverishing conditions for local wildlife, there's still plenty of birdlife in the area (see box, page 308).

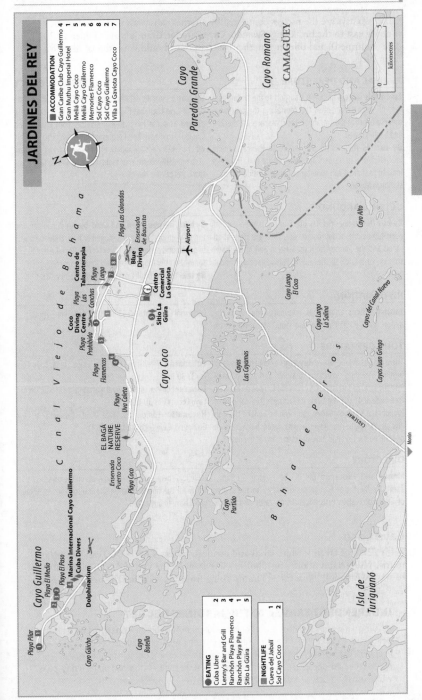

JARDINES DEL REY

■ ACCOMMODATION
Gran Caribe Club Cayo Guillermo	4
Gran Muthu Imperial Hotel	1
Meliá Cayo Coco	5
Meliá Cayo Guillermo	3
Memories Flamenco	6
Sol Cayo Coco	8
Sol Cayo Guillermo	2
Villa La Gaviota Cayo Coco	7

● EATING
Cuba Libre	2
Lenny's Bar and Grill	3
Ranchón Playa Flamenco	4
Ranchón Playa Pilar	1
Sitio La Güira	5

■ NIGHTLIFE
Cueva del Jabalí	1
Sol Cayo Coco	2

CAMAGÜEY

Cayo Paredón Grande

Cayo Romano

Cayo Alto

Cayo Largo El Coco

Cayos del Canal Nuevo

Cayo Largo La Salina

Cayos Juan Griego

Playa Las Coloradas

Ensenada de Bautista

Airport

Blue Diving

Centro de Talasoterapia

Playa Larga

Centro Comercial La Gaviota

Coco Diving Centre

Playa Las Conchas

Sitio La Güira

Playa Prohibida

Cayos Las Coyamas

Playa Flamencos

Cayo Coco

Playa Uva Caleta

EL BAGÁ NATURE RESERVE

Ensenada Puerto Coco

Playa Coco

Cayo Partido

Bahía de Perros

CAUSEWAY

Morón

Isla de Turiguanó

C a n a l   V i e j o   d e   B a h a m a

Cayo Guillermo

Playa Pilar

Playa El Medio

Playa El Paso

Marina Internacional Cayo Guillermo

Cuba Divers

Dolphinarium

Cayo Güicho

Cayo Batella

0   5
kilometres

6

6

The two cays are themselves connected by another causeway, with an offshoot running east to the breakaway **Swandor Cayo Paredón Grande** (due to open in 2022, no date confirmed), and offering another beach option should you exhaust those on the main islets.

ARRIVAL AND DEPARTURE
JARDINES DEL REY

Essentials There is no public transport to the Jardines del Rey. All road traffic enters the cays along the causeway; there's a booth at the entrance where passports are checked and a toll is levied.

By taxi As there is no bus service to the cays, many independent day-trippers opt for a private taxi. Travellers looking to share a cab sometimes gather outside the train station in Morón.

By plane Jardines del Rey airport (☎ 33 30 8228), on the east of Cayo Coco, has flights from Havana (3 weekly; 2hr), as well as some international services from Europe and Canada. From here hotel representatives whisk passengers off to their accommodation; if you haven't booked accommodation with your flight, you'll be able to take a taxi to a hotel of your choice.

GETTING AROUND

By bus The Jardines del Rey Bus Tour is a hop-on hop-off open-top double-decker bus service. There are stops at all hotels and the journey from the eastern end of the hotel strip on Cayo Coco all the way to Playa Pilar takes about 1.5hr.

By bike, moped, jeep and sand-buggy Zipping around the near-empty roads on a moped or bike, is the best way to get around on the cays. Many hotels offer bike rental, and some also offer moped, jeep and sand-buggy rental.

By taxi You can book taxis from all the hotel desks.

INFORMATION

Tourist offices Infotur has information points at the airport (☎ 33 30 9109; daily 8am–5pm) and at the Centro

Comercial La Gaviota (☎ 33 30 1001; daily 8am–5pm).

TOUR OPERATORS

There are lots of land-based **day-trips** around the cays and beyond, including excursions to Morón and a Jeep Safari into the local countryside, taking in the Laguna de la Leche (see page 304) and the Loma de Cunagua (see page 305). Broadly the same organized tours can be booked through any of the state-run travel agents listed below, which operate on the cays and have desks in many of the hotels.

Cubanacán *Hotel Tryp Cayo Coco*, Playa Larga, Cayo Coco (☎ 33 30 1215).

Cubatur Edificio 15, Villa Azul, Carretera a Cayo Guillermo, Cayo Coco (☎ 33 30 1236).

Havanatur Edificio 13, Villa Azul, Carretera a Cayo Guillermo, Cayo Coco (☎ 33 30 1371).

DIRECTORY

Money and exchange The BFI bank (Mon–Fri 9am–3pm), by the Cupet Garage mini-complex in the centre of Cayo Coco, gives cash advances on cards and cashes

travellers' cheques. There are no ATMs on the cays.

Wi-fi All the hotels have on-site internet access, though you'll have to buy a card.

Cayo Coco

With 22km of creamy-white sands and cerulean waters, **CAYO COCO** easily fulfils its tourist-blurb claim of offering a holiday in paradise. The islet is 32km wide from east to west, with a hill like a camel's hump rising from the middle. The best beaches are

---

INDEPENDENT TRAVEL TO THE JARDINES DEL REY

All foreign travellers, whether drivers or passengers, must bring their **passport** to get past the police checkpoint at the start of the causeway to the cays. Technically all beaches are open to everyone, but in reality some parts have become the exclusive domain of hotel guests – many hotels offer non-guests access to all their facilities once they've stumped up for a **day-pass**, which usually covers all meals and drinks.

COCKFIGHTING

Cockfighting has been the sport of Cuban farmers since the eighteenth century, with sizeable sums of money changing hands on bets, and thefts of prized specimens and allegations of rooster nobbling common. There is a particular breed of rooster indigenous to Cuba that exercises considerable cunning in defeating its opponent, parrying attacks and throwing false moves, and the bloodlines of these birds are protected and nurtured as carefully as those of any racehorse.

Since the **ban on gambling** introduced by the Revolution, this cruel practice has been pushed underground – although the sport itself is still legal. Nowadays cockfighting is a clandestine affair, taking place on smallholdings deep in the country at the break of dawn, when the fowl are in vicious ill-humour and at their fighting best. Unlike the shows laid on for tourists, where the cocks are eventually separated, the spurred cocks here will slug it out to the death.

clustered on the north coast, dominated by the all-inclusive hotels whose tendrils are gradually spreading along the rest of the northern coastline.

Cayo Coco's beaches

Cayo Coco's main three **beaches**, **Playa Las Coloradas** and, 3km further west, **Playa Larga** (of which **Playa Las Conchas** is a continuation) hog the narrow easternmost peninsula jutting out of the cay's north coast. More than half of Cayo Coco's hotel resorts line up along the sand, and the scene is picturesque if pretty boisterous, with watersports and activities laid on by the hotels. Technically none of these are private beaches, but you may have to go beyond the hotel grounds to get to them, unless you buy a day-pass.

If you'd prefer peace and quiet to volleyball and aerobics sessions, seek out pockets of tranquillity such as **Playa Prohibida**, hidden behind a sand dune 1km east of Playa Larga. There are also several undeveloped beaches to the far west of the cay, in the vicinity of the **El Bagá nature reserve**.

Cayo Coco's interior

Dirt roads allow easy access into Cayo Coco's lush wooded **interior**, where hidden delights include hummingbirds, pelicans, gorgeous lagoons and the re-created **Sitio La Güira** village. Toward the extreme south, the land becomes marshier but is still navigable on foot, and is a haven for herons and the **white ibis** or *coco* that give the cay its name, as well as a number of animals – it's not uncommon to see wild boar scooting out of the undergrowth and wild bulls lumbering across the road. Also keep an eye out for the colony of **iguanas** that originally floated here from other islands on coconut husks.

Sitio La Güira

Daily 9am–11pm • Free • Charge for horseriding; prices for guided walks are negotiable • ☎ 33 30 1208

In the centre of Cayo Coco, 6km from the north coast, **Sitio La Güira** is a mocked-up, early twentieth-century poorer community built to impart some idea of traditional Cuban farming culture to visitors who might never venture further than the beach. Though it's something of a novelty theme park, a number of interesting exhibits rescue it from complete tackiness. The main features are a typical **country cottage** made entirely from palms with a thatched roof, a **ranch** where charcoal is made, and a **bohío**, a triangular palm hut in which tobacco leaves are dried. There's also a small children's **playground**. Less appealing are the animal shows, put on several times a day, featuring buffalo, dogs and bulls performing tricks, as well as cockfights.

Surrounded by lush greenery, Sitio La Güira also offers **walking** and **riding tours** through the mangrove outback, which is home to woodpeckers and nightingales, and on to the lakes in the interior where waterfowl and wild ducks nest.

ACCOMMODATION · CAYO COCO; SEE MAP PAGE 307

With no towns or villages to provide *casas particulares*, accommodation on Cayo Coco is almost totally limited to all-inclusives grouped together on the main beach strip. If you haven't pre-booked into one as part of a package holiday, it's a good idea to phone the hotels directly or check with Havanatur (☎ 33 26 6342) in Ciego de Ávila to enquire about cheaper rates, as some offer rooms at a reduced cost when they're not full. Otherwise, your best bet is to seek out the cheaper options in Morón (see page 301).

Meliá Cayo Coco Playa Flamenco ⓦ meliacuba.com. This adults-only resort is the most stylish of the Cayo Coco all-inclusives, with a more intimate feel than its brasher, more sprawling neighbours. Take your pick from elegant two-storey bungalows perched over a lagoon, or cheaper (but still spacious) rooms in two-storey blocks. The grounds are glorious, the staff friendly, and the restaurants are a cut above typical all-inclusive buffet fare. $$$

Memories Flamenco Playa Flamencos ⓦ memoriesresorts.com. This hotel has an airy design and a multitude of facilities including five restaurants, children's clubs and playgrounds, and an ebullient entertainments team. Standard rooms are tasteful if a little anonymous; some have stunning ocean views. $$$

Sol Cayo Coco Playa Las Coloradas ⓦ meliacuba.com. Painted in bright tropical colours, this popular family-oriented hotel has a mini-club for kids, free non-motorized watersports, a buffet restaurant, snack bar and beach grill, and a lively atmosphere with excited children running around causing mayhem. $$$

Villa La Gaviota Cayo Coco Playa Las Conchas ☎ 33 30 2180, ⓔ Recepcion1@villagaviotacayococo.co.cu. While this isn't the flashiest all-inclusive on the cay, it's by far the cheapest and it still has its good points, like two-storey blocks laid out in spacious surroundings with sea views, and a jetty leading down to a small private beach with golden sand. $$

EATING AND DRINKING · SEE MAP PAGE 307

Lenny's Bar and Grill Playa Prohibida. This tiny, thatched beach bar serves tasty barbecued chicken, fish and lobster, as well as soft drinks and beers. $$

Ranchón Playa Flamenco Playa Flamencos. The basic but reasonably well-prepared mains here include lobster, chicken and pork, while sides range from fried green bananas to rice. $$

Sitio la Güira ☎ 33 30 1208. A ranch restaurant in the midst of the theme park, serving moderately priced spaghetti and steaks and expensive seafood; in high season only, it stages a daily *guateque*, "a farm party with animation activities and lessons on typical dances". $$

NIGHTLIFE AND ENTERTAINMENT · SEE MAP PAGE 307

If you've paid for a day-pass at one of the all-inclusive hotels, you can have dinner and go on to the **hotel disco** afterwards for no extra charge; otherwise, the hotels charge an entrance fee for non-guests.

ERNEST HEMINGWAY'S SUBMARINE HUNT

The affection that **Ernest Hemingway** had for Cuba sprang from his love of **fishing**, and numerous photographs of him brandishing dripping marlin and swordfish testify to his success around the clear waters of the Jardines del Rey. He came to know the waters well and, when the United States entered World War II, Hemingway, already having seen action in World War I and the Spanish Civil War, was more than ready to do his bit.

With the full support of the US ambassador to Cuba, Spruille Braden, he began to spy on Nazi sympathizers living in Cuba. He gathered enough information to have his 12m fishing boat **Pilar** commissioned and equipped by the Chief of Naval Intelligence for Central America as a kind of Q-ship (an armed and disguised merchant ship used as a decoy or to destroy submarines). His search-and-destroy missions for Nazi submarines off the cays continued until 1944 and he was commended by the ambassador, although according to some critics – notably his wife Martha Gellhorn – the whole thing was mainly a ruse for Hemingway to obtain rationed petrol for his fishing trips. Although he never engaged in combat with submarines, Hemingway's Boys' Own fantasies found their way into print in the novel *Islands in the Stream*.

ACTIVITIES IN THE JARDINES DEL REY

The Atlantic Ocean fringing **Cayo Coco**'s northeast coast holds one of the world's longest **coral reefs**, with shoals of angel fish, butterfly fish, nurse sharks and surgeon fish weaving through forests of colourful sponges, and alarmingly large barracudas bucking below the water line. There are over forty **dive sites** spread over the length of the reef, averaging 10m in depth but reaching 35m in places. Several diving centres operate on the cays (all listed below) but, if you're staying at a hotel, you can organize a dive, or a boat trip, through the hotel itself and most establishments give free induction classes to guests.

Cayo Guillermo has its own dive centre, as well as some of the cays' best snorkelling off of Cayo Media Luna. It's also the only place you can kite surf in the country with winds regularly reaching speeds of 20–40km/hr. The best conditions are at the northern end of Plàya El Paso and on Playa El Medio.

There are also many other activities, from **fishing** and **boat trips** to **horseriding** along the beaches and exploring the lush interior south of Cayo Coco's hotel strip on **foot**. Though you can strike off on your own – ask at the hotels about hiring horses or arranging horse-drawn carriage tours – you can also book organized excursions (see page 308).

DIVING AND FISHING

Blue Diving Playa Las Coloradas, Cayo Coco ☎ 33 30 8180. In front of the *Meliá Cayo Coco*, they offer single dives, SNSI open-water courses, open-sea fishing and fly fishing.

Coco Diving Centre Playa Larga, Cayo Coco ⓦ amazingcocodiving.com. Just west of the *Tryp Cayo Coco*, this dive centre provides all equipment and offers everything from single dives and initiation courses, to four-day SNSI open-water courses. They also run fishing expeditions for billfish, snapper and bass around Cayo Media Luna.

Green Moray International Dive Centre Playa El Medio, Cayo Guillermo ☎ 33 30 1680. Beside the *Meliá Cayo Guillermo* hotel, and offering two daily dive trips to the best sites off Cayo Media Luna.

Marina Internacional Cayo Guillermo Cayo Guillermo ☎ 33 30 1737 or ☎ 33 30 1515. Located at the eastern end of the cay, they offer a range of fishing excursions.

BOAT TRIPS

Coco Diving Centre Playa Larga, Cayo Coco ☎ 30 1620. So-called "seafari" trips in a pleasure yacht that cruises around the coast and to the cay's celebrated flamingo community, and catamaran excursions for offshore swimming and snorkelling, with lunch and an open bar.

Jungle Tours Marina Internacional Cayo Guillermo Cayo Guillermo ☎ 33 30 1515. Based on Cayo Guillermo but with representatives in all the hotels, and offering the chance to captain your own two-person motorboat on tours into the narrow canals between the dense mangrove thickets that fringe the cays.

Marina Internacional Cayo Guillermo Cayo Guillermo ☎ 33 30 1737 or ☎ 33 30 1515. At the eastern end of the cay, offering all-day yacht "seafaris", with time set aside for offshore swimming and snorkelling.

KITESURFING

Havana Kiteboarding Club ⓦ havanakiteboarding. com. Based on Cayo Guillermo, this longstanding kitesurfing outfit also offers boat and jeep safaris, and catamaran trips. If you're an experienced kitesurfer, you can rent equipment. Otherwise, they offer a range of courses.

Cueva del Jabalí 1km south of Playa Prohibida. A glittery, loud cabaret complete with fire dancers followed by a disco, all staged in a natural cave 5km inland from the hotel strip, which takes its name from the wild boar evicted to make way for the venue.

Sol Cayo Coco Playa Las Coloradas ☎ 33 30 1280. With live salsa bands playing at top volume, glitter balls and a dancefloor of illuminated tiles, the disco here is raucous, glitzy and lots of fun without being too tacky.

Cayo Guillermo

Bordered by pearl-white sand melting into opal waters, sleepy **CAYO GUILLERMO**, west of Cayo Coco and joined to it by a 15km causeway, is a quieter, more serene retreat

6

than its neighbour: a place to fish, dive and relax. The cays' colony of twelve thousand **flamingos** (celebrated in all Cuban tourist literature) gather here to feed, and although they are wary of passing traffic, you can usually glimpse them swaying in the shallows and feeding on the sandbanks as you cross the causeway. As the presence of the birds testifies, the waters around Cayo Guillermo are home to an abundance of sea life including a wealth of fish, notably marlin, and the marina here offers a range of deep-sea fishing expeditions.

At only thirteen square kilometres, Cayo Guillermo is tiny, but its 4km of **beaches** seem infinite nonetheless. **Development** has been steadily growing, and although still considerably quieter than its neighbour, it's no longer the peaceful haven it once was. However, all the hotels are fairly close together, and the rest of the cay's stunning **beaches** remain largely untouched – you'll never have a problem finding solitude.

Just after the causeway that connects Cayo Guillermo with Cayo Coco are the two main beaches, **Playa El Medio** and **Playa El Paso**, home to all the hotels. Popular with package-tour holidaymakers, both are suitably idyllic with shallow swimming areas and lengthy swathes of sand. El Medio also has towering **sand dunes** celebrated as the highest in the Caribbean, and at low tide sandbars allow you to wade far out to sea.

Playa Pilar

On the western tip of Cayo Guillermo, gorgeous **Playa Pilar** is named after Ernest Hemingway's yacht, *Pilar*, and was the author's favourite Cuban hideaway. With limpid clear shallows and squeaky-clean sand, Playa Pilar is without doubt the top beach choice on Guillermo, if not in the entire cays. Largely undeveloped but still quite popular, precisely because of its natural character, there is a growing infrastructure here, including a number of new hotels (with additional resort developments underway), a beach bar and restaurant, and a watersports club.

ACCOMMODATION

CAYO GUILLERMO; SEE MAP PAGE 307

Gran Caribe Club Cayo Guillermo Playa El Paso ☎33 30 1712. This calm and quiet hotel has snazzy blue-and-yellow bungalows spread around spacious, manicured gardens, as well as a large free-form pool, four restaurants and ample sports facilities. It's significantly less expensive than the other hotels here, and you can find good discounted deals online. $$$

Gran Muthu Imperial Hotel Playa Pilar

ⓦmuthuhotels.com. This full-on luxury affair has airy, expansive rooms with all mod cons and ample pools, tennis courts and a gym. There are seven restaurants including an Italian, Chinese, Mexican and a beach-front seafood option. Bars are equally plentiful and include a cigar snug. $$$$

★ **Meliá Cayo Guillermo** Playa El Paso ⓦmeliacuba. com. Popular with divers on account of the nearby scuba centre, this swish hotel is one of the smartest on the strip.

BIRDING IN THE CAYS

The northern cays are an avian paradise and one of the best locations in the country for birdwatchers. To see as much as possible, your best bet is to contact Paulino López Delgado (Paulino.nature@nauta.cu), an informed, amiable, easy-going local guide who offers birdwatching and wildlife excursions around the Jardines del Rey and beyond.

A half-day-trip in Paulino's fabulous 1955 American Chevrolet BelAir covers Cayo Coco and Cayo Romano, or Cayo Guillermo and Cayo Coco. Expect to see the Cuban gnatcatcher, Oriente warbler, Zapata sparrow, Cuban vireo, Cuban bullfinch, Cuban green woodpecker, Cuban flicker, West Indian woodpecker, Cuban tody, Cuban oriole, Cuban black hawk, American kestrel, Cuban emerald hummingbird, loggerhead kingbird, Cuban pewee, Western spindalis, red-Legged thrush, American flamingo, and roseate spoonbill.

Paulino (and his son, Raynier) also offer five- and seven-day-trips around Western Cuba covering Cuba's Pinar del Río, Artemisa and Matanza provinces, with a focus on the Guaniguanico mountain range and the Zapata Peninsula wetlands.

Rooms are attractive and the range of restaurants includes Italian, international and an outdoor grill. There's a high-tech gym, beauty salon and tennis courts, and a long rickety wooden pier on the beach that's perfect for sunset strolls. $$$

Sol Cayo Guillermo Playa El Medio ⓦ meliacuba.com. Small, friendly, painted in pretty pastels and patronized largely by couples and honeymooners, this hotel has a very Spanish feel with its immaculately tiled reception area full of tinkling fountains. The appealing, sunny rooms have wooden furniture, balconies and all the standard facilities. $$$

EATING AND DRINKING

SEE MAP PAGE 307

Cuba Libre Playa El Paso. This tiny beach bar between the *Iberostar Daiquiri* and *Meliá Cayo Guillermo* hotels serves fresh fish, lobster, fried chicken and drinks. Mains are around $$

Ranchón Playa Pilar Playa Pilar. Excellent but pricey barbecued fish and lobster, served up in a simple wooden lean-to with skinny cats twirling around your ankles as you eat. Opening times fluctuate depending on the whims of the chef, but you are usually guaranteed service around lunchtime. $$$

Cayo Media Luna

From Playa Pilar, speedboats ferry sunbathers and snorkellers the short distance to **Cayo Media Luna**, a tiny crescent cay just across the water, with nothing other than a small, simple café. The cay's shallow waters make it a popular destination for **snorkellers**. Deeper offshore, the kaleidoscopic **coral reef** is rich with sponges, anemone, fish and corals, and offers excellent scuba diving (see page 311), while marlin, tuna, barracuda and sailfish are the potential haul for **anglers** (see page 311).

Cayo Paredón Grande

Some 12km to the northeast of Cayo Coco and connected to it by a small causeway starting around 6km east of Playa Las Coloradas, **Cayo Paredón Grande** is a thumbnail of a cay. With a couple of clean, pleasant beaches on the northern coastline, it makes an ideal retreat if you can get there, particularly as the view over the sea as you cross the causeway is glorious. The islet's focal point is the elegant nineteenth-century **lighthouse** (no entry) on the rocky headland of the northern tip, built by Chinese immigrant workers to guide ships through the coral-filled waters. If you visit Paredón Grande on a day-trip, take provisions with you as there are no facilities. The causeway leads through the uninhabited **Cayo Romano**, which is technically in Camagüey province though usually treated as an extension of the major cays.

Jardines de la Reina

Back on the mainland, the area south of Ciego de Ávila is made up of agricultural farming areas and small one-street towns like **Venezuela** and **Silveira**, each a clutch of humble concrete houses, built since the Revolution to house workers who previously lived in shacks, plus a central grocery store and a doctor. The only reason for heading south of the provincial capital, however, is for the outstanding diving and fishing at the **Jardines de la Reina** archipelago, a cluster of over six hundred tiny virgin cays some 80km from the mainland. The jumping-off point for trips to the cays is the barren fishing village of **Júcaro**, 32km south of Ciego de Ávila. It's a miserable collection of wooden shacks and half-finished cement constructions set around the derelict-looking Parque Martí and a malodorous fishing port. Don't let this deter you, as the real beauty round these parts is hidden underwater. As the whole area was declared a National Marine Park in 1996, protected from commercial fishing and with public access strictly controlled, the only way to get out to the cays is on a fishing or diving trip, usually for a minimum of six days,

6

DIVING IN THE JARDINES DE LA REINA

The diving at **Jardines de la Reina** is considered by many to be among the best in the world. More than eighty **dive sites** around the archipelago boast caves, canyons, and wall, spur and groove **coral** formations. The real draw, though, is the phenomenal abundance of **fish**, including many large species. Spectacular **feeding shows** are staged by Avalon staff, who attract scores of sharks with scraps of fish. Also abundant are monster-sized goliath grouper, barracuda, cubera snapper and tarpon; with luck, you may see eagle rays, hammerhead sharks, lemon sharks, nurse sharks and turtles.

All diving, fishing and accommodation is organized by the Italian specialist **tour operator** Avalon, which has been granted exclusive operating rights in this area and caters for no more than seven hundred divers per year. Accommodation is provided aboard *La Tortuga*, an air-conditioned, seven-cabin floating **hotel**, or on one of five impressive yachts. More information and booking is available directly from Avalon (Ⓦavalonoutdoor.com,Ⓦcubandivingcenters. com & Ⓦcubanfishingcenters.com). You can also book with Avalon through the UK operator **Scuba Place** (Ⓣ44 7644 8252), whose local office is on the seafront in Júcaro opposite the square (Ⓣ33 98 1004).

with the Italian specialist tour operator Avalon (see box above). The cays themselves, all completely deserted, are mostly covered in scrub with one of the only significant beaches at **Cayo Caguamas**, in the waters of Camagüey, where you can see iguanas and turtles, the latter venturing out onto the sand in the moonlight.

Camagüey city

Nestled 30km from the north coast in the heart of Camagüey, the provincial capital is aptly called the city of legends, its winding streets and wizened buildings weaving an atmosphere of intrigue. On first view, **CAMAGÜEY** is a bewildering place to negotiate, with a seemingly incomprehensible labyrinth of roads that were laid out in a futile attempt to confuse marauding pirates. It is this maze-like layout, highly unusual for the Americas, which won the historic centre of Camagüey Unesco World Heritage status in 2008. An aimless wander along the narrow cobbled streets, overhung by delicate balustrades and Rococo balconies, is one of the delights of a visit, as you round corners onto handsome parks and happen upon crumbling churches.

Cuba's third-largest city, Camagüey has enjoyed significant investment over recent years. Prompted in part by its five-hundredth anniversary in 2014, the Ministry of Tourism has attempted to broaden Camagüey's capacity and appeal for foreign visitors, renovating and refurbishing museums and historic buildings while opening new bars, restaurants and hotels. There are regular free concerts in the Plaza de los Trabajadores and summer alfresco cinema screenings, and townsfolk pull out all the stops for the annual June **carnival**, the highlight of the Camagüeyan calendar.

Peppered with churches and squares, Camagüey will take a couple of days to explore fully. Many sights are in easy walking distance of **Maceo** and **República**, the two main shopping streets, both largely pedestrianized and home to several hotels. Within just a block or two of the intersection between these streets are two of the city's most interesting churches and the **Casa Natal de Ignacio Agramonte**, birthplace of Camagüey's most revered son, a martyr of the struggle for independence. South of here, past the Plaza Antonio Maceo, is the congenial **Parque Agramonte**, the main square, home to the city's **cathedral**. Further south again is the **Plaza de San Juan de Dios** which, blessed with the **Iglesia San Juan de Dios** and **Museo de San Juan de Dios**, is Camagüey's most attractive colonial square. Although the northern end of town has fewer sights, it's still worth venturing up for a breeze around the quietly impressive **Museo Ignacio Agramonte**.

Brief history

One of Cuba's seven original *villas* founded by Diego Velázquez, Camagüey was established between 1514 and 1515 on the site of a sizeable Native American village, and although the original inhabitants were swiftly eradicated, traces of burial sites and ceramics have been found in the area. The only legacy of the Indigenous people

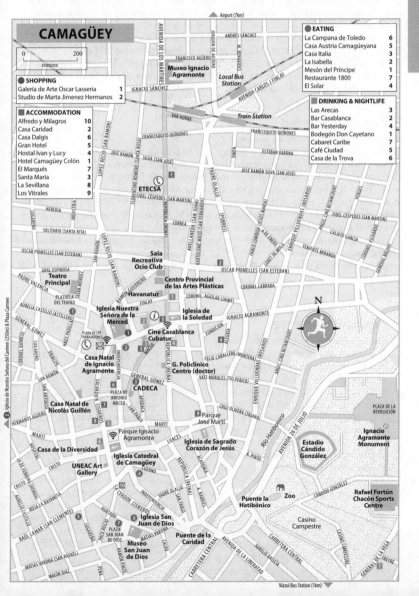

CAMAGÜEY

0 — 200 metres

● SHOPPING
Galería de Arte Oscar Lasseria	1
Studio de Marta Jimenez Hermanos	2

■ ACCOMMODATION
Alfredo y Milagros	10
Casa Caridad	2
Casa Dalgis	6
Gran Hotel	5
Hostal Ivan y Lucy	4
Hotel Camagüey Colón	1
El Marqués	7
Santa María	3
La Sevillana	8
Los Vitrales	9

● EATING
La Campana de Toledo	6
Casa Austria Camagüeyana	5
Casa Italia	3
La Isabella	2
Mesón del Príncipe	1
Restaurante 1800	7
El Solar	4

■ DRINKING & NIGHTLIFE
Las Arecas	3
Bar Casablanca	2
Bar Yesterday	4
Bodegón Don Cayetano	1
Cabaret Caribe	7
Café Ciudad	5
Casa de la Trova	6

remains in the city's name, thought to originate from the word *camagua*, a wild shrub common to the lowlands that's believed to have magical properties.

Initially known as **Santa María del Puerto del Príncipe**, the settlement was first established, in 1514, as a port town on the north coast where present-day Nuevitas lies. A year or so later, it was moved to the fertile lands of present-day Caonao on the northwestern edge of the province until, according to some sources, a rebel band of Native Americans forced the settlers out and the town moved once more, to its present site, in 1528. Straddling the Tínima and Hatibonico rivers, so as to be in the middle of the trade route between Sancti Spíritus and Bayamo, the newly settled town began to consolidate itself. During the 1600s its economy developed around sugar plantations and cattle farms, generating enough income to build distinguished churches and civil buildings in the following century. Despite intermittent ransacking by pirates, Puerto Príncipe grew into a sophisticated and elegant city, one its townsfolk fought hard to win from the Spanish during the Wars of Independence. Eventually, in 1903, following the end of Spanish rule, the city dropped its lengthy moniker and adopted the name by which it is now known.

Iglesia de la Soledad

República esq. Ignacio Agramonte • Daily 8am–noon • Free

Presiding over the intersection of Maceo and República is the **Iglesia de la Soledad**, tiered like a wedding cake and with a lofty tower that can be seen from all over the city. The **interior**, with its domed roof painted with Baroque frescoes, merits a look. There has been a church on this site since 1697 (the original was built from wood and guano), though the present structure dates from 1758. Like others in the town, the church has its very own creation myth. Apparently one rainy morning an animal carrier's cart became stuck in the mud in the road in front of the site. Everyone gathered around to push the wagon free and in the process a box bounced off the back and smashed open to reveal a statue of the Virgin. As the cart-driver could lay no claim to it, it was taken as a sign that the Virgin wanted a chapel built on this spot.

CAMAGÜEY'S PIRATES

Although not the only Cuban city to suffer constant attacks from **pirates**, irresistibly wealthy Camagüey was one consistently plagued, with buccaneers regularly rampaging through the city before retiring to the northern cays or the Isla de la Juventud to hide their spoils. To confound pirates, the centre of Camagüey was built as a web of narrow and twisted streets rather than the usual colonial city plan, with roads laid out in a regular grid pattern; however, the design did not deter the invaders, who left many legends in their wake. The first pirate to arrive was the singularly unpleasant Frenchman **Jacques de Sores** in 1555, who roamed the farms on the north coast stealing cows and cheese, as well as abducting women. (These last he would abandon violated in Cayo Coco to the mercy of the elements.) In 1668, Welsh buccaneer **Henry Morgan** – the terror of the Caribbean seas – and his men managed to occupy the city for several days before making off with a hefty booty of gold and jewels belonging to the Spanish bourgeoisie. With a dashing show of irreverence, he is also reputed to have locked the town elders into the Catedral de Santa Iglesia to starve them into revealing the whereabouts of their riches. Struggling to reassert itself eleven years later, in 1679 the city fell prey to the wiles of another Frenchman, **François de Granmont**. Nicknamed *El Caballero* (the gentleman), he sacked the city and captured fourteen women. After nearly a month of occupying the town he marched to the coast and released all the women unharmed, thus earning his nickname.

THE STORY OF EL SANTO SEPULCRO

In eighteenth-century Puerto Príncipe (as Camagüey was then known), a wealthy merchant named **Manuel de Agüero** employed a widowed housekeeper, **Señora Moya**. Master and servant each had a son of the same age, and it seemed natural for the boys to play and grow up together. Agüero paid for both to go to Havana to study at the university, and they seemed assured of bright futures. Tragedy struck when both young men met and fell in love with the same woman, and in a fit of pique Moya challenged Agüero to a **duel** and killed him.

Distraught, Agüero Senior promptly banished the murderous boy and his mother from his sight, lest his remaining sons avenge their brother's death. However, his woes were not over, as his wife, sick with a broken heart, wasted away and died soon after. Torn apart by grief, Agüero decided to become a friar, and, with his surviving sons' approval, poured their inheritance into jewels and treasures for the Church. The most splendid of all his tributes was the **Santo Sepulcro**, the silver coffin that he commissioned in readiness for his own death, now displayed in the Iglesia Nuestra Señora de la Merced. Long seen as a hero who rose above personal disaster to overcome bitterness, his is a puzzling tale of uneasy colonial values.

Centro Provincial de las Artes Plásticas

República no.289 e/ Finlay y Oscar Primelles • Daily 10am–7pm • Free

About halfway along República, the **Centro Provincial de las Artes Plásticas** stages a mixed bag of temporary exhibitions that are well worth dipping into – if only for the cool, airy space. The works featured are predominantly paintings by artists from Camagüey as well as other provinces, and are of a generally high standard, affording an insight into Cuban visual arts away from the tourist trail.

Iglesia Nuestra Señora de la Merced

Plaza de los Trabajadores • Mon 3.30–6pm, Tues–Sat 9.30–11.30am & 3.30–6pm • Free

At the western end of Ignacio Agramonte, the **Plaza de los Trabajadores** is a businesslike square beautified by some attractive colonial buildings and the **Iglesia Nuestra Señora de la Merced**, Camagüey's most impressive building. The story goes that one day in the seventeenth century, when the land here was still said to be submerged beneath a lake, the townsfolk heard shouts and screams from the thickets on the banks. Terrified to approach, they kept watch from a distance over several days until, to their amazement, a shimmering white church emerged from the water. Beckoning from the portal was a priest with a cross clasped in his hand: the Merced church had arrived. A more prosaic history tells that the church was built as a convent in 1747, and the rooms to the left of the chapel, set around a cool and attractive central patio, still serve as such today.

The church which adjoins the convent and chapel is a confection of styles following several rebuilds and extensions. Inside, the richly ornate Neo-Gothic altar imported from Spain contrasts with the delicate eighteenth-century Baroque balconies swooping above. The most intriguing item is the **Santo Sepulcro**, an ornate silver coffin, thickly coated with intertwined hand-beaten bells and flowers, made in 1762 from 25,000 molten silver coins by Mexican silversmith Juan de Benítez, and commissioned by an ill-fated merchant (see box above).

The crypt

Guided tours daily 8.30am–5pm; ask at the convent • Free

Hidden beneath the church, accessible by a tiny flight of stairs behind the main altar, is a fascinatingly macabre little **crypt**. Formerly an underground cemetery that ran all the way to López Recio, 500m away, much of it was bricked up following a fire and only a claustrophobic sliver remains. Among the musty **relics**, several life-sized statues gleam in the half-light, while embedded in the walls are the skeletal remains of a woman and her child: look carefully and you may see cockroaches skittering across the bones. There's no charge but contributions towards the upkeep of the church are much appreciated.

Casa Natal de Ignacio Agramont

Plaza de los Trabajadores • Tues–Sat 9am–5pm, Sun 9am–noon • Charge

On the south side of Plaza de los Trabajadores is the **Casa Natal de Ignacio Agramonte**, an attractive colonial house with dark-wood balustrades. Birthplace of the local hero of the first War of Independence, whose full name was Ignacio Agramonte y Loynaz, it was converted into a market after his death and later into a bar; it opened as a museum in 1973. All of Agramonte's possessions were confiscated when he took up arms against the Spanish colonial powers and, although never returned to him while he was alive, they now form part of the displays here. The standard of life enjoyed by wealthy sugar plantation owners like the Agramontes is well highlighted by their impressive furniture, including a well-crafted piano and oversized *tinajones* out in the central patio. Free piano recitals are held every Saturday night at 8.30pm.

Casa Natal de Nicolás Guillén

Hermanos Agüero 58 e/ Cisneros y Príncipe • Mon–Fri 8am–noon & 1–4.30pm, Sat 8am–noon • Charge

One block south of Plaza de los Trabajadores is the **Casa Natal de Nicolás Guillén**. An African-Cuban born in 1902, Guillén was one of Cuba's foremost poets and is renowned throughout Latin America, particularly for his eloquent pieces on the condition of Black people in Cuba, whose profile he raised and whose cause he championed in his writing. A founding member of the National Union of Writers and Artists (UNEAC), an organization responsible for much of the promotion of the arts in Cuba, and recipient of the Lenin Peace Prize, he died in 1989. The small house in which he was born has relics of his life, but nothing really gives much of an insight into his days there. There are, however, many of his poems in poster form on the walls, and a good selection of photographs to peruse.

Parque Ignacio Agramonte

At the southern end of Maceo is the bijou **Plaza Antonio Maceo**, from where it's one block south down Independencia to **Parque Ignacio Agramonte**. Filled with shady tamarind trees and marble benches, this pretty square is the town's social centre. Each corner is pegged by a **royal palm** to symbolize the deaths of four independence fighters – leader Joaquín Agüero, Tomás Betancourt y Zayas, Fernando de Zayas and Miguel Benavides – shot for treason here by the Spanish in the early struggles for independence. The men were immediately hailed as martyrs and the townsfolk planted the palms as a secret tribute, the Spanish authorities ignorant of their significance. Dominating the park's south side is the large **Santa Iglesia de Camagüey**; though its architecture and interior are unremarkable, if you climb to the top of the bell tower you'll be rewarded with panoramic views over the city.

Casa de la Diversidad

Salvador Cisneros no.69 e/ Martí y Luaces, Parque Ignacio Agramonte • Mon–Fri 10am–6pm, Sat 9am–7pm, Sun 8am–noon • Charge

One of the most striking civil buildings in the city is the **Casa de la Diversidad**, whose florid Moorish-style blue-and-white exterior frames the swirling designs of its wrought-iron window railings. Inside are murals, a lovely patio and a half-decent museum. Four exhibition rooms provide a brisk walk through the history and culture of Camagüey, with music, dance, religion, decorative art and architecture all briefly covered – don't miss the detailed murals in the bathrooms.

Iglesia de Nuestra Señora del Carmen

Plaza del Carmen • Tues–Sat 8am–noon & 3–5pm, services Sun 11am & 6pm • Free

On the western side of the old town is Camagüey's only twin-towered church, the **Iglesia de Nuestra Señora del Carmen**, completed in 1825. The simple interior is enlivened by bright panels of stained glass in red, blue and green, while the cupola ceiling painting of various saints is worth a look.

Outside the church, the photogenic **Plaza del Carmen** is peppered with rather amusing life-sized statues of local people – several of their real-life counterparts attempt to capitalize on their bronze incarnations by asking for money in return for a posed photograph.

Iglesia de Sagrado Corazón de Jesús

Plaza de la Juventud • Daily 9am–noon • Free

A few blocks east of Parque Agramonte is one of the city's only twentieth-century churches, the **Iglesia de Sagrado Corazón de Jesús**. Built in 1920, its towering Neo-Gothic structure makes a striking contrast to most of the other churches in the old town. After passing through the forbidding mahogany doorway, you'll find yourself under a Neo-Gothic crossed roof; lining the walls are four wooden altars skilfully painted in trompe l'oeil to look like marble, typical of the era. Light trickling through cracked stained glass gives this rather faded church a pleasing air of serenity.

Plaza de San Juan de Dios

Six blocks south of the Sagrado Corazón is the eighteenth-century **Plaza de San Juan de Dios**, the city's most photogenic square. A neat cobbled plaza with red-tiled pavements and little traffic, it's bordered with well-kept lemon-yellow and dusty-pink buildings, their windows hemmed with twists of sky-blue balustrades. A stall selling artisans' products can be found in the square most days.

Iglesia San Juan de Dios

Plaza de San Juan de Dios • Daily 8am–noon • Free

On the northern corner of Plaza de San Juan de Dios is the **Iglesia San Juan de Dios**, built in 1728. A single squat bell-tower rises like a turret from a simple symmetrical facade saved from austerity by soft hues of green and cream. The dark interior is richly Baroque, typical of Cuban colonial style, with rows of chocolatey wood pews and a

---

IGNACIO AGRAMONTE – REBEL AND DAREDEVIL

The son of wealthy Camagüeyan cattle farmers, **Ignacio Agramonte y Loynaz** (1841–73) studied law in Havana and then in Spain before returning in 1868 to become a revolutionary leader in the first War of Independence against Spain. Back in his homeland, he incited the men of Camagüey to take up arms against the Spanish, taking the town at the end of that year and forming a small unorthodox republic with some of the local farm owners. He was known as the **Daredevil of the Wars of Independence** for his often misguided valour – on one occasion, when one of his fighters was captured by the Spanish, he dashed off to rescue his unfortunate compatriot from the 120-strong enemy column, armed only with a machete and 34 of his most trusted men – and actually lived to tell the tale. Killed aged 32 on the battlefields of Jimaguayú, Agramonte's youth as well as his passion for his province guaranteed him a revered place as one of the local martyrs of the Wars of Independence.

gilded altar. Note the original brick floor, the only one remaining in any church in Camagüey.

Museo de San Juan de Dios

Plaza de San Juan de Dios • Tues–Sat 9am–5pm, Sun 9am–1pm • Charge

Fitted snugly to the side of the Iglesia San Juan de Dios is the old **Hospital de San Juan de Dios**. Ignacio Agramonte's body was brought here after he was slain on the battlefield; the Spanish hid his remains from the Cubans without allowing them to pay their last respects and burned him as an example to other would-be dissidents. It now houses the **Museo de San Juan de Dios**, with some early maps and photographs of the town in bygone years. The display only takes up a small corner of the hospital, and the real pleasure lies in looking around the well-preserved building, admiring the original heavy wood staircase, cracked *vitrales*, courtyard filled with *tinajones* and palms, and the view over the church tower from the second floor.

Casino Campestre

The eastern border of the colonial centre is the murky Río Hatibonico; on the other side of the river is the vast **Casino Campestre**, the biggest city park in Cuba and a refreshingly spacious and verdant contrast to the tightly packed, mostly concrete old town. Spliced by the Juan del Toro River, and dappled by royal palms, it has a children's area, a bandstand and an unimpressive zoo (best avoided), while among the shady trees are monuments to local martyr Salvador Cisneros Betancourt and former mayor Manuel Ramón Silva. The **Estadio Cándido González** baseball stadium and a sports centre sit beyond the landscaped section to the north of the park, as does the **Plaza de la Revolución** which, in keeping with all Cuban squares of this ilk, is a wide-open concrete space overseen by a large monument, this one featuring a statue of Ignacio Agramonte.

Museo Ignacio Agramonte

Avenida de los Mártires • Tues–Fri 9am–5pm, Sat 9am–4pm, Sun 9am–noon • Charge

While the north end of Camagüey has few sights, it's worth making the effort to check out the **Museo Ignacio Agramonte**, just beyond the top end of República. Also known as the Museo Provincial, it has an elegant Art Deco exterior, the unassuming white facade masking its sleek lines and the geometric lettering announcing the museum's name. While there's nothing to suggest a connection with its namesake, the museum's engaging array of exhibits includes some quality nineteenth-century **furniture**, most notably a *tinajero* washstand with a stone basin inset and some fine Sèvres china. Most impressive is the **fine art collection**, which includes a Victor Manuel García original,

---

TINAJONES

Dotted around the city, in public and private spaces, are the large bulbous clay jars known as **tinajones**. Seen throughout Camagüey, they were originally storage jars used to transport wine, oil and grain, and were introduced by the Spanish as the solution to the city's water shortage, placed beneath gutters so that they could fill with rainwater. Slightly tapered at one end, they were half-buried in earth, keeping the water cool and fresh. They soon came to be produced in the town, and every house had one outside; inevitably, they became a status symbol, and a family's wealth could be assessed by the style and quantity of their *tinajones*. They also came in handy during the Wars of Independence when soldiers escaping the Spanish would hide in them. Indeed, so proud are the Camagüeyans of their *tinajones* that a local saying has it that all who drink the water from one fall in love and never leave town.

Muchacha, and a good example of the Cuban Vanguard movement, which introduced modern art to the country between 1920 and 1960.

ARRIVAL AND DEPARTURE

By plane Daily flights from Havana arrive at the Ignacio Agramonte airport (☎32 26 1010), 7.5km northeast of the city, from where you can catch a bus (5 daily) or taxi into town.

Destinations Havana: (9 weekly; 1hr 35min).

Airlines Cubana, República no.400 esq. Correa (Mon–Fri 8am–4pm, Sat 8.30–11.00am; ☎32 29 2156).

By train The train station (☎32 29 2633) is on the northern edge of town, near the municipal bus station. Take a cheap *bicitaxi* to the centre – or you can walk to the northern end of República in five minutes. For tickets and timetables go to the terminal building opposite the *Hotel Plaza*, on the other side of Avellaneda. Timetables are unreliable and subject to frequent changes. Note that the service to Morón has been

CAMAGÜEY CITY

entirely suspended for months at a time in recent years.

Destinations Bayamo (2 weekly; 6hr); Ciego de Ávila (6 weekly; 2hr); Havana (6 weekly; 9hr); Las Tunas (1 daily; 2hr); Matanzas (6 weekly; 6hr); Morón (1 daily; 3hr); Santa Clara (2 weekly; 7hr); Santiago de Cuba (4 weekly; 6–9hr).

By bus Víazul buses (call ☎32 27 0396; Mon–Fri 10am–6pm, Sat 10am–2pm for reservations) pull in at the bus station on the Carretera Central, 3km south of the town centre. How many trips there are daily to destinations varies so it's worth calling ahead to check.

Destinations Ciego de Ávila (2 daily; 1hr 30min); Havana (5 daily; 8hr); Sancti Spíritus (2 daily; 2hr 30min); Santa Clara (2 daily; 4 hr); Santa Lucía (1 daily; 2hr); Santiago de Cuba (3 daily; 6hr); Trinidad (1 daily; 5hr).

GETTING AROUND

By car Car rental is available from Havanautos at Independencia no.210 (Mon–Sat 9am–5pm; ☎32 29 6270).

By bicitaxi There are *bicitaxi* ranks at the Plaza de los

Trabajadores, the *Hotel Camino de Hierro* on República and down by the river next to the Puente de la Caridad.

By taxi Call Cubacar (☎32 29 2550) or Transtur (☎32 27 1015).

INFORMATION, TRAVEL AGENTS AND TOURS

Tourist office National tourist information provider, Infotur, has an office at El Callejón de los Milagros, on Ignacio Agramonte (Mon–Sat 8.30am–5.30pm; ☎32 25 6794).

Camaguax Tours An excellent local travel agent, superior to any of the state-run agents, with an extensive catalogue of reasonably priced tours around the city and province. The office is at República no.155 e/ General Gómez y Padre Valencia (24hr; ☎32 28 7364, ⊛camaguax.com),

but (unofficially) you can also enquire about their tours at Infotur.

Cubanacán At the *Hotel Plaza* at Van Horne no.1 e/ Avellaneda y República (daily 9am–4pm; ☎32 29 7374). They sell maps, phonecards and flights, and organize day-trips around the province, including to the Jardines de la Reina.

Havanatur República no.271 esq. Finlay (Mon–Sat 9am–12.30pm & 1.30–5pm).

ACCOMMODATION

SEE MAP PAGE 315

Camagüey has around a dozen **hotels** and has enjoyed a spate of centrally located boutique hotels opening in the last few years. There are also a number of excellent, centrally located **casas particulares** to choose from and equal numbers of *jineteros* doing what they can to take advantage of people looking for them (see page 36).

HOTELS

Gran Hotel Maceo no.67 e/ Ignacio Agramonte y General Gómez ☎32 29 2093. Graciously faded eighteenth-century building that became a hotel in the 1930s, with well-maintained rooms; the best have balconies overlooking the busy street below, though others are a little pokey. The small pool, elegant marble dining room with panoramic views, and a dark and sultry piano bar are nice additions. $$$

★ **Hotel Camagüey Colón** República no.472 e/ San

José y San Martín ⊛melia.com. This beautiful museum of a hotel in the heart of the city was built in 1927 and has been artfully renovated, preserving its Baroque balconies, exquisite tiling, cracked marble staircase and corridors bathed in greenish light. The comfortable rooms, with reproduction 1920s furniture, are small and lack natural light, but this is more than compensated for by the building's class and character; the best rooms are arranged around a pretty patio housing a bar and a veranda where breakfast is served. $$$

★ **El Marqués** Cisneros no.222 e/ Hermano Aguero y Martí ⊛hotelescubanacan.com. A graceful, single-floor boutique hotel with two adjoining patios around which all six of the attractive, dignified rooms are arranged. The patio towards the back has sun loungers and a jacuzzi while the more central one, where breakfasts are served, is pleasingly swamped by the low-hanging branches of two small trees. $$

6

6

Santa María República esq. Ignacio Agramonte Ⓦ hotelescubanacan.com. About as central as you can get, this hotel is at its best in the ground-floor communal areas, with a peaceful café in the muted elegance of the lobby and a fountain-centred patio. Rooms are perfectly pleasant but nothing special. A safe option. $\overline{\underline{\$\$}}$

La Sevillana Cisneros no. e/ Hermano Aguero y Martí, Ⓦ hotelescubanacan.com. Opened in late 2015, this splendid Spanish-styled building is the most impressive of the city's new boutique hotels. Modern stained-glass windows imbue the place with colour, among them a glass arch between the lobby and the Neoclassical patio where a statue-topped fountain takes centre stage. There's a suntrap roof terrace and lovely rooms full of neo-colonial furniture. $\overline{\underline{\$\$}}$

CASAS PARTICULARES

Alfredo y Milagros Cisneros no.124 esq. Raúl Lamar ☎ 32 29 7436, ✉ allan.carnot@gmail.com. Very professionally run outfit, with English and French spoken. All three rooms are well appointed, with fridges, fans, a/c, private bathrooms and desks, and there are extensive menus for meals and cocktails. The owners' son, a trained masseur, offers a massage service. A pretty patio tiled in pink and green marble and a tropical fish tank complete the picture. $\overline{\underline{\$}}$

★ **Casa Caridad** Oscar Primelles no.310a e/ Bartolomé Masó y Padre Olallo ☎ 32 29 1554, ✉ caridadgarciavalera@gmail.com. Three rooms – with private bathrooms, good water pressure in the showers, excellent a/c and fully stocked minibar-style fridges –

arranged along a sunny passageway. The best feature of the spacious house is a pretty garden complete with a large *tinajon* under a flowery bower. $\overline{\underline{\$}}$

Casa Dalgis Independencia no.251 (altos) e/ Hermanos Aguero y General Gómez ☎ 32 28 5732, ✉ minerva@mmnauta.cu. This fabulous apartment overlooking Plaza Maceo is decorated with antique furniture, colourful floor tiles and chandeliers. The three rooms (one triple, one double and one single) have wrought-iron and brass bedsteads and their own bathrooms, and there's a balcony from where you can watch life go by below. $\overline{\underline{\$}}$

★ **Hostal Ivan y Lucy** Alegría no.23 e/ Ignacio Agramonte y Montera ☎ 32 28 3701, ✉ ivanlucy@gmail.com. A spacious, spotlessly clean house run by a charming family. One room, more like an apartment, occupies an entire upstairs floor, with three beds and room for four people; the other, a double, is on the ground floor next to the beautiful garden, which boasts a fountain, caged songbirds, rocking chairs, its very own bar and a pond filled with carp and terrapins. Both feature private bathrooms, minibars and top-notch a/c. An upper terrace and huge breakfasts help make this an exceptional choice. $\overline{\underline{\$}}$

Los Vitrales Avallaneda no.3 e/ General Gómez y Martí ☎ 32 29 5866, ✉ requejobarreto@gmail.com. This beautiful former convent is chock-full of antiquities and stained-glass panels, from which it takes its name. Its four bedrooms are big, with a/c, fridge and minibar. Food is excellent and the house itself a gem, but the owners have a tendency to double-book rooms. Parking available and English and Italian spoken. $\overline{\underline{\$}}$

EATING

SEE MAP PAGE 315

Camagüey has a good selection of **restaurants** and **paladars**, and there are a couple of good local specialities. At carnival time, look out for steaming pots of a meat and vegetable broth called *ajiaco*, cooked in the street over wood fires. All the neighbours pile out of the houses and chuck in their own ingredients while an elected chef stirs the concoction to perfection. You can also sample this delicacy in local eateries throughout the year.

La Campana de Toledo Plaza de San Juan de Dios ☎ 32 28 6812. This state restaurant is set in a leafy courtyard inside a pretty blue-and-yellow building with a red-brick roof and a quaint tradition of tolling the bell when anyone enters or leaves. It serves the usual quasi-international and Cuban cuisine, but the tranquil setting makes it a top choice for a mellow, moderately priced meal. $\overline{\underline{\$\$}}$

Casa Austria Camagüeyana Lugareño no.121 e/ San

CARNIVAL TIME

Camagüey is particularly vibrant during its week-long **carnival** in late June, when an exuberant parade takes place on the main streets and musicians dressed in multicoloured, frilled costumes twirl huge batons adorned with silver glitz, bang drums and clap cymbals while others dance, swig beer and quarrel with the parade officials. Floats with disco lights, bouncing speakers and unsmiling girls in home-made costumes dancing energetically bring up the rear, while running in between the different trucks are **diablitos**, men disguised head to foot in raffia, who dart into the crowd with the seemingly sole purpose of terrorizing the assembled children. Stalls selling gut-rot beer in vast paper cups (hang on to your empties – cup supplies often run out) and roast suckling pig provide refreshment.

Rafael y San Clemente ☎32 28 5580. The city's most unexpected paladar brings authentic Austrian trademarks like *Wiener schnitzel* (breaded lamb) and *Rostbraten* (beef fried with onions) to central Cuba; the Cuban offerings padding out the menu are at least as worthwhile. Bypass the slightly staid though dressed-up front room and head for the atmospheric pondside patio, perhaps a little heavy on the flashing lights but otherwise picturesque. The slightly out-of-the-way location sometimes means it's quiet here. $$

Casa Italia Calle San Ramon no. 11 esq General Gomez ☎52 712 654. A decent attempt at authentic Italian food here with pizzas cooked in a wood-burning oven and prepared with fresh ingredients. Other specialities include lobster thermidor and bruschetta to start. The restaurant itself is pleasingly atmospheric, with tables arrayed beside an interior courtyard filled with palms and a giant *tinajón*. $$

La Isabella Ignacio Agramonte esq. Independencia ☎32 24 2925. Italian restaurant where most of the substantial pizzas are very affordably priced, though it pays to add extra toppings as they can otherwise be a little plain. Fabulous Cuban cinema posters fill one of the walls while director's chairs and clapboard menus complete the movie theme. Frosted windows make it feel cut off from the outside, but the a/c can be very welcome. $$

Mesón del Príncipe Astillero no.7 e/ San Ramón y Lugareño ☎32 29 3770. Choose from shrimp, lobster, chicken, fish and pork, each cooked to some ten different recipes. Highlights are the fish fillet in *salsa caribeña*, a sweetish sauce with pineapple, onion, green and mild red chillis, or the sliced lamb in a spicy tomato sauce. Of the excellent cocktails, the sangría-like Limonada Clarete is the most refreshing. $$

★ **Restaurante 1800** Plaza San Juan de Dios ☎32 28 3619. It's rare to find a buffet outside the all-inclusives, and this atmospheric paladar offers a very good quality spread. Sit out on the square or in the pretty courtyard where you can watch the chef prepare your food on the outdoor grill to the strains of a local band. The simple á la carte options cover a nice range of Cuban cooking, from a traditional *chilindrón* lamb ste, to shredded beef, and shrimp in tomato, chilli and onion sauce. $$

El Solar Independencia no.126 e/ Pobre y Cuerno ☎32 29 7618. All the usual Cuban suspects are on the menu here, but it's a good place to try the local speciality of *ajiaco*, or the daily specials, usually announced by the raconteur owner José Ángel. There are three small dining spaces but the most fun is the front room where you eat virtually shoulder to shoulder with the punters on the other three tables, all huddled around the tiny bar from where José Ángel often holds court and a TV plays music videos. There's a more sterile upstairs room and another sociable little room downstairs. $$

DRINKING, NIGHTLIFE AND ENTERTAINMENT

The Parque Ignacio Agramonte is usually the liveliest outdoor space in central Camagüey after dark, home to one of the city's best live music venues, the Casa de la Trova, and a couple of buzzing bars. Otherwise, the majority of the bars are on República and although most are inexpensive they are also generally pretty dreary – you're generally better off at the bars and squares south of Ignacio Agramonte (the street not the square).

BARS, CLUBS AND LIVE MUSIC VENUES
SEE MAP PAGE 315

Las Arecas Gran Hotel, Maceo no.67 e/ Ignacio Agramonte y General Gómez ☎32 29 2093. Though all the big hotels have their own bars, the only one worth lingering in is this dark, atmospheric piano bar, which sometimes has live music.

Bar Casablanca El Callejón de los Milagros ☎32 28 5200. One of the city's, flashiest music venues, this is more nightclub than bar, and one of the best places in Camagüey for a proper night out. Tables on two levels, divided by arches, surround a T-shaped stage with regular live music performances, mostly salsa and jazz. Though the bar staff wear a Moroccan-style waistcoat and fez and there are a few *Casablanca* posters on the walls, the music videos projected behind the stage ensure the ambience falls a long way short of *Rick's Café*-style colonial chic. Severe air-conditioning.

Bar Yesterday República no.222 e/ Ignacio Agramonte y Callejón del Castellano ☎32 24 4943. A Beatles-themed venue in terms of the decor, but the music policy is classic pop and rock. It's a well-designed, loungey place, with low-slung, cushiony seats in the streetside bar and out back, along one side of the patio, which has its own bar and a stage where tribute bands and the like perform.

Bodegón Don Cayetano República no.79 e/ Callejón de la Soledad y Callejón Magdelena ☎32 29 1961. Immense wooden doors, tiled floors and dark-stained wooden beams all give this atmospheric bar and restaurant a taverna feel, in keeping with the tapas menu. Chorizo, prawns, tuna and *frituras* (corn fritters) are all tasty and good value. There's a pleasant cobbled outdoor area as well. Just right for early evening drinks.

Cabaret Caribe Alturas del Casino ☎32 29 8112. This cabaret-cum-club is a dark and sultry space with a music show most evenings. Tuesday and Saturday are considered the best nights; on Saturday the cabaret is followed by a banging reggaeton and salsa disco. It's worth booking a ticket in advance; ask at Infotur (see page 321).

Café Ciudad Parque Ignacio Agramonte ☎32 25 8412. This is a pretty straightforward tavern-style bar, with a restaurant out back, but the location right on the city's liveliest square ensures it's usually one of the more animated places for a drink at night.

★ **Casa de la Trova** Salvador Cisneros no.171 e/ Martí y Cristo ☎ 32 29 1357. A good place to catch live music all day long. The fun really kicks off at the weekends, when excellent local bands play in the palm-tree-fringed courtyard, getting audiences (a good mix of locals and visitors) on their feet and dancing and the place buzzing.

SHOPPING

Galería de Arte Oscar Lasseria Ignacio Agramonte no.438 esq. López Recio ☎ 54 77 2269. Original and very individual painting and sculpture, some of it quite abstract, by an artist who uses the upstairs as his workshop – his son also has some work on display here.

GAMES AND SPORTS

Estadio Cándido González Casino Campestre ☎ 32 29 3140 or ☎ 32 29 4539. The city baseball stadium, built in 1965, is where the provincial team play their national league home games.

Rafael Fortún Chacón Sports Centre Casino Campestre ☎ 32 29 4793 or ☎ 32 29 8670. Huge concrete sports centre with a swimming pool and large arena

THEATRE AND CINEMA

Cine Casablanca Ignacio Agramonte e/ República y López Recio ☎ 32 29 2244. This cinema shows a selection of Cuban, Spanish and North American films. In summer there are free outdoor screenings on a nearby wall.

Teatro Principal Padre Valencia no.64 ☎ 32 29 3048. Regular theatre and ballet performances, the latter from the excellent Camagüey Ballet Company, which are usually thoroughly entertaining. Most reliable performance time is 8.30pm Fri–Sun.

SEE MAP PAGE 315

Studio de Marta Jimenez Hermanos Agueros no. 282 e/Carmen y Honda Plaza del Carmen ☎ 32 25 7559. The creator of the human-sized statues in Plaza de Carmen has a pleasant studio close by from which you can buy her pieces – or just take the opportunity to see the artist at work.

with activities as varied as tae kwon do, basketball and trampolining. Salsa concerts are often held here too: ask for details at reception.

Sala Recreativa Ocio Club República no.278 e/ San Esteban y Finlay ☎ 32 28 7384. This games and sports arcade is likely to appal die-hard Cuba traditionalists but delight bored teenagers. Big and brash, it has a bowling

---

DIVING, FISHING AND BOAT TRIPS FROM SANTA LUCÍA

The optimistically named **Shark's Friends Diving Centre** (☎ 32 36 5182) on the stretch of beach nearest to *Hotel Brisas Santa Lucía* runs all the diving, fishing and boat trips in Santa Lucía.

DIVING

Daytime **dive trips** leave at 9am and 1pm; there are several dive sites of note here though Hurricane Irma, which ripped through the region in 2017, destroyed much of the coral. You can also dive at night, when the sea glitters with starry phosphorescence. They also offer ACUC- and SNSI-registered courses, including initiation and five-dive open water courses.

The centre's leading offer is the dive at El Nuevo Mortera, where instructors hand-feed the female **bull sharks** which use this sunken steamship as part of their breeding ground. Organizers assert that this practice has actually protected the shark population from local fishermen, who have now stopped catching them in return for a share in the profits from the dives. However, shark conservationists have expressed serious concerns both for the safety of divers – bull sharks are among the four species most likely to attack humans – and over potential upset to the ecological balance, which can be disturbed by such feeding. Although the organizers assert that the pregnant sharks are at their most benign, note that nonfatal attacks have been reported.

FISHING

Full-day excursions offer opportunities to fish for sea bream, barracuda and snapper.

BOAT TRIPS

Day-trips to Cayo Sabinal include optional diving and snorkelling, plus lunch and drinks.

alley, a pleasant but smallish outdoor pool, a billiards table, and arcade games.

DIRECTORY

Health The 24hr Policlínico Centro is on República no.211 e/ Gómez y Castellano (☎32 29 7810). For an ambulance call ☎32 28 1248. There's a pharmacy at Ignacio Agramonte no.449 e/ Maceo y Independencia, near the post office (Mon–Fri 9am–5pm, Sat 9am–1pm).

Money and exchange You can draw cash advances on credit cards, change travellers' cheques and buy pesos at the CADECA *casa de cambio*, Maceo no.10 e/ General Gómez y Plaza de Antonio Maceo (Mon–Sat 8.30am–8pm, Sun 9am–6pm), or Banco Financiero Internacional, at Independencia no.221 on Plaza Maceo (Mon–Fri 8.30am–3.30pm), where there's usually less of a queue. There are ATMs at the Banco de Crédito y Comercio at the southern end of the pedestrianized stretch of República and on the Plaza de los Trabajadores.

Police Call ☎116 in an emergency.

Post office The main post office is at Ignacio Agramonte no.461 esq. Cisneros (daily 7am–10pm).

Wi-fi ETECSA Telepuntos at República no.453 e/ Fidel Céspedes (San Martín) y Manuel Ramón Silva (San José) (daily 8.30am–7pm) and at Ignacio Agramonte no.442 y Lopez Recio (daily 8.30am–7pm) have internet access, phones and sell wi-fi cards. The public wi-fi zones are at Parque Ignacio Agramonte; you can also use the wi-fi and buy wi-fi cards in the lobby of the *Hotel Santa María*.

Camagüey's north coast

Cut off from the mainland by the Bahía de Nuevitas, 10km north of Nuevitas town, are Camagüey's north-coast **beaches**. The remote resorts of **Santa Lucía** and **Cayo Sabinal** make perfect retreats for those seeking sun-and-sea holidays. While Santa Lucía derives an infrastructure of sorts from the knot of all-inclusive hotels arrayed along the beachfront, Cayo Sabinal is castaway country – with only the most basic accommodation, it virtually guarantees solitude.

Santa Lucía

Hemmed in by salt flats on the northern coast, 128km from Camagüey, **SANTA LUCÍA** is one of Cuba's smaller beach resorts. Much more low-key than the packed resorts at Jardines del Rey, it's perfect if you want to park yourself on the sand for a fortnight, soak up some rays and indulge in a few watersports, but those looking for a more well-rounded destination may find it lacking. The road up here from Camagüey passes through the idyllic pastoral countryside that typifies this region, with lush grazing meadows, cowboys herding their cattle and meandering goats impeding the traffic, the air thick with clouds of multicoloured butterflies. Less appealing are the swarms of mosquitoes that descend at sunset.

The **resort**, such as it is, consists of little more than the beaches. Set well back from the coastal road and lined by a few hotels, these wide expanses of soft, fine sand are bordered by turquoise waters, a little sullied by seaweed drifting in from the barrier reef, and surrounded by inaccessible mangroves. The **town**, which you pass en route to the hotel strip, has nothing to offer tourists, and you will quickly get the impression that you're out in the middle of nowhere with nothing to see or do away from the sun and sea.

ARRIVAL AND DEPARTURE   SANTA LUCÍA

The cheapest, most efficient way of getting to Santa Lucía from Camagüey is the Víazul bus, but as this once-daily service arrives in Santa Lucía in the afternoon and leaves for Camagüey in the morning, you will be obliged to stay the night if you travel this way.

By taxi State-run Cubataxi charge around $1600CUP each way from Camagüey; you may be able to negotiate a cheaper private taxi fare – ask the drivers outside Camagüey's train station.

By organized transfer Camaguax Tours (see page 321) can organize day-trips from Camagüey.

ACCOMMODATION

The Santa Lucía beach scene revolves around its rather tired all-inclusive hotels, which between them carve up almost the entire beach strip. Residency at one entitles you to use the beaches (though not the facilities) of the others. All hotels offer a range of watersports, including windsurfing, snorkelling and catamarans. Cubanacán (☎ 32 29 4905) and Cubatur (☎ 32 25 4785) in Camagüey are often able to offer discounts on the rates quoted by the hotels; check with them before setting out.

HOTELS

Brisas Santa Lucía ⓦ hotelescubanacan.com. A friendly and unpretentious family-oriented hotel with excellent rooms, a pool with a swim-up bar, a gym, billiards, darts, archery, watersports and activities for children. 5̄5̄

EATING, DRINKING AND ENTERTAINMENT

Outside of the hotel restaurants, there's little in the way of independent **eating** and **drinking** in the area. Evening entertainment is also limited to the hotels, with an endless diet of jovial staff roping drunken guests into bawdy Benny Hill-type pantomimes.

La Jungla Gran Club Santa Lucía. The resort's only disco: swanky, soulless and given to playing uninspiring mainstream Cuban and international disco music at

Gran Club Santa Lucía ⓦ hotelescubanacan.com. This complex of bungalows and two-storey apartment blocks enjoys a spacious layout. With palatial rooms, ample shops, a good pool, a gym, three restaurants and a pier-end bar that's perfect for sunset-watching, this is far and away the best hotel on the strip. 5̄5̄5̄

CASA PARTICULAR

Casa Hortensia La concha no 62 Playa Santa Lucía ☎ 32 33 6381 or ☎ 52 51 2553, ✉ gaby.he@nauta.cu. Two double rooms in a pleasant and comfortable house close to the beach, each with air conditioning. Breakfast and dinner are available. 5̄

deafening volumes. There's air hockey and billiards, too. Non-guests are welcome for a charge.

Luna Mar ☎ 32 33 6146. Near the beach between the *Gran Club Santa Lucía* and *Club Amigo Caracol* hotels, this is a relatively authentic Italian restaurant that provides a welcome respite from the hotel eateries and offers pizza, pasta and lobster. 5̄5̄

Playa Coco

Eight kilometres west of Santa Lucía's main beach drag, idyllic **Playa Coco** offers a change of scene. The locals claim that it's a beach to rival the best in Cuba is stretching it a bit, but the wide arc of fine white sand and quieter atmosphere certainly makes a welcome break from Santa Lucía. On the way there, you pass salt flats teeming with flamingos and the egrets (*cocos*) that give the beach its name.

ARRIVAL AND DEPARTURE

PLAYA COCO

By minibus A minibus picks up from the Santa Lucía hotels at 10am and drops you back at 3pm.

By horse-drawn carriage Horse-drawn carriages wait outside the hotels.

ACCOMMODATION AND EATING

Playa Coco's only accommodation is in the fishing community of La Boca, basically just a string of wooden shacks at the entrance to the beach, where a few locals offer *casas particulares*.

La Bocana Chicken, fish, lobster and spaghetti are served up for reasonable prices at this wooden hut at the far end of the beach with tables on the sand where curious crabs

dance around your feet but never come too close. 5̄5̄

Bucanero At the Santa Lucía end of the beach, this is the smarter of Playa Coco's two main restaurants, with a more formal dining room and nautical decor. There's a massive range of sumptuous seafood dishes as well as brochettes and the house speciality, roast beef. 5̄5̄

Cayo Sabinal

Twenty-five kilometres west along the coast from Santa Lucía, **Cayo Sabinal** could not be more different – a deserted white-sand beach cay that's so paradisiacal it's almost eerie. The reason it's yet to be discovered by the masses is its geographical isolation, hidden away at the end of a 7km stretch of notoriously bumpy dirt-track road, part of which forms a causeway across the bay, flanked by foaming salt marshes; there's no public transport, and very little general traffic makes it this far.

All the **beaches** are on the north side, accessible by signposted turnings off the single main road, itself bordered by thick vegetation. The longest beach is pearl-white **Playa**

Los Pinos, where the sea is a clear, calm turquoise and wild deer and horses roam through the woodland that backs onto the sand. Occasionally a group of holiday-makers arrives by boat from Santa Lucía, but otherwise it's a top choice for a couple of days' total tranquillity. Just 2km further west, smaller **Playa Brava** has similar soft white sands. **Playa Bonita**, another 3km west, has a lengthy stretch of coral reef perfect for snorkelling, as well as 3km of pure white sand.

ARRIVAL AND DEPARTURE   CAYO SABINAL

By car Peppered with rocks and cavernous potholes, the road is sometimes impassable without a 4WD, especially during the rainy season, so check conditions before you set off.

By taxi A taxi from Camagüey will set you back around $1500CUP one way.

Cayo Romano

Towards the western end of Camagüey's Atlantic coastline, **Cayo Romano** is an undeveloped 90km-long mass of fragmented cays covered with marshes and woodland. With no accommodation or restaurants, it is an archetypal untamed wilderness worth exploring if you have the time and your own transport. A causeway runs from Playa Jigüey on the north coast into the centre of the cay, although you can also reach the western tip from Cayo Coco. The only feasible way to get here is to drive yourself.

Northern Oriente

GIBARA

Northern Oriente

Traditionally, the whole of the country east of Camagüey is known simply as the "Oriente", a region that in many ways represents the soul of Cuba, awash with historic sites, propaganda billboards and political passions. Running the length of the area's north coast, the three provinces that make up the northern Oriente – Las Tunas, Holguín and Guantánamo – form a landscape of panoramic pine-scented and palm-studded mountains, all fringed by flatlands where lonely railroads thrust through the vast swathes of sugar cane. Home to some of the country's most striking peaks and beaches from the flat-topped El Yunque to the stunning protected coves at Guardalavaca, Maguana and Saetía, the Northern Oriente also boasts some of Cuba's quirkiest towns – namely Baracoa, Gibara and Banes.

The smallest and most westerly of the three provinces is **Las Tunas**, often overlooked by visitors, though its unassuming and friendly provincial capital, **Victoria de las Tunas**, is not without charm.

By contrast, larger and livelier **Holguín** province has a variety of attractions. Chequered with plazas and parks, the busy and crowded provincial capital, **San Isidoro de Holguín**, manages to be modern and cosmopolitan while retaining the feel of its colonial past, with several handsome old buildings, museums and antique churches. The once mighty nineteenth-century port of **Gibara**, presiding over the north coast, also has vestiges of its former glory visible in a few fine buildings and an old fort, while the gently undulating hills around town are honeycombed with underground caves that are perfect for independent exploration. Holguín's biggest attraction is the popular **Guardalavaca** beach resort, while the province's ancient historical pedigree can be seen in the remnants of pre-Columbian Taíno culture in and around the little village of **Banes**. Further east, the exclusive beach resort of **Cayo Saetía** is a paradise of white sands and glistening sea, an idyllic place to relax. Inland, where rugged terrain dominates the landscape, the cool pine forests, waterfalls and lakes of **Mayarí** are unmatched for isolated serenity, while the sugar-farm country further south is home to Fidel Castro's prosaic birthplace at **Birán**.

Of the three provinces, the best known is undoubtedly **Guantánamo**, with the notorious US naval base at **Caimanera**. Although Guantánamo city is largely unspectacular, it forms a useful jumping-off point for the seaside settlement of **Baracoa**, one of Cuba's most beautiful and enjoyable destinations. Sealed off from the rest of the island by a truly awe-inspiring range of rainforested mountains – which are fantastic for trekking – Baracoa's small-town charm is immensely welcoming.

Victoria de Las Tunas

VICTORIA DE LAS TUNAS seems to have been built to a traditional Cuban recipe for a quiet town: take one central plaza, a small main hotel, a Revolution square and a thriving market, add a pinch of culture and bake in the sun for two hundred years. The result is a pleasant but slow-moving town where the faster pace of life elsewhere in the world seems but a rumour. The town's hub is **Parque Vicente García**, a small but comfortable central plaza hemmed by trees and cacti, which holds a number of attractions.

BAHÍA DE MIEL

Highlights

❶ Gibara This picture-perfect coastal town is the ideal base for trips to the geologically rich Cavernas de Panadernos, one of the region's treasures, and hosts a unique film festival in April. See page 341

❷ Playa Guardalavaca With over 1.5km of sugar-like sand, this beach is the crown jewel of Northern Oriente's coastline. See page 345

❸ Cayo Saetía White sands and coral reef against a backdrop of savannah wilds – complete with roaming ostrich and zebra – make for a fantastic juxtaposition. See page 350

❹ Villa Pinares de Mayarí Waterfalls, lakes and pine forests create an idyllic haven of calm at this hotel, cupped by mountains and the centre of a fairy tale-esque nature retreat. See page 352

❺ Guantánamo's musical heritage Search for Haitian heritage and the musical tradition of changüí in Guantánamo. See page 352

❻ Baracoa This vibrant small town set on Cuba's southeastern tip is surrounded by some of the country's most breathtaking mountains, rainforest and countryside. See page 356

❼ El Yunque The easily scaled El Yunque is as famous for its mention in the 1492 log of Christopher Columbus as it is for its rare orchids and ferns. See page 363

HIGHLIGHTS ARE MARKED ON THE MAP ON PAGE 332

Museo Provincial Mayor General Vicente García González

Parque Vicente García • Tues–Sat 8.30am–4.30pm, Sun 8am–noon • Charge • ☎ 31 34 8201

On the east side of Parque Vicente García, the **Museo Provincial Mayor General Vicente García González** is housed in a distinguished duck-blue-and-white colonial building adorned with an elegant clock face. The city history detailed within includes a worthy – though brief – record of **slavery**, as well as two rooms featuring art and clocks.

Plaza Martiana de las Tunas

Opposite the southeastern corner of Parque Vicente García is the **Plaza Martiana de las Tunas**, a modern art monument to José Martí made up of six white man-sized spikes, one embossed with a bust of Martí by Cuba's most famous sculptor, Rita Longa. The whole plaza forms an ingenious gigantic sundial that illuminates the bust each May 19 to commemorate the hero's death in 1895. A vigil concert is held here to commemorate José Martí's life every January. During the day the plaza is bustling with people and in the evening students and young people come to hang out here in droves.

ACCOMMODATION
Campismo El Yunque   1

HIGHLIGHTS
1 Gibara
2 Playa Guardalavaca
3 Cayo Saetía
4 Villa Pinares de Mayarí
5 Guantánamo's musical heritage
6 Baracoa
7 El Yunque

Museo Memorial Mártires de Barbados

Lucas Ortíz no.344 e/ Teniente Peisso y Mártires de Barbados • Tues–Sat 11am–7pm & Sun noon–4pm • Free • ☎ 31 347213

The most arresting museum in Las Tunas is the small but poignant **Museo Memorial Mártires de Barbados**, just west of Parque Vicente García. It commemorates the horrific **plane crash** on October 6, 1976, that wiped out the national junior fencing team. When it was later revealed that an anti-Castro terrorist linked to the CIA had planted the bomb, the incident was popularly seen as a direct attack on Cuban revolutionary youth and achievement. The museum itself is located in the tiny former home of one of the three team members from Las Tunas, and has some affecting **memorabilia**, such as photographs of weeping crowds in Havana and the victims' fencing trophies.

ARRIVAL AND DEPARTURE

VICTORIA DE LAS TUNAS

By plane The Hermanos Almejeira airport is some 3km north of Victoria de las Tunas.

Destinations Havana (2 weekly; 1hr).

Airlines Cubana at Lucas Ortiz esq. 24 de Febrero (☎ 31 37 4295).

By Víazul bus The Terminal de Omnibus is at Francisco Varona no.240 (☎ 31 34 3060), 500m south of the Parque Vicente García. From here you can get a taxi or *bicitaxi* into

NORTHERN ORIENTE

7

> ### RITA LONGA
>
> Cuba's most famous sculptor, **Rita Longa**, considered Las Tunas her second home and two of her works adorn the city. As well as the José Martí monument in Plaza Martiana de las Tunas, there's the non-functioning *Fuente de las Antillas* fountain, across the street from the Museo Memorial Mártires de Barbados, a reclining female body in the shape of Cuba, which has been much emulated by the island's contemporary artists. East of the centre, the small Galería Taller Rita Longa, Lucas Ortíz esq. Villalón (Tues–Sun 8am–noon & 1.30–4pm, Sun 8am–noon; free; ☎31 34 2969), stages temporary sculpture exhibitions and displays works by Longa and other notable artists such as Flora Fong and Sergio Martínez in rotating exhibitions.

town.

Destinations Bayamo (5 daily; 2hr 30min); Camagüey (7 daily; 1hr 50min); Havana (5 daily; 11hr); Holguín (5 daily; 1hr 10min); Sancti Spíritus (5 daily; 5hr 20min); Santa Clara (4 daily; 6hr 50min); Santiago (5 daily; 5hr); Trinidad (1 daily; 6hr 45min); Varadero (10hr 25min).

By train The train station is on Avenida Camilo Cienfuegos, 1km northeast of Parque Vicente García.

Destinations Camagüey (2 weekly; 12hr 45min); Ciego de Ávila (2 weekly; 4hr); Guantánamo (every other day; 6hr); Havana (2 weekly; 12hr); Holguín (daily; 1hr 40min); Santiago (3 weekly; 8hr).

INFORMATION

Tourist office The local Infotur office is at Francisco Varona no.298 on Parque Vicente García e/ Ángel Guardia y Lucas Ortíz (Mon–Fri 8.15am–4.15pm, plus alternate Saturdays 8.15am–4.15pm; ☎31 37 2717).

Banks and exchange There's a CADECA *casa de cambio* at Colón no.141 e/ Vicente García y Francisco Vega (Mon–Sat

8.30am–4pm, Sun 8.30–11.30am).

Wi-fi There are wi-fi hotspots at the Plaza Martiana and the Parque Maceo. You can buy wi-fi cards and use computer terminals in the ETECSA Telepunto at Francisco Vegas no.237 e/ Lucas Ortíz y Vincente García (daily 8.30am–7pm).

ACCOMMODATION

Casa de Esperanza Fresco Ave. Frank País no.62 e/ Villalón y R. López ☎31 34 5630, ✉mahilin1974@ nauta.cu. Run by the gregarious Esperanza, this is a comfortable, quiet room with en-suite bathroom and its own independent entrance. Off-street parking available. $

Hotel E Cadillac Ángel Guardia s/n ⓦislazulhotelscom. This Art Deco-style hotel has eight rooms furnished in chocolate and cream fabrics that come with TVs, fridges and a/c. The 24hr bar is the city's social hotspot. $$

EATING AND DRINKING

Caché Francisco Varona e/ Nicolás Heredia y Joaquin Aguera ☎31 915557. This flash bar and restaurant offers something daringly different to the rest of the eating scene in town: red leather seats, flat screen TVs and pre-revolutionary posters on the walls. The reasonable food is a mix of Cuban and Italian and they do a mean cocktail. $$

La Romana Francisco Varona no.331 e/ Lucas Ortíz and L. Cruz ☎31 34 7755. This paladar is by far the best place

to eat in town. Owner Franco, from Rome, uses authentic Italian parmesan and pecorino to rustle up pasta and pesto, carbonara, a delicious lasagne and hearty salads. $$

Taberna Don Juan Francisco Varona no.225. Near Parque Vicente García, overlooking the main road and Plaza Martiana, offering decent *comida criolla* and excellent local beer. $

San Isidoro de Holguín

Nestled in a valley surrounded by hills, 72km east of Las Tunas, the provincial capital of **SAN ISIDORO DE HOLGUÍN** – or Holguín for short – is a thriving industrial town balancing quieter backstreets with a busier central district of handsome colonial buildings, bicycles and horn-blasting cars. Despite having the bustling air of a large metropolis, Holguín's centre is compact enough to explore on foot and has a couple of fine eighteenth-century **churches** and some small-scale **museums** which will keep you quietly absorbed for a day. Known as the Ciudad de los Parques, there are no less than four elegant squares right in the centre, all within a few blocks of one another. These open spaces, ideal for people-watching, are central to the Holguín lifestyle, and in the evenings it seems that the whole city turns out just to sit, chat and watch their children play in one or other of them.

Brief history

The area around Holguín was once densely populated by Indigenous Taíno, but the Spanish had wiped them out by 1545, after **Captain García Holguín**, early colonizer and veteran of the conquest of Mexico, established his cattle ranch around La Loma de la Cruz. Although a small settlement remained after his death, a town wasn't fully established here for 150 years, and it was only officially named on April 4, 1720 – San Isidoro's Day – with a commemorative Mass held in the cathedral.

Being an inland town with no port, Holguín was destined to be overshadowed in importance by coastal Gibara. In spite of its rather grand blueprint, laid out in accordance with Spanish-colonial city planning laws, it developed slowly. But by the nineteenth century an economy based on sugar production and fruit growing, as well as a little tobacco cultivation, was established and the town grew accordingly. As with other parts of Oriente, Holguín province saw plenty of action during the **Wars of Independence**. Shortly after the start of the Ten Years' War, on October 30, 1868, the city was captured by General Julio Grave de Peralta's force of Mambises, who lost Holguín to the Spanish on December 6. The tides turned again four years later on December 19, 1872, when the city was recaptured by General Máximo Gómez and Holguín-born General Calixto García. After independence, the province was largely dominated by US corporations and Holguín chugged along much the same as it always had. Since the Revolution, however, it has become more of an **industrial city**, with several factories and engineering plants, and was designated provincial capital when the province was created in 1975.

Parque Calixto García

Most of Holguín's sights spread out from the central **Parque Calixto García**, an expanse of ornamental pink and green marble. In the park's centre, a square marble column is topped by a statue of war hero **Calixto García** leaning on his sword. A bushy rim of trees lines the park's outer edge and the benches beneath are packed with old men relaxing in the shade, the more garrulous of whom will gladly fill you in on the entire history of the province.

Museo Provincial de Holguín

Frexes no.198 e/ Maceo y Libertad, Parque Calixto García • Tues–Sat 8am–noon & 12.30–4.30pm, Sun 8am–noon • Charge • ☎ 24 46 3395

FESTIVALS IN VICTORIA DE LAS TUNAS

There's not much nightlife or entertainment to speak of in Las Tunas except during the summer, when the annual **El Cucalambé music festival** is held over three days in June. Based in the grounds of the otherwise unremarkable *Hotel El Cornito* (☎ 31 38 1815), about 7km out of town, the festival features live folk and salsa in a lively atmosphere awash with beer and food stalls. Other events include **rodeos**, which take place in August and December at *Hotel El Cornito*, while fireworks and parades are held every September 26 to commemorate Major General Vicente García. The city also celebrates its carnival and *semana de la cultura* in September with music, poetry and art events.

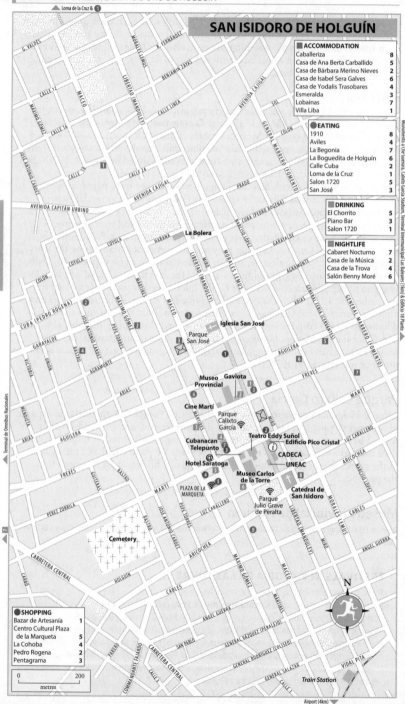

SAN ISIDORO DE HOLGUÍN

ACCOMMODATION

Caballeriza	8
Casa de Ana Berta Carballido	5
Casa de Bárbara Merino Nieves	2
Casa de Isabel Sera Galves	6
Casa de Yodalis Trasobares	4
Esmeralda	3
Lobainas	7
Villa Liba	1

EATING

1910	8
Aviles	4
La Begonia	7
La Boguedita de Holguín	6
Calle Cuba	2
Loma de la Cruz	1
Salon 1720	5
San José	3

DRINKING

El Chorrito	5
Piano Bar	3
Salon 1720	1

NIGHTLIFE

Cabaret Nocturno	7
Casa de la Música	2
Casa de la Trova	4
Salón Benny Moré	6

SHOPPING

Bazar de Artesanía	1
Centro Cultural Plaza de la Marqueta	5
La Cohoba	4
Pedro Rogena	2
Pentagrama	3

Presiding over the northeastern side of Parque Calixto García is the **Museo Provincial de Holguín**, where an assortment of exhibits is displayed in one of the town's most impressive buildings; the handsome ochre edifice was built between 1860 and 1868. Though designed as a private house, it first served as a base and refuge for the Spanish army in Holguín during the first War of Independence, the army capitalizing on its fortress-like proportions. Today, the primary draw here is still the building itself, as the historical miscellanea on display are so eclectic that the collection lacks coherence. The best section is the set of **pre-Columbian artefacts** discovered in and around Holguín, including bone fragments of necklaces, pieces of clay pots and a number of idols made of stone, bone and shell. Most impressive is a polished, olive-coloured Taíno axe, known as the **Axe of Holguín**, discovered in 1860 in the hills surrounding the city. Carved with a grimacing, crowned human figure, it was most likely used for religious ceremonies.

Museo Carlos de la Torre

Maceo no.129 • Tues–Sat 9am–noon & 12.30–5pm, Sun 9am–noon • Charge • ☎ 24 42 3935

A block south of Parque Calixto García is **Museo Carlos de la Torre**, the city's natural history museum, set in a wonderful nineteenth-century building. A fanciful lime, forest green, mustard and custard-yellow confection with a pillared portico and an entrance portal, it is exquisitely tiled in bright ceramic squares of lacquered aqua and rose, complementing the richly patterned floor inside.

Iglesia San José

Parque San José, Libertad e/ Agramonte y Arias • Mon 2–7pm, Tues–Sun 6.30am–noon & 12.30–7pm • ☎ 24 42 3155

Three blocks north of Parque Calixto García, fronting the shady, tiled Parque San José is the **Iglesia San José**, with a single weatherbeaten clocktower rising above stone arches and topped with a domed turret. The ornate Baroque **interior** is vibrant and welcoming, something of a contrast with many Cuban churches, while the rest of the church leans towards more traditional Catholic decor, with effigies of saints huddled above the altars.

Plaza de la Marqueta

The most compact and, during the day, the most subdued central square, **Plaza de la Marqueta** is dominated by a refined yellow and white market building at its centre. Beside the craft market inside and the simple art gallery, the appeal here is the cluster of bars and cafés around the edges of the square, making this the best spot in the city to kick back for a drawn-out drink or two. The best venue is the music-driven *El Chorrito* (see page 340) but there's another bar on the opposite side with a small outdoor performance space. There are occasionally musical performances in the market building itself, which dates from 1848.

Catedral de San Isidoro

Parque Julio Grave de Peralta, Libertad e/ Luz Caballero y Aricochea • Daily 7am–noon & 4–8pm • ☎ 24 42 2107 • Free

The **Catedral de San Isidoro de Holguín**, named after the city's patron saint, lords it over the stately Parque Julio Grave de Peralta, popularly known as Parque de las Flores, a couple of blocks south of Parque Calixto García. Surrounded by a walled patio, the stalwart but simple cathedral, with two turrets and a red-tiled roof, glows in the Caribbean sun. The original church on this site, completed in 1720, was one of the first buildings in Holguín; a humble affair built from palm trees, it lasted ten years until a sturdier structure was erected in 1730. The current building, containing some

7

exquisite woodwork, was finished in 1815 with some parts, like the twin towers, added later. Built as a parish church, and also used as the city crypt, it was only elevated to cathedral status in 1979, which accounts for its straightforward design and small size.

Monumento a Che Guevara

2.8km east of Parque Calixto García on Ave. de los Libertadores • Take a *bicitaxi* or taxi from the centre

The **Monumento a Che Guevara** is an impressive three-part sculpture with panels showing a silhouette of Guevara approaching, striding forward and receding. Executed in sombre stone, it's an eye-catching and accomplished piece of work, its triptych of images said to allude to, respectively, his revolutionary influence, presence and lasting legacy.

Loma de la Cruz

1.2km along Maceo from Parque Calixto García • Walk there in 20–25min from centre

Rising above Holguín, the **Loma de la Cruz**, or Hill of the Cross, is the largest of the hills that form a natural border to the north of the city. A steep, 458-step **stairway** starts from the northern end of Maceo and heads up to the summit, where you'll find a faithful replica of the hefty wooden cross erected on May 3, 1790, by Friar Antonio de Algerías, following the Spanish tradition of the **Romería de la Cruz** (Pilgrimage of the Cross). This custom commemorates the day that, according to legend, St Elena, mother of Constantine the Great, rediscovered the original cross of Christ's crucifixion. It's one of Cuba's most religious sites and when Pope Francis visited the country in September 2015 he blessed the city from its panoramic viewpoint. Every May 3, a Mass is held for the faithful – who until the construction of the staircase in 1950 had to toil up the hill the long way round – along with a low-key week-long **festival** in town, where locals gather nightly around beer stalls and food stands set up around the centre.

The hill was also used by the Spanish as a lookout during the Wars of Independence, and a bijou **fort** on the plateau set back from the cross remains as evidence. You can appreciate why they chose this point when you gaze down at the town's rigid grid below, and the panorama of lush green land on one side and dry countryside on the other, with parched and dusty hillocks visible in the distance. A small café takes advantage of the magnificent views, and there's also a restaurant up here (see page 340).

ARRIVAL AND DEPARTURE

SAN ISIDORO DE HOLGUÍN

BY PLANE

Airport The Aeropuerto Internacional Frank País handles international (☎ 24 47 4525) and domestic flights (☎ 24 47 4583). Located 9.5km south of Circunvalación, the city ring road, on the Carretera Central.

Airlines Cubana, Martí esq. Libertad (☎ 24 46 8148).
Destinations Havana (1 daily; 1hr 45min).

BY BUS OR COLECTIVO

Terminal de Omnibus Nacionales José María Pérez Capote Víazul buses arrive at Holguín's new bus terminal (opened in December 2017) on the Carretera Central opposite the Cristino Naranjo turning, 2.3km west of Parque Calixto García.
Destinations Bayamo (3 daily; 1hr 20min); Camagüey (6 daily; 3hr 10min); Havana (4 daily; 12hr); Las Tunas (6

daily; 1hr 10min); Sancti Spíritus (4 daily; 6hr 50min); Santa Clara (3 daily; 5hr); Santiago de Cuba (3 daily; 3hr 20min); Trinidad (1 daily; 8hr); Varadero (1 daily; 11hr 45min).

Conectando Cuba The hotel-door-to-hotel-door national bus service (see page 28) passes through Holguin once daily on its way to Havana (stopping at Camagüey and Ciego de Avila) and once daily on its way to Santiago (direct). Buses arrive and depart outside *Hotel Pernik*; book tickets two days in advance from any Cubanacán office (see Travel agents).

Terminal Intermunicipal Las Baleares Local intermunicipal buses leave from the Baleares terminal (☎ 24 48 1170), to the east of the centre opposite the Calixto García baseball stadium on Avenida de los Libertadores. Next door are the taxi ranks for *colectivos* travelling around the province and beyond.

BY TRAIN

Terminal de Ferrocaril Vidal The terminal is at Pita no.3 e/ Libertad y Maceo (☎ 24 42 2331), 1km south of the town centre, and is served by taxis and *bicitaxis*.

Destinations Havana (2 weekly; 14hr); Las Tunas (daily; 2hr 30min); Santiago (2 weekly; 3hr 30min).

GETTING AROUND

Car rental Havanautos/Cubacar has a desk at the airport (daily 8am–8pm; ☎ 24 46 8412), and another at Edificio Pico de Cristal, Libertad esq. Martí (Mon–Sat 9am–5pm; ☎ 24 46 8559).

Scooter rental *Hotel Pernik* (☎ 24 46 8196) rents out scooters and cars.

By taxi Cubataxi is at Máximo Gómez esq. Martí (☎ 24 42 3290). One of the most central *bicitaxi* ranks is on the east side of Parque San José.

INFORMATION, TRAVEL AGENCIES AND TOURS

The state-run travel agents in town can all book beach hotel packages and broadly the same excursions around the province and beyond.

Infotur The local branch of the national tourist information chain, Infotur, is on the second floor of the Edificio Pico Cristal, at Libertad esq. Martí (access by stairs outside; Mon–Fri 8am–4pm, plus every other Sat; ⊛ cuba.travel).

Events information A listings board outside the Fondo Bienes Cultural Centre, at no.196 Frexes, details weekly cultural and arts events in Holguín.

Festivals Holguín's carnival takes place over the third weekend in August, while the Fiesta de la Cultura Iberoamericana in October celebrates the arrival of Christopher Columbus to Cuba with a host of cultural events (⊛ facebook.com/casadeiberoamerica.hog/).

Cubanacán *La Begonia*, Maceo 176 e/ Frexes y Martí (Mon–Sat 9am–4pm; ☎ 24 47 1282).

Cubatur Based in Edificio Pico Cristal, at Libertad esq. Martí (daily 9am–4pm).

Gaviota Frexes no.220 (usually Mon–Sat 9am–4pm; ☎ 24 42 3260).

ACCOMMODATION · SEE MAP PAGE 336

There's been an upturn in recent years in the choice and quality of **hotels** in the centre of the city. Their ranks are soon to be expanded with the rescued-from-ruin, 1913-built *Hotel Saratoga* in the Maceo and Martí corner of Parque Calixto García – which is sure to be a fabulous renovation. There are numerous well-appointed **casas particulares** throughout the city, with plenty in the centre. The caution you should exercise with accommodation touts applies here just as much as it does in all the larger cities (see page 36)

HOTELS

Caballeriza Miró esq. Aricochea ⊛ hotelescubanacan. com. Very central boutique hotel opened in 2016 in a handsome building dating from 1810, the shuttered windows of its exterior clasped with iron grills. It was once a cavalry base and the long, narrow, pretty central courtyard hints at the former stables, as does the statue of a horse. Rooms are spacious, modern and understated, except for the paintings of horses in each one. ⑤⑤

Esmeralda Maceo no.112 e/ Agramonte y Arias, Parque San José ⊛ hotelescubanacan.com. One of the city's newest hotels, with just five, well-appointed rooms and facing the church across the square. This column-fronted, pastel-green edifice dates from 1864 and belonged to the mayor of the city in the nineteenth century. The beautiful restoration has accentuated a number of its colonial hallmarks, including the ornate tiled floor, saloon doors and a superb compact patio complete with vines growing up the wall, a well and rocking chairs. ⑤⑤

CASAS PARTICULARES

Casa de Ana Berta Carballido Aguilera no.163 e/ Narciso López y G. Feria ☎ 24 46 5675, ✉ anaelena90@ nauta.cu. Two double rooms each in a bright, airy house, with a bathroom, fridge, pleasant patio and a private entrance. English, Portuguese and Italian spoken. ⑤

★ **Casa de Bárbara Merino Nieves** Mártires no.31 e/ Agramonte y Garayalde ☎ 24 42 3805, ✉ babymn@ nauta.cu. Two excellent double rooms, each with a/c and its own bathroom and TV; one has a small kitchen. Use of a sunny terrace and very friendly and helpful owner make this one of the best *casas particulares* in town. ⑤

Casa de Isabel Sera Galves Narciso López no.142 e/ Aguilera y Frexes ☎ 24 42 2529. Two sizeable double rooms with fridges in a handsome and grand colonial house, with a patio, a pretty garden shaded by coconut palms and a mini Che museum. ⑤

★ **Casa de Yodalis Trasobares** Rastro no.37 e/ Agramonte y Garayalde ☎ 24 42 7069, ✉ yodalis@ nauta.cu. Three pleasantly decorated a/c rooms, all on the second floor accessed by an independent entrance. There's a balcony and a beautiful crazy-paved patio out the back where you can take home-cooked meals. ⑤

Lobainas Cervantes no.283 e/ Martí y Frexes ☎ 24 46 4475, ✉ lobainas59@gmail.com. Opening onto the plain but pleasant patio, a corridor runs through the heart of the house, past one nicely decorated mini-apartment and round to the outdoor staircase leading up to the second guest room, a wonderfully light and large room with its own

7

balcony terrace. There's a relaxed feel here. $

Villa Liba Maceo no.46 esq. Linea ☎ 24 42 3823. Two a/c rooms with TVs in an airy 1950s apartment near the Loma de la Cruz steps. Each simply furnished room has its own bathroom, plus there's a suntrap patio for eating, and a small pool. Jorge, of Lebanese descent, cooks Lebanese and vegetarian food and his wife, Mariela, gives deeply relaxing massages and teaches yoga and Reiki. Garage parking available. $

EATING

SEE MAP PAGE 336

CAFÉ

La Begonia Maceo no.176 e/ Frexes y Martí ☎ 24 42 7354. Facing Parque Calixto García, this reasonably priced open-air café serves up unexciting but decent sandwiches, beers, and ice cream. Note that this is a popular hangout for *jineteros*. $

STATE RESTAURANTS

La Boguedita de Holguín Aguilera no.249 esq. Mártires. A pleasant restaurant specializing in grilled pork, with a bar area where *trovadores* play in the evenings. The cheap prices and friendly atmosphere more than compensate for the fact that most of the menu options are usually unavailable. $

Loma de la Cruz La Loma de la Cruz. Good-value open-air restaurant at the top of the hill (to the left of the summit), featuring *comida criolla* dishes and *al dente* pasta. Friendly and unpretentious, with superb views over the city, this is a much better spot to pause for a drink than the nearby café. $$

Salon 1720 Frexes no.190 e/ Miró y Holguín ☎ 24 46 8150. With splendid decor and attentive service, this is one of Holguín's better state dining experiences and, surprisingly, everything on the menu actually appears to be available. You can relax over a *mojito* in the rooftop bar beforehand and eat either in the smart dining rooms or in the central courtyard. Options include onion soup, beef medallions or lamb chops with tamarind sauce accompanied by perfect mashed potato and lightly cooked vegetables. $$$

PALADARS

1910 Mártires no.143 e/ Aricochea y Cables ☎ 24 42 3994. A hugely popular paladar inside a columned colonial home. The standard, national Cuban *criollo* menu has been stretched to include grilled octopus in garlic sauce (a standout dish) and shrimps with caramelized pineapple, and the food is delicious and beautifully presented, though the portions are unmanageably huge. Reservations recommended. $$

Aviles Frexes e/ Miro y Morales Lemus ☎ 24 45 4373. Good, solid Cuban food presented in carefully arranged but gargantuan portions. Deliciously greasy pork cutlets in onion and garlic and some classic creole lamb dishes, including *chilindrón de carnero*, a stew with tomato, are among many other traditional favourites. The open kitchen backs on to a very pleasant half-covered patio with brick and stone walls and a couple of flourishing ferns. $$

Calle Cuba Cuba no.301 e/ José Antonio Cardet y Pepe Torres ☎ 24 42 2035. Professionally run but very simple paladar with a clean and friendly feel. More adventurous choices include pineapple chicken or chicken fajita with grilled or breaded shrimp. Unusually, Tabasco sauce is available. The flan is also par excellence. $$

★ **San José** Agramonte no.188 e/ Maceo y Libertad ☎ 24 42 4877. Succulent fish and tender meats (such as surf and turf, roast lamb or smoked pork) are cooked to order from the small kitchen on display at the back of a narrow alfresco courtyard. Dishes like chicken with green peppers and pineapple sauce and chicken fajitas in wine have a pleasant, home-cooked taste. There's air-conditioned cool in the interior dining room but it lacks the comfortable ambience of the outside space. $$

NIGHTLIFE AND ENTERTAINMENT

SEE MAP PAGE 336

BARS, CLUBS AND LIVE MUSIC VENUES

Cabaret Nocturno Carretera Central Vía Las, Km 2 ☎ 24 42 9345. Saturday is the big night at this outskirts-of-town venue, with young Holguineros descending to see the cabaret, hear the singers, compete in dancing competitions and dance to Fiesta Kaliente's techno sounds. It's a totally authentic night out, as there are few foreigners.

★ **Casa de la Música** Frexes esq. Libertad, Parque Calixto García ☎ 24 42 9561. Slick nightspot with four busy *salons* hosting great salsa and jazz bands, and a 24hr open-air bar flanking the building on Libertad. Of the four *salons*, the darkly atmospheric *Santa Palabra* has nightly live music and a Wed–Sat dance matinee, while the *Terraza Bucanero* is a lively beer-only rooftop bar, playing disco, up-tempo salsa and reggaeton. Though large tour groups often descend from nearby Guardalavaca, this doesn't detract from the generally uncontrived atmosphere.

Casa de la Trova Maceo no.174 e/ Frexes y Martí. A mixed crowd of cross-generational foreigners and Cubans fills the big wooden dancefloor for exuberant salsa and traditional trova sessions, with live bands playing daytimes and evenings.

★ **El Chorrito** Plaza de la Marqueta ☎ 24 42 6101. Part of the EGREM record label's chain of "álbum kafés", where a music shop combines with a coffee shop and alcohol is served too. This understated but cool little hang out is full of low-slung seats gathered around coffee tables and most evenings around 6.30pm there is live acoustic music.

Piano Bar Mártires esq. Frexes. Night owls in search of more mellow (and free) entertainment should head to this sultry late-night piano bar with an original 1950s counter.

Salon 1720 Frexes no.190 e/ Miró y Holguín ☎24 46 8150. The restaurant's well-stocked bar, on a romantic lantern-lit roof terrace, is the city's top choice for moonlight cocktails.

Salón Benny Moré Luz Caballero esq. Maceo ☎24 42 3399. A dance space with a large alfresco stage in the round surrounded by comfy plastic rattan sofas, and an eclectic line-up of live music. It's also a popular off-street bar during the afternoon.

SHOPPING

Bazar de Artesanía Libertad e/ Aguilera y Aría. This indoor craft market sells carved wooden ornaments, leather accessories and other souvenir-style trinkets. Mon–Sat 8am–6pm.

Centro Cultural Plaza de la Marqueta Plaza de la Marqueta ☎24 46 8697. An array of crafts for sale in a long-time market building right in the middle of the plaza. Stalls inside peddling leather goods, belts, jewellery, objects made of wood and all kinds of ornamental bits and bobs share space with a simple café.

La Cohoba Plaza de la Marqueta ☎24 46 8697. Offers a fine selection of rum.

CINEMA, THEATRE AND SPORT

La Bolera Habana e/ Maceo y Libertad ☎24 46 8812 A 10min walk from the centre, this is a popular bowling alley that has clowns and magic shows for kids on Sunday mornings.

Cine Martí Frexes e/ Maceo y Libertad. This small, intimate venue on Parque Calixto García screens Cuban and international films.

Estadio Calixto García ☎24 462014. Baseball games at Holguín's stadium, 1km east of town, take place between December and May.

Teatro Eddy Suñol Martí e/ Maceo y Libertad ☎24 45 4930. On the north side of Parque Calixto García, this attractive chocolate-coloured Art Deco theatre puts on plays, ballet and musical entertainment.

SEE MAP PAGE 336

Pedro Rogena Libertad no.193 e/ Frexes y Martí, Parque Calixto García. Sells a selection of T-shirts, CDs, postcards, Cuban art posters and socialist-themed books in English, French and Spanish. More importantly, it has the *Guia de Carreteras*, the indispensable Cuban road map book for drivers.

Pentagrama Maceo esq. Martí, Parque Calixto García ☎24 45 3135. Part of the record label EGREM's chain of music shops selling CDs, guitars and strings, maracas and other Cuban musical instruments. Staff are friendly and helpful.

DIRECTORY

Banks and exchange Banco de Credito y Comercio, Arias no.159 e/ Maceo y Libertad, Parque San José (Mon–Fri 8am–3pm, Sat 8–11am) can change travellers' cheques and give cash advances on credit and debit cards and also has two 24hr cash points. The CADECA *casa de cambio* is at Libertad no.205 e/ Martí e Luz Caballero (daily Mon–Sat 8.30am–8pm, Sun 9am–6pm).

Immigration You can extend standard tourist visas at the immigration office, Fomento no.256 esq. Peralejo, Reparto Peralta (☎24 46 2114; Mon–Fri 8am–noon).

Health Hotel Pernik and Hotel El Bosque both have medical services, while the international clinic is at the Centro Médico at Frexes no.212 (☎24 42 1176). Asistur is

also based in *Hotel Pernik* at Ave. Jorge Dimitrov (Mon–Fri 8am–4.30pm; ☎24 47 1580). Call ☎104 for an ambulance.

Police Call ☎106.

Post office The most central post office is at Libertad no.183 e/ Frexes y Martí (Mon–Sat 8am–6pm), with a DHL service. There is also a 24hr office at Maceo 114 e/ Aría y Agramonte on Parque Carlos Manuel Céspedes.

Wi-fi There are wi-fi hotspots at Parque Calixto García, Parque de las Flores and Plaza de la Marqueta. You can buy wi-fi cards and access computer terminals at the ETECSA Telepunto (daily 8.30am–7pm), facing Parque Calixto García on Martí esq. Maceo.

Gibara

Travelling 35km north from Holguín through a set of bulbous mountains, you'll reach the pleasingly somnolent fishing port of **GIBARA**, which spreads from a calm and sparkling bay into the surrounding rugged hillside. This little-visited gem is just the place to spend a few hours – or even days – enjoying the tranquil views, historical ambience, get-away-from-it-all atmosphere and lush scenery; the tiny scoops of sand at

> ### COLUMBUS AND GIBARA
>
> The name "Gibara" comes from the word *giba*, or hump, and refers to the **Silla de Gibara**, a hill which, seen from the sea, looks like a horse's saddle. Gibarans swear this is the one **Christopher Columbus** mentioned in his log when approaching Cuban shores, but although he did first land in Holguín province, the hill he wrote about is generally taken to be El Yunque in Baracoa. The spot where Columbus first disembarked in Cuba on October 28, 1492, is **Playa Blanca**, about 20km east of Gibara, in the Bahía de Bariay; it's marked today by a small monument on the hillside near the pretty, pale-sand beach.

Playacita Ballado and **Playa La Concha** are both good options for a dip after meandering through the town. Gibara is also an ideal base from which to explore the countryside and nearby pockets of interest such as the **Cavernas de Panadernos** caves.

Brief history

Founded in 1827, Gibara became the main north-coast port in Oriente because of its wide bay. During the nineteenth century the town enjoyed valuable **trade links** with Spain, the rest of Europe and the US, and was considered important enough to justify construction of a small fortification on the Los Caneyes hilltop, the ruins of which remain. Though small, Gibara was a fashionable and wealthy town, home to several aristocratic families and famed for its elegant edifices.

The glory days were not to last, however, and Gibara's importance began to slip away with the introduction of the **railway**, which could more easily transport freight around the country. The decrease in trade left the town floundering, and during the 1920s and 1930s many townsfolk moved elsewhere in search of work, leaving Gibara to shrink into today's pleasant village whose main industries are farming and fishing.

Plaza Calixto García

An enjoyable place for a wander, Gibara's streets fan out from the dainty **Plaza Calixto García**. Rimmed with large Imbondeiro African trees imported from Angola in the 1970s, the plaza is dominated by the **Iglesia de San Fulgencio**, a mid-nineteenth-century church built in a medley of styles. In the centre of the square is the marble **Statue of Liberty**, erected to commemorate the rebel army's triumphant entrance into town on July 25, 1898, during the second War of Independence. Sculpted in Italy, the statue is smaller and less austere than her North American counterpart and bears the winsome face of Aurora Peréz Desdín, a local woman considered so captivating that the town supplied the sculptor with her photograph so that he might preserve her beauty forever. The aubergine-and-yellow building on the Independencia side of the square is a **cigar factory**, where a peek inside reveals workers industriously rolling away.

Museo Historia Natural

Luz Caballero 21 e/ Independencia y Sartorio • Mon 1–4pm, Tues–Sat 8am–noon & 1–5pm • Charge • ☏ 24 84 4458

Even the smallest Cuban town has a moth-eaten collection of stuffed animals, and Gibara is no exception. The **Museo Historia Natural**, which borders Plaza Calixto García, is worth a peek, not least for its *pièce de résistance* of Cuban grotesque: a long-dead hermaphrodite chicken which was once both rooster and hen.

Museo de Artes Decorativas

Independencia no.19 • Mon–Wed 8am–noon & 1–5pm, Thurs–Sun same hours plus 8–10pm • Charge • ☏ 24 84 4687

Gibara's best museum is the **Museo de Artes Decorativas**, set in a sumptuous building built in the nineteenth century as the private residence of José Beola, a wealthy local merchant. The quietly splendid interior with its narrow staircase sweeping upstairs to the fine, though small, collection of paintings and colonial furniture is worth pausing to admire. The delicately coloured stained-glass windows are original to the house and the biggest in the province.

Cavernas de Panadernos

On the outskirts of Gibara, about 2km from the centre, the town's most rewarding feature is the **Cavernas de Panadernos**, one of 29 caves in the area. Formed from glacial movement during the ice age, the caves have gradually flooded and drained to form a labyrinth of **mineral galleries**. The caves are home to a sizeable colony of **bats** that hover above you as you pass from gallery to gallery and whose presence adds to the generally eerie air.

In all, there are several galleries stretching 11km under the Gibara hillside, though you probably won't go the whole distance. There's much to be seen in the most accessible chambers, however, including red pictographs and the largest collection of red petroglyphs in Cuba. Heading further underground, you're rewarded with a magnificent lake glinting in the Tolkienesque gloom.

You can walk to the Cavernas de Panadernos from Gibara, but you'll need a **guide**, who will provide lanterns and helmets. Nature specialist José Corella knows the caves inside out and has buckets of information on them to boot. He works at the Oficina de Monumentos Technicos, at no.7 Sartorio, next to the old theatre (☎24 84 5107, ✉gibara@baibrama.cult.cu).

ARRIVAL AND INFORMATION   GIBARA

By bus or truck Buses to Gibara leave the Baleares depot in Holguín around 7am daily and take an hour; you can also catch a private *camión* truck from the Edificio 18 Plantas nearby.
By taxi An unmetered taxi will cost around $700CUP from Holguín to Gibara, depending on the number of passengers

and how hard you bargain.
Services BPA, at Independencia no.26 (Mon–Sat 8am–3pm), offers cash withdrawals on Visa and MasterCard and exchange facilities. The post office is at Independencia no.17, just off Parque Calixto García (Mon–Sat 8am–8pm).

ACCOMMODATION

Los Hermanos Céspedes no.13 e/ Luz Caballero y J. Peralta ☎24 84 4542, ✉odalisgonzalezgurri@gmail.com. Five rooms set alongside a sunny courtyard in a very handsome colonial home. All rooms have their own bath but only one is in the old colonial section of the house. $
Hotel Arsenita Calle Sartorio No. 22 Entre Marti y Luz Caballero, ⓦiberostar.com. With a striking coral and white exterior, this 1920s-built gem is right in the heart of Gibara's historic centre. Moments from the main park, it's

friendly and intimate with a lovely lobby bar and terraces offering great views of the bay. $$$
Hotel Iberostar Gibara J. Peralta e/ Donato Mármol y Independencia ⓦiberostar.com. A splendid enormous tangerine-and-papaya-coloured building in the centre of town, also known as the *Hotel Ordoño*. Furnished in dusky blue, grey and chocolate fabrics, the super-smart rooms have TVs and plush bathrooms with rain showers. The suite is a feast, with a gloriously kitsch Cuban meringue cake

---

GIBARA'S FESTIVALS

Despite being off the tourist trail, Gibara is notable for its film festival, the biennial **Festival de Cine Pobre** (ⓦcinepobre.com), which celebrates low-budget fringe movies. Held in April, it's based at the town's cute Cine Jiba.

During Gibara's annual **Semana de la Cultura**, which takes place in mid-January, cultural, music and dance events enliven the town; while in late January, the three-day **Cine de la Cueva** festival sees the subterranean movie nights held in the Panadernos Caves.

imitation on the bedroom ceiling and a bathroom painted with a charming rural scene. There are three terraces with outstanding sea views. Rates include breakfast. $\overline{\$}\overline{\$}\overline{\$}$
La Terraza de Ileana Donato Mármol no.51A ☎ 24 84 4977, ✉ laterrazadeileana@gmail.com. One large room in a third-floor apartment with its own bathroom, kitchen with cooking facilities, sitting room and private terrace, plus a second bedroom off the main living room of the house with a tiny terrace and table. Bonuses include the shared back terrace with hill views, and a lovely host, Ileana Ramírez Ramos. $\overline{\$}$

EATING AND DRINKING

La Cueva Calle 2da no.131 ☎ 24 84 5333. On the outskirts of town, this simple thatched restaurant is the best in Gibara. Seafood dishes including crab, fried swordfish, red snapper and shrimp are plentiful and beautifully cooked. Of the meat dishes *ropa vieja* is a particular speciality. Many of the vegetables and herbs are grown in the owner's garden and he will also give you a lesson in making the perfect *mojito*. $\overline{\$}\overline{\$}$
Los Hermanos Céspedes no.13 e/ Luz Caballero y Peralta ☎ 24 84 4542. A paladar doubling as a *casa particular*, with a couple of tables set around a sunny, attractive courtyard. Service and food are both excellent, with satisfying portions of *comida criolla* and some seafood, all served with imagination and flair. $\overline{\$}\overline{\$}$
Paladar El Curujey J. Peralta no.48 e/ J. Mora y Céspedes ☎ 05 314 1785. Professionally run by Dairon Teruca, this paladar on the top terrace of a private home offers sea views and tasty seafood – lobster, crab and octopus, plus one of the best *flan de leches* in Cuba. $\overline{\$}\overline{\$}$

NIGHTLIFE AND ENTERTAINMENT

Batería de Fernando VII Eastern end of Independencia ☎ 24 84 4471. Set in the diminutive pale-yellow fort next to La Concha beach, this bar has singing and dancing shows and live music.
Cine Jiba Luz Caballero no.17 e/ Sartorio y Independencia facing Parque Calixto García ☎ 24 84 4629. The town's cinema has a large screen and a *sala de video*, and shows a mixture of Cuban and international films.
El Colonial Centro Cultural Luz Caballero no.23A e/ Sartorio y Independencia ☎ 24 84 4471. This leafy courtyard space spends most of its life as a bar but at weekends there's live music alongside the palm trees and fountain.
Mirador del Gibara Los Caneyes. For the best view over the town, head up the massive flight of steps to this hilltop bar near the fort. A regular hangout for locals, it has a certain ramshackle charm.

Guardalavaca

Despite being the province's main tourist resort, **GUARDALAVACA**, on the north coast 72km northeast from Holguín, retains a charmingly homespun air. The area's name pays tribute to a buccaneer past – Guardalavaca meaning "keep the cow safe", which is thought to refer to the need to protect livestock and valuables from marauding pirates who once used the area as a refuge point. The lively **Playa Guardalavaca** is the original resort and has the oldest all-inclusive hotel buildings, one of them dating back to the 1970s; the two exclusive satellite resorts to the west, **Playa Esmeralda** and **Playa Pesquero** (which incorporates the nearby Playa Turquesa) are popular with those seeking luxury and solitude. Surrounded by hilly countryside and shining fields of sugar cane, the **town of Guardalavaca**, which backs onto its namesake resort, is little more than a clutch of houses, many now turned into *casas particulares*.

Should you tire of sunning yourself on the beach, the surrounding area has enough sights to keep you busy for a few days, many of them reachable via tours organized by the hotels. About 6km south in the Maniabon hills, a fascinating Taíno burial ground incorporates the **Museo Chorro de Maíta** and **Aldea Taína**, a re-creation of a Taíno village that really brings the lost culture to life. Close to Playa Esmeralda, at the Bahía de Naranjo, an offshore **aquarium** offers an entertaining day out, though one of the most rewarding pastimes in Guardalavaca is to **rent a bicycle or moped** and head off into the dazzling countryside to enjoy stunning views over hills and sea; you can also do this on **horseback** with a guide.

Playa Guardalavaca

Split into two 500m-long stretches of sugar-white sand dappled with light streaming through abundant foliage, **Playa Guardalavaca** is a delight. A shady boulevard of palms, tamarind and sea grape trees runs along the centre of the beach. One of the most refreshing aspects of Playa Guardalavaca is that the beach, or at least the western half, is well used by Cubans, not just tourists, giving it a certain vitality with a lack of hustle. Midway along, the *Cafetería El Pirata* (daily 9am–9pm; ☎24 43 0239) serves fried fish and lobster meals along with drinks, and there are stands renting out **snorkelling equipment** so you can explore the coral reef offshore.

The eastern section of the beach, sometimes referred to as Playa Las Brisas, is the oceanfront of the *Las Brisas* hotel (see page 348), and non-guests are not permitted to access it via the hotel unless they purchase a day-pass. About midway between the two hotels on the opposite side of the road behind the beach, the **Centro Comercial Los Flamboyanes** comprises a few shops selling beach accessories, snacks and postcards, a *Casa del Habano* and an *El Rápido* fast-food outlet. A second mini-complex a few metres away has a more upmarket version of the same.

Playa Esmeralda

Some 5km west from Playa Guardalavaca along the Holguín road, picture-perfect **Playa Esmeralda** (also known as Estero Ciego) boasts clear blue water, powdery sand speckled with thatched sunshades and two hotels hidden from view by thoughtfully planted bushes and shrubs. To access the beach, non-guests have to buy a day-pass that covers facilities, meals and drinks.

Playa Pesquero and Playa Yuraguanal

Fifteen kilometres west of Playa Guardalavaca, the four state-of-the-art hotels (see page 347) on Playa Pesquero represent Guardalavaca's most luxurious development. Lined with gnarled and twisted sea grape trees and thatch umbrellas providing much-needed shade, **Playa Pesquero** is a 1.2km-long horseshoe-shaped bay of sparkling sand. The quieter and smaller **Playa Yuraguanal** (currently occupied by the *Hotel Memories Holguín*) is one of the most beautiful in the region. Bordered by mangrove forest at its eastern boundary, the shallow bay has a small coral reef a short swim offshore, while a strip of dense forest between the hotel and the beach makes it feel like an undiscovered paradise.

■ ACCOMMODATION			
Las Brisas	1	Playa Pesquero	11
Casa Odelsa Ricardo Caballero	5	Sol Río de Luna y Mares	8
Club Amigo Atlántico Guardalavaca	2	Villa Bely	7
Memories Holguín	9	Villa Paraiso	4
Paradisus Río de Oro	6	Villa Solymar	3
Playa Costa Verde	10		

GUARDALAVACA

● EATING	
Aldea Taína	1
El Ancla	2
La Maison	3
Villa Paraiso Restaurant	4

HORSERIDING AND DIVING AT GUARDALAVACA

Midway between *Las Brisas* hotel and *Club Amigo Atlántico*, next to the Centro Comercial Los Flamboyanes mini-complex is the state-run hire point (daily 9am–5pm) for **horseriding**. **Private horseriding** is also available from Daniel Ávila Hernández (daily 10–5pm; ☎ 05 33 89287) and his crew, who are stationed opposite the *Las Brisas* hotel entrance and have eight horses in beautiful condition. Trips include rides to the beach, into the countryside and up into the mountains.

Guardalavaca is also a good place to go **diving**; local marine attractions include parrotfish and barracuda as well as black coral. The Eagle Ray Dive Centre (Mon–Sat 8.30am–4.30pm, Sun same hours in high season; ☎ 24 43 0316) is at the western end of the beach. Dive boats leave at 9am and 11am daily. The centre also offers ACUC courses and specialist dives like diving with sharks. The *Sol Río de Luna y Mares* complex and the *Paradisus Río de Oro* resort on Playa Esmeralda share the Sea Lovers **dive centre** (☎ 24 43 0132), which offers regular dives, night dives and courses. The Blue World diving centre (☎ 24 43 0434) in front of the *Blau Costa Verde* on Playa Pesquero also offers dives and various ACUC courses.

There are no facilities outside of the hotels; both beaches can be accessed from the road, but you'll have to buy a day-pass if you want to use the hotel facilities.

Museo Chorro de Maíta

Tues–Sat 9am–5pm, Sun 9am–1pm • Charge • ☎ 24 43 0132

Some 6km southeast of the Playa Guardalavaca hotel strip in the Maniabon hills, the fascinating **Museo Chorro de Maíta** is a must-see for anyone interested in pre-Columbian history. A shallow pit in the middle of the museum holds 108 Taíno **skeletons** (mostly original, some reproductions) buried on this site between the 1490s and the 1540s, and uncovered in 1986. The most interesting aspect of the burial pit is that one of the skeletons was found to be a young male European buried in a Christian position with his arms folded across his chest.

Cabinets around the walls of the museum display fragments of earthenware pots along with shell and ceramic jewellery, while arrows positioned in the grave indicate where these were found. The area around the museum has more indigenous remains than any other part of Cuba, with villagers still unearthing artefacts and remnants of jewellery today.

Aldea Taína

Daily 9am–4.30pm • Charge

Just across the road from the Museo de Chorro de Maíta is the **Aldea Taína**, an evocative reconstruction of a Taíno village, offering valuable insight into an extinguished culture and bringing to life many of the artefacts seen in museums around the country. The painstakingly authentic little settlement features **houses** made from royal palm trees populated by life-sized models of Taínos posed cooking and preparing food or attending community rituals. Of particular note is the group inside one of the houses watching the **medicine man** attempt to cure a patient, and another group outside depicted in a **ceremonial dance**. The Taíno-themed restaurant is also pretty decent.

Acuario Cayo Naranjo

Daily 9am–3pm, marine show noon–1pm • Charge • ☎ 24 43 0439

Some 6km west of Guardalavaca beach, the **Acuario Cayo Naranjo** complex is built on stilts about 250m offshore in the shallows of the Bahía de Naranjo. Although calling itself an aquarium, it's really more of a tourist-centre-cum-marine-zoo, as its smattering of sea creatures in tanks are overshadowed by giddier attractions: yacht and speedboat "**seafari**" excursions around the bay, a saccharine **dolphin** and sea-lion show, and the chance to swim with a few of the dolphins themselves. Public concern over keeping marine mammals in captivity has gained traction in recent years, however, and you may want to read up on the issue before deciding whether or not to go (see page 54).

ARRIVAL AND INFORMATION   GUARDALAVACA

By plane Flights for visitors on package holidays land at Holguín's Aeropuerto Frank País, from where special buses ferry guests to the resorts.

By taxi or colectivo There's no public transport from Holguín to Guardalavaca, but a metered taxi will take you there for around $800CUP one way. Alternatively, *colectivo* shared taxis also run this route and leave throughout the day until about 5pm. The *colectivos* depart from Los Pozos just off the main road that heads towards the Guardalavaca stretch. Last ones heading back to Holguín leave at around 5–6pm.

Tourist information Infotur, the national tourist information provider, has an office in the *Hotel Club Amigo Atlántico*.

Services You can cash travellers' cheques at all the hotels and at the Banco Financiero Internacional (Mon–Fri 9am–3pm; last day of month 9am–noon), in the back section of the Centro Comercial Los Flamboyanes where you can also get advances on credit cards. For medical matters, there's Clínica Internacional (24hr; ☎24 43 0312), part of the *Islazul cabaña* complex set behind the Guardalavaca beach. *Club Amigo Atlántico* also has an on-site pharmacy.

GETTING AROUND

Bear in mind when making your way around Guardalavaca that some beaches are referred to by the name of whichever hotel lies on their border – Playa Yuraguanal, for example, is currently referred to by some as Playa Memories Holguín.

By car All the hotels have car rental desks, or you can visit Cubacar or Havanautos (both ☎24 43 0389), in adjacent offices next door to *Las Brisas* hotel in Playa Guardalavaca.

By scooter You can rent scooters outside *Paradisus Río de Oro* hotel at Playa Esmeralda, from *Club Amigo Atlántico* and *Las Brisas* hotels in Playa Guardalavaca, or the *Marítim* at

Playa Pesquero (all open daily 9am–5pm).

By tourist bus The Guardalavaca Bus Tour is a hop-on, hop-off service that covers a wide loop travelling from Playa Guardalavaca west to Playa Pesquero and inland to the Chorro de Maíta museum. It runs from 9am to 9pm.

By bicycle All the local hotels offer bicycles free of charge, an excellent way to get around.

By horse-drawn carriage Carriage rides are available around the Guardalavaca beach area.

ACCOMMODATION   SEE MAP PAGE 345

As a prime resort, Guardalavaca's beachside accommodation consists of **all-inclusive hotels**, mostly at the top end of the price range; the exceptions are the excellent *Las Brisas* and the lacklustre *Club Amigo Atlántico*. It's worth checking with Gaviota and Cubatur tour operators in Holguín (see page 339) before booking directly with one of the all-inclusive hotels, as they offer discounted weekend promotional offers when occupancy is low. The many **casas particulares** in Guardalavaca town and dotted around the countryside backing the coastline are a less expensive alternative.

PLAYA GUARDALAVACA

Las Brisas ⓦ brisasguardalavaca.com. This plush resort has five restaurants, two snack bars, a beauty salon, massage parlour, kids' camp and watersports, as well as mercifully restrained variety-show-style entertainment. There's a choice between rooms and suites within the hotel block or more privacy in newer bungalow-style rooms, although all are equally luxurious. $$$

Casa Odelsa Ricardo Caballero Ave. Guardalavaca,

Edificio 11, Apto 2, 2nd floor ☎24 43 0485. Two rooms with private bathroom, a/c, fridge, TV and DVD player in a spotless apartment run by the friendly Odelsa and her husband, Luis. There's also a separate two-room apartment rented out in its entirety. $

Club Amigo Atlántico Guardalavaca ⓦ hotelescubanacan.com. Although quite old and dated, this free-form complex of guestrooms, pools, bars and restaurants is a friendly and unpretentious resort. Of the various accommodation options, the premium "Villa" section is easily the most appealing, with cool, airy, pastel-painted houses with balconies and simple but attractive furnishings; the "Tropical" and "Standard" areas offer plain but decent rooms – some with a sea view – strung along shadowy corridors, while the best-avoided "Bungalow" section seems stuck in a 1970s time warp. $$$

Villa Bely No.262 Los Pozos Carretera a Guardalavaca ⓦ villabely.orgfree.com. This large, spacious house is set back off the main Guardalavaca road and accessed by turning right just before the bridge when arriving in Guardalavaca. Owners Mircelia and Asbel offer four a/c

7

7

EXCURSIONS FROM GUARDALAVACA

While you can get to most sites independently, it is usually easier to go on a tour. All excursions from Guardalavaca are organized by Cubatur (☎ 24 43 0171), Havanatur (☎ 24 43 0406), Viajes Cubanacán (☎ 24 43 0226) and Gaviota Tours (☎ 24 43 0907 ext 120), all of which have representatives in each hotel and a central office behind the Centro Comercial Los Flamboyanes.

Cayo Saetía A day-trip by catamaran to one of the most unusual resorts in the country. Enjoy the white-sand beach and take a safari through the surrounding woodland and savannah to see zebra, ostrich and the like roaming freely.

Havana You are flown to Havana for a one-night whistle-stop tour of La Habana Vieja and Vedado, with some free time for shopping. A night at *Tropicana* cabaret can be included.

Holguín A half-day jaunt to the provincial capital,

including a visit to a cigar factory to see cigars being made, a trip up the Loma de la Cruz hill, lunch and free time to explore the town centre. Although you could just as easily rent a car to get to Holguín, the tour is the only way to visit the cigar factory.

Santiago de Cuba A full-day trip to Cuba's second-biggest city. The bus ride there and back takes you through some of the region's most scenic countryside, and the trip includes visits to the Santa Ifigenia cemetery, the Castillo El Morro and a cigar factory.

---

rooms each with its own bathroom plus a terrace. Although further from the beach than those in the *edificios* on the main road, this is a quieter and exceptionally well-kept house. 5̄

Villa Paraiso Carretera Guardalavaca ☎ 52 40 2233, ✉ beatrizp94@nauta.cu. Two basic but clean, pleasant rooms each with its own bathroom and parking space in a house in the hillside with its own restaurant, a 10min walk from the beach. As there's no official address, you're best off arranging with the owners to meet you somewhere and accompany you. 5̄

Villa Solymar No.263 Los Pozos ☎ 52 77 4310, ✉ bmmesa@nauta.cu. Two rooms with their own bathroom and a pretty terrace confined by a wrought-iron fence. Set on the hillside above the beach, it's an ideal backpacker's retreat. 5̄

PLAYA ESMERALDA

Paradisus Río de Oro ⓦ melia.com. One of the best equipped hotels in Cuba, aimed at those seeking top-of-the-line though arguably anodyne Caribbean-style luxury. The attractive two-storey *villas* in muted colours are set among gardens brimming with fragrant tropical plant life. Recently remodelled rooms are attractive, with minibar, cable TV and large, smart bathrooms, including two with disabled access. The adult-only hotel boasts four excellent à la carte restaurants, including a Japanese one serving a range of sushi, as well as an airy buffet restaurant. Four beaches, three private, are within easy reach. There's a spa with a sauna as well. 5̄5̄5̄5̄

Sol Río de Luna y Mares ⓦ melia.com. This complex comprises two hotels joined together to operate as one. The more attractive "Luna" section offers spacious, light accommodation in three-storey blocks arranged around a

central pool, while "Mares" features spacious rooms grouped in a single block. There are two buffet restaurants, four à la carte restaurants, four bars and two pools. Facilities include tennis, sauna, gym and various watersports equipment. 5̄5̄5̄

PLAYA PESQUERO AND PLAYA YURAGUANAL

Memories Holguín ⓦ memoriesholguin.com. The only hotel on the exquisite Playa Yuraguanal, with extensive gardens in which the original forest habitat has been preserved. Attractions include elegant and well maintained rooms, seven restaurants including Mexican and Mediterranean, and circular swimming pools arranged in a descending series and fed by a cascade of water. The proliferation of stairs may prove a challenge for anyone with mobility issues. 5̄5̄5̄

Playa Costa Verde ⓦ gaviota-grupo.com. Popular with scuba divers, with smart if slightly sterile rooms in small blocks. There's quite a sociable atmosphere, partly due to the range of entertainment, including outdoor jacuzzis, pool tables, table football, ping pong and a disco. The beach is a few minutes' walk away over a wooden bridge spanning a mangrove lagoon. 5̄5̄5̄

Playa Pesquero ⓦ gaviota-grupo.com. This huge complex, offering the ultimate in get-away-from-it-all luxury, is one of the biggest hotels in Cuba. With a large selection of restaurants, a vast heated swimming pool, its own mini shopping mall, sports facilities and activities for all ages, this is a good option for families. The cool, stylish and ultra comfortable rooms, furnished with natural materials, are set in two-storey blocks; each has its own picturesque balcony with flower-filled window boxes and wicker furniture. 5̄5̄5̄5̄

EATING, DRINKING AND NIGHTLIFE   **SEE MAP PAGE 345**

Most visitors to the area eat most meals at their hotel **restaurants**, but there are a few alternatives and notably a clutch of decent paladars. Similarly, **bars** and **nightlife** are largely confined to the hotels, where entertainment teams host nightly stage shows in which they urge guests to take part in boisterous slapstick sketches and dances. If you've bought a day-pass to any of the all-inclusives, you can stay on for dinner and evening shenanigans.

Aldea Taína Decorated with designs found on the walls of Taíno caves, the restaurant of the museum village (see page 346) serves Taíno foods including herb teas, sweet potato and cassava bread. The recommended dish is the *ajiaco*, a tasty potato, maize and meat stew. $\overline{\$\$}$

El Ancla Playa Guardalavaca ☎ 24 43 0381. Some 100m west of *Club Amigo Atlántico* along the beach, this wind-swept, cabin-like, state-run restaurant offers standard *comida criolla* and seafood. Though the interior is a bit

soulless, the wide patio with a cracking view of the whole sweep of beach is a good place for a drink after walking along the beach. $\overline{\$\$}$

La Maison Barrio El Ancla ☎ 53480839. On the hillside overlooking the sea, the veranda here makes an ideal lunchtime spot. The simple menu focuses on seafood including grilled prawns and lobsters, clams and octopus. Friendly staff complete the picture. Access is via the stairs at the far west end of the beach. $\overline{\$\$}$

Villa Paraíso Restaurant Near the western end of Playa Guardalavaca ☎ 52 40 2233. There's only a simple handwritten menu at the restaurant adjoining a *casa particular* named *Villa Paraíso*. There is no full address: to find the restaurant follow the path up over the headland from the beach. The seafood is fresh and delicious though not everything is always available. $\overline{\$\$}$

Banes

A mix of wooden houses, dishevelled Art Deco beauties and rather more anonymous concrete buildings, the sleepy town of **BANES** lies 31km southeast of Guardalavaca. Refreshingly untouristy, it's known for its museum of pre-Columbian artefacts and for its association with the two titans of twentieth-century Cuban history – Fidel Castro and Fulgencio Batista. Castro married his first wife in Banes, and Cuba's elected president-turned-dictator was born here in 1901.

Iglesia de Nuestra Señora de la Caridad

The Art Deco-style **Iglesia de Nuestra Señora de la Caridad** sits on the edge of a central park with a neat domed bandstand. This is where, on October 10, 1948, **Fidel Castro** married his first wife, Mirta Díaz-Balart, sister of a university friend and daughter of the mayor of Banes. The couple divorced in 1954, the bride's conservative family allegedly disapproving of the young Castro, already known as a firebrand at the university. Although the church interior is fairly prosaic in itself, it's mildly interesting for the historical connection. To go inside, you'll need to ask at the priest's house next door, another handsome Art Deco building.

Museo Indocubano Bani

Avenida General Marreo no.305 • Tues–Sat 9am–5pm, Sun 8am–noon • Charge • ☎ 24 80 2487

Banes' most substantial attraction is the **Museo Indocubano Bani**, devoted to **pre-Columbian Cuban history**. While many of the fragments and representational sketches of Indigenous communities are similar to exhibits in larger museums in the country, it also has a unique gathering of **jewellery** gleaned from the Holguín region. Only a tiny selection of the 22,000 pieces owned by the museum are on display; these include the first skeleton found at Chorro de Maíta as well as its *pièce de résistance*, a tiny but stunning gold (replica) idol.

Casa de la Cultura

Avenida General Marreo no.327 • Daily 8am–10pm • Free • ☎ 24 80 2111

On the opposite side of General Marreo from the Museo Indocubano Bani, the elegant **Casa de la Cultura** is one of Banes' most outstanding buildings, with a black-and-white marble-tiled floor, pale pink and gold walls and a sunny courtyard at the back. As the town's theatre and music hall it has regular performances of traditional music and dance, and players are generally unfazed if you pass by to admire the building and catch snippets of their rehearsals during the daytime.

ARRIVAL AND DEPARTURE
BANES

By camiones and colectivo Services from Guardalavaca, Holguín, Mayarí and Santiago arrive at the bus station on Los Angeles esq. Tráfico.

By taxi Taxis from Guardalavaca resorts cost around $1200CUP for a return trip.

By workers' bus Many travellers also use the workers' transport from Guardalavaca to Holguín but you'd need a bit of Spanish to negotiate this one.

By car The road from Banes to Mayarí is in an appalling state, but it is passable in a normal hire car if you drive carefully.

ACCOMMODATION, EATING AND DRINKING

Cafetería Las Palmas Ave. General Marreo no.730 ☎ 24 80 2803. A thatched restaurant and bar that dishes up indifferent pizza, spaghetti, sandwiches, and the ubiquitous fried chicken. ⑤

Casa Las Delicias Augusto Blanca no.1107 e/ Bruno Meriño y Bayamo, Reparto Cardenas ☎ 24 80 2905. Jorge and Caridad offer a spotless, large room with its own bathroom, a small kitchen and a covered terrace. The friendly couple also run a paladar (daily noon–10pm), in an additional private dining room with a bar, offering seafood as well as spaghetti and chicken dishes. ⑤

El Latino Ave. Martí s/n ☎ 24 80 2298. Just down the road from the church, this is the smartest establishment in town, serving up *comida criolla* and tortillas in air-conditioned surrounds. ⑤

Cayo Saetía

Hidden away on the east side of the Bahía de Nipe near the village of Felton, and connected to the mainland by a drawbridge, picture-postcard, isolated **Cayo Saetía** is the most bizarre – and exclusive – resort in the country. A one-time private game reserve and beach catering to government party officials, it was opened up to the public during the 1990s, yet still retains its air of exclusivity. It's run by Gaviota, the army-owned tourist group, which may explain the vaguely military aura, notably in the ranks of jeeps and other vehicles stationed across the island. Oddly, Cayo Saetía's beauty is not diminished by the pale orange smog drifting across the bay from grimy **Nicaro**, a distinctly uneventful town wreathed in plumes of smoke from an electricity plant.

Cayo Saetía beach

Daily 9am–5pm • Charge

Cayo Saetía's northern coast offers scoops of practically deserted soft white **sand**, hemmed in by a buttery yellow rockface and sliding into the bay's sparkling turquoise green waters. Close to shore, the island's shelf makes for perfect **snorkelling**, with a wealth of brightly coloured sea life, while further out a coral reef offers even better pickings. If you want the beach to yourself, arrive early, as an invasion of tourists on catamaran trips from Playa Guardalavaca arrives from noon onwards. The beach is some 8km from the hotel.

Cayo Saetía safari park

Cayo Saetía's 42 square kilometres of woodland and savannah (unique in Cuba) are home to the most exotic collection of animals in the country – a menagerie of imported zebra, camel, antelope, deer, wild boar and even three ostriches, all freely galloping about. It's as close as Cuba gets to a **safari park** and guests are driven off-piste in a jeep safari through the lush grounds, to admire and photograph the creatures – just before sunset is the ideal time.

ARRIVAL AND ACTIVITIES
CAYO SAETÍA

By car Most people arrive on organized trips from Guardalavaca resorts. If you're travelling in a hire car; from the main-road turn-off to Cayo Saetía, it's around 21km to the hotel, passing the small town of Felton. The road is mildly bumpy but a 4WD isn't necessary.

Activities Jeep safari tours take you through the grounds and can be arranged from the hotel or at the beach restaurant. The latter also offers reasonably priced horseriding, snorkelling expeditions, day-trips around the cay by speedboat, and catamaran safaris. Pedalo and kayak usage is free for all visitors.

ACCOMMODATION AND EATING

Cayo Saetía ⓦ gaviota-grupo.com. Spread about a grassy compound on a knoll overlooking the sea is this twelve-room lodge, which offers twelve comfortable double cabins, three superior rooms and one suite. Rooms are spacious and comfortable but spartan. The lodge's restaurant cooks up exotic meats such as antelope $\overline{\underline{\$\$}}$

7

Parque Nacional La Mensura

Some 45km southwest of Cayo Saetía, the ground swells and erupts into the livid green Sierra de Cristal mountains in which lies the **Parque Nacional La Mensura**. High above the cloud line here, the beautiful **Pinares de Mayarí** pine forest is a great place for some hiking or relaxation, or a stay at the *Villa Pinares de Mayarí* (see page 352). The forest is reached from the nondescript little town of **Mayarí**, 26km to the north, from where you head south towards the Carretera Pinares and take the right-hand track where the road forks, past tiny Las Coloradas; from Holguín, it's a 2.5-hour drive. Though manageable in a rental car, the road is steep and poorly maintained so requires masterful driving, and during the wet season it's advisable to check in advance if it's passable.

The drive up the hill to the forest affords crisp views over the Bahía de Nipe and the terracotta nickel mines to the east, near Nicaro. This lofty region is also Cuba's main producer of **coffee**, with stretches of coffee plants visible along the way. At the top of the hill the sharp incline evens out into a plateau, where the lush green grass and cool air form a scene that's more alpine than Caribbean.

Saltón de Guayabo
Viewpoint daily 8am–4pm

BIRÁN: BIRTHPLACE OF FIDEL CASTRO

A vast area of swaying cane and working plantations, the whole swathe of land southwest from Bahía de Nipe and west of the Pinares de Mayarí is given over to sugar. There's nothing here for the casual visitor, though true Castro devotees may wish to make a pilgrimage to the tiny community of **Birán**, 44km southwest of Mayarí, near which, at the **Finca Las Manacas** plantation, **Fidel Castro** was born on August 13, 1926. He spent part of his youth here, until he was sent to school in Santiago, and owned the farm until his death in 2016. Home to the former school, post office, bar, butcher's, cock-fighting arena and a hotel, the tidy and well-maintained farm also holds the **Sitio Histórico de Birán museum** (Tues–Sat 9am–4pm, Sun 9am–noon, closed if raining; charge), with a collection of photographs, clothes, Fidel's childhood bed and a 1918 Ford. Near the entrance are the well-tended graves of Fidel's father Ángel Castro and mother Lina Ruz.

Finding the *finca* is something of a challenge: from Holguín follow the road east to Cueto, then turn south onto the road to Loynaz Hechevarría; turn east at the sign to Birán and carry on a further 2km north.

You can take a dip in the wide and tranquil **La Presa lake** near the *Villa Pinares de Mayarí* hotel, but there's more exhilarating swimming to be had at the foot of the majestic **Saltón de Guayabo waterfall**, a definite must-see if you are in the area. If you drive for about ten minutes back down the hill towards Mayarí, a steep and narrow dirt track on the left will get you to a **viewpoint**, which provides a splendid vista over a misty and pine tree-covered mountainside, parted here by the two turbulent cascades that comprise the Saltón de Guayabo, thundering down to a pool below. At 104m, the larger of the two is the highest waterfall in Cuba. **Guided treks** (1–2hr) along the nature trail to the foot of the falls can also be arranged at the viewpoint.

ACCOMMODATION

PARQUE NACIONAL LA MENSURA

Villa Pinares de Mayarí Pinares de Mayarí ⓦ gaviotahotels.com. Comprising several chalet-style *villas* with quaint rooms richly inlaid with wood and tiny beds (think Goldilocks visiting the three bears), this is the perfect base for exploring the nearby wilds, with guided walks available into the pine-scented mountains. Misty mornings, steamy tropical afternoons, peacocks and giant rabbits materializing around the grounds, geese supping from the swimming pool, a huge dining hall reminiscent of a giant's cabin – it all adds up to an enchanting, back-to-nature Alice in Wonderland experience. ⑤

Guantánamo city

Even though the provincial capital of **GUANTÁNAMO** is only on the tourist map because of its proximity to the US Guantánamo naval station, 22km southeast, the base plays a very small part in the everyday life of the town itself. For the most part, this is a slow-paced place marked by a few ornate buildings, attractive but largely featureless streets and an easy-going populace. Most visitors bypass it altogether, and those who don't tend to use it simply as a stepping-stone to the naval base and attractions further afield. However, it's worth visiting the **Casa del Changüí**, where changüí genre (a country music which predates son) is nurtured and performed, or taking in a performance by the **Tumba Francesa Pompadour**, an African-Haitian cultural and dance group.

Parque Martí

Guantánamo fans out around the central **Parque Martí**, a small concrete square neatly bordered by intricately trimmed evergreens with hooped gateways. On its north side is the **Parroquía Santa Catalina de Riccis**, a pretty ochre church built in 1863, while one block north, the **Palacio de Salcines** is an eclectic neo-Rococo building with shuttered windows, cherubs over the door and, on its high spire, an outstretched figure with bugle in hand, which has become the symbol of the city. The art museum and gallery inside have been closed for years as the wait for the full restoration the interior of the building so desperately needs continues.

> ### GUANTANAMERA
>
> Synonymous with the beleaguered history of the US naval base, Guantánamo province is an enduring legacy of the struggle between the US and Cuba. In name at least, it's one of the best-known places in Cuba: many a Cuban and a fair few visitors can sing the first bars of the immortal song **Guantanamera** – written by Joseito Fernández in the 1940s as a tribute to the women of Guantánamo. Made internationally famous by North American folk singer Pete Seeger during the 1970s, it has become something of a Cuban anthem and a firm – if somewhat hackneyed – favourite of tourist-bar troubadours the country over, a fitting fate for the song which includes words from José Martí's most famous work, *Versos Sencillos* ("Simple Verses").

Museo Provincial

Martí no.804 esq. Prado • Mon–Fri 8am–4.30pm, Sat 8am–noon • Charge • ☏ 21 325872

One block behind Parque Martí is the humble **Museo Provincial**. Built on an old prison site, it displays some fearsome padlocks and bolts alongside archeological remains and stuffed animals and birds. Much more interesting is the room devoted to the joint USSR and Cuban **space flight**, which sent the first Cuban (and, indeed, Latin American) astronaut – Arnaldo Tamayo Méndez – into space in September 1980. A peek inside the capsule used in their descent back to Earth is the museum's highlight.

Plaza del Mercado

Los Maceos esq. Prado

A couple of blocks northeast of Parque Martí, one of the most intriguing buildings in Guantánamo is the quite fantastical agricultural marketplace, **Plaza del Mercado**, with its big pink dome and crown-like roof bearing statues of regal long-necked geese at each corner. It was designed by Guantánamo's most famous architect, Leticio Salcines, who along with the Palacio Salcines, designed three hundred other buildings in town.

Casa del Changüí

Serafin Sánchez e/ Narcisco López y Jesús del Sol • Tues–Sun 9am–noon, 2–6pm & 7pm–midnight • Performances Fri, Sat & Sun 8pm • Charge • ☏ 21 32 4178

The **Casa del Changüí** cultural and nightlife venue is a great place to catch live shows by changüí groups, with performances by the likes of Tumbao de Monte, Universales del Son, Morenos de Changüí and Estrellas Campesinas in an alfresco courtyard decorated with colourful murals. Changüi emerged from the Guantánamo countryside as campesino music in the late nineteenth century, and is played by an ensemble that incorporates the Cuban *tres* – the only melodic instrument in the genre – the *marímbula* and a metal *guayo* as well as maracas and bongo drums.

ARRIVAL AND DEPARTURE — GUANTÁNAMO CITY

By plane Cubana has two weekly flights between Havana and the Mariana Grajales airport (☏ 21 355912), 12km southeast of town.

Destinations Havana (2 weekly; 2hr 10min).

By train The town's train station (☏ 21 325518) is centrally located in a squat Art Deco folly on Pedro A. Pérez.

Destinations Havana (2 weekly; 16hr); Holguín (2 weekly; 6hr); Las Tunas (2 weekly; 5hr) Matanzas (2 weekly; 14hr); Santa Clara (2 weekly; 11hr 30min).

By bus Víazul services (☏ 21 325780) arrive at the Terminal de Omnibus (☏ 21 325588) on Carretera Santiago, 2.5km out of town; you can walk or catch a *bicitaxi* into the centre, but as it's so remote you may want to organize a taxi or pick-up in advance.

Destinations Baracoa (1 daily; 3hr 10min); Santiago de Cuba (1 daily; 1hr 30min).

By Conectando Cuba bus Services for Baracoa depart Guantánamo city on Tues, Thurs and Sat at 9.30am.

INFORMATION, TRAVEL AGENTS AND TOURS

Both the travel agents, the information office and the hotel chain Isalzul can help you with permits and guides for a visit to Caimanera, the closest you can get to Guantánamo Bay (see page 354). They also arrange other excursions in and around the city and province, including trips to the Zoológico de Piedras (see page 356) and tours of a local sugar mill.

Infotur The information office at Calixto García e/ Emilio Giró y Flor Crombet (Mon–Sat 8.30am–5pm; ☏ 21 351993)

offers a weekly events list as well as just about every kind of visitor advice.

Cubatur Aguilera e/ Calixto García y Los Maceo (Mon–Sat 8.30am–4.30pm; ☏ 21 328342).

Havanatur Aguilera e/ Calixto García y Los Maceo (Mon–Sat 9am–noon & 2–4.30pm; ☏ 21 326365).

Islazul Aguilera e/ Calixto García y Los Maceo (Mon–Sat 9am–noon & 2–4.30pm; ☏ 21 386466 or ☏ 21 327197).

ACCOMMODATION

Casa de Lissett Foster Lara Pedro A. Pérez no.761 e/ Jesús del Sol y Prado ☏ 21 32 5970, ✉ lisset128@gmail.

com. Four clean and comfortable double rooms with a/c and private bathrooms in a large, airy, modern apartment

7

THE US AT GUANTÁNAMO

Described by Fidel Castro as the dagger in the side of Cuban sovereignty, the **US naval base at Guantánamo** is approximately 118 square kilometres of leased North American territory, armed to the teeth and planted on Cuba's southeastern coast.

The history of the naval base here dates back to Cuba's nominal victory in the Wars of Independence with Spain, whereupon the US government immediately began to erode Cuba's autonomy. Under the terms of the **1901 Platt Amendment**, the US ordered Cuba to sell or lease land necessary for a naval station, declaring without irony that it was "to enable the United States to maintain the independence of Cuba". Its primary aim, however, was to protect the nascent Panama Canal from any naval attacks. An annual rent was set at two thousand gold coins, and the base was born. In 1934 the Treaty of Reciprocity repealed the Platt Amendment but did not alter the conditions surrounding the lease; and as it's stipulated that the lease cannot be terminated without both parties' consent, it seems unlikely that Cuba will regain sovereignty of the land under its present regime. Famously, Fidel Castro never cashed a single rent cheque from the US government, preferring to preserve them for posterity in a locked desk drawer.

GITMO DEVELOPS

Although the US quickly broke off all relations with the Cuban government after the Revolution, they were less speedy to give up their territory. Known as "**Gitmo**" by US servicemen, Guantánamo base is like an American theme park inside, with stateside cars zooming along perfectly paved roads bordered by shops and suburban houses. From the 1970s until the mid-1990s, such material riches gave the base an El Dorado lustre that lured many a dissident Cuban to brave the heavily mined perimeter or chance the choppy waters to reach this ersatz chunk of North America in the hope of gaining US citizenship as a political asylum seeker. US immigration policy was changed in 1994 and now Cubans who make it into the base usually find themselves making a swift exit back onto Cuban soil via the nearest gate.

CAMP DELTA AND THE WAR ON TERROR

The base's history took another twist in December 2001 with the decision of the Bush

with a roof terrace and balcony overlooking the street, a stone's throw from Parque Martí. $

Casa de Osmaida Carlos Manuel no.811 e/ Prado y Aguilera ☎ 21 32 5193, ✉ osmaidablanco@nauta.cu. Three large spacious rooms with a kitchen and patio doors, and a smaller internal room in this helpful household, four blocks from Parque Martí. Parking available. $

Hotel Martí Calixto García esquina Aguilera 82 🌐 hotelmarti.com. This impeccable, 21-room hotel with its smart wooden desks, TVs and comfortable beds is a good central option. Those wanting a bit of grandeur should opt for room 206, with its three balconies. The top-floor bar and terrace opens Fri, Sat and Sun from 8.30pm. Rates include breakfast. $$

EATING AND ENTERTAINMENT

Sabor Melian Ave. Camilo Cienfuegos e/ Pedro A. Pérez y Martí ☎ 21 32 4422. This off-centre, friendly, candy-pink restaurant offers a large *criollo* menu but with limited availability. $

Tumba Francesa Pompadour Serafín Sánchez no.715 e/ Narciso López y Jesús del Sol · ☎ 21 381 669. The local

home of the **Tumba Francesa Pompadour,** an African-Cuban-Haitian society and dance group originally formed following the migration of French landowners, enslaved people and free enslaved people from Haiti to Cuba after the 1791 Haitian Revolution.

Around Guantánamo

Many visitors come to the Guantánamo area just to see the US base, but although you can get to the lookout point in **Caimanera** with a little groundwork, there really administration to detain Islamic militants captured as part of the "**War on Terror**". Prisoners were initially kept in the makeshift Camp X-Ray but in April 2002 were transferred to **Camp Delta**, a larger, permanent site, which comprises several detention camps, manned by six hundred soldiers as part of the Joint Task Force Guantánamo. Controversy immediately arose around the circumstances under which the men were held. Because they were classed as "**illegal combatants**" rather than prisoners of war, the US military felt they did not have to uphold the Geneva Convention and that the detainees could be held indefinitely without charge. Some 780 people (including a number of children) representing forty different nationalities have to date been held here, many without access to any court, legal counsel or family visits.

Since 2002, images of shackled detainees in orange jumpsuits – along with reports of numerous suicide attempts and persistent allegations of abuse and torture of prisoners – have provoked international condemnation, including the accusation that the detainees are being held unlawfully. While the majority of them have not been charged, those who have were tried in the **Guantánamo Military Commissions** to determine whether their crimes warrant further detention. No one has been convicted by a trial in a US court of law. To date, more than 700 prisoners have been released.

THE ON-GOING SITUATION

A decision in June 2004 by the US Supreme Court ruled that the detainees should come under the jurisdiction of US courts and that the policy of holding prisoners indefinitely without the right to judicial review was unlawful. Rather than address these charges, the Bush administration passed the **Military Commissions Act 2006**, which overrode the main objections. In January 2009, as part of a broader aim to restore the international reputation of the US justice system and foreign policies, President Obama suspended the Guantánamo Military Commissions and vowed that the detainee camp would be **closed** by January 2010 – but could not persuade Congress to approve this. President Trump declared a determination to keep the base open (one of his many reversals of Obama policy on Cuba) and in January 2018 signed an executive order to do just that. While President Biden declared an intention to close the detention centre, significant steps have yet to be taken and, at the time of writing, 37 detainees remain in the centre.

isn't a lot to see, as you cannot enter the base itself – or barely see it at all from Cuban territory. Venturing into the **countryside** around Guantánamo city is more rewarding, with bizarre contrasts between lush valleys and the weird desert scenery of sun-bleached barren trees. Just north of town is the offbeat **Zoológico de Piedras**, a "zoo" entirely populated by sculpted stone animals.

Caimanera and the US naval base

A return taxi from Guantánamo costs around $800CUP, and you will need a guide and permit (see box, page 356)

Bordered by salt flats that score the ground with deep cracks and lend a haunting wildness, **CAIMANERA**, 23km south of Guantánamo, takes its name from the giant caiman lizards that used to roam here, although today it's far more notable as the closest point in Cuba to the US naval base. Prior to the Revolution, Caimanera was the site of carousing between the naval-base officers and the townswomen: its main streets were lined with bars, and rampant sex work, gambling and drugs were the order of the day. Little evidence of that remains in today's sleepy and parochial town.

The village is a **restricted area**, which you cannot visit independently, with the ground between it and the base one of the most heavily mined areas in the world, though the US removed their mines in 1999. This hasn't stopped many Cubans from braving it in the slim hope of reaching foreign soil and escaping to the US. Visitors, meanwhile, have to have a **permit** to enter (see box). The village is entered via a checkpoint at

> ### CAIMANERA PERMITS AND GUIDES
>
> To visit Caimanera for the day or stay at the hotel, you'll need a permit, issued by the Ministry of the Interior (MININT) and a guide, both of which you should arrange through travel agencies in Guantánamo city at least 72 hours in advance. Permits are free but you'll need to present identification and complete some paperwork to obtain one. These organized visits require a minimum of two people and usually include tours around Caimanera and the surrounding countryside as well as far-off views of the US naval base. You can arrange transport through the agency too (car, train or bicycle) though if you have your own car you can use it – but you'll need to make sure there is room in the car for your guide to travel along with you. The permit is for a fixed date of entry so if, for any reason, you are late arriving to pick up your permit, you will have to apply for a further one.

7

which guards scrutinize your passport and permit before waving you through; note that taking pictures en route is not permitted.

The **lookout** in the grounds of the *Caimanera* hotel has a view over the bay and mountains to the base – though even with binoculars you only see a sliver of it. Inside the hotel is a small **museum** (opened on demand), with a history of the base, a floor model and photos.

ACCOMMODATION AND EATING   CAIMANERA

Hotel Caimanera ⓦ islazulhotelscom. The most unusual hotel in Cuba, facing the watchtowers and the US naval base. The rooms and restaurant are adequate for a one-night stay, though think twice about a bay view, as the 24hr revolving searchlights are a tortuous experience. There's a pool to while away the hours once you've finished scoping out the base. Rates include breakfast. $\bar{\underline{5}}$

Zoológico de Piedras

Altos de Boquerón, Km 27 Carretera a Yateras • Daily 9am–6pm • Charge

Roughly 20km north of Guantánamo, in the foothills of the Sierra Cristal and set in a private coffee farm, the whimsical and slightly surreal sculpture park known as the **Zoológico de Piedras** was created in 1977 by local artist Ángel Iñigo Blanco, who carved the stone in situ. Cool and fresh, dotted with lime and breadfruit trees, hanging vines and coffee plants, the park centres on a path that weaves around the mountainside, with **stone animals** peeking out from the undergrowth at every turn. Slightly cartoonish in form, the creatures bear little relationship to their real-life counterparts: a giant tortoise towers over a hippo the size of a modest guinea pig. Needless to say, it's a hit with children.

Baracoa

In the eyes of many visitors, the countryside around **BARACOA** is quite simply the most beautiful in Cuba. Set on the coast at Cuba's southeastern tip and protected by a deep curve of mountains, the town's isolation has so far managed to protect it from some of the more pernicious effects of tourism that have crept into other areas of the island. Self-contained and secluded, Baracoa vibrates with an energy surprising for such a small place, and has become a must on the travellers' circuit. It's also home to a uniquely mixed population, with many locals of Haitian and Jamaican origin – the result of late nineteenth- and early twentieth-century immigration.

Simply wandering around is one of the town's greatest pleasures. The quaint central streets are lined with tiny, pastel-coloured colonial houses with wedding-cake trim, and modern development is confined to the outskirts and the **Malecón**, where new apartment blocks were built after the Revolution.

All the sites of interest are within easy walking distance of one another, radiating out from the **Parque Central** on Antonio Maceo, where, under the shade of the wide laurel trees, generations of Baracoans gather around rickety tables to play chess and dominoes.

A festive time to be in Baracoa is for the Semana de la Cultura, held in the last week of March/first week of April, and the even bigger celebration of the Fiesta de las Aguas, between August 10/12 and 15.

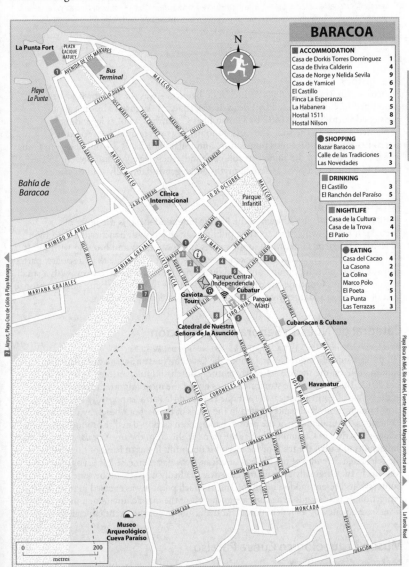

BARACOA

ACCOMMODATION

Casa de Dorkis Torres Dominguez	1
Casa de Elvira Calderin	4
Casa de Norge y Nelida Sevila	9
Casa de Yamicel	6
El Castillo	7
Finca La Esperanza	2
La Habanera	5
Hostal 1511	8
Hostal Nilson	3

SHOPPING

Bazar Baracoa	2
Calle de las Tradiciones	1
Las Novedades	3

DRINKING

El Castillo	3
El Ranchón del Paraíso	5

NIGHTLIFE

Casa de la Cultura	2
Casa de la Trova	4
El Patio	1

EATING

Casa del Cacao	4
La Casona	2
La Colina	6
Marco Polo	7
El Poeta	5
La Punta	1
Las Terrazas	3

> ## BARACOA'S FORTS
>
> As a defence against marauding pirates in the eighteenth and nineteenth centuries, the Captain of Baracoa, one Pedro Oviedo, ordered the fortifications of three forts between 1739 and 1742. **Castillo Seburuco**, which overlooks the town and El Yunque from the northern hills, has been converted into a hotel, while the Malecón is sealed by **La Punta**, now a restaurant, a door in its western wall leading down a flight of stairs to the tiny **Playa La Punta**, a good spot for a quiet dip (daily 9am–5pm). East of the centre, past the shops and the triangular Parque Maceo – complete with bust – is **Fuerte Matachín** (Mon–Sat 8am–noon & 2–6pm, Sun 8am–noon; charge), a well-preserved structure with the original cannons ranged along its walls. The cool interior now houses the town **museum**, with a good collection of delicately striped Polymita snail shells, some Native American relics and a history of the town's most celebrated characters.

Brief history

Baracoa – Nuestra Señora de la Asunción de Baracoa – was the **first town** to be established in Cuba, founded by Diego de Velázquez in August 1511 on a spot christened Porto Santo in 1492 by Christopher Columbus who, as legend has it, planted a cross in the soil. The early conquistadors never quite succeeded in exterminating the Indigenous population, and today Baracoa is the only place in Cuba where descendants of the **Taíno** can still be found. Their legacy is also present in the food and transport, as well as several myths and legends habitually told to visitors.

Parque Central

The **Parque Central**, also known as the **Parque Independencia**, is the heart of Baracoa. It's the town's most sociable public space, filled with benches, flanked by pedestrianized streets lined with modest cafés and restaurants and buzzing with locals and visitors alike, especially on weekend evenings. More a triangle than a square, part of it sits under a bushy canopy provided by its mature and attractive trees, with a small central fountain. Opposite the cathedral that occupies the whole of one side is a bronze bust of Taíno hero Hatuey by Cuba's most famous sculptor, Rita Longa.

Catedral de Nuestra Señora de la Asunción

Parque Central • Tues–Fri 8–11am & 4–7pm, Sat 8–11am & 5–9pm, Sun 8am–noon; Mass at 9am

On the east side of Parque Central stands the **Catedral Nuestra Señora de la Asunción**, built in 1807 on the site of a sixteenth-century church and fully restored between 2010 and 2012. This unobtrusive structure houses one of the most important religious relics in the whole of Latin America, the antique **La Cruz de la Parra**, supposedly the antique cross brought from Spain and planted in the sands of the harbour beach by Christopher Columbus. It's undeniably of the period, having been carbon-dated to around thirty years before the arrival of Columbus, but as the wood is also from the tree *Cocoloba diversifolia*, indigenous to Cuba, the truth of the legend is doubtful. It was in front of this cross that the celebrated defender of the Native American, Fray Bartolomé de Las Casas, gave his first Mass in 1510. Originally 2m tall, the cross was gradually worn down by time and souvenir hunters to its present modest height of 1m, at which point it was encased in silver for its protection. It now stands in a glass case to the left of the main church door, on an ornate silver base donated by a French marquis at the beginning of the twentieth century.

Museo Arqueológico Cueva Paraíso

Loma Paraíso • Daily 8am–6pm • Charge

A steep climb up the thickly forested Loma Paraíso brings you to Las Cuevas del Paraíso, a series of **caves** once used by the Taíno for ceremonies and funeral chambers, now home to Baracoa's fascinating and atmospheric **Museo Arqueológico Cueva Paraíso**. Archeologists have unearthed a treasure-trove of pre-Columbian artefacts, in the caves themselves and the surrounding countryside, left by successive Indigenous groups who made the region their home: the Guanahatabey occupied the area from about 3000 to 1000 BC, the Siboney from approximately 1000 BC until 1100 AD, and the Taíno who supplanted them until the arrival of the Spanish in the fifteenth century.

Among the most interesting exhibits are the **human remains** in the funerary chamber. The skeletons are displayed as they were found, in the traditional foetal position, and all the specimens' skulls are badly misshapen. It is thought likely that the Taíno tied heavy weights to babies' heads, flattening the forehead by pushing the bone down horizontally and extending the back of the skull. The malformed bodies were buried with *esferolitas*, small round stones used to indicate the person's age and social standing – those found here indicate that this was the resting place for important and wealthy people.

Between caves, stairs wind up to a natural platform where a path and a couple of well-positioned benches allow you to drink in the fantastic views of Baracoa and beyond.

The Malecón

A walk along the **Malecón**, a ragged collection of the backsides of houses and ugly apartment blocks, is something of a disappointment, not least because the area was ravaged by a hurricane in 2008. To the north is the town's **Plaza de la Revolución**, surely the smallest in Cuba, decorated only with one revolutionary poster.

Playa Boca de Miel

At the eastern end of the Malecón, accessed by the stone stairs to the right of an imposing stone statue of Christopher Columbus, is the main town beach, **Playa Boca de Miel**, a boisterous hangout mobbed in summer by vacationing schoolchildren. People walk their dogs along the multicoloured shingle near town, but the brilliant jade, grey and crimson of the stones fade into sand a little further along, making for a decent swimming spot. The best place for a paddle, however, lies beyond the clump of trees at the far eastern end of the beach, in the gentle **Río de Miel**, which has its own legend (see page 361).

Boca de Miel

Beyond the reaches of Playa Boca de Miel, there's an unaffected and intimate view of Baracoan life at the hamlet of **Boca de Miel**, comprising little more than a handful of

---

LA FAROLA: THE MOUNTAIN ROAD TO BARACOA

Before the Revolution, Baracoa was only accessible by sea, but the opening of the **La Farola** road in 1965 changed all that, providing a direct link with Guantánamo 120km away, and allowing a flood of cars to pour into the previously little-visited town. Considered one of the triumphs of the Revolution, the road was actually started by Batista's regime, but was temporarily abandoned when he refused to pay a fair wage to the workers, and work was only resumed in the 1960s. Today, La Farola makes for an amazing trip through the knife-sharp peaks of the Cuchillas de Baracoa mountains. However, the route should only be attempted in daylight, as the steep banks bordering the road in places, combined with a cracked and broken road surface, make it extremely dangerous in the dark.

simple, single-storey homes and, further on, the pale-sand beach at Playa Blanca. At the easternmost edge of Playa Boca de Miel, where the river reaches the sea, turn towards the river and follow the path down to the picturesque though rickety wooden bridge. Take the path to the left of the bridge and head up the hill. Here, there's a control post for the Mayajara protected area (see below), and **Playa Blanca** on the other side of a little grove of trees. You can enter for free but if you want to head up to the mirador point you must pay the waiting guard a few pesos. The tiny hoop of coarse, blondish sand makes a good spot to relax for an afternoon, though you should be very mindful of the vigorous undertow if you go swimming. There are no facilities here, so be sure to take a supply of water; locals will offer to prepare you fried fish and water coconuts.

Mayajara protected area

Daily 8am–5pm • Charge for guided walks

Just outside Boca de Miel village, and accessed from the guardpost close to Playa Blanca, the **Mayajara protected area** is riddled with caves and petroglyphs, but best known for its incredible 500m-long **Balcón Arqueológico**, an extensive elevated limestone balcony accessed by a mixture of sturdy and rickety ladders. The views through the palms to the ocean are outstanding.

ARRIVAL AND DEPARTURE

BARACOA

By plane The Aeropuerto Gustavo Rizo (☎ 21 64 5376) is near the *Porto Santo* hotel, on the west side of the bay 4km from the centre. The Cubana office is at Martí no.181 (Mon–Fri 8am–noon & 1–3pm, Sat 8–11am; ☎ 21 64 5374). Destinations Havana (2 weekly; 2hr 30min).

By Víazul bus Demand for Víazul tickets to and from Baracoa usually outstrips supply, especially in the summer, so make sure you book yours well in advance, preferably before you arrive. If you don't you could find yourself queuing early in the morning for a first-come-first-served distribution of remaining spaces and may end up waiting several days to leave. Víazul buses pull up at the bus terminal (☎ 21 64 3660) at the northern end of the Malecón; it's a 500m-walk down José Martí or Maceo to the centre, or you can take a *bicitaxi*. Destinations Guantánamo (1 daily; 3hr 10min); Santiago

(1 daily; 4hr 45min).

By Conectando Cuba bus Cuba's other national bus service runs three times a week between Baracoa, Guantánamo city and Santiago. Book tickets through the Cubanacán travel agent (see page 339). Destinations Guantánamo (3 weekly; 3hr 10min); Santiago (3 weekly; 4hr 45min).

By private bus Gaviota Tours, inside *La Habanera* hotel (daily 8am–6pm; ☎ 21 64 4115) and at *Cafetería El Parque* (daily 8am–noon & 2–6pm; ☎ 21 64 5164), runs a service to Holguín, departing at 8.30am on Sat

By car or colectivo Half the pleasure of a visit to Baracoa is the view en route through the mountains on the La Farola road (see box above). Note that the only petrol station on the coastal road between Mayarí and Baracoa is at Moa. *Colectivos* leave in the mornings from the Parque Central.

GETTING AROUND

On foot The best way to get around Baracoa is on foot, as most of the places you'll want to see are within easy reach of the centre. There's little point relying on public transport – buses are scarce and always jam-packed.

By bicitaxi or unmetered taxi If travelling further afield, you can catch a *bicitaxi* from anywhere in town, or an unmetered taxi from behind the church.

By metered taxi Call Cubataxi (☎ 21 64 3737).

By car and scooter For car rental, try Cubacar, Martí no.202 e/ Céspedes y Coroneles Galano (Mon–Sat 8am–5pm; ☎ 21 64 5225), Transgaviota at the airport (☎ 21 64 1665; Sun–Fri 8am–noon & 2–6pm) or at *Cafetería El Parque* Maceo esq. Rafael Trejo (Mon–Sat 9am–1pm & 2–6pm; ☎ 21 64 1671), where you can also rent scooters.

INFORMATION AND TRAVEL AGENTS

It's advisable to talk to one of the travel agents, or Infotur, if you are planning any trips into the nearby mountains and countryside – and essential if you don't have your own transport. The state-run agents all offer roughly the same tours around Baracoa at more or less the same price. Some should be able to book plane tickets too.

Infotur The national tourist information provider is at Maceo no.129A e/ Frank País y Maraví (Mon–Sat 8.30am–4.45pm; ☎ 21 64 1781) with general information about the area such as tours, hikes, museums and entertainment plus free maps and guides.

Cubanacán Martí no.181 e/ Ciro Frias y Céspedes (Mon–

Sat 8.30m–noon & 1.30–5pm; ☎ 21 64 4383).
Cubatur Maceo no.147 esq. Pelayo Cuervo (Daily 8am–noon & 2–6pm; ☎ 21 64 5306).
Ecotur Ciro Frías esq. Ruber López (☎ 21 64 2478).

Gaviota Tours Cafeteria El Parque, Maceo esq. Rafael Trejo, Parque Central (Daily 8am–noon & 2–6pm; ☎ 21 64 4115).
Havanatur Martí e/ Coroneles Galano y Roberto Reyes (☎ 21 64 5358).

ACCOMMODATION

SEE MAP PAGE 357

All five of the hotels in town, as well as a couple just beyond, are operated by the Cuban chain Gaviota (ⓦ gaviotahotels. com).

HOTELS

El Castillo Calixto García ⓦ gaviotahotels.com. Perched high on a hill overlooking the town, this former military post is now an intimate, comfortable and very welcoming hotel. Glossy tiles and wood finishes give the rooms a unique charm, while the handsome pool patio with views over the bay is the best place in town to sip *mojitos*. Very popular and often fully booked, making reservation essential. $\overline{\underline{SS}}$

La Habanera Maceo no.126 esq. Frank País ⓦ gaviotahotels.com. Right in the centre of town, with a pretty pink exterior and an airy reception filled with comfy sofas. The ten rooms, arranged around a courtyard, are clean and comfortable with TV, a/c and private bathrooms. Guests can use *El Castillo*'s pool. $\overline{\underline{SS}}$

Hostal 1511 Ciro Frias ☎ 21 64 5700. A charming, small hotel which has been kitted out in a simple but comfortable style. Its main attraction, however, is its lovely veranda. Rooms are comfortable, but standard ones don't have a view. Guests can use *El Castillo*'s pool. $\overline{\underline{SS}}$

CASAS PARTICULARES AND HOSTALESSEE

Casa de Dorkis Torres Domínguez Flor Crombet no.58 (altos) e/ 24 de Febrero y Coliseo ☎ 21 64 3451, ✉ dorkistd72@yahoo.es. Two modern, en-suite a/c rooms with minibar, fridge and sea view in a friendly household. A terrace next to one of the bedrooms on which to eat the delicious home-cooked meals seals the deal. $\overline{\underline{S}}$

Casa de Elvira Calderin Frank País no.19 e/ Martí y Maceo ⓦ facebook.com/casaelvirabaracoa. This spacious, central property has three pleasant, airy rooms with a/c and private bathroom, and a courtyard out back. Meals are available. Massage and salsa classes offered. $\overline{\underline{S}}$

★ **Hostal Nilson** Flor Crombet no.143 e/ Ciro Frias y Pelayo Cuervo ☎ 21 64 3123, ⓦ hostalnilson.baracoa. co. Fantastic, spacious apartment close to the centre of town, with two double rooms which have the use of a kitchen and a semi-independent apartment with a sea view. The attractive roof terrace with decorated wooden carvings of Cuban birds, *Restaurant Las Terrazas*, where the amicable owners serve up traditional Baracoan meals, makes this one of the best choices in town. $\overline{\underline{S}}$

Casa de Norge y Nelida Sevila Flor Crombet no.265A e/ Glicerio Blanco y Abel Díaz ☎ 21 64 3218, ✉ cnorge@rocketmail.com. A royal blue house with a double room and dining room accessed by an independent entrance. There's a small balcony, with sea view, for sunning out back, and Norge is a charming host. $\overline{\underline{S}}$

Casa de Yamicel Martí no.145 e/ Ciro Frias y Pelayo Cuervo ☎ 21 64 1118, ✉ neoris70@gmail.com. French colonial house built by enslaved people owners fleeing the Haitian Revolution. Yamicel carried out an outlandish extension so it now has five double rooms. The huge rooftop terrace is uncluttered and relaxing. Yamicel's husband Neoris makes a fine *mojito*. $\overline{\underline{S}}$

Finca La Esperanza Carretera a Moa Km 8 ☎ 5218 0735. On the banks of the beautiful River Toa, 4km from town, this rustic *hostal* is a delightful spot for those wanting to escape the city. There are sixteen beds across six rooms, with two shared bathrooms, and a bar and restaurant. $\overline{\underline{S}}$

EATING

SEE MAP PAGE 357

Food in Baracoa draws on a rich local heritage and the region's plentiful supply of coconuts. Tuna, red snapper and swordfish fried in coconut oil are all favourite dishes, and there is an abundance of lobster, as well as a few vegetarian

---

THE RIVER OF HONEY

Many years ago, a Taíno maiden with honey-coloured hair used to bathe daily in the waters of the **Río Miel**. One day a young sailor steered his ship down the river and spotted her. Captivated by her beauty, he instantly fell in love and for a while the happy couple frolicked daily in the river. However, as the day of the sailor's departure approached, the young girl became increasingly depressed and would sit in the river crying until her tears swelled its banks. Impressed by this demonstration of her love, the sailor decided to stay in Baracoa and marry her, from which grew the saying that if you swim in the Río Miel, you will never leave Baracoa, or that if you do you will always return.

specials. **Local specialities** include *cucurucho*, a deceptively filling concoction of coconut, orange, guava and lots of sugar sold in a palm-leaf wrap on the hillside roads leading into the town. Other treats for the sweet-toothed include locally produced chocolate and the soft drink Pru, a fermented blend of sugar and secret spices that's something of an acquired taste and is widely available from street stands.

STATE RESTAURANTS AND CAFÉS
Casa del Cacao Maceo no.129 ✆ 21 64 2125. This café-cum-museum has cabinets sparsely laid out with the tools and instruments of traditional chocolate production spaced around its elegant interior plus a small bar in the patio out back. Hot chocolate is offered straight or with rum and you can take it with mint or liqueur too. This is also the place to buy locally made chocolate bonbons and bars. $

La Punta Ave. de los Mártires, at the west end of the Malecón ✆ 21 64 1480. An elegant restaurant, detached from the rest of the town, in the grounds of La Punta fort, cooled by sea breezes and serving traditional Cuban and Baracoan food, some spaghetti dishes and the house speciality of fish cooked with coconut sauce. $$

PALADARS
La Casona Martí no.114 esq. Maraví ✆ 21 64 1122. This no-frills paladar in an emerald green colonial building is as unassuming as they come – they even ask what music you'd like to hear while you dine. The generous servings of fried chicken or platters of shrimps or octopus in tomato sauce or coconut milk come accompanied by soup, rice, salad and *chatinos* (fried plantain strips). $

La Colina Calixto García no.158 (altos) e/ Céspedes y Coroneles Galano ✆ 05 29 03651. Owner Al has a great position with his high terrace overlooking the town and the sea, and he serves up barbecued food with panache. In addition to fish in coconut sauce, try octopus in its own ink or chicken fricassee. $$

Marco Polo Malecón no.82 esq. Moncada ✆ 53553623. One of the best restaurants on the sea front, the windowside tables here look down on the waves hitting the rocks below. Plenty of above-average Baracoan classics but also a good choice of alternatives, including a selection of salads. The shiny modern interior features pink lampshades, purple tablecloths and a red feature wall. $$

★ **El Poeta** Maceo no.159 esq. Ciro Frias ✆ 21 64 3017. A smorgasbord of local delicacies, deliciously cooked and beautifully served in gourds and cacao pods. The fish in a thick coating of coconut sauce is outstanding, and the coconut ice cream, served with cacao beans to suck on, is delightful. Owner Pablo's presentation is no cover-up for mediocre food; it's all moreish and delicious. $$

Las Terrazas Flor Crombet no.143 e/ Ciro Frias y Pelayo Cuervo ✆ 21 64 3123. At the top of this three-floor *casa particular* is the town's most idiosyncratic dining room, decorated with images and symbols of African-Cuban santería, a makeshift bar, a mezzanine level and a small balcony. Decent mains, like fish or chicken in coconut sauce, hit the right notes but more notable are the great sides and accompaniments, like the delicious pumpkin soup and the succulent yet crispy fired banana. In the summer they open the roof terrace. $$

DRINKING AND NIGHTLIFE
SEE MAP PAGE 357

Nowhere else in the town can compete with the size of the crowd and the buzz around the Parque Central. Around half-a-dozen cafés and bars are huddled around the square though none has much to recommend it over the others.

Casa de la Cultura Maceo no.124 e/ Frank País y Maraví ✆ 21 64 2364. A haven of jaded charm, with live music and dancing on the patio nightly, plus regular rumba shows. Performances from 9–11pm.

★ **Casa de la Trova** Victorino Maceo no.149B e/ Ciro Frias y Pelayo Cuevo ✆ 21 64 17 47. Concerts take place in this tiny room opposite Parque Central, after which the chairs are pushed back to the wall and exuberant dancers spill onto the pavement. A lively, unaffected atmosphere makes for

one of the most vibrant and authentic nights out in town.

El Castillo Calixto García ✆ 21 64 5165. With views of El Yunque and overlooking the bay, the poolside bar of this hotel is one of the most attractive options in town for twilight cocktails.

El Patio Maceo esq. Maraví. Nightly traditional music shows at 9pm draw a crowd, while the bar does a fine trade in expertly prepared *mojitos*. Entrance is free.

El Ranchón del Paraíso Loma Paraíso ✆ 21 64 3268. Up on Paradise Hill behind Baracoa and reached by a stone staircase, this large, open-sided bar and club is popular with local youngsters as well as tourists. Disco music plays nightly and food is available.

SHOPPING
SEE MAP PAGE 357

To buy bars of chocolate head for the Casa del Cacao (see page 362). For groceries, there are several supermarkets on José Martí between Ciro Frias and Roberto Reyes.

Bazar Baracoa Martí no.197 esq. Céspedes ✆ 21 64 5373. The local ARTEX shop sells posters of Cuban art, handheld fans, ceramics, handmade bags, CDs, T-shirts and

Cuba baseball caps.

Calle de las Tradiciones Maraví y Maceo. A row of artisans' market stalls operates here daily in this tiny plaza.

Las Novedades Martí no.217 e/ Coroneles Galano y Roberto Reyes ✆ 21 64 5307. This small supermarket has the town's best selection of rum at very reasonable prices.

DIRECTORY

Banks and exchange Banco de Crédito y Comercio, Maceo no.99 e/ 10 de Octubre y 24 de Febrero (Mon–Fri 8am–3pm, Sat 8–11am), gives cash advances on MasterCard and Visa, changes travellers' cheques and has two 24hr ATMs. The CADECA *casa de cambio* at José Martí no.261 e/ Roberto Reyes y Limbano Sánchez can handle all currency exchange transactions. (Mon–Fri 8.15am–2pm, Sat 8.15–11.30am).

Health The Clínica Internacional, Maceo no.89 e/ 10 de Octubre y 24 de Febrero (daily 8.30am–8pm; ☎21 64 1038), has the town's best stocked pharmacy. There's a 24hr pharmacy at Maceo no.132 (☎21 64 2271). The general hospital, the Hospital Octavio de la Concepción y de la Pedraja (☎21 64 7100), is on the Carretera Central, the

main road out of town, 1.6km south of Parque.

Police The police station is on Martí no.26 towards the Malecón, near the bus station (☎21 64 2479). In an emergency call ☎116.

Post office Maceo no.136 (daily 8am–8pm).

Swimming pool The pool at the Hotel El Castillo is open to non-guests for a charge.

Wi-fi The local wi-fi hotspot is Parque Central. You can buy Nauta wi-fi cards at the ETECSA Telepunto at Maceo esq. Rafael Trejo (daily 8.30am–7.30pm), just off the Parque Central, where there are also nine computer terminals free to use with wi-fi cards.

7

Around Baracoa

Cradled by verdant mountains smothered in palm and cacao trees, and threaded with swimmable rivers, the Baracoan countryside has much to offer. **El Yunque**, the hallmark of Baracoa's landscape, can easily be climbed in a day, while if you have a car and a little time to spare you could take a drive east along the coast and seek out some quintessentially Cuban fishing villages, including **Boca de Yumurí**. Alternatively, just head for the **beach** – there are a couple of good options northwest of town.

El Yunque

The walk to the summit starts near *Campismo El Yunque*, 3km off the Moa road • Charge • Guided excursions can be arranged by the Ecotur office (see below)

As square as a slab of butter, 575m **El Yunque**, 10km west of Baracoa and streaked in mist, seems to float above the other mountains in the Sagua Baracoa range.

TOURS AROUND BARACOA

With an abundance of verdant countryside, exploring the surrounding area is one of the pleasures of a visit to the Baracoa region. Without your own car, the only option is to take a **guided tour**, which can be arranged through any of the travel agents in Baracoa.

Boca de Yumurí Though its tranquil nature has been damaged somewhat by tourism, Boca de Yumurí still offers splendid views and swimming spots. This excursion includes a boat ride and a tour of the local cocoa plantation, which cannot be visited any other way.

Parque Nacional Alejandro de Humboldt These lush rainforests, curving and swelling into hills above coastline tangled with mangroves, cover some 700 square kilometres of land and sea and were deservedly designated a Unesco biosphere and national park in 2001. Views are fantastic and access to secluded beaches and surrounding countryside easy. Guided tours take you through some of the most beautiful scenery on hillside hikes or boat trips around the coast and usually include a visit to Playa Maguana too.

Playa Duaba Only 6km outside of Baracoa, Playa

Duaba is set on an estuary. The beach itself is a scrubby grey, but is pleasant enough for a swim. The tour includes a short guided walk, while lunch at the *Finca Duaba* is an optional extra.

Río Toa Reached through some gently undulating rainforest filled with a cornucopia of cocoa trees, one of the country's longest rivers lies 10km northwest of Baracoa. Wide and deep, the Río Toa is one of the most pleasant places to swim in, although you should choose your spot carefully and watch out for a fairly brisk current.

El Yunque Nestling in lush rainforest is the hallmark of Baracoa's landscape, El Yunque. The area is rich with banana and coconut trees, while the views are astounding. If you are striking out alone, start your climb at the *Campismo El Yunque*.

Christopher Columbus noted its conspicuousness: his journal entry of November 27, 1492, mentions a "high square mountain which seemed to be an island" seen on his approach to shore – no other mountain fits the description as well. El Yunque is the remnant of a huge plateau that dominated the region in its primordial past. Isolated for millions of years, its square summit has evolved unique species of ferns and palms, and much of the forest is still virgin, a haven for rare plants including orchids and bright red epiphytes. The energetic though not unduly strenuous **hike to the summit** should take about two hours. A shorter and easier option is a guided trek to a waterfall within the protected area. After a 2km walk you reach a pristine lake, perfect for bathing in. An easy enough fifty-metre scramble then takes you to a pretty waterfall. It's well worth it for a short morning excursion.

ACCOMMODATION
EL YUNQUE; SEE MAP PAGE 332

Campismo El Yunque ☎ 21 64 5262. The boxy concrete cabins sleeping up to six here are scattered across a beautiful grove of palm trees near the River Duaba and starting point for climbing El Yunque. It's a perfect escape, but you'd need your own transport. Five cabins are reserved for tourists. 💲

Playa Maguana

Some 25km northwest of Baracoa along the road to Moa, **Playa Maguana** is an attractive, narrow beach with golden sand, some seaweed, plenty of shade and a reef for snorkelling. Partly bordered with the spindly though leafy *Coco thrinas* palm, indigenous to the area, it's popular with locals as well as visitors, and is less exclusive than many in Cuba. At the far end of the beach, *Villa Maguana* (see page 364) sits in its own private cove. Take care of valuables while swimming at Maguana, as there have been reports of bags being taken.

ACCOMMODATION AND EATING
PLAYA MAGUANA

Playa Maguana now offers a handful of new **paladars**, on or just off the beach, while pop-up places also open during the summer months. Alternatively, beach fishermen often approach sunbathers and will offer to cook freshly caught fish with rice and banana, served with rum-laced milk coconuts.

Beach bar Set back from the water, Playa Maguana's beach bar sells drinks and some snacks like fried chicken and spaghetti. 💲💲

Paladar El Pulpo ☎ 05 22 78598. One of several paladars on the beach; this one stays open all year serving seafood and a few plates of pasta. 💲💲

★ **Villa Maguana** Playa Maguana ☎ 21 64 1204 or ☎ 21 64 1205. The only beach accommodation in the area, this is a little idyll, with plenty of privacy and sixteen comfortable double rooms, tastefully decorated and housed in a series of tall, smart, rustic cabins overlooking a little hoop of semiprivate beach. There are two restaurants and a beach bar to boot. Well worth at least a night's stay. 💲💲

THE POLYMITA SNAIL

Along the Boca de Yumurí beach you may spot the brightly coloured shells of the **Polymita snail**. According to local Native American legend, there was once a man who wanted to give his beloved a gift. As he had nothing of his own to give, he set out to capture the colours of the universe: he took the green of the mountains, the red of the earth, the pink of the flowers, the white of the foam of the sea, the yellow of the sun and the black of the night sky. He then set all the colours into the shells of the snails and presented them to his love. Each snail is unique, ornately decorated in delicate stripes and consequently quite sought after – the Duchess of Windsor in the 1950s, for instance, had a pair encrusted with gold studs and made into earrings. Such caprices have severely depleted the snails' numbers, and although locals still sell them, buying is not recommended. A local campaign has started to raise awareness of the danger the sale of shells poses for the species – and buying them is now prohibited.

WALKS IN PARQUE NACIONAL ALEJANDRO DE HUMBOLDT

There are several **guided walks** on offer in the Humboldt national park that allow you to experience the peculiar plants and wildlife of the region. The **El Recreo** (3hr) and **Sendero Balcón de Iberia** (5hr) trails can be booked at the park gate or through travel agencies in Baracoa. Exclusive walks, which can only be booked in the national park itself or EcoTur (see page 363), include **Sendero El Copal** (4hr) and **Sendero Loma de Piedra** (6hr). An **agroecoturismo route** offers opportunities to experience local craft and honey production. Another option is the 22km, three-day **Ruta Humboldt**, but must be organized well in advance at the park headquarters at Martí opposite the bus stop (☏21 64 5289), or through EcoTur.

Boca de Yumurí

Thirty kilometres east of Baracoa, past the Bahía de Mata – a tranquil bay with a slim, shingled beach and a splendid view of the mountains – is the little fishing village of **BOCA DE YUMURÍ**, standing at the mouth of the eponymous river. Known as a place to find the highly prized Polymita snails (see box above), the rather bland, brown-sand beach is also lined with houses whose owners will offer to cook you inexpensive **meals** of fish, rice and bananas. The village has suffered somewhat from the more pernicious effects of tourism and it's more than likely you'll be besieged with *jineteros* trying to steer you towards their restaurant of choice and flog you shells from your moment of arrival. Head to the end of the beach and a wooden jetty from where you can catch a **raft taxi** further upstream, where the river is clearer and better for swimming, banked by a high rock face.

Parque Nacional Alejandro de Humboldt

Park office • Daily 8am–4pm • Charge

Some 56km north out of Baracoa on the Moa road, with an office right on the *carretera* where you pay your entry fee, the **Parque Nacional Alejandro de Humboldt** stretches across more than 32,000 hectares of mountainous rainforest and sea. Its forests are home to the world's smallest bird, bat, frog and male scorpion, and the park also includes the stunning, discus-shaped **Taco Bay**, fringed by beautiful coconut palms and hemmed in by dense mangrove and frequented by an elusive cluster of manatees. The best time to spot these unusual mammals (also known as sea cows) is November to January via a two-hour boat trip across the bay to the mangroves.

Santiago de Cuba and Granma

DRIVING TO EL COBRE

Santiago de Cuba and Granma

The southern part of Oriente – the island's easternmost third – is defined by the Sierra Maestra, Cuba's largest mountain range, which binds together the provinces of Santiago de Cuba and Granma. Rising directly from the shores of the Caribbean along the southern coast, the mountains make much of the region largely inaccessible – a quality appreciated by Fidel Castro and his rebels, who spent two years waging war here in the late 1950s. At the eastern end of the sierra is the roiling, romantic city of Santiago de Cuba, capital of the eponymous province and with a rich colonial heritage that's evident throughout its historical core. Cuba's most important urban area outside Havana, the city draws visitors mainly for its music. Developed by the legions of bands that have grown up here, the regional scene is always strong, but it boils over in July when the Fiesta del Caribe and carnival drench the town in rumba beats, fabulous costumes and song.

Within easy day-trip reach of the city, just down the coastline, is the magnificent coastal fortification of **El Morro** and, slightly further afield, the **Gran Parque Natural Baconao**; inland, there's gentle **trekking** in the **Parque Nacional de la Gran Piedra** where one of the highest points in the province, Gran Piedra itself, offers far-reaching vistas. In the lush, cool mountains west of the city, the town of **El Cobre** features one of the country's most important churches, housing the much-revered relic of the Virgen de la Caridad del Cobre. Still further west, bordering Granma province, the heights of the **Sierra Maestra** vanish into cloudforest, and although access to the **Parque Nacional Turquino** – around Pico Turquino, Cuba's highest peak – can be restricted, you can still admire from afar.

Unlike Santiago de Cuba, which revolves around its main city, the province of **Granma** has no obvious base from which to approach its highlights. The small black-sand beach resort at **Marea del Portillo** on the south coast is a favourite for Canadian visitors, but the highlight of the province, missed out on by many, is the **Parque Nacional Desembarco del Granma**. Lying in wooded countryside at the foot of the Sierra Maestra, this idyllic park, home to an assortment of intriguing stone petroglyphs, can be easily explored from the beach of **Las Coloradas**. Further north, along the Gulf of Guacanayabo, the museum at **Parque Nacional de Demajagua**, formerly the sugar estate and home of Carlos Manuel de Céspedes, celebrates the War of Independence amid tranquil, park-like grounds.

Granma's two main towns are underrated and often ignored, but the fantastic Moorish architecture in the coastal town of **Manzanillo** is reason enough to drop by; while **Bayamo**, the provincial capital, with its quiet atmosphere and pleasant scenery, appeals to discerning visitors looking for an easy-going spot to stay.

Santiago de Cuba city

Beautiful, heady **SANTIAGO DE CUBA** is the crown jewel of Oriente. Nowhere outside Havana is there a city with such definite character or such determination to have a good time. Spanning out from the base of a deep-water bay and cradled by mountains, Santiago is credited with being the most Caribbean part of Cuba, a claim borne out by its laidback lifestyle and rich mix of inhabitants. It was here that the first

BASÍLICA DE LA CARIDAD DEL COBRE, NEAR SANTIAGO DE CUBA

Highlights

❶ Santiago's summer festivals The city's musical *joie de vivre* is summed up in a cacophony of salsa, trova, conga and fabulous costumes at its double summertime fiesta bill. See page 378

❷ Museo Emilio Bacardí Moreau Based on the private collection of the son of the Bacardí empire founder, this cornucopia of artefacts is as precious as it is eclectic. See page 377

❸ El Castillo del Morro San Pedro de la Roca An impressive seventeenth-century stone fortress, built on a cliff outside Santiago to ward off pirates. See page 384

❹ Hotel Casa Granda Presiding over Santiago's main square, the reception-level terrace and

the rooftop bar of this historic hotel are perfect spots to soak up the city life. See page 389

❺ Santiago's Casa de la Trova An atmospheric music house thrumming with authentic Cuban sounds. See page 390

❻ Comandancia de La Plata A trek through verdant peaks of the Sierra Maestra to the rebels' mountain base brings the 1959 revolution to colourful life. See page 402

❼ Playa Las Coloradas The site where the *Granma* yacht deposited Fidel, Che and the other revolutionaries at the inception of the struggle is both a historic and scenic pleasure. See page 404

HIGHLIGHTS ARE MARKED ON THE MAP ON PAGES 370 AND 372

enslaved people from West Africa were brought, and today Santiago has a larger Black population than anywhere else in Cuba. African-Cuban **culture**, with its music, myths and rituals, has its roots here, with later additions brought by French coffee planters fleeing revolution in Haiti in the eighteenth century.

The leisurely pace of life doesn't make for a quiet city, however, with the higgledy-piggledy net of narrow streets around the colonial quarter ringing night and day with the beat of drums and the toot of horns. **Music** is a vital element of Santiaguero life, whether heard at the country's most famous **Casa de la Trova** and the city's various other venues, or at the impromptu gatherings that tend to reach a crescendo around **carnival** in July. As well as being the liveliest, the summer months are also the hottest – the mountains surrounding the city act as a windbreak and the lack of breeze means that Santiago is often several degrees hotter than Havana, and almost unbearably humid.

Although Santiago's music scene and carnival are good enough reasons to visit, there are a host of more concrete attractions. Diego Velázquez's sixteenth-century merchant house and the elegant governor's residence, both around **Parque Céspedes** in the colonial heart of town, and the commanding **El Morro** castle at the entrance to the bay, exemplify the city's prominent role in Cuban history. Additionally, the part played by townsfolk in the **revolutionary struggle**, detailed in several fascinating museums, makes Santiago an important stop on the Revolution trail.

One downside to a visit here is **street hustle** (see Basics, page 54) in the downtown area. The level and persistence of hassle and propositioning, especially acute around

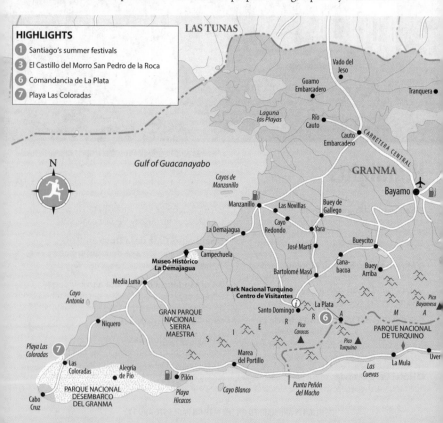

HIGHLIGHTS

1 Santiago's summer festivals
3 El Castillo del Morro San Pedro de la Roca
6 Comandancia de La Plata
7 Playa Las Coloradas

LAS TUNAS

Vado del Jeso

Guamo Embarcadero

Tranquera

Laguna las Playas

Río Cauto

Cauto Embarcadero

CARRETERA CENTRAL

Gulf of Guacanayabo

Cayos de Manzanillo

GRANMA

Bayamo

Manzanillo

Las Novillas

Buey de Gallego

Cayo Redondo

Yara

La Demajagua

José Martí

Bueycito

Campechuela

Museo Histórico La Demajagua

Bartolomé Masó

Cana-bacoa

Buey Arriba

Media Luna

Cayo Antonia

Park Nacional Turquino Centro de Visitantes

Santo Domingo

La Plata

6

Pico Bayamesa

GRAN PARQUE NACIONAL SIERRA MAESTRA

Niquero

Pico Caracas

Pico Turquino

PARQUE NACIONAL DE TURQUINO

Playa Las Coloradas

7

Las Coloradas

Alegría de Pío

Marea del Portillo

Las Cuevas

La Mula

Uver

Pilón

Cayo Blanco

PARQUE NACIONAL DESEMBARCO DEL GRANMA

Playa Hicacos

Punta Peñón del Macho

Cabo Cruz

Parque Céspedes, is among the highest in the country. More positively, the city has enjoyed a thorough makeover in recent years, both in response to the terrible damage wreaked by Hurricane Sandy in 2012 and further stimulated by the 500th anniversary of the city's foundation in 2015. Today Santiago is far cleaner, fresher-looking, more pedestrian friendly and better equipped with inner-city hotels.

Brief history
Established by **Diego Velázquez de Cuéllar** in 1515, the port of Santiago de Cuba was one of the original seven *villas* founded in Cuba. Velázquez, pleased to find so excellent a natural port near to reported sources of **gold** (which were quickly exhausted), named the port Santiago (St James) after the patron saint of Spain. With the construction of the central trading house shortly afterwards, the settlement became Cuba's capital.

After this auspicious start – boosted by the discovery of a rich vein of **copper** in the foothills in nearby El Cobre – the city's importance dwindled somewhat. Buffeted by severe earthquakes and **pirate attacks**, Santiago developed more slowly than its western rival and in 1553 was effectively ousted as capital when the governor of Cuba, Gonzalo Pérez de Angulo, moved his office to Havana.

Sugar, coffee and slavery
Santiago's physical bounty led to a new boom in the eighteenth century, when Creoles from other areas of the country poured **sugar** wealth into the area by

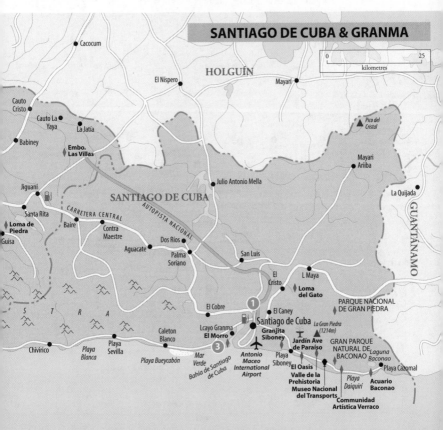

developing plantations. The cool mountain slopes around Santiago proved ideal for growing **coffee**, and French planters, accompanied by their enslaved workers, emigrated here after the 1791 revolution in Haiti, bringing with them a cosmopolitan air and continental elegance, as well as a culturally complex slave culture.

Relations with Havana had always been frosty, especially as culturally distinct Santiago had fewer Spanish-born *Penínsulares*, who made up the ruling elite. This rivalry boiled over during the **Wars of Independence**, which were led by the people of Oriente. Much of the fighting between 1868 and 1898 took place around Santiago, led in part by the city's most celebrated son, **Antonio Maceo**.

The US takeover

The Cuban army had almost gained control of Santiago when, in 1898, the **United States** intervened. Eager to gain control of the imminent republic, it usurped victory from the Cubans by securing Santiago and subsequently forcing Spanish surrender

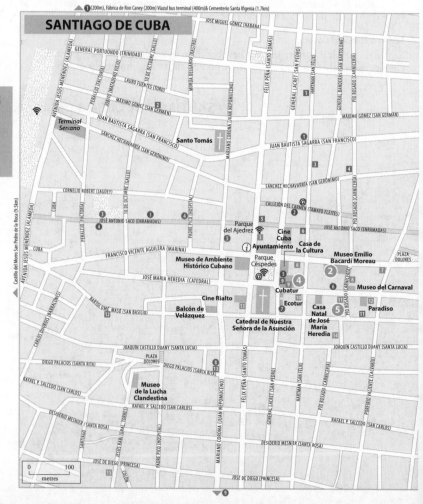

after a dramatic battle on **Loma de San Juan**. The Cubans were not even signatories to the resultant Paris peace settlement between the US and Spain, and all residents of Santiago province were made subject to the protection and authority of the US. As an added insult, the rebel army that had fought for independence for thirty years was not even allowed to enter Santiago city.

The Revolution and Santiago today

Over the following decades, the American betrayal nourished local anger and resentment, and by the 1950s Santiago's citizens were playing a prime role in the civil uprisings against the US-backed president Fulgencio Batista. Assured of general support, **Fidel Castro** chose Santiago for his debut battle in 1953, when he and a small band of rebels attacked the **Moncada barracks**. Further support for their rebel army was later given by the M-26-7 underground movement that was spearheaded in Santiago by **Frank and Josue País**. It was in Santiago's courtrooms that Fidel Castro and the other rebels were subsequently tried and imprisoned.

HIGHLIGHTS

2 Museo Emilio Bacardí Moreau

4 Hotel Casa Granda

5 Santiago's Casa de la Trova

SHOPPING	
Artesanías Art Decó	4
La Barrita	1
Callejón del Carmen	2
Galería Oriente	5
Librería La Escalera	6
Proyecto Espiral	3

NIGHTLIFE	
Casa de las Tradiciones	15
Casa de la Trova	10
La Claqueta	13
Club 300	6
Coro Madrigalista	8
Iris Jazz Club	4
Los Dos Abuelos	1
Patio Artex	12
Sala de Conciertos Dolores	5
UNEAC	11

DRINKING	
La Gran Sofía	2
Hotel Casa Granda	9
La Isabelica	7
Parque del Ajedrez	3
Taberna del Ron	14

EATING	
La Arboleda	2
Casa Micaela	5
La Fabada de Marieta	4
Jardín de Las Enramadas	3
El Morro	9
Roy's Roof Garden	8
San Francisco	1
La Taberna de Dolores	6
Thoms & Yadira	7

ACCOMMODATION	
Casa Colonial Maruchi	1
Casa Granda	9
Casa Ilia	3
Casa de Leonardo y Rosa	8
Casa Miriam	10
Casa de Nolvis Rivaflecha Martínez	12
Casa de Noris y Pedro	4
Hostal Casa Jardín	2
Imperial	5
Libertad	7
Roy's Terrace Inn	13
San Basilio	11
San Felix	6

8

SANTIAGO'S STREET NAMES

Many streets in Santiago have two names, one from before the Revolution and one from after. Theoretically, street signs show the post-revolutionary name, but as these signs are few and far between, and locals tend to use the original name in conversation, we follow suit in the text. Cuban maps, however, usually show both names, with the original in brackets; on our maps we've followed their example. The most important roads are listed below.

OLD NAME	NEW NAME
Calvario	Porfirio Valiente
Carnicería	Pío Rosado
Padre Quiroga	Clarín
Enramadas	José A. Saco
Máximo Gómez	San Germán
Reloj	Mayía Rodríguez
San Francisco	Sagarra
San Basilio	Bartolomé Masó
San Félix	Hartmann
San Gerónimo	Sánchez Hechevarría
San Pedro	General Lacret

When the victorious Castro swept down from the mountains, it was in Santiago that he chose to deliver his maiden speech, in the first week of January 1959. The city, which now carries the title "Hero City of the Republic of Cuba", is still seen – especially in Havana – as home to the most zealous revolutionaries, and support for the Revolution is certainly stronger here than in the west of the island. The rift between east and west still manifests itself today in various prejudices, with Habaneros viewing their eastern neighbours as troublemaking criminals, and considered solipsistic and unfriendly by Santiagueros in return.

Parque Céspedes

Originally the Plaza de Armas, the first square laid out by the conquistadors, **Parque Céspedes** is the spiritual centre of Santiago. There's a gentle ebb and flow of activity, as sightseers wander through between museum visits, musicians strum their instruments around the edges and impromptu performances by a brass and percussion band draw in a crowd.

The rooftop bar at the picturesque *Casa Granda* hotel, on the park's east side, provides a fantastic setting to admire the sunset as well as the surrounding sights, while the hotel's balcony bar, on the ground floor, is a great place to people-watch over a glass of fresh lemonade. Two doors down from the hotel is the old high-society **Club San Carlos**, housed in an exquisite nineteenth-century building, part of which holds an art gallery. On the south side, a small **monument** celebrates the park's namesake, Carlos Manuel de Céspedes, one of the first Cubans to take up arms against the Spanish, issuing the *Grito de Yara* (cry of Yara) and urging his enslaved workers and comrades to arm themselves (see page 399).

Facing the cathedral on the park's north side is the brilliant-white **Ayuntamiento**, or town hall, whose balcony was the site of Fidel Castro's triumphant speech in January 1959.

Catedral de Nuestra Señora de la Asunción

Parque Céspedes • Mon 8am–4.30pm, Tues–Fri 8am–7.15pm, Sat 8am–noon & 4.30–6pm; Mass Tues–Fri 6.30pm, Sat 5pm, Sun 9am & 6.30pm • ☎ 22 628202

On the south side of Parque Céspedes is the handsome **Catedral de Nuestra Señora de la Asunción**. The first cathedral in Santiago was built on this site in 1522, but repeated run-ins with earthquakes and pirates – in 1606 English privateer Christopher Myngs even stole the church bells after blowing the roof off – made their mark, and Santiagueros started work on a second cathedral on the site in 1674, only to see the building demolished by an earthquake just three years later. A third cathedral was erected in 1690 but was wiped out by another earthquake in 1766.

The present cathedral, completed in 1818, has fared better, having been built with a fortified roof and walls in order to withstand natural disasters. However, it has been shaken by quakes in 1852 and 1932, and damaged by Hurricane Sandy in 2012. The cathedral features a Baroque-style facade, its twin towers gleaming in the sunshine and its doorway topped by an imposing herald angel, statues of **Christopher Columbus** and **Bartolomé de las Casas**, defender of the Native Americans, erected in the 1920s, and four Neoclassical columns.

The interior

The **interior** is no less ornate, with an arched Rococo ceiling rising above the pews into a celestial blue dome painted with a cloud of cherubs. Facing the congregation is a modest marble altar framed by rich dark-wood choir stalls, while to the right a more ornate altar honours the Virgen de la Caridad, patron saint of Cuba. The prize piece, almost hidden on the left-hand side, is the tremendous **organ**, no longer used but still replete with tall gilded pipes. Lining the wall is a noteworthy frieze detailing the history of St James, the eponymous patron saint of Santiago.

8

Museo Ambiente Histórico Cubano

Parque Martí e/ Aguilera y Heredia • Mon–Thurs, Sat & Sun 9am–4.45pm, Fri 1.30–4.45pm • Charge

Built in 1515 for Diego Velázquez, the first conquistador of Cuba, the magnificent stone edifice on the west side of the park is the oldest residential building in Cuba. It now houses the **Museo Ambiente Histórico Cubano**, a wonderful collection of furniture, curios, weapons and fripperies which offers one of the country's best insights into colonial lifestyles, and is so large it spills over into the house next door. There are traditional music *peñas* here throughout the week. Ask for the timetable.

The first floor

Start your tour on the first floor, in the family's living quarters, where you'll find some unusual **sixteenth-century** pieces exhibited beneath stunning Mudéjar ceilings. All the windows have heavy wooden lattice balconies and shutters – intended to hide the women, keep the sun out and protect against attack – which lend the house a surprising coolness, as well as the look of an indomitable fortress. The house was strategically built facing west so that the first-floor windows looked out over the bay, and a **cannon** is still trained out of the bedroom window. The next two adjoining rooms represent the mid- and late **seventeenth century**; the first room holds a chunky, carved mahogany chest, and a delicate Spanish ceramic inkwell that has survived intact through three centuries.

The final rooms on this floor take you into the **eighteenth century**, and the furnishings seem incongruously grand, set against the plain white walls and cool tiled floors of the house. Cut into the inner wall there's the **Poyo de la Ventana**, a latticed spy window overlooking the hallway, which allowed inhabitants to check on the movements of other people in the house.

Out in the cool upstairs **hallway** you can fully appreciate the cleverness of its design in its stark contrast with the dazzling, sunny central courtyard visible below, where there's an elegant central fountain and a huge *tinajón* water jar from Camagüey. Before you venture downstairs, walk to the end of the hallway to see the remains of the stone

furnace that Velázquez built into the corner of the house so that he could smelt his own gold.

The ground floor

The rooms on the **ground floor**, where Velázquez had his offices, are now laid out with more extravagant eighteenth-century furniture and artefacts, though more impressive, perhaps, are the details of the house itself, such as the wide entrance made to accommodate a carriage and the expansive trading rooms with a stone central arch, marble flagged floor and window seats.

The annexe

The collection overflows into the **house next door**, which dates from the nineteenth century. Again, much of what's on display is imported from Europe and shows off the good life enjoyed by Santiago's bourgeoisie, but the most interesting items are native to Cuba, like the reclining *pajilla* smoking chair with an ornate ashtray attached to the arm, made for the proper enjoyment of a fine cigar.

Calle Enramadas

The longest pedestrianized street in Cuba, the fourteen colourful, boisterous blocks of Enramadas pass through the centre of the city from lofty Plaza de Marte all the way down to the port road. The paving over of Santiago's main commercial street, completed in 2016, has transformed it into a bubbling river of shoppers, hustlers, school children and tourists, flowing through little parks and squares and past front-room street-food vendors, cheap restaurants, makeshift shops, chain stores and pastel-coloured buildings. At the lower end, the half dozen blocks sloping down to the harbour area, there are several attractive hotels, indoor and open-air craft markets, the street's best restaurant and the sprawling, leafy **Jardines Las Enramadas**, the best place in the city to stop for ice cream. One block north of Enramadas, between Felix Peña and General Banderas, is the city's arts and craft market street, the **Callejón del Carmen** (see page 391).

Calle Heredia

Of the four streets bisecting Parque Céspedes, the liveliest is **Calle Heredia**, and more precisely its three blocks immediately east of the square. Here the drums emanating from the *Casa de la Trova*, *Patio Artex* and the *UNEAC* music venues (see page 390) combine with the catcalls of street vendors and the shuffling of visitors to the small museums and souvenir shops to create one of the most stimulating areas in the city.

Casa Natal de José María Heredia

Heredia no.260 e/ Hartmann y Pio Rosado • Mon–Sat 9am–7pm, Sun 9am–4pm • Charge • ☎ 22 62 5350

The handsome colonial **Casa Natal de José María Heredia** is the birthplace of one of the greatest Latin American poets. His poetry combined romanticism and nationalism, and was forbidden in Cuba until the end of Spanish rule. While not the most dynamic museum in the world, it's worth a quick breeze through the spartan rooms to see the luxurious French *bateau* bed, the family photos and the various first editions. A good time to visit is on Wednesday at 5pm, when local poets meet for (free) discussions and recitals on the sunny patio at the back of the house.

Museo del Carnaval

Heredia no.301 esq. Pio Rosadoe • Tues–Sun 9am–5pm • Charge • ☎ 22 626955 • Dance recitals Mon–Sat 4–5pm, Sun 10am–12noon

A must if you can't make it for the real thing in July, the **Museo del Carnaval** is a small but bright and colourful collection of psychedelic costumes, atmospheric photographs and carnival memorabilia. Beginning with scene-setting **photographs** of Santiago in the early twentieth century, showing roads laced with tram tracks and well-dressed people promenading through the parks, the exhibition moves on to newspaper cuttings and **costumes** belonging to the pre-revolutionary carnivals of the 1940s and 1950s. In a separate room are photographs of some of the musicians who have played at carnival accompanied by their **instruments**, displayed in glass cases. A final room shows off costumes made for post-Revolution carnivals, along with some of the immensely intricate prototypes of floats that are constructed in miniature months before the final models are made.

The flamboyant carnival atmosphere is brought to life with a free, open-air, hour-long **dance recital** called the *Tardes de Folklórico* (folklore afternoon), showcasing the dances and music of various *orishas* (deities).

Museo Emilio Bacardí Moreau

Aguilera esq. Pío Rosado • Mon–Fri 9am–4.30pm, Sat 9am–6.30pm, Sun 9am–2.30pm • Charge • ☎ 22 628402

Of all the museums in Santiago, by far the most essential is the stately **Museo Emilio Bacardí Moreau**. Its colonial antiquities, excellent collection of Cuban fine art and archeological curios make it one of the most comprehensive hoards in the country. Styled along the lines of a traditional European city museum, it was founded in 1899 by Emilio Bacardí Moreau, then mayor of Santiago and patriarch of the Bacardí rum dynasty (see page 380), to house his vast private collection of artefacts amassed over the previous decades. The exhibits are arranged over three floors.

The ground floor

The entrance floor is the most eclectic. A collection of Carlos Manuel de Céspedes memorabilia helps to illustrate the history of the fight for independence and leads into an excellent collection of Taíno artefacts – mostly Idols and petroglyphs, as well as a particularly good example of a *dujo*, the seat on which the cacique sat down for ceremonies. At the back of this level, the **Sala de Conquista y Colonización** is full of elaborate weaponry like sixteenth-century helmets, cannons and spurs, although copper cooking pots and the like add a suggestion of social history. Much more horrific are the whips, heavy iron chains and the *Palo Mata Negro* (or Kill-the-Black person stick), all used to lash and beat enslaved workers.

The lower ground floor

On the lower ground floor, accessed by a staircase at the back of the Sala de Conquista y de Colonización, the **Sala de Arqueología** contains a strange mix of artefacts from South and Central America including a shrunken head and a small Egyptian collection which features a mummy and her sarcophagus brought over from Luxor by Bacardí himself.

The first floor

The first floor has a good display of **paintings** and **sculpture**, including some fascinating nineteenth-century portraits of colonial Cubans. A surprise is the delicately executed series of watercolours – including a rather camp cavalryman and an enigmatic picador – by the multitalented Emilio Bacardí. Other highlights include the **Colección procedente del Museo del Prado**, sent over from Madrid at the end of the nineteenth century, and the rather striking *La Confronta de Billetes o La Lista de la Lotería* by José Joaquín Tejada, which was presented in New York in 1894 and described by José Martí as the tangible expression of the "new Cuban painter".

8

SANTIAGO'S CARNIVAL

The extravaganza that is **Santiago's carnival** has its origins in the festival of Santiago (St James), which is held annually on July 25. While the Spanish colonists venerated the saint, patron of Spain and Santiago city, their African enslave people celebrated their own religions, predominantly Yoruba. A religious procession would wend its way around the town towards the cathedral, with the Spanish taking the lead and the enslaved people bringing up the rear. Once the Spanish had entered the cathedral, the enslaved people took their own celebration onto the streets, with dancers, singers and musicians creating a ritual that had little to do with the solemn religion of the Spanish – the frenzied gaiety of the festival even earned it the rather derisive name **Los Mamarrachos** (The Mad Ones).

Music was a key element, and enslaved people of similar ethnic groups would form *comparsas* (carnival bands) to make music with home-made bells, drums and chants. Often accompanying the *comparsas* on the procession were *diablitos* (little devils), male dancers masked from head to toe in raffia costumes. This tradition is still upheld today and you can see the rather unnerving, jester-like figures running through the crowds and scaring children. Carnival's popularity grew, and in the seventeenth century the festival was gradually extended to cover July 24, the festival of Santa Cristina, and July 26, Santa Ana's day.

The festival underwent its biggest change in 1902 with the birth of the new republic, when politics and advertising began to muscle in on the action. It was during this era that the festival's name was changed to the more conventional **carnaval**, as the middle classes sought to distance the celebrations from their African-Cuban roots. With the introduction of the annually selected *Reina de Carnaval* (Carnival Queen) – usually a white, middle-class girl – and carnival floats sponsored by big-name companies like Hatuey beer and Bacardí, the celebration was transformed from a marginal Black community event to a populist extravaganza. With sponsorship deals abundant, the **carrozas** (floats) flourished, using extravagant and grandiose designs.

Perhaps the most distinctive element of modern-day carnival in Santiago is the **conga parade** that takes place in each neighbourhood on the first day of the celebrations. Led by the *comparsas*, almost everyone in the neighbourhood, many still dressed in hair curlers and house slippers, leaves their houses as the performers lead them around the streets in a vigorous parade. The week before carnival starts, you can see the Conga de los Hoyos practising around town and visiting the seven other city conga groups every day from 3pm to 8pm.

CARNAVAL PRACTICALITIES

Carnaval takes place every year from around July 18 to July 27. The main parade is on the first day, and is followed by smaller parades on the second, third and fourth days. On the 25th, there's a general parade from 10pm in honour of the city's patron saint; the 26th sees a grand parade, and there's prize-giving on the 27th. The parades process down Avenida Garzón, where there are seats for viewing, and the Paseo de Martí, to the east and north of the centre respectively; to buy a ticket, visit the temporary wooden booths near the seating stands earlier in the evening.

Balcón de Velázquez

Corona esq. San Basilio • Daily 9am–9pm • Free

West of Parque Céspedes, the **Balcón de Velázquez** fortification was built between 1539 and 1550 as a lookout point for incoming ships, and was originally equipped with a semicircle of cannons facing out over the bay. It was renovated in 1953, sadly without its most intriguing feature, a tunnel entered from beneath the circular platform in the centre of the patio and running for less than 1km down to the seafront. This was presumably used by the early townsfolk for making a swift exit when under siege. The modern covered entrance is lined with a history of Santiago (in Spanish) and honorary plaques to influential dignitaries, but the highlight here is the **view** over the ramshackle, red-tiled rooftops down towards the bay and the ring of mountains beyond.

El Tivolí

Occupying the hills about four blocks south of the Balcón de Velázquez is the **El Tivolí** neighbourhood, named by the French plantation owners who settled here at the end of the eighteenth century. With no real boundaries – it lies loosely between Avenida Trocha to the south and Calle Padre Pico in the north – there's not much to distinguish it from the rest of the old quarter, save for its intensely hilly narrow streets heading down towards the bay. The immigrant French made this the most fashionable area of town, and for a while its bars and music venues were *the* place for well-to-do Santiagueros to be seen. While the *Casa de las Tradiciones* (see page 390) is still a great, intimate venue, the area has definitely lost its former glory, though it is worth visiting the **Museo de la Lucha Clandestina** and climbing the **Padre Pico Escalinata**, a towering staircase of over fifty steps, built to accommodate the almost sheer hill that rises from the lower end of Calle Padre Pico.

Museo de la Lucha Clandestina

General Rabí 1 e/ Sta Rita y San Carlos • Tues–Sun 9am–4.45pm • Charge • English and Spanish guides available • ☎ 22 624689

Just west of Padre Pico, perched on the Loma del Intendente, the **Museo de la Lucha Clandestina** is a tribute to the pre-revolutionary resistance. Spread over two floors, it comprises a photographic and journalistic history of the final years of the Batista regime and is a must for anyone struggling to understand the intricacies of the events leading up to the Revolution.

The immaculate building is a reproduction of an eighteenth-century house built on the site as the residence of the quartermaster general under Spanish rule. In the 1950s it served as the Santiago police headquarters until it burnt to the ground during an assault orchestrated by schoolteacher-cum-underground-leader **Frank País** on November 30, 1956. The three-pronged attack also took in the customs house and the harbour headquarters, in an attempt to divert the authorities' attention from the arrival of Fidel Castro and other dissidents at Las Coloradas beach on the southwestern coast. The attack is well documented here, with part of the museum focusing on the lives of Frank País and his brother and co-collaborator Josue, both subsequently murdered by Batista's henchmen in 1957.

The best exhibits are those that give an idea of the turbulent climate of fear, unrest and excitement that existed in the 1950s in the lead-up to the Revolution. Most memorable is a clutch of **Molotov cocktails** made from old-fashioned Pepsi Cola bottles, a hysterical newspaper cutting announcing Fidel Castro's death and another published by the rebels themselves refuting the claim.

Plaza de Marte

At the eastern end of pedestrianized Enramadas is the lively **Plaza de Marte**, the least touristy of the central squares and a focal point for the local community. Here gaggles of game-playing schoolchildren, loudspeakers transmitting radio broadcasts, occasional live bands and plenty of benches make for an enjoyable place to spend some time; it is particularly animated on weekend evenings. The tall column, a **monument** to local veterans of the Wars of Independence, has a particular significance – the plaza was formerly the execution ground for prisoners held by the Spanish. The Smurf-like cap at its summit is the *gorro frigio*, given to enslaved people in ancient Rome when they were granted their freedom, and a traditional symbol of Cuban independence.

THE BACARDÍ DYNASTY

Don Facundo Bacardí Massó emigrated to Santiago de Cuba from Spanish Catalonia in 1829, and eventually established one of the largest spirits companies in the world. At the time, **rum** was a rasping drink favoured by pirates and enslaved workers. Bacardí, however, was swift to see the drink's potential and set to work refining it. He discovered that filtering the rum through charcoal removed impurities, while ageing it in oak barrels provided a depth that made it eminently more drinkable.

Buoyed by his successful discovery, Facundo and his brother Jos opened their first distillery on February 4, 1862. Company legend relates that when Don Facundo's wife Dona Amalia glimpsed the colony of fruit bats living in the building's rafters, she suggested they adopt the insignia of a **bat**, symbolizing good luck in Taíno folklore, as the company logo. This proved a shrewd marketing tool as many more illiterate Cubans could recognize the trademark bat than could read the name "Bacardí".

The company went from strength to strength, quickly becoming the major producer of quality rum, while the family's involvement in **Cuban politics** grew in tandem with their business interests, and they became instrumental in the push for independence and subsequent alliance with the US. Emilio Bacardí, Don Facundo's eldest son, was exiled from Cuba for anticolonial activities but later returned as a Mambises liberation fighter in the rebel army during the Second War of Independence. The Bacardís' loyalty to the cause was rewarded in 1899 when American General Leonard Wood appointed Emilio Bacardí mayor of Santiago de Cuba. While Facundito – Facundo senior's younger son – ran the company and supervised research into further refining the rum, Emilio Bacardí concentrated on public life. The **Emilio Bacardí Moreau Municipal Museum** opened the year he became mayor. The old Santiago HQ, with the bat motifs imprinted in the columns, still stands two blocks west of Parque Céspedes at Aguilera 55–59. Testimony to the family bounty stands in the fabulous 1930 Art Deco **Edifico Bacardí** on Havana's San Juan de Dios, which combined a company headquarters with an elegant bar. During World War II, the company was led by Schueg's son-in-law José Pepin Bosch, who also founded Bacardí Imports in New York City. Also a political mover and shaker, he was appointed Cuba's Minister of the Treasury in 1949 during Carlos Prío's government.

The **Revolution**, with its core aim of redistributing the country's wealth to the benefit of the underprivileged, less economically advantaged classes, completely altered the course of the Bacardí family's history. Enraged by the 1960 nationalization of its main distillery in Santiago, and later, of all its Cuban assets, the company shipped out of Cuba, relocating their headquarters to the Bahamas where sugar cane – and cheap labour – were in plentiful supply. Though no longer based in Cuba, the Bacardí family did not relinquish its desire to shape the country's destiny. Author Hernando Calvo Ospina, in his 2002 book *Bacardí, The Hidden War*, claims that Bacardí financed 1960s counter-revolutionary groups (including the attack on the Bay of Pigs), and helped found the ultra-right-wing Cuban American National Foundation (CANF). The Bacardís have denied most of these allegations but have made no secret of the fact that there is no love lost between them and the Cuban government.

Cuartel Moncada

Trinidad esq. Moncada

Several blocks north from Plaza de Marte and just off the Avenida de los Libertadores is the **Cuartel Moncada**. Scene of a bungled attack by Fidel Castro and his band of revolutionaries on July 26, 1953 (see page 382), the fort is a must-see, if only for the place it has in Cuban history. With a commanding view over the mountains, the ochre-and-white building, topped with a row of castellations, is still peppered with bullet holes from the attack. These were plastered over on Fulgencio Batista's orders, only to be hollowed out again rather obsessively by Fidel Castro when he came to power, with photographs used to make sure the positions were as authentic as possible.

Castro closed the barracks altogether in 1960, turning part of the building into a school, while the grounds outside are now used for state speeches and music concerts.

Museo 26 de Julio

Mon & Sun 9am–12.30pm, Tues–Sat 9am–7pm • Charge • ☎ 22 661157

Inside Cuartel Moncada, the **Museo 26 de Julio** boasts flashes of brilliance when it comes to telling the story of the attack, but is otherwise rather dry. Bypassing the pedantic history of the garrison, the museum gets properly under way with its coverage of the 1953 attack. A meticulous **scale model** details the barracks, the now-demolished hospital and the Palacio de Justicia, and gives the events a welcome clarity. The museum pulls no punches on the subject of the **atrocities** visited upon the captured rebels by the Regimental Intelligence Service, Batista's henchmen: a huge collage, blotted with crimson paint, has been created from photographs of the dead rebels lying in their own gore.

Thankfully, the last room has a less oppressive theme. Have a look at the **guns** used in the war, in particular the one in the final display cabinet, carved with the national flag and the inscription "*Vale más morir de pies a vivir de rodillas*" ("It's better to die on your feet than to live on your knees").

Parque Histórico Abel Santamaría

A couple of blocks west of the Cuartel Moncada, on the site of the Civil Hospital which Abel Santamaría captured during the Moncada attack, **Parque Histórico Abel Santamaría** is less of a park and more like a small field of concrete centred on a monument to the young revolutionary. Set above a onetime gushing fountain, a gigantic cube of concrete is carved with the faces of Santamaría and fellow martyr José Martí and the epigram "*Morir por la patria es vivir*" ("To die for your country is to live"). The giant grey monument is rather impressive and worth a look while you're in the area.

Monumento Antonio Maceo

Plaza de la Revolución • Museum Tues–Sat 9am–5pm, Sun 9am–1pm • Charge

Two kilometres north of the centre, on Avenida de las Américas, by the busy junction with Avenida de los Libertadores, is the **Plaza de la Revolución**, an empty space backed by a park in which stands the gargantuan **Monumento Antonio Maceo**. The 16m steel effigy, on a wide plateau at the top of a jade marble staircase, shows Maceo, the "Bronze Titan" – so named because he was of mixed race – on his rearing horse, backed by a forest of gigantic steel machetes representing his rebellion and courage. On the other side of the marble plateau, wide steps lead down behind an eternal flame dedicated to the general, to the entirely missable **Museo Antonio Maceo**, housed in the plateau basement.

Fábrica de Ron Caney: the original Bacardi factory

Ave. Jesús Menéndez esq. Gonzálo de Quesada • Shop daily 9am–6pm • ☎ 22 651212

This historic rum factory on the port road, just a few hundred metres east of the bus station, opened in 1868 as the Bacardí rum factory and now produces the Ron Caney, Ron Santiago and Ron Varadero brands. Bacardi itself, exiled since the Revolution, operates out of Puerto Rico.

Cementerio Santa Ifigenia

Calzada Crombet • Daily 8am–6pm • Charge • ☎ 22 632723

The prestige attached to the **Cementerio Santa Ifigenia**, about 3km northwest of Parque Céspedes, went up a notch in 2016 when Fidel Castro's ashes were laid to rest

THE ATTACK ON CUARTEL MONCADA

Summing up his goals with the words "a small engine is needed to help start the big engine", Fidel Castro decided in 1953 to lead an attack to capture the weapons his guerrilla organization needed and hopefully also spark a national uprising against the Batista regime. Santiago's **Cuartel Moncada** seemed perfect: not only was it the second largest in the country, but it was also based in Oriente, where support for the clandestine movement against the government was already strongest.

A three-pronged assault was planned, with the main body of men, led by Fidel Castro, attacking the barracks themselves, while Raúl Castro would attack the nearby Palace of Justice, overlooking the barracks, with ten men to form a covering crossfire. At the same time, Abel Santamaría, Castro's second-in-command, was to take the civil hospital opposite the Palace of Justice with 22 men; the two women, his sister Haydee Santamaría and his girlfriend Melba Hernández, were to treat the wounded.

The attack was an unqualified fiasco. At 5.30am on July 26, the rebels' motorcade of 26 cars set off for Santiago from the farm they had rented in Siboney. Somewhere between the farm and the city limits, several cars headed off in the wrong direction and never made it to the Cuartel Moncada. The remaining cars reached the barracks, calling on the sentries to make way for the general, a ruse which allowed the attackers to seize the sentries' weapons and force their way into the barracks.

Outside, things were going less well. Castro, who was in the second car, stopped after an unexpected encounter with patrolling soldiers and the subsequent gunfire alerted the troops throughout the barracks. Following their previous orders, once they saw that Castro's car had stopped, the men in the other cars streamed out to attack other buildings in the barracks before Castro had a chance to re-evaluate the situation. The rebels inside the first building found themselves cut off amid the general confusion, and as free-for-all gunfire ensued, the attackers were reduced to fleeing and cowering behind cars. Castro gave the order to withdraw, leaving behind two dead and one wounded.

By contrast, the unprotected Palace of Justice and hospital had been attacked successfully, but both groups were forced to withdraw or hide once their role was rendered useless.

THE AFTERMATH

The real bloodshed was yet to come, however, as within 48 hours of the attack somewhere between 55 and 70 of the original rebels had been captured, tortured and **executed** by Batista's officers after an extensive operation in which thousands were detained. The casualties included Abel Santamaría, whose eyes were gouged out, while his sister, Haydee, was forced to watch. The soldiers then attempted to pass the bodies off as casualties of the attack two days before. Thirty-two rebels survived to be brought to trial, including Fidel Castro himself. Others managed to escape altogether and returned to Havana. Although a disaster in military terms, the attack was a political triumph: the army's **brutality** towards the rebels sent many previously indifferent people into the arms of the clandestine movement and elevated Fidel Castro – previously seen as just a maverick young lawyer – to hero status throughout Cuba.

The rebels were tried in October, and despite efforts to prevent Castro appearing in court – an attempt was apparently made to poison him – he gave an erudite and impassioned speech in his own defence. A reprise of the speech was later published as a manifesto for revolution, known as "History will absolve me" (the last words of the speech). Although the declamation did little to help Castro at the time – he was sentenced to fifteen years' imprisonment – the whole episode set him on the path to leadership of the Revolution.

here. The natural simplicity of his memorial stone, a giant boulder bearing the single word "Fidel", is in marked contrast with **José Martí's mausoleum**, a grandiose affair of heavy white stone encasing a statue of the Cuban independence hero. Located near the cemetery entrance at the end of a private walkway, every half an hour there's an attention-grabbing five-minute changing of the guard ceremony here.

Another high-profile twenty-first-century arrival at the cemetery is **Compay Segundo**, a native Santiaguero, legendary singer and guitarist, member of the Buena Vista Social Club and composer of the ubiquitous *Chan Chan*. Segundo, who died in 2003 at the age of 95, was buried with full military honours in recognition of his achievements during the Revolution, long before he became famous as a musician.

The burial site of **Frank and Josué País** is flanked by the flags of Cuba and the M-26-7 movement. A former schoolteacher and much-loved revolutionary, Frank País led the movement in the Oriente until his assassination, on Batista's orders, at the age of 22. Among other luminaries buried here are Carlos Manuel de Céspedes and Antonio Maceo's widow. Guides are available to show you around in return for a tip.

Reparto Vista Alegre

East of town is the residential suburb of **Reparto Vista Alegre**, established at the beginning of the twentieth century as an exclusive neighbourhood for Santiago's middle classes. Today, its lingering air of wealth is confined to a few **restaurants** dotted around wide and regal Avenida Manduley. Most people visit for the restaurants, although a clutch of interesting museums also makes a trip up here worthwhile. Some of the handsome Neoclassical buildings lining the main road – best seen in springtime under a cloud of pink blossoms – are still private residences, while others are government offices and new government hostels. Although most of the buildings are a bit worn around the edges, they make for pleasant sightseeing, especially the madly ornate peach-coloured palace – one-time Bacardí family residence – that's now the headquarters of the children's youth movement Los Pioneros.

Museo de la Imagen

Calle 8 no.106 e/ 3 y 5 • Mon–Fri 9am–5pm, Sat & Sun 2–5pm • Charge • ☎ 22 642234

The small and quirky **Museo de la Imagen** presents a brief history of photography told through antique Leicas, Polaroids and Kodaks, and some brilliant (and odd) one-off **photographs**, such as the one showing Fidel Castro, in Native American feathered headdress, accepting a peace pipe from the leader of the White Bird people.

Casa de las Religiones Populares

Calle 13 no.206 esq. 10 • Mon–Sat 9am–6pm • Charge • ☎ 22 642387

Anyone interested in Cuba's idiosyncratic home-grown religions should head four blocks east of the Museo de la Imagen to the fascinating **Casa de las Religiones Populares**. The collection spans the different belief systems, including Santería and Voodoo, which developed in different parts of the country, each local variation shaped by the traditions of the homelands of the enslaved people and all influenced by the Catholicism of the Spanish settlers. It's striking to see how Christian iconography has been fused with some of the African culture-based paraphernalia, with the animal bones, dried leaves and rag dolls presented alongside church candles, crucifixes and images of the Virgin and Child.

Loma de San Juan

The **Loma de San Juan**, the hill where Teddy Roosevelt rode his army to victory against the Spanish, is about 250m south from Avenida Manduley, which runs through the centre of Reparto Vista Alegre. The neatly mowed lawns framing a bijou fountain, the dainty flowerbeds and the sweeping vista of mountain peaks

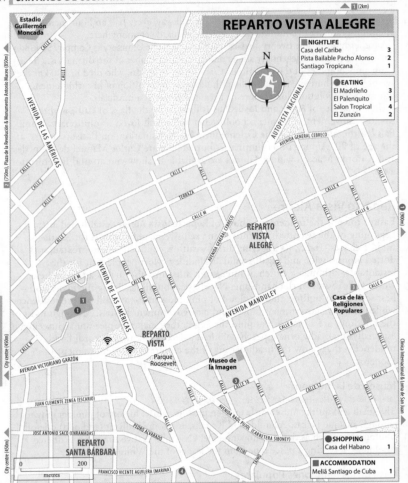

REPARTO VISTA ALEGRE

NIGHTLIFE
Casa del Caribe	3
Pista Bailable Pacho Alonso	2
Santiago Tropicana	1

EATING
El Madrileño	3
El Palenquito	1
Salon Tropical	4
El Zunzún	2

SHOPPING
Casa del Habano	1

ACCOMMODATION
Meliá Santiago de Cuba	1

beyond the city make it all look more suited to a tea party than a battle, but the numerous plaques and monuments erected by the North Americans to honour their soldiers are evidence enough. The sole monument to the Cuban sacrifice is squeezed into a corner; erected in 1934 by Emilio Bacardí to the unknown Mambí soldier, it's a tribute to all liberation soldiers whose deaths went unrecorded. The park would be a peaceful retreat were it not for the persistent attentions of the attendant crowd of hustlers.

Castillo del Morro San Pedro de la Roca

Carretera del Morro Km 7.5 • Daily 9am–5.30pm • Charge • Buses #11 and #12 leave from Plaza de la Revolución • ☎ 22 691569

Just 8km south of the city is one of Santiago's most dramatic and popular sights, the **Castillo del Morro San Pedro de la Roca**, a fortress poised on the high cliffs that flank the entrance to the Bahía de Santiago de Cuba. Designed by the Italian military engineer Juan Bautista Antonelli (whose namesake father was responsible for similar fortifications in Havana) and named after Santiago's then-governor, it was built between 1633 and 1639 to ward off pirates. However, despite an indomitable appearance – including a heavy drawbridge spanning a deep moat, thick stone walls angled sharply to one another and, inside, expansive parade grounds stippled with cannons trained out to sea – it turned out to be nothing of the sort. In 1662 the English pirate Christopher Myngs captured El Morro after discovering, to his surprise, that it had been left unguarded. Ramps and steps cut precise angles through the heart of the fortress, which is spread over three levels, and it's only as you wander deeper into the labyrinth of rooms that you get a sense of how huge it is. Now home to the Museo de la Piratería, El Morro is also notable for its daily cannon-firing ceremony, which takes place at dusk; but the real splendour here is the structure's magnificent scale, the sheer cliff-edge drop and its superb views out to sea.

Museo de Piratería
Daily 9.30am–6.30pm • Entry is included in the El Castillo del Morro ticket

Inside El Castillo del Morro San Pedro de la Roca, the **Museo de Piratería** details the pirate raids on Santiago during the sixteenth century by the infamous Frenchman Jacques de Sores and Welshman Henry Morgan. Detailed explanations in Spanish are complemented by weapons used in the era, now rusted by the passing years.

Cayo Granma
Ferries to the island depart from the jetty in Punta Gorda, half-way between the city and the Castillo del Morro San Pedro de la Roca, about six times a day from 6am to 8pm; journey time is about 15min; ferries also depart from near the cruiser terminal in town but journey times are closer to an hour.

A half-day trip out to El Morro can easily take in the diminutive **Cayo Granma**, 2km offshore, where a peaceful rural village offers an excellent spot for a meal. You can work up an appetite by walking round the tiny island, which is home to two thousand people and takes just twenty minutes to circumnavigate. The village boasts some attractive wooden buildings trimmed with ornamental fretwork, the tiny hilltop church of San Rafael and a couple of **restaurants**.

8

| **ARRIVAL AND DEPARTURE** | **SANTIAGO DE CUBA** |

BY PLANE

AEROPUERTO INTERNACIONAL ANTONIO MACEO
International and domestic flights arrive at the Aeropuerto Internacional Antonio Maceo (☎22 691052), near the southern coast, 10km from Parque Céspedes. There are at least two daily flights to Havana (1hr 30min–2hr).
Airlines Cubana has its main office at Enramadas esq. San Pedro (Mon–Fri 8.30am–4pm; ⌨cubana.cu).
Transport to and from the airport Metered and unmetered taxis wait outside the airport, though there's sometimes a bus that meets flights from Havana. You can arrange car rental at the Transtur desk at the airport (☎22 686161) or Rex (☎22 686444), or at travel agencies in town. Buses #11, #12 and #13 connect the city to the airport (see page 387) but travelling on them with bulky luggage can often be a nightmare.

BY BUS

Víazul buses Tourists are swamped by taxi drivers and touts outside the gates to the Víazul bus terminal (☎22 628484), which has moved from its long-time location near the Monumento Antonio Maceo to Paseo de Martí esq. Ave. Jesús Menéndez, near the port, opposite the train station. See page 28 for advice on booking tickets.
Destinations Baracoa (1 daily; 4hr 50min); Bayamo (5 daily; 2hr 5min); Camagüey (5 daily; 7hr 30min); Ciego de Ávila (5 daily; 8hr 55min); Guantánamo (1 daily; 1hr 25min); Havana (3 daily; 15hr 30min); Holguín (4 daily; 3hr 30min); Las Tunas (5 daily; 4hr 40min); Sancti Spíritus (5 daily; 10hr 30min); Santa Clara (3 daily; 12hr); Trinidad (1 daily; 11hr 45min); Varadero (1 daily; 15hr 25min).
Intermunicipal buses There are two intermunicipal bus stations serving destinations around the province and in neighbouring provinces. The Terminal Serrano is near the port at Ave. Jesús Ménendez esq. Sánchez Hechavarría (☎22 624325); the Terminal de Omnibus Municipales at Ave. de los Libertadores esq. Calle 4 (☎22 624325) offers buses to Playa Siboney among other places.
Conectando Cuba buses This hotel-door-to-hotel-door

service leaves at 6am daily from the Hotel Meliá Santiago de Cuba to Camaguey (5hr), Ciego de Avila (8hr), Holguin (2hr) and Havana (14hr); and three times a week to Baracoa (4hr). Book tickets through the Cubanacán travel agent.

BY TRAIN
Essentials Trains arrive at the modern station (☎ 22 62 2836) near the port, on Paseo de Martí esq. Ave. Jesús Menéndez. From here, taxis, horse-drawn buggies and *bicitaxis* can take you to the centre.

Destinations Camagüey (4 weekly; 6hr 30min); Ciego de Avila (2 weekly; 9hr); Havana (2 weekly; 16hr); Matanzas (2 weekly; 13hr); Santa Clara (4 weekly; 15hr).

GETTING AROUND

On foot Although a large city, Santiago is easy to negotiate on foot, as much of what you'll want to see is located in the historic core, particularly between Parque Céspedes and Plaza de Marte.

By taxi Taxis are the best way to reach outlying sights as the buses are overcrowded and irregular. State-registered metered taxis and *cocotaxis* wait on the cathedral side of Parque Céspedes or around Plaza de Marte. The unmetered taxis parked on San Pedro negotiate a rate for the whole journey. Touts skulk around the main streets but you'll strike a slightly cheaper deal if you negotiate with the drivers themselves. To call a state-registered taxi try Cubataxi (☎ 22 651038 & 39).

By car or scooter There are Cubacar and Havanautos car rental offices at the airport (☎ 22 686161) and at hotels *Las Américas* (☎ 22 687160), Casa Granda (☎ 22 686107) and Meliá Santiago de Cuba (☎ 22 686477). You can rent scooters from Hotel Las Américas.

By boat Local ferries operate between the city, Punta Gorda, Cayo Granma and the hamlet of La Socapa. The timetable is unreliable but there are departures around six times a day. The boat journey most frequently taken by visitors is between Punta Gorda (5km along the bay road from the city) and Cayo Granma from the city's commercial marina, the Marlin Marina Santiago de Cuba (ⓦ cubanautica.travel). Excursions from here include a boat tour of the bay (1hr, subject to minimum of 10 people). To get here take the road to El Morro (the #11 bus) and once at the village ask for the Embarcadero Cayo Granma.

By bus Most local buses are too infrequent and too crowded to bother with, but one or two run routes worth knowing about. An open-top double-decker that looks like a city-tour bus is in fact a local bus serving the community – it runs between the Plaza de Marte and the Parque de Diversiones in the east of the city and gets you to the south of the Reparto Vista Alegre. Buses #11, #12 and #13 connect the city to the airport and points along the bay towards the Castillo del Morro – pick them up at the provincial hospital or along the Ave. de los Libertadores.

INFORMATION

Tourist information and maps Infotur at Félix Peña no.562 esq. Aguilera (daily 8am–8pm; ⓦ cuba.travel), just off Parque Céspedes, provides maps and visitor information. There are Infotur offices at the Víazul bus station and airport too.

Cultural information Infotur usually has a weekly cultural calendar, while the Casa de la Cultura posts one at the Librería Renacimiento (Centro Información Cultural), Enramadas 350 e/ Carnicería y San Félix (Mon–Fri 9am–5pm; ☎ 22 655708); look out also for its copy of elusive cultural mag, *Espectro*.

Listings information Santiago's weekly newspaper, the *Sierra Maestra* (ⓦ sierramaestra.cu), available from street vendors and occasionally from the bigger hotels, has a brief listings section detailing cinema, theatre and other cultural activities.

ACCOMMODATION   SEE MAPS PAGES 372 AND 384

Accommodation in Santiago is plentiful and varied; however, it's worth booking in advance, particularly during carnival and the Fiesta del Caribe in July when the city becomes booked up. A relatively recent investment in the city centre's **hotels** has seen new openings and successful renovations, particularly along Enramadas, making it harder to find reasons to stay outside the centre unless a pool or total peace and quiet are priorities. **Casas particulares** remain abundant and make much better out-of-centre choices than the hotels for budget travellers, though many are conveniently central and several offer impressive luxury. The usual advice on accommodation **touts** applies (see page 36).

HOTELS

Casa Granda Parque Céspedes, Heredia no.201 e/ San Pedro y San Félix ⓦ iberostar.com. An attraction in itself on account of its beauty, the regal *Casa Granda* is a 1920s hotel overlooking Parque Céspedes. From the elegant, airy lobby to its two atmospheric bars, it has a stately, colonial air – and the rooms are much improved since the hotel was acquired and renovated by Iberostar. $$$

Imperial Enramadas esq. Felix Peña ⓦ iberostar.com. Reopened in late 2016, a hundred years after the hotel was built, to become the historic quarter's most luxurious and upmarket option. Rooms are large and modern though a little bland with their neutral furnishings. Communal areas

TOURS AND TRAVEL AGENTS

Tours and **excursions** around the city and throughout the province are available from any of the state-run travel agents in Santiago. They all charge similar prices for **tour options** that include a leisurely excursion to the Gran Piedra and a Santiago city tour covering the Castillo del Morro San Pedro de la Roca, Cayo Granma and El Cobre. Rates are reduced slightly according to the number of people participating; the rates quoted here are based on the minimum number of people required.

Cubanacán Calle M esq., Ave. de las Américas and in hotels Casa Granda and Meliá Santiago de Cuba, w viajescubanacan.cu.

Cubatur Parque Céspedes, Heredia esq. General Lacret; Ave. Victoriano Garzón e/ 3era y 4ta ☎ 22 687010; and in hotels Meliá Santiago de Cuba and

Las Américas, w cubatur.cu.

Ecotur General Lacret e/ Heredia y Bartolomé Maso w ecoturcuba.tur.cu.

Havanatur Calle 8 no.54 e/ 1era y 3era and in hotel Meliá Santiago de Cuba, w havanatur.cu.

---

include a street-side café and knockout roof terrace with unbeatable views. $\overline{\underline{\math$}}$ $\overline{\underline{\math$}}$ $\overline{\underline{\math$}}$

Libertad Plaza de Marte, Aguilera no.658 e/ Serafín Sánchez y Pérez Carbo w islazulhotels.com. This cosy, budget hotel dating from the 1940s offers a worn elegance and unexciting but decent a/c rooms, though some do not have windows. Its position facing the square means it's a relatively noisy option but there's an enjoyable sense of being in the thick of things; rooms at the back are quieter. $\overline{\underline{\math$}}$

Meliá Santiago de Cuba Ave. de las Américas y Calle M w meliacuba.com. Santiago's biggest, brashest hotel is a modernist, blocky, red, white and blue angular tower with the best pool in town. Other facilities include a beauty parlour, boutiques, a gym, conference rooms and bars and restaurants galore. The rooms are tastefully decorated, some with original paintings by local artists, and fully equipped with all mod cons. $\overline{\underline{\math$}}$ $\overline{\underline{\math$}}$ $\overline{\underline{\math$}}$

San Basilio San Basilio no.403 e/ Calvario y Carnicería w hotelescubanacan.com. This gorgeous little hotel has eight tastefully furnished rooms, arranged around a bright, plant-filled patio, each with cable TV, fridge and a/c. Breakfast is included. $\overline{\underline{\math$}}$ $\overline{\underline{\math$}}$

San Felix Enramadas 310-312 esq. Hartmann w iberostar.com. Formerly the *Gran Hotel*, this delightful boutique hotel is as central as they come and rooms are well equipped, inviting and warmly decorated in pastel colours. The artfully furnished lobby and comfy mezzanine bar create an instant sense of escape from the busy street outside and the roof garden bar, with great views, crowns it all perfectly. $\overline{\underline{\math$}}$ $\overline{\underline{\math$}}$ $\overline{\underline{\math$}}$

CASAS PARTICULARES

★**Casa Colonial Maruchi** San Félix no.357 e/ San Germán y Trinidad ☎ 22 620767, e maruchib@yahoo. es. Three rooms (one with its own terrace) in a magnificent colonial house. Vintage brass beds, exposed brickwork and wooden beams add romance, while a well-tended patio filled with lush plants and a menagerie of birds and other

pets is the perfect spot for the alfresco breakfast, included in the price. $\overline{\underline{\math$}}$

Casa Ilia San Félix no.362 e/ San Germán y Trinidad ☎ 22 654138, e jbdeas74@gmail.com. A pleasant house owned by a welcoming family offering two spacious, high-ceilinged, comfortable rooms with a/c and large bathroom. $\overline{\underline{\math$}}$

Casa de Leonardo y Rosa Clarín no.9 e/ Aguilera y Heredia ☎ 22 623574, e elseoclarin@nauta.cu. Four large rooms, three of which boast two comfy double beds while the fourth boasts one massive double bed, with a/c in all. Each leads onto a mini-apartment with two beds, a bathroom, a leafy patio in a wonderful eighteenth-century house featuring period ironwork, wooden walls, high ceilings and stained-glass windows. $\overline{\underline{\math$}}$

Casa Miriam Heredia no.412 e/ Reloj y Clarín ☎ 22 622328, e casamiriams@gmail.com. Three double-bed rooms each with a/c, minibar and en-suite bathroom. Cool, breezy corridor full of tastefully done hanging plants adjoins the rooms. The multi-level terrace network above offers great views over the city. $\overline{\underline{\math$}}$

Casa de Nolvis Rivaflecha Martínez San Basilio no.122 e/ Padre Pico y Teniente Rey ☎ 22 622972, e ebemezer33@nauta.cu. Three clean, a/c rooms (with independent entrance) each with two beds and its own bathroom, in a sociable house with a lively communal area. Close to the Padre Pico steps, in a quiet area of town with off-road parking, it's a good option for those with a car. $\overline{\underline{\math$}}$

Casa de Noris y Pedro Pío Rosado no.413 e/ San Gerónimo y San Francisco ☎ 22 656716, e jonicogno@ gmail.com. This lovely colonial house set back from the road has two quiet a/c rooms each with its own bathroom and fridge, plus a patio and roof terrace to share. The friendly owners cook great meals and speak a little Italian. $\overline{\underline{\math$}}$

★**Hostal Casa Jardín** San Germán no.165 e/ Rastro y Gallo ☎ 22 653720, e mariaelsa7@nauta.cu. Nicely furnished, comfortable a/c rooms in an exceptionally friendly household, also known as *Casa Jardín*. An

8

enchanting lantern-lit garden out back and a roof terrace decorated in potted plants with swings are a real bonus. $\overline{\underline{5}}$ **Roy's Terrace Inn** Santa Rita no.177 e/ Mariano Corona y General Feria ☎ 22 620522, ✉ roysterraceinn@gmail. com. A top-of-the-range inn a few blocks south of the cathedral with a lovely, plant-filled dining terrace and four spacious en-suite rooms. Roy and his partner Diego have decked each room out with all the mod cons: everything from hairdryers to umbrellas. $\overline{\underline{5}}$

EATING
SEE MAPS PAGES 372 AND 384

You won't be stuck for places to eat in Santiago, with plenty of **restaurants** and **cafés** around the centre serving meals at affordable prices. For really cheap eats head for the food stalls along Enramadas, particularly near the Plaza de Marte end. On Saturday and Sunday nights, Avenida Victoriano de Garzón is also worth checking out, with food stalls offering – among other things – whole roasted pig, with bands livening up the atmosphere.

STATE RESTAURANTS

La Fabada de Marieta Enramadas no.123 esq. Padre Pico ☎ 22 669358. Great value restaurant for straight-down-the-line Cuban creole cooking. They serve the most affordable lobster in town, plus plenty of rich stews (*ajiacos* and *potajes*). A raftered wooden ceiling, large shuttered doors, wooden slatted tables, ceiling fans, clay plates and tankards create the colonial-era tavern setting. $\overline{\underline{55}}$

★ **El Morro** Castillo El Morro ☎ 22 691576. Perched next to the fortress in a lovely, breezy spot overlooking the bay, this relatively pricey restaurant boasts a generous array of choices and serves good-quality cuisine including soups, fish, seafood, chicken and pork dishes. $\overline{\underline{55}}$

La Taberna de Dolores Aguilera no.468 esq. Reloj ☎ 22 623913. A lively restaurant serving reasonable *comida criolla*, popular with older Cuban men who while away the afternoon with a bottle of rum on the sunny patio. Musicians play in the evenings. Book to reserve a seat on the balcony overlooking the patio or street. $\overline{\underline{55}}$

El Zunzún Ave. Manduley no.159 esq. Calle 7 ☎ 22 641528. One of the classiest restaurants in town, with a series of private dining rooms perfect for an intimate dinner. Choose from an imaginative menu including pork in citrus sauce or seafood stir-fried in garlic butter and flaming rum.

There's an international wine list, too. $\overline{\underline{55}}$

PALADARS

Casa Mícaela Corona no.564 e/ Aguilera y Enramadas ☎ 22 624927. A small and friendly paladar just east of Parque Céspedes, offering up hearty *comida criolla*, barbecued platters and shellfish. An excellent bar is attached. $\overline{\underline{55}}$

★ **El Madrileño** Calle 8 no.105 e/ 3 y 5 ☎ 22 644138. This is one of the best paladars on the Santiago dining block. The pretty plant-filled patio provides a pleasant setting, and the menu includes lobster and tasty shellfish dishes such as large flamed shrimps in a whisky sauce. Try its signature Turquino Madrileño, an indulgent chocolate cake with ice cream. $\overline{\underline{555}}$

El Palenquito Ave. del Río no.28 e/ 6 y Carretera del Caney, Reparto Pastorita ☎ 22 645220. Smart tables in a garden filled with hummingbirds and hibiscus are one of the highlights of this out-of-town paladar, but the well-prepared *comida criolla*, shellfish and pasta merit the trek out here too. $\overline{\underline{555}}$

Roy's Roof Garden Santa Rita no.177 e/ Mariano Corona y General Feria ☎ 22 620522. Set back from the hustle and bustle of the city centre, this roof garden, cloaked in exotic vegetation, offers hearty suppers for meat-eaters and veggies alike. Succulent chicken fricassee and *yuca con mojo* (yuca in tomato salsa) are standouts, as are the selection of cakes and flans for pudding. $\overline{\underline{55}}$

Salon Tropical Fernando Markane no.310 (altos) e/ 9 y 10 Reparto Santa Barbara ☎ 22 641161. A long-standing paladar with a pleasant terrace for pre-dinner drinks. Chicken and prawn shish kebabs and grilled fish served with *yuca tamales* are good choices here. Round the meal

8

ICE-CREAM VENUES

Cubans love their *helado* and in Santiago there are two veritable shrines to the stuff. The choice of flavours may not be so impressive, but the temples of worship themselves demonstrate a hard-to-beat dedication to ice cream.

La Arboleda Ave. de los Libertadores esq. Garzón ☎ 22 661435; see map page 372. The local branch of the Coppelia chain offers freshly made ice cream at unbeatable prices in an outdoor café that looks like a mini-golf course. Very popular with locals, so arrive early before the best flavours of the day sell out; expect a long queue. $\overline{\underline{5}}$

Jardín de Las Enramadas Enramadas e/ Peralejo y 10 de Octubre ☎ 22 652205; see map page 372. Surrounded by gorgeous gardens occupying almost an entire block, if the bargain sundaes don't tempt you in the resplendent, leafy, tropical shade surely will. The headliner is the monster seven-scoop Gran Piedra, with the coconut flavour being the highlight. $\overline{\underline{5}}$

LIVE MUSIC AND DANCE IN SANTIAGO

The range of **musical entertainment** in Santiago is the best in the country, with an unparalleled line up of musicians and venues representing the traditional styles, especially trova and son. You don't have to exert too much effort to enjoy the best of the town's music scene; the centre is dotted with concert halls, especially around the three main squares, and music often spills onto the streets at weekends and around carnival time, when bands set up just about everywhere. This is all available for a fraction of the cost you are likely to pay back home for live music of this calibre.

Santiago has some fantastic **dance** and **folkloric groups**, too, offering mesmerizing performances. Ballet Folklórico Cutumba is an outstandingly brilliant *folklórico* group that practises and performs at the former Cine Galaxia, Trocha esq. Santa Úrsula (Tues–Fri 9am–1pm; ☎ 22 655173). Accompanied by some passionate percussive rhythms, Haitian folkloric group Tumba Francesa practise at Carnicería 268 on Tues and Thurs at 9pm.

off with crème caramel and coffee. As this is really on the outskirts of town, you'll want to arrange a taxi there and back. Reservations are advised. $\overline{\overline{\$\$}}$

San Francisco San Francisco no.441 e/ Calvario y Pio Rosado ☎ 22 628673. The best budget restaurant for a proper evening meal out. Despite the low prices, the *criolla* food is more delicately prepared than in similarly priced venues and the portions more manageable. The rooftop terrace with its trellised arch and mounted lamps is very

agreeable. $\overline{\overline{\$\$}}$

Thoms & Yadira General Lacret no.705 e/ Heredia y Bartolomé Masó ☎ 55551207. A great spot, just off Parque Céspedes, with a narrow first-floor balcony crammed with tables overlooking the street, subtly lit at night, and inside, the beautifully tiled floor of the original colonial building. The well-prepared mains focus on seafood, including fish, shrimp, octopus and langosta *enchilado* dishes. There is a wide pasta selection too. $\overline{\overline{\$\$}}$

DRINKING

SEE MAP PAGE 372

Going out for a drink in Santiago, especially at night, almost inevitably means live music too, though there are one or two noteworthy places that are for drinking only and the cafés tend less towards live music than the bars. For more drinking recommendations see the Nightlife and Entertainment section.

La Gran Sofia Plaza de Marte, Plácido e/ Enramadas y Bayamo. Outside of the hotels this café is one of the most relaxing and inviting spots for a daytime coffee or beer, up on the roof terrace looking over the square and across to the mountains. The coffee is good quality, and there is an indoor area on the ground floor full of comfy seating.

★ **Hotel Casa Granda** Heredia no.201 e/ San Pedro y San Félix ☎ 22 65 3021. The hotel's *Las Terrazas* balcony bar is both a tourist magnet and one of the best located, most congenial drinking spots in the centre, on an elegant balustraded terrace overlooking Parque Céspedes. The open-air rooftop bar has equal appeal, less atmospheric but with outstanding views over the city, bay and the surrounding countryside and is the best place from which to

watch the sun slide down behind the mountains.

La Isabelica Calvario esq. Aguilera ☎ 22 669546. Atmospheric little coffeeshop with wooden fittings and whirling ceiling fans offering a variety of coffees; the most popular come with a shot of rum.

Parque del Ajedrez Enramadas esq. Felix Peña ☎ 22 626328. A geometric concrete design and marble-topped tables with chess boards designed into them scattered around a right-angled, raised terrace give this outdoor café and bar a memorable quirkiness. A couple of cocktails, rum and a few soft drinks make up the entire drinks list but it's cheap and attracts a local clientele thanks to the wi-fi on site.

★ **Taberna del Ron** Heredia no.201 e/ San Pedro y San Félix ☎ 58327914. Below what used to be the Rum Museum is this fantastic little, low-lit dungeon bar. Sit on the barre-shaped stools, order the potent house speciality Mojito Santiaguero (made with 7-year-aged rum) and work your way through the mass of scribbled plaudits on the walls for the charismatic bartender, Eduardo.

NIGHTLIFE AND ENTERTAINMENT

SEE MAPS PAGES 372 AND 384

There are plenty of quality **live music** and **cabaret** venues in Santiago to keep your feet tapping. Music played in **clubs** and **discos** tends to be anything from Cuban and imported salsa, through reggaeton and rock to very cheesy house. They tend to draw a young, sometimes edgy and

high-spirited crowd, including many of the *jinetero* and *jinetera* types who hang out in Parque Céspedes trying to win your attention. Baseball games are played at the Estadio Guillermon Moncada (☎ 22 642655) on Avenida las Américas.

8

LIVE MUSIC VENUES AND CABARET

★ **Casa del Caribe** Calle 13 no.154 esq. 8, Reparto Vista Alegre ☎ 22 64 3609. This African-Cuban cultural and study centre hosts free traditional music performances and a Sunday rumba *peña*. Performances are either here on the patio, or at the patio of the nearby *Casa de las Religiones* (see page 383) just up the road. An informal atmosphere and enthusiastic performances make this worthy of the trip to the town outskirts.

★ **Casa de las Tradiciones** Rabí no.154 e/ Princesa y San Fernando ☎ 22 65 3892. A different trova band plays into the small hours every night in this tiny, atmospheric house where the walls have photographs and album sleeves.

★ **Casa de la Trova** Heredia no.208 e/ San Pedro y San Félix ☎ 22 65 2689. A visit to this famous venue is unmissable on a trip to Santiago, with musicians playing day and night in one or more of its three performance spaces. Audiences pack into the tiny downstairs room or hang in through the window while upstairs is more expansive but just as atmospheric. Very touristy but still the top choice in town.

La Claqueta Felix Peña e/ Heredia y Bartolome Masó ☎ 22 652243. More a get-up-and-dance than a sit-down-and-watch venue, with an open-air dance floor and stage for its nightly performing son and salsa bands. The higher energy levels attract a younger-than-average local crowd but over-40s won't feel out of place here.

Coro Madrigalista Carnicería no.555 e/ Aguilera y Heredia ☎ 22 65 9439. This homely venue, which feels much like a village hall, is home to Santiago's oldest choir, whose repertoire includes classical, sacred and traditional Cuban music. You're welcome to pop in and listen to the free daily practice session, while the *peña* features an assortment of local son and trova bands.

Irís Jazz Club Paraíso s/n e/ Enramadas y Aguilera, Plaza de Marte ☎ 22 62 7312. Santiago's best destination for live jazz is a plush and intimate space that hosts local and national acts.

Los Dos Abuelos Pérez Carbó no.5, Plaza de Marte ☎ 22 623302. A variety of local groups play son and guaracha on this bar's pretty patio, shaded by fruit trees, at around 10pm every night which attracts a busy crowd of locals and tourists. There's an extensive range of rums and snacks available.

Patio Artex Heredia no.304 e/ Calvario y Carnicería ☎ 22 65 4814. Bypass the inside bar (which unfortunately smells of fried chicken) and head to the outside patio for live bolero, rumba, son and lively salsa. There's music at 11am, 1pm, 5–7pm and 8pm–1am. It's a good place to warm up before heading on to *Casa de la Trova*, further down the same road.

Sala de Conciertos Dolores Plaza Dolores ☎ 22 62 4623. Take a break from the salsa and son drums and refresh your soul with a choral or classical concert in an elegant former church on the corner of Plaza Dolores. The Coro Madrigalista sometimes perform here. Check the door for the programme.

★ **Santiago Tropicana** Autopista Nacional Km 1.5 ☎ 22 64 2579. Not quite the *Tropicana* of the east, but a fun night out if you're with friends watching the costumed dancers perform a show. You can make reservations at Cubatur or other tour agencies.

UNEAC Heredia no.266 esq. Pio Rosado (Carnecería) ☎ 22 653465. Traditional and contemporary music *peñas* are held on the pretty and intimate patio here three or four nights a week attracting a varied crowd. Check the door for the weekly programme.

CLUBS

Club 300 Aguilera no.300 e/ San Pedro y San Félix ☎ 22 65 3532. A relaxing café by day, and buzzy bar by night, this slick and sultry little hideaway with leather seats serves cheap cocktails, quality rum and single malt whiskies. Entry is free.

Pista Bailable Pacho Alonso Teatro Heredia, Ave. de las Américas s/n ☎ 22 64 3190. Pumped-up salsa, merengue, disco and reggaeton tunes get the crowd dancing at this unpretentious local club.

THEATRES AND CINEMAS

Cine Cuba Enramadas no.304 esq. San Pedro ☎ 22 62 2225. Santiago's most important cinema with daily showings at 3pm, 5pm and 8pm.

Teatro Heredia Plaza de la Revolución ☎ 22 64 3190. The city's only large venue for plays, musicals and children's drama.

FIESTA DEL CARIBE

Taking place annually between July 3–9, the **Fiesta del Caribe**, or Fiesta del Fuego, brings academics, foreign participants and dance, music and cultural groups from across the Caribbean and Latin America to celebrate the culture and music of a designated Caribbean country or region each year. Organized by the city's Casa del Caribe, it's a highlight of Santiago's cultural calendar, with a finale celebrated via a city-wide conga and the burning of an effigy of the devil.

SHOPPING

SEE MAPS PAGE 372 AND 384

Although Santiago is no shoppers' paradise, there are still several places to sniff out an authentic bargain or curiosity, while the town's art galleries occasionally have some worthy paintings and sculptures.

ARTS AND CRAFTS

Artesanías Art Decó A misleadingly named market as there are no Art Deco items here, but there are tonnes of arts and craft stalls filling this old warehouse and more Che Guevara ashtrays than you can wave a cigar at. A great place for a cheesy souvenir.

Callejón del Carmen This thriving, densely packed, touristy street market occupies three blocks, parallel with Enramadas, between Felix Peña and General Banderas. It's full of bone and shell jewellery, figurines, maracas, drums and all the usual trinkets.

Galería Oriente San Pedro no.163 ✆ 22 65 7501. Some excellent revolutionary and carnival screen-printed posters and a few colourful surrealist oil paintings by local artists.

Proyecto Espiral Enramadas e/ Padre Pico y 10 de Octubre. There's a welcome degree of quality control at this outdoor market under a canvass dome. Particularly strong on wooden items, especially figurines, jewellery and ornamentation, leather bags, tote bags and traditional lace clothing.

CIGARS AND RUM

La Barrita Ave. Jesús Menéndez esq. Gonzálo de Quesada ✆ 22 625576. Rum aficionados will adore this shop/bar at the side of the Fábrica de Ron Caney (see page 381) with its huge selection, and its tables and chairs where you can indulge in your purchases straight away. It also sells cigars.

Casa del Habano Hotel Meliá Santiago de Cuba ✆ 22 687070. The best selection of cigars in the city is at this swanky hotel's *casa del habano*, opened for the city's 500th anniversary. There's a smoker's lounge attached and the range is superb, with Cohiba, Partagás, Montecristo, Romeo y Julieta, H. Upmann, Bolívar and others.

BOOKS AND MUSIC

Librería La Escalera Heredia no.265 e/ San Félix y Carnicería. An extraordinary little den filled with all manner of secondhand books and vinyl, as well as the eccentric owner's display of business cards and liquor bottles from around the world.

DIRECTORY

Banks and exchange There are branches of the Banco de Crédito y Comercio with 24hr ATMs on Parque Céspedes at Aguilera esq. San Pedro (Mon–Fri 8am–3pm, Sat 8–11am) and at Enramadas esq. Calvario (Mon–Fri 8am–3pm, Sat 8–11am). There are CADECA *casas de cambio* at Aguilera 508 e/ Reloj y Rabí (Mon–Sat 8.30am–8pm & Sun 9am–6pm) and the Centro de Negocios Alameda at Ave. Jesús Menéndez e/ Enramadas y Cornelio Robén (Mon–Fri 8.30am–4pm & Sat 8.30–11.30am).

Health Call ✆ 185 for a public ambulance or, for a private ambulance, the Clínica Internacional (✆ 22 71 4256) at Avenida Raúl Pujol esq. Calle 10, which also offers general medical services to foreigners. The most central state hospital is the Hospital Provincial Clínico Quirúgico Docente, at Avenida de los Libertadores (✆ 22 62 6571 to 9). Policlínico Camilio Torres is a 24hr doctors' surgery at Heredia no.358 e/ Reloj y Calvario. There are pharmacies at Enramadas no.402, *Hotel Santiago* and the Clínica Internacional. The latter also has a dental surgery.

Immigration You can renew visas at the immigration office, at Avenida Pujol e/ 10 y A, Reparto Vista Alegre (Mon & Fri 8am–noon & 2–4pm; ✆ 22 64 2557).

Police The main station is at Corona y San Gerónimo. In an emergency call ✆ 106. The tourist support group Asistur offers 24hr assistance in emergency situations (✆ 78 67 1315).

Post office The main post office is at Aguilera y Clarín. Stamps can also be bought from *Hotel Casa Granda* and *Hotel Santiago de Cuba*. The most central agent for DHL is at Aguilera no.310, esq. San Félix (Mon–Fri 8am–noon & 1–4pm, Sat 8am–11am).

Wi-Fi There are over a dozen public wi-fi hot spots around the city, including at Parque Céspedes, Plaza de Marte and Parque de la Alameda down by the port. To buy wi-fi cards and for PCs that you can use them on go to the ETECSA centres at Heredia esq. Félix Pena on Parque Céspedes (daily 8.30am–7pm), the Callejón del Carmen esq. Hartmann (daily 8.30am–7pm) and the Centro de Negocios Alameda at Ave. Jesús Menéndez e/ Enramadas y Cornelio Robén (Mon–Fri 8.30–noon & 1–4pm).

East of Santiago

Many of the attractions surrounding Santiago are east of the city, and you'll need at least a couple of days to do them justice. Cool and fresh, the mountains of the **Sierra de la Gran Piedra** make an excellent break from the harsh Santiago heat, and the giant **Gran Piedra** is an extraordinary lookout point. Nearby, there's the atmospheric

Museo Isabelica, set on one of several colonial coffee plantations in the mountains; on another former plantation is the lovely **Jardín Ave del Paraíso**, a small but exquisite botanical garden. Spanning the east coast is the **Gran Parque Natural Baconao**, not so much a park as a vast (and still hurricane-raddled) collection of beaches and other tourist attractions, among them a vintage **car collection** and the **Comunidad Artística Verraco** – home, gallery and workplace for several local artists.

GETTING AROUND	EAST OF SANTIAGO
By car If you've got your own transport, head east out of the city towards the Loma de San Juan, then take the road south	down Avenida Raúl Pujol, from where it runs straight towards the coast and the turn-off for the Sierra de la Gran Piedra.

Parque Nacional de la Gran Piedra

There's no public transport on the mountain road, but an unmetered taxi from Parque Céspedes in Santiago will charge around $500CUP to take you to the foot of the Gran Piedra staircase

Just east of Santiago, the mountains of the **Parque Nacional de la Gran Piedra** are some of the most easily accessible peaks in the country. Eleven kilometres along the coastal road from town, a turn-off inland leads you up a steep, curving mountain road. As the route ascends, temperate vegetation such as fir and pine trees gradually replace the more tropical palms and vines of the lower levels.

Jardín Ave de Paraíso

Daily 8am–4pm • Charge

Approximately 13km along the Gran Piedra road are the manicured flowerbeds and shrubberies of the **Jardín Ave del Paraíso**. The lofty grounds are spread over the ruins of one of the sierra's many colonial coffee plantations, divided up by flagstone pathways and affording scenic views of the surrounding terrain. Densely packed and bursting with life, you can see heavy-scented white gardenias, assorted orchids, the flame-coloured rainfire bush and countless others. The prize of the collection is the spectacular blue-and-orange Bird of Paradise flower, from which the garden takes its name.

La Gran Piedra

Daily 8am–4pm • Charge • ☎ 22 686147

Around 15km along the road into the Parque Nacional de la Gran Piedra, a purpose-built staircase leads up from the visitors' centre to **La Gran Piedra**, or "The Big Rock", sculpted by ancient geological movement from surrounding bedrock and now forming a convenient viewing plateau 1234m above Santiago de Cuba, with views out to the sea on clear days. It's an easy though still invigorating climb to the top, through woodland rich in animal and plant life, including over two hundred species of fern, and is best made before noon, when you've a better chance of clear views.

Museo Isabelica

Daily 8.30am–4pm • Charge

Around 1km or so along the mountain road from La Gran Piedra, a left turn leads to the **Museo Isabelica**, set in the grounds of the Cafetal Isabelica, a coffee plantation established by an immigrant French grower who fled the Haitian slave revolution of 1791. Housed in a restored, small, two-storey estate house covered in red lichen and surrounded by ferns, the museum's collection contains original furniture. The main reason to come here, though, is the atmosphere, with the mountains' mist-shrouded hush broken only by birdsong and the tapping of sheep crossing the stone area used to dry coffee beans. You can explore the overgrown paths leading off round the house into the derelict plantation and inspect what is left of the disused mill – now just a stone wheel and a few wooden poles.

Gran Parque Natural Baconao

Most visitors to the park come by private taxi or on an organized excursion with one of Santiago's travel agents

A mountainous stretch of attractive countryside interspersed with an eclectic set of tourist attractions, the **Gran Parque Natural Baconao**, 25km southeast of Santiago, makes for a good day out but is hardly the rugged wilderness suggested by its name. Its appeal lies in its relative proximity to the city, the gentle beauty of the landscape and the variety of its attractions.

Granjita Siboney

Carretera Siboney s/n Km 13.5 • Daily 9am–5pm • Charge • ☎ 22 39 9168

Some 2km along the park road past the La Gran Piedra turn-off is the **Granjita Siboney**, the farm that Fidel Castro and his rebel group used as their base for the Moncada attack. The pretty little red-and-white house, pockmarked by bullet holes (perhaps from target practice, as no fighting actually took place here), now holds a **museum** that largely reproduces information found in bigger collections in the city, with newspaper cuttings, guns and bloodstained uniforms presented in glass cabinets.

Playa Siboney

Just beyond the Granjita Siboney is **Playa Siboney**, 19km from Santiago and the closest beach to the city. Overlooked by a towering cliff, this brown-sand, partially pebbly beach is hardly the stuff of archetypal Caribbean picture-postcards but there's a likeable unkemptness and untouristy quality to it. A scattering of *casas particulares* and restaurants complete the picture.

8

ACCOMMODATION AND EATING	PLAYA SIBONEY
Casa de Ovidio González Sabaldo Calle Banco no.1 e/ Ave. Serrano y Montenegro, Alto de Farmacia ☎ 22 39 9340. A *casa particular* with a sea view right in the village centre offering four rooms, just two minutes from the beach. Rooms are comfortable with private bathrooms and a/c. $	**La Rueda** Just behind Playa Siboney ☎ 22 39 9325. State restaurant offering inexpensive fried chicken, tasty fish and good lobster. There's a pleasant top-terrace on which to eat, while the bar below is less appealing. Order ahead if you want to eat after 6pm. $$

Finca El Porvenir

Carretera Baconao Km 4 • Daily 9am–5pm • ☎ 22 629064

A few kilometres east of Playa Siboney a signposted turn left (north) down a potholed track leads to this rustic countryside spot, which makes a pleasant stop for lunch. A stone staircase descends the hillside to the reasonably priced bar-restaurant, where tables are shaded by mango and palm trees, and sun loungers surround a swimming pool. There's horse riding available here too (prices negotiable).

Valle de la Prehistoria

Carretera Baconao Km 6.5 • Daily 8am–6pm • Charge • ☎ 22 39 9239

Five kilometres east from Playa Siboney along the coastal road you'll come across one of the area's quirkiest attractions, the **Valle de la Prehistoria**, populated by practically life-sized stone models of dinosaurs and Stone Age men. While essentially a bit kitsch, it's worth a look for those with kids.

Museo Nacional del Transporte

Carretera Baconao Km 8.5 • Daily 8am–4pm • Charge • ☎ 22 39 9197

About 4km east of the Valle de Prehistoria, the **Museo Nacional del Transporte** is one of Baconao's biggest attractions, with an excellent collection of vintage cars and a formidable display of 2500 toy cars. Outside in the car park sits a 1929 Ford Roadster belonging to Alina Ruz, Fidel Castro's mother; Benny Moré's ostentatious golden

Cadillac; and the 1951 Chevrolet that Raúl Castro drove to the attack on the Moncada barracks (see page 382).

Playa Daiquirí

Close to the Museo Nacional del Transporte is the turning for **Playa Daiquirí**, the beach where the US army landed when they intervened in the War of Independence in 1898 and which gave its name to the famous cocktail. Home to a holiday camp for military personnel, the beach is closed to foreign visitors.

Comunidad Artística Verraco

Playa Verraco

Ten kilometres east from the Museo Nacional del Transporte on the main coast road, in an attractive clearing beneath tall trees next to the local Playa Verraco, the unique **Comunidad Artística Verraco** is a highlight of a trip out to Baconao. A small artists' community that's home to nine sculptors, painters and potters, you can tour the individual home-studios, and there's a small communal gallery where their work is on sale.

Acuario Baconao

Carretera Baconao Km 27.5 • Tues–Sun 9.30am–4pm • Dolphin shows 10.30am & 3pm • Charge • ☎ 22 35 6264

Some 8km east of the Comunidad Artística Verraco on the coast road, the **Acuario Baconao** suffered terribly from the ravages of Hurricane Sandy; damage to its hydraulic system led to the death of most of the marine collection, which included seven sharks. The aquarium has not yet fully recovered, though the dolphins, fish and tortoises have been replenished. You may want to read up on the welfare of marine mammals kept in captivity in Cuba before you go, though (see page 54).

Playa Cazonal

Playa Cazonal, just under 1km east of Acuario Baconao, is the most appealing beach east of Santiago, though it's no secluded paradise despite being a long way from the city. Backed by a huge, congenial all-inclusive hotel, the small stretches of off-white sand compete with vast blankets of tiny shells and broken coral dotted by randomly spaced palms. Most people come for the snorkelling and diving on the nearby coral reef. To pre-arrange diving excursions, contact the Carisol Corales Diving Center (✉ mercado@marlin.scu.tur.cu).

ACCOMMODATION

PLAYA CAZONAL

Club Amigo Carisol-Los Corales Carretera Baconao Km 54 ⊕ hotelescubanacan.com. All-inclusive hotel spread across a large swathe of beach in two separate buildings. The most pleasant section of beach fronts the Los Corales building, which also houses the complex's only junior suites. Staff are pleasant and friendly and the dining area of the *Carisol*, in particular, is very attractive. Day-passes available for non-guests. $$$

Laguna Baconao

Tues–Sun 9am–4.30pm • Charge for boat hire and to access the Sendero el Cimarron trail • ☎ 22 35 6198

Roughly 3km from Playa Cazonal, **Laguna Baconao** is a serene spot from which to enjoy the unaffected beauty of the surrounding mountains. There are sad caged crocs and flamingos but you can take in a more natural scene by hiring a **boat** to row on the lake and a guide to walk the area's **trails**, such as the Sendero el Cimarron. Bizarrely, there are three dolphins living in the semi-saltwater lake and the lagoon's managers are waiting to see if they'll reproduce in this environment. Laguna Baconao marks the end of the line for easy independent travel; a checkpoint here prevents cars travelling into Guantánamo province due to the US naval base.

West of Santiago

Although there are few sights to see west of Santiago, those that exist are interesting enough to warrant a visit if you have a spare day. The **Basilica de la Caridad del Cobre**, presiding over the town of El Cobre in the hills to the northwest, is one of the most important – and most visited – churches in the country. The **beaches** west of the city are mostly smaller than those on the eastern side, and correspondingly less developed and more intimate, the playgrounds of Cubans rather than foreign visitors. In contrast, the resort of **Chivirico** is dedicated to international tourism, with two large hotels dominating its fine-sand beach.

There is no reliable public transport west of the city, so you'll need to hire a taxi or take your own transport.

Basilica de la Caridad del Cobre

El Cobre daily 6.30am–6pm; Mass Mon 10am, Tues–Fri 8am & 10.15am, Sat 8am, Sun 8am & 10am • ☎ 22 34 6118

A lovely structure nestling in palm-studded forest 18km northwest of Santiago, the imposing cream-coloured, copper-domed **Basilica de la Caridad del Cobre** houses the icon of **Nuestra Señora de la Caridad**, Cuba's patron saint, and is one of the holiest sanctuaries in the country. Pleasingly symmetrical, with three towers capped in red domes, the present basilica was constructed in 1927, on the site of a previous shrine. Inside, the icon has pride of place high up in the altar, and during Mass looks down over the congregation; at other times she is rotated to face into an inner sanctum reached by stairs at the back of the church, where another altar is always garlanded with floral tributes left by worshippers.

Soon after her discovery, local mythology endowed the Virgin with the power to grant wishes and heal the sick, and a steady flow of believers visits the church to solicit her help. A downstairs chamber holds an eclectic display of the many **relics** left by grateful recipients of the Virgin's benevolence, including a rosette and team shirt from Olympic 800m gold medallist Ana Fidelia Quirot Moret, as well as college diplomas, countless photographs and, poignantly, an asthmatic's ventilator.

The western beaches

The drive along the coast west towards Chivirico and beyond, with the seemingly endless curve of vivid mountains on one side and a ribbon of sparkling shallow sea on the other,

---

NUESTRA SEÑORA DE LA CARIDAD

Nuestra Señora de la Caridad, also known as La Virgen de la Caridad del Cobre (the Virgin of Charity), and just "Cachita", is so much more than just Cuba's patron saint: source of succour, icon and artists' muse, her presence is embedded in the cultural, religious and social life of Cubans of all colour and creed.

Legend relates that in 1612, a statue of the Virgin was found floating in the Bahía de Nipe, off Cuba's northern coast, by three sailors (or salt workers depending on which storyline you adhere to) from El Cobre town on the verge of being shipwrecked. They claimed not only that the icon – a mother and child figurine – was completely dry when drawn from the water but also that the sea was instantly becalmed. Inscribed with the words *Yo soy la Virgen de la Caridad* ("I am the Virgin of Charity"), the icon became the most important image in Cuban Roman Catholicism, gaining significance by becoming the alter ego of **Ochún**, the Santería goddess of love, whose colour, yellow, mirrors the Virgin's golden robe. In 1916 the Virgen de la Caridad became the patron saint of Cuba, following a decree by Pope Benedict XV. Her saint's day is September 8, when an annual pilgrimage is held.

is one of the most fantastic in the country, though potholes and hurricane damage make it somewhat treacherous after dark. About 15km from the city, don't be put off by **Playa Mar Verde**, a small, rather grubby hoop of roadside shingle-sand with a café and restaurant; instead, carry on along the coastal road for another couple of kilometres to **Playa Bueycabón**. Here, an orderly lawn dotted with short palms stretches almost to the sea, and with its calm, shallow waters and narrow belt of sand it is altogether an excellent little spot to pass the day. There is a café here, but no other facilities.

Chivirico

Nearly 70km from Santiago, **CHIVIRICO** is a quiet coastal village and an interchange point for buses and trucks running between Pilón and Santiago. Other than that, the main action, such as it is, centres on a micro-resort of hotels capitalizing on good brown-sand beaches and impressive mountain views. This is a better place to stay rather than visit on a day-trip, as the most appealing beach is now the domain of an all-inclusive resort which charges non-guests for the privilege of using it.

Access to **Playa Sevilla** (daily 9am–5pm), the easternmost beach of the three, is controlled by the beachfront *Brisas Sierra Mar* hotel. Location of the *Motel Guáma*, the central **Playa Virginia** is narrower but free to enter. Tiny mangrove-coated cays lie not far offshore, though there can be dangerous undertow currents. Finally, **Playa Chivirico** is the private preserve of the attractive hilltop *Hotel Los Galeones*, the secondary outpost of *Brisas Sierra del Mar*.

8

ARRIVAL AND DEPARTURE   CHIVIRICO

By taxi A private taxi from Santiago to Chivirico will cost around $1800CUP, less if you negotiate.

ACCOMMODATION

Brisas Sierra Mar Carretera a Chivirico Km 60, Playa Sevilla ⓦ hotelescubanacan.com. A large, attractive all-inclusive hotel offering spacious, comfortable rooms and a full complement of watersports, including diving, plus five bars and several restaurants. $̄$̄$̄

Bayamo

On the northern edge of the Sierra Maestra mountains in the centre of Granma, provincial capital **BAYAMO** is one of the most peaceful towns in Cuba. Its spotless centre is based around a pleasant park; there are near-zero levels of hassle on the streets; and, with the streets pedestrianized, even the cars are silenced.

A fire destroyed most of Bayamo's colonial buildings in 1869, and though the splendid **Iglesia San Salvador de Bayamo** still presides over the cobbled **Plaza del Himno**, only remnants of it pre-date the fire. Elsewhere, neat rows of modern houses, dotted with pretty tree-lined parks, stand testament to a well-maintained town. Bayamo is smaller than you'd expect a provincial capital to be, and you could cram its few sights into one day; but if you've no agenda, it's better to do some gentle sightseeing, eat well and match the town's unhurried pace.

Brief history

The second of the original seven Cuban towns or *villas* founded by Diego Velázquez de Cuéllar in November 1513, Bayamo flourished during the seventeenth and eighteenth centuries when, along with its neighbour Manzanillo, it was heavily involved in dealing in contraband goods. Bayamo became one of the most prosperous towns in the country and by the nineteenth century had capitalized on the fertile plains to the west of the city, becoming an important sugar-growing and cattle-rearing area.

Influential figures like wealthy landowner Francisco Vicente Aguilera and composer Pedro Figueredo established a revolutionary cell here in 1868 to promote their call for independence from the Spanish. They were joined by **Carlos Manuel de Céspedes**, another wealthy local plantation owner, who freed his enslaved people and set off to war. By the end of October 1868, Céspedes' modest army of 147 had swelled to 12,000 and he had captured Bayamo and Holguín. Rather than relinquish the town, after three months of fighting, the rebels set fire to it on January 12, 1869, and watched the elegant buildings burn to the ground. Bayamo's glory days were over.

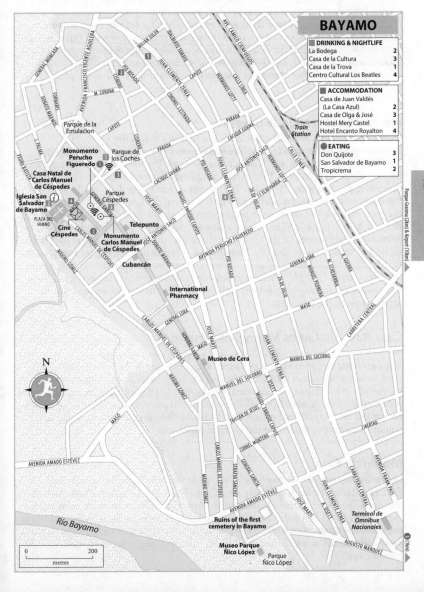

BAYAMO

DRINKING & NIGHTLIFE 2
La Bodega
Casa de la Cultura 3
Casa de la Trova 1
Centro Cultural Los Beatles 4

ACCOMMODATION
Casa de Juan Valdés
  (La Casa Azul) 2
Casa de Olga & José 3
Hostel Mery Castel 1
Hotel Encanto Royalton 4

EATING
Don Quijote 3
San Salvador de Bayamo 1
Tropicrema 2

Bayamo moved into the twentieth century without fanfare, continuing to support itself by producing sugar and farming cattle. The town's last memorable moment was the unsuccessful attack on the army barracks on July 26, 1953 (see page 382), timed to coincide with Castro's attack in Santiago – though this happened over half a century ago, it still keeps several old-timers gossiping today.

Parque Céspedes

Most of the sights in Bayamo are within view or easy walking distance of the central **Parque Céspedes** – also known as Plaza de la Revolución – a shiny expanse of marble fringed with palm trees, where children play and queue for rides in the goat-pulled pony cart. At the northern end is a small three-panel tribute to **Perucho Figueredo**, a local independence fighter principally remembered for writing the patriotic poem *La Bayamesa* in 1868, which later became the Cuban national anthem, still sung today. The monument to **Carlos Manuel de Céspedes**, at the southern end of the plaza, is rather more grandiose.

Iglesia San Salvador de Bayamo

Plaza del Himno • Mon–Fri 9am–noon & 2.30–4.30pm, Sat 9am–noon, Sun (Mass) 9–10.30am • Free

The showpiece of Bayamo architecture is the repeatedly reconstructed **Iglesia de San Salvador de Bayamo**, which dominates the small Plaza del Himno. Though the original church was built in 1516 it was completely destroyed and rebuilt three times over the following 250 years. The current construction dates partly from the eighteenth century, and although this was one of the few buildings to survive the great fire of 1869, it has since been restored multiple times, most significantly in 1919, when much of what you see today was fashioned. Inside, apple-shaped portraits of the Stations of the Cross line the walls. The impressive **mural** over the main altar depicts an incident on November 8, 1868, when Diego José Baptista, the parish priest, blessed the rebel army's newly created flag before a mixed congregation of Cuban rebels. This piece is unique in Latin America as an ecclesiastical painting with political content – the imagery indicates that the new republic received the approbation of the Church.

Casa Natal de Carlos Manuel de Céspedes

North side of Parque Céspedes • Tues–Fri 9am–5pm, Sat 9am–2pm & 8–10pm, Sun 10am–1.30pm • Charge

The **Casa Natal de Carlos Manuel de Céspedes** is a survivor of the fire of 1869, and contains a hotchpotch of exhibits relating to the nineteenth century in general and to the life of Carlos Manuel de Céspedes, born here in 1819. Céspedes' ceremonial sword is displayed on the ground floor, while upstairs is the *pièce de résistance*: a magnificent bronze bed with ornate oval panels, inlaid with mother-of-pearl and depicting a fantastic coastline at the foot of the bedhead panel.

Museo de Cera

Calixto García no.259 e/ Masó y Manuel del Socorro • Tues–Fri 9am–5pm, Sat 10am–1pm & 7–10pm, Sun 9am–noon • Charge

General García, the main shopping street, is a pleasant place to stroll and catch the flavour of the town; its muted pedestrianized marble walkway makes a good foil for the fun sculptures of giant tubes of paint and the sinuous benches. Halfway down is the **Museo de Cera**, a waxworks gallery, featuring models which include indigenous birds and animals as well as personalities like Compay Segundo and Ernest Hemingway.

Museo Parque Ñico López

Tues–Fri 9am–noon & 1–5pm, Sat noon–8pm, Sun 8am–noon • Charge

Bayamo's spacious walled garden, **Museo Parque Ñico López**, landscaped with swaying palms and intersected with layers of marble steps, was arranged in the grounds of the Bayamo barracks as a tribute to Ñico López, one of the 28 men who tried to storm and capture the building on July 26, 1953.

The attack was synchronized with the assault on the Moncada barracks in Santiago (see page 382), partly to secure weapons for the rebel cause but primarily to prevent more of General Batista's troops being drafted in from Bayamo to Santiago. The attempt failed when the whinnying of the cavalry horses, alarmed at the sound of the rebels scrambling over the wall, aroused the sleeping soldiers, and though López escaped, later meeting up with fellow rebels in exile in Mexico, several other men died in the attack. López returned to Cuba aboard the yacht *Granma* in 1956, only to be killed a few days later in an early skirmish. The garden honours both his contribution to the cause, and, probably more crucially, his status as the man who introduced Che Guevara to Fidel Castro in 1955. López himself is commemorated by a **sculpture** in the grounds.

Inside the barracks is a rather poor **museum** giving a scant account of events accompanied by photographs of the men involved and a cutting from the following day's newspaper. You'd be better off giving it a miss and instead striking up a conversation with the old men who sometimes sit in the park, several of whom remember the attack.

ARRIVAL AND GETTING AROUND   BAYAMO   8

By plane Domestic flights arrive from Havana (2 weekly; 2hr) at the Aeropuerto Carlos M. de Céspedes (☎23 42 7514), 10km northeast of the centre on the Holguín road, where unmetered taxis wait to bring you into town.
Airlines Cubana, Martí no.52 esq. Parada (Mon, Wed & Thurs 8am–4pm; ☎23 42 7514).
By bus and colectivo Bayamo is well served by three

main roads from Las Tunas, Holguín and Santiago de Cuba; interprovincial buses pull in at the Terminal de Omnibus Nacionales (☎23 42 7482) in the eastern outskirts of town, on the Carretera Central towards Santiago de Cuba. From here, *bicitaxis* will take you into the centre. *Colectivos* also use the terminal as their unofficial base.

Destinations Camagüey (5 daily; 4hr 10min); Ciego de

CARLOS MANUEL DE CÉSPEDES

A key figure in the fight for independence, **Carlos Manuel de Céspedes** is much lauded in Cuba as a liberator. A wealthy plantation owner, he freed his enslaved people on October 10, 1868, and called for the abolition of slavery – albeit in terms least likely to alienate the wealthy landowners upon whose support he depended. Giving forth his battle cry, the *Grito de Yara*, which summoned Cubans, whether enslaved or Creole, to take arms and fight for a future free of Spain, he marched in support of the independence movement. Céspedes summed up the dissatisfaction that many Cubans felt in a long declaration which became known as the **October 10th manifesto**, nationally credited as the inception of Cuban independence because it was the first time that Cubans had been talked about in terms of a nation of people.

The newly formed army set out with the intention of capturing the nearby town of Yara, but were overtaken by a column of the Spanish army and utterly trounced, reduced to a fragment of the original 150-strong force. Undefeated, Céspedes proclaimed, "There are still twelve of us left, we are enough to achieve the independence of Cuba."

Céspedes is most remembered for the death of his son, Óscar, captured by the Spanish and subsequently shot when Céspedes refused to negotiate for peace under Spanish conditions. This act earned him the title "Padre de la Patria" (Father of the Homeland): as he famously replied to the letter requesting his surrender, "Óscar is not my only son. I am father to all the Cubans who have died to liberate their homeland."

Ávila (5 daily; 5hr 10min); Havana (3 daily; 13hr); Holguín (4 daily; 1hr 15min); Las Tunas (5 daily; 2hr 35min); Sancti Spíritus (5 daily; 7hr); Santa Clara (3 daily; 9hr 30 min); Santiago de Cuba (5 daily; 2hr 20min); Trinidad (1 daily; 9hr 30min); Varadero (13hr 10min).

By train The train station is about 1km east of the centre on Línea esq. José Antonio Saco (☏ 23 42 3056).

Destinations Camagüey (2 weekly; 5hr 30min); Havana (2 weekly; 13hr); Manzanillo (2 daily; 3hr); Matanzas (2 weekly; 14hr); Santa Clara (2 weekly; 11hr); Santiago de Cuba (1 daily; 4hr 15min).

By taxi Cubataxi is at Martí no.480 esq. Armando Estévez (☏ 23 42 4313).

By car Cubacar is based at *Hotel Sierra Maestra* (☏ 23 48 2990).

INFORMATION AND TOURS

Tourist information Infotur on Plaza del Himno esq. José Joaquín Palma (Mon–Fri 8.30am–5pm; ⊕ cuba.travel) is the best bet for general information and maps.

Tours and travel agents Anley Rosales Benitez at Bayamo Travel, opposite the Víazul bus station at Carretera Central no.478 (⊕ bayamotravelagent.com, prices listed in euros), organizes drivers and accommodation in and around the Sierra Maestra and beyond, and offers tours, including trips to La Comandancia (€95 per person for two people), two-day hikes up Pico Turquino (€165 per person for two people), and a five-hour tour around Granma that takes in the Desembarco del Granma National Park, Manzanillo city

and the La Demajagua and Celia Sanchez memorials (€80 per person for two people). Ecotur (see page 387) in the *Hotel Sierra Maestra*, on the Carretera Central to the south of the town (☏ 23 48 7006), also provide details on excursions into the Sierra Maestra.

Festivals From Jan 6, Bayamo celebrates its Semana de Cultura which culminates on Jan 12 with a commemoration and a re-enactment of the day the locals set fire to the town in 1869. The Fiesta de la Cubanía takes place between October 13–20 with fiestas, music, dancing and other cultural events.

ACCOMMODATION SEE MAP PAGE 397

HOTEL
Hotel Encanto Royalton Maceo 53 e/ J Palma y D Mármol ⊕ islazulhotels.com. This lemon-yellow hotel in a mid-twentieth-century edifice is right on the main square. It offers several dozen smart and simple rooms, arrayed around a central courtyard and fitted out with TVs, fridges, a/c and a minibar. The choice rooms are the four at the front, with balconies overlooking Parque Céspedes. Rates include breakfast. $̄$̄$̄

CASA PARTICULARES
Casa de Juan Valdés (La Casa Azul) Pio Rosado no.64 e/ Ramírez y N López ☏ 23 42 3324, ⊕ melanienogueras04@gmail.com. One well-appointed a/c room with fancy bedspread, pink marble floor and a

large bathroom. There's a large living room, small kitchen area and roof terrace for guests to use, too. $̄

Casa de Olga & José Parada no.16 (altos) e/ Martí y Mármol ☏ 23 42 3859, ⊕ olgacr@nauta.cu. Olga and José run a first-class B&B with two comfortable rooms off the living room of the main house. They have a great balcony from where to people-watch or drink the night away. Olga is very helpful with excursions. Wi-fi from the park below reaches the balcony. $̄

Hostel Mery Castel Zenea no.56A e/ William Soler y Capote ☏ 23 42 4051, ⊕ mery2906@nauta.cu. There's room for seven guests here across three rooms, the best of which is at the top of the house, with its own terrace. Great food and wi-fi too. $̄

EATING SEE MAP PAGE 397

Surprisingly, for such a small town, Bayamo boasts several good **paladars**. Around the park end of General García are several stalls selling **snacks** – some of them, like the corn pretzel-style cracker, are unique to Bayamo.

Don Quijote Ave. Antonio Maceo no.116 e/ Segunda y Mendive ☏ 23 48 2781. A pleasant new paladar serving up a huge spread of *comida criolla*, and seafood and shellfish. Try the house cocktail – it's a lurid blue colour but it goes down a treat. To get there, take the turning opposite the *Hotel Sierra Maestra* and then the third turning on the left; the house is immediately on the left. $̄$̄

San Salvador de Bayamo Maceo no.107 e/ Martí y

Mármol ☏ 23 42 6942. This colonial-style paladar with dusty pink Moorish arches serves up a good honest spread of shellfish, kebabs, pork chops in rum, a tasty fish fillet in sweet and sour sauce, and lamb chops with raisins and ginger. Pizzas and lasagne also feature on the extensive menu. The coconut ice cream served in a coconut is a treat. $̄$̄

★ **Tropicrema** Figueredo e/ Libertad y Céspedes ☏ 23 42 2606. Pleasant, open-air ice-cream parlour, sometimes serving up cake as well. Tables are shared with the next person in the queue and everyone waits for everyone else to finish before leaving the table. Oddly, if they run out of ice cream, they'll occasionally substitute Spam rolls. $\overline{\underline{\underline{5}}}$

DRINKING AND NIGHTLIFE
SEE MAP PAGE 397

★ **La Bodega** Plaza del Himno ☏ 23 42 1011. An eternally popular spot behind the church, where there's beer and dancing until 2am in an intimate courtyard with a striking view over the Río Bayamo. During the day, it's often taken over by tour groups tucking into pre-booked meals.

Casa de la Cultura General García ☏ 23 42 5917. Stroll in during the day to view art exhibitions or occasional evening theatre and dance performances later on (check the board outside for weekly listings).

Casa de la Trova Maceo no.111 ☏ 23 42 5673. This is an excellent live-music venue in a bijou colonial house. The daily programme of traditional Cuban sounds is posted inside.

Centro Cultural Los Beatles Zenea e/ Figuero y Saco ☏ 23 42 1799. Named for the life-size statues of the Fab Four outside; live music is followed by a disco at weekends.

DIRECTORY

Banks and exchange The Banco de Crédito y Comercio at General García 101 esq. Saco (Mon–Fri 8am–3pm, Sat 8am–11am) and the CADECA at Saco no.105 e/ General García y Mármol (Mon–Sat 8.30am–4pm) change travellers' cheques and give cash advances on Visa and MasterCard. ATMs are located outside the bank.

Cinema Cine Céspedes, on Parque Céspedes just next to the post office, shows a mix of Cuban and international films.

Health Call ☏ 104 for a public ambulance. Bayamo's general hospital is Carlos Manuel de Céspedes, at Carretera Central (Vía Santiago) y 3ra, ☏ 23 42 5012. The most central 24hr *policlínico* doctors' surgery is on Pío Rosado, and there's

a 24hr pharmacy, Piloto, at General García no.53 e/ Maceo y Saco as well as an International Pharmacy at General García s/n e/ Figueredo y Lora (daily 8am–noon & 1–5pm; ☏ 23 42 9596).

Police In an emergency call ☏ 116.

Post office The post office on Parque Céspedes (daily 8am–8pm) has a DHL service.

Wi-fi There are wi-fi hotspots at Parque Céspedes and Parque de los Coches. You can buy wi-fi cards and use computers at the ETECSA Telepunto at General García no.109 (daily 8.30am–7pm).

8

The Sierra Maestra

Cuba's highest and most extensive mountain range, the **Sierra Maestra** stretches along the southern coast of the island, running the length of both Santiago and Granma provinces. The unruly beauty of the landscape – a vision of churning seas, undulating green-gold mountains and remote sugar cane fields – will take your breath away.

Access to the mountains is strictly controlled (see box opposite), but there are some excellent trails, most notably through the stunning cloudforest of the **Parque Nacional Turquino** to the island's highest point, Pico Turquino, at 1974m. Although a considerable part of the Sierra Maestra falls in Santiago province, Parque Nacional Turquino included, the best chance you have to do any **trekking** is to base yourself in Bayamo, where you can arrange a guide and suitable transport (see box, see page 402).

The main trails begin at the lookout point of **Alto del Naranjo**, 5km southeast of *Villa Santo Domingo*, which marks the start of the mountains proper. When the mountains are off limits this is as far as many people get, but at 950m above sea level, the panoramic views are awe-inspiring. Most people, especially those planning to trek further into the mountains, make the journey up the immensely steep ascent road to Alto del Naranjo in a sturdy jeep provided by Cubataxi or Ecotur.

Pico Turquino trail

At 1974m above sea level, **Pico Turquino** stands proud as the highest point in Cuba. From Alto de Naranjo it's approximately 12km to the summit, and while it's possible to ascend and return in a day, you are better off arranging with your guide to stay overnight at the very rudimentary *Campamento de Joaquín* mountain hut and stretching the trek over a day and a half. This is not a trek for the faint-hearted: the final kilometre is a very steep slog, though not dangerous. Take something warm to wear, as temperatures plummet after nightfall and even the days are cool in the high cloudforest.

The Pico Turquino is overhung with plants and ancient tree ferns, the forest air exuding an earthy dampness and the ground oozing with thick red mud. Through the breaks in the dense foliage you can occasionally see blue-green mountain peaks and birds circling lazily above the gullies. Just before the final ascent, a short ladder to the left of the path gives a panoramic view over the surrounding landscape; it's worth grabbing the opportunity at this stage in your trek, as the summit itself is often shrouded in thick clouds.

Comandancia de La Plata trail

A less taxing alternative to the Pico Turquino trail is the trek to the **Comandancia de La Plata**, 3km west of Alto de Naranjo, where Fidel Castro based his rebel headquarters during the Revolution. The trail is well marked and you can complete

---

EXPLORING THE SIERRA MAESTRA

Visitors are not permitted to go trekking in the **Sierra Maestra** without a guide – if you head into the mountains on your own, you risk landing yourself in serious trouble with the authorities. Having a guide will not always guarantee entrance, however, as the routes are sometimes **closed** for various reasons – from bad weather to reports of epidemics in the coffee plantations.

INFORMATION, ACCESS AND ORGANIZED TOURS

The only places to get reliable **information** on access to the Sierra Maestra, including the areas in Santiago province, are the Ecotur offices, in *Hotel Sierra Maestra* in Bayamo (Mon–Fri 8am–5pm & Sat 8am–noon; ☎ 23 48 7006), and the **Parque Nacional Turquino Centro de Visitantes** (daily 7.30am–4pm; ☎ 23 56 5568), run by Flora y Fauna and located at the foothills of the mountains next door to *Villa Santo Domingo*. Ecotur also runs an office at the *Villa Santo Domingo*. However, if you book a hike through Bayamo-based agent Bayamo Travel (see page 400), you will save yourself the bother of having to get the latest on hiking conditions and you can leave the arranging of permits and travel to them too. They can arrange excursions from Santiago de Cuba, Holguin and Bayamo itself.

Permits from Flora y Fauna to reach Comandancia de La Plata include guide, entrance fee and water. The jeep to Alto de Naranjo, from where the Comandancia de La Plata walk begins, is paid separately if you book a Flora y Fauna tour. Flora y Fauna charges around $1500CUP to scale Pico Turquino in one night including transport, food, accommodation, guide and park's entrance, with the return to Santo Domingo. A two-night Turquino trek crossing the mountain finishing at Las Cuevas on the Carretera del Sur also costs in the region of $1500CUP including food, accommodation, guide and park's entrance.

Ecotur also runs excursions into the mountains, including one-night trips to Pico Turquino and packages that include nights in the *Villa Santo Domingo*.

HIKING PRACTICALITIES

You must **arrive between 7.30 and 10.30am** on the day that you want to visit or else you may be turned back (guides arrive early to be allocated to their visitors for the day but leave swiftly if there is no one waiting). The last daily departure to the Comandancia is at 1pm (11am in the wet season). The last departure for Pico Turquino is at 9.30am year-round.

Note that the obligatory jeep transport from the Centro de Visitantes to Alto de Naranjo is cheaper booked through Flora y Fauna if you have not bought an Ecotur hiking package. Trekkers must bring their own sleeping bag for the overnight trips and sugary snacks for this trip. Everything else is provided.

the reasonably strenuous climb in around four hours return. The headquarters are spread over two or three sites, the first of which is the very basic **hospital** (it's little more than a wooden hut) that Che Guevara founded and ran. The second site comprises the guard post, a small but worthy **museum** and the grave of a rebel who fell in battle.

Most evocative are the wooden huts where the rebels lived and ate, which were covered with branches to protect them from enemy air strikes. **Castro**'s small quarters consist of a rudimentary bedroom with a simple camp bed, a kitchen, a fridge, a study and a secret trap door to escape through if he was under attack. Those wanting to take pictures of the rebel camp will need to pay extra at the Casa Medina rest stop, halfway along the walk.

Buey Arriba and the Comandancia de Che

Excursions to Buey Arriba and the Mando de Puesto de Che are available from Bayamo Travel

Fifty-four kilometres southwest of Bayamo in the Sierra Maestra is the small town of **BUEY ARRIBA**, where the **Comandancia de Che** is the starting point for a 45-minute walk uphill to the hamlet of **La Otilia**, the last rebel command post (Mando de Puesto de Che) of Che Guevara before he was dispatched to Villa Clara during Fidel Castro's 1956–59 rebel campaign. There are panoramic views of the Sierra Maestra all the way up, while the small command post is now the **Casa Museo La Otilia** (daily 9am–4.30; charge), with displays of artefacts from Che's short stay.

In Buey Arriba itself, the **Museo Municipal** (Tues–Fri 9am–5pm, Sat 9am–1.30pm & 8–10pm, Sun 9am–2pm; charge; ☎23 42 4125) exhibits a white stuffed mule used by Camilo Cienfuegos.

ACCOMMODATION	SIERRA MAESTRA

Campismo La Sierrita Beside the Río Yara, 50km southeast of Bayamo and 14km before Santo Domingo ☎23 56 5584, ✉sierrita@grm.campismopopular.cu. This rural and idyllic spot has 15 cabins available to non-Cubans, with self-contained bathrooms. If you cannot make direct contact in advance, call in at the Agéncia de Reservaciónes de Campismo in Bayamo (General García no.112 e/ Saco y Figueredo; Mon–Fri 8–11am & 3–7pm & Sat 9–12pm; ☎23 42 2425) to make sure the campsite is open and book. You can also book through the Agéncia de Reservaciónes de Campismo in Havana (☎7 832 1116). $̄

Casa Sierra Maestra Carretera La Plata Km 16, on the opposite side of the river to the Villa Santo Domingo, Santo Domingo ☎05 26 10846, ✉casasierramaestra@gmail.com. This is a welcoming house with basic facilities; to get there, cross the river on the large stones downhill behind the Flora y Fauna office. There are two rooms inside

the house with shared bathrooms (there's no hot water) and four more rooms in two-storey cabins. Owners Ulises Junco and his wife Esperanza offer delicious food. Trekking excursions and horseriding) can also be arranged. $̄

El Mirador de Arcadia en la Montaña Next door to Ecotur, Santo Domingo. Three bedrooms with a/c, hot water, and fridge in each. You can book mountain excursions at Ecotur next door (see page 387). Reservations made through Bayamo Travel (see page 400). They offer breakfast and dinner. $̄

Villa Santo Domingo About 68km southwest of Bayamo ☎23 56 5635. The best place to stay in the mountain area, in the foothills of the mountains (but not in a restricted area). Set on the banks of the Río Yara, the picturesque cabins (which now include twenty alpine-style *villas*, for which rates include breakfast) make an ideal spot to relax even if access to the mountains is denied. Cabins $̄, villas $̄$̄

Manzanillo

Though run down and ramshackle, **MANZANILLO**, 64km west from Bayamo and 75km up the coast from Playa Las Coloradas, still possesses some charm. Now a fairly pedestrian coastal fishing village, it was established around its harbour at the end of the eighteenth century and for a time enjoyed a brisk trade in contraband goods. The sugar trade replaced smuggling as the primary business hereabouts in the nineteenth century, but the town's heyday had passed and it never grew much bigger.

Manzanillo's sole attraction these days is its fantastic **Moorish architecture**, dating from the 1910s and 1920s. The sensual buildings, all crescents, curves and brilliant tiles, are best seen in the town's central **Parque Céspedes**. Most eye-catching is the richly decorated gazebo presiding over the park, giving an air of bohemian elegance well suited to the sphinx statues in each corner and the melee of benches, palm trees and faux-nineteenth-century streetlamps. Opposite the park, the pink **Edificio Quirch** is no less splendid, with its crescent arches and tight lattice design.

Museo Histórico La Demajagua

Mon–Sat 8am–5pm, Sun 8am–noon • Charge • No public transport; a taxi from Manzanillo costs around $500CUP return.

Ten kilometres south of town, the **Museo Histórico La Demajagua** is a pleasant place to while away an hour or two. It was from the **grounds** of this former sugar plantation that **Carlos Manuel de Céspedes** set out to win Cuban independence from Spain (see page 399), and with splendid views over the bay and the cane fields, it's a picture of serenity. The small building housing the museum was built in 1968 (the centenary of the uprising), the original plantation having been completely destroyed by shells from a Spanish gunboat on October 17, 1868. The museum itself is depressingly sparse, with a brief history of the plantation forming the main part. The highlight is the first Cuban flag ever made, hand-sewn by Céspedes' mistress. Look out for the Demajagua bell, built into a dry-stone wall on the far side of the lawn, with which Céspedes summoned his enslaved people to freedom.

8

ARRIVAL AND DEPARTURE   MANZANILLO

By plane The Aeropuerto Internacional Sierra Maestra (☎23 57 7401) is 7km from Manzanillo on Carretera a Cayo Espino, and has flights to Havana (1 weekly; 2hr 30min).

By train The station is 1km east of the centre.
Destinations Bayamo (2 daily; 3hr); Havana (2 weekly; 15hr); Santiago de Cuba (1 daily; 6hr).

By colectivo There are no tourist buses from Bayamo and Pilón; if you're coming from Bayamo you'll have to catch one of the *colectivo* taxis.

By taxi A one-way taxi ride from Bayamo will cost around $900CUP.

INFORMATION

Information Infotur is at Maceo no.75 e/ Merchán y José Miguel Gómez (Mon–Fri 8.15am–noon & 1–4.45pm, plus alternate Saturdays; ☎23 57 4412, ⓦcuba.travel). There's also an office in the Aeropuerto Internacional Sierra Maestra (☎23 57 4434). Both branches offer basic information.

Currency exchange Should you need to change money, head to the CADECA at Martí no.184 (Mon–Sat 8.30am–6pm, Sun 8am–1pm). There are also now ATMs at Merchán e/ Saco y Dr Codina.

ACCOMMODATION

Casa Adrián and Tonia Mártires de Viet Nam no.49 esq. Caridad ☎23 57 3028, ⓔato700714@gmail.com. A good *casa particular* offering four rooms and an independent apartment with a kitchen. 💲

Casa d' Ruben León no.256 e/ San Salvador y Concordia ☎23 57 5160, ⓔcasadruben@nauta.cu. Three decent double bedrooms each with their own bathroom, garage, a/c, a good terrace on which to take breakfast and dinner. 💲

Parque Nacional Desembarco del Granma

Daily 8am–6pm • Charge

South of Niquero on the coastal road, the province's southwestern tip is commandeered by the **Parque Nacional Desembarco del Granma**, which starts at **Campismo Las Coloradas** (open to Cubans only), and stretches some 20km south to the tiny fishing village of **Cabo Cruz**. The forested interior of the park is littered with trails, but its main claim to fame is that it was here, on the park's western coastline just south of Playa Las Coloradas, that the *Granma* yacht deposited Fidel Castro on December 2, 1956 (see page 405).

THE GRANMA

Under constant surveillance and threat from the Batista regime following his release from prison, Fidel Castro left Havana for exile in Mexico in the summer of 1955. Along with other exiled Cubans sympathetic to his ideas, he formed the **26 July Movement** in exile – the Cuban counterpart was run by Frank País – and began to gather weapons and funds to facilitate the return to Cuba.

Castro was anxious to return as soon as possible. Leaks within the organization had already resulted in the confiscation of arms by the Mexican government and there was an ever-present threat of assassination by Batista's contacts in Mexico. By October the following year Castro had gathered enough support and money and declared himself ready to return. He bought a 58ft yacht called **Granma** from a North American couple for $15,000, and hatched a plan to sail it from Tuxpan, on the east coast of Veracruz in Mexico, to Oriente, following the tracks of José Martí – who had made a similar journey sixty years before.

At around 1.30am on November 25, 1956, with 82 men crammed into the eight-berth yacht, the *Granma* set off for Cuba. Because of the stormy weather all shipping was kept in port and the yacht had to slip past the Mexican coastguard to escape. Foul weather, cramped conditions and a malfunctioning engine meant that the journey that was supposed to take five days took eight. The plan had been to come ashore at Niquero, where Celia Sánchez, a key revolutionary, was waiting to ferry them to safety, but on December 2 they ran out of petrol just 35m from the coast, and at 6am the *Granma* capsized just south of Playa Las Coloradas. As Che later commented: "It wasn't a landing, it was a shipwreck."

Exhausted, sick and hungry, the 82 young men waded ashore only to find themselves faced with a kilometre of virtually impenetrable mangroves and sharp saw grass. They eventually made camp at Alegría de Pío, a sugar cane zone near the coast, with the intention of resting for a few hours. It was to be a baptism of fire as Batista's troops, who had been tipped off about their arrival and had been strafing the area for several hours, came across the men and attacked. Completely unprepared, the rebels ran for their lives, scattering in all directions. Thanks to the efforts of Celia Sánchez, who had left messages at the houses of poorer communities sympathetic to the rebels' cause, the rebels were able to regroup two weeks later. It was hardly a glorious beginning, but the opening shots of the Revolution had been fired.

Monumento Portada de la Libertad

Daily 8.30am–6pm • Charge

South of Playa Las Coloradas, which is named after the murky red colour the mangrove jungle gives to the water here, is the exact spot of the landing where Fidel Castro's rebels waded ashore marked by the **Monumento Portada de la Libertad**. Flanked on either side by mangrove forest hedged with jagged saw grass, the kilometre-long path to the monument (which starts a short way from the museum) makes a pleasant walk even for those indifferent to the Revolution, although even the most jaded cynics will find it hard to resist the guides' enthusiasm for the subject, their compelling narrative (in Spanish) bringing to life the rebels' journey through murky undergrowth and razor-sharp thicket.

The tour also takes in a life-size replica of the **yacht**, which guides can sometimes be persuaded to let you clamber aboard; and a rather spartan **museum** with photographs, maps and an emotive quotation from Castro on the eve of the crossing.

El Guafe

Mon–Fri 8.30am–5pm, Sat & Sun 8.30am–2pm

The interior of the Parque Nacional Desembarco is made up of idyllic woodland that skirts the western verge of the Sierra Maestra. From Las Coloradas you can walk to the

---

DRIVING THE SOUTHERN COAST ROAD

The lonely **Southern Coast Road** between Pilón and Santiago de Cuba offers one of the most exhilarating drives in Cuba, with the Sierra Maestra rearing up directly from the roadside, and the ocean swirling from a Caribbean postcard-blue to an indigo black. The road undulates up and down the mountainside and, at one point, due to persistent damage, has fallen into the sea; it is sometimes passable by negotiating the track and the sea. Sometimes passing inches from the ocean, skirting rockfalls and crossing or diverting via broken bridges, this is a hair-raising route, and you should always seek out local advice before setting out to drive it, either in Niquero or Pilón in the west, or in Santiago. The journey from Pilón to Santiago (where the last petrol station is) takes 6–7 hours because of the state of the road.

---

start of **El Guafe**, one of the four trails in the park, celebrated for the intriguing stone petroglyphs found in the vicinity, the remnants of Native American culture. It's an easy and reasonably well-signposted walk – roughly a 3km circuit – which you can do on your own, although the guides have extensive knowledge of both the history of the area and the cornucopia of birds and butterflies, trees and plants you'll see along the way. Look out for the ancient cactus nicknamed "Viejo Testigo" (the Old Witness), thought to be five hundred years old and now so thick and twisted it has formed a robust, tree-like trunk.

The small, human-form **petroglyphs**, sculpted with haunting, hollowed-out eyes, are in a low-roofed cave musty with the smell of bats, probably used as a crypt by the Aboriginal Native Americans, who carved the idols as guardians. Fragments of ceramics and a large clay jar decorated with allegorical characters were also found, supporting the theory. A second cave close to the exit of the trail houses another petroglyph known as the **Idolo del Agua** (the Water Idol), thought to have been carved into the rock to bless and protect the sweet water of the cave – a rarity in the area. Along the walk, look out for the cute little *cartacuba* (Cuban tody). Often found in pairs, this gem-like bird has vivid green upperparts, a crimson throat, fluffy pink sides and a pale grey belly.

Parque Nacional Desembarco del Granma trails

Ecotur in Bayamo (☎ 78 48 7006)

Parque Nacional Desembarco del Granma's **other trails** run along the southern coastline 20–30km east of El Guafe. Highlights include the **Agua Fina cave**, roughly 20km from El Guafe and, some 7km further east, the **Morlotte** and **El Furstete caves** as well as **Las Terrazas**, a natural coastline shelf sculpted by geographic formations to look like man-made terraces.

ACCOMMODATION   **PARQUE DESEMBARCO DEL GRANMA**

Hotel Niquero Martí no.100 e/ Céspedes y 2 de Diciembre, Niquero ⊛ islazulhotels.com. A basic, quiet and serviceable hotel 13km north of the park and the closest accommodation for visitors to the park. Rates include breakfast. $̄

Pilón

Tiny sugar town **PILÓN**, 37 kilometres southeast of Niquero, a second-rate beach resort, and 8km west of Marea del Portillo, is like a remnant of past times, with open-backed carts laden with sugar cane zigzagging across the roads and the smell of boiling molasses enveloping the town in its thick scent. The most useful establishment in town is the local service station on the Marea del Portillo road, which sells petrol, sweets, snacks and cold drinks. It's also a good place to ask whether the Carretera del Sur to Santiago is passable.

Casa Museo Celia Sánchez Manduley

Mon–Sat 9am–5pm • Charge

The small but engaging **Casa Museo Celia Sánchez Manduley**, erstwhile home of revolutionary Celia Sánchez, offers a ragbag of exhibits, including Taíno ceramics, shrapnel from the Wars of Independence and a photographic history of Pilón.

Pilón's beaches

There's little else to see in Pilón and even less to do, but the two beaches, **Playa Media Luna**, with beautiful views over the Sierra Maestra and a rocky coastline good for snorkelling, and the narrow white-sand **Playa Punta**, have an unruliness that's refreshingly different from the smarter resort beaches.

8

Isla de la Juventud and Cayo Largo

SUNRISE ON CAYO LARGO

9 Isla de la Juventud and Cayo Largo

About 100km south of the mainland, the little-visited Isla de la Juventud (Island of Youth) is the largest of over three hundred scattered emerald islets that make up the Archipiélago de los Canarreos, a fantasy paradise of pearl-white sand and translucent, coral-lined shallows. Extending from the island capital of Nueva Gerona in the north to the superb diving region of Punta Francés, 70km to the southwest, the comma-shaped Juventud is bisected by a military checkpoint designed to control access to ecologically vulnerable swampland in the south, which is rich in wildlife; the northern region is mostly farmland, characterized by citrus orchards and mango groves. Although it has an air of timeless somnolence, Isla de la Juventud was actually once a pirate haunt, ruled over for three centuries by French and English buccaneers and adventurers. Development here has been unhurried, and even today there are as many horse-drawn coaches on the roads as there are cars or trucks.

It probably won't be your first choice for a beach holiday, although it's a good place to unwind once you've visited the more flamboyant – and hectic – sights elsewhere in Cuba. With little tourist trade, Juventud's charm is anchored to its unaffected pace of life and pleasant beaches, and the lack of traffic and predominantly flat terrain make **cycling** an excellent way to explore. The single real town, **Nueva Gerona**, founded in 1830, has few of the architectural crowd-pullers that exist in other colonial settlements, and is a refreshingly low-key place, easily explored over a weekend or even just a day. Beyond the town, there are some intriguing pre-Columbian **cave paintings** in the south and, close to the capital, the museum at the abandoned **Presidio Modelo**, a prison whose most famous inmate was Fidel Castro. With a couple more small but worthy museums, some of the country's best offshore **dive sites** and one beautiful white-sand beach, Isla de la Juventud is one of Cuba's best-kept secrets.

A necklace of islets streaming 150km east, the cays of the **Archipiélago de los Canarreos** are mostly too small to sustain a complex tourist structure, though **Cayo Largo**, the archipelago's second-largest landmass after La Isla, is arguably Cuba's most exclusive holiday resort – if only in terms of accessibility. Completely devoid of a genuine local population, the resort was created in 1977 and capitalizes on its flawless, 22km-long ribbon of white sand and features a marina, dive centre and a growing clique of all-inclusive hotels.

Isla de la Juventud

A vision of fruit fields and soft beaches, it is little wonder that **Isla de la Juventud**, or "La Isla" as it's known in Cuba, allegedly captured Robert Louis Stevenson's imagination as the original desert island of *Treasure Island*. Although Christopher Columbus chanced upon the isle in 1494, the Spanish had scant use for it until the nineteenth century and development unfolded at an unhurried pace. Even today the quiet, underpopulated countryside and placid towns stil have the air of a land waiting to awaken from its slumber.

MUSEO PRESIDIO MODELO

Highlights

❶ Sierra de las Casas The short, easy and enjoyable trek up these low hills rewards with some of the best views over the Isla de la Juventud. See page 418

❷ Museo Presidio Modelo Take in its forbidding atmosphere and grim but compelling history on a walk around the huge ruined cell blocks of the "Model Prison". See page 420

❸ Diving at Punta Francés One of the premier diving areas in Cuba, with over fifty dive sites – from shipwrecks and caves to coral walls and tunnels – and some stunning marine life. See page 422

❹ Cuevas de Punta del Este These atmospheric caves, once home to the Siboney people, hold significant examples of early pre-Columbian art, while the nearby beach completes a day-trip. See page 423

❺ Playa El Francés With its silver sands and limpid waters, this is the best beach on Isla de la Juventud, beautifully located on a remote peninsula. See page 425

❻ Boat trips from Cayo Largo Hop on a catamaran or a yacht to the outlying cays around Cayo Largo to see the iguana colonies and snorkel at coral reefs and deserted beaches. See page 427

HIGHLIGHTS ARE MARKED ON THE MAP ON PAGE 412

9

The main focus for the island's population is in the **north**, where you'll find many of the sights and the capital, **Nueva Gerona**. Nestling up against the Sierra de las Casas, this town is satisfyingly self-contained, ambling along perpetually behind developments on the mainland. Spread around it is a wide skirt of low-lying fields, lined with orderly citrus orchards, fruit farms and two of the island's modest tourist attractions. Both are former prison buildings, a testament to Juventud's long-standing isolation. **El Abra** is a delightfully located hacienda that once held captive the nineteenth-century independence suffragist José Martí, while the **Presidio Modelo**, set up in 1926 to contain more than six thousand criminals – most famously Fidel Castro – is a contrastingly ominous-looking place. Deserted, but still a dominating presence on

HIGHLIGHTS

1 Sierra de las Casas

2 Museo Presidio Modelo

3 Diving at Punta Francés

4 Cuevas de Punta del Este

5 Playa El Francés

6 Boat trips from Cayo Largo

ISLA DE LA JUVENTUD & CAYO LARGO

ISLA DE LA JUVENTUD

■ **ACCOMMODATION**
Hotel Colony   **1**

the island's mostly flat landscape, the prison and its museum make for a fascinating excursion. There are also a couple of brown-sand beaches, **Playa Bibijagua** and **Playa Paraíso**, within easy reach of Nueva Gerona.

South of the capital are several sights that can be explored in easy day-trips. To the west of the island's second-biggest town, the rather mundane **La Fe**, a compact nature reserve, **La Jungla de Jones**, is a place for simple pleasures, with short trails and picnic spots. South of La Fe is a **crocodile farm** offering an excellent opportunity to study the creatures at close range. Further south still is the **military checkpoint** at Cayo Piedra, in place to conserve the marshy southern region that forms the **Siguanea Nature Reserve**, access to which is strictly controlled. South of the checkpoint on the southeast coast is one of the island's most intriguing attractions, the pre-Columbian paintings in the **Punta del Este caves**. On the west side of the south coast is the tiny hamlet of **Cocodrilo**, set on a picturesque curve of coastline and an ideal spot for swimming, while close to hand is the picture-perfect white-sand beach of **Playa El Francés**. Just offshore you can enjoy the island's celebrated dive sites, including underwater caves and a wall of black coral, but to do so you'll need to set off from the **Marina Siguanea**, north of the protected area near one of the island's several mediocre hotels, the **Colony**.

Brief history

The Isla de la Juventud's earliest known inhabitants were the **Siboney** people, who are thought to have settled here around a thousand years ago. They lived close to its shores where they could fish and hunt, eschewing the pine-forested interior. Tools and utensils made from conch shell and bone have been found at Punta del Este, suggesting that the Siboney based themselves around the eastern caves.

By the time **Christopher Columbus** landed here in June 1494, on his second trip to the Americas, the Siboney had disappeared. Though Columbus claimed it for Spain, the Spanish Crown had little interest in the island over the next four centuries. Neither the mangrove-webbed northern coastline nor the excessively shallow southern bays afforded a natural harbour to match the likes of Havana, while the Golfo de Batabanó, separating the island from mainland Cuba, was too shallow for the overblown Spanish galleons to navigate. Official colonization would not begin for another three centuries.

Pirates and prisons

Left outside the bounds of Spanish law enforcement, the island attracted scores of **pirates** between the sixteenth and eighteenth centuries. It came to be known as the **Isla de Pinos** – after its plentiful pine trees, ideal for making masts and repairing ships – and, informally, as the **Isla de las Cotorras**, for its endemic green parrot population. Lurid stories of wine, women and warmongering were enough to keep all but the most determined settlers away, and so the pirates ruled the roost right up until the early nineteenth century, when Spanish interest in the island was renewed. However, despite a massive push by Spanish royal decree for whites to populate this remote territory, there was comparatively little response. The Spanish authorities decided to capitalize on the island's isolation, using it as a convenient **offshore prison** during the nineteenth-century Wars of Independence.

US interests

By the early twentieth century, the Spanish were rueing their indifference, as much of the property had fallen into the hands of shrewd **North American** businessmen and farmers who had waited in the wings during the troubled years. When Cuba won its independence from Spain in 1898, the island's small population allowed the North Americans to muscle in and start development unimpeded. By the 1920s a US-funded infrastructure of banks, hotels and even a jail – the vast Model Prison – was already in

9

place. By the time of the Revolution the island had become a popular North American **holiday resort**.

A fruitful future

The North Americans departed following the Revolution, and the history of the island took another turn when the state's drive to create arable land established it as one of the country's major producers of fruit for export. In 1966 it became a centre for experimental **agriculture**, to which a flood of students came to work the fields and study. In 1976 the government extended this free education to **foreign students** from countries with a socialist overview and, until the Special Period curtailed the flow, thousands of students arrived from countries like Angola, Nicaragua and South Yemen. When Cuba hosted the eleventh World Youth and Student Festival in 1978, the government changed the island's name from Isle of Pines to **Isle of Youth**, shedding the final trace of the island's rebellious past, although islanders still refer to themselves – and their national-league baseball team – as Pineros.

GETTING AROUND   ISLA DE LA JUVENTUD

By car or jeep Isla de la Juventud's bus network is skeletal, with no services in the southern protected zone, so you'll need to rent a car or jeep to explore the whole island. Cubacar is the only rental outfit in Nueva Gerona, at José Martí esq. 32 (☎ 4632 4432).

By bus Buses are a reasonably reliable way of getting around the north of the island; the routes below cover the places you're most likely to visit. You can board them at the bus station on Calle 39A at the northern end of town, along Calle 41, the main thoroughfare through Nueva Gerona, or Calle 47.

Nueva Gerona to Playa Bibijagua Bus #204 (4 daily each way; 30min), via Chacón (for Museo Presidio Modelo (4 daily each way; 20min).

Nueva Gerona to La Fe Bus #431 and #436 (10 daily each

way; 45min).

Nueva Gerona to Hotel Colony Bus #440 (4 daily each way; 2hr).

By taxi There's the state taxi company Cubataxi (☎ 4632 3121); alternatively, you'll find private taxis at the Parque Guerrillero Heroico in Nueva Gerona, or ask in a *casa particular*.

By bicycle Bikes are a great way to navigate the north end of the island; there are no rental outlets, but *casas particulares* owners are often willing to loan you the family bicycle for a small charge.

By bicitaxi A good option for getting to the outlying areas of Nueva Gerona, *bicitaxis* can be flagged down throughout the centre.

Nueva Gerona

Isla de la Juventud's only sizeable town, **NUEVA GERONA** lies in the lee of the Sierra de las Casas, on the bank of the Río Las Casas. Whether you travel to the island by plane or boat, this is where you'll arrive and where you're likely to be based. According to an 1819 census, the population stood at just under two hundred and it boasted just "four guano huts and a church of the same". While the town has certainly moved on since then, it's still a small and quirky place, with a cosiness more suited to a village than an island capital, and a sleepy peacefulness offset by the hub of action around the central streets. Even half a day here breeds a sense of comfortable familiarity, and much of the town's attraction lies in wandering its relaxed streets hassle-free. Basing yourself here and exploring the hillsides, beaches and museums around Nueva Gerona can easily keep you occupied for a couple of days.

Architecturally, Nueva Gerona floats in a no-man's-land between old-style colonial and modern urbanity. Many of its concrete one- and two-storey buildings are painted in pastel colours, and its few older buildings add an elegant touch.

Calle José Martí

Nueva Gerona's heart lies on **Calle José Martí** (also known as Calle 39 and often referred to simply as Martí), the amiable central street that gives the town its defining character and which holds the majority of shops and restaurants. It's a good-looking strip worthy of a stroll, with the verandas of the low buildings offering welcome respite from the sun. At the northern end of the pedestrianized section, sometimes referred to as Boulevard, is a small green space, the **Parque de las Cotorras**.

Museo Municipal del Deporte Juan Pedros Heredia

Calle José Martí e/ 22 y 24 • Tues–Sat 8am–noon & 1–5pm • Free

A couple of blocks south of Parque de las Cotorras, the tiny **Museo Municipal del Deporte Juan Pedros Heredia** serves as a modest tribute to local sports heroes, with sweatshirts and trophies worn and won by baseball players and other successful athletes from the island.

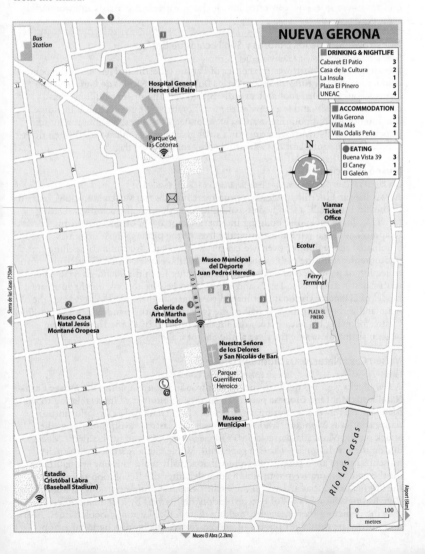

NUEVA GERONA

Bus Station

Hospital General Heroes del Baire

Parque de las Cotorras

N

Víamar Ticket Office

Ecotur

Museo Municipal del Deporte Juan Pedros Heredia

Ferry Terminal

Galería de Arte Martha Machado

Museo Casa Natal Jesús Montané Oropesa

Nuestra Señora de los Delores y San Nicolás de Bari

PLAZA EL PINERO

Parque Guerrillero Heroico

Sierra de las Casas (750m)

Museo Municipal

Río Las Casas

Estadio Cristóbal Labra (Baseball Stadium)

Airport (6km)

0   100
metres

Museo El Abra (2.2km)

DRINKING & NIGHTLIFE	
Cabaret El Patio	3
Casa de la Cultura	2
La Insula	1
Plaza El Pinero	5
UNEAC	4

ACCOMMODATION	
Villa Gerona	3
Villa Más	2
Villa Odalis Peña	1

EATING	
Buena Vista 39	3
El Caney	1
El Galeón	2

9

Galería de Arte Martha Machado
Calle José Martí esq. Calle 26 • Daily 8am–10pm • Free

The **Galería de Arte Martha Machado** has a small space for exhibitions of local art, mostly from the Naïve school, some of which is for sale. The gallery is associated with the internationally renowned artist **Kcho** (aka Alexis Leyva Machado), who was born in Nueva Gerona. If you're in luck, your visit may coincide with a temporary exhibition of his work.

Parque Guerrillero Heroico

At the southern end of Calle José Martí, past the pedestrianized centre, is the **Parque Guerrillero Heroico**. Although unspectacular in itself – it's basically a wide slab of plaza – it's bordered by some picturesque buildings such as the handsome, pastel-yellow *villa* on the western side, now converted into a school, with elegant arches and wonderful stained-glass windows.

Nuestra Señora de los Dolores y San Nicolás de Barí
Parque Guerrillero Heroico • Mon–Fri 8.30am–noon • Free

Presiding over the northwestern corner of Parque Guerrillero Heroico is the ochre-coloured church of **Nuestra Señora de los Dolores y San Nicolás de Barí**, boasting a curvaceous red-tiled roof and a sturdy bell-tower. The present building was completed in 1929 and is a copy of the San Lorenzo de Lucina church in Rome. The interior is disappointing: a sparsely decorated sky-blue shell houses a huddle of pews – it's only worth entering for a swift glance at the **altar** to the Virgen de la Caridad, the patron saint of Cuba, backed by the national flag.

Museo Municipal
Calle 30 e/ 37 y 39 • Tues–Sat 9am–noon & 1–4.45pm, Sun 8am–noon • Charge • ☎ 46 32 3791

Across Parque Guerrillero Heroico from the church is the **Museo Municipal**, housed in the old town hall, a stately colonial building with a small clocktower. Dating to 1853, this is the oldest building in Nueva Gerona. On display are portraits, weapons and naval relics illustrating the lives of the **pirates** whose activities dominated the region for over two centuries. There are also some compelling **photographs** from the early years of the twentieth century, and a wonderfully retro collection of pamphlets and advertisements dating from the island's heyday as a tourist destination in the 1940s and 1950s. Also be sure to look for the intricate model of **El Pinero**, the boat that ferried passengers and supplies to and from the mainland throughout the first half of the twentieth century, and which carried Fidel Castro following his release from the Presidio Modelo in 1955. The real thing can be seen sitting alongside the river at the end of Calle 26.

Museo Casa Natal Jesús Montané Oropesa
Calle 24 e/ 43 y 45 • Tues–Sat 9.30am–5pm, Sun 8.30am–noon • Free • ☎ 46 32 4582

A few blocks west from Martí, the modest wooden house holding the **Museo Casa Natal Jesús Montané Oropesa** packs in a surprising number of items relating to the islanders' part in the revolutionary struggle. Many relate to Isla de la Juventud's native son Jesús Montané, who was among Fidel Castro's revolutionaries at the attack on the Moncada Barracks in 1953 (see page 382) and in the Sierra Maestra during the revolutionary war (see page 440). While Cuba is stuffed with such museums, there are a couple of exhibits that actually make this one special. Look for the commemorative **photo album** compiled after the Revolution to celebrate the original band that arrived on the yacht *Granma*, Montané among them. Each page features photographs of two revolutionaries framed by a dramatic line-drawing depicting their struggles, making them look like comic-book heroes. Also noteworthy are the 1960s **photos** of excited crowds celebrating nationalization outside banks and factories and, best of all, an ingenious fake cigar used by the rebels to smuggle messages.

ARRIVAL AND DEPARTURE

NUEVA GERONA

BY PLANE
Essentials Two daily flights (45min) from Havana arrive at Rafael Cabrera Mustelier Airport (☎ 4632 2300), 10km south of the town centre. See ⦿ cubana.cu for details and to book. On landing, have some change ready for the buses that meet the planes and run to the town centre, or take a taxi.

BY FERRY
Arriving by ferry The daily catamaran ferry (2hr 45min, with a cheaper 5hr service also available) to Isla de la Juventud leaves from the ferry terminal at Batabanó, on the southern coast of Mayabeque province. It docks at the terminal (Mon–Fri 8.30am–4pm; ☎ 46 32 4406) on the Río Las Casas in Nueva Gerona. From here it's a 5min walk to the centre, or you can jump on one of the army of *bicitaxis* or horse-drawn carriages that wait to pick up passengers.
Tickets Most visitors set off for the journey to Batabanó (daily; 1hr 30min) from Havana. Be sure to buy in advance

in Havana. To do so, you should make an early visit (ideally before 9am) to the Oficina de la Naviera booth at Havana's Terminal de Omnibus Nacionales (daily 7.30am–12.30pm; ☎ 7878 1841; see page 113), where staff will sell you a bus ticket and reserve your boat ticket – payment for the latter is taken at Batabanó. You'll need your passport to be allowed to travel. Return journeys are hideously oversubscribed, so buying a return ticket is highly recommended.

Leaving by ferry Leaving the island by ferry can be problematic. If you don't already have a ferry ticket, you must go to the ticket office (☎ 4632 4415) near the ferry terminal two and a half hours before the scheduled departure time on the day you plan to travel; boats leave daily at 8am, plus 1pm on Fri & Sun. You'll need to put yourself on the waiting list (*lista de espera*), and then wait, sometimes several hours, until the number of no-shows (*fallos*) has been established. If there are no *fallos* then you won't be able to travel, but there are usually at least a few.

INFORMATION AND TOURS

Tourist information The only place for visitor information in town is the Ecotur office next to the ferry terminal (Mon–Fri 8am–4.30pm; ☎ 4632 7101, ✉ reservas.ij@occ.ecotur.tur.cu).
Travel permits and tours Visitors are not permitted to pass the military checkpoint at the entrance to the protected southern part of the island without a guide and permit. To explore the area, you need to arrange an organized excursion with Ecotur (see above); tours are not available at the checkpoint itself, so you must book at the Nueva Gerona

office in advance. All tours include the necessary permit, as well as the cost of renting a jeep (the cavernous potholes and long stretches of unpaved road necessitate a 4WD). Prices depend on the number of people, so it's worth trying to go with a group and splitting the cost. Ecotur organize excursions to Criadero Cocodrilo, the Cuevas de Punta del Este, La Fe, La Jungla de Jones, and Punta Francés for diving. For information on diving you could also ring the *Hotel Colony*, on the island's southwest coast.

ACCOMMODATION

SEE MAP PAGE 415

Unless you've come for the diving, in which case you'll be based on the west coast at *Hotel Colony* (see page 422), Nueva Gerona is the only base for a stay on Isla de la Juventud. Given that the small clutch of tatty hotels in and around the town has little going for them, you're better off in one of the excellent **casas particulares** in the town itself, often somewhat cheaper than on the mainland.
★ **Villa Gerona** Calle 35 no.2410 e/ 24 y 26 39 ☎ 4631 2962. An outdoor jacuzzi and bar in the impressive backyard patio elevate this central, modern house above most of its competitors. Quality meals are offered as is transport for getting around the island – all at additional costs. Three straight-forward but comfortable and well maintained double rooms, each with a/c, TV, minibar and its own bathroom. 𝕾
★ **Villa Más** Calle 41 no.4108 e/ 8 y 10, apto. 7 ☎ 4632

3544. Situated behind the hospital on a dusty track where the block layout gets a bit jumbled, this hard-to-find first-floor apartment offers spotlessly clean, stylishly decorated rooms with TV and fridge. It's well worth searching out as you'll be rewarded with two fabulous levels of roof terrace, one with a matted roof and barbecue grill, the other with views over the city and out to sea. The owner is a qualified chef and will provide meals. 𝕾
Villa Odalis Peña Calle 10 no.3710 esq. 39 ☎ 4632 2345. Big, friendly household surrounded by pretty gardens and offering two comfortable, well-appointed rooms with a/c, each of which has its own minibar and bathroom with an electric shower. Good food is available and, unusually, vegetarian and vegan meals are a speciality; opt for the breakfast. Around 300m out of town but a good choice nonetheless. 𝕾

9

EATING
SEE MAP PAGE 415

Casas particulares are generally the best places for a meal in town. A small concentration of uninspiring but very cheap **café/restaurants** lies on José Martí, many of them closed by 8pm despite advertising longer opening hours. For **snacks**, there's the local branch of Coppelia, the ice-cream café chain, at Calle 37 e/30 y 32, and several options on the pedestrianized section of José Martí, including a supermarket between Calle 22 and Calle 24

★ **Buena Vista 39** Calle José Martí no.2416A e/ 24 y 26 ⊛ buenavista39.com. With a balcony overlooking the Boulevard, an intimate, comfortable upstairs dining room inside, a half-decent bar and some of the best food in the city, this is as good a place to eat as any. Fish dominates the mains. $\overline{\underline{\textbf{S}}}$

El Caney Calle 3ra. no.401 e/ 4 y 6 ☎ 4632 5547. Open sides and a thatched roof give this lively paladar an airy feel, while the typical Cuban cuisine includes pork and chicken, with seafood the speciality, most of it cooked to a turn on an open grill within view. Portions are generous and complemented by a very friendly owner. $\overline{\underline{\textbf{SS}}}$

★ **El Galeón** Calle 24 no.4510 e/ 45 y 47 ☎ 5 3509128 (mobile). A pirate ship-themed paladar with a large open-air rooftop deck where diners nosh on fabulous, fresh grilled fish and slightly less noteworthy greasy chicken and pork standards. With attentive service, this is the most professionally run paladar in town. $\overline{\underline{\textbf{S}}}$

DRINKING AND NIGHTLIFE
SEE MAP PAGE 415

Not a lot happens after dark in Nueva Gerona between Monday and Wednesday, but weekends can be surprisingly lively, with most of the action taking place around the half-dozen blocks north of Parque Guerrillero Heroico between José Martí and the river.

Cabaret El Patio Calle 24 e/ José Martí y 37 ☎ 4632 2346. Hosts live singers and a fabulously camp small-scale cabaret in a dark and moody hall for an enthusiastic crowd.

★ **Casa de la Cultura** Calle 24 esq. 37 ☎ 4632 3591. Entertainment most nights, with two floors of performance spaces, ranging from singing troupes and African-Cuban dancing to burlesque pantomimes and daytime children's shows. This is also the spot for catching live traditional Cuban music such as trova, son and bolero, and is most reliably lively during the week.

La Insula José Martí esq. 22 ☎ 4632 1825. The straightforward bar at this restaurant is open some evenings, and is liveliest on Sundays when it hosts a karaoke night.

Plaza El Pinero Calle 33 e/ 26 y 28. Crowds gather at this open space next to the river where bands perform at weekends on a large concrete stage. Popular with a young crowd and one of the main venues for visiting bands from Havana.

UNEAC Calle 37 e/ 24 y 26. The local branch of this national cultural institution has a small patio for all kinds of live music performances by aspiring and seasoned musical talent, from reggaeton and rock to guitar-strumming troubadours.

DIRECTORY

Bookshop Librería Frank País at José Martí esq. 22 (Mon–Sat 8am–7pm) has a range of books in Spanish and the occasional English title.

Health The only hospital on the island is the Héroes del Baire, on Calle 41 e/ 16 y 18. For an ambulance call ☎ 4632 4170. The state hotels have medical posts, while the most accessible pharmacy is in the hospital grounds, facing the entrance.

Money and exchange Banco de Crédito y Comercio, José Martí no.39 esq. 18 (Mon–Fri 8am–3pm, Sat 8–11am; ☎ 4632 2256) offers foreign currency transactions and an ATM; CADECA *casa de cambio* at José Martí no. 20 (Mon–Sat 8am–6pm, Sun 8am–1pm) for foreign exchange. There's

also an ATM at the Banco Popular de Ahorro at José Martí esq. 26.

Police Call ☎ 106.

Post office The main post office is on José Martí e/ 18 y 20 (Mon–Sat 8am–6pm). There's a DHL desk in the stationery shop at José Martí s/n e/ 22 y 24 (Mon–Fri 8am–noon & 1–5pm, Sat 8am–noon).

Wi-fi Public wi-fi spots in town include the pedestrianized section of José Martí, Parque de las Cotorras and around the Estadio Cristóbal Labra. You can buy wi-fi cards at the Telepunto office at Calle 41 esq. 28, near Parque Guerrillero Heroico (daily 8.30am–7.30pm), where you can use the computer terminals to access the internet using your card.

Sierra de las Casas

The best way to appreciate Nueva Gerona's diminutive scale is to take the short but exhilarating climb up into the hills of the gently undulating **Sierra de las Casas** range, just to the west, for a bird's-eye view over the town and the surrounding countryside. It's under an hour's easy climb up to the highest summit, beneath which are spread the town's orderly rows of streets, curtailed by the stretch of blue beyond. To the east, below the cliff-edge, the island's flat landscape is occasionally relieved by a sparse sweep of hills; to the south, you can see the gleaming quarry which yields the stone for so many of Cuba's marble artefacts.

To get to the hills, head 500m west from Neuva Gerona's centre down Calle 24; take the first left turn and carry on another few hundred metres along a well-trodden path until you reach the foot of the first hill, marked by two lone concrete poles poking out of the ground.

Cueva del Agua
24hr • Free

Before heading back to town from the Sierra de las Casas, make time to explore the underground **Cueva del Agua**, whose entrance is at the foot of the hill. The steep, narrow staircase cut from the rockbed can be slippery, so take care descending and bring a torch. There's a natural lagoon and captivating rock formations but the real treat here lies along a narrow tunnel on the right-hand side just before the mouth of the pool, where intricate, glittery stalactites and stalagmites are slowly growing into elaborate natural sculptures.

Museo El Abra
Tues–Sun 9am–5pm • Charge • ☎ 4639 6206

Around 2km southwest of Nueva Gerona, on the Carretera Siguanea – the continuation of Calle 41, which heads towards *Hotel Colony* (see page 422) – a signposted turning leads to the **Museo El Abra**, the Spanish-style hacienda where José Martí spent three months in 1870. Nestling at the foot of the Sierra de las Casas, the whitewashed farmhouse – with Caribbean-blue balustrade windows and a charming stone sundial from Barcelona – has rather more style than substance. Inside is a collection of inconsequential artefacts from Martí's life. Letters and documents vie for attention with his bed and a replica of the manacles from which Martí was freed on his arrival.

Although just 16 at the time of his arrest, Martí had already founded the magazine *La Patria Libre*, and his editorials contesting Spanish rule had him swiftly pegged as a dissident. On October 21, 1869, he was arrested for treason. His original sentence of six years' hard labour was mitigated and he was exiled to El Abra. Here he was permitted to serve out his sentence under the custody of family friend and farm owner José María Sardá, but within three months the Spanish governor expelled him from Cuba altogether. During his time on the island he wrote the essay *El Presidio Político en Cuba* (*The Political Prison in Cuba*), which became the seminal text of the independence struggle.

Presa El Abra
Charge to rent kayaks and pedal boats

Around 5km southwest of Nueva Gerona, and a further 3km south along the Carretera Siguanea from the Museo El Abra, **Presa El Abra** is an artificial but very natural-looking lake, with idyllic grassy, tree-lined shores and a decent restaurant to help focus a visit. It's a great place for whiling away an afternoon, easily reachable by bike and affordable by taxi from the town. Lots of locals come here at weekends and during holidays to swim and relax along the shore, where there are several picnic spots, and to paddle about in kayaks and pedal boats.

EATING	PRESA EL ABRA

El Abra Presa El Abra ☎ 4632 4927. Open-air *El Abra* restaurant, whose inexpensive *comida criolla*, like roast pork and grilled fish, has a home-cooked quality, is enhanced by the lakeside setting, mountain backdrop and panoramic views. ⑤

9

Museo Presidio Modelo

Mon–Sat 8am–4pm, Sun 8am–noon • Charge • ☎ 4632 5112 • To get here, turn off the road to Playa Bibijagua at the small housing scheme of Chacón

The looming bulk of the **Museo Presidio Modelo** lies 2km east of Nueva Gerona. Although this massive former prison has housed a fascinating museum for over thirty years and is now one of the most-visited sights on the island, its forbidding atmosphere has been preserved. Surrounded by guard towers, the classically proportioned governor's mansion and phalanx of wardens' *villas* mask the four circular cell buildings that rise like witches' cauldrons from the centre of the complex.

Commissioned by the dictator Gerardo Machado, the "Model Prison" was built in 1926 by its future inmates as an exact copy of the equally notorious Joliet Prison in the US. At one time it was considered the definitive example of efficient design, as up to six thousand detainees could be controlled with a minimum of staff, but it soon became infamous for unprecedented levels of corruption and cruelty. The last prisoner was released in 1967 and the cell blocks have long since slid into decay, serving to increase the sense of foreboding inside.

The cell blocks

Unmanned by museum staff and falling into disrepair, the four huge, cylindrical **cell blocks** still feel as oppressive as they must have been when crammed with inmates. The prisoners, housed two or more to a cell, were afforded no privacy, constantly on view through the iron bars. Note the gun slits cut into the grim tower in the dead centre of each block, allowing one guard and his rifle to control nearly a thousand inmates from a position of total safety. To really appreciate the creepy magnitude of the cell blocks, you can take the precarious narrow marble staircase to the fifth-level floor.

The prison museum

Less disturbing than the cell blocks, the **prison museum** is located in the hospital block at the back of the grounds. Knowledgeable Spanish-speaking guides take you around and will expect a small tip. The most memorable part of the museum is the dormitory where **Fidel Castro** and the rebels of the Moncada attack were sequestered on the orders of Batista, for fear of them inflaming the other prisoners with their firebrand ideas. Above each of the 26 beds is the erstwhile occupant's mug shot and a brief biography, while a piece of black cloth on each sheet symbolizes the rags the men tore from their trouser legs to cover their eyes at night, when lights were shone on them constantly as torture.

On February 13, 1954, **Batista** made a state visit to the Presidio Modelo. As he and his entourage passed their window, the rebels broke into a revolutionary anthem. As a result, Castro was confined alone in the room that now opens off the main entrance but was at the time next to the morgue, within full view of the corpses. For the early part of his forty-week sentence he was forbidden any light. Despite the prohibition, a crafty home-made lamp enabled Castro to read from his small library and to perfect the speech he had made at his defence, which was later published by the underground press as *La Historia me Absolverá* and became the manifesto of the cause.

Playa Paraíso

To get here, take the road east of Nueva Gerona; after 2km, take the left-hand turn north, from where it's a further 2km to the beach

East of Nueva Gerona, and an easy bike ride from town, **Playa Paraíso** beach is popular with locals, who call it "El Mini". The small hoop of rather grubby, seaweed-strewn sand is somewhat redeemed by its friendly atmosphere and a striking hill behind, whose shadow lengthens over the beach in the afternoon.

Playa Bibijagua

Some 6km east along the main road from Nueva Gerona, **Playa Bibijagua** has an attractive grassy approach through the remains of an old hotel that's used exclusively by Cubans. Billed as a black-sand beach, it's actually a mottled brownish colour, the result of marble deposits in the sand. Although not the prettiest beach on the island, the view over a curve of coastline enveloped with pine trees is picturesque, and it has a lively atmosphere. Make sure you bring plenty of insect repellent to ward off the vicious sandflies.

La Fe

The island's second-largest town, **La Fe**, also known as **Santa Fe**, is 27km south of Nueva Gerona. Not much more than a handful of streets lined with housing blocks built after the Revolution, it is also the site of some mineral springs, the **Manantial de Santa Rita**, which surface at the northeastern end of town. You can join the queue of locals filling up their water bottles here from three free-flowing taps, each producing a different mineral water.

La Jungla de Jones

Daily 8am–8pm • Charge • Ecotur (see page 417) run organized excursions from Nueva Gerona

Around 4km west of La Fe, along the road that bisects the island, **La Jungla de Jones** is more a nature reserve than the "botanical garden" it is sometimes described as. Even before it suffered severe storm damage in 2008 the sense of landscaping was minimal and it retains an appealingly natural feel, though the impressive variety of trees is not actually as natural as it might seem. Established by a couple from Chicago, Helen Rodman and Harry Sanford Jones, in 1902, there are all kinds of tropical fruit trees, including some 20 varieties of mango tree, plus coconut palms, tea and coffee plants and an impressive, swaying bamboo cathedral. You can picnic here and pick your way through the unkempt grounds, crisscrossed by a web of leaf-littered trails and the Río Los Almácigos.

Playa Roja

Almost exactly 40km along the road south from Nueva Gerona is **Playa Roja**. Often referred to as Playa El Colony, it's the only decent beach on the west coast, and lies within the grounds of the only hotel in the whole southern half of the island. Built in the 1950s by the Batista regime as a casino hangout for American sophisticates, **Hotel Colony** was abandoned just weeks after its opening when Batista fled the Revolution. You can spend the day here by paying for a **day-pass**, but however long you spend at the resort, make sure you come with insect repellent as mosquitoes and sandflies are ever present.

A high proportion of guests here come for the daily diving trips to Punta Francés, which are organized by the **Marina Siguanea**, also known as Marina El Colony (see box below), 1.5km south of the hotel. Small and strictly functional, the marina is not somewhere to pass the time: there are no services other than the dive facilities and a medical post.

ARRIVAL AND DEPARTURE   **PLAYA ROJA**

By bus There are currently four public buses from Nueva Gerona to *Hotel Colony*. There is also a workers' bus ferrying hotel staff back and forth, which you can flag down on Calle 41 in Nueva Gerona. Wait for buses opposite the ETECSA Telepunto, on the corner of Calle 41 and Calle 28, in Nueva Gerona.

By taxi A taxi from Nueva Gerona to the hotel should cost about $900CUP one way.

DIVING OFF THE ISLA DE LA JUVENTUD

All the **diving** on Isla de la Juventud is arranged through the **Marina Siguanea**, commercially known as **Marina El Colony** (✉ comercial@marlin.cls.tur.cu). A five-day SNSI course includes a training day in the swimming pool, plus three dives. If you already have certification, discounted multi-dive packages are available. A minimum of two paying divers are required per trip unless you are prepared to make up the extra cost. Snorkelling excursions are also offered.

DIVE SITES

Isla de la Juventud has over fifty **dive sites**, all offshore of a 6km strip of coast between Punta Francés and Punta Pedernales, at the western tip off the island's southern coastline and in the protected zone. There are also two shipwrecks close to Cayos Los Indios, about 30km out from the hotel. The following sites are among the highlights.

El Cabezo de las Isabelitas 5km west of Playa El Francés. This shallow (15m) site has plenty of natural light and a cornucopia of fish, including goatfish, trumpetfish and parrotfish. An uncomplicated dive, ideal for beginners.

Cueva Azul 2km west of Playa El Francés. Reaching depths of 42m, this site takes its name ("the blue cave") from the intensely coloured water. Although there are several notable types of fish to be seen, the principal thrill of this dive is ducking and twisting through the cave's crevices.

El Escondito del Buzo 4km west of Playa El Francés. Coral gardens (at 15m) skirted by a wall (at 30m) in an area populated by schools of jacks and blue chromis as well as by, typically, stingrays, groupers and jewfish, among others.

Los Indios Wall 5km from Cayos Los Indios. A host of stunning corals, including brain, star, fire and black coral, cling to a sheer wall that drops 30m to the sea bed, while you can see stingrays on the bottom, some as long as 2m. A supplement must be paid for this dive and you need a minimum of five people.

Pared de Coral Negro 4km northwest of Punta Francés. The black coral that gives this dive its name is found at depths of 35m, while the rest of the wall is alive with colourful sponges and brain corals, as well as several species of fish and green moray eels.

ACCOMMODATION   SEE MAP PAGE 412

Hotel Colony ⓦ grancaribehotels.com. The only place to stay with access to Punta Francés, this blocky hotel, with its old-fashioned decor, feels a bit dated, but there is a reasonable swimming pool and a pleasant strip of palm-studded beach, and the sunset view from here is spectacular. Rooms are split between the main block and separate chalets (not all have sea views), and are generally clean and spacious, though with only basic facilities. $$

Criadero Cocodrilo

Daily 7am–5pm • Charge; bring small bills as keepers rarely have change • ☎ 4632 7101

South of La Fe, a subtle change begins to come over the terrain as the road opens up, the potholes increase and the prolific fruit groves gradually become marshy thicket. Just past the settlement of Julio Antonio Mella, 12km on, you'll come to a left turn heading to the **Criadero Cocodrilo**. Looking more like a swampy wilderness than a conventional farm, this crocodile nursery is actually, on closer inspection, teeming with reptiles. The large white basins near the entrance form the nursery for a seething mass of 4-month-old, 25cm-long snappers, surprisingly warm and soft to the touch. Nearby, what at first looks like a seed bed reveals itself to be planted with a crop of crocodile eggs that are removed from the female adults once laid, and incubated for around eighty days before hatching. Larger specimens cruise down enclosed waterways choked with lily pads and teeming with birds and butterflies. The crocodiles are endemic to the area, but were in danger of extinction until the farm's creation. It keeps around four hundred crocodiles at any one time, and periodically releases them into the southern wilds when they reach seven years of age, at which point they measure about 1m in length.

The southern protected zone

Although rumours abound concerning the purpose of the military presence in the southern third of the island, its primary function is simply to conserve and restrict access to the **Siguanea Nature Reserve**. Parts of the reserve are completely closed to the public – you need a pass and a guide to go south of the military checkpoint at **Cayo Piedra** (see box below) – as the luxuriant vegetation of the area shelters such **wildlife** as wild deer, green parrots and the *tocororo*, Cuba's national bird.

The flat land south of the checkpoint conforms to the storybook ideal of a desert island, with caves and sinuous beaches fringing a swampy interior of mangroves and thick shrubs. It's also home to one of the most impressive sights on the Isla de la Juventud: the **pre-Columbian cave paintings** at **Punta del Este**, believed to date back some 1100 years, making them among the oldest in the Caribbean. Along with the caves, the main reasons for a visit here are the fine-sand **beaches** at Punta del Este and **Punta Francés**, on opposite sides of the southern coastline, which many visitors get to by boat from the *Hotel Colony*, situated just north of the military border on the west coast, rather than by land.

Near Punta Francés on the island's western hook is **Cocodrilo**, a tiny hamlet whose pleasant charms are increased by a rugged granite-rock coastline that forms natural pools ideal for snorkelling. Whichever part of this area you visit, be sure to bring insect repellent with you.

Cuevas de Punta del Este

No set hours • Charge • The caves are 25km down a dirt track leading east of the checkpoint at Cayo Piedra

Half buried amid overgrown herbs and greenery, the **Cuevas de Punta del Este** contain significant examples of early pre-Columbian art, pointing to an established culture on the island as early as 900 AD. These paintings are among the few remaining traces of the **Siboney** – among the first inhabitants of Cuba – who arrived from South America via other Caribbean islands between three and four millennia ago; they are thought to have died out shortly after the paintings were made.

This area is also great for birdwatching, with over 160 species recorded here, including a clutch of attractive Cuban endemics, among them the Cuban trogon, Cuban tody and the Cuban green woodpecker.

The six caves, only two of which are accessible, were discovered by accident at the turn of the twentieth century by a North American named Freeman P. Lane, who disembarked on the beach and sought shelter in one of them. The discovery made archaeologists reconsider their assumption that Siboney culture was primitive, as the paintings are thought to represent a solar calendar, which would indicate a sophisticated cosmology.

CROSSING THE MILITARY BORDER

To pass the military checkpoint at Cayo Piedra you will need a one-day **permit** and the services of a **registered guide**, which you must arrange in advance at the Ecotur office in Nueva Gerona (see page 417); tours include permit and transportation by jeep to and from Nueva Gerona. You shouldn't encounter any difficulties at the checkpoint as long as you avail yourself of the necessary documentation – there are usually only one or two guards there to wave you past the hut; however, should you arrive at the checkpoint without a guide and pass, you will be unceremoniously turned back.

9

Caves One and Two

On March 22 each year, the sun streams through a natural hole in the roof of **Cave One**, the largest of the group, illuminating the pictographs in a beam of sunlight. Being linked to the vernal equinox, the effect is thought to celebrate fertility and the cycle of life and death. When bones were excavated here in 1939, it became apparent that the caves' function was not only ceremonial – they had also been used for habitation and burial.

Of the 230 pictographs, the most prominent are the tight rows of concentric red-and-black circles overlapping one another on the low ceiling of Cave One. Despite creeping erosion by algae, the fading images are still very visible. Major excavation work got under way in the 1940s, when five more caves were discovered, though the paintings within are in a far worse state of repair and you'll need a keen eye to spot them. Even so, you should take a look at **Cave Two**, 500m away, where more fragments of circles are outshone by the fragile remains of a painted fish.

Playa Punta del Este

Just 200m east of the Cuevas de Punta del Este the tufts of undergrowth give way to beach. The small white-sand strand of **Playa Punta del Este**, sown with sea grass and rimmed by mangroves, is a good spot for a refreshing dip, though it can't compare to the beauty of the other southern beaches to the west.

Playa Larga

Some 20km south, the road from the Cayo Piedra checkpoint meets the coast at the narrow wedge of sand that comprises **Playa Larga**. Though not really the best spot for a swim, it's a popular place with local fishermen from Cocodrilo, to the west, and the pretty pine-backed stretch of sand is littered with golden-pink conch shells. The beach was the landing site for several Camagüean *balseros* (rafters) intent on emigrating to the US, who arrived here in 1994 after a turbulent journey from the mainland, jubilantly believing themselves to be on North American soil, only to discover that they had not left Cuban territory.

Carapachibey lighthouse

About 5km west of Playa Larga you can take a quick detour down a pine-lined drive to **Carapachibey lighthouse**. Although Art Deco-like in its straight-lined simplicity, it wasn't built until 1983. At 63m in height it is supposedly the tallest lighthouse in Latin America and it's worth asking the keeper if you can make the steep climb up 280 steps

---

LE CLERC'S TREASURE

The beach at Punta Francés is named after the French pirate **François Le Clerc**, who frequented the Ensenada de la Siguanea, on the north side of the spit of land. In 1809 he captured two Spanish ships laden with gold and jewels, and made swiftly for the Isla de la Juventud's southern coast to hide, rightly deducing that the theft was unlikely to pass unavenged. With just enough time to bury his **treasure**, Le Clerc was captured by North Americans and sent to Kingston, Jamaica, where he was promptly executed for piracy.

The whereabouts of the treasure has haunted bounty hunters ever since. The night before his execution Le Clerc is supposed to have written a note to his fellow pirate Jean Lafitte, cryptically hinting that the hoard was buried ninety paces "from the mouth of the boiling spring", but Lafitte never received the note and the treasure is still hidden. Though unlikely to be anything more than romantic fancy, legend has it that the booty is buried somewhere in the waters of the Ensenada de la Siguanea, offshore of the southern protected zone's west coast.

to enjoy the views over the rocky coastline and turquoise sea; after dark, you can see the lights of Grand Cayman.

Cocodrilo

Some 20km west of the Carapachibey lighthouse, the dusty road takes you to a tiny village called **COCODRILO**. This peaceful haven boasts just a few palm-wood houses and a school in front of a village green that backs on to the sea. Isolated from the north of the island by poor transport and the military checkpoint, it's a fairly rustic community seemingly unaffected by the developments of the twentieth century, albeit healthy and well educated thanks to the Revolution. Originally named Jacksonville, after one of its first families, the hamlet was founded at the beginning of the twentieth century by Cayman Islanders who came here to hunt the large numbers of turtles – now much depleted – that once populated the waters and nested along the southern beaches (there's now a rudimentary turtle centre just outside the village). Some of the village's older residents still speak the English of their forefathers.

At the north end of the hamlet, cupped by a semicircle of rocky cliff, the electric-blue water of a natural **rock pool** is an excellent place to spend a few hours. It's about a 2m drop to the water below, but take care if jumping, as the pool is shallow. If you've brought equipment, it's also worth heading offshore to snorkel among the tiny, darting fish.

Punta Francés

Northwest of Cocodrilo, a 10km track heads toward the island's most remote spot, **Punta Francés**, an upturned hook of land where you'll find the island's top beach, **Playa El Francés**. There is over 3km of beach in all, split by a sandy headland into two broad curves of silver, powdery shore ringed on one side by the lush green of a woody, palm-specked thicket and on the other by the glassy, brilliant turquoise of the Caribbean Sea. The deserted tranquillity of this private world is all part of what makes it exceptional, though this is sometimes destroyed by hordes of cruise-ship visitors. Equally attractive is the excellent **diving** offshore (see page 422). There is no food and drink available at the beach, as the ranch-house restaurant that once stood here was destroyed by hurricanes, though a couple of small jetties remain. A slightly easier way to get to the beach is to catch a boat from *Hotel Colony* (see page 422). Although you will be in the protected part of the island, you don't need a permit to visit Punta Francés by boat – though you are strictly prohibited from going any further than the beach.

ARRIVAL AND DEPARTURE
PUNTA FRANCÉS

By boat The boat used for diving excursions from the marina at the *Hotel Colony* also acts as a ferry between the hotel and the beach. It leaves from the hotel most days at 9am, returning at around 5pm, and you must book your journey in advance through the hotel itself.

Cayo Largo

Separated from the Isla de la Juventud by 100km of sea, **Cayo Largo**, a narrow, low-lying spit of land fringed with powdery beaches and no permanent local population, is geared entirely to package holiday-makers. The tiny islet, measuring just 25km from tip to beachy tip, caters to a steady flow of international tourists who flock here to enjoy its excellent watersports, diving and all-inclusive hotels. For a holiday cut adrift from responsibilities and the outside world, this is as good a choice as any. But while Cayo Largo is undoubtedly the stuff of exotic holiday fantasy, it's not a place to meet Cubans. There are no born-and-bred locals and the hotel staff only live on the island in shifts, so though people are as friendly as elsewhere in Cuba, the atmosphere is more than a little contrived.

Development of the cay began in 1977 when the state, capitalizing on its extensive white sands and offshore coral reefs, built the first of the small set of hotels that currently line the western and southern shores. Although Cayo Largo is being steadily developed, it has a long way to go before being spoilt; indeed, for some the cay won't actually be developed enough, its sparse infrastructure meaning you have to rely heavily on the hotels for entertainment and eating options. There is a small artificial "**village**" on the west of the island, which has a distinctly spurious air, consisting of just a shop, restaurants, a museum, a bank and, behind the tourist facade, blocks of workers' accommodation. The **interior** is a mixture of grassland, rocky scrub and crops of pine trees, but there is not much to see.

Isla del Sol village

Built on Cayo Largo's southwestern coast – to optimize the pleasant view over cay-speckled waters – the artificial **Isla del Sol village** doesn't offer much of a reason to leave the resorts. Among the red-roofed ochre buildings ranged around the small but attractive **Plaza del Pirata** you'll find the obligatory tourist trappings: a shop selling cigars, postcards and sunscreen, plus a bank, museum, bowling alley, restaurant and bar. The main focal point is the **Marina Cayo Largo**, west of the plaza, an area that bustles with activity when motorboats dock to collect or release the sunbathers, snorkellers and divers en route to and from dive sites and beaches. For the rest of the day, the village sinks into an easy somnolence, though its **museum** and **Turtle Rescue Centre and Farm** offer diversions.

Casa Museo

Daily 9am–6pm • Charge

A short way west of Isla del Sol's marina, and set in a small bungalow, the **Casa Museo** aims to portray Cayo Largo in its historical and biogeographical context. There isn't much to go on, but exhibits include some remnants of tools supposedly used by the cays' original inhabitants, plus photos depicting touristic developments here, some taken by construction workers, as well as hurricane damage.

Turtle Rescue Centre and Farm

Daily 8am–noon & 1–5pm • Charge • The farm is just off Plaza del Pirata, some 100m west of the marina

Part tourist attraction, part conservation project, Isla de Sol's **Turtle Rescue Centre and Farm** works to protect the green, loggerhead and critically endangered hawksbill turtles

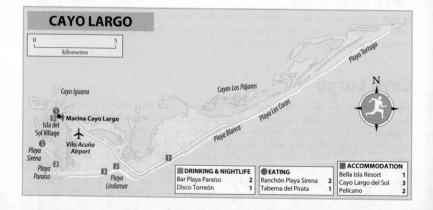

CAYO LARGO DIVING, FISHING AND BOAT EXCURSIONS

With over thirty **dive sites** in its clear and shallow waters, Cayo Largo is deservedly well known as one of Cuba's best diving areas. Particularly outstanding are the coral gardens fringing the islet, while other highlights include underwater encounters with hawksbill and sea-green turtles. The cay's **dive centre** (daily 7am–7pm; ☎ 4524 8214) at the Marina Cayo Largo offers week-long open-water SSI courses, and discounts for multi-dive packages. They can also provide transport to the site and all equipment.

The marina also runs a variety of day-long **excursions** (usually 9am–4pm) to the surrounding cays, including tiny Cayo Iguana, the nearest islet to Cayo Largo (where the eponymous reptiles can be fed by hand), Cayo Rico and the Cayos Pedrazas, 12km from the western tip of Cayo Largo. Most excursions include snorkelling at one of the surrounding coral reefs and a visit to a "natural swimming pool" where the water is only 1m deep, along with a lobster lunch and an open bar.

The waters around the cays also make for excellent **fishing**. All fishing around Cayo Largo is managed by Avalon (🌐 cubanfishingcenters.com), in partnership with the Marina Cayo Largo. They offer high-sea expeditions and fly-fishing trips. Huge tarpon are a big draw between March and June.

that populate the waters around the archipelago. Each year, the staff here collect turtle eggs from the most vulnerable beaches around the cays and bring them to the farm for incubation. Soon after hatching, the restless baby turtles are released into the sea on a safe beach – an unforgettable ceremony visitors can take part in.

Cayo Largo beaches

The southern coast of Cayo Largo boasts some of the very best beaches in Cuba, with warm, shallow waters lapping onto a largely narrow ribbon of pale downy sand. Protected from harsh winds and rough waves by the offshore coral reef, and with over 2km of white sands, **Playa Sirena**, at the western tip of the cay, enjoys a deserved reputation as the most beautiful of all the beaches on Cayo Largo, and is consequently the most popular; it's also the base of all the beach watersports facilities. Further south along the same strand, **Playa Paraíso** is almost as attractive and popular as Sirena, with the added advantage that its shallow waters are ideal for children. Heading east, **Playa Lindamar** is a serviceable 5km curve of sand in front of the *Lindamar*, *Pelícano*, *Soledad* and *Coral* hotels, and is the place to come if you're looking for some surf and wind.

For real solitude, you need to head off up to the eastern beaches. **Playa Blanca**, occupied at its western extremity by the *Bella Isla Resort*, boasts over 6km of deserted, soft sand, backed by dunes, and staking out your own patch shouldn't be a problem (though you'll need to bring your own refreshments as there's not an ice-cream stand in sight). Further east still, the lovely **Playa los Cocos** is seemingly endless, while far-flung **Playa Tortuga** is similarly deserted.

Uniquely in Cuba, there are a number of **nudist beaches** on Cayo Largo, though none is officially designated as such. The nudist sections have evolved thanks to a policy of tolerance rather than outright endorsement from the Cuban authorities. Generally they are found at one end or another of each beach, as opposed to right in the middle.

ARRIVAL AND DEPARTURE

CAYO LARGO

By plane All national and international flights to Cayo Largo arrive at the tiny Vilo Acuña airport (☎ 4524 8207), 1km from the main belt of hotels; courtesy buses meet every flight and whisk passengers off to their accommodation. Direct scheduled international flights to and from Cayo Largo have fluctuated somewhat in recent years. Air Canada and Cubana have operated weekly services between the island and Montréal, though charter airlines are the more regular link between the Vilo Acuña airport and other international airports, mostly in Canada. All domestic flights are from Havana (2 daily; 40min); note that if you come independently, you will need to book accommodation when you arrange your flight. A quicker option is to take a day-trip from Havana, which you can arrange through a number of the national travel agents (see page 34).

By boat As there is no boat service between the islands, only yacht owners – for whom the clear shallow seas, excellent fishing and serviceable marinas make it a favourite destination – can breeze in by water to the main Marina Cayo Largo on the village coastline. Although only 140km away, there is no way to get here from Isla de la Juventud.

GETTING AROUND

Cayo Largo is small enough to negotiate easily, with a single asphalt road linking the airport and the village, just 1km apart, with the hotels. The beaches to the east and west of the hotel strip are accessible via dirt tracks running within a few hundred metres of the shore.

By shuttle bus Shuttle buses (free to guests) connect all the hotels with the western beaches, including Playa Sirena, and run three times daily in both directions, with the last departure from the beaches at 5pm.

By ferry A ferry (leaves from the marina in the village to Playa Sirena and Playa Paraíso twice daily at 9.30am and 11am, returning at 3pm and 5pm.

By jeep or scooter Jeep and scooter rental is available at the hotels, the latter only available for cash.

By taxi It's best to book taxis with your hotel. They also wait outside hotels and the marina, though demand often exceeds availability in high season.

INFORMATION

Tourist information Though there is no main tourist office on the cay, you should be able to get all the information you need from the travel agents based at the larger hotels and the hotel staff. The *Pelícano* hotel (see below) has representatives from all three major Cuban travel agents: Cubatur (☎ 4524 8258), Havanatur (☎ 4524

8215) and Cubanacán (☎ 4524 8391).

Services There's a bank (Mon–Fri 8.30am–noon & 2–3.30pm, Sat & Sun 9am–noon) and a pharmacy (daily except Wed 8am–noon & 1–8pm, Wed 8am–noon & 4–10pm) at the Isla del Sol village.

ACCOMMODATION

SEE MAP PAGE 426

Cayo Largo's **hotels** tend to be block-booked by overseas tour operators at a specially discounted rate, but are not cheap if you make your booking in Cuba. If you're not on a package booked from abroad then you'll have to choose your accommodation when you buy your flight in Havana, as flights and prebooked accommodation in Cayo Largo are sold as a deal by tour operators. At the 2022 International Tourism Fair in Varadero. it was announced that the Canadian hotel chain Blue Diamond Resorts and the Cuban Gran Caribe Group will jointly manage all tourism facilities on Cayo Largo from the 2022–2023 winter season. Renovated hotels, an expansion of the airport, and development of the marina are on the cards for future visitors.

Bella Isla Resort ⑩ bellaislaresort.com. Previously known as the *Playa Blanca*, this is one of the quieter, more secluded options, situated 1km east from the main cluster of hotels. Rooms are of a high standard and are split between accommodation blocks and prettier two-storey *villas* dotted around the attractive grounds. There's a very simple pool, and the wooden terrace on a rocky seaside ledge is a nice touch. $\overline{\$\$\$}$

Cayo Largo del Sol ⑩ grancaribehotels.com. An appealing, buzzy, Caribbean-themed hotel with airy rooms painted in tropical colours set around palm trees and rather parched lawns. With an all-inclusive buffet, beach grill and à la carte restaurants, plus two swimming pools, free non-motorized watersports, a health centre, tennis courts and a football field, this is the biggest and plushest place on the cay. A road train ferries guests to Playa Sirena and Playa Paraíso. $\overline{\$\$\$}$

Pelícano ⑩ hotelsolpelicano.com. A family-friendly luxury hotel characterized by mock-colonial architecture and a fetching five-floor lookout tower. There's a dedicated play area and children's entertainment, four all-inclusive restaurants, two swimming pools and bold two- and three-storey *villas*. $\overline{\$\$\$}$

EATING, DRINKING AND ENTERTAINMENT

SEE MAP PAGE 426

RESTAURANTS
Ranchón Playa Sirena Playa Sirena. This decent open-air restaurant offers lobster in hot sauce, a lobster and shrimp mixed grill, and several cheaper meat dishes such as

pork loin steak. $\overline{\$\$\$}$

Taberna del Pirata Isla del Sol village. Tiled-roof bar and basic restaurant with a terrace overlooking the picturesque harbour. A good spot to enjoy the cooling sea breezes while the sun sets, with great value sandwiches, pizza and beer. ⑤

NIGHTCLUB
Bar Playa Paraíso Playa Paraíso. Snacks, cocktails, beers and soft drinks at this simple beach bar on Playa Paraíso.
Disco Torreón Isla del Sol village. A fortress-like building of grey stone whose rather plain interior is the scene for nightly music and dancing.

MARCHING ON REVOLUTION SQUARE TO CELEBRATE MAYDAY

Contexts

History

The strategic and geographical importance of Cuba to the shifting global powers of the last five centuries has dictated much of the Caribbean island's history. Formerly a stepping stone between Spain and its vast American empire, Cuba has struggled to achieve a real and lasting independence ever since, passing from Spanish colony to US satellite and, despite the nationalist Revolution of 1959, relying on economic support from the Soviet Union until the 1990s. At the start of the twenty-first century Cuba is at a crossroads, with its revolutionary, socialist ideals and achievements set firmly against survival in a capitalist global economy.

Pre-Columbian Cuba

Unlike Central America with its great Maya and Aztec civilizations, no comparably advanced societies had emerged in Cuba by the time Columbus arrived in 1492. Although people from ancient cultures – Native Americans who had worked their way up through the Antilles from the South American mainland – had inhabited the island for thousands of years, they lived in simple dwellings and produced comparatively few artefacts and tools. It's estimated that at least one hundred thousand Native Americans were living in Cuba on the eve of the first European voyages to the Americas.

The **Guanahatabey** were the first to arrive and were almost certainly living in Cuba by 3000 BC. These hunter-gatherers were based in what is now Pinar del Río, often living in cave systems such as the one in Viñales. The **Siboney** arrived later and lived as fishermen and farmers, but it wasn't until the arrival of the **Taíno**, around 1100 AD, the last of the Native American groups to settle in Cuba, that the cultural make-up of the islanders reached a level of significant sophistication. Settling predominantly in the eastern and central regions, they lived in small villages of circular thatched-roof huts known as *bohíos*; grew tobacco, cassava, *yuca* and cotton; produced pottery; and practised religion. Though it's been suggested that the Taíno enslaved some of the Siboney or drove them from their home territory, evidence suggests that they were a mostly peaceful people, unprepared for the conflict and brutality they were forced to face once the Spanish arrived.

The conquest

On October 27, 1492, **Christopher Columbus** landed on the northeastern coast of Cuba, probably in the natural harbour around which the town of Baracoa was later to emerge, though the exact spot where he first dropped anchor is hotly disputed. This first short expedition lasted only seven days, during which time Columbus marvelled at the Cuban landscape, briefly encountered the locals (who fled on seeing the new

3000 BC	2500 BC	1100 AD	1492
Guanahatabey hunter-gatherers settle in Cuba	The Siboney arrive from either modern-day Venezuela or Florida	The Taíno become the last Native American culture to settle in Cuba	Christopher Columbus disembarks on the northern coast of modern-day Holguín province

HATUEY: THE FIRST CUBAN REBEL

The most legendary Taíno in Cuba was **Hatuey**, a bold chief who, like many others, had been forced to flee from Hispaniola after the Spanish took over the island. He led the most concerted resistance effort against the advancing colonists. The Native Americans fought fiercely but their initial success was cut short by the Spanish capture of Hatuey. Before burning him at the stake the Spaniards offered him salvation if he would convert to Christianity, an offer met with a flat refusal as Hatuey declared that heaven would be the last place he'd want to spend eternity if it was full of Christians.

arrivals) and left a wooden cross now preserved in the Catedral Nuestra Señora de la Asunción in Baracoa.

Columbus made a second voyage of discovery in 1494 but the first colonial expedition did not begin until late 1509, when **Diego Velázquez** – a rich settler from neighbouring Hispaniola, and the man charged with the mission by the Spanish Crown – landed near Guantánamo Bay with three hundred men. By this time the Native Americans were wary of the possibility of an invasion, word having spread via refugees from already occupied Caribbean islands.

The Indigenous population did not last long once the Spanish arrived, and were either slaughtered or enslaved as the conquistadors worked their way west across Cuba. By the end of the sixteenth century, there was almost no trace of the original Cuban population left. Meanwhile, the colonizers had exhausted the small reserves of gold on the island, and interest in Cuba quickly died out as Spain expanded its territories in Central and South America, where there was far greater mineral wealth. However, as Spain consolidated its American empire, Cuba gained importance thanks to its location on the main route to and from Europe, with ports like **Havana** becoming the principal stopping-off points for ships carrying vast quantities of gold, silver and other riches across the Atlantic.

Colonization

By 1515 Velázquez had founded the first towns in Cuba, known as the **seven villas**: Baracoa, Santiago de Cuba, Bayamo, Puerto Príncipe (now Camagüey), Sancti Spíritus, Trinidad and San Cristóbal de la Habana. The population grew slowly, consisting mostly of Spanish immigrants, many from the Canary Islands, but also Italians and Portuguese. Numbers were also increased as early as the 1520s by the importation of enslaved Africans, transported to replace the dwindling Indigenous population. Still, by the seventeenth century, Havana, the largest city, had only a few hundred inhabitants.

Agriculture takes hold

Many of the early settlers created huge cattle ranches, but the economy came to be based heavily on more profitable **agricultural farming**. Cassava, tropical fruits, coffee and increasingly tobacco and sugar were among the chief export products on which the colony's trade with Spain depended. As Europe developed its sweet tooth, the

1509	1512	1514	1519
Diego Velázquez leads the first Spanish colonization and conquest expedition to Cuba	The Spanish kill Taíno chief Hatuey and establish Cuba's first village, Baracoa	The Spanish complete their conquest of Cuba	Havana is founded at its current location, having been moved from further south

Spanish Crown saw its potential selling power: by the early seventeenth century the **sugar** industry had been afforded preferential treatment, subsidized and exempted from duties, and an estimated fifty sugar mills constructed.

The commercial value of **tobacco**, on the other hand, was more immediate and needed no artificial stimulus. As tobacco farming expanded across the island it served to disperse the population further inland, in part because farmers sought to escape the fiscal grip of the colonial government, whose relatively scarce resources to regulate and tax the crop were concentrated in the towns and whose jurisdiction did not, effectively, apply to the Cuban interior.

Despite these developments the economic and political structure of Cuba remained relatively unchanged throughout the late sixteenth and seventeenth centuries. The island continued to be peripheral to the Spanish Empire and life evolved somewhat haphazardly, with contraband an integral part of the economy, removed from the attentions and concerns of the monarchy in Spain.

TOBACCO

Tobacco is one of the most intrinsic elements of Cuban culture. Not as vital to the economy as sugar (Cuba's most widely grown crop), tobacco farming and cigar smoking are nonetheless more closely linked with the history and spirit of this Caribbean country. When Columbus arrived, the Indigenous islanders had long been cultivating tobacco and smoking it in pipes that they inhaled through their nostrils rather than their mouths. When the leaf was first taken back to Europe it received a lukewarm reaction, but by the nineteenth century it had become one of the most profitable Spanish exports from its Caribbean territories. As early as the sixteenth century Cuban peasants had become tobacco farmers, known as *vegueros*, during an era in which sugar and cattle-ranching were the dominant forces in the economy.

As it became more profitable to grow tobacco, so the big landowners, most of them involved in the sugar industry, began to squeeze the *vegueros* off the land, forcing them either out of business altogether or into tenant farming. Many took their trade to the most remote parts of the country, out of reach of big business, and established small settlements from which many communities in places like Pinar del Río and northern Oriente now trace their roots. There nevertheless remained a conflict of interest which, to some extent, came to represent not just sugar versus tobacco but *criollos* versus *Península res*. The tensions that would eventually lead to the Cuban Wars of Independence first emerged between **criollo**, or Cuban-born, tobacco growers and the Spanish ruling elite, the **Península res**, who sought to control the industry through trade restrictions and price laws. Thus the tobacco trade has long been associated in Cuba with political activism. Today, when you visit a cigar factory and see the workers being read to from a newspaper or novel, you're witnessing the continuation of a tradition that began in the nineteenth century as a way of keeping the workers politically informed.

For an even broader perspective on the tobacco industry it's worth attending the annual **Festival del Habano**, which takes place principally in Havana and the Vuelta Abajo region (see page 175).

1526	1555	1607
Enslaved Africans are brought to the island to work on sugar plantations	French corsair Jacques de Sores ransacks Havana in an era of frequent pirate attacks on Cuba's Spanish settlements	Havana is formally established as the capital of Cuba

The impact of the Bourbons

When, at the beginning of the eighteenth century, the **Bourbon Dynasty** took over the throne in Spain, it sought to regain control of Spanish assets overseas, particularly in the Caribbean. The Bourbons stepped up their monopoly on trade, and in 1717 ordered that all tobacco be sold to commercial agents of the Crown sent from Spain, who added insult to injury by paying artificially low prices. Resentment from the Cuban-born tobacco farmers soon bubbled over into revolt among the growers. The subsequent **uprisings** were easily repressed by the colonial authorities, and even more restrictive measures were introduced in 1740. Discontent increased as profits for Cuban producers dropped, and the lines drawn between the *criollos* (those of Spanish descent but born in Cuba, who tended to be small-scale farmers or members of the emerging educated urban class), and the *Península res* (those born in Spain, who made up the ruling elite) became more pronounced.

The first half of the eighteenth century saw Cuban society become more sophisticated, as wealth on the island slowly increased. Advancements in the **cultural character** of Cuba were particularly notable during this era, partly as a result of encouragement from the Bourbons but also as a consequence of an emerging Cuban identity, unique from that of Spain. By the end of the century the colony had established its first printing press, newspaper, theatre and university.

The British occupation of Havana

Economic progress had been severely held back by the restrictive way in which Cuba, and indeed the whole Spanish Empire, was run by the Crown, forcing the colony to trade exclusively with Spain and draining the best part of the wealth away from the island into the hands of the colonial masters. This was to change in 1762 with the **British seizure of Havana**. Engaged in the Seven Years' War against Spain and France, the British sought to weaken the Spanish position by attacking Spain's possessions overseas. With Spanish attention focused in Europe, the British navy prepared a strike on the Cuban capital, control of which would strengthen their own position in the Caribbean and disrupt trade between Spain and its empire. After a six-week siege, Havana fell to the British, who immediately lifted the disabling trade restrictions and opened up new markets in North America and Europe.

Within eleven months Cuba was back in Spanish hands, exchanged with the British for Florida, but the impact of their short stay was enormous. A number of hitherto unobtainable and rarely seen products, including new sugar machinery and consumer goods, flowed into Cuba, brought by traders and merchants who were able to do business on the island for the first time. Cubans were able to sell their own produce to a wider market and at a greater profit and, even in such a short space of time, standards of living rose, particularly in the west where much of the increased commercial activity was focused. So much had changed by the time the Spanish regained control that to revert back to the previous system of tight controls would, the Bourbons realized, provoke fierce discontent among large and powerful sections of the population. Moreover, the new Spanish king, Charles III, was more disposed to progressive reforms than was his predecessor, and the increased output and efficiency of the colony did not pass him by. **Free trade** was therefore allowed to continue, albeit not completely unchecked, transforming the Cuban economy beyond recognition.

1713	1762	1763
The Bourbons assume power in Spain and introduce strict reforms in their colonies, centralizing power in Madrid	The English capture Havana, and occupy the city for eleven months	The English trade Havana for Florida; Spanish control of Cuba resumes

SLAVERY IN CUBA

Early Spanish colonial society was based on the **encomienda** system, whereby land and enslaved workers were distributed to settlers by the authorities. The proportion of enslaved people in Cuba up until the British occupation of 1762, however, was lower than almost anywhere else in the Caribbean. Most of the enslaved worked as servants in the cities and the smaller plantations. Unlike the English, who allowed their colonies to develop their own independent codes of practice, the Spanish applied the same laws governing slavery in Spain to their territories overseas. Though this did not necessarily mean that the Spanish master fed his enslaved workers any better or punished them less brutally, it did grant them a degree of legal status unheard of in other European colonies. Enslaved workers in the Spanish Empire could marry, own property and even buy their freedom, this last right known as *coartación*. By the eighteenth century there was a higher proportion of **free Black people** in Cuba than in any other Caribbean island of comparable size. Nevertheless, the life of an enslaved worker, particularly in the countryside, was a miserable existence, and for the Spanish Crown their rights were incidental at best. Spanish ordinances did as much to perpetuate slavery as they did to allow individuals their freedom. Laws were passed banning the enslaved from riding horses or from travelling long distances without their masters' permission, and preventing enslaved women from keeping their children.

As the size of the **enslaved population** swelled in the late eighteenth and early nineteenth centuries so the conditions of slavery, particularly in the sugar industry, worsened, fuelled by the plantation owners' insatiable appetites for profit. Some enslaved people in the countryside continued to work on coffee and tobacco farms, but most were involved in sugar production, where **conditions** were harshest. Where before the enslaved had lived in collections of small huts and even been allowed to work their own small plots of land, now they were crowded into barrack buildings and all available land was turned over to sugar cane. Floggings, beatings and the use of stocks were common forms of **punishment** for even minor insubordinations, and were often used as an incentive to work harder. The whip was in constant use, employed to keep enslaved workers on the job and to prevent them from falling asleep, most likely during the harvest season, when they could be made to work for eighteen hours of every day for months at a time.

A large proportion of the enslaved in Cuba during this period were West African Yoruba, a people with a strong military tradition, who launched frequent and fierce revolts against their oppressors. Uprisings were usually spontaneous, and frequently very violent, often involving the burning and breaking of machinery and the killing of whites. A minority of slave rebellions were highly organized and involved whites and free Black people.

The sugar boom

After 1762, sugar's profitability increased with the expansion of trade, causing the industry to begin operating on a much larger scale and marking a significant development in Cuban society. In 1776 the newly independent US was able to start trading directly with Cuban merchants, at the same time that the demand for sugar in Europe and the US increased.

In 1791 **revolution in Haiti** destroyed the sugar industry there and ended French control of one of its most valuable Caribbean possessions. Cuba soon

1790	1796	1812	1837
The first Cuban newspaper, the *Papel Periódico de La Habana*, is established	The steam engine is introduced to Cuba and employed in sugar production	The antislavery movement emerges in Cuba	Cuba's first railway begins operating

took advantage of this and became the largest producer of sugar in the region. Thousands of French sugar plantation owners and coffee growers fled and settled in Cuba, bringing with them their superior knowledge of sugar production. These developments – combined with scientific advances in the sugar industry and improved transportation routes on the island – transformed the face of Cuban society. With ever-increasing portions of the land taken over for the planting of sugar cane, labour, still the most important component in the production of sugar, was needed on a vast scale. In the 1820s some sixty thousand **people** were enslaved and transported to the island, with numbers exceeding 350,000 during the first half of the nineteenth century.

Reform versus independence

In the final decade of the eighteenth century and the first few decades of the nineteenth, a number of new cultural and political institutions emerged, alongside new scientific developments, all aimed specifically at improving the lives of Cubans. Though most of these changes affected only a small number of citizens, they formed the roots of a **national identity**, a conception of Cuba as a country with its own culture, its own people and its own needs, separate from those of the Spanish minority ruling class.

Slave rebellions became more common as each decade of the nineteenth century passed, symptomatic of an increasingly divided society, one which pitted *criollos* against *Península res*, black against white, and the less developed eastern half of the country against the more economically and politically powerful west. The sugar boom had caused Cuban society to become more stratified, creating sharper lines between the landed elite, who had benefited most from the sugar revolution, and the smaller landowners, petit bourgeoisie and free Black people who had become increasingly marginalized by the dominance of large-scale sugar production.

The American Revolution of 1776 proved to be a precursor to the Wars of Independence that swept across mainland Spanish America during the initial decades of the nineteenth century. However, Cuba's own bid for self-rule was held up, partly by a period of economic prosperity, but also because most *criollos* identified more closely with the Spanish than with the enslaved Black population who, by the start of the nineteenth century, formed a larger part of the total population than in any other colony. *Criollo* calls for reform were tempered by a fear of the enslaved people gaining any influence or power. The economy in Cuba relied more heavily on slavery than any of the South American states, with the livelihood of *criollos* and *Península res* alike dependent on its continued existence.

Nevertheless, a **reformist movement** – albeit fragmented – did emerge. There were calls, predominantly from big businessmen and well-to-do trade merchants, for fiscal reform within Spanish rule; separatists who wanted total independence; and another group still that formed an **annexationist movement** whose goal was to become part of the US, the biggest single market for Cuban sugar. There was growing support for this within the US, too, where it was felt that Cuba held tremendous strategic importance.

With the wealthier *criollos* and the *Península res* unwilling to push for all-out independence, the separatist cause was taken up most fervently by *criollos* of modest

1868	1878	1886	1895
The First War of Independence begins	The Pact of Zanjón ends the First War of Independence	Slavery is abolished	The Second War of Independence commences; José Martí is killed in combat

social origins and by free Black people. Their agenda became not just independence but social justice and, most importantly, the abolition of slavery. As the reformist movement became more radical, Spanish fear of revolution intensified; following slave rebellions in Matanzas and elsewhere in the country in the early 1840s, the colonial government reacted with a brutal campaign of repression known as **La Escalera** (the ladder), which involved tying those accused of conspiracy to a ladder and whipping them. In an atmosphere of hysteria fuelled by the fear that a nationwide slave uprising was imminent, the Spanish authorities killed hundreds of enslaved and free Black suspects and arrested thousands more. At the same time, the military presence on the island grew as soldiers were sent over from Spain, and the governor's power was increased to allow repression of even the slightest sign of rebellion. The reform movement and the abolition of slavery became inextricably linked, and this fusion of ideas was embraced by reformers themselves. In 1865 the **Partido Reformista** (Reformist Party) was founded by a group of *criollo* planters, providing the most coherent expression yet of the desire for change. Among their demands were a call for Cuban representation in the Spanish parliament and equal legal status for *criollos* and *Peninsulares*.

The Ten Years' War

The life of the Reformist Party proved to be a short one. Having failed to obtain a single concession from the Spanish government, it dissolved in 1867, while the reform movement as a whole suffered further blows as a new reactionary Spanish government issued a wave of repressive measures, including banning political meetings and censoring the press. Meanwhile, pro-independence groups were gaining momentum in the east, where the proportion of *criollos* to *Peninsulares* was twice that in the west.

From 1866 onwards, a group of landowners, headed by **Carlos Manuel de Céspedes**, began to plot a revolution; but it had got no further than the planning stage when the colonial authorities learned of it and sent troops to arrest the conspirators. Pre-empting his own arrest on October 10, 1868, Céspedes freed the enslaved people working at his sugar mill, La Demajagua, near Manzanillo, effectively instigating the **Ten Years' War**, the first Cuban War of Independence. The size of the revolutionary force grew quickly as other landowners freed their enslaved people, and soon numbered around 1500 men. Bayamo was the first city to fall to the rebels and briefly became the headquarters of a revolutionary government. Their manifesto included promises of free trade, universal male suffrage (though this meant whites only) and the "gradual" abolition of slavery.

Support for the cause spread quickly across eastern and central parts of the country, as two of the great heroes of the Wars of Independence, the mulatto **Antonio Maceo** and the Dominican **Máximo Gómez**, emerged as military leaders. A much smaller insurgency movement emerged in the west, where, on the whole, the landowners remained on the side of the colonial authorities. In Havana, a teenaged **José Martí** (see page 105) was arrested and exiled after challenging Spanish rule in the newspaper *Patria Libre*. Then, in 1874, Céspedes was killed in battle and the revolutionary movement began to flounder, becoming increasingly fragmented as divisions between

1898	1899	1901
The scuppering of the US battleship *Maine* in Havana harbour triggers the start of the Spanish–American War	Spain signs the Treaty of Paris and officially relinquishes control of Cuba; the US begins its military occupation	The Cuban Constitution is ratified, but includes the Platt Amendment

criollos and the peasants and ex-enslaved people who fought on the same side fermented distrust.

Seizing on this instability, the Spanish offered what appeared to be a compromise. The **Pact of Zanjón** was signed on February 10, 1878, and included a number of concessions on the part of the Spanish, such as increased political representation for the *criollos*. However, sections of the rebel army, led by Maceo, refused to accept the pact, asserting that none of the original demands of the rebels had been met. In 1879 this small group of rebels reignited the conflict in what became known as the **Guerra Chiquita**, the Small War. It petered out by 1880, and Maceo (along with José Martí and others) was forced into exile.

The Second War of Independence

Over the course of the next fifteen years, the reformists – among them ex-rebels – became increasingly dismayed by the Spanish government's failure to fulfil the promises made at Zanjón. Though the first phase of the **abolition of slavery** in 1880 seemed to suggest that genuine changes had been achieved, this development proved to be something of a false dawn. Slavery was replaced with the apprentice system, whereby former enslaved workers were forced to work for their former owners, albeit for a small wage. It was not until 1886 that slavery was entirely abolished, while in 1890, when universal suffrage was declared in Spain, Cuba was excluded.

These years saw the independence movement build strength from outside Cuba, particularly in the US. From his base in New York, Martí worked tirelessly, visiting various Latin American countries trying to gain momentum for the idea of an independent Cuba, appealing to notions of Latin American solidarity. In 1892 he founded the **Partido Revolucionario Cubano**, or Cuban Revolutionary Party (PRC), aiming to unite the disjointed exile community and the divided independence movement on the island.

On February 24, 1895, small groups in contact with the PRC mounted armed insurrections across Cuba, beginning the **Second War of Independence**. Then, on April 1, Maceo landed in Oriente, followed a fortnight later by Martí and Gómez, who mobilized a liberation force of around six thousand Cubans. In May of the same year at Dos Ríos, Martí was killed in his first battle. Undeterred, the revolutionaries fought their way across the country; by 1897, almost the entire country (save for a few heavily garrisoned towns and cities) was under rebel control.

Riots in Havana gave the US the excuse they had been waiting for to send in the warship **Maine**, ostensibly to protect US citizens in the Cuban capital. On February 15, 1898, the *Maine* blew up in Havana harbour, killing 258 people; the US accused the Spanish of sabotage and so began the **Spanish–American War**. Whether the US blew up its own ship in order to justify its intervention in the War of Independence has been disputed ever since, but whatever the true cause of the explosion, it was the pretext the US needed to enter the war. Many Cuban nationalists, believing that victory was already in their grasp, were hostile to US involvement and suspicious of its intentions, fearing an imperial-style takeover. Attempting to allay these fears, the US prepared the **Teller Amendment**, declaring that they did not intend to exercise any political power in Cuba once the war was over, their sole aim being to free the country from the

1902	1903	1906
Tomás Estrada Palma becomes the first President of the new Republic of Cuba	The lease giving the US control over Guantánamo Bay naval base is signed	US military intervention in Cuba reinstated in line with the Platt Amendment, and lasts three years

colonial grip of Spain. Despite these promises, when the **Spanish surrendered** on July 17, 1898, Cuban troops were prevented by US forces from entering Santiago, where the victory ceremony took place.

The pseudo-republic

On December 10, 1898, the Spanish signed the **Treaty of Paris**, thereby handing control of Cuba, as well as Puerto Rico and the Philippines, to the US. Political power on the island lay in the hands of **General John Brooke**, who maintained a strong military force in Cuba while the US government decided what to do with the island they had coveted for so long. The voices of protest in Cuba were loud and numerous enough to convince them that annexation would be a mistake, so they opted for the next best alternative. In 1901 Cuba adopted a new constitution, devised in Washington without any Cuban consultation, which included the **Platt Amendment**, declaring that the US had the right to intervene in Cuban affairs should the independence of the country come under threat – an eventuality open to endless interpretation. The intention to keep Cuba on a short leash was made even clearer when, at the same time, a **US naval base** was established at Guantánamo Bay. On May 20, 1902, under these terms, Cuba was declared a **republic** and Tomás Estrada Palma became the first elected Cuban president.

With the economy in ruins following the war, **US investors** were able to buy up large stakes of land and business relatively cheaply. Soon three-quarters of the sugar industry was controlled by US interests, and few branches of the economy lay exclusively in Cuban hands as the North Americans invested in cigar factories, railroads, the telephone system, electricity, tourism and other industries.

The Machado era and the Depression

The first two decades of the pseudo-republic saw four corrupt Cuban presidents come and go and the US intervene on a number of occasions, either installing a governor or sending in troops. In 1925 **Gerardo Machado** was elected on the back of a series of promises he had made to clean up government. Though initially successful – he was particularly popular for his defiance of US involvement in Cuban politics – his refusal to tolerate any opposition wrecked any legitimate efforts he may have made to improve the running of the country. In 1925, strikes by sugar mill and railroad workers led by **Julio Antonio Mella**, founder of the **Partido Comunista Cubano** (Cuban Communist Party), led to the assassinations of a host of political leaders. In 1928 Machado changed the constitution, extending his term in office and effectively establishing a dictatorship.

The **global economic crisis** that followed the Wall Street Crash in 1929 caused more widespread discontent, and opposition became increasingly radical. Machado ruthlessly set about trying to wipe out all opposition in a bloody and repressive campaign. Fearing a loss of influence, the US sent in an ambassador, **Sumner Welles**, with instructions to get rid of Machado and prevent a popular uprising. As Welles set about negotiating a withdrawal of the Machado administration, a general strike across the country in late 1933, together with the loss of the army's support, which had long played an active role in informal Cuban politics, convinced the dictator that

1924	1929	1933
Gerardo Machado begins his first presidential term	Having altered the constitution, Machado begins a second term, his presidency effectively becoming a dictatorship	Machado's dictatorship is overthrown, Fulgencio Batista leads a military revolt and Ramón Grau takes up the presidency

remaining in power was futile and he fled the country. Amid the chaos that followed emerged a man who was to profoundly shape the destiny of Cuba over the following decades.

The rise of Fulgencio Batista

A provisional government led by Carlos Manuel de Céspedes y Quesada filled the political vacuum left by Machado, but lasted only a few weeks. Meanwhile, a young sergeant, **Fulgencio Batista**, staged a coup within the army and replaced most of the officers with men loyal to him. Using his powerful military position, he installed **Ramón Grau San Martín** as president, who went on to attempt to nationalize electricity, which was owned by a US company, and introduce progressive reforms for workers. This was too much for US President Franklin Roosevelt, who accused Grau of being a communist and refused to recognize his regime. Not wanting to antagonize the US, Batista deposed Grau and replaced him in January 1934 with **Carlos Mendieta**. Batista then continued to prop up a series of Cuban presidents until in 1940 he was himself elected.

Some of Batista's policies during his earlier years of power were met with widespread support and, despite the backing he received from the US, he was no puppet. In 1934 he presided over the dissolution of the Platt Amendment, which was replaced with a new agreement endowing Cuba with an unprecedented degree of real independence. In a move designed to harmonize some of the political groupings in Cuba and appease past opponents, in 1937 Batista released all political prisoners, while using the army to institute **health and education programmes** in the countryside and among the urban poor. By the time he lost power in 1944, ironically to Ramón Grau, Cuba was a more independent and socially just country than it had been at any other time during the pseudo-republic.

Grau showed none of the reformist tendencies that he had demonstrated during his previous short term in office and was replaced in 1948, after proving himself no less corrupt than any of his predecessors. **Carlos Prío Socarrás**, under whom very little changed, led the country until 1952 when Batista, who had left the country after his defeat in 1944, returned to fight another election. Two days before the election was to take place, Batista, fearing failure, staged a **military coup** on March 10 and seized control of the country. He subsequently abolished the constitution and went on to establish a dictatorship bearing little – if any – resemblance to his previous term as Cuban leader. Fronting a regime characterized principally by violent **repression**, **corruption** and self-indulgent **decadence**, Batista seemed to have lost any zeal he once had for social change and improvement. Organized crime became ingrained in Cuban life, particularly in Havana, where notorious American gangster Meyer Lansky controlled much of the gambling industry. During these years living conditions for the average Cuban worsened as investment in social welfare decreased.

Fidel Castro and the revolutionary movement

Among the candidates for congress in the 1952 election was **Fidel Castro**, a young lawyer who had seen his political ambitions dashed when Batista seized power for himself. Effectively frozen out of constitutional politics by Batista's intolerance of organized opposition, Castro and around 125 others, a year after the military

1934	1940	1944	1952
Batista deposes Grau and appoints Carlos Mendieta as president	A new constitution is drafted and Batista becomes president	Ramón Grau is elected president	Batista seizes the presidency by means of a military coup

CUBA BEFORE CASTRO

On the eve of the Revolution, Cuba was among the most **prosperous** Latin American countries. Culturally and economically it had become intricately tied to the US, importing most of its manufactured goods from across the Florida Straits, including cars, clothes and electrical equipment – even the telephone system was North American – while the US benefited from cheap sugar, the reward for massive investment in the agricultural industry. The American **Mafia** had also gained a strong foothold in the country, predominantly in Havana, where it controlled much of the tourist industry, including the cabarets, casinos and many of the hotels. The capital was also home to a significant-sized middle class. Outside the cities, however, the rural population lived in abject **poverty**, with no running water, electricity, healthcare or education, and hunger was not uncommon. Peasant wages were desperately low and those working on sugar farms would only draw a wage for a few months of seasonal work a year.

coup, on July 26, 1953, attacked an army barracks at **Moncada** in Santiago de Cuba in a bid to topple the regime. Castro regarded the attack "as a gesture which will set an example for the people of Cuba". The attack failed miserably and those who weren't shot fled into the mountains, where they were soon caught. Castro would certainly have been shot had his captors taken him back to the barracks, but a sympathetic police sergeant kept him in the relative safety of the police jail. A trial followed in which Castro defended himself and, in his summing-up, uttered the now immortal words, "Condemn me if you will. History will absolve me." He was sentenced to fifteen years' imprisonment but had served fewer than three when Batista, feeling confident and complacent, released him, along with the other rebels, and he went into **exile**.

Now based in Mexico, Castro set about organizing a revolutionary force to take back to Cuba; among his recruits was an Argentinean doctor named **Ernesto "Che" Guevara**. They called themselves the **Movimiento 26 de Julio**, the 26th of July Movement (often shortened to **M-26-7**), after the date of the attack at Moncada. In late November 1956 Castro, Guevara and around eighty other revolutionaries set sail for Cuba in a large yacht called the *Granma*. Landing in the east at Playa Coloradas, in what is today Granma province, they were immediately attacked and suffered heavy casualties, but the dozen or so who survived headed directly for the Sierra Maestra, where they wasted no time in building up support for the cause among the local peasantry and enlisting new recruits into their army. Waging a war based on **guerrilla tactics**, the rebels were able to gain the upper hand against Batista's larger and better-equipped forces.

As the war was being fought out in the countryside, the base of support for the Revolution grew wider and wider, and an insurrectionary movement already established in the cities began a campaign of sabotage aimed at disabling the state apparatus. By the end of 1958, the majority of Cubans had sided with the rebels and the ranks of the revolutionary army had swelled. The US, sensing they were backing a lost cause, had withdrawn military support for Batista, and there were **revolts within the army**. Realizing that he no longer exercised any authority, on January 1, 1959, Batista escaped on a plane bound for the Dominican Republic. The army almost immediately surrendered to the rebels, and Fidel Castro, who had been fighting in the east, began a

1953	**1956**	**1959**
Fidel Castro and a band of rebels attack the Moncada military barracks in a failed attempt to start a revolution	Castro and 82 others disembark from the yacht *Granma* in eastern Cuba to begin a guerrilla war against Batista's regime	The revolutionary war is won on January 1, Batista having fled the country on New Year's Eve

victory march across the country, arriving in Havana seven days later on January 8, 1959.

The Cuban Revolution: the first decade

Though the Revolutionary War ended in 1959, this date marks only the beginning of what in Cuba is referred to as the Revolution. The new government appointed as its president Manuel Urrutia, but the real power lay in the hands of Fidel Castro, who, within a few months of the revolutionary triumph, took over as prime minister.

Early reforms

Fidel Castro's new government began to implement a vast programme of social and political transformation, passing more than 1500 laws in its first year. This tidal wave of change was felt most keenly in the countryside, with the intellectual and economic empowerment of rural peasants at the heart of the Revolution's objectives. The first **Agrarian Reform Law** of May 1959 established the **Agrarian Reform Institute** (INRA), which soon became a kind of government for the countryside, administering most of the rural reform programmes, including new health and educational facilities, housing developments and road construction, as well as redistribution of much of the land into the hands of the rural population and the state. By 1961 over forty percent of Cuba's farmland had been expropriated and reorganized along these lines. In 1962, in a push to eradicate **illiteracy**, the government sent more than 250,000 teachers, volunteers and schoolchildren into the countryside to teach reading and writing to the peasants. By the end of 1962 illiteracy had been slashed from 23.6 percent to 3.9 percent.

Free education for all was another key revolutionary objective, as private schools were nationalized and education until the sixth grade made compulsory, with a new programme of learning based on anti-imperialist Marxist ideology implemented. Universities proliferated, as numbers of teachers and schools multiplied. **Health**, too, saw great gains in the early years of the Revolution. A free national health service was created, and new hospitals and health centres were built, most notably in rural areas where institutional healthcare had been all but non-existent. A new emphasis was put on preventive medicine and care in the community, while there was also investment in medical research.

Opposition and emigration

While these very real gains for large sections of the Cuban population ensured continued popular support for the new regime, not everyone was happy, and the Revolution was not without its victims in these early years. Many of those who had served under Batista, from government officials to army officers, were tried, and – with little regard for their legal rights – executed, sometimes for ideological crimes. Many moderates and liberals became increasingly **disillusioned** and isolated from the political process. Under Castro, the government had little sympathy for the constitutional framework in which the liberals felt it must operate and, appealing to what it regarded as the higher ideals of social justice and the interests of the collective over the individual, swept much of the legal machinery aside in its drive to eliminate opponents of the Revolution and carry out reforms. As the decade wore on, the regime became

1961	**1962**	**1965**
A counter-revolutionary contingent attack Castro's forces at the Bay of Pigs and are defeated in 72 hours; the US declare a trade embargo on Cuba	The US and Soviet Union are brought to the brink of nuclear conflict in the Cuban Missile Crisis	The Cuban Communist Party (PCC) is created

increasingly intolerant of dissenting voices, which were characterized as counter-revolutionary. By the end of the 1960s there are estimated to have been over twenty thousand **political prisoners** in Cuban jails. Gay people, whose sexuality was deemed to be a product of capitalist society, were also persecuted throughout the 1960s and 1970s, with many homosexuals imprisoned and placed on "reform" programmes.

For the first few years after the rebel triumph, as Cuban-US relations soured and the Revolution radicalized, swathes of the upper and middle classes – among them landowners, doctors, lawyers and other professionals – sought refuge overseas, predominantly in the US. Between 1960 and 1962 around 200,000 **emigrants**, most of them white, left Cuba, forming large exile communities, especially in **Miami**, and setting up powerful anti-Castro organizations, intent on overthrowing Castro and returning to Cuba.

Cuba enters the Cold War

As huge sectors of Cuban industry, much of it US-owned, were **nationalized**, Washington retaliated by freezing all purchases of Cuban sugar, restricting exports to the island and then, in 1961, breaking off diplomatic relations. Counter-revolutionary forces within Cuba, some mounting terrorist campaigns in the cities, received US backing. Then, with the blessing and backing of President John F. Kennedy, an invasion was prepared. On April 17, 1961, a military force of Cuban exiles, trained and equipped in the US, landed at the **Bay of Pigs** in southern Matanzas. The revolutionaries were ready for them and the whole operation ended in failure within 72 hours (see page 224).

It was not until December 1961 that Fidel Castro declared himself a **Marxist–Leninist**. Whether opportunistic or, as Castro himself declared, a statement of beliefs he had always held, there was no doubt whose support he coveted at the time of his declaration, and the **Soviet Union** was only too happy to enter a pact with a close neighbour of its bitter Cold War adversary. The Soviets agreed to buy Cuban sugar at artificially high prices while selling them petroleum at well below its market value. Then, in 1962, on Castro's request, the Soviets installed over forty **missiles** on the island. Angered by this belligerent move, Kennedy declared an embargo on any military weapons entering Cuba. Soviet Premier **Nikita Khrushchev** ignored it, and Soviet ships loaded with more weapons made their way across the Atlantic. Neither side appeared to be backing down and nuclear weapons were prepared for launch in the US. A six-day stalemate followed, after which a deal was finally struck and the world breathed a collective sigh of relief – the **Cuban Missile Crisis** had passed. Khrushchev agreed to withdraw Soviet weapons from Cuba on the condition that the US would not invade the island. This triggered the tightening of the trade embargo by the US.

Economic policy in the 1960s

Reducing Cuba's dependence on sugar production was one of the central **economic policies** of the new Cuban government, and efforts were made to expand and diversify industry. However, at times revolutionary ideals outweighed realistic policy and planning. The **mass exodus of professionals** during the early years of the decade made the transition from an essentially monocultural capitalist economy to a more diverse,

1967	1976	1980
Che Guevara is killed in Bolivia	The socialist Cuban Constitution is promulgated	Castro opens the port at Mariel to anyone wanting to leave the country; an exodus of 125,000 Cubans follows

THE POLITICS OF A ONE-PARTY STATE

Though it had several predecessors, the **Partido Comunista Cubano** or Cuban Communist Party (PCC) – the only political party in post-Revolution Cuba – was not founded until 1965, six years after Fidel Castro's victory, and did not hold its first Congress until 1975. The following year a new constitution was drawn up and approved. Castro's position as head of state became constitutionalized, thus doing away with the last vestiges of democracy. Attempts were made, on the other hand, to decentralize power by introducing an extensive system of **local government**. However, as agents of central government these local assemblies had little or no real independence.

Countless **mass organizations** provide, in theory, further avenues for grievances and the raising of issues. Widespread membership of the Committees for the Defence of the Revolution (CDR), the Union of Young Communists (UJC) and the Federation of Cuban Women (FMC), among other bodies, is portrayed by the government as an expression of popular support for the Revolution and its ideals. Local branches of these organizations hear local grievances and representatives pass them up to elected members at the legislative assembly. They also spearhead local campaigns, like organizing blood donation, arranging street parties and rounding up local truants. For detractors of the government, however, these organizations are the watchdogs of the regime, ensuring that at every level people are behaving as good citizens.

industrialized yet highly centralized one extremely problematic. Until more were trained, there were simply not enough workers with the skills and experience necessary to realize such ambitious plans. Furthermore, the impact of the US embargo had been severely underestimated: the Americans had supplied machinery, raw materials and manufactured goods easily, quickly and inexpensively and, despite subsidies from the Soviet Union, the greater distances involved and less sophisticated economy of Cuba's new suppliers could not fill the hole. Following a significant drop in agricultural output, **rationing** was introduced in 1962. Attempts to produce the type of industrial goods and machinery that had previously been imported had largely failed and, following Castro's visit to the Soviet Union in 1964, during which the Russians promised to purchase 24 million tonnes of sugar over the next five years, the focus for the economy shifted back to **sugar**. Ambitious targets were set for each harvest, none more so than in 1970, when Castro declared that Cuba would produce ten million tonnes of sugar. This blind optimism was to prove disastrous, as the impossible production targets were not met, while other areas of the economy suffered from neglect and underinvestment, leaving Cuba even more dependent on sugar than it had been prior to the Revolution.

Shifting sands: the 1970s and 1980s

The 1970s saw a complete reappraisal of **economic policy** and planning. A more realistic programme replaced the heady idealism of the 1960s, striking a more even balance between the role of the state, which still controlled heavy industry and the major pillars of the economy, and the private sector, which was expanded. With

1989	1990
The Soviet Union scales back its trade with Cuba and reduces its subsidies to the country	Castro announces a series of austerity measures as part of the Special Period

rises in the price of sugar on the world market in the first half of the decade and increased Soviet assistance, there were tangible advances in the country's economic performance. The policy changes were carried on into the next decade as the economy continued to make modest improvements.

As more private enterprise was permitted, Castro became alarmed at the number of people giving up their state jobs, and concluded that he had made a mistake. In 1986 he issued his **Rectification of Errors and Negative Tendencies** and the economy returned to centralization. With increasing sums being ploughed into defence, the economy survived only through heavy Soviet support.

The Special Period: the 1990s

The **collapse of the Soviet bloc** and subsequently the Soviet Union itself between 1989 and 1991 led to a loss of over eighty percent of Cuba's trade. In 1990, as the country stumbled into an era of extreme shortages, Fidel Castro declared, euphemistically, the beginning of the **Special Period in Times of Peace**, usually referred to simply as the Special Period (*Periodo Especial*). Food rationing became stricter, timed power cuts frequent and public transport deteriorated dramatically as the country lost almost all of its fuel imports. At the risk of undermining the Revolution's ideological basis, in August 1993, the **US dollar** was declared legal tender and the floodgates to investment from international companies were opened, most notably in the tourist and mining industries. All but the most basic products and services were sold in dollars, as the state tried to acquire hard currency through restaurants, hotels, supermarkets and other dollar stores. Small-scale **private enterprise** was also legalized as the face of modern-day Cuba began to take shape. Private farmers' markets became the norm, small home-based restaurants known as paladars emerged, and house owners began renting out their bedrooms to tourists.

Seizing on this moment of weakness, the US government tightened up the trade embargo even further in 1992. Thousands of Cubans risked their lives trying to escape the country across the Florida Straits in makeshift craft, and the Cuban exile

---

THE MARIEL BOATLIFT

In March 1980, several Cubans rammed the gates of the Peruvian embassy in Havana seeking asylum. With the Peruvian authorities reluctant to hand over the perpetrators, Castro promptly removed police protection from the grounds and within 48 hours over 10,000 **asylum seekers** had crammed themselves inside the gates. Responding to this obvious build-up of tension, and seeking to rid the island of potential agitators, Castro announced that the port at Mariel bay, 25km west of Havana, would be open to anyone who wished to leave for the US. In what became known as the **Mariel Boatlift**, hundreds of small vessels crossed the straits from Miami to fetch waiting Cubans. Ever the opportunist, Castro seized on the exodus to rid Cuba of large numbers of its criminals and mental patients, releasing them from prisons and institutions to swell the ranks of exiles. Some 125,000 Cubans fled the island between April and October of 1980; the Carter administration and Castro finally agreed to end the exodus on October 31, 1980.

1996	1998	2006
The US trade embargo on Cuba is tightened under the terms of the Helms–Burton Law	Pope John Paul II visits Cuba	Fidel Castro is taken seriously ill and his brother Raúl Castro assumes temporary presidential responsibilities

community in Miami, by now consisting of a number of well-organized and powerful political groups, rubbed its hands with glee, anticipating the imminent collapse of the Revolution and the fall of Fidel Castro.

Tales of survival from the era are by turns grotesque, comic and heroic. While stories of vendors replacing pizza cheese with melted condoms and CDR meetings called with the express purpose of ordering people to stop dining on the neighbourhood cats and dogs may be urban myths, they nonetheless represent the very desperate living conditions during the Special Period.

Emerging from crisis

As Cuba entered the new millennium it appeared to have weathered the worst of the economic storm that threatened to destroy the regime in the 1990s. However, chronic **shortages** of basic foodstuffs, household goods and medicines remained, while the advent of private enterprise allowed more distinct class-based divisions to creep back into society, still apparent today. But new **international allies** emerged, most notably Venezuela and, as left-wing governments came into power all over South and Central America, other Latin American states including Bolivia, Ecuador and Nicaragua, all then diplomatically and politically closer to Cuba than to the US. The special relationship with Venezuela brought increased investment and aid, crucially in the supply of oil to the island. Despite recent instability within its own borders, in 2019 Venezuela represented $2.2 billion of Cuba's annual two-way trade and supplied it with some 115,000 barrels of oil per day. Some of this is financed by the doctors-for-oil programme that sees around 20,000 Cuban doctors and teachers working in Venezuela under an exchange initiative.

Since the 2000s there has also been a significant increase in investment from Canada, Brazil, India and especially China. The latter is now Cuba's largest trading partner, having overtaken Venezuela, and has invested over US$1 billion in Cuba's nickel industry, as well as substantial amounts in tourism and public transport.

Raúl Castro and the new Cuba

In July 2006, with Fidel Castro convalescing after intestinal surgery, his younger brother **Raúl Castro** took over his responsibilities. In February 2008, having acted as president for eighteen months, Raúl formally took over the presidency. In charge of the military since 1959, Raúl Castro had a reputation as a ruthless military mastermind, a dour man compared with his charismatic older brother, portrayed as a contradictory mixture of hardliner and pragmatist. However, Raúl Castro's presidency, which lasted from 2006–2018, was characterized as much as anything by limited but significant **reforms** that reduced centralization and bureaucracy and increased the roles and freedoms of the private sector. Very early on in his presidency, restrictions were lifted on the private purchase of electrical consumer goods, including computers, DVD players and mobile phones. Farmers were allowed to cultivate unused state-owned land for personal profit, but more importantly to increase productivity. Cubans were permitted to buy and sell houses, and no longer needed state permission to leave the country, just a passport.

2008	2012
Raúl Castro officially becomes Cuban president and embarks on a series of liberalizing economic reforms	In October, Hurricane Sandy hits eastern Cuba; eleven people lose their lives, and 200,000 buildings are damaged

In September 2010 Raúl Castro and his government announced the biggest **reduction to the size of the state** since the Revolution, determining that one million state-sector jobs would be cut. The effects remain tangible all over Cuba. Many industries, particularly small-scale businesses, were turned over to the private sector, making bosses and managers owners overnight. Hairdressers, driving instructors, art restorers and other small workplaces became legitimate private businesses. Workers were encouraged to set up their own businesses in one of the many professions given legal status in the private sector, from travel agents and roofers to manicurists and carpenters, and Cubans now habitually employ other Cubans who are not their relatives for the first time since the Revolution.

A new era of trade and foreign relations

In recent years Cuba has become increasingly open to foreign business and trade, more so than at any time in its revolutionary history. The foreign investment law of 2014, for the first time since the Revolution, permitted 100 percent foreign ownership investment in the country, while a port and business zone in Mariel, outside Havana, was built especially for foreign business investment opportunities. At national level the burgeoning private-enterprise sector has brought noticeable changes to the commercial landscape, where privately owned business is flourishing in Havana and other large cities, allowing money to percolate through the economy. There are also gradual improvements being made to the country's infrastructure, such as investment in public transport.

Changes on the international stage have proved equally significant. During the second term of US President Obama's office there was a definite **thawing in relations** between the two countries. Obama had long been an advocate of improving the relationship between Cuba and the US and in July 2015 the US embassy finally reopened, marking the formal restoration of diplomatic ties. In a nicely choreographed piece of synchronicity, at the reopening ceremony held in August that year the flag was raised by the same three US marines who had presided over its lowering in 1961.

In March 2016 Obama made a well-publicized state visit to Cuba. His speech at the Gran Teatro in Havana emphasized the need for the two countries to put the Cold War past to rest and move forward. While he was careful to keep references to infringements of human rights opaque, and made conciliatory remarks about the social and political problems in the US about which Raúl Castro has in turn expressed concerns, he made it clear that the US was in favour of Cuba moving towards a Western-style democracy.

Post-Castro Cuba

On 25 November 2016, the indefatigable and iconic Cuban leader, Fidel Castro, died at the age of 90. His body lay in state for two days before he made the final journey (the reverse of his 1959 victory march from Santiago de Cuba to Havana) through streets and roads lined with supporters in a camouflage green hearse to the Santa Ifigenia Cemetery in Santiago where he was buried. It

2013	2016
Raúl Castro declares he will stand down at the end of his second term in 2018	Raúl Castro welcomes US President Obama on a state visit; the first by a sitting US president for 88 years. Fidel Castro dies on 25 November; he has a state funeral amid national mourning

marked the end of an era for Cuba, but as the presidency had been ceded to his brother a decade before, political and socially there was none of the instability that foreign Cuban watchers had predicted decades before.

Cuban politics continues to evolve according to its own agenda rather than that of any other country. In 2018 Raúl Castro stepped down as President and **Miguel Díaz-Canel** was selected as the only candidate to succeed him; he was sworn in the same year. Formerly Cuba's vice president, Díaz-Canel is largely seen as a safe pair of hands who will continue the path upon which Raúl Castro has set the country. For a time, Raúl Castro remained at the heart of government, occupying the powerful positions of First Secretary of the Communist Party of Cuba and the commander-in-chief of the Cuban Revolutionary Armed Forces.

Before retiring and stepping down as head of Cuba's Communist Party in April 2021, Raúl Castro was instrumental in the drafting of the **new Cuban constitution**, the approval of which was put to a referendum vote in February 2019. Turnout in this historic ballot was large – with 81 percent of those eligible voting – and the results were overwhelmingly in favour of passing the constitution. Nevertheless, the proposed constitution has been highly divisive. In an unprecedented show of opposition the conservative forces of the Methodist, Baptist and Pentecostal churches banded together to campaign against the new constitution, which they feared could open the door to gay marriage. Díaz-Canel has openly declared himself in favour of same-sex marriage, however he backed down in response to the backlash and amended the constitution's wording from stating that marriage was a union "between two people". In effect, the government sidestepped the issue, which will now be dealt with under family law instead.

The lobbying success of the church marks a significant achievement by an orchestrated right-wing movement in Cuba. In common with the rest of the Americas – both North and Latin – right-wing Evangelism is on the rise and playing an increasing role in influencing populist politics. Meanwhile, despite the new constitution continuing to enshrine the one-party state, there are some important changes which are a departure from the past. There is now a five-year, two-term imposition on the presidency, and candidates must be 60 or younger when first elected. Private ownership of businesses is now also recognized. In addition, 2022 will see Cubans vote in a referendum on the Family Code, which includes a gender-neutral definition of marriage, thus allowing the possibility of same-sex marriage. The Code also seeks to strengthen women's rights through reinforcing sexual and reproductive rights.

Developments elsewhere in society are equally apparent: greater access to the internet, international news and social media is reflective of the state loosening its stranglehold on freedom of information. And, while the plight of political prisoners still remains a concern for international human rights organizations, in 2015 the state did release several dozen political prisoners as part of a deal between the US and Cuba. However, fundamental questions remain, not least over the lack of social, political and artistic freedom. In July 2018 President Díaz-Canel signed the contentious **Decree 349**, which prohibited all musicians, artists and performers from operating in public or private spaces without prior approval from the Ministry of Culture. With little opportunity to demonstrate or organize political opposition, feelings of powerlessness and disenfranchisement remain ever-present.

2017	**2018**
Hurricane Irma battered Cuba's north central coast, killing ten people and affecting 200,000 households.	Miguel Díaz-Canel becomes President of the Council of State and the Council of Ministers on 18 April

Indeed, July 2021 saw Cubans take to the streets to protest a shortage of food and medicine, and the government's handling of the Covid-19 pandemic. While Cuba's management of the pandemic might be considered strong, with the island developing and manufacturing their own vaccines, and sending doctors to support medical practitioners in fifteen countries (52 Cuban doctors went to Italy; closer to home, Cuba sent doctors to Dominica, Haiti, Jamaica, Suriname, Venezuela, Nicaragua, and St. Kitts and Nevis), the economy was hit hard. The loss of income from tourism coupled with the momentous move to a single currency on 1st January 2021, a long-discussed project that saw the unification of the Cuban peso (CUP) and the Cuban convertible peso (CUC), created a tinderbox of economic uncertainty. In response to the protests, President Biden was quick to impose sanctions on Cuba's defence secretary and an interior ministry special forces unit.

Cuba's relationship with the US continues to yo-yo. Under President Trump's administration the rhetoric swang from Obama's conciliatory position to a hostile far-right narrative. In April 2019 Trump announced a new series of restrictions, including limiting non-family travel to Cuba, restricting how much money Cuban-Americans can send in remittance to the island and allowing exiles to sue for property seized under the Castro regime. Yet despite the bluster, there was little concrete change in Cuba-US relations, US visitors increased in numbers, and although the embargo remains intact, many US companies signed agreements to start trading with Cuba.

In May 2022 the Biden administration announced "measures to support the Cuban people". Though Biden has yet to take significant constructive steps, it

RACE RELATIONS IN CUBA

At the onset of the Revolution in 1959, Fidel Castro declared that he would eradicate racial discrimination, establishing the unacceptability of **racism** as one of the core tenets of the Revolution. He carried through his promise with legislation that threw open doors to previously white-only country clubs, beaches, hotels and universities and, more importantly, established equality in the workplace.

However, the question of race in Cuba is still a problematic issue. Official statistics put the **racial mix** at 66 percent white (of Hispanic descent), 12 percent Black, 21.9 percent mulatto (mixed-race between Hispanic and Black) and 0.1 percent Asian. There is, however, an obvious disparity between figures and facts, and the claims by some that as much as 70 percent of the population have some trace of Black heritage seem to be closer to the truth. Some critics of the official figures claim they are a way of downplaying the importance of the Black heritage.

Although institutional racism has been somewhat lessened, its existence is still apparent in the lack of Black people holding the highest positions across the professional spectrum. A more recent dimension in the race question has arisen from the tourist trade. *Jineteros* and *jineteras* (hustlers, escort girls and sex workers) are nationally perceived as exclusively African-Cuban, and this in turn has led to the stereotype of wealthy African-Cubans as sex workers, pimps and touts, while white Cubans with money are generally assumed to be supported by relatives in Miami.

2019	2021
US President Trump announces plans to clamp down on "veiled tourism" to Cuba	Cuba became the smallest country in the world to develop and produce its own Covid-19 vaccines; Cuba ended its dual-currency system; Raúl Castro retired; Cubans engage in widespread protests at food and medicine shortages

seems Cuba is on his agenda. This came in the wake of members of the Caribbean Community (CARICOM) countries making a fresh call for the US to end the economic and trade embargo against Cuba, with Dominica's Prime Minister, Roosevelt Skerrit, explaining, "it is not an anti-America position, it is a matter of justice and fairness, that's all".

Cuba's future holds many challenges, not least steering itself through switching to a single currency and strengthening the economy with a long-term plan for success. And all such issues must be addressed under the hawkish eye of US relations.

In the Caribbean island that always confounds expectations, one constant holds true: Cuba always finds a way to endure. The future is likely to be no different.

2022

Heavy rains from the remnants of Pacific Hurricane Agatha caused widespread flooding in western and central Cuba, killing three people in Havana; President Biden states an intention to introduce "measures to support the Cuban people".

Cuban music and musicians

Cuba is the musical powerhouse of Latin America, the birthplace of a multitude of influential musical styles – from rumba and son to mambo and chachachá. The staggering success of the Buena Vista Social Club reminded the world of this rich musical heritage, but Cuban musical influence stretches beyond these traditional homegrown styles, with claims to roles in the history of American jazz, African rumba, Spanish and Latin American folk music and most recently Caribbean reggaeton.

The origins of most traditional Cuban musical styles are found in the east of the country, particularly in and around Santiago de Cuba, though Havana can also claim to have given birth to a number of influential music genres, and Matanzas has its own significant musical claims to fame too.

Rumba

Not to be confused with the rumba of ballroom dancing, the frenetic rhythms and dances of Cuban **rumba** are the closest contemporary Cuban music has to a direct link with the music brought to the island by African enslaved people. A raw music driven by drums and vocals, it emerged from the docks and sugar mills in Havana and Matanzas in the late nineteenth century. Black workers developed songs and dances by playing rhythms on cargo boxes and packing cases. Once the music became more popular, these rudimentary instruments were subsequently replaced with conga drums of several different sizes and tones along with two different kinds of wooden sticks (*claves* and *palitos*), a metal shaker (*maruga*) and specially manufactured boxes (*cajones*).

Rumba is very distinct and can sound like a cacophony of rhythm to the uninitiated, making it perhaps one of the less accessible musical styles to the foreign ear, with so many percussive elements and an absence of brass, string or wind instruments. On the other hand, rumba performances are engaging and energetic and the vocal sections, involving a leader and a responder, can be quite hypnotic. Improvisation is an integral part of the art of rumba, as is call-and-response, while the dance calls on its performers to display explosive levels of energy.

Modern rumba divides into three main dances. The **guaguancó** is a dance for a couple in a game of seduction and sexual flirtation; the **yambú** is slower and less overtly sexual, while the **columbia** is a furiously energetic solo male dance.

Rumba at its most authentic is informal and spontaneous, but the music has been extensively recorded and is widely performed. Many of the biggest names in contemporary rumba, such as **Los Muñequitos de Matanzas**, **Claves y Guaguanco** and **Los Papines**, are legendary groups formed decades ago but still going strong.

Danzón

In contrast to rumba, **danzón** is a more formal strain of Cuban music, less spontaneous and with none of the improvisations of rumba; it best represents the musical traditions brought to Cuba by the Europeans, a kind of cross between classical music and African rhythms. Danzón was born out of the instrumental music known in Cuba as **contradanza**, a style performed in ballrooms and at formal events during the nineteenth century by recreational versions of military bands.

The contradanza was adapted and reinterpreted during the course of the nineteenth century until, in 1879, a Cuban band leader in Matanzas, Miguel Failde, composed what

CHARANGAS, CONJUNTOS AND ORQUESTAS TÍPICAS

The evolution from contradanza to danzón was by equal measure the transformation of **orquestas típicas** to charangas. *Orquestas típicas* were brass bands dating back to the eighteenth century and most popular in Cuba in the nineteenth century, before the success of danzón. They comprised a cornet, trombone, clarinets, a kind of elaborate bugle known as an ophicleide, violins, kettledrums, double bass and a *güiro* (a kind of scraper). These bands tended to play at formal occasions, for lines of dancers facing one another, but fell out of favour once the danzón turned the line-dance into a couple-dance, a development considered by some contemporaries as obscene and scandalous.

Though sometimes mistakenly used to denote a genre of music, a type of rhythm or a kind of dance, the term **charanga** actually describes a particular kind of band line-up. In Spanish a *charanga* is a brass band but the Cuban spin on the word has a much more specific meaning, referring to a particular set of instruments. Charanga orchestras emerged with the development of danzón in the early twentieth century and were originally known as *charangas francesas*. These bands traditionally consisted of flute, violin, piano, double bass, *güiro* and *timbal* (a type of drum). Charanga line-ups developed over the course of the twentieth century and the term is still in popular use today, though the modern-day interpretation has changed quite radically – the look and sound of La Charanga Habanera, one of the most successful salsa and timba acts of recent years, is a long way from the danzón charangas of the 1930s and 1940s. Cuban bands since the 1940s have also been referred to as **conjuntos**, though these have usually been son and subsequently salsa bands. A conjunto implies a larger, expanded version of traditional son sextets and septets, and the line-up can include congas, bongos, *claves*, piano, double bass and guitars as well as trumpets.

is generally considered to be the very first danzón, though there is some dispute over this. More upbeat and tuneful than contradanza, danzón orchestras nevertheless maintained the same basis of brass and string instruments, though the flute was given greater prominence. Various other innovations were made as the style developed during the early decades of the twentieth century, evolving alongside and influencing the sound of jazz in New Orleans and elsewhere in the US. The piano later became an essential ingredient, while congas have also been incorporated, taking the style closer to what is now known as son. Notably, traditional danzón has no singing parts and is, strictly speaking, a purely **instrumental** music. It has long since fallen out of fashion, and though it is still popular with elderly Cubans who meet up at weekends in dancehalls for collective dances organized in couples, it was son that really took off and came to define the Cuban sound.

One of the all-time great Cuban bands, **Orquesta Aragón**, started out playing danzón in the 1940s before moving on to other styles in subsequent years, including cha-cha-chá and son. They still perform today both in Cuba and abroad, having toured the UK and Canada among other countries in recent years. Similar to Orquesta Aragón but formed just over sixty years later, **Charanga de Oro** set out to re-establish some of the neglected traditional styles of Cuban music and, along with other revival groups including Buena Vista Social Club and **Orquesta Barbarito Diez**, have been mainstay performers at the International Danzón Festival, which takes place in Havana around April every year.

Son

Son is the blood running through the veins of Cuban popular music. More than any other music style it represents an intrinsically Cuban blend of African and European musical elements, though it has undergone so many innovations and spawned so many subgenres that it's difficult to talk of it as an individual musical style at all. Though a large proportion of bands making music in Cuba today could legitimately be described as son groups, references nowadays tend to be traditional son, with its signature sound provided by the Cuban guitar, known as the **tres**. The upright double bass and vocals, *claves*, maracas, a scraper and bongos also feature in this traditional sound.

The origins of son are in eastern Cuba and the late nineteenth century. The earliest groups to popularize the sound were sextets and subsequently, with the addition of a trumpet in the 1920s, septets. The sound was transformed in the 1940s and 1950s by **Arsenio Rodríguez**, considered by many to be the father of the modern African-Cuban sound. He added extra trumpets to his son band, brought in the piano and added a conga drummer, moving son closer to the sound produced by modern salsa bands, a transformation which was cemented in the 1970s by pioneering groups such as Los Van Van. Bands consisting of this larger, expanded line-up became known as conjuntos (see page 452). This same period marked the rise of **Beny Moré**, cited by many as Cuba's greatest ever *sonero*, who was known as the "Barbarian of Rhythm". Traditional son is now in vogue again, thanks to the Buena Vista Social Club.

Mambo

One of the most popular danzón orchestras in Cuba in the 1930s and 1940s was Arcaño y sus Maravillas, led by Antonio Arcaño. Among the orchestra's musicians was Orestes López who, in 1938, composed a tune for the band called *Mambo*. A variation on the standard danzón formula, the tune had a more African-sounding rhythm, incorporating elements of son, and was at first met by a lukewarm reaction from the Havana crowd. Within a few years, however, the sound had taken off, so much so that the Cuban pianist and bandleader **Pérez Prado** was successfully promoting his music as **mambo**, the first musician to do so.

Mambo fever hit much greater heights abroad than it ever did in the motherland, and is a rarely performed style in contemporary Cuba. Its current obscurity on the island means there are no high-profile mambo bands today, though one of the most universally loved and successful Cuban singers of all time, Beny Moré, was a prolific mambo singer. He joined Prado's band in Mexico City but returned to Cuba where he continued performing until his death in 1963. Unlike many musicians, he chose to stay in Cuba following the Revolution.

Mambo became synonymous with big bands and is a racier, louder, less elegant sound than danzón. Congas and *timbales* drums were added to danzón line-ups to create mambo orchestras. One of the biggest mambo orchestras was Beny Moré's Banda Gigante, consisting of over forty members, though performances would often involve no more than sixteen musicians. The band was hugely popular in Cuba, toured Latin America and the US and even played at the Oscars ceremony.

Chachachá

In the late 1940s and early 1950s several members of Arcaño y sus Maravillas defected to the more recently established **Orquesta América**, including the violinist Enrique Jorrín. Orquesta América, like most popular Cuban bands of the day, wrote mambo and danzón songs. It was while composing a danzón that Jorrín, having made several key adjustments to the structure of the song, came up with *La Engañadora*, the first ever **chachachá**. Orquesta América subsequently became known as the creators of the chachachá and were the ambassadors for the sound throughout the 1950s and beyond, as more and more bands, including Orquesta Aragón, adopted the sound. It was as the world's top chachachá band that Orquesta Aragón hit the heights of their international fame in the 1950s.

Like mambo, chachachá was tremendously popular beyond Cuban shores, particularly in the US. Jorrín himself said he composed *La Engañadora* with US audiences in mind and wanted to provide Americans with something they would find more manageable on the dancefloor, having seen them struggle with other more complex and faster Cuban dance

SON VETERANS: BUENA VISTA SOCIAL CLUB

"This is the best thing I was ever involved in," said **Ry Cooder** on the release of *Buena Vista Social Club*, the album of acoustic Cuban rhythms he recorded in Havana. Since then, *Buena Vista* has sold more than two million copies, won a Grammy award and become a live show capable of selling out New York's Carnegie Hall. Yet Cooder is the first to admit that *Buena Vista* is not really his album at all. He rightly wanted all the glory to go to the legendary Cuban veterans who were rescued from obscurity and retirement, and assembled in Havana's Egrem studio to record the album over seven days in March 1996. "These are the greatest musicians alive on the planet today, hot-shot players and classic people," Cooder said. "In my experience Cuban musicians are unique. The organization of the musical group is perfectly understood, there is no ego, no jockeying for position, so they have evolved the perfect ensemble concept."

The role of composer and guitarist **Compay Segundo** (1907–2003) was central to the project. "As soon as he walked into the studio it all kicked in. He was the leader, the fulcrum, the pivot. He knew the best songs and how to do them because he's been doing them since World War One."

Initially a clarinettist, Segundo invented his own seven-stringed guitar, known as the *armonico*, which gives his music its unique resonance. In the late 1920s he played with **Nico Saquito** before moving to Havana where he formed a duo with Lorenzo Hierrezuelo. In 1950 he formed **Compay Segundo y su Grupo**, yet by the following decade he had virtually retired from music, working as a tobacconist for seventeen years.

Rúben González (1919–2003) is described by Cooder as "the greatest piano soloist I have ever heard in my life, a cross between Thelonius Monk and Felix the Cat". Together with Líli Martínez and Peruchín, González forged the style of modern Cuban piano playing in the 1940s. He played with Enrique Jorrín's orchestra for 25 years, travelling widely through Latin America. When invited to play on *Buena Vista*, González did not even own a piano. However, after the release of his first solo album, González toured Europe and recorded his second solo album in London. *Chanchullo* was released in 2000 to wide acclaim as critics across the board favoured the lusher, more elaborate and rhythmic material.

Other key members of the Buena Vista Club included **Omara Portuondo** (born 1930), the bolero singer known as "the Cuban Edith Piaf"; **Eliades Ochoa** (born 1946), the singer and guitarist from Santiago who leads Cuarteto Patria; and the *sonero* **Ibrahim Ferrer** (1927–2005), whose solo album Cooder produced on a return visit to Havana.

Archive footage of Segundo and González can be seen in Wim Wenders' full-length documentary feature **film**, *Buena Vista Social Club*, filmed in Cuba and at the Buena Vista concerts in Amsterdam and New York in 1998.

rhythms like mambo. The name is said to have been born out of the sound made by the dancers' feet at the now defunct Silver Star club in Centro Habana when they danced to this new rhythm, their feet grazing the floor on three successive beats.

Trova

Another Cuban musical tradition to have emerged from the east of the island, **trova** grew out of the troubadour tradition of travelling musicians who would disperse news or tell stories through song. The early Cuban troubadours relied on nothing more than their voice, guitar and imagination, composing lyrics based on both romantic and patriotic themes. Nowadays, trova is typically sung with two voices in harmony and one or two guitars, and although no longer at the forefront of Cuban music, it can still be heard throughout the island in *casas de la trova*. This simple guitar-based musical tradition gave birth to the song **Guantanamera**, perhaps the best-known Cuban song, and certainly the most familiar to visitors who have spent any time in tourist bars and restaurants.

Its creator was a man named **José Pepe Sánchez**, born in Santiago de Cuba and known as the father of trova. One of his protégés, **Sindo Garay**, became a leading trova singer during the General Machado dictatorship in the 1930s and 1940s. Garay was a fixture at the *Bodeguita del Medio* bar and restaurant in Habana Vieja (see page 121), historically a meeting place for trova singers. Other greats of Cuban trova like Carlos Puebla played there, and in the run-up to the Revolution it was a popular meeting place for intellectuals and critics of Batista. There is no better place to hear the sound nowadays, however, than Santiago's *Casa de la Trova* (see page 390), where groups like Septeto Santiaguero, Hermanas Ferrín and Septeto de la Trova are among the regular modern performers of traditional trova.

Bolero

An offshoot of trova, Cuban **bolero** (unrelated to the Spanish musical style of the same name) is another guitar-based style but has a more lyrical, poetic and romantic slant. Like trova, it is typically performed by guitar duos and two voices in harmony. It originated in Santiago de Cuba in the latter part of the nineteenth century and is said to have been the first kind of Cuban music to gain international renown. A song composed by José Pepe Sánchez, the father of trova, *Tristeza* is credited as the first ever bolero.

In the 1920s bolero had become popular in Havana cafés and dancehalls, and performers began to include a piano in their compositions. By the 1950s, during one of its most successful decades, bolero had become more popular in Mexico than in Cuba – indeed, the centre of the bolero industry remains in Mexico to this day. Still popular in Cuba, Ibrahim Ferrer, one of the original Buena Vista Social Club singers, was an expert exponent of the bolero, as is Omara Portuondo, whose renditions of one of the classic bolero songs, *Dos Gardenias*, have enjoyed a resurgence in popularity following the Buena Vista explosion.

Feelin'

The curiously named musical style known as **feelin'**, also referred to as filin, emerged in Cuba – and most particularly in Havana – during the 1940s, as a response to trends in the US jazz scene. Taking elements of American jazz and inspired by the likes of Nat King Cole and Ella Fitzgerald, Cuban musicians combined that imported sound with some of the instrumentation and structure of bolero. Where the backing track for the bolero singer is supplied by a guitarist, the archetypal feelin' soundtrack is provided by a pianist and would be categorized today as easy-listening jazz, featuring crooning singers delivering slow-paced, romantic and bluesy ballads. The English name is said to have been taken from a song sung by the American jazz vocalist Maxine Sullivan, called *I Gotta Feeling*, whose music, along with countless numbers of her contemporaries like Sarah Vaughan and Cab Calloway, reached Cuban shores via shows on the Mil Diez radio station and with Black American sailors who would sell jazz records to an eager local following. Feelin' initially developed in private homes, particularly in the Cayo Hueso neighbourhood in Centro Habana, among enthusiasts who would gather together for domestic jam sessions before the style became widely popular.

Compared with trova and bolero, the two styles with which it shares the closest heritage, feelin' is underexposed in Cuba nowadays. You are most likely to hear it in those same venues where it was originally performed and which are still operating today, most usually at *El Gato Tuerto*, in the capital's Vedado district, where feelin' had its heyday during the 1950s and 1960s.

Salsa and timba

Arguably **salsa** is not a musical style at all but a catch-all term for music born and bred in the Spanish-speaking Caribbean and the Latin communities of the eastern US. Though there are countless definitions of what salsa actually is, the term was popularized as a description of a specific kind of music in the 1960s and 1970s in New York, Puerto Rico and Cuba and is undeniably a product of son. Modern salsa was created in the 1970s following innovations to son bands made by **Adalberto Alvarez**, and his band **Son 14**, and by **Juan Formell** and his legendary group **Los Van Van**, introducing changes by adding a trombone, synthesizer and drum. Cuban salsa has been tweaked in recent years to create **timba**, a version of salsa strongly associated with Havana.

Salsa and timba bands, along with reggaeton artists, dominate Cuban popular music. At the forefront of the scene nowadays, and still churning out hits after a decade at the top, are **Alexander Abreu** and his band **Havana D'Primera**, with their blend of timba and jazz, and **Maikel Blanco y Su Salsa Mayor**, both of whom draw huge crowds and tour internationally. They belong to a generation of salseros whose evolution can be traced back to bands like **NG La Banda**, founded in 1988 but still going strong, and pioneers of a louder, more aggressive salsa, with grittier lyrics and a more streetwise vernacular. In common with many modern-day salsa bands, they have combined salsa with elements of other music, from hip-hop and reggaeton to nueva trova and jazz. Among the most recent successes of this salsa fusion are **El Niño y La Verdad** whose music carries the influence of traditional and modern Cuban music but whose attitude harks back to a gentler era.

Cuban jazz

There have been **jazz bands** in Cuba, and particularly in Havana, almost as long as they have existed in New Orleans – but quintessentially Cuban jazz, as opposed to jazz made by Cubans, emerged in the 1940s, marked by the success of the band African-Cubans and their lead singer Frank "Machito" Grillo. The African-Cubans, however, moved to New York to establish themselves in the wider consciousness of American jazz, leaving Cuban jazz as performed and developed on the island to really find its feet in the 1970s with the formation, in 1973, of the great Cuban jazz pioneers **Irakere**. Without doubt the godfather of Cuban jazz is composer and pianist **Jesús "Chucho" Valdés** who, along with Paquito D'Rivera and Arturo Sandoval, formed the backbone of Irakere. Cuban jazz tends to incorporate elements of son and other African-Cuban music styles. Percussion is an integral part of the sound, with the conga and bongo drums lending it its unmistakeable trademark rhythm.

Though D'Rivera and Sandoval both defected from the island in the 1980s, Havana-based Irakere is still going strong and regularly performs live. Among the leading lights of the newer generation of Cuban jazz artists are internationally renowned pianist **Harold López-Nussa** and virtuoso composer **Roberto Fonseca**, master of several instruments.

Nueva trova

Nueva trova refers to the post-Revolution generation of folksy singer-songwriters who first came to prominence in the late 1960s and 1970s on a basic template of vocals and solo acoustic guitar. Nueva trova artists nowadays are a mix of solo acoustic guitar players in the traditional trova and folk moulds, as well as bands producing a slightly harder-edged sound, crossing over into rock. The style is sometimes referred to as **nueva canción** ("new song").

Nueva trova songs encompass protest and politics as well as romance and relationships, in keeping with the trova tradition. Artists have tended to be patriotic but reflective and sometimes critical of the regime. The two giants of nueva trova, considered among the founders of the movement, are **Pablo Milanés** and **Silvio Rodríguez**, both hugely popular throughout the Spanish-speaking world and still active today. Though at times critical of the regime, Milanés and Rodríguez have in fact been staunch supporters of the Revolution.

Other big names on the current nueva trova circuit are **Carlos Varela**, whose songs express some of the frustrations of the younger generation in Cuba, and **Sara González**.

Cuban rock

Rock music was actively discouraged and heavily frowned upon by the Cuban authorities in the early years of the Revolution, perceived as Yankee music and antirevolutionary. This attitude mellowed very slowly and had softened sufficiently by 2001 for Welsh rockers the Manic Street Preachers to be able to perform at the Teatro Karl Marx in Havana, a significant breakthrough at the time. Cuba today has its share of rock musicians, and though one or two Cuban rock bands have been given record deals, on the whole they are underexposed and perform at low-key venues. As elsewhere they can be split into numerous subgenres from soft rock to heavy metal, though the most characteristically Cuban take on rock takes its influence from the nueva trova movement. Many nueva trova artists, including Silvio Rodríguez, have written what could be described as crossover rock songs.

Santa Clara has emerged as the unofficial capital of Cuban rock, with an annual rock festival and a significant share of the country's heavy metal groups. Havana natives Santiago Feliú and Carlos Varela are among the rockier of the nueva trova artists still performing today, while Gerardo Alfonso and David Blanco are worth a listen for the latest Cuban twists on the rock formula. For something a little closer to classic rock check for Los Kent, long-time performers on the Havana rock scene.

Cuban hip-hop

Cuban hip-hop represents a refreshing alternative to the violence, misogyny and bling that have come to dominate modern hip-hop in the US and elsewhere. The music and particularly the lyrics are generally closer to the political and socially conscious rap of late 1980s and early 1990s New York hip-hop, and nothing like the formulaic gangster lyrics and ultra-polished sound of the current hip-hop celebrity. A lack of resources dictated the early Cuban sound, with bedroom producers drawing on whatever samples they could get their hands on, from traditional Cuban music to existing hip-hop tracks – turntables and scratch DJs were, and still are, pretty much nonexistent.

Just when Cuban hip-hop artists seemed to be building some momentum and gaining exposure in the late 1990s and early 2000s, reggaeton exploded and split the scene, pushing back those who maintained a truer, rawer hip-hop sound and elevating the more commercially friendly reggaeton groups to superstars. A slowly growing number of hip-hop artists within Cuba are now releasing full albums, though they generally remain firmly outside the mainstream. Among those to have already built up a significant catalogue of recordings are Obsesión, Ogguere, Telmary Díaz, Los Aldeanos, Anónimo Consejo, Doble Filo and the excellent **Mano Armada**.

Reggaeton and cubaton

For a while it looked as though the explosion of Cuban hip-hop groups over the last decade was going to put hip-hop firmly on the Cuban musical map. However, the momentum built up by the initial surge of rappers in Havana and elsewhere on the island was seized upon by **reggaeton** artists and it is they who have gained the recognition and radio airplay the hip-hop artists so craved. The sound is a combination of modern R&B, watered-down commercial reggae and dancehall with rapped lyrics. A home-grown, salsafied version of reggaeton, known as **cubaton**, is equally popular, and this kind of music is now a staple on the Havana club scene. Lyrics frequently revolve around sexual themes and have attracted controversy for their perceived vulgarity.

The first wave of Cuban reggaeton artists was led by **Eddy K** in the early 2000s and since then an unrelenting stream of reggaeton groups have flooded the Cuban market and radio airwaves but the undisputed superstars of the genre, having emerged in that early wave, remain **Gente de Zona**.

Cuban sport

Since the 1959 Revolution Cuba has eight times finished among the top twenty in the Olympic Games' medals tables, and competes at the highest international level in an impressive number of sports. Yet uniquely, this nation of just eleven million people has achieved these levels of global success on an amateur ethos, without the kind of sponsorship, commercialization and funding common to the other world powers in sport.

Cuban sport before the Revolution

Cuba was among the first nations to take part in the **Modern Olympic Games**, competing as one of the twenty countries present in Paris in 1900. It was at these games, the second of the modern era, and four years later in St Louis, that twelve of just fourteen Olympic medals collected by Cuban competitors before the Revolution were won. All twelve medals were in **fencing**, a sport at which Cubans continue to excel, and the hero was Ramón Fonst, the first man in Olympic history to win three individual gold medals.

Most of the Cuban population, however, was alienated not only from these successes but from organized sport in general, as only the privileged classes had access to athletic facilities. The sporting infrastructure was based predominantly on private clubs, from which Black Cubans were almost always banned. Class and race determined participation in sports like fencing, tennis, golf and sailing, all the exclusive domain of aristocratic organizations such as the Havana Yacht Club or the Vedado Tennis Club. Many of the most popular spectator sports, though accessible to a broader cross-section of the population, were inextricably tied up with tourism and corruption. The appeal of horse racing, dog racing, cock fighting, billiards and boxing derived mainly

---

THE FIDEL CASTRO FACTOR

According to **Fidel Castro** himself, had he not been a sportsman he would never have been a revolutionary, asserting that it was his physical training as an athlete that had allowed him to fight as a guerrilla in the revolutionary war. As early as January 1959, within a month of the rebel victory, Castro made a lengthy speech in Havana's Ciudad Deportiva and declared: "I am convinced that sporting activity is necessary for this country. It's embarrassing that there is so little sport…The Cuban results in international competitions up until now have been shameful."

Castro's own sporting prowess, attested to in widely published photographs, many of them displayed in museums and restaurants around the country, can be traced back to his high-school days at the Belen school in Havana. Castro played in Belen's basketball and baseball teams, and in 1944 was voted the top high-school athlete in the country. In his early university years the future leader continued to play basketball and baseball as well as training as a 400-metre runner, and was a proficient boxer too.

It would be naive to suppose that there was no political motivation behind Castro's commitment to sport, but his involvement went well beyond political gimmickry. As well as making countless speeches down the years promoting the values of sport, Castro considered the achievements in sport since the Revolution a matter of intense pride, and until ill health restricted his movements he rarely missed a chance to greet a winning team's homecoming from an overseas tournament. On more than one occasion, Castro involved himself in disputes over scandals implicating Cuban sports stars. Following the confiscation of medals from four Cuban athletes at the 1999 Pan American Games he personally appeared in a two-day televised hearing, demanding that the medals be returned.

from **gambling**, particularly during the 1940s and 1950s when the Mafia controlled much of the infrastructure. Furthermore, on the eve of the Revolution there were only eight hundred PE teachers in a population of ten million, while just two percent of schoolchildren received any kind of formal physical education at all.

It was in **boxing** and **baseball** that popular sporting culture was most avidly expressed. These were genuinely sports for the masses, but though Cuba had one of the world's first national baseball leagues and hosted its own boxing bouts, the really big names and reputations were made in the US. Indeed, both baseball and boxing were brought to Cuba by North Americans and owe much of their popularity to North American commerce and organization. With such close links between the two countries during the years of the "pseudo-republic", very few talented sportsmen went unnoticed by the fight organizers and league bosses on the opposite side of the Florida Straits. Almost all the biggest names in these two sports during this period – baseball players like **Tony Pérez**, **José Cardenal** and **Tito Fuentes** and boxers such as **Benny Paret** and **Kid Chocolate** – gained their fame and fortune in the US.

Sport and the Revolution

With sport prior to 1959 characterized by corruption, social discrimination and a generally poor standing in international competitions, the revolutionary government had more than enough to get its teeth into. Led by Fidel Castro himself, who has always been a keen sportsman (see page 458), the new regime restructured the entire system of participation.

The new ideology of sport

Like the Russians before them, the Cubans developed a new ideology around sport and its role in society. Though borrowing heavily from the Soviet model, this ideology was very much a Cuban creation. Rather than looking to Marx as a guide, the revolutionaries chose the ideas of **Baron Pierre de Coubertin**, the Frenchman responsible for the revival of the Olympic Games in 1896. Coubertin believed that one of the reasons the Ancient Greeks had reached such high levels of social and cultural achievement was the emphasis they placed on physical activity. Rejecting the neo-Marxist argument that the competitive element of sport promotes social division and elitism, the Cubans adopted Coubertin's basic premise that participation in sport was capable of bridging differences in politics, race and religion, thus encouraging feelings of brotherhood and social equality. Believing that it is not the nature of sport but the way in which it is approached and practised that would determine its effect, the Cuban state made sport one of the priorities in the transformation of society.

Sport and physical education were considered inseparable from the process of development towards Che Guevara's concept of *El Hombre Nuevo* – the New Man – one of the cornerstones of Cuban communist theory. The Cubans claim that as well as promoting better health and fitness, organized physical activities and games encourage discipline, responsibility, willpower, improved social communication skills, a cooperative spirit and internationalism, and generally contribute to a person's ethical and moral character.

Sport for all

The transformation of post-revolutionary Cuban sport began in earnest on February 23, 1961, with the creation of **INDER** (National Institute of Sport, Physical Education and Recreation), the government body responsible for carrying out programmes of sport for the masses. The first campaign was aimed at diversifying the number of sporting activities available to the public, eliminating exclusivity and involving every citizen in some kind of regular physical activity.

Sport is an integral part of the "cradle-to-grave" social welfare system born of the Revolution, and no time is wasted in introducing **children** to the benefits of physical exercise. Under the banner of slogans like "the home is the gymnasium", INDER encourages parents to actively pursue the physical health of their children, with classes in massage and physical manipulation offered for babies as young as 45 days old. Early in the morning during term time, it is common to see groups of schoolchildren doing exercises in the local parks and city squares with their teachers. These places are also where the so-called **circulos de abuelos** meet – groups of elderly people, usually past retirement age, performing basic stretches together.

In 1966 legislation was passed guaranteeing workers paid leisure time for recreational activities, and in 1967 entrance charges to sport stadiums and arenas were abolished. Today prices are well within reach of the entire population. By 1971 the number of students actively involved in one sport or another had risen from under forty thousand to just over a million, while it was estimated in a Unesco-backed report that a further 1.2 million people were participating in some kind of regular physical exercise. The right of all Cubans to participate in physical education and organized sports was even included in several clauses of the 1976 Cuban Constitution.

Making champions

Mass participation in sport was to form the base of the Coubertin-inspired **pyramid** that underpins Cuban sport and accounts, to a large extent, for the tremendous success

BASEBALL IN CUBA

The most American of sports is also the most Cuban. It was introduced to the island in the late 1800s by American students studying in Cuba and by visiting sailors who would take on the local workers in Cuban dockyards. The first officially organized game took place between the Matanzas Béisbol Club and the Havana Béisbol Club on December 27, 1874; four years later, the first elite baseball league to be founded outside the US and Canada was established on the island. Frowned upon by the Spanish colonial rulers, who even banned the game for a period, baseball really took off following the end of the Spanish–American War in 1898.

US DOMINANCE

Though a national league had been established, the **Major League** in the US dominated the fortunes of the best players. Cuban and American baseball developed in tandem during the pre-revolutionary era, as the island became a supply line to the US teams with players like Adolfo Luque, who played twelve seasons with the Cincinnati Reds from 1918, and Conrado Marrero, a pitcher with the Washington Senators in the 1950s, among the numerous Cubans to be won over by the US Major League. These were almost exclusively white players, as Black Cubans suffered discrimination in both countries and were mostly restricted either to the Black leagues or the Cuban league, in which Habana, Almendares, Marianao and Santa Clara were the only teams competing.

REVOLUTIONARY BASEBALL

Since 1959, Cuban baseball has transformed itself from the stepchild of the US Major League to one of the most potent forces in the game. The **national league** now consists of sixteen teams instead of four and the **national team** dominated international baseball for decades, taking three of the five **Olympic titles** between 1992 and 2008, becoming ten-time victors of the **Intercontinental Cup** and winning all of the biennial **World Cups** between 1984 and 2005. However, these were, strictly speaking, amateur baseball tournaments that excluded many of the world's top professionals. In 2006 the inaugural **World Baseball Classic** allowed both amateur and professional players to compete for their national teams, including, for the first time, Major League representatives. Cuba made the final in that first tournament but was knocked out in the second round in 2009 and 2013. Cuba's amateurs first tested themselves against the major leaguers in 1999 when the national team played two exhibition games of Cuban sportsmen and -women over the last thirty years. From primary schools to universities, physical education is a compulsory part of the curriculum and the progress of all pupils is monitored through regular **testing**. Thus, as early as 7 or 8 years of age, the most promising young athletes can be selected for the **EIDE** (Escuelas de Iniciación Deportiva Escolar) sports schools, of which there is one in every province. Here, physiological tests, trainers' reports and interprovincial competitions all form a regular part of school life; pupils remain until they are 15 or 16. The best EIDE pupils are then selected for the **ESPA** (Escuelas Superiores de Perfeccionamiento Atlético), the elite sports schools, one stage below the National Team, which sits at the top of the pyramid. Using this structure, the Cubans have demonstrated the reciprocal relationship between the top and the bottom of the pyramid: mass participation produces world champions and, in turn, success in international competitions encourages greater numbers to practise sport.

The nurturing of potentially world-class athletes is taken so seriously in Cuba that each individual sport has to be officially sanctioned before it is recognized as suitable for competition standard. The basic principle behind this is specialization, and since the Revolution the Cubans have made sure each of their major sports is developed to a high international standard before another is introduced.

Many of the **coaches** in Cuba during the first two decades of the Revolution were supplied by other Communist bloc countries, but INDER now has its own home-grown

against the Baltimore Orioles, an unprecedented event amid a tense political climate between the US and Cuba; the good-spirited miniseries was drawn one win each.

In 2016 the second historic match between the Cuba national team and the US Major League Baseball side the Tampa Bay Rays was played under the watchful eyes of none less than President Obama and Raúl Castro themselves. It was a star-studded match with **Pedro Luis Lazo**, part of the 2000 Olympic team and **Luis Tiant**, Major League veteran, pitching for Cuba. On the other side was Cuban defector **Dayron Varona**, who opened for the US team. It was a charged game played in an exuberant but friendly stadium which saw the Rays win 4-1.

The rapprochement was not to last. In April 2019, the US cancelled an agreement, signed in December 2018, which allowed Cuban and Major League Baseball to develop their relationship by allowing Cuban baseball players to sign with US teams. Relations within US-Cuban sport, as with many areas of social and political life between the two nations, have taken a giant step back.

DEFECTIONS

That Cuban players are among the world's best is perhaps most poignantly demonstrated by the success enjoyed by a significant number of defectors to the US Major League over the years. Among the highest-profile are **Liván Hernández**, who defected in 1995 to sign a six-million-dollar contract with the Florida Marlins, subsequently taking the team to World Series victory in 1997 and named the World Series Most Valuable Player. His brother Orlando, who was denied a place on the 1996 Olympic team that went to Atlanta as punishment for his sibling's defection, followed Liván by defecting in 1997, signing with the New York Yankees and pitching for the team in their three World Series victories between 1998 and 2000.

A record number of ballplayers left Cuba in 2015, said by some to be as high as 150, and a particularly damaging double defection took place in February 2016 when one of the hottest young prospects in Cuban baseball, **Lourdes Gourriel Jr**, and his older brother **Yulieski**, considered one of the best players on the island, disappeared from the Cuban team hotel in the Dominican Republic's capital Santo Domingo, after competing in the Caribbean Series tournament. More recently still, **Víctor Víctor Mesa Ríos**, who played for the National team in the 2017 World Baseball Series, defected with his younger brother in 2018. Nevertheless, significant talents have chosen to stay in Cuba, most notably **Omar Linares**, one of the greatest Cuban players of all time, who rejected offers of millions of dollars from Major League clubs in favour of staying with his beloved Pinar del Río in the 1990s.

experts. Cuban coaches have had almost as much success as the athletes they have trained, working in over forty countries, particularly Spain and throughout Latin America.

World beaters

Between the Montréal Olympics in 1976, when Cuba finished eighth, and the Atlanta Games in 1996, Cuba never fell out of the top ten in the **Olympic Games** medals tables, placing as high as fourth and fifth at Moscow 1980 and Barcelona 1992 respectively. Perhaps equally impressive has been Cuba's habitual second place, behind the US, in the **Pan American Games**, a championship contested by all the countries of both North and South America.

Cuban boxers are among the most respected in the world, absent from the professional game on principle but kings of **amateur boxing**, reigning supreme at the AIBA World Boxing Championships since they began in 1974 and a dominant force at the Olympics for decades. Among the greats are heavyweight **Félix Savón**, six-time world champion and gold medallist at three consecutive Olympics, from 1992 to 2000; **Mario Kindelán**, a lightweight who collected two Olympic and three World Championship golds between 1999 and 2004; and the formidable heavyweight **Teófilo Stevenson**, three-time Olympic Champion and one-time potential opponent of Muhammad Ali. Stevenson was prevented from fighting the self-proclaimed "greatest of all time" by the governing body of the sport during the 1970s, which ruled it illegal for an amateur to fight a professional. Even Ali himself, in a visit to Havana in 1996, admitted that had the two ever met it would have been a close-run contest. More recently, three of Cuba's five gold medals at the 2016 Rio de Janeiro Olympics were won by boxers.

Cuba also has an impressive record in **track and field athletics** since the Revolution. This small island nation has long made the result of the **Central American and Caribbean Athletics Championships** – in which Mexico, Colombia, Venezuela and Puerto Rico, among others, compete – almost a foregone conclusion, having failed to finish first only three times since 1967. One of the first Olympic track champions was **Alberto Juantorena**, who remains the only man in history to win both 400-metre and 800-metre events at the Olympic Games, achieved in Montréal in 1976. The 1990s were a successful time for Cuban athletes in the jumping events, with long jumper **Ivan Pedroso** winning his event at four consecutive World Championships and taking Olympic gold in Sydney 2000, while **Javier Sotomayor** – The Prince of Heights – has been the high-jump world record holder since 1988 and took the Olympic gold medal in 1992. More recently, Cuban hurdlers have been taking the world by storm, first with **Anier García** in Sydney 2000 and then the bespectacled **Dayron Robles** in Beijing 2008, both victorious in the 110-metre hurdles. Robles looked set to take gold again 2012, but was disqualified in the final.

Countless other sporting disciplines have given Cuba world and Olympic champions, including the **women's volleyball team**, Olympic gold medallists at three consecutive Games (1992, 1996 and 2000), numerous **martial arts** disciplines, **wrestling** and **weightlifting**.

A dip in form

The Special Period in the 1990s took its toll on Cuban sport just like it did on everything else in the country, and following years of underinvestment, deteriorating conditions and wilting infrastructure, results at international tournaments in many sports have been disappointing. To add insult to injury, the economic crisis led to fresh waves of defections and departures, with countless sportsmen and women seeking careers abroad (see page 460). At the 2008, 2012, 2016 and 2020 Olympic Games Cuba finished 28th, 16th, 18th and 18th respectively, its worst placings since 1968. These medal tallies nonetheless represent a country still punching way above its weight in world sport.

Books and film

There are more books on almost any Cuban subject outside of Cuba than there are on the island itself. Bookstores in Cuba are half-empty and are, of course, all run by the state, so between them offer very little variety. What's more, the state-run publishing industry, brought to its knees during the economic crisis of the 1990s and still suffering from shortages, is very selective about the books that make it to print, for both practical and political reasons. Outside Cuba, Castro and Guevara have been the subjects of countless biographies by foreign authors, while you could fill a whole library with accounts and assessments of the Revolution. There's also a rich line in expat writing, from fiction to political commentary.

Cuban **films**, on the other hand, can be hard to track down outside Cuba, and on a visit to the island it's well worth delving into the Cuban cinematic works available on DVD. Since the Revolution, the Cuban film industry has become one of the most sophisticated and highly regarded in Latin America.

The ★ symbol indicates titles that are especially recommended.

HISTORY AND POLITICS

★ **Harlan Abrahams and Arturo López-Levy** *Raúl Castro and the New Cuba*. One of the most engaging and intelligent assessments of Cuba since Raúl Castro took over, offering a contemporary take on Cuban politics, economics and society untainted by dogma but written with a lively sense of opinion. Very readable and made more so by a broad and engaging set of interviewees that includes an artist, an academic and a gay Cuban emigrant.

Philip Brenner, Marguerite Rose Jiménez, John M. Kirk and William M. Leogrande (eds) *A Contemporary Cuba Reader: The Revolution under Raúl Castro*. A superb and varied anthology on Cuban politics, economics, foreign policy, culture and social change since 2006. The collection's biggest strength is its diversity, with accounts covering the Cuban blogosphere, the country's new generation of entrepreneurs, contemporary Cuban art, the national film industry and forty-two other essays on modern-day Cuba.

★ **Alfredo José Estrada** *Havana (Autobiography of a City)*. Although at times the writer lets his anti-Castro bias flavour his outlook, that doesn't detract from this meticulously researched social and architectural history, rich in fascinating vignettes in which the author traces the lineage of the city from its earliest incarnation to modern times.

Mark Frank *Cuban Revelations: Behind the Scenes in Havana*. Written by a US journalist who has lived in Havana for most of the last thirty years, this is an extremely well-informed, sensitive account of Cuba since the Special Period, with a focus on the changes that have taken place since Raúl Castro became president.

★ **Richard Gott** *Cuba: A New History*. Few histories of Cuba flow off the page as fluently as this. The author has a great instinct for interesting anecdotes and information but ties his facts together so seamlessly that you never lose track of the wider narrative. Having visited Cuba regularly for five decades, Gott also writes with considerable authority.

★ **Guillermo Cabrera Infante** *Mea Cuba*. A collection of writings on Cuba from 1968 to 1993 by a Cuban exile and opponent of the current regime. His vehement criticisms of Fidel Castro are uncompromising and can make for rather heavy reading, but there are plenty of thoughtful and eyebrow-raising commentaries from a man who is clearly passionate about his subject matter.

Louis A. Pérez, Jr. *Cuba: Between Reform and Revolution*. Superbly researched and very readable, this complete history covers pre-Columbian Cuba up to the present. It tends towards economic issues, though it's far from one-dimensional.

Rosalie Schwartz *Pleasure Island – Tourism and Temptation in Cuba*. This readable and lively book charts the history of tourism and its relationship to political change in Cuba during its pre-Revolution days, drawing comparisons with its modern-day incarnation. Sex work is examined and there is a fascinating account of the role played by the Mafia.

Julia Sweig *Cuba: What Everyone Needs To Know*. An excellent, accessible introduction to Cuban politics, history and culture, covering a wide range of topics and themes but concentrating particularly on Cuba since 1959 and relations with the US. Balanced and thoughtful.

★ **Hugh Thomas** *Cuba: A History*. Now in its fourth decade of publication, this weighty tome remains one of the definitive histories of Cuba. Begins with the English occupation of 1762, but despite this late start this is an authoritative and exhaustive text, meticulously researched and full of fascinating facts.

Helen Yaffe *Che Guevara: The Economics of Revolution.* While much of what is written about Che Guevara focuses on his military campaigns, Yaffe's erudite account looks at the massive impact Guevara had on Cuba's economic management as a member of the Cuban government between 1959 and 1965.

BIOGRAPHY AND AUTOBIOGRAPHY

Carlos Acosta *No Way Home.* Acosta excels as a writer almost as much as he does as a ballet dancer. His detailed autobiography covers his early life in Cuba, including his childhood in the suburbs of Havana, and subsequent successes in dance companies throughout the world. The chapters that capture the feel of life in Cuba for a child in the 1980s are particularly enjoyable.

Jon Lee Anderson *Che Guevara: A Revolutionary Life.* Guevara's amazing life certainly makes a great story and, in this case, a very long one – there can be few biographies of the man as extensively researched as this. Happily this book is not ideologically driven and subsequently Guevara is portrayed in all his complexity.

Reinaldo Arenas *Before Night Falls.* Arenas's daring autobiography, smuggled out of Cuba and published abroad, is a fascinating portrayal of gay life played out under the sexually repressive mantle of 1960 and 1970s Cuba. By turns poetic, bitter and funny, the visceral and powerful prose blazes from every page.

Daisy Rubiera Castillo *Reyita: The Life of a Black Cuban Woman in the Twentieth Century.* Told in the first person to the subject's granddaughter, this simple biography creates a full picture of a life typical of many others. She relates growing up in poverty in eastern Cuba, the aftermath of slavery and racial prejudice of the 1920s and 1930s, as well as life after the Revolution.

Fidel Castro with Ignacio Ramonet *My Life.* The result of over a hundred hours of interviews with the Cuban leader between 2003 and 2005 in which Castro discusses subjects as diverse as his childhood, his revolutionary influences, his memories of Che Guevara, globalization, the environment, terrorism and the future of the Revolution. An unprecedented insight.

★ **Leycester Coltman** *The Real Fidel Castro.* Succeeds where so many biographies of the man fail in being both a balanced and a highly readable account of Castro's extraordinary life. Refreshing in its political neutrality and its animated, non-academic style, this is also a highly accessible insight into the Cuban Revolution itself.

CULTURE AND SOCIETY

★ **Peter C. Bjarkman** *Cuba's Baseball Defectors.* Bjarkman is probably the world's leading non-Cuban authority on Cuban baseball having followed the game from the inside for many years. His latest excellent book weaves the compelling narratives of Cuban ballplayers who have defected to the US to play in the major leagues. He explores the wider contexts within which these defections have taken place, in particular US–Cuba relations and life under the Castros, while also charting a fascinating history of the game itself on the island.

Stephen Foehr *Waking Up In Cuba.* An entertaining portrait of contemporary Cuba as reflected in its music and musicians. This lively account is based on the author's own encounters with a wide and intriguing range of music makers, from rappers and reggae artists to pioneers of the nueva trova movement and the Buena Vista Social Club.

★ **Rosa Lowinger and Ofelia Fox** *Tropicana Nights: The Life and Times of the Legendary Cuban Nightclub.* A thoroughly researched and expertly told story of the fabled Havana cabaret nightclub, woven into a grander narrative of the first years of the Revolution and the decade or so leading up to it. Based on testimony from an impressive list of interviewees, this is a brilliant account of how people on the ground experienced these years, and offers a compelling insight into the world of 1950s Cuban showbusiness.

Ian Lumsden *Machos, Maricones and Gays.* One of the few available books that discusses homosexuality in Cuba. A thorough and sensitive treatment, covering the history of homophobia in Cuba and such complex issues as the Cuban approach to AIDS.

Robin D. Moore *Nationalizing Blackness: Afrocubanismo and Artistic Revolution in Havana, 1920–1940.* A clear and compelling analysis of the cultural and artistic role of Black Cubans during an era of prejudice, this is a good introduction to Black culture in Cuba.

★ **Pepe Navarro** *La Voz del Caimán.* This engaging collection of short encounters with Cubans from all walks of life aims to portray the lives, opinions and aspirations of a society in all its complexity. Encompassing a strikingly diverse set of occupations and lifestyles, with all kinds of fascinating anecdotes and insights into modern Cuba.

Yoani Sánchez *Havana Real: One Woman Fights to Tell the Truth about Cuba Today.* Yoani Sánchez is arguably the most high-profile critic of the Cuban government still resident in Cuba. Her views, expressed via her Generation Y blog, are well written and passionate and more than a little vituperative. In this book she uses her diarist style of portraits of daily encounters with friends, foes and family to give her account of life on the underside of modern revolution.

★ **Pedro Peréz Sarduy and Jean Stubbs** (eds)

AfroCuba: An Anthology of Cuban Writing on Race, Politics and Culture. Essays and extracts written by Black Cuban writers covering religion, race relations, slavery, plantation culture and an absorbing variety of other topics. There are excerpts from plays, novels, poems and factual pieces, but some of the quality of the texts is lost in the occasionally stilted translations.

Madelaine Vazquez Galvez and Imogene Tondre *Cuba: the Cookbook*. If you fancy enjoying a slice of Cuba at home this book serves up the goods. The beautiful photography is matched by well-thought through and easy-to-follow recipes. All highlight the best of Cuban cuisine.

TRAVEL WRITING

Louis A. Pérez, Jr (ed) *Slaves, Sugar and Colonial Society: Travel Accounts of Cuba 1801–1899*. Covering a range of topics, including religion, crime, sugar and slavery, these accounts, written predominantly by US and British visitors to Cuba, provide a broad overview of Cuban society during the nineteenth century.

★ **Alan Ryan** (ed) *The Reader's Companion to Cuba*. Twenty-three accounts by foreign visitors to Cuba between 1859 and the 1990s. A broad range of writers, including Graham Greene and Langston Hughes, covers an equally broad range of subject matter, from places and people to slavery and tourism.

Stephen Smith *The Land of Miracles: A Journey Through Modern Cuba*. Entertaining accounts of all the attention-grabbing aspects of Cuban culture – from classic cars and Santería to love hotels and Guantánamo – are surpassed by Smith's ability to pinpoint the foreigner's experience in Cuba.

NATURE AND ORNITHOLOGY

★ **Orlando H. Garrido and Arturo Kirkconnell**, *Birds of Cuba*. With colour illustrations of 354 species, 51 colour plates depicting male, female and juvenile plumages, and detail on habitats, range, conservation, status and voice, this exhaustive Helm field guide is an essential tool.

Guy Kirwan, Arturo Kirkconnell and Mike Flieg, *A Birdwatchers' Guide to Cuba, Jamaica, Hispaniola, Puerto Rico and the Caymans*. With exhaustive detail on key birding sites provided by expert birdwatchers who really know the region, this tells you what to see where, and when, with practical information on the likes of transport, access, regulations and seasonal variations. The maps and complete species list are handy, too.

★ **Nils Navarro**, *Endemic Birds of Cuba A Comprehensive Field Guide*. Smartly-designed and resplendent with the Cuban author's colour illustrations of every Cuban endemic bird (with a series of silhouettes of each species further aiding identification), this is as beautiful as it is practical. Alongside detail on the birds themselves, the photo-rich chapters on habitats and conservation are enlightening.

Alfonso Silva Lee, *Natural Cuba / Cuba Natural*. With 112 colour photos, this handy bilingual (Spanish and English) guide to Cuba's key flora and fauna provides information on Cuba's geological history and development. It also covers the island's remarkable diversity of endemic species, from the world's smallest bird, the bee hummingbird, to all manner of lizards, frogs, snakes, snails, insects, reef fish, butterflies and orchids.

ART, PHOTOGRAPHY AND ARCHITECTURE

Gianni Basso and Julio César Pérez Hernández *Inside Cuba*. Four hundred pages of exquisite photographs of Cuban architecture and interiors, providing not just eye-catching images but a memorable illustration of all sorts of facets of Cuban life. Dilapidated peasant housing, cigar factories, stylish civic buildings and urban residential apartments all feature.

Nathalie Bondil (ed) *Cuba: Art and History from 1868 to Today*. Produced to accompany an exhibition at the Montreal Museum of Fine Arts, this overview of modern Cuban art history is an excellent reference book, beautifully illustrated and broken down into an accessible selection of essays about key art movements and seminal artists such as Wifredo Lam.

John Comino-James *A Few Streets, A Few People*. Depicting everyday street scenes and people in the run-down Cayo Hueso district of Havana, this photo collection captures the essence of Centro Habana life, so much of it lived outdoors and on view.

Kevin Kwan *I Was Cuba*. A showcase of the fantastic photographic archive of collector Ramiro Fernández, a Havana native who left Cuba in 1960 and settled in the US. A treasure-trove of images portraying pre-Revolution Cuba, wonderfully evocative of a bygone era reaching back to the nineteenth century. Unparalleled in its content.

Christophe Loviny *Cuba by Korda*. This collection of photographs taken by Alberto Korda, the man behind the iconic portrait of Che Guevara, features numerous other classic shots, like those of Castro and his rebels in the Sierra Maestra during the Revolutionary War as well as lesser-known photos, including dramatic scenes during the Bay of Pigs invasion.

Hermes Mallea *Great Houses of Havana*. Shot by a descendant of Cuban immigrants, this beautiful coffee-table book focuses on the exquisite buildings maintained by the state as museums and "protocol houses" for foreign diplomats. As well as highlighting some design detail and architectural prowess, the photographs blow away the dusty opinion that all Cuba's colonial buildings are crumbling away.

Andreas Winkler and Sebastiaan Berger (eds) *What's New in Cuba: Images from 'Cuba: Contemporary Art'*. Many of the artists who appear in this lavishly illustrated book have shown their work at Cuba's biennial and internationally, and are considered seminal in the contemporary Cuban art movement. While there is little context on art movements within Cuba the works featured – including paintings, installations, sculpture and multimedia – give a valuable insight into which names to watch, from Tania Brugera to Felipe Dulzaides.

CUBAN FICTION

Alejo Carpentier *The Lost Steps*. One of the best-known novels by the most revered Cuban author of the twentieth century, this is a captivating story of a musician living in New York, who travels to the South American jungle and becomes enveloped in a world lost in time and cut off from civilization. Broad in scope, it's a poignant examination of the nature of happiness and the trappings of society.

★ **Edmundo Desnoes** *Memories of Underdevelopment*. In this novel set in 1961, the jaded narrator takes the reader through early revolutionary Cuba after his family has fled for Miami. Its bleak tone and unrelenting existentialism are in stark contrast to the euphoric portrayal of the era generally offered by the state.

Cristina García *Dreaming in Cuban*. Shot through with wit, García's moving novel about a Cuban family divided by the Revolution captures the state of mind of the exile in the US, and beautifully describes a magical and idiosyncratic Cuba.

Pedro Juan Gutiérrez *Dirty Havana Trilogy*. Disturbingly sexy and compelling, this is the story of life under Castro through the eyes of poverty-stricken Gutiérrez. Unlikely ever to be acclaimed by the Cuban Tourist Board, the narrative is as candid as it gets, airing untold stories of vice and poverty in the heart of Cuba. Very, very dirty.

Leonardo Padura *The Mario Conde Mysteries*. These award-winning detective novels broke new ground in Cuba with their gritty, truthful depictions of Havana life and of their flawed protagonist, Lieutenant Mario Conde, revitalizing a genre characterized previously by party-line-towing detectives. The plots serve as a vehicle for exploring the human condition as much as for creating suspense.

Juana Ponce de León and Esteban Ríos Rivera (eds) *Dream With No Name*. A poignant and revealing collection of contemporary short stories by writers living in Cuba and in exile. Mixing the established talent of Alejo Carpentier and Reinaldo Arenas with the younger generation of writers, this anthology covers a diversity of subjects from rural life in the 1930s to lesbian love in modern Cuba.

Yoss *Planet for Rent*. This poignant and witty collection of interrelated science-fiction short stories takes place in a world where aliens have invaded and Earth's inhabitants are at the mercy of wealthy alien colonizers. It's an allegorical tale critiquing modern Cuba.

FILM

El Cuerno de la Abundancia (2008; dir. Juan Carlos Tabío). *The Horn of Abundance* is an insightful depiction of modern Cuban society and the pernicious effects of money on it. The story follows the inhabitants of a fictitious town who believe themselves to be poised to inherit a fortune from Spanish ancestors abroad.

Fresa y Chocolate (1994; dir. Tomás Gutiérrez Alea and Juan Carlos Tabío). The tale of an unlikely friendship between a gay artist and a pro-government student was one of the most successful Cuban films of the 1990s. Groundbreaking and controversial in Cuba – not just because one of the protagonists is gay, but because he is disillusioned with elements of life in Cuba and critical of zealous party officials. Set in Havana, this personal and political story is told with subtlety and sensitivity.

Lucía (1968; dir. Humberto Solas). Divided into three parts set respectively in 1895, 1932 and in an unspecified year in the 1960s, "196...", this seminal Cuban film traces the country's political emancipation from colonialism through the ages as seen through the eyes of three women called Lucía. Though not a polished piece of cinematography, the film is an important contribution to the Third Cinema movement of 1960s and 1970s Latin America.

La Muerte de un Burócrata (1966; dir. Tomás Gutiérrez Alea). A classic of early post-Revolution Cuban cinema from one of its most lauded directors, making it past the censors despite its critical take on the madness of Cuban bureaucracy. In this high farce the wife of a dead man buried with his work card discovers she needs the card to claim benefits she is entitled to. The plot unfolds as she seeks to exhume the body.

★ **Sons of Cuba** (2009; dir. Andrew Lang). Following the ups and downs of a group of young boxers at the renowned Havana Boxing Academy, this unforgettable documentary reaches way beyond its immediate subject matter – though that in itself is highly engaging – and offers a touching and sensitive portrayal of growing up in Cuba, family relationships, friendships and personal sacrifice.

Suite Habana (2003; dir. Fernando Pérez). An artful yet truthful depiction of a day in the life of thirteen Havana residents, cinematically shot but technically a documentary and, most notably, completely without dialogue. Following the routines and struggles of a broad cross-section of society, this apolitical film is a touching portrait of humanity.

¡Vampiros en La Habana! (1985; dir. Juan Padrón). An entertaining and bawdy animated film set in the 1930s, which has the unlikely premise of warring European and American vampires fighting to get their fangs on a Cuban-produced formula that stops sunlight harming vampires.

Spanish

Though you are very unlikely to encounter any hostility for speaking English to Cubans, and you will usually find plenty of locals willing to attempt a conversation in English, it makes sense to learn a few basic phrases in Spanish as proficient English is not widely spoken. This is especially true if you are using local buses, as the complete lack of information means you will almost certainly have to ask for help.

Cuban Spanish bears a noticeable resemblance to the pronunciation and vernacular of the Canary Islands, one of the principal sources of Cuban immigration during the colonial era. Students of Castilian Spanish may find themselves a little thrown by all the variations in basic vocabulary in Cuba. However, though the language is full of Anglicisms and Americanisms, like *carro* instead of *coche* for car, or *queic* instead of *tarta* for cake, the Castilian equivalents are generally recognized. Be prepared also for the common Cuban habit of dropping the final letters of words and changing the frequently used -ado ending on words to -ao.

Despite these areas of confusion, the rules of **pronunciation** for all forms of Spanish are straightforward and the basic Latin American model applies in Cuba. Unless there's an accent, all words ending in d, l, r and z are stressed on the last syllable, all others on the second last. All vowels are pure and short.

a somewhere between the A sound in "back" and that in "father".

e as in "get".

i as in "police".

o as in "hot".

u as in "rule".

c is soft before E and I, hard otherwise: **cerca** is pronounced "serka".

g works the same way: a guttural H sound (like the ch in "loch") before E or I, a hard G elsewhere: **gigante** becomes "higante".

h is always silent.

j is the same sound as a guttural G: **jamón** is pronounced "hamon".

ll is pronounced as a Y: **lleno** is therefore pronounced "yeno".

n is as in English, unless it has a tilde (accent) over it, when it becomes NY: **mañana** sounds like "manyana".

qu is pronounced like the English K.

r is, technically speaking, not rolled but you will frequently hear this rule contradicted.

rr is rolled.

v sounds more like B: **vino** becomes "beano".

z is the same as a soft C: **cerveza** is thus "servesa".

SPANISH LANGUAGE BASICS

ESSENTIALS

yes sí
no no
please por favor
thank you gracias
sorry disculpe
excuse me permiso, perdón
Mr señor
Mrs señora
Miss señorita
here aquí/acá
there allí
this esto
that eso
open abierto/a
closed cerrado/a

with con
without sin
and y
good buen(o)/a
bad mal(o)/a
big grande
small pequeño/a, chico/a
more más
less menos
the toilets los servicios, los baños
ladies señoras/damas
gentlemen caballeros
I don't understand No entiendo
I don't speak Spanish No hablo español
I don't know No sé
help! ¡ayudame!

NUMBERS AND DAYS

0 cero
1 uno/una
2 dos
3 tres
4 cuatro
5 cinco
6 seis
7 siete
8 ocho
9 nueve
10 diez
11 once
12 doce
13 trece
14 catorce
15 quince
16 dieciséis
20 veinte
21 veitiuno
30 treinta
40 cuarenta
50 cincuenta
60 sesenta
70 setenta
80 ochenta
90 noventa
100 cien(to)
101 ciento uno
200 doscientos
201 doscientos uno
500 quinientos
1000 mil
2000 dos mil
first primero/a
second segundo/a
third tercero/a
fourth quarto/a
fifth quinto/a
Monday lunes
Tuesday martes
Wednesday miércoles
Thursday jueves
Friday viernes
Saturday sábado
Sunday domingo

GREETINGS AND RESPONSES

goodbye adios/chao
hello hola
Good morning Buenos dias
Good afternoon/night Buenas tardes/noches
See you later Hasta luego
Pleased to meet you Mucho gusto
How are you? ¿Cómo está (usted)? or ¿Cómo andas? (informal)
Not at all/You're welcome De nada/por nada
My name is… Me llamo…
What's your name? ¿Cómo se llama usted? or ¿Cómo te llamas? (informal)
I am English Soy inglés(a)
…American …americano(a)
…Australian …australiano(a)
…Canadian …canadiense(a)
…Irish …irlandés(a)
…Scottish …escosés(a)
…South African …surafricano(a)
…Welsh …galés(a)
…a New Zealander …neozelandés(a)

PUBLIC TRANSPORT AND TAXIS

airport aeropuerto
bicycle taxi bicitaxi/ciclotaxi
bus (usually a local city bus) guagua
bus (used more to refer to long-distance bus) omnibus
bus station terminal de ómnibus
bus stop parada
communal taxi (operates more like a bus service) taxi colectivo; almendron
every other day (seen on bus and train timetables) días alternos
to hitchhike coger botella
juggernaut-style bus camello
non-state taxi taxi particular; máquina
train station estación de ferrocarriles
truck (a commonly used alternative to long-distance buses) camión
I'd like a (return) ticket to… Quisiera boleto/ pasaje (de ida y vuelta) para…
Is this the stop for…? ¿Es está la parada para…?
Is this the train for Havana? ¿Es éste el tren para La Habana?
Take us to this address Llévenos a esta dirección
What time does it leave (arrive in…)? ¿A qué hora sale (llega a…)?
When is the next bus to…? ¿Cuándo es la próxima guagua para…?
Where can I get a taxi? ¿Dónde puedo coger un taxi?
Where does the bus to… leave from? ¿De dónde sale la guagua para…?
Where is a good place to hitchhike? ¿Dónde hay buen lugar para coger botella?

CAR RENTAL, DRIVING AND ROADS

car carro
Could you check…? ¿Puede usted comprobar…?
…the oil …el aceite

...the water ...el agua
...the tyres ...los neumáticos
crossroads cruce
driver's licence carné de conducir
Fill it up please Llénelo por favor
Give way Ceda el paso
I'd like to rent a car Quisiera alquilar un carro
Is the petrol/gasoline included? ¿Está incluida la gasolina?
main road carretera principal
map mapa
motorway autopista
petrol station gasolinera
pothole bache
railway crossing crucero
road carretera
roundabout rotonda
traffic light semáforo

ASKING DIRECTIONS

Carry straight on Siga todo derecho/recto
How do I get to...? ¿Por dónde se va para llegar a...?
How far is it from here to...? ¿Qué distancia hay desde aquí hasta...?
Is it near/far? ¿Está cerca/lejos?
Is there a hotel nearby? ¿Hay un hotel aquí cerca?
Is this the right road to...? ¿Es esta la carretera para...?
Next to Al lado de
Opposite Frente/enfrente
Turn left/right Doble a la izquierda/derecha
Where does this road take us? ¿A dónde nos lleva esta carretera?
Where is...? ¿Dónde está...?

NEEDS AND ASKING QUESTIONS

Can you help me please? Por favor, ¿me puede ayudar?
Could you speak slower please? Por favor, ¿puede usted hablar más despacio?
Do you accept credit cards/travellers' cheques here? ¿Aceptan aquí tarjetas de crédito/cheques de viajero?
Do you have...? ¿Tiene...?
Do you know...? ¿Sabe...?
Do you speak English? ¿Habla usted inglés?
Give me... Deme...
How much is it? ¿Cuánto cuesta?
I'd like Quisiera
I want Quiero
(one like that) (uno así)
There is (is there)? (¿)Hay(?)
What...? ¿Qué...?
What does this mean? ¿Qué quiere decir esto?
What is there to eat? ¿Qué hay para comer?
When...? ¿Cuándo...?

What's that? ¿Qué es eso?
What's this called in Spanish? ¿Cómo se llama esto en español?
Where...? ¿Dónde...?

TIME

a day un día
a month un mes
a week una semana
afternoon tarde
half past two dos y media
It's one o'clock Es la una
It's two o'clock Son las dos
later más tarde or después
morning mañana
night noche
now ahora
quarter past two dos y cuarto
quarter to three tres menos cuarto
today hoy
tomorrow mañana
tonight esta noche
What time is it? ¿Qué hora es?
yesterday ayer

ACCOMMODATION

air-conditioning aire acondicionado
balcony balcón
boutique hotel hostal
cabin complex campismo
cabin or chalet cabaña; bungaló, bungalow (not necessarily single storey)
Can one...? ¿Se puede...?
... camp (near) here? ¿...acampar aqui (cerca)?
Do you have a room? ¿Tiene una habitación?
...with two beds/double bed ...con dos camas/cama matrimonial
...facing the sea ...con vista al mar
...facing the street ...con vista a la calle
...on the ground floor ...en la planta baja
...on the first floor ...en el primer piso
Do you have anything cheaper? ¿No tiene algo más barato?
fan el ventilador
hot/cold water agua caliente/fria
house with rooms to rent casa particular
It's fine, how much is it? Está bien, ¿cuánto es?
It's for one person/two people Es para una persona/dos personas
...for one night ...para una noche
It's too... Es demasiada/o...
...expensive ...cara/o
...dark ...oscura/o
...noisy ...ruidosa/o

key llave
laundry service servicio de lavandería
reception carpeta
room service servicio de habitación
safety deposit box caja de seguridad
swimming pool piscina
switchboard pizarra
The TV/radio doesn't work No funciona el televisor/ el radio
toilet/bathroom baño
village complex villa
We have booked a double room Hemos reservado una habitación doble

SHOPPING, BANKS AND EXCHANGE

agromercado/ agropecuario market selling fresh produce
artesanía arts and crafts
bodega a grocery store only open to those with a corresponding state-issue ration book
bolsa negra black market
cambio bureau de change
casa de cambio a bureau de change
casa comisionista Cuban equivalent to a pawnbroker
en efectivo in cash
guardabolso cloakroom for bags (usually outside shops)
habanos Cuban cigars
humidor box for storing and preserving cigars

SCUBA DIVING

coral reef barrera coralina/ arrecife de coral
coral wall pared coralina

depth profundidad
depth gauge profundimetro
dive sites sitios de buceo
diver buceador
diving gear equipo de buceo
fins aletas
mask máscara
open water mar abierto
regulator regulador
scuba diving buceo
shipwreck barco hundido
snorkel snorkel
tank tanque
tunnel túnel

ARCHITECTURAL AND GEOGRAPHICAL TERMS

balneario health spa; seaside resort
cordillera mountain range
embalse reservoir
finca ranch; country estate
ingenio sugar refinery
malecón seaside promenade
mirador place, usually at the top of a hill or mountain, from where there are good views
mogote boulder-like hills found only in Pinar del Río, particularly in Viñales
municipio division of a city equivalent to a borough or electoral district
reparto city district/ neighbourhood
taller workshop
vega tobacco farm
vitrales arched stained-glass windows, unique to Cuba

CUBAN MENU READER

FOOD AND RESTAURANT BASICS
aceite oil
ají chilli
ajo garlic
almuerzo lunch
arroz rice
azúcar sugar
bocadillo/bocadito sandwich
cena dinner
cereal cereal
combinaciones set meals
comida criolla Cuban/Creole food
comidas ligeras light foods
cuenta bill
desayuno breakfast
ensalada salad
entrantes starters
entremeses starters

guarnición side dishes
huevo eggs
huevos fritos fried eggs
huevos hervidos boiled eggs
huevos revoltillos scrambled eggs
mantequilla butter or margarine
mermelada jam (UK); jelly (US)
miel honey
mostaza mustard
pan bread
perro caliente hot dog
pimienta pepper
platos combinados set meals
platos fuertes mains
potaje soup, stew
queso cheese
sal salt
sopa soup

tortilla omelette
tostada toast
vinagre vinegar

TABLE ITEMS

botella bottle
carta menu
cuchara spoon
cucharita teaspoon
cuchillo knife
cuenco bowl
mesa table
plato plate
servieta napkin
tenedor fork
vaso glass

COOKING STYLES

al ajillo fried with lots of garlic
a la brasa braised
a la jardinera with tomato sauce
a la parrilla grilled
a la plancha grilled
agridulce sweet and sour
ahumado/a smoked
al horno baked
asado/a roast
bien cocido/a well done (meat)
caldoso/a cooked with lots of stock
cazuela stew, casserole
churrasco grilled meat
crudo/a raw
empanadilla puff pastry/pie
enchilado/a cooked in tomato sauce
estofado/a stewed/braised
frito/a fried
grillé grilled
guisado/a stewed
hervido/a boiled
lonjas slices/strips
poco cocinado/a rare (meat)
regular medium (meat)
revoltillo scrambled
tostado/a toasted

CUBAN DISHES

ajiaco rich stew featuring corn and varied meats and vegetables
aporreado beef stew with tomato and garlic
bistec uruguayo steak covered in cheese and breadcrumbs
chicharrones fried pork skin/pork scratchings
congrí rice and red beans (mixed)
empanada pastry stuffed with meat or sometimes cheese or guava
langosta enchilada lobster in a tomato sauce
lechón roast pork suckling
moros y cristianos rice and black beans
palomilla steak fried or grilled with lime and garlic
ropa vieja shredded stewed beef
tamale Mexican-influenced local dish made with steamed cornflour
tasajo shredded and jerked stewed beef
tostones fried plantains

STREET VENDOR SNACKS

churros long curls of fried batter covered in sugar, similar to doughnuts
coquitos sweets made from shredded coconut and sugar
empanada de guayaba guava jam in pastry
fritura de maíz corn fritter
maní molido ground-peanut bar
pan con lechón roast chicken sandwich
papa rellena balls of deep-fried mashed potato stuffed with mincemeat
rositas de maíz popcorn
torreja eggy sweet bread in syrup
tortica shortbread biscuit
turrón de maní peanut and syrup bar

FISH (PESCADOS) AND SEAFOOD (MARISCOS)

aguja swordfish
anchoas anchovies
arenque herring
atún tuna
bacalao cod
calamares squid
camarones prawns, shrimp
cangrejo crab
espada swordfish
langosta lobster
merluza hake
pargo red snapper (tilapia)
pulpo octopus
salmón salmon
tetí small fish, local to Baracoa
trucha trout

MEAT (CARNE) AND POULTRY (AVES)

albóndigas meatballs
bistec steak
brocheta kebab
buey beef
cabra/chivo goat
carnero mutton

cerdo pork
chorizo spicy sausage
chuleta chop
conejo rabbit
cordero lamb
costillas ribs
escalope escalope
hamburguesa hamburger
hígado liver
jamón ham
lacón smoked pork
lomo loin (of pork)
masas de cubed (pork)
oveja mutton
pato duck
pavo turkey
pechuga breast
picadillo mince
pierna leg
pollo chicken
rana frog's meat
res beef
ropa vieja shredded beef
salchichas sausages
sesos brains
solomillo sirloin
ternera veal
tocino bacon
venado venison

FRUITS (FRUTAS) AND NUTS (FRUTOS SECOS)

aguacate avocado
albaricoque apricot
almendra almond
avellana hazelnut
cereza cherry
ciruelas prunes
coco coconut
fresa strawberry
fruta bomba papaya
guayaba guava
lima lime
limón lime/lemon
mamey mamey (thick, sweet red fruit with a stone)
maní peanut
manzana apple
melocotón peach
melón melon (usually watermelon)
naranja orange
papaya papaya (or pawpaw)
pera pear
piña pineapple
plátano banana

toronja grapefruit
uvas grapes

VEGETABLES (VERDURAS/VEGETALES)

aceituna olive
berenjenas aubergine/eggplant
boniato sweet potato
calabaza pumpkin
cebolla onion
champiñón mushroom
chícaro(nes) pea (pulse)
col cabbage
esparragos asparagus
frijoles black beans
garbanzos chickpeas
habichuela string beans/green beans
hongos mushrooms
lechuga lettuce
malanga starchy tubular vegetable
papa potato
papas fritas french fries
pepino cucumber
pimiento capsicum pepper
quimbombo okra
rábano radish
remolacha beetroot
tomate tomato
yuca cassava
zanahoria carrot

SWEETS (DULCES) AND DESSERTS (POSTRES)

arroz con leche rice pudding
...en almíbar ...in syrup
flan crème caramel
galleta biscuit/cookie
helado ice cream
jimaguas two ice-cream scoops
queik cake
queso cheese
merengue meringue
natilla custard/milk pudding/ mousse
pasta de guayaba guava jam
pay pie (fruit)
pudín crème caramel or hard-set flan
torta de queso cheesecake
torta Santiago almond tart
tortica shortbread-type biscuit
tres gracias three ice-cream scoops

RUMS (RONES) AND COCKTAILS (COCTELES)

Cuba Libre rum and Coke

Cubanito white rum, lemon juice, salt, Worcester sauce, hot sauce and crushed ice

Daiquirí white rum, white sugar, lemon juice, maraschino and crushed ice

Daiquirí Frappé white rum, maraschino (cherry liqueur), white sugar, lemon juice and crushed ice

Habana Especial white rum, maraschino, pineapple juice and ice

Mulata dark rum, white sugar, lemon juice and cacao liqueur

Presidente white rum, curaçao, grenadine and sweet white vermouth

ron…

…añejo dark rum, aged 7 years

…carta blanca (ron blanco) white rum, aged 3 years

…carta oro dark rum, aged 5 years

…gran reserva dark rum, aged 15 years

Ron Collins white rum, lemon juice, white sugar and soda

OTHER DRINKS (BEBIDAS)

agua water

agua mineral mineral water

…(con gas) …(sparkling)

…(natural/sin gas) …(still)

batido milkshake

café coffee

café con leche coffee made with hot milk

cerveza beer

chocolate caliente drinking chocolate

ginebra gin

guarapo sugar cane pressé

jerez sherry

jugo juice

leche milk

limonada natural lemonade (fresh)

prú fermented drink flavoured with spices

refresco pop/fizzy drink

refresco de lata canned pop

té tea

té manzanillo camomile tea

vino blanco white wine

vino rosado rosé wine

vino tinto red wine

vodka vodka

whisky whisky

Idiom and slang

Cuban Spanish is rich in idiosyncratic words and phrases, many borrowed from English. Some of the slang is common to other Latin American countries, particularly Puerto Rico, while there are all sorts of **cubanismos** unique to the island. A number of everyday Cuban words, particularly for items of clothing, differ completely from their Castilian equivalent. These are not slang words, but equate to the same kind of differences that exist between North American and British English.

CLOTHING

blúmer knickers

camiseta vest

chor shorts

chubasquero cagoule

guayabera traditional lightweight shirt, often with four pockets

overol dungarees

pitusa jeans

pulover T-shirt

saco a suit

tenis trainers, sneakers

yin jeans

MONEY

baro dollar

divisa hard currency (used in an official capacity, eg in a bank or shop)/dollars/convertible pesos

fula dollar/s, convertible peso/s

kilo/s cent/s or centavo/s

un medio five cents or centavos

moneda efectivo cash, convertible pesos

moneda nacional national currency, Cuban pesos

una peseta twenty cents or centavos

HISTORICAL TERMS

bohío thatched-roof hut as made and lived in by pre-Columbian peoples on the island

cabildo town council during the colonial era

casino Spanish social centre in the nineteenth century

cimarrón escaped enslaved person

criollo/a a pre-independence term to describe a Cuban-born Spanish person; also used to describe something as specifically or traditionally Cuban

mambí member of the nineteenth-century rebel army fighting for independence from Spain

palenque a hideout or settlement occupied by runaway enslaved people during the colonial period

peninsular/es Spanish-born person/s living in Cuba prior to independence

trapiche machine used in colonial era to press sugar cane

MISCELLANEOUS

asere similar to "mate" or "buddy" (usually used as an exclamation)

barbacoa two rooms created from one by building in a floor halfway up the wall to create an upper level (a popular Cuban practice)

bárbaro/a excellent, great

bolsa negra black market

casa particular private home where rooms are rented to guests

CDR (Committee for the Defence of the Revolution) neighbourhood-watch groups devised to root out counter-revolutionaries

chao goodbye (never hello)

chopin convertible-peso shop, often a supermarket (an appropriation of the English "shopping")

¿Cómo andas? How's it going?

compañero/a comrade (formal); friend, mate, pal (informal)

consumo consumption; used with entrance costs to denote an entitlement of food or drink included in cost

guajiro/a person who lives in a rural area/peasant

guapo criminal or street hustler

gusano/a Cuban refugee or counter-revolutionary (pejorative)

jinetera female hustler who specifically targets tourists; sex worker

jinetero male hustler who specifically targets tourists

orisha A deity in African-Cuban religions like Santería

pa' for (shortened version of para)

paladar privately run restaurant located in the owner's home

peña musical group, jam or small concert

pepe/a tourist

pila a lot; Hay una pila de gente aqui – "There are a lot of people here"

prieto/a dark-skinned

ponchera puncture repair and bicycle maintenance workshop

posada short-term hotel renting rooms for sex

¿Qué bolá? What's up?, How's it going?

reparto neighbourhood or area of a city

sala de video venue where films are shown to the public on a television screen

socio/a mate, buddy

tonga a lot

trigueño/a light-brown-skinned

veguero tobacco farmer

Small print and index

A ROUGH GUIDE TO ROUGH GUIDES

Published in 1982, the first Rough Guide – to Greece – was a student scheme that became a publishing phenomenon. Mark Ellingham, a recent graduate in English from Bristol University, had been travelling in Greece the previous summer and couldn't find the right guidebook. With a small group of friends he wrote his own guide, combining a contemporary, journalistic style with a thoroughly practical approach to travellers' needs.

The immediate success of the book spawned a series that rapidly covered dozens of destinations. And, in addition to impecunious backpackers, Rough Guides soon acquired a much broader readership that relished the guides' wit and inquisitiveness as much as their enthusiastic, critical approach and value-for-money ethos. These days, Rough Guides include recommendations from budget to luxury and cover more than 120 destinations around the globe, from Amsterdam to Zanzibar, all regularly updated by our team of roaming writers.

Browse all our latest guides, read inspirational features and book your trip at **roughguides.com**.

Rough Guide credits

Editor: Zara Sekhavati
Cartography: Carte
Picture editor: Thomas Smyth

Layout: Pradeep Thapliyal
Head of DTP and Pre-Press: Katie Bennett
Head of Publishing: Kate Drynan

Publishing information

Ninth edition 2023

Distribution

UK, Ireland and Europe
Apa Publications (UK) Ltd; sales@roughguides.com
United States and Canada
Ingram Publisher Services; ips@ingramcontent.com
Australia and New Zealand
Booktopia; retailer@ booktopia.com.au
Worldwide
Apa Publications (UK) Ltd; sales@roughguides.com

Special Sales, Content Licensing and CoPublishing

Rough Guides can be purchased in bulk quantities
at discounted prices. We can create special editions,
personalised jackets and corporate imprints tailored to
your needs. sales@roughguides.com.
roughguides.com

Printed in China

Help us update

We've gone to a lot of effort to ensure that this edition of
The Rough Guide to Cuba is accurate and up-to-date.
However, things change – places get "discovered", opening
hours are notoriously fickle, restaurants and rooms raise
prices or lower standards. If you feel we've got it wrong
or left something out, we'd like to know, and if you can
remember the address, the price, the hours, the phone
number, so much the better.

Please send your comments with the subject line
"Rough Guide Cuba Update" to mail@uk.roughguides.
com. We'll credit all contributions and send a copy of the
next edition (or any other Rough Guide if you prefer) for
the very best emails.

Acknowledgements

Joanne Owen: Special thanks to Paulino López Delgado for his insightful bird and nature guiding around Jardines
del Rey, and to Stephen Saunders for being the best partner in life, at home, and on roads, rivers, rainforest trails and
mountaintops around the Caribbean – here's to taking flight at Hummingbird Heights.

ABOUT THE AUTHOR

Joanne Owen is a Pembrokeshire-born writer with a special interest in Wales and the
Caribbean. The author of several books for children and *The Rough Guide to Responsible Wales*,
she's worked on *The Mini Rough Guide to St Lucia* and *The Rough Guide to Cuba*, and contributed
to *The Rough Guide to the 100 Best Places on Earth* and *The Rough Guide to the 100 Best Places in
the USA*. Joanne also writes for ⓦ roughguides.com.

Photo credits

(Key: T-top; C-centre; B-bottom; L-left; R-right)

Index

W

Y

Z

Map symbols

The symbols below are used on maps throughout the book

▪▬▪	Provincial boundary	◆	Point of interest	ᐱᐱ	Spring	🐊	Crocodile park
– – –	Chapter boundary	◆	National park/reserve	⊤	Garden	🐘	Zoo
	Motorway	ⓘ	Tourist information office	⚘	Waterfall	⛳	Golf course
	Road	ⓒ	Telephone office	⤳	Dive site	☀	Viewpoint
	Pedestrianized road	@	Internet	▲	Peak	⬭	Stadium
■-■-■	Unpaved road	🛜	Wi-fi hotspot	⌂	Mountain range		Building
▥▥▥▥	Steps	✉	Post office	◠	Cave		Church
– – –	Path	⊞	Hospital	Ⅺ	Campsite/campismo		Park
⊠▦▦	Railway	Ⓟ	Parking	♦	Military checkpoint		Mudflats
– –	Ferry route	✈	Airport	♚	Museum		Mangrove swamp
	Wall	⛽	Fuel station	⚔	Castle		Beach
		⊙	Statue/memorial	⚲	Lighthouse		Cemetery

Listings key

- ▪ Accommodation
- ● Eating
- ▪ Drinking/nightlife
- ● Shopping